A Cultural History of Causality

A Cultural History of Causality

Science, Murder Novels,
and Systems of Thought

STEPHEN KERN

PRINCETON UNIVERSITY PRESS

PRINCETON AND OXFORD

Copyright © 2004 by Princeton University Press
Published by Princeton University Press, 41 William Street,
Princeton, New Jersey 08540
In the United Kingdom: Princeton University Press,
3 Market Place, Woodstock, Oxfordshire OX20 1SY

Second printing, and first paperback printing, 2006
Paperback ISBN-13: 978-0-691-12768-2
Paperback ISBN-10: 0-691-12768-9

The Library of Congress has cataloged the cloth edition of this book as follows

Kern, Stephen.
    A cultural history of causality : science, murder novels, and systems of thought /
    Stephen Kern.
        p. cm.
    Includes bibliographical references and index.
    ISBN 0-691-11523-0 (alk. paper)
    1. Causation in literature. 2. Murder in literature. 3. Causation. 4. Fiction—19th
century—History and criticism. 5. Fiction—20th century—History and criticism.
I. Title.

  ⌄ PN56.C38K47 2004   )0) ⎾
    809'.93384—dc22
                                                                    2004044676

British Library Cataloging-in-Publication Data is available

This book has been composed in Janson

Printed on acid-free paper. ∞

pup.princeton.edu

Printed in the United States of America

10 9 8 7 6 5 4 3 2

For Mary

Contents

Acknowledgments

SOME OF THE RESEARCH on this book was supported by a National Endowment for the Humanities Fellowship during 1998–1999 and a sabbatical leave from Northern Illinois University in 2001.

Thanks to Kevin Anderson, Harold Brown, K. Codell Carter, Paul Croce, Otniel Dror, William Everdell, Claudio Fogu, Michael Gelven, Thomas Haskell, Ursula Heise, Linda Henderson, Richard John, David Joravsky, Tomis Kapitan, Gerald Karp, Samuel Kinser, Robert Markley, Richard Metzner, Robert Nye, Laura Otis, Arkady Plotnitsky, Brian Richardson, George Roeder, Ronald Schleifer, and Martin Sklar who read individual chapters relating to their respective areas of expertise. They were an invaluable source of encouragement, direction, and scholarly control. Sander Gilman and Anson Rabinbach read the manuscript in preparing it for press. While writing this book I occasionally felt like Icarus. Robert Brenner was always there to control my altitude but still not limit the broad scope that this undertaking demanded. I am also indebted to my editor, Brigitta van Rheinberg, who supported this project early on and made several key suggestions about its scale and shape. Thanks also to the history department at Ohio State University which gave me a leave of absence during the first year of my tenure there so that I could accept a Guggenheim Fellowship in 2002–2003 that enabled me to complete the writing.

I am particularly grateful to three people who read all the emerging chapters with meticulous care. Rudolph Binion critiqued my evidence and coherence, Sean Shesgreen tempered my literary voice, while my wife Mary Damer had a keen eye for what did not belong or did not make sense. Over the years it has become increasingly difficult to identify a readership as the field of cultural history moves with the shifting currents of scholarly interest. It has been my great pleasure to share with her on a regular basis the piloting of this book through those rough waters.

Ohio State University
Columbus, Ohio

THE QUESTION behind all other questions is the "why?" of human experience. The newborn's mind gropes for primordial understanding of the causal links between reaching out and human touch, crying and a mother's soothing voice, sucking and relief from hunger. Causal inquiry drives children's endless why questions as they try to make sense of life. While scientists try to limit themselves to the how of phenomena, an ultimate why lies behind all their observations and experiments. The concept of causality grounds physicists' study of subatomic events and astronomers' probing of the cosmos. Theologians look to God for ultimate first and final causes, while believers pray to God to modify miraculously the course of everyday causality. Psychiatrists struggle to discover why their patients become ill, just as historians investigate why wars break out and why civilizations rise and fall. Novelists build stories around motivation, which is the driving force for their characters' thoughts and actions. Causality is thus a centerpiece of the inquiring human mind, so fundamental to human understanding and so universal in its explanatory function that it would seem to transcend any historical development. This book ventures into such a history.

In the years since 1830, European and American thinkers transformed understanding of the causes of human behavior. These changes are evident in novels as well as in genetics, endocrinology, physiology, medicine, psychiatry, linguistics, sociology, economics, statistics, criminology, law, philosophy, and physics. Other researchers have studied changing ideas about causality in these specific areas, but no one has tackled a broad cultural history of this concept as my book undertakes to do.[1]

The thought of writing a history of causality first occurred to me in 1970, when I read an article by Henri Ellenberger on three types of mental illness that philosophically oriented psychiatrists interpreted in terms of defining causal modes.[2] A causality of determinism dominates the depressed person, for whom everything seems to result from the pressure of circumstances over which he or she has no control. A causality of chance dominates the manic, for whom nothing happens according to any deterministic order and the future looms fraught with possibility—unpredictable and anxiety-provoking. A causality of intentionality dominates the paranoid, for whom nothing is the result of chance and everything is caused by menacing thoughts and deeds directed toward the patient.

Ellenberger's speculation that a mental breakdown might be related to the way causality was experienced suggested the deep constitutive power of causal understanding. His notion that individuals experience causality in different ways suggested that historical eras might experience it and try to understand it in distinctive ways. A literary source base for a history of changing ideas about causality occurred to me when I realized that the novelists who did most to define literary modernism—James Joyce, Marcel Proust, and Virginia Woolf—rejected the plot-driven novel and created novels that instead concentrated on the inner life of characters. Their work diminished the role of external pressures and specific motives such as those that had structured the naturalist novels of Émile Zola and Thomas Hardy, in which characters are governed by social, biological, and psychological forces. That literary shift suggested a cultural pivot for a history of causality.

But causal factors and motives were too broad a focus, because there are so many of them for countless possible human actions. For more than fifteen years, while working on two other books, I searched for a way to deal with the many causal determinants for the myriad human behaviors that historical experience includes. I eventually realized that such a history would have to focus on a single act in order to document historically distinctive thinking about its causes. But what was that act?

I discovered it in Roy Jay Nelson's study of causality in the French novel, which briefly discussed a novel by André Gide, *Lafcadio's Adventures* (1914), about an unusually motivated murder.[3] While reading that novel I realized that murder suited my analytical purposes because, compared with other acts, it is exceptionally vivid and important and in most cases sharply focused in time and space. Murder superbly illustrates the various characteristics that action theorists offer to explain human behavior, because it is strongly intentional, highly motivated, full of meaning, the result of a desire or a "trying," directed at a clear goal, and usually "done for a reason."[4] By focusing on murder, an act that remains relatively consistent over time, I could focus on historically changing ideas about its causal factors. Murder further lends itself to historical analysis because in life and literature after 1830 it attracted increasing attention to its causal circumstances and motives among a number of new professionals: criminologists, sociologists, detectives, statisticians, and forensic psychiatrists, as well as writers of detective fiction (whodunits) and crime novels (whydunits). The history of ideas about the causality of murder over these years also includes a number of new explanatory concepts: monomania, moral insanity, diminished responsibility, irresistible impulse, born criminal, sadism, unconscious determination, and childhood sexual trauma.

In Gide's novel the hero attempts to break the conventional path to murder by intentionally killing without a motive, or at least without a conventional motive such as money or revenge. While sitting in a train, Lafcadio realizes that to kill the stranger who appears in his compartment, he has only to release the door latch and give a push and the man will plunge to his death. Inspired by the prospect of committing a "motiveless crime" (*crime immotivé*), Lafcadio flicks the latch and pushes the man to his death. In contrast to Zola's murderers, who kill because of an irresistible hereditary taint or overwhelming biological, psychological, or social forces, Gide's hero kills for the sole reason of killing without a reason. Gide further challenged Zola's explanatory technique through another character, the novelist Julius, who, in expressing his literary aim to Lafcadio, articulates Gide's own approach: "I used to demand logic and consistency from my characters, . . . [but] it wasn't natural." People are neither logical nor consistent. With respect to murder, Julius specifies, "I don't want a motive for the crime—all I want is an explanation of the criminal. Yes! I mean to lead him into committing a crime gratuitously—into wanting to commit a crime without any motive at all."[5] Here Julius overstates his case, because Lafcadio's murderous act is indeed motivated, but the motive is, as Gide subsequently explained, not subject to the sort of "ordinary psychological explanation" that occurs in naturalist novels.[6]

Later Gide clarified misunderstanding about his notion of the "gratuitous act" and rejected the notion that it might explain a crime. "I personally do not believe in the gratuitous act, an act motivated by nothing. That is essentially inadmissible. There are no effects without causes. The words 'acte gratuit' are a *provisional* label [étiquette *provisoire*] that seems convenient to designate acts which escape ordinary psychological explanations, the gestures not determined by simple personal interest (and it is in this sense, in playing with words a little, that I can speak of *disinterested* acts)."[7] Julius's explanatory excess highlights Gide's main goal, which was to dramatize the unpredictable nature of human action in contrast to the way the characters in naturalist novels behave when governed by external circumstances or driven by inner motives.[8] Thus Lafcadio's odd murderous act was an event of enormous cultural historical significance, which became clearer as I explored its larger context in the work of Gide and beyond.

In addition to assailing the strong determinism of the naturalist novel with his literary efforts, Gide's life and thought challenged a spectrum of causal foundations of Western civilization: political, religious, sexual, familial, monetary, and legal. Born into a patriotic and pious French Protestant family, Gide abhorred imperialism and became an atheist. He defied sexual convention as the first prominent French intellectual to acknowledge his homosexuality in print. He married a cousin but never had sex with her and later intentionally sired a child out of wedlock. His novels questioned the privileges of patriarchal authority by mocking cold and menacing fathers. In *The Counterfeiters* (1925), he subverted conventional family values when he wrote that he preferred to see his characters as orphans, "unmarried, and childless."[9] That novel also exposed the artifice of the gold standard by suggesting that the art of the novel is analogous to counterfeiting and that art, like money— even gold—has no real backing, no guaranteed frame of reference.[10] His novels about crime challenged the French legal system that his father embodied as a professor of law at the Sorbonne. By presenting Lafcadio's murder as not determined by "simple personal interest" (or "disinterested"), Gide subverted the conventional narrative strategies of the naturalist novelists and underscored the open-ended nature of human action.[11] These innovations from a man who grew up at the center of French high culture suggested a broad source of evidence for a history of causality. Perhaps, I thought, other murder novelists might have also challenged the received deterministic ideas relating to causality that Gide challenged in his novel and have offered new ways of rendering the causes and motives for human action. Perhaps a survey of murder novels might reveal some unifying logic to this history.

In reading over a hundred murder novels, I found that nineteenth-century novelists typically crafted clear and strongly deterministic causal factors, either singly or in clusters. Some of their murderers are driven by a single dominant factor, frequently described with the new diagnostic category of monomania, which the French psychiatrist J.-E.-D. Esquirol identified early in the century and which one character in Dostoevski's *Crime and Punishment* (1866) used to explain Raskolnikov's act of murder. That tag suggesting a strong linear determinism was used by other novelists to explain a murderous impulse, as in *Moby Dick* (1851) where Melville repeatedly describes Ahab as a monomaniac, and Ahab himself explains that "the path to my fixed purpose is laid with iron rails whereon my soul is grooved to run" (147). Other nineteenth-century novelists explained murders as the result of interlocking deterministic causal factors such as poverty and revenge in Dickens's *Oliver Twist* (1838) or heredity and sexual perversion in Zola's *La bête humaine* (1890).

In contrast, modernists complicated and subverted these causal factors in many ways. In *Heart of Darkness* (1899), Joseph Conrad characterized the intentions behind Kurtz's acts of killing and head-hunting as "inscrutable" and "incomprehensible," and he repeatedly referred to the murderous imperialist venture itself as "absurd." In Robert Musil's *The Man without Qualities* (1933), the motives of the deranged murderer Moosbrugger are a chaotic mixture of self-defense, self-definition, and sexual panic. Jean-Paul Sartre questioned the motive underlying a political assassination when in *Dirty Hands* (1948), Hugo explains, "I killed him because I opened the door," and then wonders, "Where is my crime? Does it exist?"

While modernist detective stories are more concerned with who did it than why, they nevertheless also subvert conventional plotting, which in earlier detective stories was based on a clear motive trail of cause and effect leading ineluctably to the murderer as in the tidy concluding explanations of Sherlock Holmes. Thomas Bernhard's *The Lime Works* (1970) clouds any clear understanding of the motives for a murder by basing an entire murder investigation on unreliable hearsay accounts from characters whose senses are flawed and whose accounts are contradictory. In Carlo Emilio Gadda's *That Awful Mess on Via Merulana* (1957), about a grisly murder that never gets solved, the detective believes that crimes are never the consequence of single motives but are "like a whirlpool, a cyclonic point of depression in the consciousness of the world, towards which a whole multitude of converging causes have contributed." He elaborates that investigative theory into a more general philosophical claim that we must "reform within ourselves the meaning of the category of cause" (5). Friedrich Dürrenmatt's *The Pledge*, subtitled *Requiem for the Criminal Novel* (1958), is indeed just that, because it fatally ridicules the entire rational framework of such novels—coherent plots, clear motives, genius detectives, even causal reasoning itself—and in the end the murders are solved by nothing more than dumb luck.[12]

Reading these novels revealed that from the nineteenth century to the twentieth century understanding of the causes of murder in them shifted in five interrelated ways. That multifaceted shift is the thesis of this book—namely, that causal understanding moved in the direction of increasing specificity, multiplicity, complexity, probability, and uncertainty.

The historical significance of these changes can be seen if they are viewed against the dominant thinking about causality in the preceding period, which I begin to trace in 1830, when August Comte published the first volume of his *Course in Positive Philosophy*, an influential statement of the positivistic epistemology and determinist philosophy of science that dominated Victorian thought.[13] In that same year Charles Lyell published *Principles of Geology*, which demonstrated that geological phenomena are caused by gradual and uniform forces acting according to continuously operating laws. Soon thereafter, social researchers applied positivist methods to show that "moral facts" were subject to behavioral laws similar to physical laws.[14] The first cited reference to *determinism* in the *Oxford English Dictionary* is dated 1846. Balzac underscored the deterministic philosophy that informed his novels. "In this world," he wrote, "every effect has a cause and every cause a principle, every principle is dependent upon a law. The principles which have created extraordinary men can be studied and known."[15] In 1851 the novelist George Eliot expressed her confidence in a deterministic causal order of nature in terms of "undeviating law in the material and moral world," an "invariability of sequence," and an "inexorable law of consequences."[16] A materialist-determinist causality dominated much scientific research, in accord with the view of the German physiologists Emil du Bois-Reymond and Ernst Brücke in 1842 "that in the organism no other forces are effective than the purely physical-chemical." Five years later they were joined by the biophysicists Hermann von Helmholtz and Carl Ludwig and collectively resolved to "constitute physiology on a chemico-physical foundation and give it equal scientific rank with physics."[17]

While there was spirited resistance to such a materialistic determinism that would reduce explanation of all phenomena to matter in motion, especially explanations of human behavior, it nevertheless shaped thinking throughout the remainder of the century.[18] In England, as Frank Turner noted, it was "part of a general cult of science that swept across Europe during the second half of the nineteenth century and that was associated with the names of Renan, Taine, Bernard, Büchner, and Haeckel."[19] An evolutionary determinism was reinforced by the enormous impact of Darwin's theory beginning in 1859. A materialistic determinism applied to mental life peaked with the "mental physiologists" such as Henry Maudsley, who, in 1874, argued that "lunatics and criminals are as much manufactured articles as are steam-engines and calico-printing machines."[20] The French essayist and fictionist Paul Bourget elaborated such thinking in his novel *The Disciple* (1889), which ridiculed the extreme positivism of one arrogant character, who updated Pierre Laplace's famous determinist hypothesis of 1814 in speculating that "if we could know correctly the relative position of all the phenomena which constitute the actual universe, we could, from the present, calculate with a certainty equal to that of the astronomers the day, the hour, the minute when England will evacuate India . . . or when a criminal, still unborn, will murder his father."[21] A physics based on classical mechanics, thermodynamics, and electrodynamics filled out the determinist model with an explanatory system that could account for, and in many cases predict, a spectrum of phenomena such as planetary orbits, tides, trajectories, heat, light, and magnetism. Hard determinists believed that biological and even psychological and social phenomena could be reduced to matter in motion governed by lawlike mechanical forces in addition to electromagnetic, thermodynamic, and gravitational forces. These philosophical and scientific ideas were the foundation for the spectacularly successful positivist-determinist framework of nineteenth-century economy and society as well as its life and thought.

Against this sketch of the highlights of nineteenth-century positivism, reductionism, determinism, and materialism, I offer, by way of introduction, a sampling of evidence for my thesis about the increasing specificity, multiplicity, complexity, probability, and uncertainty of causal understanding that challenged this earlier model.[22] These changes are evident in the murder novels as well as in the history of science and systems of thought.

Increasing specificity includes modern novelists' invocation of the explanatory knowledge of new professional specialists such as forensic scientists, endocrinologists, sociologists, and neuroscientists. In these and other areas, the increasing specificity includes more precise and in some instances more valid causal explanations, such as the way modern genetics specified more precisely and accurately the causal action of chromosomal DNA in contrast to the invalid nineteenth-century theory that hereditary traits are transmitted by mixing male and female sexual fluids. Specificity was also a function of the increasing division of labor in academic disciplines and professions. In addition to those new disciplines concerned with the causes of murder, already mentioned, others emerged that analyzed causality more broadly: molecular biology, biochemistry, nerve electrophysiology, bacteriology, epidemiology, existential phenomenology, and modern probability theory.[23]

These new specialists identified an *increasing multiplicity* of causal factors from their respective sciences and systems of thought.[24] In 1907 Henry Adams described a new "multiverse" brought about by modern science. "The child born in 1900 would, then, be born into a new world which would not be a unity but a multiple."[25] He was referring to the newly discovered forces and processes at work in a human being, but the new sense of living in a "multiverse" came from the identification of many new forces and causal factors from new ways of thinking. In subsequent years, linguists probed new causal functions of language in structuring basic concepts and individual behavior. Sociologists identified multiple ways in which society impinges on behavior from the immediate environment to broad social forces. In biological sciences increasing multiplicity included the identification of new causally acting entities, such as the approximately thirty thousand genes, several hundred hormones and peptides, and fifty neurotransmitters. Forensic psychiatrists, beginning with Richard von Krafft-Ebing, identified new varieties of sexual pathology that led to bizarre sex crimes. Modern criminal profilers drew on increasingly precise and enormous data banks to reconstruct the etiology of murder for purposes of police investigation. Psychoanalysis elaborated a detailed nomenclature of psychosexual etiology which influenced how some novelists made sense of their characters' behavior. In some areas, however, modern science reduced the number of causal factors. Many nineteenth-century medical and psychiatric researchers elaborated long lists of causes of diseases because they had no clear understanding of their specific etiology. The contribution of the germ theory of disease reduced the causes of diseases to single specific organisms, offering one particularly clear example of the progress of causal understanding as a reduction and simplification rather than a multiplication of causal factors. It should be added, though, that in identifying specific germs, scientists vastly increased the number of specific etiologies for an increasing number of specific diseases. The larger picture is therefore one of a dramatic increase in the number of causal factors identified ever more precisely by new sciences (such as genetics and sex endocrinology), as well as new systems of thought (such as psychoanalysis and sociology).

Increasing complexity was a consequence of efforts to integrate these new causally acting entities and forces in comprehensive systems. In 1902 the French physicist Henri Poincaré connected the increasing specificity and complexity of recent scientific knowledge in noting that "we are continually perceiving details ever more varied in the phenomena we know, where our crude senses used to be unable to detect any lack of unity. What we thought to be simple becomes complex, and the march of science seems to be towards diversity and complication."[26] A few years later Henry Adams listed the many causal forces that must be taken into account in addition to electrical forces: thermal, magnetic, chemical, osmotic, cohesive, elastic, vibratory, capillary, and sexual. Science has found that forces "sensible and occult, physical and metaphysical, simple and complex, surround, traverse, vibrate, rotate, repel, attract, without stop." He concluded that "a historian after 1900 would think in complexities unimaginable to an earlier mind."[27] More recently the historian of science Gerald Holton concluded that "it is as if after a successful search for simplicities and harmonies in science over the last three centuries, the search has turned to a more direct confrontation of complexity and derangement, of sophisticated and astonishing relationships among strangely juxtaposed parts."[28]

Around the mid–twentieth century researchers began to explore complex feedback systems under the general rubric of cybernetics. Modern systems theory and, later, chaos theory were based on the interactive causal action of complex systems. In the last thirty years computers have enabled scientists to solve nonlinear problems and to understand more fully the complex systems of such phenomena as heart fibrillations, population ecology, and weather patterns. In consequence, as Alan Beyerchen noted, "the rise of an aesthetic of complexity in science" has made "a significant challenge to the primacy of simplicity."[29] Some researchers applied a nonlinear causality to the human sciences, emphasizing that culture emerges as a series of causally interactive feedback loops, making it possible for individuals to "transform nature or society in dramatic and unpredictable ways."[30] Prior to around 1980, complexity referred to something complicated, with many layers of meaning that are difficult to sort out; after that time it began to refer to the specific science of adaptive and self-organizing systems in which the whole is greater than the sum of its parts. In 1984 the Santa Fe Institute was founded to explore such complex systems.

Modernist fiction, as David Lodge argued, "eschews the straight chronological ordering of its material [and] tends toward a complex or fluid handling of time, involving much cross-reference back and forward across the temporal span of the action."[31] In 1925 Virginia Woolf made a classic statement among modernist novelists on the need to move from a linear to a nonlinear narrative form that does justice to the complexity of experience: "If a writer were a free man and not a slave, if he could write what he chose, not what he must, if he could base his work upon his own feeling and not upon convention, there would be no plot, no comedy, no tragedy, no love interest or catastrophe in the accepted style. . . . Life is not a series of gig lamps symmetrically arranged; but a luminous halo, a semi-transparent envelope surrounding us from the beginning of consciousness to the end. Is it not the task of the novelist to convey this varying, this unknown and uncircumscribed spirit, whatever aberration or complexity it may display?"[32] Joseph Conrad and Ford Madox Ford made similar appeals.[33] The novels of Proust and Joyce attempted to capture the luminous halos of life across time and space in ways that would have been unthinkable to earlier realists. Later in the twentieth century Vladimir Nabokov, Jorge Luis Borges, and Thomas Pynchon explicitly invoked scientific field models for causal action to create novels based on what N. Katherine Hayles subsequently characterized as a "cosmic web."[34]

The increasing specificity, multiplicity, and complexity of causal knowledge was made more calculable with the computer and made more visible by other new research technologies, beginning with X rays around the turn of the century. Later, with the widespread use of electron microscopes in the 1950s, biologists were suddenly able to observe numerous subcellular structures that had been invisible through light microscopes. Within a decade they amassed an array of high-resolution photographs of different types of cells, revealing a vast new realm of life processes. Since that time researchers worked to understand the causal functions of the structures that first appeared in these early electron micrographs along with other causally significant processes. More causally acting entities and processes throughout the body and the brain were revealed by the electroencephalogram (EEG) in 1929 and a series of breakthroughs in the 1970s: computerized axial tomography (CAT), magnetic resonance imaging (MRI), and positron emission tomography (PET).[35] These technologies produced more exact knowledge of ever smaller structures and functions never before viewed so precisely, and in so doing they raised questions about complex interactions that constitute the cellular and molecular springs of human behavior and thought.

Increasing probability refers to new interpretations of chance in the novel and to probabilistic explanations in science. In the nineteenth-century novel, chance or coincidence was invariably a sign of some transcendent controlling destiny if not divine plan.[36] In the modern novel, chance is more often evidence of life's fundamentally stochastic nature and the absence of any ultimate designing mind.[37] Nineteenth-century sciences were themselves increasingly probabilistic. The kinetic theory of gasses, Darwin's theory of evolution, Mendel's experiments on hereditary transmission, and sociological studies of suicide and crime by means of "moral statistics" all involved probabilistic calculations. Modern probability theory refined the statistical techniques for dealing with such probabilistic explanations. For example, early nineteenth-century phrenologists believed that enlarged "organs" of the brain directly cause the increasing activity and importance of the individual faculty supposedly located in them. Modern neuroscientists exposed such erroneous confusions of correlation with causation and made probabilistic causal analyses of the relative causal role of brain anatomy, neuropeptides, neurotransmitters, and environmental stimuli in the determination of behavior. Such calculations were made possible by what historians of science have called "the probabilistic revolution," which centered on developments among statisticians who, in the generation around 1900, refined and developed a number of new techniques for calculating probabilities, including standard deviation, the chi-square, analysis of variance, and the t-test and its distribution.[38] These techniques revolutionized social science and made it possible to assign magnitudes to a variety of causal factors impinging on single events and thereby determine the statistical probability of their respective causal roles. Relating to the causality of murder, researchers conducted statistical analyses of the causal significance of reduced levels of the neurotransmitter serotonin relative to other neurobiological agents and social factors among incarcerated men to help explain why they committed murder. With such calculations, causal explanations throughout the physical as well as the natural sciences became increasingly probabilistic.

Nineteenth-century physicists conceived of probability as dealing with limits in the knowledge of what they believed to be phenomena that ultimately, at least in theory, could be reduced to deterministic, lawlike processes. In the twentieth century, quantum physicists theorized that some phenomena were irreducibly indeterministic and that the world was therefore ultimately explicable with only a probabilistic causality, at least at the subatomic level.

Increasing uncertainty is a function of increasing multiplicity, complexity, and probability, which modern novelists dramatized in their narratives and which scientists studied in their research. Philosophers in the sway of pragmatism and pluralism, contextualism and historical relativism, abandoned the earlier absolutist "quest for certainty."[39] Modern novelists reveal a greater willingness to accept open-ended stories with less satisfying closure than one finds in the Victorian novel, which typically was governed by what Thomas Vargish called "the providential aesthetic"—a belief in some guiding transcendent destiny or ultimate meaning to life.[40] In contrast, modern philosophers and novelists were more willing to accept higher levels of uncertainty in understanding the causes of behavior, while some such as Nietzsche, Sartre, Gide, Bernhard, and Pynchon reveled in it.

In 1911 Karl Pearson, a pioneer of modern probability theory, wrote, "Nobody believes now that science *explains* anything; we all look upon it as a shorthand description, as an economy of thought."[41] A year later Bertrand Russell underscored that skepticism, specifically with regard to causal knowledge: "The word 'cause' is so inextricably bound up with misleading associations as to make its complete extrusion from the philosophical vocabulary desirable. . . . The reason why physics has ceased to look for causes is that, in fact, there are no such things. The law of causality, I believe, like much that passes muster among philosophers, is a relic of a bygone age, surviving, like the monarchy, only because it is erroneously supposed to do no harm."[42] Later in the century the uncertainty of knowledge of events in the physical world became a defining feature of modern science, formalized by Werner Heisenberg's uncertainty principle. It maintained that it is impossible to know with unlimited precision both the position and momentum of an electron or any subatomic particle at the same instant. The product of the error or uncertainty in these two measured values is approximately equal to a constant (discovered by Max Planck in 1900)—a small but discrete magnitude that appears in many places in quantum physics and functions in the physical world as an insurmountable margin of error in all measurements. This further limit on deterministic causal understanding fueled speculation, sometimes rather loosely, that uncertainty was a defining feature of modern life and thought.[43]

My book draws on a wide range of sources—from quantum theory and genetics to existential philosophy and murder novels—to track changing thought about the increasing specificity, multiplicity, complexity, probability, and uncertainty of causal knowledge across 170 years. Some of these changes begin well back in the nineteenth century or well into the twentieth century and vary widely in their extensive range and intensive depth among different sciences and systems of thought. They proceed with different paces and magnitudes for each discipline and science and so preclude any broad chronological ordering of them across the entire cultural record, although the turn-of-the-century period produced a great many new ideas and is generally the historical pivot for this history. I am describing the logic of a general development in many areas, a gradational shift, not a specific turning point in the history of ideas or a single paradigm change. In some places I refer to this shift as going simply from Victorian to modern modes without qualification. Such renderings are usually a shorthand formulation of what is more precisely a gradational change unless otherwise specified, as in those occasional instances when a later idea is absolutely unprecedented (e.g., Freud's theory of the causal role of child sexual trauma) or when an earlier idea is flatly rejected (e.g., hereditary traits passed through the blood).

The scope of this undertaking obliged me to combine these five developments into a single argument that readers could grasp with a single concept and visualize with a single image. That argument is a variant of the epistemological cliché that the more we know, the more we realize how little we know; or, specifically applied to causality, the more causes we understand, the more we realize how many more causes there are to discover and how little we actually know about the causes we think we know. I refer to this argument as the *specificity-uncertainty dialectic*. I use the terms *specificity* and *uncertainty* because they come closest to expressing the positive and negative aspects of this interaction, but they each stand for a cluster of concepts. Specificity may also imply precision and validity, while uncertainty may imply multiplicity, complexity, and probability.

The specificity-uncertainty dialectic embraces the interdependence of the two main concepts. Thus, as researchers sharpened their understanding of causal factors in the physical, biological, and social sciences, they also disclosed new areas of ignorance about what they did not know and new sources of uncertainty about what they did know, and those areas of ignorance and uncertainty suggested new projects for more specific inquiry. The visualizability of the concept is suggested by my use of the image of areas or realms of ignorance to refer to the palpable volume of all that was not known, which was increasingly delineated by ever more specific accounts of those causal agents and causal processes that were known. This expanded realm of ignorance suggested to some observers that causal knowledge was increasingly complex and uncertain. And because that realm seemed to grow in size in comparison to the area of empirically verifiable and causally acting biochemical substances and psychosocial determinants, causal understanding seemed to many observers to be moving toward greater uncertainty. Early on, Oliver Weldell Holmes noted the dialectical interaction of knowledge and ignorance and used a spatial metaphor to illustrate it: "Science is the topography of ignorance. From a few elevated points we triangulate vast spaces, including infinite unknown details. We cast the lead, and draw up a little sand from abysses we may never reach with our dredges. The best part of our knowledge is that which teaches us where knowledge leaves off and ignorance begins."[44] Similar formulations can be found at will throughout the modern period, such as one about the impact of computer modeling on the study of oceans made by the oceanographer Jochem Marotzke in 2002: "We are in a state now where the more we know, the more it becomes clear how little we really understand about the system."[45] Arkady Plotnitsky ran the dialectical argument the other way—from the unknowable to the knowable—in maintaining that in quantum theory the impossibility of knowing certain things about subatomic events has "shaping effects upon what can be known."[46] In mathematics and science generally, he concluded, "the threshold of the unknown, and even the unknowable . . . defines all significant knowledge."[47]

A graphic example of the specificity-uncertainty dialectic is the human genome. The discovery that it is made up of three billion pairs of nucleotides snaking around one another in double helixes enormously increased the specificity of scientific knowledge of the complex interaction of a great number of new causally acting entities in the process of hereditary transmission. At the same time, it opened vast realms of uncertainty about what exactly all of these causally acting entities do and how they do it. Modern novelists were increasingly aware of the complexity of genetics but less inclined to explain behavior based on it in contrast to a number of nineteenth-century novelists who eagerly invoked "hereditary taints" flowing "in the blood" to make sense of their characters' acts of murder.

In the modern period novelists rarely explained behavior in terms of cellular and, even less frequently, molecular processes. They occasionally mentioned genes, hormones, and neurotransmitters to suggest that a detective, forensics expert, or scientist was aware of current knowledge, but causally acting biochemical entities play an insignificant role in explaining the motive for murder or any other behavior. I found no references to neuropeptides by their technical name, although their aliases as opiates do cause numerous murders indirectly by addicts who kill to get money to buy drugs, such as heroin, that initiate the same physiological response as neuropeptides. Nevertheless, I include the history of understanding of these causally acting biological substances for four reasons: (1) because understanding of their causal function is distinctive to the modern period and therefore offers compelling evidence for historical change, (2) because these substances account for human behavior at the most basic level and as such imply the most basic causal explanation, (3) because theories about their causal role make vivid historical contrasts with less precise nineteenth-century theories about gemmules, germ plasm, body humors, vital forces, and imagined ultimate atoms of life, and (4) because the history of their discovery, which opened up vast new realms of the unknown, offers compelling evidence for my argument about the specificity-uncertainty dialectic.

That argument raises a major evidentiary problem, however, because increasing specificity implies progress, not in a moral or aesthetic sense, but according to the standards of scientific research. One can claim that the history of science, and especially the history of medicine, progresses in understanding the causes of ever more numerous and precise aspects of observed phenomena. The accomplishments of Newton, Darwin, Mendel, Pasteur, Koch, Einstein, Heisenberg, Crick, and Watson mark unmistakable progress in the direction of increasing accuracy, detail, and verifiability in explaining phenomena. But one cannot argue that causal understanding in novels progresses—that explanatory understanding of characters or even of specific acts of murder in Dreiser or Don DeLillo is more valid than, or represents progress over, such understanding in

Dickens or Zola. Without making such a claim, I believe that one can integrate evidence from the history of science and literature in support of an argument about the specificity-uncertainty dialectic based on six considerations.

1. Modern science is more precise and valid than Victorian science.[48] The emergence of the germ theory of disease in the 1870s is a hallmark of modern medicine, which is clearly more effective than was earlier medicine in diagnosing, preventing, and curing illnesses.[49] Today anyone practicing Victorian science would be incompetent, and anyone practicing Victorian medicine would be subject to malpractice suits. If a contemporary physician treated a tubercular patient 1830s-style by opening a vein in the neck, he or she would be indicted for assault. One early-nineteenth-century medical organization estimated that in 1810 there were nine quacks in England for every regular doctor.[50] At the turn of the twentieth century, Sherlock Holmes's detecting was supposed to be based on the latest and best science, and Conan Doyle invented for Holmes some scientific breakthroughs of his own, which themselves represented progress over earlier investigative methods. The first words Holmes utters are "I've found it!"; and "it" refers to a test for the presence of blood. In investigating murders it is useful to be able to test for blood, and any discovery that makes such identification possible is evidence of progress toward achieving that result. Modern pharmacologists have discovered drugs that target specific enzymes with minimal negative side effects. Twentieth-century physicians, psychologists, sociologists, and criminologists improved on earlier methods of data collection and statistical analysis to make their probabilistic causal explanations more reliable. Modernist novelists' ability to draw on that science gave them a more precise understanding of specific causal processes and also helped identify their work as distinctly modern.

2. I compare not whole novels but parts of novels, which I draw on as if they were criminological or psychiatric case histories. Dreiser in total did not understand the causes of behavior better than did Zola in total, because each novelist understood behavior according to the current level of knowledge and explanatory categories of their respective times. Nevertheless, specific parts of their dramatizations of human causality are historically marked, and the more modern explanations—to which Dreiser had access, and Zola did not—were better able to explain more precisely the function of such causally acting entities as genes and hormones. Dreiser was particularly influenced by current

theories about tropisms and hormones, and while one cannot argue that his novels represent progress in artistic expression, one can argue that specific parts of them explained behavior based on more verifiable science than was available to Victorian novelists.

3. Modern novelists had the benefit of hindsight in that they were able to draw on as well as critically evaluate the novels of their predecessors. Gide criticized the psychological and social determinisms in Zola and Bourget, while Alain Robbe-Grillet targeted Balzac for similar reasons. Virginia Woolf registered her disappointment with the subject matter of H. G. Wells, Arnold Bennett, and John Galsworthy, concluding forcefully that "the sooner English fiction turns its back upon them ... the better for its soul."[51] Such criticism suggested that the novel was moving beyond earlier conventions in ways that were historical and directional, if not progressive. Many modernist novelists viewed themselves as an avant-garde, by which they meant a group that led the way into formerly tabooed topics and new artistic strategies that improved on outmoded traditions and conventions. The historian Christopher Butler noted that insofar as the development of new paradigms for art is seen "to derive from innovative technical breakthroughs, they are by definition 'progressive,' because if you can imitate the technique, you can do something that you could not do before." Butler dissociated himself from the claim of progress in art by putting the word in quotation marks, but his study documents the pervasive sense among avant-garde artists that they were breaking new ground in a positive direction. Some modernists, like the German expressionists, emphasized the social and political aspect of that emancipatory role from the grip of "bourgeois" morality and oppressive family psychodynamics. Others emphasized their contribution as technical and formal, but they shared a sense of surpassing what had gone before, at least during the heyday of their stylistic triumphs.[52] The benefit of hindsight that the moderns enjoyed did not in itself enable them to understand or explain human behavior any better than their predecessors, to be sure, but it did create a sense of historical development, however difficult it may be to define precisely its meaning or logic.

4. In writing about causality, modern novelists and scientists used rhetorical techniques and explanatory models that are closer to our own, and they therefore addressed some issues that may seem more germane and responsive to contemporary scientific and artistic concerns, if only for their more up-to-date rhetoric, subject matter, value judgments, and methods. The language that novelists, critics, and especially scientists

used to contrast past and present work was shot through with value judgments implying a sense of progress, because later as opposed to earlier work avoided the deficiencies of exhausted topics, dated material, passé attitudes, outmoded styles, refuted theories, and obsolete research methods.

5. Evolution and human history suggest kinds of progress or at least directed change. Evolution produced more complex living forms with human brains instead of primitive nerve nets, offering a controversial but compelling model of the progress of higher forms of organization and consciousness throughout the eons. In the first edition of *On the Origin of Species*, Darwin claimed that "as natural selection works solely by and for the good of each being, all corporeal and mental endowments will tend to progress towards perfection."[53] In history the Judeo-Christian tradition offered the hope for worldly perfection, the fulfillment of the millennium. History generally was a story of movement toward goals resulting in more complex social organizations and indisputable progress in at least one area—knowledge of the time span of history itself. A sense of progress lies behind the grand historical narratives of nineteenth-century thought: Hegel's view of history as the realization of the idea of freedom, Comte's theory of the three progressive stages in the history of knowledge (theological, metaphysical, positivist), Kierkegaard's three progressive stages on the way to true Christian faith (aesthetic, ethical, religious), Marx's theory of the dialectical advance of history toward communism, Darwin's theory of evolution in the direction of what is increasingly well adapted and reproductively successful, and Spencer's notions of the survival of the fittest and evolution from simple to complex. Although Nietzsche rejected any collective historical improvement of human life, his exhortative positive philosophy charted a way to the "higher man," or overman, as a way to an increasingly meaningful existence. The purpose of Freud's psychoanalytic therapy was to make progress toward mental health, while Jung viewed individual life as a process of increasing individuation.

6. Human beings individually experience progress in many simple acts such as drinking in order to quench thirst, studying in order to pass an exam, or practicing a musical instrument in order to improve.

Thus, the tendency to view history, evolution, and individual lives in matters big and small as stories of progress, or at least of accomplishment, is an abiding temptation. Although that temptation has sometimes substituted for careful argumentation and led to crudely self-congratulatory Whiggish history, it is built into the primordial intentionality and purposiveness of human experience and shapes the way we view our own life in time as well as the larger sweep of history. We judge as progressive whatever satisfies our immediate desires, resolves our daily challenges, and realizes our endlessly projected goals. The widespread belief in some such design to life is further evidence of this insistent explanatory instinct.

These six considerations address the difficult problem of integrating the history of science, which clearly progresses in some aspects, with the history of literature, which does not reveal even an overriding direction or meaning, let alone a story of progress. They also apply to another body of evidence, the systems of thought that make other historically distinctive contributions to the understanding of causality—psychoanalysis, linguistics, philosophy of language, sociology, cybernetics, systems theory, and existential philosophy. These systems of thought aspired to the rigor of observational sciences but based their explanations more on interpretations, philosophical arguments, and historical narratives. Freud, Saussure, Wittgenstein, Derrida, Durkheim, Weber, Nietzsche, Wiener, Bertalanffy, and Sartre contributed to the specificity of causal understanding of various human behaviors and experiences by raising awareness, redirecting attention, and clarifying thought about a host of issues and therefore must be characterized as progressive.

Although these considerations justify using scientific, philosophical, and literary evidence together in support of my argument about the increasing specificity of causal knowledge, these clashing sources nevertheless generated interpretive instability that, I must concede, would not go away. However, to generalize about the history of such a complex concept as causality across almost two centuries demands a broad evidentiary base and bold interpretations. Without the novels, this history would lack dramatic action to flesh it out in observable movements and lack the voices of the past in dialogue to articulate its living actuality; without the systems of thought, it would lack evidence from some of the most probing and influential examinations of the human condition made during the years of this study; and without the science, it would lack concrete evidence for the essentially progressive movement of historical change that an argument about increasing specificity implies. The discoveries of germs, genes, hormones, peptides, and neurotransmitters were specific, datable events that—yes—improved the way scientists understood the causes of disease, hereditary transmission, sexual desire, emotion, and neural transmission. Novelists from both periods were perceptive observers of scientific achievements in their own times, but only the moderns had access to such findings of modern science that made it possible to understand these phenomena more precisely and fully.

The novels I use for evidence to make that argument are not so much typical of their time as representative. By this I mean that novels render the causes of murder in ways that are historically marked in that some of the causal analyses in them are unlikely, if not inconceivable, in other historical periods.[54] Thus in Zola's *Germinal* (1885), Etienne kills because of a hereditary taint from his remote human ancestors, an explanation that is unlikely in a serious modern novel. Conversely, in *Compulsion* (1956), Meyer Levin explains a murder by two young men as caused by their childhood sexual traumas, an explanation that appears nowhere in the cultural historical record before Freud, as far as I have been able to determine.

Another reason for viewing these novels as representative of the times in which they were written or set is that many of their authors took pains to craft a sense of historical verisimilitude and create murderers based on real people—beginning with Stendhal's *The Red and the Black*, subtitled "Chronicle of 1830" and based on a real-life model for Julien Sorel. A few of the many other fictional murderers with actual models include Vautrin in *Old Goriot*, Raskolnikov in *Crime and Punishment*, Pozdnyshev in "The Kreutzer Sonata," Clyde Griffiths in *An American Tragedy*, Moosbrugger in *The Man without Qualities*, Bigger Thomas in *Native Son*, Jame Gumb in *The Silence of the Lambs*, and the titular murderers in *Eugene Aram*, *The Count of Monte Cristo*, *Thérèse Raquin*, *The Picture of Dorian Gray*, and *Lafcadio's Adventures*.[55] In the modern period a new genre also appeared—"nonfiction novels" based closely on actual murders, as in Levin's *Compulsion* and Truman Capote's *In Cold Blood*.

These novels also document historical change in that they function as a filter for current scientific explanations of behavior. Reductive scientific explanations deaden fiction, so novelists glean scientific ideas from wide reading and everyday experience to understand how they are disseminated in popular culture and shape everyday understanding of human action; then they sift and adapt those ideas to make their novels plausible. Dreiser, for example, studied new theories about tropisms and hormones, which he wove into his rendering of Clyde's murder of Roberta in *An American Tragedy* in order to evoke a sense of contemporary historical actuality and draw authority from the current state of scientific understanding. In *Berlin Alexanderplatz: The Story of Franz Biberkopf* (1929), Alfred Döblin explained one murder, ironically, with reference to the causal action of the pituitary, thyroid, suprarenal, and prostate glands. DeLillo invoked neurotransmitters to help explain a murder in *White Noise*. Dozens of novelists drew on Freud to explain how adult character and actions derive from childhood experiences and are shaped by unconscious mental processes, while Thomas Pynchon satirized Pavlovian sex conditioning in *Gravity's Rainbow* (1973). In *A Philosophical Investigation* (1992), Philip Kerr mined Wittgenstein's philosophy of language in crafting a main character, actually named Ludwig Wittgenstein, who attempted to put into practice the philosopher's ideas (grotesquely misinterpreted) by committing serial homicide.

I rely primarily on novels by male authors about male murderers, because my method is comparative and requires controlling variables to focus on historical change. To add female writers and female murderers would have multiplied those variables and reduced the sharpness of the historical comparisons. Moreover, in fact and fiction the majority of murderers are male, as are almost all serial murderers. I do, however, include a few female novelists or female murderers when the evidence is clearly marked historically: for example, the female author Mary Braddon, who used Victorian theories of heredity and insanity to explain the attempted murder by a female in *Lady Audley's Secret* (1862); and the female serial murderer in Laurence Sanders's *The Third Deadly Sin* (1981), who kills men and mutilates their genitals at twenty-seven-day intervals because of hormonal problems that are detected by endocrinological and hematological analyses that would have been impossible a century earlier.

The interpretive problem of authorial distance further challenged my synthetic objective. Historically revealing ideas can be uttered by a character in a novel who speaks for the author (Pozdnyshev in "The Kreutzer Sonata"), by a character who does not speak for the author (Bill Sikes in *Oliver Twist*), by a character who explicitly subverts the author's ideas (Edouard in *The Counterfeiters*), by two characters who formulate the author's ideas in dialogue (Julius and Lafcadio in *Lafcadio's Adventures*), by a first-person narrator (Humbert Humbert in *Lolita*), by a third-person narrator (in Kafka's *The Trial*) who occupies varying distances from the author's "actual" view, by the author in an interview about a novel (DeLillo in "American Blood"), by a journal entry (Gide in his

Journals), or by a subsequent essay that explains what the author had in mind (Richard Wright in "How 'Bigger' Was Born"). While I was aware of the different evidentiary value of these various sources, I did not make a systematic assessment of them, which would have enormously complicated my synthetic task and cluttered my presentation of evidence.

This book is organized in chapters on changing ideas from Europe and America about causal factors. Their classification and ordering is based on three guidelines: the chronology of when factors effect their causal action (ancestry before childhood and language), physical factors before mental (sexuality and emotion before ideas), and individual factors before collective (mind before society). Of course, these orderings are arbitrary and these distinctions are not absolute: language is acquired in childhood, sexuality and emotion have a mental aspect, and society shapes mental development just as it shapes social pressure. These ordering principles and the classifications they determine are therefore approximate and interrelated, neither precisely delineated nor mutually exclusive. Changing ideas about these factors emerged in nineteenth- and twentieth-century modes, which, for purposes of conciseness, I refer to as *Victorian* and *modern*. Victorian does not denote specifically English developments or any sexual morality; I use it because the period to which it refers, 1837–1901, approximates my periodization of this earlier stretch of time, 1830–1900. Modern denotes the entire twentieth century, including developments that some critics call postmodern.

Each chapter surveys changing ideas about a different causal circumstance or motive for murder in novels supported by developments in the new sciences or disciplines that are its intellectual pivot. These shifts are about causality in general, not just the causality of murder, and so they are drawn from the natural and social sciences, as well as from novels and systems of thought. Their groupings in my chapters are: ancestry with genetics, childhood with psychoanalysis and psychohistory, language with philosophy of language and linguistics, sexuality with sexology and endocrinology, emotion with economics (for greed) and physiology (for emotion generally), mind with neuroscience and psychiatry, society with sociology, and ideas with existential philosophy (primarily Nietzsche's).

Causality, or causation (the terms are used interchangeably), is a metaphysical (or ontological) concept that refers to actual cause-and-effect relations between events or to dynamic interactions and processes in the world; it is also an epistemological concept that refers to knowledge involved in answering "why" questions about those interactions and processes. These two definitions are circular, because causality is a fundamental aspect of human existence in the sense that all human beings necessarily have some elementary causal understanding, such as, for example, that dropping an object will cause it to fall or that running into a tree will cause pain. The philosopher and historian of causality in science and medicine K. Codell Carter concurred emphatically in noting "how totally pointless, hopeless, and downright silly it is to think one can ever state *precisely* what it is for one thing to cause another."[56] Although that elemental sense is universal, elaborations of it vary culturally and emerge in historically changing ways which are the focus of my study. *Human causality* refers to causes of human action and ways of understanding them. Other terms in this study refer to aspects of human causality. *Motives* are inner impulses toward action, while *intentions* are object-oriented plans for fulfilling the motive. Causal understanding can also include *purposes* for actions directed toward the realization of goals. *Reasons* are the rational grounds for behavior and may form part of *explanations* that answer causal questions. Explanations may include a broad range of factors such as universal covering laws and a specification of initial conditions, a single decisive factor such as an icy road in a car crash, or a mix of factors such as heredity, desire, belief, childhood background, and social pressure.

Causal knowledge is most specific at the molecular level, less so at the cellular level, and extremely complex and uncertain at the behavioral level, generating in the modern period many new unanswered questions about the way in which molecular or cellular entities cause gross behavior. This increasing uncertainty at higher levels of complexity is also a function of the phenomenon of emergent properties. This concept refers to the fact that at higher levels of complexity properties emerge that cannot be predicted from lower levels. For example, a precise understanding of the properties of protons, neutrons, and electrons would not enable one to predict the properties of combinations of those subatomic components into atoms of oxygen and hydrogen, and a precise understanding of the properties of those atoms would not enable one to predict the properties of molecules of water such as its surface tension and boiling point, and so on to cells, individual behavior, and group behavior. The phenomenon of emergent properties reveals a central methodological problem in this history: the impossibility of achieving a fully integrated history of causal analysis that would include subatomic, atomic, molecular, biological, individual psychological, and collective social causation.

That problem is further complicated by the different sorts of phenomena treated by novelists, philosophers, natural scientists, and social scientists. While they are all concerned with causality, they approach it in radically different ways with different purposes and different criteria for precision, evidence, and argumentation. A few novelists draw on scientific findings, while the arrow of influence almost never goes the other way.[57] Formal thinkers such as Darwin, Spencer, Lamarck, Mendel, Weismann, Nietzsche, Freud, Wittgenstein, Sartre, and Derrida exert some direct influence on murder novelists, and I have been attentive to such influences.

This study is primarily an interpretive history of changing ideas about causality (the epistemology of causality), but such a history cries out for some causal explanation of those changing ideas based on changing ways in which people actually experienced causality (the ontology of causality). While my primary focus is on those ideas, in every chapter (usually at the end) I do consider concrete historical developments that helped shape new experiences of causality as well as thinking about it. The major concrete historical influence is the increasing division of intellectual labor and analytical precision that resulted from the rise of new academic disciplines in universities and from the increasing specialization among professionals such as doctors and lawyers, whose diagnoses and briefs rested ultimately on causal analysis. A related influence is the increasing complexity and interdependence of social relations and market activities in cities, which also increased reliance on a wide range of highly specialized professionals. The expansion of capitalism in scale and scope brought more remote and complex productive and distributive forces to bear on local activities. Industrial production became the consequence of ever more temporally and spatially remote psychological, social, technological, and economic determinants, creating a potential market for new professionals who were trained to analyze specific causal actions.

Among the most concrete historical influences on the experience of causality are the new transportation and communication technologies. Across the years of my study the telegraph, railroad, telephone, automobile, airplane, cinema, radio, television, computer, and Internet accelerated communication and transportation across time and space to create new paths and variable speeds of transportation and information flow, including computerized global communications networks, which reworked the experience of causality for everyone. The same communication and transportation technologies that expanded the spatial and temporal range of causal action in social relations and economic undertakings also revolutionized how individuals became motivated to commit murder and carried it out. A number of fictional murderers, and especially serial murderers, found their victims or became worked up about something they learned about them from modern communication technologies such as newspapers, movies, and television—media they also used to follow investigations into their own murderous acts and observe their growing public reputations afterward. In Richard Wright's *Native Son* (1940), Bigger Thomas first becomes attracted to the woman he will eventually kill when he and his friends masturbate while looking at her in a newsreel shown in a movie theater, and he commits a cover-up murder of someone else in reaction to the attack on him in the newspapers while he is still at large.[58] One murderer from Truman Capote's *In Cold Blood* (1965) dreamed of "fast money" from finding hidden treasures he learned about in travel magazines and movies such as *The Treasure of Sierra Madre*, which he had seen eight times. The serial killer in Kerr's *A Philosophical Investigation* (1992) revels in the fact that "you kill enough people, you get your story in the papers all the time" (176). In DeLillo's *Libra* (1988), Lee Harvey Oswald targets JFK by watching him on television and then imagines himself being seen live on TV as he is being shot by Jack Ruby. In Thomas Harris's *Red Dragon*, a serial killer finds his victims from the home movies he processes in the laboratory where he works and makes a movie of his slaughter of a family, which he then uses to arouse himself for subsequent killings.[59]

In real life, the causal role of media technology is operative in copycat killings, terrorism, and the murder of media celebrities and political leaders—including, most famously, the assassination of John Lennon in 1980 by Mark David Chapman and the attempted assassination of Ronald Reagan in 1981 by John Hinckley, who was morbidly inspired by the movie *Taxi Driver* and the movie actress Jodie Foster. After seeing the movie *A Clockwork Orange*, Arthur Bremer changed his assassination target from Richard Nixon to George Wallace. The motivation for September 11 was likely shaped in part by the conspicuous American values, economy, foreign policy, and lifestyle that were communicated around the world by television and movies and symbolized by the World Trade Center.

Sometimes the most important things in history are the most obvious. I had mixed feelings about my argument for this huge subject turning out to be as obvious as a cliché—that the more one knows, the more one realizes how little one knows. Its obviousness meant that it was easy to grasp, although it also suggested that the argument might be trivial. But the force of my argument about the specificity-uncertainty dialectic is not its unexpected nature but its broad applicability, which implies that there just might be a unifying sense to the history of such a fundamental concept as causality that grounds many natural and social sciences and also shapes how novelists over the past 170 years made their characters' actions plausible. My argument integrates the various modes of changing thought about the increasing specificity, multiplicity, complexity, probability, and uncertainty that are evident in a wide range of sources from genetics, neuroscience, and psychoanalysis to sociology, existential philosophy, and murder novels. That integration also embraces a set of concrete developments in the ontology of causality, as it was shaped by the increasing division of labor among research professionals, the increasingly complex and interdependent life in modern cities and industrial capitalism, and new technologies of communication and transportation. Making that argument involved a comparative cultural history of thinking about the nature of causal explanation across two ages—Victorian to modern. The scale of that undertaking obliged me to focus on the act of murder. That approach made it possible to identify a coherent evidentiary base for a broad cultural history of causality, and while the overall argument about that history was as simple as a cliché, its elaboration proved to be richly varied and endlessly surprising.

1

Ancestry

IN THE COURSE of the nineteenth century, as industrialism and urbanism transformed life beyond recognition and beyond conventional explanations, new disciplines emerged that looked increasingly to the past for causal understanding of human origins and the meaning of life. Geologists and paleontologists found evidence of evolution in the earth's strata and the fossil record; anthropologists and archaeologists dug information out of buried civilizations; philologists charted the emergence of modern languages from ancient ones; biologists looked for the origins of human anatomy in embryological development; and psychologists sought the origins of adult mental life in the mind of the child. The century's most influential thinkers developed historical approaches to knowledge; Hegel, Comte, Marx, Darwin, Spencer, and Freud interpreted how things came to be as a result of conflict and resolution out of the way things were. The scale of this shift has been forcefully assessed by Carl Schorske: "Never in the history of European culture had Clio enjoyed such preeminence—not to say hegemony—as in the mid-nineteenth century. . . . History's mode of thought and its temporal perspective penetrated most fields of learning, while models of the past inspired the nineteenth century's arts."[1]

Victorian personal lives were rooted in an ancestry of dynastic pedigrees and family genealogies, of portrait galleries and photo albums.[2] Expert thinking about the mechanism of ancestral influence diverged widely, but it centered on the erroneous belief that some blending of parents' sexual fluids transmitted to children a blending of their inherited as well as acquired characteristics. The causal force of ancestry loomed large among Victorians, whose ignorance about the mechanism of hereditary transmission fueled exaggerated fears about how children will inherit their ancestors' birth defects, diseases, and vices along with their ideas, property, and social standing. A few of the many Victorian fictional characters who inherit plot-turning financial legacies include Jane Eyre, Pip, Dorothea Brooke, and Jude Fawley, while legacies of degeneration pass to Jonas Chuzzlewit, Jean Des Esseintes, Little Father Time, and Hanno Buddenbrook. Thomas Hardy explained how a simple genealogy could inspire a novelist to flesh out such complex stories: family trees "may be transformed into a palpitating drama . . . and anybody practiced in raising images from such genealogies finds himself unconsciously filling into the framework the motives, passions, and personal qualities."[3] More recently, the critic Patricia Tobin documented the pervasiveness of "the genealogical imperative" in the Victorian novel in which "the individual member is guaranteed both identity and legitimacy through the tracing of his lineage back to the founding father, the family's origin and first cause."[4]

On the ancestral causes of murder, Victorian novelists and researchers explored five periods of time prior to birth: animal ancestry, remote human ancestry, recent human ancestry, moment of conception, and pregnancy.

ANIMAL ANCESTRY

The idea that human beings inherit traits from animal progenitors was supported by recapitulation theory and Darwin's theory of evolution.

Recapitulation emerged in Germany in the early nineteenth century among "teleo-mechanists" who sought to find laws of purposive development based on the differentiation of structures in the developing embryo to show how individual life (ontogeny) paralleled the history of the species (phylogeny).[5] In 1821 Johann Meckel argued that the embryonic development of complex animals recapitulates and ascends the hierarchy of the organizational forms of lower animals from fish to reptile to mammal. "The development of the individual organism obeys the same laws as the development of the whole animal series: that is to say, the higher animal, in its gradual evolution, essentially passes through the same permanent organic stages which lie below it."[6] In 1836 the American biologist Louis Agassiz extended recapitulation into a triple parallel between fossil history, embryological development, and rank in classification, all of which documented the animal origins of human existence.[7] In 1857 he concluded, "The phases of development of all animals correspond to the order of succession of their extinct representatives in past geological times."[8]

Some scientists viewed recapitulation as a function of a divine purpose or life force inherent in organic matter; for others it came from the repetition of simple chemical or biological processes repeated in ever more complex patterns. But in spite of all the controversy, recapitulationists agreed that human instinct, anatomy, intelligence, and memory derive from animal ancestors, are recapitulated during embryological development, and are retained with modifications in adult human beings.

Recapitulation enjoyed broad support in the last third of the nineteenth century. Its most famous German proponent was Ernst Haeckel, whose *General Morphology* (1866) was based on a biogenetic law that ontogeny is a compressed recapitulation of the adult stages of ancestry and therefore is caused by phylogeny.[9] His *Natural History of Man* (1868) depicted an evolutionary tree pasted over with markers for human ancestors ranging from tiny organisms at the bottom of the trunk up to humans at the top branches. The English read about recapitulation in Henry Maudsley's *Body and Mind* (1870): "every human brain does, in the course of its development, pass through the same stages as the brains of other vertebrate animals, [and] the stages of its development in the womb may be considered the abstract and brief chronicle of a series of developments that have gone through countless ages in nature."[10]

Animal ancestry became downright threatening after the appearance of *On the Origin of Species* in 1859. This book, which revolutionized conceptions of human nature, had, amazingly, only one sentence about humans: "Light will be thrown on the origin of man and his history."[11] The rest was primarily about animals, but many Victorians were shocked by its implications about the origin of human beings.

To some troubled observers, Darwin replaced the creative hand of God with the germ plasm of an ape. In place of a comforting belief in the divine creation of each species, Darwin proposed a discomforting first cause by common descent from some ape-like ancestor or even, before that, from some microorganism drifting through primeval ooze.[12] All species may have "one progenitor," Darwin hypothesized, and may "have descended from one ancient but unseen parent."[13] Thomas Huxley linked the human brain phylogenetically to a rat's by arguing in *Man's Place in Nature* (1863) that "Nature has provided us . . . with an almost complete series of gradations from brains little higher than that of a rodent, to brains little lower than that of man" (115).

The abundant evidence for evolution from an ape-like ancestor radically demoted human beings from their traditional position as the pinnacle of all life. Some evolutionists became obsessed with finding the "missing link" in the ancestral chain, which could complete the line back to that transition creature between animal and man. To that end, much excitement was generated in 1857, before *Origin of Species*, by the discovery of the Neanderthal skull with prominent eyebrow ridges, which the paleontologist Richard Owen concluded were similar to gorilla eyebrow ridges and therefore proof that the missing link was ape-like. The even more primitive Java man was discovered by Eugene Dubois in 1891. In *The Expression of the Emotions in Man and Animals* (1872), Darwin linked humans to animals with pictures of frightened cats with bristled fur and angry dogs showing bared teeth. In between man and animals, he speculated, "our semi-human progenitors uncovered their canine teeth when prepared for battle, as we still do when feeling ferocious."[14] Following Darwin, the field of comparative psychology began comparing human mental activity with that of lower animals.

Many Victorians associated animal origins with the instinct to kill. Before Darwin, Tennyson's *In Memoriam* (1850) evoked the killing ground of nature with a disturbing image of "Nature, red in tooth and claw." While natural selection was phrased in euphemistic terms about favorable adaptations and chances of survival, it could more accurately have been termed evolution by a killing of the weak, sick, and congenitally deformed. Darwin offered a striking example: "It may be difficult," he wrote, "but we ought to admire the savage instinctive hatred of the queen-bee, which urges her instantly to destroy the young queens her daughters as soon as born . . . for undoubtedly this is for the good of the community."[15]

Hugo invoked animal atavism in *Les Misérables* (1862) to explain the behavior of his thief Jean Valjean: "it was not the man who had stolen; it was the animal which, from habit and instinct, had brutally set its foot on the coin" (117). Atavistic murderous impulses wreak havoc over generations in Zola's novels about the Rougon-Macquart family. The title of one of them, *La bête humaine* (1890), refers to the animal in humans as well as humans' beastly nature. The novel's main character, Jacques, inherited a homicidal impulse that is triggered by sexual arousal, but its deep source is a hereditary taint that originated with an event from the time of his animal forebears: "he had been carried away by inherited violence, the instinct for murder that in the primeval forests had hurled one beast onto another" (332). His lovemaking with Séverine, whom he eventually kills, is a search for sexual release in killing achieved "with the same agonizing pleasure as beasts disembowelling each other in mating" (235). Elsewhere Zola suggests that the taint may derive from sometime later "when man strangled wild beasts in the forest," a time of "women-devouring savages" reenacting some "resentment passed down from male to male since the first betrayal in the depths of some cave" (237, 66, 67).

REMOTE HUMAN ANCESTRY

The causal function of remote human ancestry figured large in Victorian novels, which drew on Lamarck, Darwin, Lombroso, and theorists of organic memory.

Lamarck's theory of the hereditary transmission of acquired ancestral characteristics and experiences in evolution is a checklist of Victorian values; it holds that evolution follows from human intentions and efforts of the will and from the accumulated residue of utilitarian use and disuse to give a meaningful direction and overall purpose to the progressive achievement of accumulated habits and traditions from distant ancestry to the present.[16] Although this "soft" theory of heredity based on the transmission of acquired characteristics was challenged by Darwin's "hard" theory of natural selection through random selection, which did not allow for the transmission of acquired characteristics, Lamarckism prevailed throughout the century. Darwin himself repeatedly contradicted his own hard formulation to include explanations of how parental experiences might be transmitted.

The theory of organic memory relied on a Lamarckian mechanism of hereditary transmission and on recapitulation theory to argue that new living forms remember and in some compressed form recapitulate the experiences of their ancestors.[17] Organic memory was popularized in Germany in a lecture by Ewald Hering in 1870, *On Memory as a General Function of Organized Matter*, which defined memory as a basic reproductive capability of all living matter. The theory aligned memory with heredity and suggested that the entire history of the race was evident in the individual memory, which retains and succinctly recapitulates life experiences of ancestors. In 1878 the British novelist Samuel Butler incorporated the theory in arguing that the small ovum from which we have sprung "has a potential recollection of all that has happened to each one of its ancestors."[18] In 1880 Butler quoted from

Hering's article to underscore the ancestral foundation of organic memory, which he eventually incorporated into his fiction: "We must bear in mind that every organized being now in existence represents the last link of an inconceivably long series of organisms, which come down in direct line of descent, and of which each has inherited a part of the acquired characteristics of its predecessors."[19] The theory grounded human causality in a dynamic embodied memory that united mind and body in a sequential development through species, races, nations, and family ancestries.

Darwin's original formulation of natural selection was a theory of ancestral influence based on the progressive accumulation of slight and successive variations. Although he accepted that some variations were random, he could not accept that all were random, unaffected by ancestral experience. The first edition of *Origin of Species* held that no acquired characteristics were inherited, but subsequent editions and later publications became increasingly Lamarckian. He explained this channel of inheritance with his theory of pangenesis. In sexual reproduction, every cell in the body produces tiny gemmules that register the experience of that cell and then flow through the blood to the gonads, where they form germ cells that contain gemmules from all other body cells, at all periods of development, even from past generations. During fertilization these gemmules are somehow combined from the male and female parent to produce progeny. In 1868 he wrote, "It is probable that hardly a change of any kind affects either parent without some mark being left on the germ."[20] Like so many Victorians, he was unable to believe that the prodigious efforts of a lifetime become extinct with the individual's death.

With solid Darwinian influence, British psychiatry affirmed clear ties between heredity and crime. Darwin had applied his theory of atavism to warn that "some of the worst dispositions which occasionally . . . make their appearance in families, may perhaps be reversion to a savage state."[21] In 1870 the Scottish prison surgeon J. B. Thomson argued that there is a distinct criminal class of "demi-civilized savages" who are "born into crime." These hereditary criminals frequently inherit other disorders such as epilepsy and insanity and tend to be incurable.[22] In 1873 Maudsley held that "in consequence of evil ancestral influences individuals are born with such a flaw or warp of nature that all the care in the world will not prevent them from being vicious or criminal. . . . No one can escape the tyranny of his organization."[23] In 1893 W. Bevan Lewis wrote that a large proportion of criminals "are the degenerate relics of an ancestry who have passed through the more acute stages of mental derangement."[24] Such overheated rhetoric of ineluctable hereditarian etiology can be found at will in late Victorian journals dealing with mental illness and crime.

Italy produced Europe's most influential theorist of the hereditary causes of crime, Cesare Lombroso. In *L'uomo deliquente* (1876) (*Criminal Man*), he adduced massive evidence to argue that evolutionary atavisms cause the notorious "born criminal," who reveals animal ancestry with visible "stigmata" such as ape-like pointed ears and a protruding jaw. Victorians were eager to displace the etiology of crime from current social conditions to remote human or even animal ancestral origins over which modern society had no control and for which it bore no responsibility. With such a theory, officials could treat born criminals as a race apart, their blood tainted by sins committed in the distant past.

Victorian novels are rife with causal accounts of murderers based on remote ancestry backed by the theories of Lamarck, Hering, Darwin, or Lombroso. To explain the murderous personality of Jonas Chuzzlewit, Dickens claimed that "the more extended the ancestry, the greater the amount of violence." Throughout English history "the Chuzzlewits were actively connected with diverse slaughterous conspiracies," and the arch-traitor Guy Fawkes himself might have been "a scion of this remarkable stock" (51–52). In *The House of Seven Gables* (1851), Nathaniel Hawthorne invoked a two-century-old curse of Matthew Maule that God would give his unjust persecutor, Colonel Pyncheon, blood to drink. The colonel dies, choking on his own blood in an apoplectic fit, as does his equally evil descendant, Jaffrey Pyncheon, while sitting under the portrait of the colonel, whom he resembles. Although Hawthorne indicated that these deaths may have been from natural causes, he implied some remote ancestral etiology with the symbolism of family resemblance in old portraits and with revenge for a two-hundred-year-old injustice through the fulfillment of a blood curse. The preface made explicit Hawthorne's moral purpose to show "that the wrong-doing of one generation lives into the successive ones."

In Paul Bourget's *The Disciple* (1889), the murderous hero, Robert Breslou, confesses that he harbors "hates formerly felt by those whose sons we are and who continue to pursue, through us, combats of heart begun centuries ago" (181). Elsewhere he identifies his hereditary origins: "Persuaded as I am of the laws of prehistoric atavism, I aroused in myself . . . the rudimentary mind of the ancestral brute, of the man of the caves from whom I, as well as the rest of mankind, am descended" (245). The hero of Zola's *Germinal* (1885) kills a rival as the "blood lust rose up in him and his will-power was swept away before the onrush of his hereditary taint" (478). In *Nana* (1880), Zola's heroine is "descended from four or five generations of drunkards, her blood tainted by a cumulative inheritance of poverty and drink." Her heredity has taken the form of an exaggeration of the sexual instinct which leads to death, if not murder, as she becomes "a ferment of destruction, unwittingly corrupting and disorganizing Paris between her snow-white thighs" (221). Frank Norris invoked Zolaesque rhetoric in *McTeague* (1899), about a man driven to murder by his remote ancestry. Below the good in McTeague "ran the foul stream of hereditary evil." "The vices and sins of his father and of his father's father, to the third and fourth and five hundredth generation, tainted him. The evil of an entire race flowed in his veins" (19).

In *Dracula* (1897), Bram Stoker exploits the imagery of predatory impulses inherited from ancient times through the blood with Count Dracula, who assimilated his urge to attack from the four-hundred-year-old ancestral blood that flowed in his veins. The pedigree of his murderous instinct hovers between ancient human and animal, as in one vampire outing he changes into a bat and crawls like a lizard down the wall of his castle. His victim Lucy devolves into a savage beast who sucks the blood of children. Although Dracula ingests his victims' blood rather than transfuses it, Stoker implies that somehow it got into his veins. For all the dangers explored in *Dracula*, Stoker was unaware of the danger of a transfusion from someone with a different blood type. The specificity of blood types was pioneered within four years of the publication of the novel by an Austrian researcher who distinguished blood types, labeled A, B, and O, which explained why fatalities following blood transfusions were so common throughout the nineteenth century.[25]

Hardy's *Tess of the d'Urbervilles* (1891) is about a Victorian murderess harking back to remote ancestors. Parental pressure sets tragedy in motion after Tess's father learns that he is descended from an ancient aristocratic family. First she is raped by Alec, posing as her "cousin" and a d'Urberville. For her rape by a sham relative Hardy offers an ironic explanation: "doubtless some of Tess d'Urberville's mailed ancestors rollicking home from a fray had dealt the same measure even more ruthlessly towards peasant girls of their time" (119). Since Alec is no blood relative, this explanation is invalid, even by nineteenth-century ways of thinking, but still Hardy offered it as part of the explanatory mix. Tess's husband Angel Claire tells her of the legend that some d'Urberville of the sixteenth or seventeenth century committed a dreadful crime, and later she learns that it concerned "a murder, committed by one of the family, centuries ago" (280, 437). On their wedding night Angel takes Tess to one of her family's dilapidated mansions where she sees a portrait gallery of her ancestors with treacherous narrow eyes and large teeth. After learning of her rape, Angel charges that "decrepit families imply decrepit wills" and accuses Tess of being "the belated seedling of an effete aristocracy" (302). After learning that she killed Alec, Angel wonders "what obscure strain in the d'Urberville blood had led to this aberration" (475).

In 1890, while writing *Tess*, Hardy read August Weismann. There he could have found scientific evidence against the Lamarckian notion that an actual murder centuries earlier could influence anyone in a later generation to commit a specific deed such as a murder. Still, in successive revisions of the novel, he made Tess increasingly subject to hereditary degeneration.[26] Nine months after publishing the novel, Hardy told an interviewer: "The murder that Tess commits is the hereditary quality . . . working out in this impoverished descendant of a once noble family."[27] Although Hardy distanced himself from Angel's theorizing about ancestral destiny causing a specific murder, he endorsed popular views that governed the Victorian belief that the force of ancestral influence somehow coursed through the blood and determined the workings of fate.

Recent Human Ancestry

The causal role of recent ancestry derived from the theories about remote ancestry as well as degeneration theory. Historians and politicians made depressing analyses of current problems and dire predictions for the future, drawing evidence of degeneration from physics, medicine, evolutionary biology, sociology, psychiatry, and criminal anthropology.

In a stunning essay of 1852, the physicist William Thomson (Lord Kelvin) generalized the second law of thermodynamics into "a universal tendency in nature to the dissipation of mechanical energy." In conclusion he made the ominous claim that "within a finite period of time past, the earth must have been, and within a finite period of time to come the earth must again be, unfit for the habitation of man as at present constituted, unless operations have been or are to be performed, which are impossible under the laws to which the known operations going on at present in the material world are subject."[28] This law hypothesized that the entropy of the universe is increasing and consequently that warm bodies tend to lose heat to cooler bodies. As a result, the sun will cool, and life on earth will freeze to death. In medicine, discoveries about contagion from the 1860s to the 1880s revealed how germs were supposedly pooling in ever greater concentrations and virulence, causing hereditary degeneration. The apparent rise in tuberculosis and syphilis, spiked by what many thought to be an overworked and oversexed population, seemed to demonstrate the spread of killer bugs everywhere from congested cities to the individual bloodstream, from crowded brothels to marriage beds. In a letter of 1881 the influential French historian Hippolyte Taine wrote of "the morbid germ which entered the blood of a diseased society [and] caused fever, delirium, and revolutionary convulsions."[29] Evolutionary theory, specifically Darwin's theory of reversion to earlier forms, was also used to explain degenerative tendencies. Social thinkers believed that environmental poisons and social pressures somehow made their way into germ cells (whatever they were), further intensifying degeneration from parent to child. From about 1885 to World War I, as Robert Nye concluded, degeneration theory "asserted practically an imperialistic sway over all public and professional discourse concerning individual and social pathologies."[30]

Psychiatrists in France, United States, Germany, and England saw degeneration progressively corrupting ancestral lines with physical, mental, and moral deterioration. In 1857 the French psychiatrist B. A. Morel introduced the term *dégénérescence* in a treatise that outlined how a family line could die out over four generations, beginning with nervousness and moral depravity in the first generation, neurosis and alcoholism in the second, defective intellect and mental disorders in the third, and congenital deformities and sterility in the fourth.[31] This sequence was caused by myriad biological and social factors and could effect most anything—hernias, alcoholism, impotence, suicide, moral corruption, insanity, and crime. This confusion of pathological scenarios was shunted through a theory that centered on the explanatory concept of degeneration, which became a catchall for the apparent ills of the age: overwork and laziness, hyperrefinement and primitivism, hypernervousness and nervous exhaustion, boredom and mania, premature senility and infantilism, English homosexuality and French infertility. Charles Féré applied it to crime in *Dégénérescence et criminalité* (1888), which added a poisonous environment along with a hereditary lesion to the mounting list of factors liable to cause a hereditary taint in "the neuropathic family" that breeds insanity and crime.[32] As the historian Daniel Pick concluded, *dégénérescence* became "the ultimate signifier of pathology. . . . It explained everything and nothing as it moved back and forth between the clinic, the novel, the newspaper, and the government investigation."[33]

Etiologies of degeneration abound in period fiction: Huysmans, Laforge, Maeterlinck, and Péladan. Source material on degeneration came from psychiatric case histories and court records, from Baudelaire's poems and the Goncourts' journals, from Bourget's essays and Zola's novels.[34] The murderess in Zola's *Thérèse Raquin* (1867) has inherited the "degenerative" blood of her dangerously seductive mother. Thérèse burns for revenge against the aunt who adopted her and made her live with her sickly son, whom Thérèse is forced to marry (and ultimately murders), fulfilling a degenerate ancestral destiny.

American psychiatry also emphasized somatic etiology along with hereditary degeneration. Researchers fused these approaches by claiming that heredity caused structural malformations, if not actual lesions, that created a susceptibility to physical disease and pathogenic social pressures, which in turn could trigger crime. In 1872 Charles Brace offered such a grab-bag causal explanation of a nine-year-old with criminal tendencies: "The 'gemmules' or latent tendencies, or forces, or cells of her immediate ancestors were in her system and working in her blood, producing irresistible effects on her brain, nerves, and mental emotions."[35] In *"The Jukes": A Study in Crime, Pauperism, Disease, and Heredity* (1877), Richard Dugdale made one American family synonymous with hereditary degeneration. He traced reversion and atavism in the Juke family, all with "Juke blood," that produced a "criminal stock" including 1,200 bastards, beggars, prostitutes, syphilitics, thieves, and murderers.[36] References to the Jukes were common among later thinkers who recommended removing the hereditary taint in society by forced sterilization of criminals, a procedure later called negative eugenics.[37]

In 1900 August Drähms, the resident chaplain at San Quentin Prison, explained the genesis of an "instinctive homicidal proclivity" with an adaptation of Weismann's theory of the continuity of the germ plasm: "In almost every instance it is the direct entailment of a pre-criminalistic stock whose antecedent moral ideals were low, and whose nature had already received the inviolable impress of the pregenital taint to be transmitted to the descendant with the unerring certainty characteristic of Nature in all her ways." The "congenital offender," he concluded, "is the entailed inheritance from ancestral germ-plasm . . . carrying in its current and inoculating that new life with the very germs of theft and murder already stirring in the blood of its progenitor ages back."[38] Such protracted speculation, using ten synonyms for hered-ity in a single sentence, strained to channel the complex etiology of crime through the single concept of hereditary degeneration, supplying medico-psychiatric prestige for a repetitious monocausal explanation. Lacking specific knowledge of the causes of crime based on experimen-tal evidence, Victorians sometimes compensated with rhetorical excess. In 1897 another American psychiatrist linked the singularity of heredi-tary etiology with its universality: "the laws of heredity are fixed and unchangeable as those of gravitation, heat, light, or any others known; and one of those is that like begets like."[39]

In Germany, Max Nordau listed in his immensely popular alarmist tract, *Degeneration* (1892), the signs of cultural and moral decline. With-out the restraint of any clear understanding of the causes of hereditary degeneration, Nordau was free to elaborate a long list of its causes leading to such diverse effects as neurasthenia, immorality, sacrilege, and anarchy as well as Nietzsche's megalomania, Verlaine's erotomania, Huysmans' decadence, Wagner's graphomania, Wilde's aestheticism, and Maeterlinck's mysticism.[40] German playwrights Richard Voss and Wolfgang Kirchback explored the consequences of familial degenera-tion, as did Hauptmann in *Before Sunrise* (1889), which dramatized the effects of familial degeneration from recent ancestry.[41]

In England the essayist George Henry Lewes surveyed research on animals and humans to support the hereditary transmission of acquired habits. To evidence from breeders on how horses transmit acquired "vicious dispositions," Lewes added that "the 'thieving propensity' is transmitted from father to son through generations," and "murder, like talent, runs in families."[42] Maudsley stressed recent ancestry in the causes of degeneration that led to mental illness and crime: "The differ-ent forms of insanity that occur in young children . . . are always trace-able to nervous disease in the preceding generation."[43] He combined Lombroso's criminal anthropology, Morel's stages of *dégénérescence*, and

Darwin's theory of regression with a broad indictment of the increasingly pathogenic effect of urban life.

English fiction abounds with explanations of murder from degenerative ancestors. In *Lady Audley's Secret* (1862), Elizabeth Braddon invoked it to explain the insanity that caused the murderous acts of her heroine: "a hereditary disease transmitted to her from her mother, who had died mad." Audley's secret *is* the hereditary disease that had emerged in her mother at the moment of her birth. When Audley's own child is born, she explains, "the crisis which had been fatal to my mother arose for me . . . the hereditary taint that was in my blood." Later she refers to it as "the hidden taint that I had sucked in with my mother's milk" (348, 393). Her confusion about when she inherited her taint was typical in an age when experts were confused. In a morbid circularity of ancestral causation, she attempts to kill because of a hereditary taint in order to keep secret her hereditary taint.

Even light-handed Oscar Wilde indulged in some heavy-handed ancestral explanation for his murderer in *The Picture of Dorian Gray* (1890). Dorian believes that his "flesh was tainted with the monstrous maladies of the dead." He wanders through a family portrait gallery of beautiful, sensuous women and evil, sinister men "whose blood flowed in his veins" and wonders about his own ancestry: "Had some strange poisonous germ crept from body to body till it had reached his own?" (157, 158). For the Victorians, such speculations were indeed metaphorical, but, compared with moderns, these were taken more seriously and energized by confused theories of heredity. Wilde interrupts the conventional causal scenario of the nineteenth-century portrait, in which real faces determined the images of them in paintings, with a unique portrait of Dorian that itself does the aging and shows the effects of his dissolute life while his actual face remains young and beautiful. Years later, Dorian murders the portrait artist after he asks to see the portrait that Dorian has kept hidden. Dorian suspects that letting the artist discover that the now degenerate face on the portrait has miraculously substituted for the actual degeneration of his own face might somehow end the miracle and restore his actual face to its deservedly degenerate condition marked by his own evil deeds.

Several murderers hunted by Sherlock Holmes are tainted by degenerate ancestry. In "The Speckled Band" (1892), Dr. Roylott, who murders his stepdaughter to prevent her from inheriting money upon her marriage, is the last survivor of one of the oldest Saxon families in

England, which went into progressive decline in "four successive heirs" over a century (possibly modeled after Morel's four generations of *dégénérescence*). The surviving daughter tells Holmes that "violence of temper approaching mania has been hereditary in the men of the family." In "The Final Problem" (1894), Holmes explains that his archrival, Professor Moriarty, "has hereditary tendencies of the most diabolical kind." In *The Hound of the Baskervilles* (1901), a reversion to ancestral evil motivates the murderer Stapleton, who kills the family patriarch for an inheritance. Holmes discovers a portrait of the original bad Baskerville, Hugo, from 1647 with "a lurking devil in his eyes" that resembles Stapleton, "an interesting instance of a throw-back" to primordial family evil (139).[44] In "The Empty House" (1903), Holmes draws on evolutionary reversion to explain the ancestral origins of the murderer Colonel Moran: "There are some trees, Watson, which grow to a certain height and suddenly develop some unsightly eccentricity. You will see it often in humans. I have a theory that the individual represents in his development the whole procession of his ancestors, and that such a sudden turn to good or evil stands for some strong influence which came into the line of his pedigree."

Conrad's *The Secret Agent* (1907) is transitional between Victorian degeneration theory and more modern views of criminal motivation, because it explains the murder with Victorian hereditarianism but mocks the degeneration theory on which it was based. Winnie Verloc stabs her husband to death after she learns that he accidentally killed her mentally retarded younger brother, Stevie, while the two were on an anarchist mission. Conrad's account of Winnie's homicidal act suggests her remote ancestral heritage. "Into that plunging blow . . . Mrs Verloc had put all the inheritance of her immemorial and obscure descent, the simple ferocity of the age of caverns, and the unbalanced nervous fury of the age of bar-rooms" (234). "The age of caverns" is from Victorian theorizing about animal atavisms, although Conrad concentrated on more recent motives, beginning with Winnie's emotional reaction to overhearing how Stevie was blown to bits by the premature explosion of Verloc's bomb. In the end Conrad mocks degeneration theory by presenting it through the cowardly anarchist Ossipan, groping to rationalize his betrayal of Winnie by taking her money and then abandoning her: Ossipan "gazed scientifically at that woman, the sister of a degenerate, a degenerate herself—of a murdering type. He gazed at her and invoked Lombroso" (259). In the twentieth century the idea of explaining any murder from animal ancestry or Lombroso's hereditary criminal type became suspect, and murderers typically did not look the part. In place of the Victorians' linear and positivist explanatory models, moderns offered more multiple, complex, and probabilistic explanations and drew spiritual and artistic sustenance from the increasing uncertainty.

MOMENT OF CONCEPTION

While most Victorian thinkers screened their confusion about ancestral causality by displacing its source to shadowy stretches of family history, remote antiquity, or even caveman times, some focused on the state of the parents during sexual intercourse, which most also believed to be the moment of conception. The historian Charles Rosenberg concluded that in America, "both popular and scientific treatises warned throughout the century of the need to conceive children only when both parents were relaxed, well-rested, and affectionate. Tension, hostility, even exhaustion during intercourse could result in weak and unhealthy offspring."[45] The father was thought to contribute body stature and intellect, while the mother contributed inner organs and temperament. In *Transmission; or Variation of Character through the Mother* (1877), the American essayist Georgiana Kirby argued that both parents' condition during the sex act was important. As she urged hopeful mothers, "Never run the risk of conception when you are sick or over-tired or unhappy; or when your husband is sick, or recovering from sickness, exhausted, or depressed," she warned, "for the bodily condition of the child, its vigor and magnetic qualities, are much affected by conditions ruling this great moment."[46] In 1879 the popular moralist J. H. Kellogg maintained that "the moment of the performance of the generative act" can be a source of crime, because "the unhappy or immoral thoughts of one alone at the critical moment when life is imparted may fix for eternity a foul blot upon a character yet unformed."[47] Others argued that if a mother were intoxicated at the moment of conception the offspring would be an alcoholic; if she were overly aroused, the offspring would be demented. In *The Strange Case of Dr. Jekyll and Mr. Hyde* (1886), Stevenson suggested how seriously Victorians worried about the state of mind of a father at the moment of conception. In a dark-comedic account (no doubt unintended) Dr. Jekyll laments the troubled circumstances of the moment of his "conception" of his perverse double, Mr. Hyde: "had I risked the experiment while under the empire of generous or pious aspirations, all must have been otherwise, and from these agonies of death and birth I had come forth an angel instead of a fiend" (45). Although we have no idea what is in the mixture that brings about the transformation, Stevenson's account strains even Victorian fantasies of generation to suggest that Hyde would have come out generous and pious if Jekyll's mood had been different when he concocted the drug that brought Hyde's character into being.

Victorians emphasized the moment of impregnation, when a lifelong accumulation of physical and psychic experience of both parents was somehow channeled into offspring. Misunderstanding of the mechanism of that process was sometimes veiled by overblown Victorian rhetoric, such as O. S. Fowler's in a popular marriage manual: "And it is this *combined and concentrated*, as well as *high-wrought*, inter-communion of *every physical, every intellectual, every moral element and function of humanity* in generation as it is *by constitution*, which renders the pleasure attendant on this *double* repast so *indescribably* exalted and beatific to those who *spiritually love* each other or in proportion thereto; besides being *the* ONLY means of augmenting and perfecting the intellectuality and morality of its product—redoubling more and more as its handmaid love becomes more and more perfect, and thereby enhances, and also unites, in this holy alliance, faculty after faculty, till finally, when both love and generation have their perfect, and of course *united*, work, they embrace within the wide range of their sanctified enjoyment, every animal, every intellectual, every moral, organ and function, and element of man's entire constitution!"[48] Fowler's frenetic prose replicates the sex act itself: Laced with italics and prolonged as though he could not bear to bring his sentence to an end, it strains to convey the exclusivity and totality of a marriage yielding an offspring that embodies the parents' thoughts, morals, emotions, and physical traits all in proportion to the intensity and spirituality of their love, united under the witness and sanction of God.

PREGNANCY

Even though motherhood was a defining experience of a Victorian woman's life, pregnancy was obscured by the conspiracy of silence about sex.[49] And because pregnancy was the only period without ancestral or direct paternal influence, research on it, conducted mainly by men, was skewed to minimize fears about the father's irrelevance and to maximize concerns about the mother's responsibility.

The idea that the fetus is affected by the mother's thoughts and emotions had appeared in philosophy and fiction since antiquity. Without a clear understanding of sexual reproduction, Victorian experts speculated wildly about how during pregnancy the fetus can also be affected by its mother's blood and sex organs as well as her food and drink. In 1868 William A. Hammond, a New York physician, cited more than a dozen writers who gave examples of pregnant women seeing something shocking and then imprinting a mark of that shock on their baby. One saw a leech on someone's foot and then bore a child with the "mark of a leech" on the same spot. Although Hammond conceded that there was no general acceptance that the mother's mind can directly affect the fetus, "many of the most eminent physiologists hold to it, and among the people at large throughout the civilized world . . . it is received with unquestioning faith." He suggested an explanation: "The blood which circulates through [the fetus's] body is separated from her blood by an exceedingly thin membrane and is thus impressed with the mental characteristics . . . which arise from her brain and nervous system." He therefore urged pregnant women to avoid anger, sexual desire, or envy, as these might adversely affect their children. As he noted, "Within the womb a new connection is set up between the ovum and the mother— that of the blood; and it is through this medium that all impressions from her mind to her offspring must pass."[50]

One pregnant woman's emotional shock explains the genesis of a murderer in E.T.A. Hoffmann's "Mademoiselle de Scudéry" (1816). René Cardillac is a brilliant goldsmith who develops an uncontrollable compulsion to kill customers and repossess the exquisite jewels he has created and sold to them. On being caught, he explains that when his mother was pregnant with him, she had been captivated by an ornately jeweled Spanish cavalier who attempted to seduce her. A struggle ensued and he died. Her resultant trauma caused the unborn child's subsequent homicidal mania. In Oliver Wendell Holmes's novel *Elsie Venner* (1859), a monstrous child is born to a pregnant woman terrorized by a snake, this being "an ante-natal impression which had mingled an alien element in her nature."[51]

For other thinkers, a child could be shaped by its mother's experiences prior to pregnancy, especially a former pregnancy. This supposed causal influence fascinated breeders and researchers beginning in 1820, when Lord Morton reported to the British Royal Society that his chestnut mare had bred two generations of foals with stripes that came not from her or the black Arabian that sired them but from the sire of her first foal, a striped horse called a quagga.[52] In 1892 Weismann named the phenomenon *telegony*, meaning offspring at a distance, or, more precisely, the direct influence of male gametes on a female's reproductive system and consequently on all of her subsequent offspring.[53] "The concept of telegony," wrote Harriet Ritvo, "was almost universally believed by nineteenth-century breeders and fanciers and widely accepted within the zoological community."[54]

Victorian researchers offered two scenarios for telegony: (1) the direct impact of a pregnancy, possibly even mere intercourse, on a female's sex organs, which subsequently affects a second fetus (called *maternal infection*), and (2) the indirect impact of the sire's hereditary characteristics on a fetus, which pass to the mother during pregnancy and then are transmitted to any subsequent fetus, possibly through maternal-fetal blood exchange (called *maternal inoculation*).

A distinguished proponent of maternal infection was Louis Agassiz, who believed that a first pregnancy permanently "affects the whole system, the sexual system especially; and in the sexual system the ovary to be impregnated hereafter is so modified by the first act that later impregnations do not efface that first impression."[55] Darwin risked undermining his theory of natural selection with his efforts to explain telegony by gemmules from the sire of a mother's earlier pregnancy collecting in her gonad's germ cells and then being passed to her subsequent fetus. In 1868 he maintained that Lord Morton's studhorse affected the character of the offspring subsequently delivered by his mare. He concluded that in general "it is certain that [the mother's] ovaria are sometimes affected by a previous impregnation, so that the ovules subsequently fertilized by a distinct male are plainly influenced in character."[56]

While Zola's hereditary killers are tainted from remote ancestry, if not animal forebears, some of his other characters are tainted by a prior pregnancy. He was influenced in this thinking by the hereditarian theory of Prosper Lucas and by the popular psychology of Jules Michelet, both of whom argued that a pregnancy imprints a woman forever and leaves traces that may appear in her subsequent children sired by another man.

Lucas accepted such instances, provided they were considered atypical.[57] Michelet believed them to be typical, arguing that "woman, once impregnated, carries her husband everywhere in herself. . . . A widow with a second husband often has children who resemble the first."[58] Zola went further back in time with a heroine in *Madeleine Férat* (1868) who is physiologically tainted not from a pregnancy, but from her earlier defloration. "When Madeleine had forgotten herself in Jacques's arms, her virgin flesh had received the ineffaceable imprint of the young fellow's nature . . . [and] the fatality of physiological laws had bound her closely to him and filled her blood with his." As a result her first child resembles her first lover Jacques instead of her first husband, its biological father.[59] In a later Zola novel, Dr. Pascal's analysis of the Rougon-Macquart family's heredity includes "one example of transmission by influence, Anna [actually Nana in *L'Assommoir*], the daughter of Gervaise and Coupeau, who bore a striking resemblance, especially in her childhood, to Lantier, her mother's first lover" (108). The Austrian philosopher Otto Weininger drew exceptional attention to maternal infection when he committed suicide just after publishing his dissertation, *Sex and Character* (1903), which maintained that the woman is "impregnated not only through the genital tract, but through every fiber of her being. All her life makes an impression on her and throws its image on her child."[60] Such anxious theorizing about what is and is not exchanged between mother and fetus fueled a host of Victorian anxieties about virginity, sexual exclusivity, and family pedigree.

The second explanation, maternal inoculation, is that a sire somehow imprints its traits on the fetus, and during pregnancy the mother's body absorbs those traits from the fetus and subsequently transmits them to other offspring. Lacking a clear understanding of how the placental barrier blocks the exchange of blood between mother and fetus, theorists suspected that mothers share some fetal blood, if not all of it. Therefore the father's character traits flow in the veins of a fetus and consequently in the veins of the mother before and after delivery. Thereafter, any subsequent child she might have with another man will bear some trace of the father of the first child, because she will pump his residual character traces into the blood of her second fetus.

William Hammond argued that "the offspring has received certain physical or mental impressions from the father; it conveys them through its blood to the blood of the mother, and the latter in turn gives them through the blood to a subsequent fetus in her womb." The consequences of this phenomenon were ominous: "it is not uncommon to see the children of a widow by her second husband resemble in mind and body her first husband, provided she has had children by him."[61] Alexander Harvey offered evidence of maternal inoculation in a medical tract bearing what had to be a frightening title for pregnant women: *On the Foetus in Utero as Inoculating the Maternal with the Peculiarities of the Paternal Organism* (1886). He argued that "the fetus, partaking, as it must, of the character or peculiarities of its father *inoculates* therewith the blood, and, generally, the system, of its mother."[62]

August Strindberg was tormented by fear of maternal infection and inoculation, which convinced him that his children had been contaminated directly and indirectly by the infidelity of his wife, who, he claimed, drove him mad with uncertainty about his fathering role. Insane jealousy led to his distressed reasoning: "My heart's blood transmitted through my wife's uterus into the veins of their [his children's] small bodies."[63] But if his blood could get into the veins of his children and then circulate back into his wife's veins, so could that of any of his wife's previous lovers, a fear he explored in several plays. In *The Father* (1887), the Captain, beginning to question whether his daughter is really his own, asks a doctor, "Is it true that if you cross a mare with a zebra you get striped foals?" Panicked about a phenomenon identical to Lord Morton's mare and obviously aware of that specific example, the Captain asks further, "if the breeding is then continued with a stallion, the foals may still be striped?" The doctor assures him that such hereditary influence by a previous sire is possible. Strindberg dramatized those anxieties in *The Creditors* (1888) by having a woman's first husband return to haunt, and eventually destroy, her second marriage. Her second husband is in anguish because "when the child was three years old it began to look like him, her former husband."

Strindberg also believed in psychic telegony, as did Henrik Ibsen. In *The Lady from the Sea* (1888), Ellida thinks she sees in her child the eyes not of its father but of a mysterious seaman who had intrigued her years before. In *Ghosts* (1881), Mrs. Alving believes that her son's mouth resembles not that of his father but of a pastor with whom she was infatuated before her marriage. An article titled "Ibsen, Strindberg, and Telegony" surveyed both Scandinavian playwrights' use of psychic and physiological telegony in a number of major plays in which children show the influence of an earlier intense but thwarted love or in which adults believe that traces of some amorous predecessor flow in their own veins. In Strindberg's *To Damascus*, a former husband challenges his male successor directly: "Your child shall be mine, and I shall speak through its mouth. . . . I am in your blood—your lungs—your brain."[64]

The German philosopher Eduard von Hartmann wrote in 1895 that during pregnancy the mother experiences "an interchange of blood with a second body, whose composition is only half-conditioned by qualities inherited from the mother, the other half being contributed by paternally inherited characteristics." Some of the father's traits therefore "lie dormant within her but can manifest themselves all the more strikingly in the children of a later marriage. . . . The husband of a widow does not therefore find a clean page, but one written over by his predecessor, with whose hereditary tendencies his own must enter into conflict."[65] For the Victorians with such a view of heredity, virginity had enormous biological as well as characterological significance.

Telegony may have been on the mind of Thomas Hardy when he created *Tess of the d'Urbervilles* and was reading Weismann. In the novel the contaminating effects of a previous pregnancy surface in the explanation for murder, because Tess not only inherited her remote ancestor's destiny to kill ("a murder, committed by one of the family, centuries ago"), but she presumably also absorbed some traces of her rapist Alec, who left her pregnant with a child who died in infancy. On her wedding night her husband Angel is shocked to learn of her former pregnancy and rejects her in disgust, charging that she is not the woman he thought she was. He means this characterologically, but perhaps also biologically if he suspected that she had absorbed Alec's essence from the pregnancy and was therefore forever tainted, because he tells her that any child they might have together would be tainted, adding: "You were one person; now you are another." Angel returns to this obsession with the bitter question: "How can we live together while that man [Alec] lives? He being your husband in Nature, and not I." If he married her, their children would become "wretches of our flesh and blood growing up under a taunt" (313). Angel's chilling emphasis, "while that man lives," suggests another possible motive for Tess to murder Alec. Angel's word *taunt* also suggests *taint*, as if in his mind any children he might have with Tess would be exposed to taunts because of their taint. Angel's despair is a culmination of the anxiety about impure blood and hereditary taints that plagued the Victorians in their ignorance of genetics.

GENETICS AND MEDICINE

Genetics is the pivotal science for this chapter. It came into prominence at the turn of the twentieth century and profoundly shaped thinking about the causal role of ancestry.[66] In 1865 Gregor Mendel published the results of experiments crossing pea plants with different characteristics that revealed four features of hereditary transmission which, when ultimately accepted, demolished Victorian hereditarianism: (1) Characteristics of parent plants are transmitted in discrete units of inheritance (genes) that are present as pairs (alleles) throughout life. During reproduction, members of each pair of genes segregate into different reproductive cells. This being so, Victorian notions of a blending of parents' traits from a blending of their reproductive units or fluids became untenable. (2) A trait, such as blood type, derives from the influences of both male and female alleles, although one allele is often dominant and the other recessive. This finding, that both parents contribute equally, refuted a cluster of Victorian theories about specific traits coming exclusively from the mother or the father. (3) According to Mendel's law of independent assortment, hereditary influence on one trait is independent of influence on another trait. This independence undercut the notion that complex behaviors, such as an instinct to commit murder based on many genetically determined traits, could be inherited *in toto*. (4) When first-generation hybrids self-fertilize, individual traits in the next generation occur in fixed ratios, roughly 3:1, further refuting any multiple-particle theory such as Darwin's pangenesis.

Recent scholarship has suggested that Mendel was not fully understood in 1865 because his generation was committed to a paradigm that made it impossible to grasp the significance of his findings. His contemporaries were more concerned with breeding new species by hybridization than with understanding the mechanism of heredity and so could not detach evolution from individual ontogenic development, a crucial distinction for the emergence of scientific genetics. Further, Mendel himself thought of hereditarian influence in terms of Aristotelian opposing essences and so was unable to develop the key concept of paired material particles as the decisive agent in hereditary transmission.[67] This construction of Mendel supports my larger argument that this new approach to hereditary transmission was part of a broad cultural shift in thinking about the causes of human experience generally. The inability to grasp and accept Mendelism in full, even by Mendel himself, is evidence of the importance and tenacity of the concepts he challenged; the accurate interpretation of his results undercut Victorian notions of hereditary continuity, blending of sexual fluids, male or female primacy, inheritance of complex behaviors, and an evolution-designing mind.

After 1865 scientists concentrated on finding the nature and location of reproductive units within the cell. This research was facilitated by the invention of the oil immersion lens (1870), along with the newly invented microtome, aniline dyes, and stains, which made possible more detailed observations and precise explanations. In 1875 Oscar Hertwig observed that only a single sperm is involved in the fertilization of a sea urchin, not a swarming of male sexual fluid causing a hereditary blending. In 1879 Hermann Fol actually observed a sperm penetrating an egg and the fusion of the two nuclei. These findings demolished preformation of the embryo in either the egg or the sperm along with other Victorian theories that fertilization is caused by some mechanical or chemical force exciting the egg to develop.[68]

Beginning in the 1880s researchers focused on the behavior of material in the nucleus, which during cell division formed threadlike structures that were believed to carry out the reproductive function. By 1888 Theodore Boveri named them *chromosomes*. In 1885 Weismann announced "the continuity of the germ plasm" and its independence from influence by the body cells (soma), thereby severing hereditary transmission from any influence of acquired characteristics.[69] He argued for a continuity of mindless germ plasm instead of a continuity of mindful soma. Five years later George J. Romanes summarized Weismann's theory for English readers and challenged the intractable Lamarckism that had for so long justified Victorians' confidence in the hereditary continuity of their hard-earned acquired characteristics. Romanes was triply blunt: all acquired variations are "ruled out as regards the species," "blocked off in the first generation," and "entirely lost to progeny."[70]

In 1900 Mendel was rediscovered by Hugo De Vries, Carl Correns, and Erich von Tschermak. The next year De Vries introduced the term *mutation* to account for variations but erroneously thought that mutations involved a sudden change in the phenotype rather than a change at the genetic level, and he had no clear understanding of how they occurred. William Bateson coined the term *genetics* in 1905. Four years later W. L. Johannsen coined *gene* for the material basis of heredity.

That same year Thomas Hunt Morgan researched mutations in fruit flies, which clarified the mechanism for variation (mutation) and showed that genes reside on chromosomes. Two years after that Morgan introduced the term *crossing over* to account for unexpected combinations of traits in offspring coming from a breakdown in linkage during sexual reproduction. Since the extent of recombination was determined in part by the distance that separates genes, he reasoned that recombination frequencies offered a way to map genes on the chromosomes. Subsequent gene mapping vividly illustrated modernists' increasing specificity of causal understanding of ancestry, although filling out the map proved to be difficult, and mapping itself charted a vast molecular realm that geneticists did not understand along with what that they did understand. Morgan's work also increased the complexity of genetics by showing that a trait can be influenced by several different genes, that a single gene may affect more than one trait, and that any gene's influence could be modified by neighboring genes. Genes not only affect traits from scattered segments of their chromosome (or another chromosome) but they do so at different stages of development. By 1910 researchers had concluded that DNA molecules contained four nucleotides—guanine, adenine, cytosine, and thymine—although it took another forty-three years before James Watson and Francis Crick discovered how they were intertwined into a double helix that provides the biological information for sexual reproduction and cellular differentiation.

Over the past 135 years, conceptions of the nature of the gene underwent dramatic revision, as the techniques for probing gene structure became increasingly refined: the gene was defined as an abstract unitary factor (Mendel, 1865); a chromosome-bound element (Sutton, 1903); a mutable element (Morgan, 1909); a specific portion of a chromosome whose position can be mapped (Sturtevant, 1911); a visible band on a chromosome (Painter, 1930s); a segment of DNA (Avery, 1944); and a sequence of codons that determines the amino acid sequence (Nirenberg, 1961).[71]

Revolutionary developments made by geneticists since the 1970s increased the precision of DNA analytic techniques and the specificity of understanding how genes affect anatomy, development, pathology, health, and behavior. These developments involve gene mapping, recombinant DNA technology, DNA sequencing and cloning, and genetic engineering, which includes the creation of genetically modified plants and animals that may lack specific genes or carry extra copies of genes bearing specific mutations.[72] The increasing specificity of genetic explanations has sharpened causal understanding in developmental biology, immunology, endocrinology, neurobiology, and every other discipline of the medical sciences. Yet with all the increasingly precise knowledge has come more uncertainty. In an interview in 2000, Craig Venter, chief scientific officer of the Celera Genome Group, explained to a reporter what was being accomplished in a roomful of powerful new computers working on sequencing the human genome: "There are three people working in this room. A year ago this work would have taken one thousand to two thousand scientists. With this technology, we are literally coming out the dark ages of biology. As a civilization, we know far less than one per cent of what will be known about biology, human physiology, and medicine. My view of biology is 'We don't know shit.'"[73]

The spectacular increase in the specificity of genetic understanding coupled with an expanding sense of its uncertainty are related historically to developments in theories of disease, which eventually became based in part on genetics. While not at first directly concerned with heredity, the rise of a causal theory of disease sharpened standards for explanation that influenced hereditarian thinking and eventually included genetically caused diseases. As K. Codell Carter noted, early nineteenth-century physicians who explained disease by too many causes (miasma, tainted water, contaminated soil, poor living, sleeping while intoxicated, etc.) actually had no causal theory at all.[74] Since around 1835, researchers began to discover that diseases were caused by specific microorganisms, beginning with fungi, parasites, and decaying organic matter. This research eventually focused on the causal role of bacteria. The word "germ" to refer to organic bodies that cause disease came into medical use in 1876 in a letter from Joseph Lister to Louis Pasteur, which the latter quoted in a book of that year.[75] During the 1880s Pasteur developed vaccinations for anthrax and rabies based on the causal role of specific bacillus germs. In 1882 Robert Koch announced his discovery of the tuberculosis bacillus and challenged the prevailing miasmatic theory that disease was caused by pathological states of the atmosphere, full of noxious exhalations from putrescent organic matter or stagnant water. In opposition to miasmatic theory, Koch wrote: "It was once customary to consider tuberculosis as the manifestation of social ills. . . . But in the future, the fight against this terrible plague will no longer focus on an undetermined something, but on a tangible parasite, whose living conditions are for the most part known."[76] He also developed three criteria, known as Koch's postulates, for establishing a specific etiology. To prove that a microorganism causes a disease one must (1) detect it in all cases of the disease, (2) show that it does not occur in other diseases or does so nonpathologically, and (3) purify it in a culture and cause the disease by introducing a pure culture of it into a healthy organism. As Carter concluded, "by the 1880s, we find a full-blown research programme focusing on the identification of universal and necessary causes [for disease]."[77]

In the course of the twentieth century, medical diagnoses became ever more precise in identifying diseases caused by genetic and molecular malfunctions, often expressed as enzyme deficiencies in metabolic pathways. In 1902 Archibald Garrod first identified the disease alkaptonuria as a congenital metabolic abnormality. Subsequent genetic diagnoses became increasingly specific as well as numerous and complex, while relying increasingly on probabilistic data. Since the first genetic diagnosis was made for Down syndrome in 1958, researchers have made many others: sickle-cell anemia (1978), Duchenne muscular dystrophy (1987), Tay-Sachs disease (1987–88), cystic fibrosis (1989), and an inherited form of breast cancer (1994). One medical text of 1995 lists the genetics, biochemical bases, and clinical symptoms of about five hundred disorders caused by a single anomalous gene.[78] In recent years researchers have been able to identify the exact "address" of the genetic abnormality on the single linear DNA molecule that makes up a chromosome. The first such precise address for a disease was found for Huntington's disease in 1983, located between genes D4S127 and D4S180, on the distal end of the short arm of chromosome 4.[79]

But all this increasingly specific technique and knowledge also disclosed vast uncertainty. As Ernst Mayr admitted in 1982: "The role of nucleosomes and the various proteins in the eukaryote chromosomes is understood only in a rudimentary way. The role of introns, transposons, and supposedly 'silent' DNA is mysterious. New phenomena are discovered almost every month that pose new puzzles."[80] Because the gene is considered the most fundamental heredity-bearing causal entity, I have dwelled on theories about its complex nature, which show how much of its causal role remains uncertain. As with the other biological causal entities that I will consider (hormones, peptides, and neurotransmitters), the gene has come to be viewed as increasingly multiple and complex, and its causal actions increasingly probabilistic and uncertain, even as understanding of its multiple causal functions has become increasingly precise.[81] In recent years hereditarian factors have further complicated thinking about the causes of disease. The etiological model of singular causal explanations of disease has increasingly been expanded to include elements of probability and uncertainty with new explanations such as multicausality, risk factors, and causal webs.[82]

INTO THE MODERN PERIOD

The historical significance of new thinking about hereditary causality can be assessed against the preceding sketch of the emergence of modern genetics. It demonstrated that the parents' state of mind or body during coitus or at the moment of conception had no effect on the genetic makeup of offspring. It also showed that although the circumstances of pregnancy might affect a baby's health and perhaps its character, they had no effect on its hereditary acquisition or on the mother's subsequent offspring. As Richard Burkhardt concluded, modern geneticists "purged from the domain of their concerns such dubious phenomena as maternal impressions, the inheritance of acquired characters, and telegony."[83] Thus, the moment of conception and the period of pregnancy ceased to be taken seriously as sources of ancestral influence. On the other hand, knowledge of animal and human ancestry became more precise but also more complex and probabilistic. As that knowledge grew, it increasingly generated a huge realm of uncertainty. That epistemological dialectic continued to structure the way modern researchers and novelists viewed animal and human ancestry.

It is ironic that Victorians should have generated so much anxiety over the animal origins of the instinct to kill, because, aside from a few exceptions (cases of infanticide and cannibalism), adult animals do not kill other members of their own species. Into the twentieth century, that fact became more clearly appreciated, although the subject of instinctual aggression continued to attract scholarly interest from Freud on. The idea that a human could inherit from animal ancestors something as complex as the impulse to strangle a sexual rival became untenable as the understanding of heredity became more precise, and such gross recapitulation of animal behavior was removed from serious research protocols. In the twentieth century, particularly relating to the genome project, ethologists continued to look for evolutionary connections between animals and humans embedded in instinctual behavior but with increasing awareness of the complexity of hereditary transmission and the uncertainty of causal understanding of the process at the genetic level.

Since the mid-nineteenth century, knowledge of the biological source of animal ancestry focused on ever smaller heredity-bearing substances, from sexual fluids to germ plasm to chromosomes to genes to DNA. Current research shows that roughly 98.5 percent of human DNA matches chimpanzee DNA. The precision of that number is misleading, however, because most DNA does not perform functions that account for differences between apes and humans, while some small portions of DNA have enormous significance, such as the DNA that determines intellectual capacity. Still, scientific knowledge of similarities between humans and animals has become increasingly specific. That knowledge also reveals a vast realm of uncertainty, because with all the impressive new technologies and theories, geneticists still have no idea how specific genes cause the similarities or the differences between chimpanzees and humans.[84]

The Victorians' panic at the thought that they may have descended from apes has evolved into modern wonder that such an enormously complex evolutionary process was able to occur at all. Modernist artists and intellectuals embraced a primitivism that included human as well as animal origins, which they viewed as essential to fulfillment rather than as sources of degeneration or criminality. Expressionist writers and artists sought release from bourgeois conformism in a revitalizing primitivism. Freud found an "archaic heritage" energizing the human unconscious and driving the primordial id, while Jung based his psychology on individuation, a process of becoming aware of the psychic residue of ancestral experience that includes the archetype of the primitive, shadowy element of the psyche. In 1923 D. H. Lawrence inverted Victorian disgust about animal as well as remote human ancestry by arguing that "unless we proceed to connect ourselves up with our own primeval sources, we shall degenerate."[85]

That increasingly favorable estimate of our animal heritage has left a mark on the murder novel. Modernists may have referred to a primitive, murderous impulse raging in the blood, but only as a metaphor for a dark urge or a bloody past rather than as a specific biological carrier of animal ancestry. Of all of the modernist novels I have read, none seriously attempted to explain a murder as a direct consequence of animal ancestry.

Three Failed Theories

The changing role of both remote and human ancestry can be tracked in the fate of three failed theories: criminal anthropology, negative eugenics, and the XYY male.

Lombroso's theory of the hereditary origins of the "born criminal" lingered into the twentieth century under attack from supporters of environmental causation. The theory became unsupportable after the triumph of Mendelian genetics and its laws of segregation and independent assortment, and Lombroso himself included a multiplicity of other causes in later versions. The three-volume fifth edition of *L'uomo delinquente* (1896–97) was more than 1,900 pages. It included in addition to hereditary causes numerous environmental causes, such as climate, rainfall, religion, laws, sex, race, food, diseases, education, money, age, profession, newspapers, and politics. The table of contents of his last major book, *Crime: Its Causes and Remedies* (1911), included 129 separate causal factors listed under the "Aetiology of Crime."

Nineteenth-century theorists, with scant understanding of the actual workings of heredity, thought it to be as linear as the concussive causal action of one ball striking another and as cumulative as the amassing and transmission of a family fortune over successive generations. In contrast to such Victorian emphasis on direct and linear hereditarian etiology, modernist research began to envision more indirect, multiple, and complex causal explanations that included human heredity but also interaction with environmental factors.

The rise of modern sociology further diminished the role of hereditarian etiology and Lombroso's criminal anthropology. In 1893 Emile Durkheim announced that "faith in heredity, formerly so intense, has today been replaced by an almost opposed faith." His own research (discussed below in chapter 7) emphasized social over hereditary causes, including the causes of crime. He conceded to Lombroso that "the propensity toward evil in general is often heredity" but rejected the notion of a hereditary "criminal type."[86]

In 1865 Francis Galton began publishing his findings on inheritance, which were elaborated in *Hereditary Genius* (1869). It began with the claim that "man's natural abilities are derived by inheritance" and then recommended that "it would be quite practicable to produce a highly-gifted race of men by judicious marriages during several consecutive generations."[87] He coined the term *eugenics* in 1883 for his new science of improving the human race by applying statistical mathematics and probability theory to populations and by instituting reforms to increase the ratio of superior to inferior individuals. Around 1910–15, British and American eugenicists were applying, with increasing confidence, single-gene explanations of mental disorders such as feeblemindedness and seeking a way to eradicate them.[88] Some findings seemed to show that crime was statistically correlated with certain families, hence its hereditarian nature. Galton reasoned that since plants and animals could be bred for superior species, so could humans. Positive eugenics encouraged the reproduction of such superior human beings, while negative eugenics aimed to eliminate inferior ones by sexual abstention or sterilization.

Negative eugenics policies were instituted in the early twentieth century to carry out these objectives. In America, thirty-three states passed sterilization laws mainly for the mentally ill and sex criminals. Some countries in western Europe also passed laws restricting immigration, marriage, or racial mixing. The Holocaust dramatized the atrocity of negative eugenics practices based on theories of heredity, specifically the Nazi theory that Jews were causing Germany's misfortunes by poisoning "pure" German blood.

In disrepute in the post-Nazi years, hereditarian theories attracted renewed attention in 1965 from an article about a supposedly disproportionate number of men in an Edinburgh correctional institution who had an anomalous XYY sex chromosome, which, the researchers speculated, might predispose them to aggression.[89] The theory explained aggressive behavior on the basis of a single anomalous chromosome, and it surged into popularity in 1968 when an article reported incorrectly that the psychopath who killed eight nurses in Chicago, Richard Speck, was XYY. In subsequent years the myth of the XYY male flourished in sensationalist articles on "criminal chromosomes" and "criminal genes."[90] Although scientists were eager to document this causal connection, rigorous scholarship exposed its flaws. In 1974, a survey of more than 200 articles on the subject maintained that the research connecting the XYY male and aggression or criminality was methodologically flawed and concluded that "the frequency of antisocial behavior of the XYY male is probably not very different from non-XYY persons of similar background."[91]

The strongly hereditarian emphasis of criminal anthropology, negative eugenics, and the XYY male was rejected not only by modern anthropologists, sociologists, and geneticists but also by modern novelists.

They avoided structuring novels around hereditarian explanations of characters impelled by atavistic survival of animal or human ancestry flowing in the blood and erupting in criminal types fated to kill. They also avoided establishing motivation based on modern genetics. The hereditary action of chromosomal DNA just does not make for intriguing character motivation. Modernist writers shifted their emphasis toward the inner life of character and away from overbearing plots, especially those based on a hereditary destiny. A few tried to incorporate bits of modern genetics, but most either mocked hereditarian explanations or relegated them to the margins.

As experts came to absorb Weismann's message and accept the independence of sex cells, novelists were increasingly less inclined to rely on ancestry to explain murder, or at least less inclined to rely on hereditary features passed through the "blood." Friedrich Dürrenmatt suggested a microscopic biological trigger for his serial murderer in *The Pledge* (1958). A psychiatrist explains to the detective that "it does not matter whether the feeble-mindedness is inborn or develops later," because such persons have no control over their impulses. Their resistance to those impulses is small, and "it takes damnably little—altered metabolism or a few degenerate cells—and such a human being becomes a beast" (86). For the Victorians, by contrast, it generally took a long ancestral pedigree, not "damnably little" genetic material to cause a murder. Dürrenmatt's murderer is a product of a genetic fluke or metabolic misrouting, not generations of ancestral misdeeds. The author of *The Bad Seed* (1954), explains a murder by eight-year-old Rhoda Penmark as a result of a hereditary taint, but it is one caused by a minute particle, a bad seed, not bad blood. One character does suggest that the taint may have come from remote ancestors five thousand years ago, before a moral sense developed, though short of the full Victorian pedigree of a cumulative inheritance of the entire life experience of her ancestors. Rhoda's hereditary influence also skips a generation—her mother is virtuous, her grandmother a serial killer. The causal mechanism reveals shades of Victorian thinking, because the impulse to kill was transmitted in toto, but otherwise the account agrees with modern genetics, specifically the particulate nature of hereditary transmission, the function of recessive characteristics, and an appreciation for the complexity and probabilistic mix of environmental and hereditarian factors.

In *Lafcadio's Adventures* (1914), Gide was especially intent on stigmatizing the nineteenth-century convention of reconstructing a character's ancestry back several centuries and the naturalist convention of motivating characters with overbearing hereditary taints. He satirized both conventions by tracing Lafcadio's origins back to an irrelevant ancestor "who in 1514 married his second wife Filippa Viconti, a few months after the annexation of the Duchy to the Papal States." In the midst of this tedious elaboration of the family's history, Gide critiques himself: "it would be easy, though not very interesting, to trace the family fortunes up till 1807" (14). So he skips the two centuries and resumes his account with equally tedious recent family background. He completes the assault on gratuitous lineages by having the novelist Julius express his philosophy of *inconséquence*—that individuals ought to act freely in response to the dynamics of the moment and not in a way determined by their ancestors' pasts.

Robert Musil tore up ancestral determinism by the roots. In *The Man without Qualities* (1930), the title character, Ulrich, lacks the conventional characteristics of the typical European. He has no clear profession, social status, moral values, marital inclinations, or personal identity. He struggles to find some compelling reason for being the way he is in opposition to the "already petrified carapace of the self of [his] predecessors, a pseudo self, a loosely fitting soul" (1:138). Ulrich feels remote from his family but strangely akin to a sex murderer, Moosbrugger, who, like himself, is not determined by tradition to be anything and who is defined in terms of what he lacks. Moosbrugger is an orphan, and his ancestry can only be guessed at, but the conventional observers represented by reporters, psychiatrists, gossips, lawyers, and a judge insist on creating a criminal ancestry for him in order to explain his brutal murder of a prostitute and so convict him. On the other hand, from Moosbrugger's perspective the murder was a desperate and confused act of self-definition. In this novel, ancestry is uprooted or disjoined from these two main characters, who are defined negatively as essentially without any conventional antecedent causes, including heredity.

William Faulkner despised the mythic ancestry that was responsible for those aspects of southern tradition that corrupted individuals, and he dramatized its erosive effect as the motive for murder in *Absalom, Absalom!* (1936). Thomas Sutpen's lack of aristocratic ancestry and obsessive desire to establish a great family dynasty generate the corrupt values that his son Henry vows to protect. That corruption is dramatized in the cruel way Thomas treats everyone, which deprives him of any genuine respect from others. Ironically, his hunger to establish an

ancestral line is the cause of his own downfall, because it leads his unworthy legitimate heir Henry to kill his more worthy illegitimate heir
Charles, who personifies the lifestyle, if not the biological pedigree, of
the aristocratic ideal that Thomas aspires to emulate. The impending
marriage of Charles to Judith Sutpen triply threatens Thomas's dynasty: it involves bigamy because Charles is already married, it involves
incest because Judith is Charles's half-sister, and it involves racial mixing because Charles's mother was one-eighth Negro. When Thomas
learns of the engagement, he manipulates Henry to kill Charles. Henry
thus "inherits" his father's obsession with racial purity as a foundation
for family respectability, which inspires him to protect the family's
tradition by killing its most impressive member.

In the context of evolving views of heredity, Faulkner's novel is an
interpretive challenge, because it was published in 1936 but treats a
murder committed in 1865 that is subsequently interpreted by several
narrators in 1909. I view it as a modernist critique of nineteenth-
century views about ancestry, dramatized in characters whose identities are shaped by a commitment to a world that is destined to moral
failure because of its reliance on slavery, itself built on the obliteration
of one race's ancestry. Charles's Negro blood is indeed the cause of
the downfall of Thomas's dream of establishing a great dynasty, but
not for any reason that Thomas could have fathomed. Faulkner believed that identity cannot be tainted by racial mixing and that whatever nobility there might have been in the old South had nothing to
do with pure blood. Faulkner makes no mention of genetics, but his
exposé of a mythic old South based on aristocratic dynasties and obsession with pure bloodlines reflects the increasingly precise grasp of
hereditarian theory available to him in the 1930s. Fears of racial mixing and tainted blood in the American South persisted well into the
twentieth century, to be sure, but serious modern novelists of the
South would not likely use them as the motivation for murder.

In *Being and Nothingness* (1943), Jean-Paul Sartre relegated the causal
role of ancestry to an essential but marginal element of human existence, which he called facticity—a set of defining characteristics of an
individual, such as height and weight and hereditary endowments that
are causally determined by circumstance and cannot be changed but do
not identify what is distinctive about an individual. His philosophy of
existence affirmed that at the core of every individual is nothing determinate, like a hereditary endowment, but rather a *concrete nothingness*,

a gaping void of possibility and freedom that we try to avoid (some-times with ideologies based on causal determinisms) but are con-demned to confront and somehow fill with meaning throughout life.

In 1939 Sartre insisted that the proper goal of the novelist was to avoid any deadening determinism and instead re-create a world of gen-uine expectation about a future full of surprise. "If I suspect that the hero's future actions are determined in advance by heredity, social in-fluence, or some other mechanism," he wrote, "my own time ebbs back into me; there remains only myself, reading and persisting, confronted by a static book. Do you want your characters to live? See to it that they are free."[92] In 1943 he celebrated Camus's novel *The Stranger* (1942), about a murderer, Meursault, who is uniquely devoid of con-ventional values and emotional responses. Sartre focused on Camus's staccato prose, which resists determination and thereby preserves the vitality and uncertainty of the present. In Camus's writing, "all causal links are avoided lest they introduce the germ of an explanation. . . . A nineteenth-century naturalist would have written 'A bridge spanned the river.' M. Camus will have none of this anthropomorphism. He says, 'Over the river was a bridge.'" Sartre related the new technique to a subversion of determinism. "In this world that has been stripped of its causality and presented as absurd, the smallest incident has weight. There is no single one which does not help to lead the hero to crime and punishment."[93] Sartre downplayed the importance of overbearing causes and highlighted a new range of small incidents that open out to-ward future possibilities. That redistribution of the weight of deter-ministic and circumstantial causal factors creates the situation that he and Camus defined as the absurd. But far from being a condition of meaninglessness, the rejection of determinism is central to understand-ing human existence as absurd; to look at existence more fully one must avoid reductionist explanations, including ancestry.

Murderers fascinated Sartre and Camus because the acts cry out for the sort of determinist causal explanations that existentialists avoided. Everyone wants to know why the murderer did it. The scandal of *The Stranger* emerges as the reader suspects first that Meursault will refuse to answer that question in any conventional way, then that he may not actually know the answer, and finally that there may be no answer, at least none that will satisfy the determinist parameters of the legal sys-tem. The central buildup of conflict is over Meursault's resistance to explaining to the prosecutor why he killed the Arab, and its climax is

Meursault's famous reply to the judge that he pulled the trigger "because of the sun." That reply marks a sea change in the rendering of
causality in the modern murder novel. Victorian readers accustomed
to the overdetermined murderers driven by hereditary taints would
never have accepted such an explanation as carrying enough causal
clout. It is hard to imagine a nineteenth-century murderer such as
Tess explaining that she stabbed Alec because of the sun.

Sartre and Camus accord with Gide because they also made explicit
the rejection of a determinist causality as the way to a fuller dramatization of human existence. For them, overbearing causal explanations
based on heredity or even social circumstance obscured the free, creative,
and unpredictable nature of existence. Literary critics have concurred
with this interpretation. For Jacques Guicharnaud, violent action in
Sartre and Camus "takes on a new value in that their philosophy consists in destroying the importance traditionally accorded to motives."[94]
What counted for them were not reasons for action but the act itself.
Meaning did not boil down to causes, and the search for them obscured
the fullness of the act itself.[95] For these existentialists, characters who
acted definitively because of any hereditary influence were incomplete
characters. They did not make genuine existential choices in recognition of their responsibility for actions but made excuses for them based
on causal analyses of their previous circumstances. Sartre's famous definition of the central tenet of existentialism—that existence precedes
essence—reversed the causal order of the Victorian world, in which ancestral essence along with a host of conventions and values preceded
and determined existence.

Since 1830, understanding of the five aspects of ancestral causation
that I have traced shifted in the direction of increasing specificity, multiplicity, complexity, probability, and uncertainty. Scientists rejected
the Victorians' ancestral influences such as animal atavisms, organic
memory, recapitulation, telegony, maternal infection, maternal inoculation, and Lamarckism. In particular, geneticists' explanations of the
biological carrier of ancestral traits focused on ever smaller and more
specific substances from sexual fluids and germ plasma to genes and
DNA. Their explanations also involved ever more complex biochemical processes with an increasing number of active biological agents,
such as proteins, amino acids, and enzymes, with even more precise
phenomena at the molecular level. Along with all this increasing specificity of causal understanding, the realm of uncertainty also expanded.

As early as 1930, Karl Pearson identified this historical movement in admitting that "during the last 25 years we seem scarcely nearer the exact knowledge of the laws of heredity; the farther we advance the more complex does the problem become."[96]

While scientists were drawn to make ever more precise causal explanations of behavior with specific causal agents, novelists were wary of such explanations; they needed to rely on a conscious human being, not chromosomal DNA, making acts occur. Their murder novels were more plausible when centered on murderers who were intentionally motivated, aware that what they were doing was wrong, and responsible for their acts, otherwise their actions would lack depth and plausibility. While most novelists resisted making precise scientific explanations for their murderers based on the increasing specificity of knowledge such as modern genetics, they did incorporate the increasing uncertainty about behavior that included the increasing multiplicity, complexity, and probability that became defining characteristics of the modernist conception of human nature. This literary response to increasing specificity helps explain why the argument in this chapter is based on missing evidence, that is, a dearth of hereditarian explanations of murders in modernist novels. Aside from Dürrenmatt and March, the other modernists I surveyed—Gide, Musil, Faulkner, Sartre, and Camus—mocked, rejected, or omitted ancestry to explain the actions of a murderer.

Three historical developments play a decisive role in explaining these changing ideas about the value and importance of ancestry for causal understanding. The most important explanation is the increasing division of labor and specialization in science, which included a plethora of new specialities concerned with the causal phenomena of hereditary transmission: evolutionary biology, cytology, genetics, population genetics, biochemistry, biophysics, microbiology, electron microscopy, bioengineering, and molecular biology. A second explanation is the development of new technologies that facilitated the detection of ever more minute biological processes. The electron microscope and new techniques such as DNA fingerprinting and gel electrophoresis sharpened the increasing specificity of causal understanding but at the same time posed new questions and defined new areas of uncertainty.

The final explanation is the increasing secularization of thought, which subverted God as the first cause of life and therefore as the first ancestor. It also allowed (or in some cases forced) researchers to do without a designing mind behind creation and evolution. The loss of a divine and primordial ancestral pedigree forced both scientists and novelists to find other sources of meaning in life and other ways of understanding experience. Scientists responded by finding more specific causes, while novelists created characters who acted in a world of increasing uncertainty. Modernism was forged out of those reciprocally related developments that are the scientific and literary outcome of the specificity-uncertainty dialectic.

2

Childhood

In *Red Dragon* (1981) Thomas Harris introduced a character who became the most notorious serial killer in twentieth-century literature and cinema—Hannibal Lecter. At the beginning of the novel, Hannibal was already imprisoned for several brutal murders involving cannibalism. In Harris's next novel, *Silence of the Lambs* (1988), Hannibal escaped and murdered two police officers in acts that were presented as those of a deranged monster. In the conclusion to these novels, Harris provided motives for the serial killers who are the main target of investigation, but not for Hannibal himself. Finally, in *Hannibal* (1999), Harris made it clear that the motivation originated in a gruesome childhood trauma.

Critics of *Silence of the Lambs* speculated freely that Hannibal's motivation was homosexual or religious or psychopathic—as one put it, "yet another dangerous pervert" like Jeffrey Dahmer.[1] Delacorte Press gave Harris a multimillion-dollar advance for *Hannibal* without having a clue to why Hannibal did what he did. Fascination with Hannibal was enhanced by the riveting performance of Anthony Hopkins in the movie of *Silence of the Lambs*, but Hopkins had no idea why Hannibal did what he did, or at least no idea what Harris thought the reason was. For eighteen years, readers and movie viewers were intrigued by a character whose motivation for committing vicious murders remained a mystery. I will postpone revealing the traumatic childhood origins of Hannibal's pathology until later in this chapter to suggest the long delay until those origins are typically revealed during individual psychoanlyses and to re-create the sustaining interest generated in crime novels by the narrative technique of postponing the disclosure of those origins until the end of the story.[2]

Freud's conception of the childhood determination of adult mental life is the turning point in this chapter, because across the years of my study he influenced thinking about childhood causality more than anyone else. Psychoanalysis revolutionized popular ideas about nursing, toilet training, masturbation, exhibitionism, voyeurism, sadism, and family psychodynamics; it magnified the importance of childhood for the social sciences, literary criticism, and art history; it revamped biography; and it transformed child and adult psychiatry. Among modern murder novelists Freud was the psychiatrist of choice in part simply because as the most widely known psychiatrist, his theories were available for popular understanding. But more important, novelists writing about serial murderers in particular relied on the Freudian model for its substance, because a solidly entrenched cause—such as a childhood sexual trauma germinating over many years at the deepest levels of mental life— provided the most plausible explanation for the obsessional focus and frantic energy necessary to motivate increasingly brutal acts of murder, sometimes involving matricide, torture, dismemberment, necrophilia, and cannibalism.[3]

VICTORIAN CHILD CAUSALITY

Under Freud's influence the causal role of childhood shifts along two interpretive gradations: from passivity to activity and from sexual innocence to sexual motivation. My survey of the Victorian view of childhood that Freud revolutionized draws on four major sources: Christianity, Romanticism, Darwinism, and, as a sampling of the fictional sources, the novels of Charles Dickens.

Christianity viewed the child as a passive recipient of original sin that has to be absolved for all of humankind by the Crucifixion, washed away in infants by baptism, and warded off throughout life by stringent religious and moral discipline. Growth to adulthood takes shape around that discipline. The passive transmission of original sin condemns children to struggle actively to become moral Christian adults. Preoccupation with a such a defining event inclines the subsequent causal role of childhood to be singularly focused, in that it begins to operate with that unique event and functions continuously throughout life by instilling obedience to the moral precepts of the one and only God.

The Romantics emphasized the child's innocence and passivity. Rousseau viewed the child as born innocent but prone to guilt stemming from sexual desire that threatens to disrupt his education during puberty. Rousseau's treatise on education, *Emile* (1762), urged that the model child, Emile, learn from nature and become self-reliant, but in fact he remains a passive recipient of moral and intellectual instruction by a private tutor throughout childhood and into adolescence. The innocence of the child was further captured in Romantic art, which mostly depicted children as miniature adults with faces reflecting angelic souls, untainted and uncomplicated by experience. The Romantic poet William Wordsworth believed that nature, which dominates the world of childhood, is benevolent and that man is inherently good, blessed by a divine creator: "Trailing clouds of glory do we come / From God who is our home: / Heaven lies about us in our infancy!"[4] In *The Prelude* he viewed "our simple childhood" as a time of cognitive receptivity. "The Child is father of the man," he wrote, although that reverse parenting happens only after the grown-up retrieves and redefines childhood experience.[5] For the Romantics, childhood was passive, shaped by external sensation, and innocent in that it was devoid of sexual desire.

Darwin conceived of the child as a passive recipient of evolutionary prehistory, seen in action as the growing child manifests in stages the mental and physical traits of lower species. In *The Descent of Man* (1871), he theorized about how such recapitulation applied to the mind: "We daily see these faculties developing in every infant; and we may trace a perfect gradation from the mind of an utter idiot, lower than that of an animal low in the scale, to the mind of a Newton."[6] The first serious German child psychologist, Wilhelm Preyer, tracked that evolutionary development as he observed his child day by day over his first three years and published an analysis of it in 1881.[7] In *Mental Evolution in Man* (1888), the English psychologist George Romanes observed mental recapitulation in childhood, which he illustrated with a chart comparing the first fifteen months of human mental development week by week with the adult mentality of organisms from one-celled animals to the higher apes. In 1900 the English psychologist Alexander Chamberlain applied an evolutionary scheme with a grotesque racist twist in arguing that the expression of a Caucasian child in pain "resembles that of a monkey or a negro, while in a child of three, with its few speech-gestures, we have before us the picture of a savage."[8]

Most of late-nineteenth-century child psychology was undertaken to verify evolutionary theory. But with eons of evolution feeding into and governing whatever was supposed to cause the child's mind to evolve into the adult mind, child psychology was awash with wildly speculative comparisons between the mental life of animals, "savages," and children and was less interested in exploring how the specific experience of particular children determined their individual adult mental life. The huge impact of Darwinian theory tended to swamp the uniqueness of actual childhood experience under a formulaic recapitulation of the prehistory of the species. Darwinian child psychology focused backward toward that prehistory and viewed the child as passive in receiving its evolutionary payload rather than looking forward from childhood toward the active determination of particular adult characteristics.

Dickens, who pioneered the novel about childhood, viewed children as passive victims of social neglect and personal abuse, who struggle mightily but still need the goodness of others to prevail. *Oliver Twist* (1839) was the first novel in English that focused on the life of a child, and it became the model for depictions of child abuse. Oliver is neglected by a mother who dies shortly after bearing him, is starved in the workhouse where he spends his first years, and is abused in his first employment with a casket maker who makes him dress in mourning clothes and attend children's funerals. Oliver escapes to London, where a gang of child thieves force him to commit a burglary during which he is shot and left in a ditch. He is then betrayed by his half-brother, who is in cahoots with the leader of the thieves. Periodically Oliver is rescued from various scrapes by kindly Mr. Brownlaw, sympathetic Rose Maylie, and saintly Nancy. For the Victorians, Oliver was the quintessential passive victim of child abuse.

Compared with post-Freudian views of children as driven by powerful inner desires stemming from their earliest experiences, complicated by traumas and fixations, childhood causality for Victorian thinkers was more passive and sexually innocent. It was more passive for the Christian child born stigmatized by sin, for the Romantic child shaped by external sensations, for the Darwinian child as a recipient of evolutionary prehistory, and for the Dickensian child rescued by others. It was also far more innocent. Freud rejected the prevailing conviction of the child's asexuality along with the corresponding moral-religious model; instead he offered a medical-psychoanalytic model of childhood sexuality as the normal and universal foundation for character development.

Freudian Childhood Causality

Freud's conception of childhood causality is centered in his theory of psychosexual development. An examination of how long he took to discover and then accept the causal role of child sexuality suggests how original and unsettling his theory was.

When Freud started practicing psychiatry in the early 1880s, most experts believed that mental illness was caused organically by heredity or by a physical shock such as a railway accident or blow to the head. In 1885, under the influence of Jean Charcot, Freud shifted his explanations of neurosis toward psychic causes, but still ones arising from adult experience.[9] In 1888 he first referred to adult sexuality as a cause of neurosis but did so incidentally and not as a general theory. By 1892 he came to believe that all neuroses were directly or indirectly caused by "a disturbance of the sexual factor" that occurred "before the age of understanding."[10] Over the next several years he pushed the upper age limit for that determinative sexual trauma back to puberty, then to the age of the Oedipus complex (five to six years), and finally to the age of three. Later he recalled how his search for the cause of mental illness carried him "further and further back into the patient's life and ended by reaching the first years of childhood. . . . Since these experiences of childhood were always concerned with sexual excitations and the reaction against them," he wrote, "I found myself faced by the fact of *infantile sexuality*—once again a novelty and a contradiction of one of the strongest human prejudices. Childhood was looked upon as 'innocent' and free from the lusts of sex."[11] By 1896 he believed that all neuroses were caused by traumatic sexual seductions in childhood. Freud's important shift in 1897, from that first seduction theory of neurosis to the psychoanalytic theory, can best be understood historically against a survey of his theory of normal child sexuality.

Victorian thinking about child and adult sexuality was confused. Victorians believed that normal children have no sexual desires. Only sexually abused children have sexual desires, which are caused by seductions which they experience passively. Thus, whether children have innate sexual desires depends on an experience that is not innate. Throughout the Victorian period, sexuality in adults meant genital excitation. Freud expanded sexuality temporally back to childhood and expanded it anatomically to include more complex excitations associated with the erotogenic zones of the mouth, anus, and genitals. These zones have enormous psychosomatic force because they are made up of sensitive tissues that cause intense pleasure and are located at parts of the body that perform vital functions necessary for survival and reproduction and so are impossible to ignore. Freud's child sexuality also includes the eroticism of smell associated with erogenous zones, the eroticism of vision from looking at or exposing stimulating parts of the body, the sexuality of pain linked with sadism and masochism, and cultural sources from jokes, myths, literature, art, and religion. Adult character is forged in stages during childhood when pleasure is focused at each of the erotogenic zones. During the oral stage the child develops character traits that resemble the anatomical functions of pleasurable sucking, nursing, nutrition, and later biting. These traits include the ability to relate to and love others (derivative of the infant's primordial relation to the breast and then the mother), the ability to trust (derivative of the reliability of the breast and then the mother being accessible when needed), the ability to learn (derivative of feeding), and the ability to inflict pain (derivative of biting the nipple).

A child traumatized during the oral stage will remain fixated at it, incapable of developing the normal character traits associated with that stage or of proceeding normally to the next stage. An oral trauma is caused when frustration and anxiety related to nursing surcharge the child with stimulations that its tiny ego is unable to process. Over the years, the energy that should fuel loving and trusting is wasted in defending the mind from the repressed memory of the precipitating trauma and in creating psychic mechanisms that operate at the unconscious level to generate mental illness. For a child traumatized by an anxious and rejecting mother or by an overprotective and smothering mother, the resulting disturbance will center on the inability to love or trust and may surface as intense hatred and mistrust, addictions and feeding disorders, or oral compulsions and sexual fetishes. Children fixated at the oral aggressive stage after teething may manifest verbal or physical rage, oral sadism, or, in extremely pathological cases, cannibalism.

The anal stage centers on toilet training, when the child develops more traits that are analogous to the vital psychosomatic function that it must learn to perform—withholding or releasing dirty but valuable feces in cooperation with or against the wishes or demands of the beloved or feared mother. Other polar character traits that may emerge in adulthood include willfulness or lack of will, stinginess or profligacy, and cleanliness or slovenliness. The typical compulsive and retentive "anal character" may also be excessively pedantic or forgetful, punctual or procrastinating, and secretive or gossipy, all analogous to various aspects of the socially vital and complex function of learning to defecate at the right time in the right place with socially acceptable attitudes about hygiene, privacy, and authority. Anal fixation and trauma may cause exhibitionism, voyeurism, sodomy, coprolagnia, urolagnia, and flagellation among murderers as well as compulsive trophy collecting of clothing or body parts among serial killers.

These polar character possibilities for both the oral and the anal stage added complexity to Freudian causal thinking. Especially evident in dream formation, such polarities function at the unconscious level during waking, sometimes alternating with one another, substituting for one another, or fusing in a single image, which Freud called *condensation*. Feelings of love can switch to hate, which he tagged *reaction formation*. Other unconscious processes include *projection*, which involves attributing to others what comes from the self, or its opposite, *introjection*. *Displacement* involves shifting ideas and emotions associated with one person or object onto another person or object.

Any assessment of Freud's historical role must include both his originality and his influence. At the end of this chapter I will consider his influence on psychohistory and murder novels. Here I turn to the originality of his thinking about oral, anal, phallic, and Oedipal sexuality by comparing it with that of his early contemporaries, who, after around 1880, began to theorize how character is shaped by the child's nursing, toilet training, masturbation, and family relations.[12] While late Victorian views increased the specificity of causal understanding compared with previous studies, Freud's would be considerably more specific.

Freud cited an article in 1879 by the Hungarian pediatrician S. Lindner as the first serious work to view infants' sucking as sexual and consider its characterological consequences. Lindner argued that the impulse to suck is inherent in every infant and may lead to a pathogenic "delirious sucking" (*Wonnesaugen*).[13] Two years later Preyer warned that any sucking beyond nutritional needs was a "vicious and highly reprehensible practice."[14] Most experts believed that allowing children to enjoy sucking led to lack of self-control and ultimately adult sexual perversion and that the use of a pacifier was as dangerous as masturbating children or using drugs to quiet them. Freud's originality was in documenting the intense sexuality of sucking and its far-reaching characterological consequences and in challenging Victorian moral values by arguing that sucking for pleasure was a natural sexual instinct, had no degenerate consequences, and should not be restricted.

Victorian literature on toilet training shows a similar mixture of sketchy understanding of its characterological consequences and fear of its moral perils. Some early professionals studied how toilet training shapes character traits such as cleanliness, orderliness, punctuality, discipline, and will.[15] Others noted a connection between the anal region and sexual excitation, specifically warning that corporeal punishment might lead to adult sexual pathology or homosexuality.[16] Several viewed the anus as an erotogenic zone, though they regarded any sexual arousal of it as pathological.[17] Discussions of toilet training and anal excitation urged crushing the child's interest in anal eroticism. In contrast, Freud viewed the child's anal as well as oral experiences as important sources of sexual pleasure stemming from necessary stages of psychosexual development and warned against premature, overly severe, or anxious weaning or toilet training to avoid oral or anal fixations.

More childhood determinants of character were implied by Freud's concept of polymorphous perversity. Freud's use of *perverse* was misleading, because it had no conventional moral connotation. He took the term from outmoded degeneration theory but used it to label any sexual activity that did not have as its goal heterosexual intercourse and orgasm. And since children did not normally aim at intercourse and were incapable of orgasm, their sexuality was perverse only in that precise sense and not degenerate or immoral. In a letter of 1896 he wrote that "during childhood sexual release would seem to be obtainable from a great many parts of the body."[18] By 1905 he elaborated that idea into his theory of the "polymorphous perverse disposition," which referred to the way children are able to receive sexual stimulation over the entire surface of their body at just about any time, almost endlessly, in contrast to the postpubertal privileging of genital excitation terminating with orgasm.[19] Compared with the Victorians' denial of normal child sexuality, the expanded anatomical terrain of polymorphous perversity increased the multiplicity and complexity of the normal child's bodily sources of sexual excitation as well as their subsequent causal roles.

In the phallic stage, boys and girls develop distinct sexual traits beyond the bisexuality of the oral and anal stages. The immense Victorian literature on this subject generally viewed the penis and vagina or the sperm and egg as the biological determinants for adult sexual traits, interpreted those traits as polar opposites, and focused on how to prevent masturbation and its myriad pathological consequences. Freud challenged all three notions. He argued that the penis and clitoris determine the characterological consequences of the phallic stage because they are the bodily zones involved in childhood masturbation. He also challenged Victorian gender theorizers who argued that males are active like sperm cells, while female are passive like eggs, because men and women do not experience sperm cells and eggs consciously the way they do their external genitals. Freud derived sexual theorizing from sexual embodiment that *is* mediated by consciousness—specifically the penis and vagina, which determine strikingly different sexual character traits as a consequence of the way these parts of the sexual apparatus are experienced neurologically and psychologically during childhood masturbation and then even more differently during adult intercourse. Second, although he saw sexual divergence in this period as a consequence of those contrasting masturbatory activities with the penis and clitoris, he also insisted on the fundamental bisexual disposition of both sexes. In 1915 he wrote that "in human beings pure masculinity or femininity is not to be found either in a psychological or a biological sense. Every individual on the contrary displays a mixture of the character-traits belonging to his or her own and to the opposite sex."[20] Finally, he argued that masturbation was healthy and dismissed warnings about its dangers.

During the Oedipal stage, boys and girls experience intense ambivalence toward both parents, which is normally resolved as they pass into latency. For the boy especially, this ambivalence may lead to murder, because it includes the boy's strong identification with his father mixed with murderous rage. Freud named the Oedipal stage after the character in Sophocles' play, who unwittingly carries out the two impulses that Freud believed motivated all young boys, sexual desire for the mother and murderous rage toward the father. Most boys resolve the rage in a healthy and nonviolent manner, but a few act it out.

Victorian evaluations of the family glossed over its internal conflict and emphasized its harmony. That view was crystallized by John Ruskin in describing the home in 1865 as "the place of Peace; the shelter, not only from all injury, but from all terror, doubt, and division . . . a temple of the hearth watched over by Household Gods."[21] Such hyperbole denied the tensions that began to peak after around 1880 in plays by Ibsen, Strindberg, Chekhov, and Shaw as well as novels by Butler, Zola, and Gide. Sons especially began to feel the explosive intimacy of family emotions, which came from increasing parental pressure for the child to study or work hard in order to enable the family to rise socially or from the son's belief that he had been fated by heredity to inherit his parents' vices or diseases.[22] No major writer before Freud argued that family conflict originated in childhood sexual traumas. Dostoevsky hinted at a mother–son relationship motivating a murder in *The Brothers Karamazov* (1880) when Dimitry is driven to murderous rage against his father Fyodor out of sexual rivalry with his father's mistress Grushenka. But this novel is transitional: Grushenka is not Dimitry's mother, he does not actually kill Fyodor, and his love does not originate with any childhood sexual experience.

Although many Victorians explored family psychodynamics, none argued as did Freud that intense, sexually charged family feelings existed from early childhood and were normal in all children. Victorians tended to view a son's sexual feelings for his mother or hatred of his father as perverse. Freud argued that such feelings, when not excessive, are normal, and that the familial emotions that Victorians worked so diligently to repress are the very ones that need conscious recognition and expression. Pre-Freudian analyses and dramatizations of the family were vaguely aware of sexual tension and conflict, but not on the scale or with the degree of explicitness that such emotions had in Freud's theory of the Oedipus complex. Without any acknowledgment, let alone clinical understanding, of childhood sexual traumas, Victorians were unable to trace any direct lines of causal influence from those traumas into adult mental life. One of the main reasons for Freud's historical influence is that he charted those causal lines through complex but intelligible unconscious mental processes. His single most important clarification of that causal action was in 1897.

THE PSYCHOANALYTIC THEORY OF NEUROSIS

In 1895 Freud first shared with his friend Wilhelm Fliess his incipient theory that neurosis was caused by prepubertal sexual experience.[23] On April 21, 1896, in a lecture before the Viennese Psychiatric and Neurological Association, Freud made that theory public and scandalized his audience by presenting what he believed to be the source of neuropathology. Drawing on analyses of six men and twelve women, he theorized about a common causal factor. "Sexual experiences in childhood consisting in stimulation of the genitals, coitus-like acts, and so on, must therefore be recognized, in the last analysis, as being the traumas which lead to a hysterical reaction to events at puberty and to the development of hysterical symptoms." These seductions were made by other children, usually siblings, or by adult strangers or caretakers, not parents. The seductions did not become pathogenic in childhood but only later when they became "aroused after puberty in the form of unconscious memories." That arousal was usually triggered by subsequent abuse that reawakened "the sensory content of the infantile scenes." Freud admitted, however, that he imperfectly understood the mechanism of that subsequent symptom formation.[24]

The difficult circumstances of Freud's discovery, documentation, and public presentation of the seduction theory of neurosis illustrate how stunningly original it was. He himself resisted the theory, his colleagues were outraged by it, and his patients recoiled from it. Indeed, he insisted that all this resistance to the theory was further evidence of its credibility. He never claimed that his patients consciously recalled and directly admitted seductions, rather that he and they pieced them together, usually against great resistance on the part of the patient, from the direct reports of other people and from indirect, fragmentary evidence based on the interpretation of his patients' dreams and from the neurotic symptoms themselves. Still he was convinced that the only way to make sense of the symptoms was on the basis of the repressed memory of a traumatic childhood seduction.

After risking his reputation with such an outrageous theory, he disclosed to Fliess in a letter of September 21, 1897, that it had to be scrapped for several reasons, most importantly because it implicated many fathers as sexual abusers (even though fathers were not mentioned in the original formulation), and also because it was difficult to distinguish his patients' fantasies of seduction from reality. As he explained, "there are no indications of reality in the unconscious, so that one cannot distinguish between truth and fiction that has been cathected with affect, . . . [and] only later experiences stimulate fantasies, which then hark back to childhood."[25] Mulling over these two main reasons eventually led him to a new theory of neurosis with causal roles attributed to children as well as to their caretakers and to fantasized as well as to real seductions. Moreover, the fantasies did not obscure causes but provided material with which Freud and his patients were able to unravel them.

That new theory was the psychoanalytic theory of neurosis, which Freud announced in late 1897. It revolutionized thinking about childhood causality by affirming the pathogenic force of fantasized seductions, by viewing those fantasies as full of sexual desire, by insisting that that desire was mixed with hostility, and by generally transforming the metapsychological structure of childhood causality.

In affirming the role of fantasy as emanating from the child's psychosexual development, Freud greatly increased the number of individual factors and the complexity of his causal explanation of neurosis. His discovery of the role of fantasies coincided with his discovery that in the unconscious there is no distinction between fantasy and reality. A fantasy of seduction could be just as pathogenic as an actual seduction, if not more so, because with fantasies the child is the originator.

Although Freud questioned the frequency of real seductions, he never questioned that they occurred.[26] He knew full well that some adults abuse children sexually and thereby activate their budding eroticism. But in 1897 he was concerned with documenting a shift in the child's role in such awakenings from passivity to activity according to the new psychoanalytic theory that viewed all normal children as full of nascent but powerful sexual desires associated with erotogenic zones and undifferentiated polymorphous perverse stimuli augmented by erotogenic sights and smells. In 1898 he wrote, "We do wrong to ignore the sexual life of children entirely; in my experience, children are capable of every psychical sexual activity, and many somatic sexual ones as well."[27] It is ironic that Freud should be blamed for downplaying his patients' sexual seductions when he was the first major thinker of his time to take them seriously and make sense of them while also having to fight his patients' resistance and public censure. His originality lay in arguing that such seductions can be experienced as sexual by the child only because the child harbors nascent sexual desires and sexual fantasies of its own. Why some children are traumatized by seductive experiences and become neurotic while others do not remains an unanswered question, but the focus on that question in the psychiatric community is a legacy of Freud's psychoanalytic theory.

Compared with the seduction theory, the psychoanalytic theory also interpreted the child as more responsible for neuroses, because it held that the child's fantasies, generated around its normal sexual desires, play an active role in the formation of neuroses. Sexual abuse, however severe, can be processed psychologically by the child only because it corresponds psychodynamically with the child's own sexual desires and aims. In 1905 Freud theorized that "in *everyone*" there is something innate behind perversions—"the innate constitutional roots of the sexual instincts." Freud stunned his readers by concluding that the roots of adult perversions originate in all children. "This postulated constitution containing the germs of all the perversions, will only be demonstrable in *children*, even though in them it is only with modest degrees of intensity that any of the instincts can emerge."[28]

The child's active role in processing the seduction becomes morally stigmatized as its sexuality becomes censured during normal development when it abandons, as it must, the childhood modes of sexuality— the oral mode during weaning, the anal mode during toilet training, the phallic mode in shifting from masturbation to object relations, and the Oedipal mode in capitulating to anxiety generated by castration threats and guilt stemming from the incest taboo. Those instinctual renunciations take place under the overwhelming pressures of parents and society, so the child's internal sources of sexual desire become morally suspect simply because they must be abandoned. That uncompromising suppression of the child's own sexual constitution, which previously energized its most basic physical pleasures and its earliest intense love relation with the mother, lays a foundation for a lasting stigma of moral censure surrounding any subsequent sexual relationship. And so even malevolent seductions are grounded in the normal child's sexual disposition. Those seductions do involve actual hostility directed against a child, but they can be registered in the child's psyche only because the child harbors powerful hostile impulses of its own. Freud became convinced that children normally harbor aggression toward both parents even in the absence of seduction or abuse, sometimes triggered simply by witnessing adult sexuality but always motivated by the need to become an independent self by separating from parents with whom they identify strongly and whom they love intensely.

In the boy especially, hostility toward the father reaches murderous proportions during the Oedipal stage, which Freud discovered over a number of years of psychoanalyzing patients and himself. In May 1897 he wrote to Fliess, "Hostile impulses against parents (a wish that they should die) are also an integrating constituent of the neuroses."[29] By October he generalized such feelings to all normal children; he had discovered love of his mother and jealousy against his father and considered it "a universal event in early childhood," which explained "the gripping power of *Oedipus Rex*." The patricidal impulse in boys comes from a "compulsion which everyone recognizes because he senses its existence within himself."[30] In *The Interpretation of Dreams* (1899), Freud documented the boy's normal "death-wishes against his parents" and interpreted dreams of the death of a parent as evidence of that hostility, which he elaborated with an extended interpretation of the Sophoclean play. In 1910 he first used the term *Oedipus complex*.[31] Eighteen years later he offered an Oedipal interpretation of the parricide in *The Brothers Karamazov*.

The psychoanalytic theory of neurosis also transformed thinking about the metapsychological aspects of childhood causality from passive to active, conscious to unconscious, simple to complex, external to internal, linear to interactive, reactive to expressive, and sexually innocent to sexually responsible. The new theory reinterpreted the way the seduction occurred, from the child's passive victimization experienced at the conscious level to the child's active complicity experienced at the unconscious level. Instead of generalizing about chronic abuse, it focused on a specific trauma or series of traumas and the subsequent mix of pathogenic sequelae. As he explained in the first full-length case history that applied the new theory—the case of Dora—he was "anxious to show that sexuality does not simply intervene, like a *deus ex machina*, on one single occasion, at some point in the working of the processes which characterize hysteria, but that it provides the motive power for every single symptom."[32] The basic structure of the causal action also shifted from a linear series of sequential events to a field of interactive creations triggered by external events but also energized by the child's normally developing sexual desires and fantasies. Instead of seeing symptoms as merely a defense against external pain, the new theory saw them as a product of the repression of psychosexual desires and of an effort to transcend that repression and communicate the desires to others. Finally, the new theory placed more responsibility on the sexually motivated patient. In Dora's case, Freud concluded that although she was indeed the victim of adult abuse, she was also partly responsible for her neurosis, and the possibility of cure depended on her understanding and accepting her share of responsibility.[33]

Thus, from the Victorian period to the modern, the role of childhood in the determination of adult mental life shifted along a set of gradations from passive to active, from simple to complex, and from sexually innocent and inert to psychosexually experienced and motivated. These shifts can be seen in psychohistory and murder novels.

PSYCHOHISTORY

Psychohistory is the use of psychological theory to explain the behavior of individuals or groups. An early attempt can be found in the German philosopher Wilhelm Dilthey, who in the 1880s urged that history should center on intellectual history based on the great minds of the past. His psychological history ignored the childhood of these thinkers and of course their sexuality. Until the 1930s, biographers generally devoted more introductory pages to ancestral origins than to childhood experiences; references to child sexuality were unthinkable.

In contrast, Freud's psychohistory centered on determinative psychosexual experiences from the childhood of major figures, real and fictional. He explained the murderous plots against Moses and, later, Jesus as the collective rebellion of sons against fathers. He speculated that civilization began with a primordial family in which sons envied the powerful father's monopoly of the women, conspired to kill him, ate him to assimilate his potency, felt remorse at their act, and reenacted it ritually while invoking stringent taboos against its recurrence of their own real or fantasied crimes of murder, cannibalism, and incest that became the foundation of civilized morality. In 1910 he viewed Leonardo da Vinci's art as the product of a childhood desire to remain in a passive homosexual relationship with his mother and viewed his scientific research as a sublimation of childhood impulses to know and to see.[34] Modern psychohistory since these early efforts has been based on Freud or on thinkers who used explanatory concepts that derive from aspects of his developmental psychology: C. G. Jung's "individuation," Alfred Adler's "inferiority complex," Erik H. Erikson's "identity crisis," Heinz Kohut's "narcissistic transference," and Jacques Lacan's "mirror stage."[35]

By the 1950s psychoanalysis achieved considerable influence in literature, popular culture, and the social sciences.[36] In 1957, in his presidential address to the American Historical Association, William Langer urged historians to use psychoanalysis to understand human motivation and thereby deepen their causal explanations. Langer conceded that "the experiences of earliest childhood are no longer rated as important for later development as was once the case," but he emphasized the value of the other defining feature of psychoanalysis—its charting of unconscious mental processes, specifically "repression, identification, projection, reaction formation, displacement, and sublimation."[37] Langer's manifesto underscored the increasing complexity and depth of causal analyses of human behavior made possible by the new "depth psychology."

A response to Langer's recommendation for the profession was under way as he spoke. The next year Erikson published his influential psychobiography *Young Man Luther: A Study in Psychoanalysis and History.*

Erikson credited Freud with challenging the excessively teleological orientation of much nineteenth-century biography but criticized him for going to an opposite extreme by reducing all explanations to what came earliest.[38] Instead Erikson saw Luther's break with Catholicism and the Papacy as caused not by a childhood trauma but by an adolescent identity crisis, energized by rebellion against his father. The debt to Freud is illustrated by Erikson's interpretation of Luther's association of the anus with the devil's face. Erikson saw himself supplementing Freud's theory of anality with his own theory of autonomy, which, he conceded, included Freudian anal characteristics of defiance and stubbornness.

Erikson explained an important chapter of Western history—the Protestant Reformation—as caused in part by Luther's adolescent identity crisis in which "much that he had to say to the devil was fueled by a highly-compressed store of defiance consisting of what he had been unable to say to his father and to his teachers; in due time he said it all, with a vengeance, to the Pope."[39] In spite of the emphasis on adolescence over childhood, the basic structure of Erikson's argument is Freudian, in that anal traumas and intense family dynamics determine adult behavior by means of mental processes operating at the unconscious level.

Erikson warned against making facile connections between Luther's anal preoccupations or his adolescent identity crisis and the rise of Protestantism. Still, he made audacious causal connections between one child's psychosexuality and an enormously important historical event. In so doing he violated a respected rule among traditional historians—that big events must have big causes.

Since the 1960s physicists have studied chaos phenomena, whereby minute differences in input cause enormous differences in output. This process is characterized as "sensitive dependence on initial condition" or, more commonly, "the butterfly effect," after the illustrative hypothetical example of a butterfly's wing motion generating a hurricane around the globe.[40] But historians have resisted explaining huge outputs from tiny inputs. That resistance is especially strong against psychohistorical explanations of the Holocaust, such as that of Rudolph Binion, who in *Hitler among the Germans* argued that two traumas from Hitler's early manhood laid the foundation for his subsequent obsession with killing Jews, both grounded in an initial childhood trauma.[41] Binion's book is highly controversial, positively infuriating to some readers who think it trivializes the Holocaust by explaining it ultimately from the accidents of Hitler's life. I include the following detailed reconstruction of its argument, because it is a prime example of the new research specialty of psychohistory that was generally based on psychoanalytic theory, and it specifically connected childhood experience with adult life, which in the case of Hitler was that of a serial mass murderer.

The origins of Hitler's childhood trauma began even before his birth, because shortly before his conception his mother Klara lost her three young children to diphtheria. Deeply grieved by those deaths and feeling that she was somehow guilty, that her milk might be inadequate or even poisonous, she overfed and overprotected Hitler during his oral stage. She also deserted her husband emotionally as she smothered Adolf with love. She delayed weaning so long, Binion estimated, that Hitler's nursing lasted into the teething stage when he was learning to talk and getting pleasure by biting and inflicting pain on his mother's breasts. Klara traumatized Hitler orally by communicating to him her massive grief and guilt over the loss of her other children while nursing him inordinately long. His oral trauma and subsequent oral fixation were energized positively by his attachment to Klara's unconditional and overwhelming maternal love, tainted by her feelings of guilt and inadequacy, and they were energized negatively by his anger because her overprotection ill prepared him to outgrow her consuming love and learn to deal with life on his own. The evidence for that crippling trauma of satiety, guilt, anxiety, helplessness, and aggression is abundant, if largely retrospective, as interpreted psychohistorically in Hitler's craving for sweets, frenzied tirades, loud speaking at Nazi rallies, dictatorial rule, and lust to conquer more German feeding ground. It is also evident in disguised references to it in speeches to the effect that "the 'Germanic mother' could not feed her children adequately," and, as when justifying ruthless territorial conquests to feed an expanding German population, Hitler noted, "the child does not ask, when it drinks, whether the mother's breast is being tortured" (58). The abiding lessons of his first trauma were that the most important object is a mother's breast and that the greatest danger is starvation.

Hitler's second trauma literally cut off his mother's breasts and introduced an imaginary danger—Jews. On January 14, 1907, when Hitler was seventeen years old, Klara was diagnosed with breast cancer by the Jewish doctor Eduard Bloch. He recommended a double mastectomy, which was performed by a Christian surgeon in the presence of Bloch, who afterward pronounced her cured. By October the cancer returned, and Bloch diagnosed it as incurable. Frantic, Hitler urged Bloch to

prescribe iodoform for his mother against Bloch's advice that it was useless, painful, and toxic. Iodoform is a pungent-smelling drug applied
topically in presoaked strips of gauze. In the patient it causes headaches,
fever, burning thirst, and inability to drink, and is so painful that it is
often accompanied by morphine injections. When inhaled it creates a
burning sensation in the nostrils and eyes. Hitler moved into his
mother's tiny quarters in Linz where for seven weeks he watched her
suffer day and night while himself inhaling the burning, nauseating
stench from iodoform packed into suppurating postsurgical scars over
what had been his mother's breasts. Bloch reapplied the iodoform daily
from early November until her death on December 21, probably from
iodoform poisoning. He collected his fee from Hitler on Christmas Eve.

One source of evidence for a link between this trauma and Hitler's
later killing of Jews is that all the terms of abuse that Hitler subsequently used against Jews over the years reduce to three terms that
characterize Hitler's distorted interpretation of Bloch's role: "the Jewish cancer," "the Jewish poison," "the Jewish profiteer." Hitler knew
that cancer is not Jewish, that iodoform is not Jewish, that Bloch was
not the cause of the cancer, and that the use of the "poison" (iodoform)
was Hitler's own idea, which Bloch opposed. Bloch's Christmas eve
"profiteering" was an accident of the calendar. Still, these expressions
of anti-Semitism all associate Hitler's hatred of the Jews with his
mother's treatment for breast cancer and death, which drew psychic
force in Hitler's mind from the infantile oral trauma that preceded it.

The first trauma involved a hypercathexis of his mother's breasts.
The second trauma involved those breasts being horribly diseased,
then surgically removed, then reinfected with cancer—a traumatic sequence capped by Hitler's own responsibility for "poisoning" them
with a desperate treatment that probably killed her.

Hitler's third trauma magnified the first two into a world historical
event. On October 15, 1918, while serving in the German army, Hitler
was hit by British mustard gas, which burned his skin and temporarily
blinded him. Until early November he convalesced in a hospital where
his eyesight slowly returned. There, upon learning of the armistice he
relapsed into a psychosomatic (hysterical) blindness accompanied by a
seizure and a vision during which he heard a voice, possibly that of his
psychiatrist, summon him to deliver Germany from defeat while himself being cradled in a nurse's arms. He emerged from the hospital
burning with rage against Jews and with a mission to get revenge.

The shock of the gassing and the trauma of defeat triggered Hitler's intense anti-Semitism, because he imagined Jews to be behind both events. In 1907 he had imagined a Jew behind his mother's poisoning and his own physical suffering from iodoform fumes. But that imagining took much unconscious processing, because in fact he was behind her poisoning as well as his own physical suffering. In 1918 the mustard gas reactivated the somatic source of his earlier trauma because he experienced both of them as a burning of his own flesh, especially in the nose and eyes, which also effected a further identification with his mother, who had suffered from the "Jewish cancer" and then the "Jewish poison." Along with other Germans he also imagined Jews to be behind the military defeat, sharing the widespread delusion that German armies had not really lost the war but had been stabbed in the back by civilians, most conspicuously Jews. Over the years, Hitler plotted to get revenge against Jews by pursuing domestic and foreign policies that would eventually enable him to conquer new living space, invade Russia, relocate Jews outside Germany, cleanse Germany of her poisoners, set up extermination camps, and finally kill Jews with a poisonous gas.

Binion argues that Hitler was able to get the German people to help him with this revenge because his third trauma coincided in time and in content with a collective German trauma. The two traumas coincided in time because both were triggered by the shock of defeat in November 1918. They coincided in content because both had oral significance. For Hitler the oral content came from the stinging mustard gas, which reactivated somatically the stinging iodoform vapors and recalled his traumatic loss of the maternal breasts from cancer, mastectomy, iodoform poisoning, and death, a loss that was doubly traumatic because it reactivated his infantile oral trauma at those same breasts. For Germany the trauma came from the masses having experienced sudden and unexpected defeat after a glorious victory in the east, while the western front was still in France, and in anticipation of a final victorious offensive in the west by Ludendorff. That trauma of defeat had oral significance because it was preceded by food shortages arising out of the stress of warfare and the increasing effectiveness of the British "hunger blockade"; then, after the Treaty of Versailles, it was exacerbated by the territorial loss of feeding ground (*Lebensraum*) on Germany's frontiers and its colonial empire overseas.[42] Hitler was able to inspire German support because his rhetoric, fulminating with oral aggression from a massive oral trauma that started in infancy and was potentiated years later, hit a sympathetic chord among Germans who were also traumatized orally in the months before and after the shock of defeat in November 1918. They responded especially to Hitler's aggressive campaign to get revenge against the "November criminals" who signed the armistice and against those who gave away German *Lebensraum* with the Treaty of Versailles.

Binion's evidence includes birth records, documents about nursing customs, Bloch's medical records, a case history by Hitler's psychiatrist, a novel about that case history, memoirs, and archival records; but the most convincing evidence are the psychohistorical interpretation of Hitler's writings and speeches as reworkings of his last two traumas, which themselves went back to his infantile oral trauma. For example, in 1928 Hitler justified his own drastic program for Germany with words that barely disguised his frantic reasoning with Bloch in 1907 over iodoform: "To cure the national body of deep and grave illnesses is not a matter of finding a prescription that is itself completely nontoxic, but frequently of fighting one poison with another. To remove a condition recognized as deadly, one must have the courage to impose and enforce even decisions that themselves harbor dangers" (16). Binion reads such comments as a political reworking of Hitler's traumatic past: his revenge against Jews would be a courageous attempt to cure the German national body of the grave effects of the Jewish poison with an even more potent poison of his own that would pose deadly dangers to Germany in the process. Or again, Binion sees the 1907 trauma behind another of Hitler's comments in 1932, implying Hitler's identification with Bloch as the responsible doctor: "Every plight has a root. So it is not enough . . . for me to doctor around its edges and try now and again to lop off the cancerous growth, but I must get down to its source." (117). Here Hitler saw himself doctoring his way to the cancerous root of the maternal breast projected onto the geopolitical sphere. Such unconscious reworking of his traumatic past led Hitler to develop a foreign policy intended to get at the source of the "Jewish cancer" in Russia and to root it out with the "Final Solution," which he implemented with a directive that a doctor (i.e., Bloch) must always be present to order the gassing.

Although Binion emphasizes an adult trauma over a childhood one, his explanation of Hitler begins with a classic oral trauma and includes Oedipal material in arguing that Hitler's relationship with his mother was a "breast-and-mouth incest" that "unsuited him for any normal erotic relationship" (56, 22). Hitler slept with his mother's picture over his bed and claimed that he could not marry because he was married to the Motherland. The ultimate outcome of his Oedipus complex was violent and murderous, because just after he finally did marry, after resigning as Führer, he poisoned his wife and shot himself while the Fatherland, which he alone called the Motherland, went up in flames.

Binion also explains by using Freudian unconscious mechanisms. Hitler *repressed* the infantile source of later traumas and behavior, so he did not consciously link his mother's cancer in 1907 with what happened in his infancy and did not know that when he expanded Germany territorially to acquire feeding ground he was trying to recapture the blissful abundance of his mother's love when nursing. He *displaced* his love for his mother onto Germany, which made it possible for him to *sublimate* his tabooed infantile love for his mother's breast into a socially acceptable adult love for his Motherland. He further displaced the causes of his misfortunes in obsessing over the "Jewish cancer" and the "Jewish poison," because Jews were responsible for neither. His attempts to poison the poisoner and reverse the defeat of 1918, although manifested with conscious words and deeds, were processed at the unconscious level by the mechanism of *undoing*. His private *denial* was reinforced by the collective national denial that the German army had not really lost the war but had been "stabbed in the back" by civilians. His traumatic reliving of the trauma of 1918 itself involved further *regression* back to his infantile experience of being coddled; these moments additively energized his compulsion to reexperience 1918 in order to revise it as well as repeat it. He *projected* his responsibility for prescribing iodoform onto Bloch while also denying it. His attitude toward Bloch, and behind him Jews, involved a *reaction formation* (the turning of an emotion into its opposite, for example love into hate), because the Jewish doctor actually tried to protect Hitler's mother by warning Adolf about the dangers of iodoform. Reaction formation also accounts for his unconscious transformation of an impulse to save Germany (i.e., his mother) into an impulse to destroy Germany. He did this on the conscious level by killing Jews and invading Russia, which drained military resources and corrupted morale, and, in the last weeks of the war, by ordering the destruction of key installations in Germany without regard for the safety of German citizens. The mechanism of *incorporation*, along with regression, accounts for the mustard gas causing Hitler to "suffer his mother's martyrdom in his own flesh" (21). His conscious policy of expanding Germany's frontiers for feeding ground *symbolized* his unconscious desire to recapture the maternal breast.

I have reconstructed Binion's argument in detail because it illustrates every feature of my larger argument about the specificity-uncertainty dialectic applied to childhood causality. It shows how psychoanalysis increased the specificity, multiplicity, and complexity of causal understanding by tracking specific stages of psychosexual development, multiple characterological consequences for each stage, the complex interdependencies of unconscious mental processes, and the numerous points of trauma and fixation which can cause adult neurosis by endlessly complex psychic pathways. It also reflects the incomplete and uncertain nature of psychoanalytic interpretation. Freud was a psychic determinist, insisting that every psychic event has a cause. What he did explain is not uncertain, but the many new determinants he identified raised new questions and created an additional sense of uncertainty or at least inconclusiveness to his interpretations. Similarly, Binion offered decisive determinative causes for Hitler's central goal of killing Jews, but his last chapter, titled "Loose Ends," conceded candidly that "every insight is tentative and every connection between insights tenuous" (129). Finally, Binion also explained how a childhood trauma can help explain a life of enormous historical significance that was based on murder, which is my focus.

Literary dramatizations of how childhood experience affects adult mental life shifted gradationally from passive to active, simple to complex, chronic to acute, and sexually innocent to sexually motivated.

Orientation: Passive to Active

In Victorian murder novels children are acted upon by others and shaped by passive experiences of abuse or neglect with a minimum of their own activity, as if they were Locke's blank tablets. In Washington Irving's "The Story of the Young Italian" (1824), the murderer's first-person narrative is in the passive voice about how an "irritable temperament" was given to him at birth and then further provoked in childhood by the wickedness of others. He was "looked upon with indifference by [his] father" and sent to a convent where he heard dismal stories about evil spirits and "was taught nothing but fear and hatred." These influences fated him to avenge his victimization by murdering a rival for a woman in a diabolical plot that stretched back to his childhood persecution.[43] In Hugo's *Notre-Dame of Paris* (1831), Claude Frollo's childhood is one of indoctrination under the authority of Catholicism. Its restrictive morality repressed his sexuality, which later erupted in murderous jealousy over the gypsy dancer Esmeralda. The narrator who is the murderer in William Simms's *Guy Rivers* (1834) explains his mother's overbearing influence during his formative years: "She taught me the love of evil with her milk—she sang it in lullabies over my cradle—she gave it to me in the playthings of my boyhood; her schoolings have made me the morbid, the fierce criminal." He concedes that she did not explicitly instruct him to do evil but influenced him in that direction by her own example and by neglect of his moral education.[44]

In *Martin Chuzzlewit* (1844), Dickens's murderous Jonas is schooled in vice by his own father, shaped "in the precept and example always before him to engender and develop the vices that make him odious, . . . and justified from his cradle in cunning, treachery, and avarice" (39). When Jonas's father discovers his son's intention to poison him for an inheritance, he realizes his own responsibility and forgives Jonas because, he explains, "it began when I taught him to be too covetous of what I have to leave" (863). The murderous passion of Zola's heroine in *Thérèse Raquin* (1867) is cultivated in the hothouse atmosphere of the squalid room where as a child she had been forced to share a bed with her sickly cousin Camille, whom she is subsequently obliged to marry and later murders. Zola acknowledged the "stored-up energy and passion lying dormant in her quiescent body," but it is a vague energy and passion, far less specific than overt Freudian psychosexuality. In Wilde's *The Picture of Dorian Gray* (1890), the arrogant hero is passively destined for vanity because of his mother's exquisite beauty, destined for violence as a consequence of a plot to kill his father shortly after his birth, and destined for evil and murder from early victimization under "the tyranny of an old and loveless man" (42).

These Victorian murderers receive the seeds of the murder impulse passively: Frollo from Catholic dogma, Rivers from lullabies and his mother's milk, Chuzzlewit from precepts and examples, Raquin from the oppressive atmosphere of her aunt's home, and Gray from a tyrannical old man. Of course, for these passive influences to result in murder they had to be internalized and then activated. In the Victorian novel, those processes are ignored or explained imprecisely as the result of moral deficiency, errant destiny, or inherent evil. In the modern novel, children respond to external influences more actively, and the complex circuitry from childhood trauma to adult murder is explained more specifically as the product of unconscious mental processes.

The formative experiences of the adult murderer in Horace McCoy's *Kiss Tomorrow Goodbye* (1948) are triggered by others but registered in and elaborated by means of his emerging sexual desires. Ralph Cotter's first-person narration probes the origin of his own murderous impulses, which are unknown to him at the outset of the story and revealed at the end as a series of childhood sexual traumas. At one and a half years of age he was walking to the outhouse, which he referred to as the *cloaca*, suggesting sewer or vagina. He was accompanied by his grandmother, whom he thought was his mother. When he became traumatized by the sound of horses mating, she playfully sheltered him under her large black dress. His more active role began when this innocent game turned serious as he came to long for her protective dress whenever his grandfather tried to find him and punish him, and, he narrates, "all the time I was growing up and getting bigger and wondering about things" (336). His sexual wondering became traumatic when he saw his grandfather castrate a ram. His sexual desires were aroused around the age of six when he pretended to be afraid, crawled under his grandmother's skirt, "and finally started exploring her legs." She got angry and threatened to have his grandfather do to him what he did to the ram (337). Terrified, he hit her on the head with a rock to silence her but accidentally killed her. These childhood traumas involved a number of causally decisive psychosexual experiences in which the child played an active role: pregenital association of anality and sexuality (the outhouse/cloacal setting), witnessing the primal scene displaced to animals (horses mating), castration anxiety (grandfather's castration of the ram and threats against him), and an Oedipus complex (playing with grandmother's/mother's legs under her dress and the grandfather's threat).

The title of Meyer Levin's novel *Compulsion* (1956) refers to the active impulses motivating Artie Strauss and Judd Steiner that originated in their childhood. In this novel, based on an actual murder by Nathan Leopold (Artie) and Richard Loeb (Judd), a psychoanalyst speculates on the childhood origins of their murder compulsion. Artie had sibling rivalry with his baby brother, and so he chose a young boy for a victim. In college Artie was impotent with women and therefore chose a taped chisel for a weapon, which symbolized a big hard penis to compensate for his phallic insecurity. Judd's murder compulsion also went back to childhood. His parents had wanted a girl instead of a boy, and after his birth his mother's health began to fail. The psychoanalyst explains, "This child feels his birth killed his mother, but his father killed her first. It's the classic complex, the Oedipus . . . the boy in love with his mother, hating his father" (305). Judd was the one who chose to pour acid on the face and genitals of the victim and then stuff him into a cistern. These acts symbolically undo Judd's own identity, sex, and birth by obliterating the victim's face and genitals and then stuffing the body, which symbolized himself as a naked and bloody, newborn baby girl, back into a tube from which water was slowly flowing. "This child had been placed naked in a womb, returned to pre-birth. And the womb was a sewer—the way he had always thought of females" (407). Levin's explanation includes a cluster of traumatic childhood origins in which both boys' emergent sexuality plays an active role: Artie's sibling rivalry, phallic insecurity, and castration anxiety; Judd's birth trauma, troubled gender identification, and Oedipal guilt.

Levin wrote in the 1950s, when psychoanalysis peaked in influence before the assaults from some feminists and postmodernists in the 1970s. But Freud's influence continued especially among novelists who needed to establish powerful motivation for serial killers driven to commit violent, sadistic murders by compulsions originating in childhood and germinating over many years. Although the traumas to these children were committed by adults, the child victims responded with their own emerging sexuality far more actively than their comparatively more passive childhood predecessors in Victorian murder novels.

This modern emphasis on the child's active complicity, however, does not diminish the reality of the traumas. An exceptionally brutal child abuse triggers a child's increasingly emotional reactivity in Shane Stevens's *By Reason of Insanity* (1979). Thomas Bishop was conceived during his mother's rape by a man who, she later came to believe, was the convicted serial rapist Caryl Chessman. She cultivated a maniacal hatred of men and sex, which she displaced onto Thomas. She beat and burned him and told him bedtime stories about male monsters, sometimes named Chessman, who did hideous things to female victims. As Thomas matured she hated him for his growing masculinity and tormented him accordingly. The beatings became sadomasochistic orgies: "Horror-filled eyes huge now, mouth foaming, she would scream at him. . . . Blood demons pouncing, crushing, wrenching muscle from bone. Insane paws ripping flesh apart, huge gaping mouths gulping whole intestines, heart, liver, kidneys slit open strap beating beating screaming both of them screaming now in nameless terror slowly sinking eyes unseeing frenzy-flushed pain-pleased bodies slowly sinking sinking softly into silent sleep" (40). One night he snapped and put his mother, still conscious, in the wood stove and watched her burn to bones. The prologue to the novel is his reaction to this atrocity: "Silent now but for a gurgling singsong moan from somewhere deep in his throat, his eyes maniacal in the red glow of the fire, the boy watched his mother's body burn." When he grew up he became a serial killer shaped by this traumatic past: he fancied himself raping like his "father" Chessman, beating and torturing like his mother, but going one better: after killing her once he killed her again and again, mutilating his victims and then having sex with them while he strangled or stabbed them.

In Thomas Harris's novels child sexual traumas are the earliest acting and deepest-lying causes for his characters becoming serial killers. In *Red Dragon* (1981), Francis Dolarhyde's life began with an oral trauma when he was born with a cleft palate. His mother screamed when she saw him and abandoned him in the hospital. His deformity also made it impossible to suck or nurse, and later other children called him "cunt-face." His grandmother retrieved him from an orphanage and raised him. To cure his bed-wetting she pinched his penis in a pair of scissors and threatened to cut it off if he wet the bed again. Once he and a local girl stripped to see each other naked, and as he squatted to see her genitals, a recently decapitated chicken that was running around spattered blood on her legs. His grandmother saw this, sent him to his room, and told him to take off his pants and wait for her get the scissors. He never ceased that anxious waiting. Once he fantasized rescuing his grandmother from burglars to win back her love and lift the castration threat, but since he was too small to protect her from real burglars, he wrung the neck of a chicken instead. After his mother remarried, his stepbrother teased him for being ugly, once smashing his face into a mirror and smearing it with his own blood and mucus.

Each of these traumas contributed to the modus operandi of his serial killing. He could not suck as an infant, so he made a replica of his grandmother's dentures to fit in his surgically altered mouth and bite victims. But he did not suck or bite the wounds for pleasure or to eat his victims; his goal was pure oral aggression. The boy who had been called cuntface by the other boys in his orphanage ejaculated on the faces of his female victims. He had been abandoned by his mother, so he killed families out of attraction for the mother. He had been caught under the gaze of his watchful grandmother and had had his face smashed into a mirror, so he put shards of broken mirror in the mouth, vagina, and eyes of the dead mothers he killed so they could "see" him murder the rest of their family. He had been punished for being wet and later smeared with blood and mucus, so he punished his victims by making them wet with blood and semen. He compensated for the castration anxiety and poor self image of his childhood by fantasizing that while murdering he was becoming the red dragon in a William Blake painting, titled *The Red Dragon*, which had a huge, muscular phallic tail.

Killers in nineteenth-century novels did not reach this level of brutality and did not have such horrific childhoods. The causal role of Dolarhyde's birth deformity suggests a comparison with the creature in *Frankenstein*, who was also driven to murder because people recoiled from his frightening appearance. But Mary Shelley's creature was not abused as a child and did not kill because the act of killing in itself fulfilled some deep-rooted sadistic need for murder that originated with his own emergent sexuality in response to childhood traumas.

Thomas Harris crafted another traumatic childhood behind the serial killer in *The Silence of the Lambs* (1988). Jame Gumb had an intense, but largely fantasized, relationship with his mother, who became an alcoholic and abandoned him to a foster home when he was two. He remembers her with a VCR tape made from newsreel footage of her parading in a bathing suit in the Miss Sacramento beauty contest back in 1948, when she was one month pregnant with him. As an adult he became aroused watching the videotape before killing women to "harvest" their skin with which to make a vest-like suit that he would wear to effect a symbolic identification with his long-lost mother. Harris also added a childhood trauma for the detective Clarice Starling, who as a young girl discovered that her stepfather bred horses and lambs for slaughter. Her horror over killing innocent animals for food creates a bond with Hannibal, whose horror at killing the innocent for food also originated in a childhood trauma, which Harris finally disclosed in *Hannibal*.

Hannibal was the son of a Lithuanian count. He was six years old in 1944 when retreating German panzers shelled their estate, killing his parents. Then he witnessed some starving German deserters who shot and brutally dismembered a deer for food. A few days later they were again ravenous and came for one of the children huddled in the barn. After feeling Hannibal's skinny thigh they passed him by and went instead for his chubby two-year-old sister Mischa. They pulled her out of his desperate grasp, breaking his arm as they slammed the barn door. His fervent prayer that he would see Mischa alive again was interrupted by the sound of an ax and then horribly disappointed a few days later when he saw her teeth in the Germans' reeking stool pit. Hannibal's subsequent killing and cannibalism originated with this trauma. He killed and ate people who were cruel to animals or children, and he protected Clarice because she had a similar trauma from seeing innocent creatures slaughtered for food.

Thus, a comparison of Victorian and modern murder novels reveals the shift from passive victimization to more active complicity emanating from the child's emerging passions and sexual desires. Modernists writing about serial murder in particular needed a plausible explanation for brutal acts that were often driven by raging sexual instincts and repeated with increasing frequency and destructive force. Childhood sexual traumas provided the most plausible explanation for such acts, and so novelists were drawn to the Freudian model. This shift is not, however, absolute: the moderns retained elements of child passivity, and the Victorians acknowledged some active complicity. The moderns adapted more of Freud's earlier seduction theory than his psychoanalytic theory because they wanted to dramatize more directly how horrible things actually done to children, rather than fantasized, caused them to do actual horrible things in turn. But compared with Victorians, the moderns still emphasized more active sexual desire coming from the child in response to those horrors. On the other hand, the Victorians acknowledged some active complicity by the child, but they accounted for it with vague concepts such as tainted heredity, moral evil, or errant destiny, whereas the moderns explained the action of the traumas with more precise accounts of an increasingly complex network of causal factors.

EXTENT: SIMPLICITY TO COMPLEXITY

In arguing for a second shift from simplicity to complexity, we must avoid two misunderstandings. First, while Victorian explanations of childhood determination were simpler than the modernists', they were not simplistic. Victorian novelists such as Flaubert and Eliot were exquisitely sensitive to subtleties and complexities of human thought and emotion and their origins in memory. But Victorian explanations of the specific childhood determination of adult mental life were not as precise, detailed, or lengthy as those by later writers, especially those aware of Freud. Second, the argument about modernist complexity also invites misunderstanding. Throughout the years of my study, *complex* could mean chaotic or confused. Many moderns struggled to clarify more precisely the elements of an increasingly complex causal analysis. Mindful of these clarifications, I can abundantly document a measured argument about a gradational shift from simpler to more complex accounts of child causality.

The passivity of Victorian childhood abuse that I traced in the preceding section meant that the determinative experience worked in a uniform way as a direct consequence of the conscious intentions and outward behavior of the abuser toward the child. The lack of reciprocity from the child also meant a relative lack of complexity. Thus Frollo's childhood experience came from the single channel of religious discipline, Rivers's came from lack of parental discipline, Chuzzlewit's came from his father's sowing of evil, and Raquin's came from an oppressive aunt. In a study of homicide in American fiction, David Brion Davis noted how in many Victorian novels, overdrawn characters had simplified "good" or "bad" motives deriving from schematic childhood origins: "good brothers uncovered the villainy of bad brothers' fathers, and good sons rescued hidden mothers and cleared the reputation of murdered good fathers." Davis concluded that "moral values were simplified and clarified in this literature by a disproportional emphasis on family ties and sexual attraction."[45] But the family ties and sexual attractions in Victorian novels did not emanate from the sorts of powerful fixations and deep instinctual drives that Freud believed were present in every normal child and that modern novelists adapted to motivate their murderers.

In modern novels, childhood development is a network of psychosexual complexity. In *An American Tragedy* (1925), Dreiser spent the first third of this long novel on the childhood and youth of the murderer Clyde Griffiths. Dreiser implied a multifaceted childhood causality, characterizing Clyde's family as one that "presented one of those anomalies of psychic and social reflex and motivation such as would tax the skill of not only the psychologist but the chemist and physicist as well, to unravel" (13). One might add the theologian, economist, and social historian to that list of specialists, because Dreiser elaborated Clyde's motivation in this *American* tragedy as deriving from his childhood and youth out of a network of psychosocial factors as complex as American society itself.

As I have noted, the childhood determinants of Ralph Cotter in *Kiss Tomorrow Goodbye* include anal sexuality from the cloaca associated with the sound of mating horses, tactile eroticism from playing with his grandmother's legs under her dress, and visual anxiety from witnessing an actual castration magnified by his grandmother's castration threats. To these interacting agencies McCoy added a haunting smell which eventually discloses the childhood origin of Ralph's homicidal impulse. His lover Margaret Dobson exudes an odor that he recognizes but cannot place. When he finally identifies it as the perfume *Huele de Noche*, she insists that she is not wearing perfume. His search for the meaning of that odor combines theories of forgetting and recollecting from Proust and Freud. As he narrates, "I was close to remembering something, that I vaguely knew I did not want to remember, but . . . like a clap of thunder there was a bright blinding light inside my head and through it I could feel the cold wind tunnelling from many, many years away and when it passed it left in focus only a white, white face, and black, black hair, and there was my grandmother stretched stiffly in the coffin in the parlor . . . and the room was filled with the smell of the big *Huele de Noche* bushes which had grown around the house" (113). Then he realizes that he was not smelling Margaret's perfume but his own imagination of it. "Her face was the same whiteness as my grandmother's, and her hair of the same blackness, and . . . this was what had done it." To this Proustian involuntary memory, Ralph adds a Freudian repressed memory. The imagined odor is a "symbol that belongs to . . . the infantile world of shameless libidinous fantasy that I have just left" (115). When he is with Margaret he imagines the odor, which triggers increasingly violent sexual impulses. During a climactic confrontation he tries to make love to Margaret and resist the murder impulse from his traumatic past, which is now clear. "I killed you once," he pleads, "do not make me kill you again" (339). McCoy underscored the complexity of childhood origins by combining a Proustian search for the expanding intricacies of lost time with a Freudian search for the childhood determinants of a repressed traumatic memory triggered by an odor in addition to anal-erotic, tactile, and visual stimuli.

In *Compulsion*, Levin's account of the complexity of childhood determinants expands as the boys' lawyers hire specialists to find more causal factors to increase the extenuating circumstances for the murder in their legal defense. Neurologists, endocrinologists, and cardiologists test for aberrations that may account for the homicide. They use cardiograms, X rays, Rorschachs, thematic apperception tests, and "newfangled metabolism tests" to look for motives. The lead attorney insists on completeness: "The whole past life of the patient, his diseases and accidents, his schooling, environment, and character, and the entire history of his antecedents should be examined" (340). The tactic is to overwhelm the judge with the complexity of the boys' hereditary and environmental circumstances and their consequently varied and confused motives in order to create reasonable doubt about their criminal intent and thus avoid a death sentence.

While *Compulsion* fictionalized the complex childhood origins of two real murderers in Chicago in 1924, Caleb Carr's *The Alienist* (1994) projected the complex childhood of an imaginary serial murderer in New York back to 1896, the critical year when Freud published the seduction theory. One investigator in the novel is the psychiatrist Laszlo Kreizler, and his causal analysis draws from Freud's seduction theory as well as his psychoanalytic theory of neurosis. While Kreizler is uncertain whether the determinative traumas had been real and imposed from without or partly fantasized in childhood by the serial killer he is hunting, he is confident they occurred in childhood. As he explains to his co-investigator, a newspaper reporter, "The creature you seek was created long ago. Perhaps in his infancy—certainly in his childhood" (68). Kreizler locates his analysis historically by explaining that he intends to find the murderer by following a psychological determinism leading back to childhood. His new causal analysis will reject older explanatory concepts such as "evil and barbarity and madness; none of these concepts would lead us any closer to him" (160). The elaborate sadism of the murders points to the perpetrator's own victimization as a child. The first three victims were boy prostitutes found with their eyes gouged out, their inner organs exposed from knife cuts, and their genitals cut off and stuck in their mouths. Kreizler speculates that the victims are "a representation of what [the murderer] felt had been done to him—even if only psychically—at some point in his deep past" (193). Kreizler dates his theoretical approach more precisely by explaining, "The recent findings of

Breuer and Freud on hysteria point to prepubertal sexual abuse by the *father* in nearly every case." But then he adds, "Freud began by assuming sexual abuse as the basis for all hysteria, but recently he seems to have altered that view, and decided that *fantasies* concerning abuse may be the actual cause" (253). Carr fudged the chronology slightly here, because the story begins and ends in 1896, while only in 1897 did Freud abandon the seduction theory for the psychoanalytic theory.

As the investigation proceeds, the causal analysis combines Freud's earlier and later theories, starting with actual parental abuse but then augmented by the boy's fantasies. Kreizler is able to speculate about those fantasies after interviewing the murderer's older brother, who reveals the murderer's name, Japeth Dury, and explains that their mother detested sex. The brother heard her scream the night Japeth was conceived, and Japeth grew up to symbolize her husband's lust. So she weaned and toilet trained Japeth as early as she could and scolded him for bed-wetting. She seared his heart with her cruel eyes and lied to him that he was the child of "red Indians—dirty, man-eating savages" (421). While still a boy Japeth responded to this abuse with sadism when he began to cut up live animals. At age eleven he was sexually molested by a hired hand named George Beecham. In reaction, as an adult Japeth changed his name to Beecham and victimized young boys just as he had been victimized by the original Beecham, as well as by his mother and the Indians who were supposed to have been his parents. The link between the childhood traumas and the adult serial killing is revealed when Kreizler finds in Japeth's apartment a photograph of an Indian massacre, showing a dead man who has been scalped, eviscerated, emasculated, and left eyeless. Japeth's victims reenacted and reversed his own childhood trauma, with himself playing the victimizer.

Temporality: Chronic to Acute

The argument about the shift from chronic to acute causality is based partly on missing evidence, because I did not find a single Victorian novel with a murder stemming from a specific childhood trauma. In William Simms's *Guy Rivers* (1834), Colonel Munro speculates about the causes of Rivers's penchant for murder. "I was always inclined to think that circumstances in childhood . . . such as a great and sudden fright to the infant, or a blow which affected the brain, were the operating influences." But, as David Brion Davis noted, "the colonel could not account for Rivers's extreme malignity by such a theory."[46] Even this unusual Victorian theorizing about a decisive childhood trauma makes no reference to sexuality and does not explain the murderer.

The concept of trauma itself became more integral to psychological causal explanations in the 1880s, when its source began to shift from the physical (typically train wrecks) to the mental. Those Victorian murderers whose childhoods were given greatest attention were shaped by chronic "cruelty to children" in the form of protracted moral neglect (Guy Rivers, Jonas Chuzzlewit, and Dorian Gray) or chronic monomaniacal zeal (Claude Frollo, Thérèse Raquin, and McTeague). For the modern period, in addition to the acute traumas in McCoy, Harris, and Carr already surveyed, William Faulkner, Jim Thompson, and Truman Capote also relied on traumas to establish compelling motivation.

In Faulkner's *Absalom, Absalom!* Thomas Sutpen's childhood trauma is the mainspring for murder. When he was a young boy, Thomas's father sent him to "the big house" with a message. A Negro in livery answered the door and told him to go around back (192). Faulkner provided three defining aspects of this trauma for young Thomas: "he was seeking among what little he had to call experience for something to measure it by, and he couldn't find anything" (188); "he knew that something would have to be done about it in order to live with himself for the rest of his life" (189); and "it finally told him what to do that night he forgot about it and didn't know that he still had it" (192). Thus, although the trauma is not sexual, it conforms to three other key aspects of Freud's theory of the trauma: it is too powerful to be processed by normal psychological means, it is a determinative core of his emerging personality, and it is repressed but remains active enough to motivate a murder.

The trauma motivates Thomas's plan to make certain that such a thing could never happen again: he resolves to become wealthy and own a big house, have his own slaves, marry into a respectable family, and sire a distinguished dynasty. The plan is threatened when he learns that his first wife is part Negro. He divorces her, but years later their son Charles comes into his life by chance and successfully courts Thomas's daughter Judith from his "respectable" second marriage. When Thomas discovers that Charles is his own racially mixed son, he realizes that Charles's marriage to Judith would involve incest and miscegenation. To prevent this social catastrophe, he instills his son Henry with his own dynastic aspirations and motivates him to murder Charles. Although Faulkner set the trauma in the Victorian era, his literary use of it is unmistakably modern, if not directly influenced by Freud.

The source of the homicidal urge of the serial killer Lou Ford in Thompson's *The Killer Inside Me* (1952) is a traumatic discovery that the housekeeper who had initiated him into sex as a youth had once been his father's mistress. Ford's first-person narration reconstructs the shock of recognition as he examines an old photograph he discovered stuck in his father's book: "It was a woman's face, not pretty exactly, but the kind that gets to you without your knowing why. . . . Offhand it looked like she was peering through the crotch of a tree. . . . She was looking through a crotch, all right. But it was her own. She was on her knees, peering between them. And those crisscross blurs on her thighs weren't the result of age. They were scars. The woman was Helene, who had been Dad's housekeeper so long ago." That painful discovery clarifies the meaning of the violent confrontation he had overheard when his father fired Helene after discovering her seduction of his son. The interpretation of the photograph transformed Ford's recollection of that disturbing confrontation into a devastating trauma by a mechanism that Freud called trauma by deferred action (*Nachträglichkeit*). Later Ford realizes that two of his female murder victims looked like Helene (105–8).

In Capote's nonfiction murder novel, *In Cold Blood* (1965), Perry Smith does the killing of the Clutter family, starting with the father. The foundation for that murder went back to childhood traumas. The first was one of terror and shame, as Perry watched his father beat his mother after catching her with a sailor. She became increasingly promiscuous and alcoholic and eventually choked to death on her own vomit. Perry grew up as a "hated, hating half-breed child" living in a California orphanage, where he was traumatized again when nuns whipped him savagely for bed-wetting. In a second orphanage, as Perry recalled, the cottage mistress "would throw back the covers and furiously beat me with a large black leather belt—pull me out of bed by my hair and drag me to the bathroom and throw me in a tub and turn on the cold water and tell me to wash myself and the sheets" (309). She also put burning ointment on his penis and encouraged the other children to call him a sissy.

Perry's childhood was marked by traumatic brutality and neglect, which resulted in his insecurity about being teased and inability to control anger. A minor insult could trigger blinding rage, which happened when he killed Mr. Clutter and the rest of his family after breaking into their home. The sudden impulsiveness of Perry's slitting Mr. Clutter's throat matches the suddenness of the childhood traumas that established the mental foundation for it.

A fuller explanation of the connection between the childhood traumas and the murder is made by the psychiatrist hired to testify about Perry's sanity. When Perry killed Mr. Clutter, he was "deep inside a schizophrenic darkness, for it was not entirely a flesh-and-blood man he 'suddenly discovered' himself destroying, but 'a key figure in some past traumatic configuration'" (338–39). As a child, Perry had been traumatized by his parents' fights and neglect and by the punishments and teasing he suffered because of his enuresis, which caused him to develop a fragile ego, a debilitating sense of sexual inadequacy, and a hair trigger on his anger.

To support this analysis, the psychiatrist cited an article, "Murder without Apparent Motive," which further explained seemingly "unmotivated" acts such as Perry's as the result of unconscious reworkings of repressed childhood traumas. The article, written by four psychiatrists in 1960, summarized the current thinking about the childhood origin of such murders. "The history relating to *extreme* violence, whether fantasied, observed in reality, or actually experienced by the child, fits in with the psychoanalytic hypothesis that the child's exposure to overwhelming stimuli, before he can master them, is closely linked to early defects in ego formation and later severe disturbances in impulse control." In the four murderers studied, there was evidence of violence in childhood, emotional deprivation by parents, physical or sexual deficiencies (all were called "sissies"), and in some cases severe oral deprivation.[47]

The description of murders as "without apparent motive" implies a historical dating, because the lack of "apparent" motivation refers to the expectations of pre-Freudian analysis of murder by researchers who expected to explain conscious actions based on readily apparent motives such as greed or revenge. Axiomatic for Freudians is that "apparently" purposive behavior is caused by factors that are not readily apparent—mainly repressed childhood traumas that are reworked by unconscious mental processes and only become apparent after psychoanalysis.

Embodiment: Sexually Innocent to Sexually Motivated

The first three shifts—toward increasing activity, complexity, and temporal acuteness—concern the structure of childhood causality. The final shift concerns the content of childhood traumas, which in the modern era was often sexual, as is especially evident in the relationship between male murderers and their mothers.

In the Victorian novel, mothers are a source of love, goodness, and faith, and murderers are usually raised without a mother's care or affection. Jonas Chuzzlewit, Claude Frollo, and Irving's Italian murderer are raised away from their parents. When mothers do play a role, it is sexually innocent, as in *Crime and Punishment* (1866). Raskolnikov's anguished mother love has roots in the past and plays a role in his decision to commit murder, but readers get no specifics about his childhood or any hint of its sexual content. Raskolnikov is incensed when he learns that his mother is urging his sister to compromise herself by agreeing to marry an unworthy older rich man to help him financially, and his decision to kill the pawnbroker for money is motivated in part by his humiliation and anger over their sacrifices. His mother love resurfaces in the end when he returns to Christian faith and appeals to his mother, "Let me make the sign of the cross over you and bless you!" (436). Then he kisses her feet and they embrace tearfully.

In modern murder novels, the sexual content of a son's relationship with his mother plays an increasingly prominent role evident in three main scenarios: some mothers seduce with overt sexuality, some mix love with aggression, while others create psychological havoc by emotional neglect. Although the victimized boy is largely passive, in each of these scenarios he is the source of some active response even if merely in providing the psychosexual foundation that enables him to experience and process the mother's seduction, aggression, or neglect as traumatic. This he can do because he feels a nascent version of her desire toward him. For example, he knows what it is like for her to feel pleasure in touching him, because he has himself enjoyed her touch.

In *Kiss Tomorrow Goodbye*, Cotter's grandmother first aroused him sexually by hiding him under her dress, where he explored his own sexual desire by touching her legs. The classic modern novel about a sexually exploitive mother activating the pathological response of a serial killer is Robert Bloch's *Psycho* (1959). At the beginning of the story the reader assumes that Norman Bates is living with his mother and running a motel. Bloch narrates the mother's role as if she were alive, giving Norman advice, calling him impotent, chastising him for sins, and analyzing his problems with direct quotations: "Psychology, he calls it! A lot *you* know about psychology! I'll never forget that time you talked so dirty to me, never. To think that a son could come to his own mother and *say* such things!" (17). But the reader begins to suspect that this dialogue is going on in Norman's mind between the revengeful persona of his mother Norma and his own submissive little-boy self. He explains to one motel guest that after his father abandoned him, his mother raised him by herself and imposed strict controls. After the guest urges him to put his mother in a home, he flies into a rage and later stabs her in the shower, while dressed as his mother and assuming her crazed personality.

A psychiatrist explains the childhood origins of Norman's murders. When Norman's overprotective mother prevented him from expressing normal sexual desires, he became a transvestite. When she threatened to disrupt their intimacy by marrying another man, Norman poisoned them. While writing her fake suicide note, he took on her personality. Then he missed her so much that he dug up her body and preserved it with his taxidermy skills. The person who murdered was a composite of three selves: the adult Norman who ran the hotel, the little boy Norman who still craved his mother's approval, and the mother avenging anyone who threatened him as an adult.

Another seductive mother raises a murderer in Don DeLillo's *Libra* (1988), a fictionalized novel about the Kennedy assassination. It traces the motives of Lee Harvey Oswald back to his traumatic childhood with his overprotective mother, who stunted his normal sexual development. Lee slept in his mother's bed until he was eleven and shared a small bathroom with her. Their intimacy was tactile and olfactory in the cloacal settings of childhood sexuality. "He could smell the air she moved through, smell her clothes hanging behind a door. . . . He entered the bathroom in the full aura of her stink." His mother did not use deodorant, and their relationship was so oppressive that "something in him turned to murder at the sight of her" (38). When she worked as a nurse, her uniform triggered fantasies of an "angel of terror and memory sweeping down from the sky. . . . All this love and pain confused him" (227). Like the other murderers with overtly seductive mothers, Oswald's violence came from a need to define himself as an individual out of the suffocating intimacy with his overprotective mother.

The second scenario of determinative child sexual trauma comes from a mixture of maternal love and aggression. In *The Alienist* Dury's mother hated him for being male and brutally punished him for bed-wetting, while in *By Reason of Insanity* Bishop's mother blamed him for being the child of her rape and beat him until the two of them fell asleep together. In *Red Dragon* the one person who loved Dolarhyde as a child, his grandmother, threatened to cut off his penis for bed-wetting.

The title of Robert Bloch's novel *The Scarf* (1947) refers to a maroon scarf that Daniel Morley uses to strangle women who remind him of his sexually provocative and verbally aggressive mother, who laughed at him for bed-wetting, accused him of trying to seduce his sister, and ridiculed him for sex play with a neighbor. She also told him that sex was vile and tied his hands to bedposts with strips of red flannel to keep him from "polluting" himself by masturbating (23). One night, after discovering his parents having sex, he ran back to his bed in terror and slipped his hands back in the flannel bonds. In a journal, he recalled the connection between that moment and his murders: "You hated your mother from then on, although you didn't know then that it was hate. . . . You weren't a pretty pair: the dumbly resentful son; the frustrated and antagonistic mother, unconsciously, unremittingly seeking revenge for something, not knowing what it was" (24). The night his schoolteacher gave him the scarf he tied her up with it, attempted to rape her, and then turned on the gas in an attempt to conceal his crime by killing her and himself, although they both survived. His strangulation victims were a displaced revenge against his mother, while the red strips and the maroon scarf linked her traumatization of him to his later murders.

The third scenario is of murderers who were neglected or abandoned by mothers. In *The Stranger* Meursault seems indifferent to the death of his mother, as the famous opening lines reveal: "Maman died today. Or yesterday maybe, I don't know." Camus does not explain Meursault's killing out of childhood neglect, but he does begin the novel with evidence of it. The professional killer in Graham Greene's *This Gun for Hire* (1936) is obsessed with the memory of his mother's suicide. The killer in Musil's *The Man without Qualities* is an orphan, as is the serial killer in *The Pledge*, in which Dürrenmatt suggested a traumatic childhood sexual origin because the murderer married a woman who was thirty-two years his senior and called her "Mommy." In *Compulsion* both murderers had to fight for their mother's love—one out of gender confusion, the other out of sibling rivalry. The mother of Jame Gumb abandoned him to a foster home when he was two. The serial killer's mother in Lawrence Sanders's *The First Deadly Sin* (1972) was a drunk who never kissed him with her lips and instead would only brush his face with her cheek. Daniel Blank grew up in a "silent, loveless, white-tiled house" with "tiled emotions." One of his victims manages "to peel clean what had always been in him but had never been revealed" and helps him come alive sexually as a force of evil by performing fellatio on his impotent penis while he describes his vicious murders (59). He rewards her for liberating his sexuality and his penchant for evil by hacking her to death with an ice ax.

Modern thinkers following Freud viewed the causal role of childhood as more active, complex, acute, and sexual. They explored the active causal role of the child's many sexual desires in the etiology of neuroses and saw more of those desires in normal children. They noted the complex interactions of pain and erotic pleasure that energize values and character traits associated with nursing, feeding, weaning, defecating, toilet training, scopophilia, and ambivalence toward parents. In discerning more sharply the connection between adult perversions and normal psychosexual development, they were better able to understand how perversions are possible in adults and why adults desire to seduce children. In arguing that perversions come ultimately from trauma and fixation out of the child's normal sexual impulses and fantasies, Freud scandalized many in his generation and after, but he charted new modes of causal understanding for researchers and novelists. Although psychoanalysis was widely criticized, it continued to provide the basic terms of analysis for theorizing about childhood causality and remained the preferred explanation among novelists trying to make sense of murder.

These historical shifts about childhood causality also accord with my larger argument about the increasing specificity, multiplicity, complexity, and uncertainty of causal understanding in general. Compared with the Victorians, moderns made a sharper delineation of the many specific sources and causal consequences of child sexuality that Freud traced to the interplay of developing erotogenic zones, polymorphous perversity, Oedipal psychodynamics, and nonlocalized components of vision and smell. Psychoanalysis expanded the number of motives for adult behavior that derive from childhood. As Frank Manuel noted in a 1988 assessment of the historical significance of psychohistory, "From now on human conduct can no longer be explained in terms of plain utilitarian motives, as it was by nineteenth-century writers."[48] Psychohistorians hold that people are motivated not merely by the desire to maximize "pleasure" or "happiness" or to realize conscious pragmatic goals but also by a host of new motives that emerge from earliest infancy. In 1936 Walter Benjamin also argued that psychoanalysis increased the precision of causal understanding of behavior similar to the way movies enriched the perceptual field. Just as fifty years earlier, he argued, "a slip of the tongue passed unnoticed, ... since *Psychopathology of Everyday Life* [1905] things have changed." Like psychoanalysis, movies offer multiple points of view as well as slow-motion and close-up techniques that make the perception and analysis of human behavior more precise.[49]

Moderns also more precisely understood the complexities of unconscious mental processes. Victorians knew that the mind can condense, displace, project, incorporate, sublimate, symbolize, undo, deny, somatize, censor, and symbolize; but they had no formal theory such as Freud provided for tracking how such mental processes working at the unconscious level transform childhood impulses, wishes, and memories into adult character traits. The key difference between Victorian and modern thinking centered on the concept of repression (*Verdrängung*). Victorians occasionally used the term, but it referred to what Freud called suppression (*Unterdrückung*), that is, the conscious and intentional suppression of painful thoughts. In all the nineteenth-century works in which I found the word *repression*—and it was commonly used—it invariably referred to conscious suppression.

The increasing specificity also expanded the realm of uncertainty, which Freud acknowledged explicitly with his concept of *overdetermination*. The term refers to the way every mental event, from a simple dream image to complex neurotic behavior, is determined by more than enough causes to make it occur.[50] While Victorian philosophy of science going back at least to John Stuart Mill had analyzed multiple causal factors producing a single effect, Freud's concept of overdetermination was different. He emphasized not just the confluence of many causal factors impinging on a single event, as a vector of forces at a single point and a single moment in time, but a unique aspect of mental life that involves multiple associative pathways and layers of unconscious processes that direct or energize abundant and sometimes contradictory mental material over an extended period of time to create a single mental image or event. Overdetermination occurs in dreams when multiple past traumatic events or situations cause a single dream image. With such multiple determinants only partially represented in the dream recalled upon waking, any interpretation of it is necessarily fragmentary and incomplete, because there is no way to know whether every determinant has been disclosed or is even fully represented. Freud's concept of overdetermination was a significant event in the history of thinking about human causality. Compared with the Victorians, Freud raised more questions than he answered and added increasingly complex networks of conjectures to his causal explanations, which in turned opened up vast new realms of uncertainty.

Murder novels also document the four shifts in accord with the specificity-uncertainty dialectic. Modern novelists gave more details about the formative childhood experiences of murderers and related those details to more active, complex, acute, and sexually motivated experiences. Those greater details provided more material for explaining how and why children grow up to become murderers, as well as specific childhood determinants for the choice of victim, murder weapon, mode of killing, and treatment of the corpse. In many modern novels, detectives hired psychiatrists or themselves invoked psychological explanations that were often specifically Freudian. Levin's fictional attorney hired a psychiatrist who quotes Freud, McCoy's murderer-narrator relied on Freudian "libido" theory, Capote's explanation was based on psychoanalytic theory, while Carr set his novel in the precise year when Freud was moving from the seduction theory to the psychoanalytic theory and explained the killer's actions in terms of those theories. More novels based on psychoanalytic explanations of the childhood origins of a murderer can be found at will.[51] Yet, with all the increasingly precise accounts of childhood determinants, modernists also left the reader with greater uncertainty. The delightfully arrogant concluding explanations by Sherlock Holmes are mementos of a lost era that expected "scientific" causal explanations based on "objective" evidence and "rational" thinking about a "natural" order and was less inclined to question those concepts. In the modern period, Holmes came to symbolize an age that was overly confident about its causal explanations.

THE MAIN HISTORICAL explanation for these changing ideas about childhood causality is the increasing division of research labor. In the twentieth century, a host of new fields probed specific aspects of childhood causality—psychoanalysis, psychohistory, childhood and family history, child and adolescent psychology, pediatric neurology, endocrinology, social psychology, and cultural anthropology, with a variety of subspecialties in learning, intelligence, sensory capacity, motor performance, emotion, and language. I conclude this chapter with two foci of these subspecialties—multiple-personality disorders and serial homicide—because much of the research on them focused on the causal role of child sexual abuse.

The Victorian conspiracy of silence about sex in general blocked any serious consideration of child sexual abuse. In *Child Sexual Abuse in Victorian England*, Louise Jackson showed that the language Victorians used to describe such abuse relied on vague euphemisms such as "molestation," "tampering," "moral outrage," and "unlawful carnal knowledge." Analyses were further clouded by moralizing and circular reasoning. Girls victimized by incest or enforced prostitution were innocent of the precipitating incident but afterward were judged to be guilty, a danger to other children, and destined to perversion and moral corruption.[52]

Modern researchers became obsessed with establishing a causal connection between child abuse and multiple-personality disorders. Victorians were concerned about child molestation from outside the family, while moderns became increasingly concerned about sexual abuse and incest within the home. A turning point in modern research was an article of 1962 on "the battered-child syndrome," which drew attention to physical abuse that was documented by shocking X rays of broken bones in three-year-olds.[53] After that article appeared, experts focused their research more precisely. In the early 1970s, the issue of child abuse rallied feminists concerned about the way patriarchy and male violence caused children to develop multiple personalities. In 1973, Flora Schreiber's *Sybil* traced a patient's multiple personalities to anal sadistic child abuse by her mother.[54] By the mid-1970s child abuse was increasingly considered sexual and incestuous, as researchers reprised Freud's earlier seduction theory. Throughout the 1970s radiologists, orthopedists, pediatricians, and social workers joined with child psychologists and child psychiatrists to investigate child abuse and consider its long-term consequences.

Some researchers concluded that people with multiple personalities were victims of traumatic abuse as children. When subjected to overwhelming pressures, these children developed alternative personalities for each pressured situation, and consequently each adult alter ego had a specific traumatic childhood origin. This explanation began with a concise causal source—a single trauma or related pattern of traumas. The causal role of trauma in mental life is analogous to the role of the gene in hereditary transmission and the role of germs in disease. Whereas genes and germs are materially compact, a trauma is psychologically compact.[55] Like germs and genes, traumas are precisely defined nuclear entities with a specific structure that enables them to generate a wide range of consequences over many years by means of complex interactions with the environment.

According to Ian Hacking, "The linkage between childhood trauma and multiple personality . . . came into being almost suddenly in the 1970s" (86). Researchers announced their new causal understanding with bravado. In 1989 the president of the newly formed International Society for the Study of Multiple Personality and Dissociation announced, "Never in the history of psychiatry have we ever come to know so well the specific etiology of a major illness" (81). That etiology was proposed by researchers looking to isolate single causes, although much of their theorizing was more wishful thinking than verifiable science.[56] Such thinking fueled a panic in America from 1985 to 1994 among some child therapists who coerced children into "remembering" sex abuse by parents. Recent studies emphasized the complexity of the linkage stemming from the way child abuse is socially constructed.[57] For these critics child abuse is a *Rashomon*-like construction of different perspectives by specialists with different theoretical presuppositions, criteria for evidence, explanatory concepts, religious outlooks, and political agendas. Psychiatrists, social workers, and feminists not only define child abuse with different terminology but actually constitute the reality of it differently.

Since the discovery of the battered-child syndrome in 1962 and the related attention to child sexual abuse, specialists have increasingly looked for childhood origins of murderers and especially serial killers. In 1963 John M. Macdonald found that among one hundred persons convicted of homicide, a significant number had common experiences as children: "great parental brutality, extreme maternal seduction, or the triad of childhood firesetting, cruelty to animals, and enuresis."[58] In the 1970s feminists probed the sexual motivation of serial killers and identified child sexual abuse among its causes. Criminologists, psychologists, sociologists, and FBI profilers explored the causes of the serial killings that began to mount alarmingly in the late 1970s, and among these specialists the idea that child abuse played a significant causal role became axiomatic.

Although not all serial killers had traumatic childhoods, some notorious ones did. Henry Lee Lucas's mother forced him to be in the same room with her when she had sex with her clients, and in 1960 at the age of twenty three he began his serial killing by stabbing her to death in her bed. In the early 1950s Edmund Kemper's shrill and belittling mother locked him a cellar for eight months and berated him repeatedly. Later, after killing her, he cut out her larynx and put it in the garbage disposal. As a boy, Albert DeSalvo, the Boston Strangler, watched his alcoholic father knock out his mother's teeth and break her fingers one by one. DeSalvo took out his anger on women after his wife rejected him.[59] But there is no statistically significant correlation between child sexual abuse and serial killing. The demands on murder novelists to provide tidy concluding explanations has led them to imagine horrendous childhoods to explain their characters' actions, but researchers have found no significant correlation. Recent studies by Mark Selzer and Philip Jenkins focused on the broader social construction of serial killers by various professionals trying to justify their research specialty or careers.[60] Again, the increasingly specific research has opened up larger realms of investigation.

Ever since Freud, psychologists, criminologists, and novelists have been unable to resist the temptation to explain adult behavior, especially pathological or criminal behavior, as a result of some simple and visualizable cause from deep in an individual's past. The history of thinking about childhood causality has been energized by that temptation, which has also led researchers into uncharted realms from which they consistently looked for intelligible explanations based on childhood trauma. That theoretical round-trip repeatedly led them to embrace childhood causality with an abundance of sexual detail that Victorians did not dare explore.

After two novels and eighteen years, Thomas Harris could not resist providing such a singular and visualizable cause of Hannibal Lecter's character, which is distinctly twentieth-century in the extent to which it was determined by the traumatic death of his sister Mischa. What happened to six-year-old Hannibal in the barn behind his burned-out home and its lurid consequences are unimaginable in a Victorian novel. His trauma was not sexual, but it did occur in childhood, did involve his sister, and ultimately governed his adult love relations and mode of killing. Harris was able to use such a traumatic childhood causality so plausibly in a story that would have been outrageous in the previous century because popular and scholarly analyses of the childhood determinants of adult mental life had specified many new pathways of its operation and affirmed their causal force.

3

Language

FROM 1830 to the early twentieth century, most leading thinkers believed that language was a challenging but adequate instrument for communicating ideas.[1] Although they knew that specific vocabularies and grammars dictated how ideas were expressed, they did not seriously consider that those linguistic elements substantially shaped the substance of their ideas and, even less, the nature of the very experience that they used that language to describe. In that sense they believed that language communicated rather than generated experiences and ideas. Romantics had celebrated the creative (or, to use a modern term, "performative") function of language following Kant's theory of the creative role of the mind in constituting reality, but that thinking was primarily limited to philosophers and poets and did not influence the realist novelists.[2] The realists were acutely aware of the difficulty of finding the right words, as Flaubert acknowledged in *Madame Bovary* with an unforgettable image: "Human speech is like a cracked kettle on which we tap crude rhythms for bears to dance to, while we long to make music that will melt the stars" (216). But even though he struggled mightily to express himself, he did not think that the structure of language itself played a major role in constituting the thoughts he used it to convey.[3]

The growing awareness of the causal role of language in understanding and experiencing the world came to be known among philosophers as "the linguistic turn."[4] This movement originated with Bertrand Russell, G. E. Moore, Rudolf Carnap, and Ludwig Wittgenstein, who came to see philosophy not as a direct study of thought and reality but as a study of the ways that thought and reality are constituted by language. Historians of philosophy commonly date this turn from Wittgenstein's statement in 1922, "All philosophy is a 'critique of language.'"[5] Its enormous significance was noted by George Steiner, who concluded that until the late nineteenth century, the most biting skeptics remained confident in the ability of language to put their case in the form of intelligible propositions. One of the great skeptics about the epistemological status of causal understanding itself, David Hume, was "thoroughly at home in the house of language."[6] He never doubted that he could critique causal knowledge in language that would clearly convey his doubts. Like all previous skeptics he accepted the contract with language. "It is my belief," Steiner argued, "that this contract is broken for the first time, in any thorough and consequent sense, in European, Central European, and Russian culture and speculative consciousness during the decades from the 1870s to the 1930s. *It is this break of the covenant between word and world which constitutes one of the very few genuine revolutions of spirit in Western history and which defines modernity itself.*"[7] That revolution is the pivot for this chapter.

This break between word and world underscored the causal or constitutive function of language. Scholars increasingly questioned the representational or mimetic function of language and focused on the way language shapes and generates human experience. That shift is evinced in murder novels, which evolved from the Victorian preoccupation with the causal role of education, especially moral education, to the modern preoccupation with the causal role of language itself.

Victorians believed that a major cause of crime was deficient moral education. Recent historical studies of crime in nineteenth-century Europe and the United States concur that the related circumstances of poverty, parental neglect, illiteracy, and moral depravity from lack of proper religious and moral education play a major causal role. As Richard Evans concluded in a study of German crime, "At the beginning of the nineteenth century, police, penal philosophers and bureaucrats thought of law-breaking in terms of the individual moral 'turpitude' of the 'villain,' the culmination of a downward moral career which had begun with neglected education and childhood disobedience."[8] Victorian murder novelists dramatized such careers beginning with the obvious lack of moral education in characters such as Bill Sikes and Thérèse Raquin.

In addition to deficient moral education, two other modes of impaired moral education include the emotionally crippling religious education of Claude Frollo in Hugo's *Notre-Dame of Paris* (1831) and Bradley Headstone in Dickens's *Our Mutual Friend* (1864–65) as well as the explicitly immoral education of Jonas Chuzzlewit, Martin Faber, and Paul Clifford. As Dickens explained, the first word Jonas learned was "gain." "Long taught by his father to over-reach everybody . . . from his early habits of considering everything as a question of property, he had gradually come to look with impatience on his parent as a certain amount of personal estate [that] ought to be secured . . . in a coffin, and banked in the grave" (117). William Simms explained that his novel about Martin Faber was intended to show "the necessity of proper and early education" and "the ready facility with which the natural powers may be perverted to the worst purposes." The source of that immoral education is his parents, as Simms adds: "every now and then, in his narrative, the reason—the true cause—the parent germe of his error and his crime—is permitted to appear."[9] In the 1848 preface to *Paul Clifford* (1830), Edward Bulwer-Lytton wrote: "We see masses of our fellow-creatures—the victims of circumstances over which they had no control—contaminated in infancy by the example of parents—their intelligence either extinguished, or turned against them, according as the conscience is stifled in ignorance, or perverted to apologies for vice." These three causal roles can be schematized with three typical Victorian explanations for murder in terms of moral education that has been deficient, excessive, or intentionally corrupted.

Victorians and moderns divided sharply on the causal role of education and language. Victorians did not explain murder as a consequence of language, and moderns were reluctant to explain it as a consequence of faulty moral education. For the title of this chapter I have deferred to the modern conceptualization in terms of language, and not the Victorians' analogous focus on education, because the modern term identifies the direction in which this historical shift moved. In many modernist novels people kill for reasons having to do with their command of language in ways analogous to the causal role of education in the Victorian novel. That is, they kill or commit other crimes because their understanding of language is either deficient, excessive, or dynamically generative (instead of intentionally corrupted). I have organized the following discussion according to these three functions to sharpen the historical contrasts.

Deficient Language

The classic modernist fictional work in which a lack of knowledge of the language of the law plays a causal role in crime is Kafka's *The Trial* (1925). Although Josef K. never learns the charge against him, he is treated as the perpetrator of a crime, at least to the extent that in the end he is executed for it, which implies that his crime is a capital offense, if not murder. He is also a victim of a capital crime in the sense that he is executed by the authorities in the name of the law, even though he never understands that law or his crime. His treatment by everyone is nevertheless consistent with his having committed a crime, a notion which he fuels with his own growing guilt. The cause of both his "crime" and his victimization is embedded in the language of the law about which he becomes increasingly confused as he tries to fathom it.

That language pursues K. through characters who are governed by it but do not understand it. The two men who arrest him are ignorant of the language of the law they serve and terrified by the hierarchy of officials in the labyrinthine bureaucracy that administers it. Everyone involved has only fragmentary knowledge of the law they are bound to serve blindly. K.'s defense generates self-incrimination because he does not understand the language of the law. The charge sheets are inaccessible to him, so he does not know the charges against him. He has to guess what might be relevant to his case, and so whatever information he submits to the court is irrelevant. His lawyer, who is supposed to understand the language of the law, is incompetent. The proceedings are kept secret from K. and his lawyer, and court officials are corrupt. No one in the unfathomably complex and shifting system of legalistic signs understands it as a whole, as officials work on cases without knowing their source or terminus. If they did, they would not tell the accused, and if they told him, they would be wrong because everyone is misinformed.

A moment of hope occurs when K. enters a dark cathedral and sees a lone candle: "It was lovely to look at, but quite inadequate for illuminating the altarpieces, which mostly hung in the darkness of the side chapels; it actually increased the darkness" (204). His effort to see into the darkness of the cathedral is a search for illumination that actually increases his awareness of the surrounding darkness, just as his efforts to understand the language of the law increase his ignorance and guilt and may lead to his execution. This spot of light symbolizes the specificity-uncertainty dialectic: as his inquiry reveals more precise detail, the law proves increasingly complex, and his understanding of his crime and its motives grows more uncertain. The more K. learns, the more he realizes how little he knew about what he thought he knew and how much more there is to know that he will never be able to fathom.

Deficient command of language plays a different but distinctly modern causal role in Musil's *The Man without Qualities*. Ulrich rails about how "the ready-made language not only of the tongue but also of sensations and feelings" overwhelms him with qualities he is struggling to reject (1:135). But Moosbrugger has more basic problems with language. Like many a Victorian murderer, he is poor, parentless, and uneducated, although Musil did not saddle him with a deficient moral faculty, because he rejected such diagnostic categories. Moosbrugger's problems are with language itself. He often hears voices calling to him and thinks that educated people ought to have their tongues cut out (1:254). "His own words seemed to stick to his gums to spite him just when he needed them most" (1:257). Unaccustomed to conventional metaphors, he breaks language into elements or puts it together improperly. Musil narrates how Moosbrugger said to a girl, "'Your sweet rose lips,' but suddenly the words gave way at their seams and something upsetting happened: her face went gray, like earth veiled in a mist, there was a rose sticking out of it on a long stem, and the temptation to take a knife and cut it off, or punch it back into the face, was overwhelming" (1:259). The night he stabbed the prostitute, her pleading words attached themselves to his fragile ego, and he was unable to detach himself from them. He was compelled to cut away the source of her predatory words with a knife in a desperate act of self-definition, mutilating her in the process. Deficient language played a casual role in the murder in two related ways: Moosbrugger's literalism sets off confusion and fear in others and panic and rage in himself. In John Steinbeck's *Of Mice and Men* (1937), a similar character, Lenny, is unable to express his feelings to a woman, and when she reacts in fear to his overtures of affection he panics and breaks her neck.

Deficient command of language also drives DeLillo's fictionalized Lee Harvey Oswald to plot the killing of JFK in *Libra*. In this novel Oswald has a form of dyslexia that makes it impossible for him to read with comprehension or explain himself to posterity (166). Being "word-blind," he nevertheless persists in trying to write a historical diary. But he cannot "find order in the field of little symbols [or] clearly see the picture that is called a word." He tries phonetic spelling, but the language tricks him with its inconsistencies. "He watched sentences deteriorate, powerless to make them right." The description of his writing as "cramped, fumbling, deficient" could also apply to Oswald's ego (210–11). To compensate for his dyslexia, inability to write coherent sentences, and failure to make sense of his life in a historical diary, he defines the meaning of his existence historically in big bold letters by shooting Kennedy.[10]

Whereas Oswald acts because he cannot write, another modern kills because she is ashamed to admit she cannot read. In Bernhard Schlink's *The Reader* (1995), Hanna Schmitz became an SS guard of female prisoners because it was a job she could perform without anyone learning that she was illiterate. In 1965 she is brought before a war crimes court because one night three hundred prisoners in her charge were locked in a church that was hit by an Allied bomb and caught fire. Along with four other female SS guards, she is accused of not unlocking the doors while the women burned to death. During the trial, rather than submit her handwriting for analysis, which would reveal her illiteracy, she takes the blame for the report on the incident, which she could not possibly have written. She would rather be convicted of a crime against humanity than reveal she cannot read. Her deep shame over her illiteracy defines her entire life—her subsequent love affair with the narrator, her urging him to read her stories, her poor self-defense before the court, as well as her actions as an SS guard. While other factors also paralyzed her during the fire, her inability to read was the decisive one that led her to be there in the first place and then reduced her capacity for independent action while the women burned.

The novel is about Hanna's profound appreciation for the language she can neither read nor write, her respect for the classics of literature that she eventually learns to read after her conviction, and her acceptance of full responsibility for the three hundred deaths. Language is a powerful force that she cannot control and therefore dominates her life. Her linguistic deficiency does not affect her "moral faculty," and her crime is a consequence of the workings of a huge institution that she joins not out of nationalist fervor or professional ambition but to hide her linguistic deficiency. In the end she hangs herself in her cell the morning she is to be released after eighteen years of prison to complete her atonement for crimes deriving from illiteracy, estranged from the world whose scripted secrets she could not fathom.

In contrast to the Victorian novels in which murderers' deficient moral education leads to a stunting of their moral faculty, in these modernist novels language assumes functions that are causally more complex and more fundamental. The causal function of language is more complex than that of moral education, because it is not limited to a single moral faculty and a specific moral code. Josef K.'s search for his motives along with his crime leads him into an ever more convoluted self-inquiry about all variety of human values and purposes that are increasingly tangled in a maze of language games. The language of law that he cannot fathom holds the secret of his crime, and it is as varied as it is impenetrable. The causality of language is also more fundamental than the causality of moral education because it involves the most basic concepts people use to understand their existence. Language constitutes not just the moral code but all codes and values. It is the medium by which people define themselves as selves with values and meaning. Moderns kill not because of moral codes they have not learned to follow but because of their inability to learn altogether or to think clearly or understand the world, especially their relationships with others. The narrator in Samuel Beckett's *Molloy* (1955) beats to death a charcoal-burner whom he meets in the forest, offering as explanation the observation that "either I didn't understand a word he said, or he didn't understand a word I said" (113). In Thomas Bernhard's *The Lime Works* Konrad may have killed his wife (no one knows for certain) in part because he cannot write his book.

Excessive Language

Victorian moral education taught that good and evil were the fundamental categories of specific moral judgments. For some, that basic distinction was a gift of moral wisdom from God and the basis of original sin. For others it was the fundamental distinction on which all ethical philosophy was based and the foundation for civilized society. The excessive imposition of moral education, especially zealous religious education, might produce clerics such as Frollo and Headstone who become sexually obsessed and uncontrollably jealous, which in turn could lead to homicidal rage. The highly educated Robert Wringham in James Hogg's novel *The Private Memoirs and Confessions of a Justified Sinner* (1824), kills out of fanatical religious conviction, victimizing people whom he believes to be doing evil.

In place of overzealous moral and religious education, which was more typical among the Victorians, the moderns envision new ways that language constitutes experience. That constitutive function kills quite literally in Kafka's story "In the Penal Colony" (1919), about an imaginary society in which law and order are maintained with executions by an instrument that cuts the text of the law that is violated into the body of the prisoner. At the beginning of the execution the prisoner is ignorant of his sentence. The instrument "teaches" the commandment by engraving it ever deeper into his flesh over a twelve-hour period until just as the condemned man dies, he thoroughly understands the precise letter of the law and the true meaning of what he has done. Deep understanding is literally inscribed deep into his body. The particular crime punished in the story is that of a man who fell asleep while guarding the door of his master, and so he must have written into his body, "Honor Thy Superiors!" This moral education comes not through his eyes but through wounds, so that in the moment of ultimate justice the condemned man will achieve absolute understanding.[11] For Kafka, language was no transparent medium but an instrument for control and domination, whether exasperatingly elusive as in Josef K.'s world or horribly intrusive as in the penal colony.

Sartre underscored the constitutive function of language, which, along with the gaze of others, generates meaning in human existence. His biography of Jean Genet turns on a defining moment when the meaning of Genet's life and the subsequent preoccupation of his art were determined by a single word labeling his crime. Sartre imagined this moment as ten-year-old Genet might have been caught stealing from a kitchen drawer: "Beneath this gaze the child comes to himself. He who was not yet anyone suddenly becomes Jean Genet. Suddenly 'a dizzying word / From the depths of the world abolishes / the beautiful order.' A voice declares publicly: 'You're a thief.'"[12]

In this moment Genet realizes that he *is* a thief. Before he heard the word he was merely searching for something in the drawer, possibly with intent to steal, but in that instant the single word defines him in a way that "is going to determine his entire life" (18). He will be a thief not only when he steals but always—when he sleeps or kisses his foster mother. In Genet's beginning is the word, and that word is *evil*. He is evil because he is a thief, as defined by others. In reaction he chooses to will for himself what was defined by others, which requires making evil come from himself. He intends to create evil, however, not in deed but in word, by turning the language that tagged him evil into an instrument for describing the world itself as the source of evil. The entire system of conventional ethical values depends on the distinction between good and evil, which Genet will sabotage with shockingly explicit accounts in novels and autobiographical fictions about inversions of conventional values and norms—aberrant sexuality and vicious crimes culminating in sadomasochism, homosexual rape, and murder. He makes black white, as in calling the black savage in *Deathwatch* (1949) "Snowball"; he turns the moral order topsy-turvy with the murderer graced. In that play the illiterate Green Eyes is awaiting execution for the murder of a young girl he carried out because of an unspoken command from on high, and he must have letters from his girlfriend read to him by Lefranc. While Lefranc may make fine phrases, the illiterate murder snarls, "*I am* a fine phrase" (123).

Sartre's Genet will be the cause of himself by taking charge of language in novels through which he will re-present himself to those who labeled him in an underworld of crime and sex where the labels of good and evil are laughable. The objectified thief will steal conventional meanings away from the objective norm, raping syntax for his poetic purposes. Sartre's study presents the acquisition of creative linguistic potency in place of deficient or corrupted moral education in the development of a criminal mind.

Dynamically Generative Language

Victorians created corrupt murderers such as Jonas Chuzzlewit, Martin Faber, and Paul Clifford by explicitly teaching them to be evil and commit crimes. Moderns questioned the validity of any single moral code and explored how all value systems are embedded in language. Moderns kill not because they have improperly learned a public moral code but because they are disoriented by the language that gives their life meaning, or they are hyperoriented to language and overwhelmed by its generative powers. An early, pivotal disruption in the reliability and transparency of language was World War I, when propaganda was invented to enlist the moral support of the masses and make palatable the nauseating destruction of trench warfare. In *A Room of One's Own*, Virginia Woolf saw masculinist language behind the murderous impulses that caused World War I, while over the last thirty years feminists have documented the dynamic and sometimes murderous nature of "patriarchal language" in fiction and society.[13] One of Capote's murderers from *In Cold Blood* educates himself with a personal list of words that he thought were "beautiful" but incited his fear and anger, words such as *thanatoid* (deathlike), *facinorous* (atrociously wicked), *omophagia* (eating raw flesh), *depredate* (pillage), and *myrtophobia* (fear of darkness) (169). The dark world in which Perry kills is shaped by such dark words. In Julio Cortázar's "Continuity of Parks" (1963) a man is literally killed by the language of a text, when he is fatally stabbed by a character in the novel he is reading.[14] The thugs led by Alex in *A Clockwork Orange* (1962) experience their antisocial views with a language they bastardized from Russian, which includes such words as *tolchock* (a beating), *pyahnitsa* (drunk), and *oobivat* (to kill).

In *The Names* (1982), DeLillo envisioned a cult of assassins who worship the power of the word and kill out of reverence for it. Their offering to God is language, and the logic of their killing, one of them explains, "is a book" (212). They select a victim by matching his or her name's initials with the initials of the name of the place where they happen to be living. Then they create a text of mortal wounds on their victim's body using implements of earlier writers—stones, blades, hammers. One of the cult explains this transcendent experience: "It had to be that. . . . I knew it was right. It had to be. Shatter his skull, kill him, smash his brains." It had to be done "with our hands, in direct contact" (209). Unlike the victims of Kafka's penal colony, whose textual executions make known to all observers the meaning of their crime, this cult hides the meaning of its murders from anyone but its own members. As one critic concluded, "The cult's 'text'—their murdered victim—is isolated, detached, absolutely controlled, and wholly original."[15]

THE LINGUISTIC TURN

The first modern philosopher to scrutinize seriously the causal function of language was Nietzsche. His critique of language was based on extensive research in philology and classical languages, which enabled him to trace the affinity between Indian, Greek, and German philosophizing to their origin in a common language and their "unconscious dominion and guidance by similar grammatical functions."[16] That guidance worked deeper and more fundamentally than most philosophers had understood. They often noted how language could be used to distort the truth intentionally and oppress people with demagoguery, but they neglected the more basic way that the coining of words and the rules of grammar distort truth and lie in a "nonmoral (*aussermoralischen*) sense."

He explored this aspect of language in "On Truth and Lies in a Nonmoral Sense" (1873). By creating ways of thinking and being, language also "lies" by narrowing and distorting what we take for experience. We name things with words according to metaphors that express only partial and accidental relations between things and ourselves. The genesis of language from nerve stimulus to image to sound and word is a series of partial and distorted translations of the original experience. Nietzsche's critique of the "truth" of words leads logically to a critique of concepts. The concept *bird*, for example, comes from forgetting the particularity of an individual bird, a further removal of language from rendering the world (the living bird) as it truly is. The arbitrary and metaphoric origin of words and the disjunction of concepts from their experiential origin undermine the possibility of complete truth in language. Truth is rather "a movable host of metaphors, metonymies, and anthropomorphisms: in short, a sum of human relations which have been poetically and rhetorically intensified, transferred, and embellished, and which, after long usage, seem to people to be fixed, canonical, and binding. Truths are illusions which we have forgotten are illusions."[17] Thus language does not so much represent the world as it creates our experience of it.

Nietzsche's specific analysis of the causal function of language focuses on three key concepts: the subject-object distinction, free will, and causality. The first is a linguistic creation of Indo-European languages with their basic grammatical structure of subject, verb, and object that allows one to distinguish artificially between the doer and the deed. But human existence is not an ego acting on a world of objects; it is a will to meaning that we experience as a unity from inside to outside, from self to other, and from past to present to future. It is a "driving, willing, and effecting; and only owing to the seduction of language which conceives and misconceives all effects as conditioned by something that causes effects by a 'subject' can it appear otherwise." There is no being behind doing or willing. "'The doer' is merely a fiction added to the deed—the deed is everything." Scientists double the deed when they say the "lightning flashes" or the "force causes," and popular usage "still lies under the misleading influence of language and has not disposed of that little changeling, the 'subject.'"[18]

The second conceptual creation of language is free will. For Nietzsche, humans have only strong and weak wills. Free will versus determinism is a metaphysical dichotomy that has been reified into two entities that do not really exist. The concept of free will denies the causal efficacy of ancestors, society, chance, and God, and places all willing power in the self as a cause of itself. But self-causation is a self-contradiction. To be truly self-caused would take "more than Münchhausen's audacity, to pull one self up into existence by the hair, out of the swamps of nothingness."[19] By believing in such fictions, people fail to see to what extent they are governed not only by other persons and external forces but by words and grammar.

The third artificial linguistic creation is the linked concept of cause and effect, which impoverishes human experience by atomizing it. To make experience comprehensible we invented cause and effect. "The separation of the 'doer' from the 'deed,' of the event from some- one who produces events, of the process from something that is not a process but enduring substance, thing, body, soul, etc.—the attempt to comprehend an event as a sort of shifting and place-changing on the part of a 'being,' of something constant: this ancient mythology estab- lished the belief in 'cause and effect' after it had a firm form in the functions of language and grammar."[20]

Nietzsche drew attention to the causal logic of language to unmask the naïveté of philosophers who offer linguistic constructs as profound truths. Language is not natural and does not reflect the real world. It is an artificial construction of words that only partially convey the expe- riences which prompt them. Concepts are metaphors that convey only a minimal part of the experience to which they refer, and when they become reified into entities such as subject and object or cause and ef- fect, they diminish the fullness of being. In 1874 Nietzsche wrote that language itself is responsible for modern atomization and alienation. People are "fragmented and in pieces, dissociated almost mechanically into an inner and an outer . . . suffering from the malady of words and mistrusting any feeling of [their] own which has not yet been stamped with words." Most people are an "unliving and yet uncannily active concept-and-word factory."[21] He sees people as all chained, stricken, or trapped by words. In 1876 he wrote, "Language has everywhere be- come a power in its own right which now embraces mankind with ghostly arms and impels it to where it does not really want to go." People are "seized by the madness of universal concepts," plagued by a lack of mutual understanding, and dominated by "the hollowness of those tyrannical words and concepts."[22] People are manipulated into making war on their neighbors not only by conscious political demagoguery but by the nature of the subject-object structure of language itself that makes it possible to see oneself as an essential subject and see a foreigner as a nonessential object. No doubt individual murders could be produced similarly.

In exposing the fictions created by arbitrary words and grammars, Nietzsche sought to shatter the illusion that human experience took place in the one and only real world and was based on "the truth." For a society in which moral authority was based ultimately on the word of God, subversion of the representative function of language conjured up nihilism—the loss of all values and authority. Nietzsche the antinihilist subverted that authority not only by pointing out how people were finding it increasingly difficult to believe in the literal word of God as the absolute truth but, even more seditiously, by detaching the word itself from the world. The two iconoclasms are related because they shattered two pillars of Christian cosmology and faith that were unified in Saint John's account of creation: "In the beginning was the Word, and the Word was with God, and the Word was God." In denying that the connection between words and things is necessary and in affirming rather that it is arbitrary, Nietzsche demolished the causally grounding cosmology that linked the origin of time, existence, and language with God who caused all things to exist necessarily by creating and by naming them—and also by being *the* Word. If the creation of words is arbitrary, the Word could not have been in the beginning, God could not have created the Word, God could not be the Word, and no words could have sacred authority. Nietzsche underscored the strength of the equation between Word and God by noting the resistance to disjoining them: "I fear we are not getting rid of God because we still believe in grammar."[23] The need to retain the grammatical foundation for the subject of all sentences lies behind the abiding belief in the existence of the ultimate subject and author—God.

By attacking the representational theory of language and offering instead a theory of language as a creative network of unstable metaphors and partial truths, Nietzsche exposed the specific causal function of language but at the same time disclosed a vast realm of uncertainty implied by it. He delineated that realm with a series of mocking questions about what this new uncertain universe might be like, posed by the unnerved listeners to the "madman" who announces the death of God in *The Joyful Wisdom*. In such a world, they wonder, "Is there still an above and below? Do we not stray as through infinite nothingness? Does not empty space breathe upon us? Has it not become colder? Does not night come on continually, darker and darker?"[24] If *the* Word was not in the beginning, then we have no certain beginning, and everything must be sustained in meaning by words that individuals create. While Nietzsche subverted conventional notions about the representational function of language and related it to the collapse of absolute values implied by the death of God, he also offered a life-affirming philosophy in which language played a crucial role. In *Thus Spoke Zarathustra* he embodied that role in the figure of the overman—modeled variously as philosopher, artist, and poet—whose positive philosophy of existence is presented as a challenging gift that is rejected, mocked, parodied, and misunderstood by his various listeners. The overman nevertheless struggles to say yes to life in the face of mind-numbing rituals and nihilism. For a thinker who affirmed perspectivism and chance, this new conception of the causal role of language accorded with his general philosophy of human existence as, in the final analysis, wondrously complex, probabilistic, and uncertain.

Modern Sciences of Language

Nineteenth-century linguistics or philology was mainly concerned with the history of languages, the rediscovery of languages such as Proto-Indo-European from which modern languages derived, and the laws that governed the changes that shaped those derivations. This research was structured around the scientific models of physical mechanics and evolutionary theory. Studies of language that used these models tried to explain why languages were structured the way they were and why they changed over time.

The laws of motion in physics provided a model for philologists' laws governing sound shifts. In 1847 Helmholtz argued that in the exact sciences, phenomena must be reduced to attractive and repellent forces whose intensity depends only on the distance between the mass points affecting one another. In 1872 Emil du Bois-Reymond applied this approach to language, arguing that valid knowledge must reduce complex linguistic phenomena to simple changes of basic elements moving in accord with universally valid laws. This approach was elaborated by Hermann Osthoff and Karl Brugmann, who introduced their six-volume study of morphemes (1878–1910) with a methodological statement of hard determinism according to universal law: "All phonic change, in so far as it occurs mechanically, follows laws without exception, i.e., the direction of phonetic movement . . . is always the same in all members of a linguistic family, and all words in which the syllable subject to the phonetic movement appears under like conditions will without exception be affected by the change."[25] Researchers using this paradigm assumed that language change is governed by deterministic causal laws.

Other historical philologists thought of languages as governed by phenomena analogous to biological processes. In 1827 the German philologist Franz Bopp wrote that "languages must be regarded as organic bodies formed in accordance with definite laws; bearing within themselves an internal principle of life, they develop and gradually die out."[26] Some philologists saw progress in the development of languages. In 1848 August Schleicher followed a Hegelian scheme in arguing that languages progress from lower to higher as they become more inflectional and versatile, and twenty-five years later he argued that evolutionary theory applies to languages.[27] In 1893 Jan Baudouin de Courtenay argued that languages became progressively humanized as the beastlike sounds formed far back in the mouth and throat became more human sounds formed nearer the teeth and lips.[28]

In the late nineteenth century, theorists explained sound shifts in accord with the dominant evolutionary paradigm, employing various "natural" selective pressures. The substratum theory held that shifts occurred when the language of a conquering nation clashed with that of the vanquished population. Grimm explained shifts in terms of the national psychology of different nations, while Osthoff argued for the causal role of changing vocal organs of different races. Another selective pressure was geographical influence manifesting itself in the more energetic breathing of people living in hilly regions.[29] While these explanations accounted for some shifts, none provided a scientific explanation of language development according to universal law. As Geoffrey Sampson concluded, "By the end of the century the data for historical linguistics came to seem a mere assembly of sound shifts which had occurred for no good reason and which tended in no particular direction."[30] With the failure to find some overarching historical explanation of sound shifts, linguistics turned away from history.

The leading thinker in this turn was Ferdinand de Saussure, a founder of modern linguistics. His early research had been in historical linguistics, so he was well aware of the historicity of language, and he became convinced that a science of linguistics must distinguish the historical aspect of language (diachronic) from its nonhistorical aspect (synchronic). Linguistics must focus on synchronic and purely linguistic phenomena and not on historical, social, or geographical factors that are external to language. In *Course in General Linguistics* (1915), he criticized the "absurd reasoning" of comparative linguists, who based studies of language on organic metaphors and compared two languages "as a naturalist might look upon the growth of two plants" with each having to pass through linguistic stages as plants pass through stages of organic growth.[31]

He also rejected views of language as a naming process. Language is not a nomenclature of words that represent concepts in a one-to-one linear manner; it is rather a system of interdependent signs. Saussure defined the sign as a combination of a signifier (a spoken or written word, e.g., *tree*) and a signified (the concept to which it refers, e.g., the concept "tree"). That combination is "unmotivated," that is, the signifier has "no natural connection with the signified" (69). No natural reason compels the concept tree to be signified by the English word *tree* and not by the French word *arbre*. Some signs are partly natural. Onomatopoeia produces quasi-natural connections between signified and signifier, but they are not universal. The Chinese do not use *bow-wow* for a dog's bark. Symbols (scales for justice) and interjections (the word *ouch* for pain) suggest a natural connection between signified and signifier, but these connections vary among cultures and thus rely ultimately on arbitrary conventions.

This first sense of the arbitrariness of the sign is obvious, and many other thinkers had observed it. But Saussure also argued more originally that the signified itself is arbitrary because languages structure *concepts* arbitrarily, or at least not according to any "natural" or universal logic. "Distinctions of time, which are so familiar to us, are unknown in certain languages." Not all languages have a separate term for *sun*, and "in some languages it is not possible to say 'sit in the *sun*'" (116). "Without language, thought is a vague, uncharted nebula. There are no pre-existing ideas, and nothing is distinct before the appearance of language" (112).

The arbitrariness of the sign means that words are not simple positive terms that achieve their meaning and value by representing a pre-existing essential reality. Words rather achieve their meaning and value only as part of a system of signs. Other systems of meaning and value may have fixed referents, but not language. In economics, by contrast, the value (or meaning) of land is rooted in the value of its productivity, but language has no value or meaning except in a system of relations among words. In no other system, Saussure believed, are values so essentially interdependent. The system of language is based entirely on the opposition of its elements. That is, no sound or concept has any significance except in contrast to a different sound or concept. For example, the English word *red* is arbitrarily related to the concept of red and is meaningful only in a system in which it is different from other words for other colors. It has no meaning by itself. For someone who did not know what red meant, one could point to a hundred red objects, and that person still would not understand *red* until those red objects were contrasted with differently colored objects. Language is unique among all systems of meaning in that it is the basis of meaning in those systems, but its units have no natural or positive referent outside of the system of signs. "Concepts are purely differential and defined not by their positive content but negatively by their relations with the other terms of the system. Their most precise characteristic is in being what the others are not" (117).

In conclusion, Saussure argued that language is subject to social pressures that function like the accidental environmental pressures on the evolution of species. No rules of linguistic evolutionary change are unvarying, and no patterns are permanent. Phonetic modifications are caused by "blind evolution," to which the mind then attempts to find some overriding logic, but all patterns are the result of chance, and continuity results from "sheer luck" (229–31).

Saussure employed four main arguments to detach language from being a direct representation of an essential reality: that the connection between signified and signifier is arbitrary, that the system of signifieds is itself arbitrary, that the system of signs is made up of units that have no positive content independent of the system, and that the changing structure of languages is caused by chance social-historical pressures. Ironically, by depriving language of any reason for being the way it is, he accorded to language an unprecedented causal role in generating human thought and experience.

Saussure moved understanding of the causal function of language in the direction of every major aspect of the specificity-uncertainty dialectic. He rejected the imprecise organic theorizing of comparative philologists and founded the science of linguistics by focusing it more specifically on purely linguistic factors.[32] In basing that science on the system of signs, he underscored the complexity of interdependent linguistic units from phonemes and morphemes to words and phrases. Language functions as a system of units that generate meaning as a field of causally acting forces, producing meaning from their interdependent differences and oppositions.[33] The lack of any positive referents, the arbitrariness of the sign, the arbitrariness of the signified, and the reliance on a system of interactions implied that knowledge of the causal role of language would be probabilistic and uncertain.

Saussure's demonstration that the system that underlies all other systems of value and meaning—the system of language—is based on an arbitrary division of underlying concepts suggested that many critically important signs that were believed to be natural and universal might rather be arbitrary and conventional. Most unsettling was the implication that the ultimate originary sign, the sign of God, was also arbitrary. That possibility further undermined the Christian notion that "In the beginning" was the primordial linguistic sign—the Word of God—because according to Saussure, in the beginning as well as at all subsequent times language was always a system of signs, and no one word could determine any meaning, let alone create the world, without the interaction of the entire system of signs. "Language has neither ideas nor sounds that existed before the linguistic system" (120). Therefore in the beginning no single word could even have been a word by itself, let alone *the* Word. The lack of any natural causal connection between signifier and signified detached the word from the world, thereby detaching the system that underlies all other systems from any natural reason for being what it is. That stunning detachment implied the disjunction from any natural or universal grounding of all historical narratives, ethical philosophies, social norms, religious beliefs, aesthetic conventions, or even conceptual categories. These ideas might be argued for on the basis of specific premises, but then they were not natural or universal. The arbitrariness of the sign also implied that understanding of linguistic causation as well as any system of meaning based on linguistic signs is provisional. Sound shifts and meaning changes have most definite causes, but they are a result of evolutionary pressures working throughout the system of signs beyond the control of any particular individuals or groups, and they are sustained by "sheer luck." Therefore knowledge of the action of those causes must be at best probabilistic.

Saussure proposed that a science of signs, which he called semiotics, might be used to understand sign systems other than language. In the 1940s Claude Lévi-Strauss began to apply semiotics to interpret social structures in kinship rituals and myths. In "The Structural Study of Myth" (1955), he applied a structural semiotics to discover the core meaning among the several versions of the myth of Oedipus, which he believed was not evident in any single version by itself and could not be explained historically. Its meaning only became apparent when a number of the versions were broken down into their basic recurrent units (mythemes), arranged in structural patterns, and interpreted semiotically.[34]

In the modern period, semiotics was used to study other systems of signs based on distinctions such as good and evil, innocent and guilty. Since these systems were based on language, Saussure's linguistics was suggestive. From his perspective, any sign system involving murder, for example, becomes defined by the interrelation of its units (murderer, victim, witness, detective, judge, punisher) as well as the interrelation of every term of analysis with its binary opposite (self and other, subject and object, normal and abnormal, innocent and guilty, responsible and irresponsible). Sartre's account of the interdependent meanings of good and evil in Genet reads like an application of Saussure's view of language as a system of interdependent signs. Sartre argued that a thief cannot see himself as a thief in isolation. The notion of thief "is of social origin and presupposes a prior definition of society, of the property system, a legal code, a judiciary apparatus and an ethical system of relationships among people."[35] Such an interdependent analysis contrasts with Victorian positivist criminology, which viewed individuals as murderous souls in and of themselves and distinguished them as a race apart.[36] A prime example of the Victorian conviction of *non*arbitrary signs is Lombroso's theory of the born criminal, who was the natural signified par excellence, literally denoted by "natural" visible signs of criminality such as pointed ears and large jaws.

In addition to Nietzsche and Saussure, other modern thinkers also underscored the causal role of language. In 1901 Fritz Mauthner, an Austrian linguist, published a 2,200-page critique of language, which opened with a statement of his goal "to redeem the world from the tyranny of language."[37] Language governs thought by reifying abstract concepts such as force, energy, God, natural law, and causality and by structuring every thought. His emphasis on the dominion of language over thought directly influenced Samuel Beckett and James Joyce, who assailed that dominion with entirely new narrative techniques and linguistic functions.[38] In the 1930s the Russian critic Mikhail Bakhtin argued that language is fundamentally dialogic, generating experience between individuals. In the novel, meaning is not something that is possessed and then expressed by the author to the reader but is rather constructed dialogically between characters, between the author and his characters, or between characters and the reader.[39]

In the late 1930s the American linguist Benjamin Lee Whorf explored how language structures thought and reality.[40] Like Saussure, Whorf saw his research contributing to a new science of language that would surmount the deficiencies of the evolutionary model that viewed Indo-European languages as the pinnacle of development. The evolutionary theory, he insisted, was "dumped upon modern man," while understanding of the connection between language and thought was based on only a few languages out of hundreds. He dismissed the association between "primitive" languages and the mental functioning of "inferior societies."[41] "In our armchair generalizations about grammar and the related fields of logic and thought-psychology," he wrote, we are in the same position as pre-Linnaean botany, and so current provincial linguistic prejudices have produced a "grandiose hokum" (84). His own research was better able to discern more specific linguistic capabilities of scarcely known languages.[42] He probed how thought is shaped by the most basic structures of language: ways of creating plurality and tense or the division of language into parts of speech. The Hopi language, for example, does not have "imaginary plurals." It can say "ten men" because the men can be perceived, but it cannot say "ten days" because they cannot be perceived, and so in Hopi the phrase "they stayed ten days" must be "they stayed until the eleventh day" (140).

Since the seventeenth century, Western science had been the model for valid science all over the world, and it provided compelling evidence for universal concepts such as time, force, and causality. Western scientists believed that although different languages had different words for these concepts, the underlying concepts were more universal than the words used to express them, especially because many of them could be expressed mathematically, without language. But Whorf attempted to show that languages constitute even these basic concepts and the human experiences to which they refer in fundamentally different ways.

Those differences are evident with the concepts of time and causality. The closest the Hopi language comes to a word for abstract time is something equivalent to "becoming later." Hopi has "no words, grammatical forms, constructions or expressions that refer directly to what we call 'time,' or to past, present, or future, or to enduring or lasting" (57). It has no word for, and therefore no conception of, continuous movement in empty space through a uniform time apart from the dynamic processes inherent in people and things. In place of abstract time Hopi has two basic categories roughly equivalent to *objective* and *subjective*. The objective refers roughly to both the English present and past tenses, while the subjective refers to what English renders as future tense but also to what exists in the mind and heart of humans as well as in animals, plants, and things.

Hopi also has no word for abstract causation. An approximate equivalent is the Hopi concept of the subjective realm, which is "quivering with life, power, and potency" (60). Hopi renders *causation* with the subjective form that embraces the future as well as a realm "of expectancy, of desire and purpose, of vitalizing life, of efficient causes" (60). The Hopi equivalent of *causation* is distributed between the subjective and objective realms of activity that are expressed with two verb forms. The *expectant* form borders the subjective tending toward the objective and refers to what is beginning to emerge, including the sense of wanting and intending. The *inceptive* form functions at the edge of objectivity and points in the reverse direction to the end of causation. The single word that comes closest to *causation* is *tunátya*, which means desire, thought, and hope as well as the entire realm of the subjective and the "unmanifest, vital and causal aspect of the Cosmos" (61).

Whorf's linguistics illustrates the specificity-uncertainty dialectic. He laid the foundation for a new science of linguistics which refined understanding of the causal function of languages by studying many more languages and the ways their structures produced thought and behavior. On the other hand, the new science also disclosed enormous uncertainty in understanding the generative role of language as is illustrated in Whorf's struggle to translate into Hopi the English phrase "the food is being eaten." In Hopi the phrase must mean that "whatever causation is behind it is ceasing; the causation explicitly referred to by the causal suffix is hence such as we would call past time, and the verb includes this and the incepting and the decausating of the final state (a state of partial or total eatenness) in one statement. The translation is 'it stops getting eaten'" (61). Whorf generally wrote clearly, but *incepting*, *decausating*, and *eatenness* are dubious coinages. The increasing uncertainty from this approximate translation shows the difficulty of an English speaker grasping precisely what these words signify in Hopi. Scholars have questioned Whorf, or the "Sapir-Whorf hypothesis" as it is known, in arguing that these differences in ways of referring to time are the result of mistranslations or misinterpretations of language and are not truly experiential.

Still Whorf's essays were a reminder that seemingly universal foundations of experience such as past, present, and future may themselves vary culturally and historically. His study underscored not merely the difficulty of translating ideas from one language to another but a deeper source of uncertainty that stemmed from the causal function of language in constituting the most fundamental metaphysical concepts underlying human experience such as time, space, force, and causality.

The Letter Killeth

Recognition of the causal function of language in philosophy and science is analogous to, and in some cases directly influenced, how some novelists rendered the causality of murder. These various connections are evident in pairings between Ludwig Wittgenstein and Philip Kerr, Niels Bohr and Alain Robbe-Grillet, and Jacques Derrida and Umberto Eco. Put together they suggest the broader cultural dissemination of the modern recognition of the constitutive function of language. These major figures shared the distinctly modern notion, as Bohr put it, that "we are suspended in language."

In *Tractatus Logico-Philosophicus* (1921), Wittgenstein explored how language defines the limits of thought and the world. He argued that *"the limits of my language* mean the limits of my world" (56). Those limits of thought and the world in language are not fixed but a maze of shifting boundaries on the other side of which is nonsense. He used this boundary to distinguish meaningful and meaningless propositions and to challenge the intelligibility of most traditional philosophical inquiry: "Most of the propositions and questions to be found in philosophical works are not false but nonsensical," and they "arise from our failure to understand the logic of our language" (19). That logic is fundamentally causal in structuring what can be properly thought and experienced as the world.

He further challenged readers by arguing that "it is impossible for there to be propositions of ethics" (1). Ethical propositions do not pass muster as meaningful because they are not analytic or do not convey empirically verifiable information. His famous concluding sentence— "What we cannot speak about we must pass over in silence"—suggested that rigorous philosophy must pass over ethical propositions because they exceed the limits of what can be said meaningfully. But in a letter of 1919, he explained the intent of the *Tractatus* that he omitted from its preface: "I wanted to write that my work consists of two parts: of the one which is here, and of everything [else] which I have *not* written. And precisely this second part is the important one. For the Ethical is delimited from within, as it were, by my book; and I'm convinced that strictly speaking it can ONLY be delimited in this way. All of what many are babbling today, I have defined in my book by remaining silent about it."[43] The babble referred to wartime moralizing and possibly also Bertrand Russell's didactic tracts. Wittgenstein omitted from his book the most important part by locating the limit of language which can only be known by the vantage point of that which is beyond it in silence. His own silence on ethics became one of the most audible ethical voices of twentieth-century philosophy, suggesting that the abuse of language is the source of the heartlessness and stupidity of his time.

For Wittgenstein, language played a causal role by establishing the limits of truth and reality, by banishing conventional philosophical propositions to the realm of the nonsensical, and by tagging ethical propositions as lacking any propositional force while also elucidating what ethics might mean by remaining eloquently silent about it. In the end he advises readers to view his propositions as a ladder to be climbed and then discarded: "Anyone who understands me eventually recognizes [my propositions] as nonsensical, when he has used them—as steps—to climb up beyond them. (He must, so to speak, throw away the ladder after he has climbed up it)." That final image provides the title for *Wittgenstein's Ladder* by Marjorie Perloff, a study of the philosopher's influence on poetry and the novel. For Perloff, the ladder symbolizes an ordinary, everyday instrument for the way ordinary language elevates thought in a movement whose origin "is as equivocal as its destination." The ladder also suggests the way his numbered, step-by-step propositional language creates a repeated beginning toward an unreachable goal through propositions that are endlessly different and creative.[44]

While the *Tractatus* affirmed a uniform logical structure to all languages, Wittgenstein's *Philosophical Investigations* (1953) argued that languages structure experience by language games which follow rules and utilize symbols of ordinary language. Several of his ideas are aspects of the linguistic philosophy that influenced the serial killer in Philip Kerr's novel *A Philosophical Investigation* (1992): that language limits and determines thought, that much of what we say may be nonsense, that after we say whatever does make sense the rest should be silence, that ethical propositions are beyond the limit of the sayable, that philosophical thinking is like a ladder that we must discard after using, and that language is like a game.

The story is set in 2013, when a British intelligence unit is identifying potential violent criminals. Its acronym LOMBROSO stands for Localization of Medullar Brain Resonations Obliging Social Orthopraxy. The localizations are made by PET scans to identify men whose brains lack a Ventro Medial Nucleus (VMN), which controls aggression, and who are therefore at risk to turn violent. The social orthopraxy involves monitoring the men to prevent them from killing. One of these men, who is given the code name Ludwig Wittgenstein, is traumatized by his evaluation and naming, similar to the trauma that Sartre imagined for Genet on being called a thief. As Wittgenstein explains, "Names are like points; propositions like arrows—they have sense" (49). His naming turned him into a pariah one afternoon when he found himself suddenly transformed into a potential violent criminal as the naming gave him "the mark of Cain" (50). His account of the causal function of language centers on naming. Names are "replete with mystical significance." They have power, and so, he explains, "I have become a name" (105).

He internalizes the logic of LOMBROSO and breaks into the data bank to learn the identity of the other VMN-negatives, so he can find them and carry out his own social orthopraxy by killing them. The logic of his killing derives from the philosophy which his code name signifies. The female detective on his case, nicknamed Jake, sees the connection as she studies the philosopher Wittgenstein to understand the role of language. "It was something people, especially policemen, tended to take for granted, even though it provided the very stuff of man's inner life. Even more important than Wittgenstein's attempt to explain what language was capable of—or so it seemed to Jake—had been his attempt to explain what language was incapable of" (118). The murderer's acts on the border between what can and cannot be known or uttered are similar to the acts of the detective searching at the limits of the known. He comes to see his and her communication as a language game, with new limits and rules created by each killing. "Yes," he concludes, "a game with Policewoman is a fine idea" (132).

He keeps two notebooks, like his philosopher namesake; his Brown Book is a journal about his life, while his Blue Book details the murders (121). His game of life and death is intended to enact Wittgenstein's philosophy of language, as he explains, "I have spent some considerable time in attempting to think of what cannot be thought" and "trying to say what cannot be said." He pushed beyond these borders of thought and speech by doing what he is not supposed to do—kill men. He lives at the limits of language and thought with "unspeakable" acts of murder that he speaks about in accord with Wittgenstein's philosophy of the limits of language.

Wittgenstein the philosopher argued that "it is impossible for there to be propositions of ethics." Wittgenstein the serial killer claims that his murders cannot be judged because "all propositions are of equal value and there are no such things as propositions of ethics." And so, he concludes, "I kill because there is no logical reason not to" (134). He writes to Jake, "Language and its limitations prevent me from saying more. . . . Remember, when eventually we communicate in a real sense you and I will be doing Philosophy." He signs the letter, "Yours Bloodily," which is how the philosopher himself signed correspondence to close friends (151). Also like the philosopher, the killer becomes dissatisfied with his earlier writings: "my squeamishness with regard to the use of the word 'murder' now seems to me to have been mistaken." He decides to "let the earlier work stand," because alongside his new notes they "will serve to present a kind of dialectic" to illustrate the "ambiguities of language" (232).

As the police close in, Wittgenstein attempts suicide. His account of it echoes the final lines of the *Tractatus*, as he makes clear. "Anyone who understands these stories eventually recognizes them as nonsensical when he has used them as steps to climb up beyond them. Just as, in a few minutes, I will use some steps to climb up and put my head in a noose. Like me, you must also, so to speak, throw away the ladder after you have climbed up it. You must transcend the story as a mere proposition, and then you will see the world aright. I regret that circumstances prevent me from saying any more than this, however what we cannot speak about we must pass over in silence" (312). The story of his murders is a narrative ladder that he has made Jake climb, again and again (hence the serial killings), only to see that it ultimately leads nowhere and must be thrown away as nonsense. Thus, doing philosophy, killing, and detecting are all searches for truth dependent on knowing the limits of language. These "philosophical investigations" must be conducted with the conviction that there are no ultimate truths about life just as there are no ultimate reasons for murder.

Jake rushes into Wittgenstein's room and, in order to cut him down from the noose, must climb the ladder that he had just kicked away. He survives for a final exchange with her in which he tries to explain the killings. In years past, people explained heinous murders by saying that God told them to do it, but nowadays such explanations are evidence of insanity. He offers an explanation "better suited to these modern times." It was not the voice of God that made him do it, but "the voice of Logic . . . the ministers of Reason." He killed in order to have a reason to do something—anything—inspired by the voice of logos, which means logic, reason, and language.

The novels of Robbe-Grillet were influenced by quantum mechanics, in particular the theory of complementarity, which held that seemingly incompatible views of reality based on different experimental arrangements can only be understood in complementary languages that describe those experiments and the mathematics that makes sense of them.[45] These different views are not just different perspectives on an event, which could be reconciled within classical mechanics, but rather fundamentally different conceptions such as those used to describe the wave-particle duality of light.

Complementarity was first elaborated by Niels Bohr. His philosophy of language was recorded by his fellow quantum theorist Aage Petersen, who explained that for Bohr philosophical problems were "neither about existence or reality, nor about the structure and limitations of human reason. They were communication problems." When challenged with the view that language is only a picture of a singular reality, Bohr would reply, "We are suspended in language in such a way that we cannot say what is up and what is down."[46] Basic directions are confused because we are locked into the language of classical mechanics which cannot render the quantum world at the atomic level where objective measurement is impossible, the initial conditions of any system cannot be precisely determined (making precise predictions impossible), basic entities have seemingly contradictory properties (the wave-particle duality of light), and mechanical causality cannot be used to explain phenomena.

Robbe-Grillet rejected the world of classical physics that was the setting for the representational Balzacian novel, in which the author knew the initial conditions of the setting of the story, his characters' motives, and the entire plot from the outset of writing and communicated that "objective" truth to a reader, who in the end learned why characters acted the way they did. He also rejected the traditional detective novel, in which everything is "resolved in a banal bundle of causes and consequences, intentions and coincidences."[47]

Bohr's view that we are suspended in language could have been the motto for the novels of Robbe-Grillet, which lifted complementarity into the macro world of human experience. Robbe-Grillet used complementary languages in novels about murder and located the generative source for those acts in the language of his text by means of "textual generators."[48] This literary device is evident in his detective story *The Erasers* (1953) where inner emotional determinants of a character are replaced by the textual generators of the plot. Robbe-Grillet wants to subvert the reader's expectation of a rational explanation of the murder by some psychological drive or ultimate destiny as was typical of the Balzacian novel. He refuses to allow characters to be pushed along by psychological drives or social forces. The only effective causal force comes from the text, and it is unsettling, because Wallas has no motive for killing Dupont and only does so because of characters in the text who come to suspect his guilt: the landlady who had seen a man in a raincoat similar to Wallas's in front of Dupont's house before the murder, a café proprietor who takes Wallas for the man in the raincoat, another detective who suspects Wallas because his gun is like the murder weapon. These characters play a major role in causing him to kill because they "erroneously" suspect him. *Erroneously* is in quotes because it means contrary to the truth, but in Robbe-Grillet there is no truth beyond the text.

An Oedipal theme underlying the story further generates the murder textually. Wallas and Dupont are modern-day versions of Oedipus and his father, and the fateful destiny of the Greek tragedy functions causally in *The Erasers* not as an actual supernatural destiny but as a textual force of the Oedipal myth generated over centuries of retellings, reprintings, and revisions. In addition, the many parallels between Wallas and Oedipus suggest that, at least for readers steeped in literary tradition and with conventional expectations about destiny, Sophocles also determined Wallas to be the killer.[49]

In later Robbe-Grillet novels, language activates murder even more directly with textual generators such as images, words, or even single letters. Since antiquity, writers had used literary techniques such as rhyme, meter, and anagrams to generate textual form and content, but for Robbe-Grillet and other modern novelists, textual generators determine character and plot far beyond the causal function of such strategies by their predecessors.[50] In *Topology of a Phantom City* (1976), the murder narrative is generated in part by the letter *v* associated with the image of the dead body of a prostitute who reappears in several narrative variants with different meanings and in different places and times, triggering different consequences. In one version she is the goddess Vanadé, and the first letter of her name generates much of the text according to a complex set of textual generators.

The ancient city Vanadium was destroyed in 39 B.C. by a volcano that ejected a stone that wounded the goddess Vanadé with a V-shaped wound. A ship appears flying a banderole with a red letter G which somehow "yields [causes] the following series" (*donne la série suivante*) centering on the letter *v*:

> vanadis—vigil—vessel
> danger—water's edge—diviner
> plunge—in vain—carnage
> divan—virgin—vagina
> gravid—engenders—david. (37)

This phonological matrix of words involving *v* generates the story, which includes a number of murders. The story takes place in Vanadium where a virgin keeping vigil at a port sees a vessel and senses danger as the boat approaches the water's edge. An oracle (diviner) advises the women to plunge into the water to defend themselves against male sailors, but, except for the woman who gave the warning, all are massacred (carnage) and the sea fills with blood. On a divan the virgin is raped and her V-shaped pubic area covered with blood. She plunges into the water bloodied by the other victims, emerges pregnant, and gives birth to David. Thus does v generate the story, including the massacre of many young women as well as the lone survivor. Her appearance covered with blood links her to the murder victim described earlier, even though in this version she survives to give birth to David, who is also the murderer, the producer of his own play *The Birth of David*, and a hermaphrodite and so self-generating like the text itself.

The letter v continues to generate narrative as Robbe-Grillet plays with the name Vanadé, who is given other V-generated names such as Vanessa or Veronica and given alliterative epithets such as Vanadé the Victorious, the Vampire, and the Vanquished. Visual creations from v include triangles which also generate persons and objects. The first Greek letter of the name of Vanadé's brother David is a delta, a triangle, and his name itself is a v flanked by two deltas. The city of Vanadium is full of triangles: the pediment on the temple, the crossed swords of conquering soldiers, umbrellas, volcanos, and female pubic triangles.[51]

The original matrix of V-generated words is the origin of the plot. As the literary critic Ursula Heise concluded, "the text converts a pattern of repetition into a pseudo-causal chain that emphasizes that the words do not so much refer to extratextual referents as they are generated by intratextual principle." The story pretends that it is not created by the author but emerges "out of a linguistic schema, an arrangement of signifiers."[52] Later in the novel Robbe-Grillet applies another textual generator to a series of murders based on a geometrical schema that determines (or at least seems to determine—we are never certain) where the murders were committed. In the last section, titled "The Criminal Already on My Trail," the narrator-detective finds his hands covered with blood and is pursued by an assassin, and a policeman finds "clues gathered from the text" (132), hence the detective, the narrator, or the text itself may be the murderer.

Robbe-Grillet gave language unprecedented causal muscle because he wanted to challenge the Balzacian novel in which language was a transparent instrument for communicating thoughts without affecting their content and was used to valorize bourgeois society, which still governed character, plot, and moral-religious values.[53] In "New Novel, New Man" (1961) Robbe-Grillet charged that the world of the Balzacian novel, with a God-like omniscient narrator and a man-centered universe, was no longer credible, and his own *nouveau roman* must reflect changing circumstances. Lives are created by contemporary human beings, and no narrators have a privileged point of view on the truth.

After Hitler, Stalin, Hiroshima, and the world wars, the old cause-and-effect explanations and narrative accounts of history are untenable. "The significations of the world around us are no more than partial, provisional, even contradictory, and always contested." The modern novel should be an exploration "which itself creates its own signification as it proceeds."[54]

In pushing the causal function of language to its limit, however, Robbe-Grillet pushed readers beyond the limits of their understanding. His omissions, contradictions, and wild shifts were maddening. Still the novel drew attention to new causal functions of language and pressed readers to assume unprecedented levels of responsibility for making that language intelligible, even for generating the narrative.

In three influential books published in 1967, Jacques Derrida affirmed the causal role of language with his philosophy of deconstruction that targeted the metaphysics of presence. He argued that since Plato, the history of Western metaphysics was a search for some ultimate foundation for reality that he called the transcendental signified, some concept to transcend the fleeting play of appearances and signify existence essentially. To provide such an ultimate source of meaning, metaphysicians postulated concepts such as God, reason, being, substance, truth, and the self. Derrida criticized this extended search for the absolute center or fixed origin of reality. The concept of a centered structure involves "a fundamental immobility and a reassuring certitude."[55] It can also be called the origin. Whether transcendental signifieds ground existence as a material substance, spiritual essence, spatial center, temporal origin, or ultimate goal, they all function causally in the determination of what is real and true.

Derrida called the affirmation of a center in language "logocentrism." This philosophy is based on the several meanings of the Greek word *logos*, which is the first breath of existence and life, possibly also the first word of God, if not God himself, a word that also means reason, logic, or justification, as well as language and word. Historically logocentrism was based on phonocentrism, a theory of the privileged value of speech over writing. The relation between these major forms of language is one of many binary pairs which his deconstructionist method views hierarchically. Thus each of the candidates for transcendental signified is the first named and privileged term of a corresponding binary pair: God/human; reason/unreason; being/nonbeing; essence/accident; substance/void; and truth/falsehood. The first term is privileged because it is more real and therefore is closer to being a transcendental signified. It also has more causal efficacy. Derrida deconstructed these pairs by finding them in various texts, reversing their hierarchical ordering, and then reconstituting them in a nonhierarchical way with deeper meaning generated out of the interplay between them.

Deconstruction of the speech/writing hierarchy was the first task of his new science of language, which he called grammatology. Phonocentrism privileges speech as more present than writing, because it supposedly comes directly from spirit as an ultimate ground of existence and is beyond everything sensory, while writing is delayed and devalued as a mere copy of thought. Writing is also produced by an author who is absent. It is reproducible and therefore open to multiple interpretations which diminish its unity and presence.

Derrida deconstructed the speech/writing hierarchy by reversing it and then showing how meaning arises from the differences and similarities between the two terms. The reversal is, however, only momentary and partial. It remains unstable, because writing and speech contaminate each other with traces of each other just as good always contaminates evil, and truth contaminates falsehood. The terms of binary pairs draw meaning from differences between each other and from deferrals of their meaning until other terms have been drawn into the interpretation. Derrida coined the term *différance* to refer to this dual creation of meaning in writing out of (spatial) differences between words and (temporal) deferrals between them.[56] *Différance* reverses the two key binary opposites of speech/writing and presence/absence that underlie logocentrism. It refers to the slippage and movement of interpretive strategies that do not have any single meaning, interpretive resting point, logical center, or point of origin.

The generative function of writing as an endless play of words is the subject of Derrida's essay "Plato's Pharmacy," on Plato's dialogue *Phaedrus*, a critique of writing and the classic source of Western phonocentrism.[57] In Plato's dialogue Socrates begins with the myth of a young maiden who is killed when she is playing with another maiden named Pharmacia and blown into an abyss. Pharmacia's name is associated with several meanings. In the myth it suggests a playful seduction and deadly distraction. "Through her games, Pharmacia has dragged down to death a virginal purity and an unpenetrated interior" (70). *Pharmacia* can also signify "the administration of the *pharmakon*, the drug: the medicine and/or poison." A *pharmakon* can heal, but it can also be "a criminal thing, a poisoned present" (77). A *pharmakeus* can be a magician, sorcerer, herbalist, or poisoner (117). *Pharmacia* also means writing, while *pharmakos* means scapegoat, as writing can make one "stray from one's general, natural, habitual paths and laws" (70). Thus writing can play with meanings, seduce the innocent, lead astray, invoke magic, heal the sick, or be a deadly poison. Socrates himself criticized the written word and philosophized only by speech, but he was still made a scapegoat and executed by poison.

Although Derrida celebrated the life-affirming functions of writing over speech, he also probed the prejudices against writing and the fear of its toxicity. The contemporary semiotician Umberto Eco crafted such a fear as the motive for murder in his historical novel *The Name of the Rose* (1980), in which the original means of killing is poison from the pharmacy of a fourteenth-century Italian monastery.[58] The man behind the poisoning is the monk and head librarian Jorge of Burgos, who instigates the killings to prevent anyone from reading a secret book on laughter by Aristotle that he found in the library.

Jorge explains to the man investigating the murders, William of Baskerville, that Jesus used language to reveal the single and absolute truth of God and never spoke comedically, because laughter foments doubt (130). Jorge believes that librarians should guard the indubitable divine Word and suppress any corruption of it by comedy. Their purpose is to preserve knowledge of God, which "is complete and has been defined since the beginning in the perfection of the Word." Jesus said that he was *the* way and *the* truth, and knowledge is nothing but inspired commentary on that divine wisdom. Jorge justifies his murder with the final lines of the Bible: "If any man shall take away from the words of the book of this prophecy, God shall take away his part out of the book of life." Jorge sees himself doing God's work by killing anyone who wants to use Aristotle to make fun of the literal truth of the Bible.

Speaking to his companion Adso, William challenges Jorge's views by arguing that language is not a representation of fixed truth but a system of arbitrary signs created in the interplay of experience. Wisdom is most fully realized with the play of comedy and metaphor and is not given once and for all time, unambiguously and infallibly by God. "Books are not made to be believed," he claims, "but to be subjected to inquiry." Language is a network of signs rather than a literal representation of the truth. William would like to be able to go from the signs to reality if possible, just as he would like to go from the clues to the murderer, but such inquiries require "the help of other signs" (317). Language is a network of shifting interdependent signs, and the source of the murders turns out to be a network of motives and accidents among several perpetrators. Their detection follows a network of clues and traces that ultimately refer to many causal factors and several interdependent murderers, not a single guilty culprit with a single clear motive.

Adso, the narrator of the detective story, wonders whether in this network of signs relating to other signs there is not some real thing, some first cause, to which the sign refers ultimately. He appeals to William for a transcendental signified: "the final something, the true one—does that never exist?" William's answer—"Perhaps"—underscores the fundamental contingency of truth and causal understanding in the modern period (317). Truth is found in the surfacing of the incidental behind the fundamental, the marginal beyond the central, and the many voices that surface around ecclesiastical disputations. In the play of thought, traces of good and evil intermix. As the monastery herbalist Severinus tells William (no doubt echoing Derrida's essay "Plato's Pharmacy"), "the line between poison and medicine is very fine; the Greeks used the word 'pharmacon' for both" (108). Just as William cannot find a single culprit behind the murders, Adso cannot find any ultimate authority for his narrative of the murderers, as he laments: "Correct interpretation can be established only on the authority of the fathers, and in the case that torments me, I have no auctoritas to which my obedient mind can refer, and I burn in doubt" (248).

In a final clash with William, Jorge explains his fear of Aristotle's book on comedy. Each of Aristotle's books had destroyed a part of Christian learning. "The fathers had said everything that needed to be known about the power of the Word, but then Boethius had only to gloss the Philosopher [Aristotle] and the divine mystery of the Word was transformed into a human parody of categories and syllogisms" (473). Aristotle's newly found book on comedy threatens to overturn the image of God himself with laughter that frees people from a healthy fear of the devil. Sinning creatures need the divine gift of the fear of eternal damnation. Laughter threatens the entire theocentric view of creation, as he warns: "On the day when the Philosopher's word would justify the marginal jests of the debauched imagination, or when what has been marginal would leap to the center, every trace of the center would be lost. The people of God would be transformed into an assembly of monsters belched forth from the abysses of the terra incognita, and at that moment the edge of the known world would become the heart of the Christian empire" (475). Jorge fears the loss of what Derrida called the metaphysics of presence, with its promise of the origin, the center, and the ultimate reference for all things good, true, and sacred.

This novel enacts Paul's maxim that "the letter killeth" in a number of ways. Language kills against the background of the Inquisition, which tortured people into confessing sins, took their confessions as true, and then executed them on the basis of their own words and in the name of the text of the law. It kills because Jorge poisons the pages of Aristotle's book on comedy because he does not want anyone to learn the value of laughter in interpreting religious texts. The poison is made in the monastery's pharmacy, no doubt a reference to Plato's "Pharmacy," perhaps also a nod to Derrida's essay on the subject, which drew a semantic link between writing and poisoning. Jorge justifies his killing by citing the final lines of the Bible in which God threatens to kill anyone who tampers with his words. Language is indirectly responsible for some of the murders as a result of a misreading of clues by William, who guesses erroneously that a single murderer was killing according to the sequence of the seven trumpets of the Apocalypse by such means as hail and fire, a sea of blood, a scorpion's bite, etcetera. Jorge learns of William's mistaken theory based on a misreading of the biblical language and exploits it, making several subsequent murders conform to its logic. The word also kills Jorge himself, who literally eats his own murderous words, because in an act of suicide he eats the poisoned pages. In the end the entire library burns down, killing a number of monks as well as looters searching for relics among the still dangerous smoking manuscripts. The letter indeed killeth, but in an ultimate Derridean textual play, it also creates metaphorical life and meaning out of the murders and burned texts by making them into a story in which readers can come to life back in the fourteenth century.

IN PLACE OF the Victorians' emphasis on the causal role of deficient, excessive, or corrupted moral education, modern novelists gave unprecedented attention to language itself as a cause of murder in a variety of innovative ways sometimes directly influenced by philosophers, scientists, or literary critics. Some of the modernists' fictional characters kill because their language is deficient. Josef K. is ignorant of the language of the law, and that language itself, which is responsible for his ultimate execution, is secretive and confused. Moosbrugger is linguistically retarded, Oswald is dyslexic, and Schmitz is illiterate. Others kill from an excess of language imposed by others. The authorities in Kafka's sadistic penal colony execute victims literally with the letter of the law. Genet creates murders in his writings to escape from the tyranny of being named a thief. Sartre exhausts his vocabulary to express the force of language that causes Genet to become what he is: Genet is caught, defined, signified, crushed, penetrated, haunted, trapped, encased, paralyzed, condemned, and punished by language.

Others kill because of dynamic generations out of language: Konrad's frustrated literary ambitions, Perry's morbid lexicon, and Alex's bastardized Russian. The cult of assassins in *The Names* is obsessed with language, the serial assassin named Wittgenstein is motivated by his namesake's philosophy of language, while Wallas's act of murder is generated by the text of the novel in which he appears. In another of Robbe-Grillet's novels the letter v is a textual generator of the slaughter of virgins. Finally, Jorge kills out of a desire to keep others from reading what he considers to be a dangerous book on how to read and kills himself by the poisoned pages of that text.

AMONG THE HISTORICAL causes of changing ideas about causality that I am tracking, two play a major role in the causal role of language: intellectual specialization and new technologies. Throughout this chapter I have emphasized the first of these, the increasing division of intellectual labor in philosophies of language by Nietzsche, Wittgenstein, and Derrida, as well as contributions to new linguistic sciences by Saussure and Whorf. Their contributions to understanding the causal role of language evince the specificity-uncertainty dialectic. The increasing specificity of these new disciplinary investigations disclosed huge areas of probabilistic and uncertain knowledge, as in Whorf's documentation of the approximate nature of translations between different languages, Saussure's theory of the arbitrariness of the signified, and Derrida's strategy of endlessly deconstructing texts. A vivid image of my argument as applied to language is Wittgenstein's ladder, which symbolizes ascent to higher knowledge by means of a philosophy that must be discarded precisely as it becomes increasingly effective. The higher one ascends with his elucidating propositions, the more dependent one becomes on them and so the more necessary it becomes that they be thrown away. Analogously, the more one understands the causal function of language, the more one must realize how little one knows about it. In the modern period, Wittgenstein's identification of what we cannot speak of and must pass over in silence becomes an ever-increasing realm for many other thinkers and writers.

A second explanation for the increasing appreciation of the causal role of language is the new communication technology that revolutionized the power, range, and varieties of communication. The telegraph, telephone, wireless, movies, radio, television, and Internet increased the number of places from which language could be sent or received and the distance and speed of those transmissions, which also were progressively enhanced with the voices and faces of senders. With movies, radio, and television, the receivers of messages became increasingly numerous, diverse, and geographically remote, while the messages themselves became more precise, with electronically recorded and transmitted communications. At the same time they also became more probabilistic and uncertain in terms of who was sending and receiving messages, as they went beyond the specificity of earlier face-to-face communications and later the linear, point-to-point messages of telegrams to the field-like networked distributions of radio and television broadcasts and, most recently, to the Internet. A number of modern murderers are motivated to kill by something they read in a newspaper, or see on the Internet, or see and hear on television or in a movie. In *Red Dragon*, Dolarhyde is motivated by home movies he develops in a photography lab; in *The First Deadly Sin*, Daniel Blank sees himself as his computer; while Hannibal Lecter checks the FBI home page on the Internet for information about himself and his victims. DeLillo's Lee Harvey Oswald is motivated to kill by what he sees and hears on television, and in the end imagines himself being murdered live on television.

Another causal influence embraced new research specialties and new communication technologies that were developed in the United States following a series of conferences from 1943 to 1954, when several scientists pooled their expertise. Claude Shannon developed a theory of information that codified the essential communicative function of language as a probability function divorced from any content and therefore generalizable to a wide range of contexts. Warren McCullough viewed neurons as information-processing systems, John von Neumann adapted computer binary codes to process information about biological systems, and Norbert Wiener elaborated the larger significance of these theories to the tasks of communication and control with a theory he called cybernetics.[59]

Wiener began electronic feedback research in 1942, coined the term *cybernetics* in 1947, and popularized it with his book on the subject in 1948, where he applied it to the entire new field of control and communication theory in machines and living beings.[60] There he recounted how his wartime research drew on pioneering research into autoregulatory machines ranging from early thermostats to the new antiaircraft guns that received radar readings from a moving airplane, instantaneously computed its trajectory, anticipated where it would be in that trajectory when a projectile would reach it, and helped to aim the gun and trigger it at the right instant to hit its intended moving target.

Cybernetics and robotics in the postwar period were made possible by new computers which were capable of receiving unprecedented amounts of information instantaneously from numerous sensors, converting that information into a binary digital code, making calculations on it, and discharging instructions electronically to any number of electronically controlled effectors. Already in 1948 Wiener could list several automatic machines that relied on some instantaneous feedback mechanism: photoelectric cells, pressure gauges, thermostats, radar systems, self-propelled missiles, and antiaircraft guns. These prototypes of later more complex machines involved a nearly instantaneous processing of information. Modern cybernetics developed when the feedback loop was reconceived as a flow of information, and the causality of language shifted from nineteenth-century linear action to modern nonlinear reflexivity in a field of networked messages. As a result, by the end of the twentieth century, language as information came to be viewed as the generative agent in a spectrum of interdigitated functions from reproductive processes in DNA and the functioning of the human brain to the workings of ATMs and the World Wide Web. N. Katherine Hayles, following Donna Haraway, labeled these developments *informatics*, which refers to the myriad modern "technologies of information as well as the biological, social, linguistic, and cultural changes that initiate, accompany, and complicate their development." Hayles underscored the increasing uncertainty created by these new research specialties and communication technologies: "Carrying the instabilities implicit in Lacanian floating signifiers one step further, information technologies create what I will call *flickering signifiers*, characterized by their tendency toward unexpected metamorphoses, attenuations, and dispersions."[61]

The impact of such new technology and its attendant philosophy has been reconstructed by Jeremy Campbell, whose main argument is suggested by his arresting title, *Grammatical Man*.[62] The dominant nineteenth-century theory of entropy held that the universe as well as human existence is governed by a tendency that causes concentrations of energy to go from order to disorder and systems of organization to go from coherence to chaos. Just as the operation of entropy in heat systems tends toward equal distribution of heat throughout the system, entropy in language tends toward random words and dispersion of meaning or noise. Opposite the entropy principle is the information principle that is inherent in life and language. Just as life contradicts entropy as it increases organization, a sentence generates meaning as it proceeds across a line. Information theory suggests that order is natural and that "grammatical man inhabits a grammatical universe" (12). Information is the creative force in human history; it tells cells to divide and species to reproduce, and it shapes gross human behavior by training, instructing, and inspiring.

The meaning generated by language in any sentence is a model of the specificity-uncertainty dialectic. The sentence creates a specific meaning that increases the number and complexity of ideas it communicates as it proceeds while at the same time revealing a vast realm of unuttered words and meanings that it might have generated but did not. A sentence is an island of coherence in a sea of probability, uncertainty, and noise. The cultural historical significance of information theory and cybernetics is that language plays a historically unprecedented causal role in making human beings what they are.

Social scientists accorded an increasingly prominent role to the productive forces of knowledge and information, hence of language. Early on, the sociologist Daniel Bell criticized the ascendancy of language over mind in the "postindustrial society" as a source of modern alienation and uncertainty.[63] More positively, in 1980 George Lakoff and Mark Johnson explored how metaphors "structure how we perceive, how we think, and what we do."[64] Recently the social historian Perry Anderson argued that postmodern society is "a web of linguistic communications" in which the social bond is composed of many different games with incommensurable rules and agonistic interrelations, all energized by "machines transmitting discourses that are wall-to-wall ideology."[65] New information technologies drive productive forces, shape personal tastes and aesthetic sensibilities, establish moral norms, entertain the masses, influence politics, and even define religious ideals. Human consciousness is increasingly shaped by government propaganda and advertising agencies monitored by daily polls, creating an information feedback loop of self-regulating and self-generating discourses. The geographer David Harvey underscored the view of Lyotard that knowledge is the main driving force of production in the postmodern world.[66] In the writings of Michel Foucault and the countless scholars influenced by him, language as "discourse" is the defining function of human existence and, when elaborated into successive epistemes, the driving force of history.

In addition to novels about murder, another popular literary genre, science fiction, offers further evidence for the causally active role of language in countless murders by extraterrestrial aliens and partly human cyborgs who kill out of a variety of motives implemented by information technologies working through electronic, chemical, biological, or other fantastic means. Perhaps most familiar is the cyborg in James Cameron's movie *The Terminator* (1984) who is programmed to kill. His digitalized instructions that appear on screen as if through his own eyes enable him to find targets using futuristic cybernetic technology. John Badham's movie *War Games* (1983) climaxes with a runaway computer that plays its own deadly language games and in the process almost starts a nuclear war. Into the modern period new communication technologies dramatized the causal potency of languages by imagining their potential destructive capability. Aliens and cyborgs are frightening not so much because of their advanced weapons as because of what they know. A final image of ever more precise research disclosing vast realms of uncertainty about the power of language is one of the thousands of computers around the world working at blazing speed to invent digitalized languages in the hope of contacting other beings in the most unfathomable realm imaginable, the infinite reaches of outer space.

4

Sexuality

SEXUAL DESIRE is the biological deep wiring of causal activation and a powerful force behind a range of behaviors from basic relatedness to complex love. Its immediate goal is release of sexual tension and a heightening of sexual pleasure, which may involve a sexual partner. Its long-term goal is the production of offspring, which requires a partner and usually involves relationships that begin long before offspring appear and continue after they are born. These protracted social relationships may lead to competition and thus aggression. In some people, mainly men, that mix of desire and aggression can become spiked by jealousy or emotional corruption and motivate murders involving rape, torture, mutilation, necrophilia, or cannibalism.

Since the Victorian period, novels described such murders with increasing detail and specificity, drawing on findings that emerged around the turn of the century from a number of new disciplines, such as sexology, sexual science, forensic psychiatry, and psychoanalysis.[1] The new science of sex endocrinology identified specific sex hormones, which further clarified the causal action of sexual desire. As with the discovery of genes, the discovery of sex hormones and its elaboration into other new specialties such as psychopharmacology and neuroendocrinology sharpened understanding of the causal role of sexual desire while also expanding the realm of uncertainty about complex causal interactions between genes, peptides, hormones, neurotransmitters, and the brain.

Across the years of my study, descriptions of the bodily sources and causal circuitry of desire in love novels shifted from Victorian circumspection to modern directness. While Victorian novelists traced sexual desire from imprecise sources in the soul, spirit, or heart, moderns traced specific bodily sources in the mouth, nipples, genitals, anus, and the entire surface of the skin as well as in stimuli from impulses, fantasies, and vision. Earlier novelists' discretion about sex, routine with George Eliot and Henry James, became unthinkable with D. H. Lawrence and James Joyce.

In the modern period, explicit renderings of sexual desire that in the nineteenth century and earlier had been confined to pornography and had sketched mainly superficial relationships with casual partners or prostitutes appeared for the first time in serious literature to re-create more complex and abiding relationships between mature lovers. Moderns also probed more precise origins of desire deep within a lover's body. In Hardy's *Tess of the d'Urbervilles*, for example, Angel's desire is described with conventional Victorian metaphor, as a vision of Tess's lips "sent an aura over his flesh, a breeze through his nerves" (127). By contrast, in Lawrence's *Women in Love* Ursula puts her arms around Rupert's loins, her face against his thigh, and with her fingertips traces down his flanks, establishing "a rich new circuit . . . at the back and the base of the loins." The desire generated by stimulating Rupert is also reciprocal as a thrill runs through her, "flooding down her spine and down her knees." Ursula then probes desire with her fingers to its genital-anal source with a frankness unthinkable for a Victorian heroine, "from the strange marvelous flanks and thighs, deeper, further in mystery than the phallic source, came the floods of ineffable darkness and ineffable riches" (306). In *Ulysses* Joyce re-creates the intensity of Molly's fantasies about sex with Boylan and its aftermath: "he made me spend the 2nd time tickling me behind with his finger I was coming for about 5 minutes with my legs round him I had to hug him after O Lord I wanted to shout out all sorts of things fuck or shit" (754). Henry Miller's *Tropic of Cancer* (1934) explores sexual desire in a twelve-page peroration about writing, fucking, and the history of the universe that shifts from brutal realism to joyous surrealism, ransacking Western culture for images of creation and passion, anything that flows from the primordial source of desire. Serious modern novelists explored more bodily sources of sexual desire and their effects in increasingly complex networks of sexual possibilities.

Victorian novelists created some of the most powerful love stories of the Western world, but that power was in part a function of the enormous constraint that lovers in their novels had to surmount. These fictional characters were modeled after real-life Victorians who constrained sexual desire by *oppression*, a limiting pressure imposed on an individual from without, and by *suppression*, an internal conscious mental pressure by which one tries to keep oneself from thinking about or acting on something. Victorian novelists also suppressed details of the specific ways that sexual desire may motivate murder, in contrast to modern murder novelists who described the causal role of a greater number of increasingly complex and powerful motivating sexual desires and at the same time revealed the uncertainty about causal processes in the gruesome world of sex killers. Before comparing novels from these two periods, I will trace some breakthroughs in sex research that provided the context for their respective works.

SEXOLOGY AND MURDER

The starting point of serious thinking about the causal role of sexual desire in killing is Darwin, whose theory of sexual selection, introduced in *The Descent of Man* (1871), postulated an inherited aggressive instinct wired into sexual desire as the driving force behind competition between males for females. Nature's reward for a male's killing or at least scaring off male rivals is pleasure followed by more progeny. Late Victorian fiction, especially that of Bourget, Zola, Stoker, Norris, and London, contains many characters who are driven by such animal instincts to commit murder. But in these novels, as compared with later ones, causal explanations based on sexual desire are noticeably lacking in detail. As Zola explained in *Thérèse Raquin*, "Thérèse and Laurent are human animals, nothing more." They are drawn to murder "by the inexorable laws of their physical nature," and "their remorse [leading to their suicide] really amounts to a simple organic disorder, a revolt of the nervous system when strained to breaking-point" (22).

Popular thinking identified prostitutes as the most common link between sexual desire and violent crimes. Victorians routinely drew causal arrows from hereditary degeneration to female masturbation to nymphomania to prostitution to alcoholism and finally to murder and suicide. Whether prostitutes committed crimes, were the victims of crimes, or inspired killing between males, their sexuality was somehow the root cause. The classic scientific elaboration of this all-purpose scenario of the "female born criminal" was Cesare Lombroso's *La donna delinquente, la prostituta e la donna normale* (1893).

In the 1870s and 1880s researchers began to identify more precisely the multifarious sources and manifestations of sexuality in more complex combinations, creating vast nomenclatures of sexual inventiveness (or perversion, depending on the perspective), which also underscored the complexity and uncertainty of causal understanding. *Homosexuality* was coined by Karl Maria Kertbeny in 1869, *exhibitionism* by Ernest-Charles Lasègue in 1877, *sexual perversion* by Valentin Magnan in 1885, and *fetishism* by Alfred Binet in 1887.[2] During that time the next major contribution to sexology was Richard von Krafft-Ebing, whose influential *Psychopathia Sexualis*, first appeared in 1886 and went through many revisions with substantial additions by the twelfth and last edition in 1902. Its subtitle, "With Especial Reference to the Antipathic Sexual Instinct—A Medico-Forensic Study," outlined the connections it would make between sexual pathology, disease, and crime, which established it as a pathbreaking work in forensic psychiatry. His stated goal was "to record the various psychopathological manifestations of sexual life in man and reduce them to their lawful conditions" (xiii). Although he did not formulate any convincing laws, and his causal explanations were limited by preoccupation with hereditary degeneration, he did sharpen understanding of the causal links between desire and murder by defining many new diagnostic categories of sexual pathology and suggesting how they figure in the etiology of crime. These include masochism, which he coined in 1890, and sadism, which he popularized, together with voyeurism, fetishism, rape, pederasty, and lust-murder. These pathologies were richly documented for that time, with fifty-one case histories in the first edition and expanded to more than three hundred by the last edition, all taken from his own psychiatric patients, defendants in criminal courts, earlier medical literature, and reports from colleagues too embarrassed to publish their own case studies.[3]

While he emphasized the hereditary origin of sexual pathology, he insisted on the purely psychic origin of sadism, which he identified as *the* causally acting perversion par excellence, because it "represents the most intense effect that one person, either with or without coitus, can exert on another" (141–42). His survey of fetishes further expanded the number of triggers for sexual pathology to include hair, hands, feet, breasts, underclothing, handkerchiefs, furs, velvet, silks, animals, and odors, all of which could lead to sex murders, as, for example, the fetishism for fine white skin which can provoke cannibalism (156).

Krafft-Ebing also discussed the sexual pathology of lust-murder, which can involve mutilation of a woman's face, breasts, and sex organs. In one such case a murderer ripped open his victim's abdomen, tore out an ovary and pieces of her intestine, and put other severed body parts around her corpse. The only explanation Krafft-Ebing offered for such crimes was degeneration, citing Lombroso as authority. Subsequent sexologists would suggest more specific explanations based on closer examination of individual case histories, but this first work greatly expanded awareness of a wide range of activities that generate sexual desire and raised new questions about how various modes of sexual desire lead to murder and how the killing itself may enact or seek to fulfill them.

The archetype of the serial sex murderer took shape in Western culture around five brutal murders of prostitutes in the Whitechapel district of London in 1888 by a man who was never found and came to be known as Jack the Ripper. The incidents became a media bonanza, as newspapers reported the ghastly details and in turn received thousands of letters from people purporting to be the Ripper. Recent feminist scholars concerned about the rise of male sexual violence against women have focused on these murders as the moment when such acts entered popular consciousness with graphic accounts of how the body was mutilated, which organs he cut out, and where he put them.[4] Such unprecedented descriptive detail was already noted in *Lancet*, in October 1888, between the fourth and fifth murders: "Today, the press takes care to report at inordinate length, and often with objectionable minuteness, the details of the latest murder, . . . gruesome descriptions of the victims, [and] elaborate conjectures as to the precise mode and motive for the crimes."[5] The many historically dated conjectures about motive were that the Ripper was an evolutionary throwback, a born criminal, an upper-class lunatic taking revenge on the lower classes, an aristocratic libertine, a reader of Zola's novels, a religious fanatic, a mad surgeon or gynecologist, a vengeful medical student who caught syphilis from a prostitute, a multiple personality such as French psychiatrists had been studying, an anarchist, a Jewish ritual slaughterman, a vivisectionist looking for organs to sell, or an imitator of Stevenson's Dr. Hyde.[6]

The most popular motive was sexual, because the Ripper's victims were all sexually mutilated prostitutes. As Colin Wilson concluded, the case "inaugurated the age of the sex crime."[7] While some sexual explanations identified the motive as active male desire aggressively seeking a perverted outlet, others analyzed the motive along class lines as male defensiveness against the threat of female sexuality, symbolized in upper-class culture by the *femme fatale*, in middle-class culture by the more sexually demanding "New Woman," and in lower-class culture by the streetwalker.

As Judith Walkowitz argued, the imputed sexual motives of this period, which were elaborated into discourse largely by men, concealed and self-deceived as much as they revealed and self-disclosed.[8] Late-Victorian "narratives of sexual danger" were indeed larded with quasi-causal explanations that did as much to rationalize men's anxiety and vent their growing resentment as they did to identify plausible motives for action. Still, the proliferation of discourses circulating around these acts broadened the range of ideas, fantasies, and practices that could be considered sexual motivations for murder.

The first important "modernizer" of sex in the twentieth century, as Paul Robinson argued, was Havelock Ellis, who was followed by Alfred Kinsey, William Masters, and Virginia Johnson. Against Victorian ideas that most sexual desires and activities are unhealthy, immoral, sinful, or illegal, the sex modernizers viewed an expanded realm of sex as healthy and virtuous, one that ought to be free from excessive moral and legal restraint. The sex modernizers "sought to broaden the range of legitimate sexual behavior" beyond the Victorians' "exclusive commitment to adult, genital, heterosexual intercourse."[9] Ellis's mammoth *Studies in the Psychology of Sex*, which appeared in six volumes between 1897 and 1910, popularized and expanded thinking about "normal" sexual desire and its conventional goals of courtship, marriage, heterosexual intercourse, and reproduction.[10] He stretched the sexual imagination of readers by finding sexual motives behind such diverse activities as blushing, laughing, dancing, singing, dreaming, nursing, dressing, midnight bonfires, and religious conversions.

In 1900 Ellis coined the value-free term *auto-erotism* for a wide range of practices previously stigmatized by moralists as *self-abuse* or the *solitary vice*, and by ecclesiastics as *onanism*. With the zeal of a revolutionary liberated by a philosophy of sexual toleration, he found signs of auto-erotism most everywhere, especially among females, which is of particular historical significance, because it undercut frantic Victorian warnings about female self-abuse. Ellis found evidence for it from all over the world, assisted by dildos made from clay, glass, leather, ivory, or hard red rubber, some capable of injecting warm fluid at the moment of orgasm. More evidence of widespread female masturbation and the variety of techniques are the objects that he reported surgeons removed from women's vaginas: cucumbers, pencils, forks, candles, corks, compasses, crochet needles, toothbrushes, and toothpicks. Females also masturbated by grinding coffee between their knees, riding hobbyhorses and bicycles, sitting cross-legged on moving trains, even rapidly working the pedal of a sewing machine (166–82). Although Ellis conceded the possibility of "morbid" excess, he generally viewed masturbation and other sexual activities as healthy. His major interpretive shift was from Victorian concern about the problems of sexual excess (satyriasis and nymphomania) to modern concern about the problems of sexual failure (impotence and frigidity).

Ellis made three indirect contributions to thinking about the causal role of sexual desire in murder. His broadly enthusiastic view of all sexual expression cut the causal links that Victorians imagined in arguing that hereditary degeneration is the main cause of solitary vice that may result in social vices and lead to violent crimes. He also rejected earlier causal scenarios leading from homosexuality to sex crimes by arguing that all human beings are basically bisexual, that sexual inversion is innate and therefore not a vice, and that for many it generates artistic inspiration and moral value precisely because it must overcome so many external obstacles to its fulfillment. Third, his study of sadism concluded that deeply rooted sexual sources for the desire to inflict pain might drive some deranged individuals to murder. In a hundred-page section on "Love and Pain" he traced the evolution of that desire back to animal courtship involving displays of force, demonstrations of prowess in hunting, and mock combats that can cause pain and may lead to real combat and even killing. He assumed that natural selection created "savages," who measured manliness by the ability to hunt and fight, as, for example, in African cultures where "the chief incentive for head-hunting is the desire to please the woman" or among the Masai, who believe that "a man is not supposed to marry until he has bloodied his spear" (57). In some primitive societies, marriage by capture resembles animal courtship, which has evolved in higher civilizations where women become sexually aroused by being hurt, and both sexes become sexually aroused by love bites, flagellation, sadism, and masochism. He did not sanction sexual violence but viewed it as an aberrant outcome of universal and normal sex impulses.

Ellis rejected a sharp dichotomy between male sadism and female masochism, because sexual desire is more complexly distributed between the sexes. He preferred the term *algolagnia*, introduced by Schrenck-Notzing in 1899, which effaced the disjunct between sadistic males and masochistic females and referred rather to a bisexual *love of pain* among males and females who both enjoy hurting one another and being hurt.[11] Males as well as females enjoy strangling the object of sexual desire and being strangled, although his specific examples divide these anomalies between the sexes: the sadistic man who strangles a woman during coitus and the masochistic woman who "will do anything to have her neck squeezed by her lover till her eyeballs bulge" (152). The desire to link sexual pleasure with pain, he theorized, is strongest in people with a "deficient nervous organization" who need extra stimulation to become sexually aroused. "The parched sexual instinct greedily drinks up and absorbs the force it obtains by applying abnormal stimuli to its emotional apparatus" (176).

Ellis sharpened understanding of the causal role of sexual desire by specifying a variety of new activities that could be considered sexual and by defining more precisely their origin in human physiology and their evolution in human history. He expanded the number of such activities and traced their causal role into more complex activities through hundreds of richly documented case histories including rape, sadism, cannibalism, and sexual mutilation. In arguing for a continuum between the normal and the pathological, he expanded the realm of uncertainty about understanding the possibilities of sexual inventiveness and sexual pathology.

Modern sexology orchestrated a symphony of sexual sensations, as compared with the solo compositions of Victorian psychiatry, which narrowly limited sex to primarily genital excitation and narrowly explained its deviations by degeneration theory. Freud was the first major composer of that complexity. His hundred-page case histories vastly exceeded in detail and depth of analysis the sexual case histories of Krafft-Ebing and Ellis, which were rarely more than a few paragraphs. His clinical therapies, lasting many years, made possible the understanding of new complex tempos of sexual etiology moving according to at least five interrelated orderings: the chronological sequence of events in the patient's life, the order in which they subsequently became traumatic and pathogenic, the order in which the patient related them to the psychoanalyst, the order in which the patient dealt with them in treatment, and the order in which Freud reconstructed them in his retrospective case histories. Freud's theory of powerful unconscious drives originating in childhood added deeper percussion to the compositions of modernist sexology, while his theory of sexual perversion added new dissonances.

The presentation of the latter theory in a long chapter at the beginning of his major formulation of a developmental psychology transformed thinking about the nature of sexual perversion. Titling that chapter "The Sexual Aberrations" (*Die sexuellen Abirrungen*) avoided the moralistic term "*Perversionen*," which he did use elsewhere to convey the negative moral judgment so common in his time. "Aberration" suggested oddity or statistical anomaly, not pathology or degeneracy. He defined perversions as "sexual activities which either (a) extend, in an anatomical sense, beyond the regions of the body that are designed for sexual union, or (b) linger over the intermediate relations to the sexual object which should normally be traversed rapidly on the path towards the final sexual aim."[12] But this definition of practices such as anal erotism (anatomical extension) and hair fetishism (temporal lingering) raised new questions about what extensions are abnormal and how long lingering is. Moreover, he noted, the frequency with which "normal people" sometimes engage in such activities shows "how inappropriate it is to use the word perversion as a term of reproach" (160).

Freud expanded the realm of sexuality and sharpened analysis of its elements by distinguishing their sources, objects, and aims, which had been conflated by Victorian theorizers. He expanded sexual sources beyond the genitals to include the erotogenic zones (oral, anal, phallic), and he distinguished the sexual aim (looking, touching, intercourse) from the sexual object (a man or a woman). These distinctions necessitated more precise definitions of sexuality and more flexible judgments about "normalcy" because, as with male homosexuals for example, some may be instinctually aroused from within by a normal erotogenic source (the penis) and may desire the normal sexual act of penetrating a bodily orifice, but they may desire to do it with an abnormal sexual object (someone of the same sex) or by using an abnormal orifice (the anus).

While Freud retained the popular term *invert*, he exposed its vagueness. Previous thinkers saw inverts as inverted throughout their being—sexually as well as in all character traits, intellectual abilities, and social roles. Thus, for the Victorian sex theorist, male inverts will not only desire male lovers but will also have high voices, act effeminately, and love cats; while female inverts will wear pants, smoke cigars, dislike needlework, and be good at the uniquely masculine skill of whistling. For the Victorians, Michel Foucault argued, homosexuality "was everywhere present in him: at the root of all his actions because it was their insidious and indefinitely active principle; written immodestly on his face and body because it was a secret that always gave itself away."[13] George Chauncey's analysis of the shift "from sexual inversion to homosexuality" drew on Foucault and identified Freud's role in rejecting the diagnostic value of inversion and offering a more precise definition of homosexuality. By "sexual inversion," nineteenth-century theorists "referred to a broad range of cross-gender behavior," and so "in the Victorian system . . . a complete inversion (or reversal) of a woman's sexual character was required for her to act as a lesbian." Chauncey concluded that by 1900 "a fundamental shift in conceptualization was under way, as medicine began to specify and narrow the definition of the sexual and to distinguish and classify sexual deviations in ever more discrete categories." The more precise differentiation of homosexual desire from the mass of behaviors generally lumped together as inversion "reflects a major reconceptualization of the nature of human sexuality."[14] Freud's more precise definition of sexual perversion and his distinction between sexual sources, objects, and aims are keys to that intellectual shift.

While Freud did not discuss the role of sexual desire in murder, he did consider "the most common and the most significant of all the perversions—the desire to inflict pain upon the sexual object, and its reverse [masochism]" (157). Without conventional judgment, he argued that "sadism would correspond to an aggressive component of the sexual instinct which has become independent and exaggerated and, by displacement, has usurped the leading position" (158). He further speculated that sadism might be the result of an unraveling of normal sexuality into the components that are normally assembled during psychosexual development; these may include hereditary instinctual aggression, an innate "impulse for cruelty," oral aggression that accompanies teething, anal aggression normally associated with defecation and possibly exaggerated by traumatic toilet training, transformations of love into hate by means of unconscious reaction formation, and angry reactions to child sexual trauma.

Freud's provocative theory of the grounding characterological role of perversions came out of a simple clinical question that no one had posed so directly and that once asked would not go away: what was the source of all the adult perversions that he discovered in his patients' dreams, fantasies, and neuroses? His answer was the most shocking thing he ever wrote: "This postulated constitution, containing the germs of all the perversions, will only be demonstrable in *children*, even though in them it is only with modest degrees of intensity that any of the instincts can emerge" (172). That final qualifier generated little protective cover from the avalanche of criticism that this announcement triggered. Although he was not arguing that all children are perverts, to many critics he seemed to be. He was intent rather on showing how sexual perversions among adults, including sadism, are aberrant extenuations of impulses that develop normally in all children. But by arguing that children normally have an impulse to inflict pain and be hurt that accompanies their psychosexual development, he at once seemed to humanize loathsome criminals and remove the halo of sexual innocence from childhood. That double outrage to popular thinking was at the heart of what became known as "the sexual revolution." By tracing the roots of the most hideous adult sexual pathologies and violent crimes to corrupted prolongations of normal child psychosexual development, Freud created the basic orientation toward such adult acts as they became elaborated in twentieth-century psychiatry, popular culture, and literature, and, with notable consistency, in novels about sexually motivated murder.

The Discovery of Hormones

The discovery of sex hormones offers another example of the specificity-uncertainty dialectic.[15] From the time of Hippocrates in the fifth century B.C. to 1792, when Luigi Galvani discovered bioelectricity, medical researchers believed that four cardinal bodily humors (blood, yellow bile, black bile, phlegm) determined the four main character traits (sanguine, choleric, melancholic, phlegmatic). Others attempted to relate these humors to the four seasons, four parts of the day, four cardinal geographic points, and specific diseases. In the mid-Victorian period, humoralism was revived in various homeopathic medicines until it gave way under pressure from more specific explanations in cell theory and hormonal theory. Still, Balzac drew on the four humors to classify and explain characters. In *Old Goriot* he wrote, "Though melancholic men may need the stimulation of flirtatious rebuff, the nervous or sanguine may be put to rout if resistance lasts too long. In other words, the paean of victory is as essential to the choleric temperament as the mournful, pleading, elegiac strain is to the lymphatic" (160).

The murderer Vautrin was a sanguine-choleric type.[16] For several millennia, experts also believed that the seat of femaleness was the uterus, but around the middle of the nineteenth century several researchers—including Rudolf Virchow, who narrowed the diagnosis of numerous diseases to specific cells—announced that the seat of femaleness was rather the ovaries, although Virchow believed that the ovaries acted through the nervous system, not internal secretions.[17] It was not until the years 1896 and 1900 that two Viennese gynecologists, Emil Knauer and Josef Halvan, identified chemical secretions from the ovaries and suggested that they, and not nervous impulses, determined female characteristics.

The idea that testes determined masculinity was dismissed as medical folklore until 1889, when the French physiologist Charles-Edouard Brown-Séquard reported increased vigor from injecting himself with extracts of guinea pigs' and dogs' testicles. He erroneously assumed that the determinative masculine secretions circulated in the semen, but his work inspired research on "internal secretions," and new treatments with "organotherapy" fueled further experimentation on extracts from animal organs.

While Victorian researchers traced the source of sexual characteristics to the gonadal organs, researchers in the early twentieth century traced them more precisely to chemical substances, the sex hormones. In 1905 the British physiologist Ernest Starling coined the word *hormone* and speculated about how these "chemical messengers [are] carried from the organ where they are produced to the organ which they affect, by means of the blood stream."[18] The new science of sex endocrinology identified specific male and female sex hormones and shifted explanation of the main mechanism of causal action in the body from nervous regulation to chemical messengers flowing through the blood. In the 1910s geneticists and sex endocrinologists distinguished their disciplines with their respective theories about genes causing sexual difference at birth and hormones causing sexual differentiation during development. Throughout the 1920s biochemists studied the chemical composition of sex hormones, which they identified more precisely as steroids.

The history of hormones is not merely a story of the increasing specificity of causal understanding but also of increasing complexity and uncertainty, as researchers identified more than one single sex hormone for males and females and attempted to understand their interaction with other hormones, proteins, neurotransmitters, and the brain. From 1905 to around 1920, scientists viewed hormones as sexually dichotomous in origin and function, with one hormone per sex, in accord with the idea that the two sexes are biological, emotional, and intellectual opposites. Thus men are polygamous, strong, and rational and able to expend great quantities of energy in short bursts for vital activities, while women are monogamous, weak, and intuitive and capable of sustained low energy yield which destines them to build nests and nurture others. The classic Victorian survey of such fanciful polarities is John Ruskin's essay "Of Queens' Gardens," which ran fifty pages. Such thinking persisted into the early twentieth century as the discovery of specifically male and female sex hormones seemed to provide scientific affirmation for a dichotomous sexual polarity.

That polarity was elaborated into an antagonism with the early notion that male and female sex hormones not only stimulate male and female characteristics but depress opposite-sex characteristics. In 1926 the Viennese gynecologist Eugen Steinach argued that "sex hormones simultaneously stimulated homologous sexual characteristics and depressed heterologous sexual characteristics."[19] Thus a lowering of the male hormone in a man causes not only a decrease in male potency but an increase in female bodily features and character traits; that is, his libido should get weaker and his voice higher.

The first challenge to hormonal sexual polarity and antagonism came in 1921, when the Viennese gynecologist Otfried Fellner published an article describing experiments showing that extracts from rabbit testes caused uterine growth similar to the effect of ovarian extracts, suggesting that the testes also contained female sex hormones.[20] In 1930, Dutch researchers isolated one female sex hormone originating in the follicular fluid of the ovaries, which they called estrogen. In 1934 they isolated a second female sex hormone from another part of the ovaries, which the Second Conference on the Standardization of Sex Hormones in 1935 agreed to call progesterone. In 1934 the German gynecologist Bernhard Zondek reported finding in horse testes the richest source of female sex hormone ever located, and other researchers found male sex hormones in female organisms.

After 1935, hormones were no longer considered sex-specific but rather heterosexual chemicals that caused manifold synergistic effects in men and women. The first identification of heterosexual hormones was the discovery in 1937 that the adrenal glands of both sexes produce male and female sex hormones. This proliferation of the bodily sources of sexually determinative substances refuted the idea that maleness and femaleness are polar opposites or are governed biochemically solely by the gonads. Also in the 1930s researchers discovered an endocrine feedback system between the sex hormones of the gonads and the gonadotropic hormones secreted by the pituitary gland, with the two sorts of hormones working together to generate the prostate gland and seminal vesicles in males and the uterus and the opening of the vagina in females. By the end of the 1930s biologists believed that the characteristics of maleness and femaleness were not mutually exclusive and certainly not antagonistic but rather intermixed and generated by the same hormones produced in several different parts of male and female bodies in addition to the gonads, but at different times and rates and in different amounts.

Thus, from 1905 to around 1940, developments in hormonal research transformed thinking about the biological origin of sexual characteristics from being in the entire body to specific organs to sex hormones and finally to causally acting chemicals produced by both sexes in male and female gonads as well as other glands. These discoveries shattered older notions of sexual dualism determined by single organs or even single hormones and expanded the fluidity and complexity of sexual differences; and since sex hormones determined sexual desire, ideas about male and female modes of that desire became increasingly complex and uncertain.

These developments in hormone theory were the scientific focus of many changing ideas about sex and gender, which, as Thomas Laqueur has shown, were also integral to changing epistemological, social, and political ideas that governed the sex-gender distinction.[21] Early nineteenth-century advances in embryology documented the common origins of both sexes, but such a view was not as broadly influential because it was not as "culturally relevant" as the later dual-sex theories, such as that of the Scottish biologist Patrick Geddes, who argued that sexual differences were deeply grounded in biology, with women "more passive, conservative, sluggish and stable," and men "more active, energetic, eager, passionate, and variable."[22] As sexological research refined understanding of the reproductive system of both sexes, and as social and political developments created the context for women to challenge conventional male rights, privileges, and laws, the rigid sex dichotomy of Victorian theoreticians gave way to increasingly specific explanations of the causal role of ovaries, testicles, and hormones in the determination of sexual differences and sexual desires. These contributions shifted the location of the sex-gender distinction in the direction of greater cultural malleability and theoretical complexity.[23]

HORMONES AND MURDER

To explain a murder, modernist novelists were as reluctant to use hormones as they were to use genes or DNA, because such biochemical substances simplify causal explanations and short-circuit the intriguing dramatizations of motivation crucial for effective literary development of character. Nevertheless, I did find a few novels that fleshed out causal understanding with some reference to hormonal action.

For twenty years Dreiser prepared to write *An American Tragedy* by collecting newspaper reports of actual murders similar to the one that Clyde attempts to commit. During those years Dreiser also researched three new disciplines concerned with biochemical causal agents—Freud's psychoanalytic study of "chemisms," Jacques Loeb's physiochemistry of tropisms, and Max Schlapp's neuropathology of hormones.

In the novel, Dreiser explained Clyde's motivation and his sister's self-destructive sexual desires as a result, in part, of hormones acting together with tropisms, a composite causal agency he referred to as a *chemism*. Dreiser took the term from the first English translation of Freud's *Three Essays on Sexual Theory* by A. A. Brill, who was Dreiser's personal friend. In the first edition of 1905 Freud used the German word *Chemismus*, which Brill translated into English as *chemism*, to identify the biological substance that is produced in the sex glands, which are activated by arousing the erotogenic zones and stimulate sexual activity. In the 1920 edition Freud cited recent experiments by Eugen Steinach on hormonal secretions of the interstitial tissue of the gonads and the thyroid that activate sexual desire.[24] Dreiser used the term to explain how Clyde's sister Esta was driven to ruin by a "chemism of dreams" and by "those rearranging chemisms upon which all the morality or immorality of the world is based" (20). He also explained Clyde's desire for Roberta as "a chemic or temperamental pull," a passion "inflamed by the chemistry of sex" (254, 239).[25]

Tropism refers to the directional growth of plants in response to a stimulus such as gravity, light, or chemicals. The phenomenon was attributed only to plants until the French biologist Jacques Loeb used it to explain human behavior in a series of publications, which Dreiser began to read avidly around 1900.[26] In the novel, Dreiser explained Roberta's alluring effect on Clyde by the powerful action of her "actinic rays," meaning the tropistic force of light to produce biochemical change (315). Dreiser also adopted Loeb's mechanistic model of living organisms as subject to physiochemical laws of behavior and driven toward goals by external or internal forces they are unable to resist.

Dreiser's interest in chemisms and tropisms centered in his fascination with hormones, which he learned about from his friend Edward Smith. In 1919 Smith met a professor of neuropathology at New York University, Max Schlapp, who was studying the hormonal origins of mental illness, abnormal behavior, and crime. They collaborated on *The New Criminology: A Consideration of the Chemical Causation of Abnormal Behavior* (1928), which Dreiser learned about while writing his novel.[27] Schlapp and Smith argued confidently, without sufficient evidence, that a "criminal imperative" can be "completely accounted for under physico-chemical laws."[28] The sex glands contain cells that produce sperm and ova as well as interstitial cells that produce sex hormones. "The interstitial type of man is over-aggressive, foolhardy, ruthless, violent, combative" and a candidate for criminality (99). Their speculative reconstruction of a typical murderer driven by abnormal hormones prefigures the plot of Clyde's murder attempt in a nutshell: "He conceives a hatred for some person who stands in his way.... The concept of killing this enemy comes into his mind. . . . The normal man rejects the idea almost as quickly as it is formed. . . . But the man capable of murder is disturbed in his glands, cells and nerve centers.... No doubt he struggles back and forth, drawn to his victim and away from the deed of blood by the contentions of his emotions and of his inhibitory brain parts.... [But] the time comes when he can no longer resist. The idea has taken possession of him. He makes his plans, always under strong emotional excitement, lies in wait, strikes the blow and makes an attempt to direct suspicion from himself" (202–3). Schlapp and Smith concluded with the unfounded, but scientific-sounding, claim that "individuals in whom the excess of interstitial and suprarenal hormone is dominant are likely to be of the violent criminal type" (204).

In *Berlin Alexanderplatz: The Story of Franz Biberkopf*, Alfred Döblin surveyed the physiological causes of sexual desire, including hormonal activity, to help explain a brutal murder: "Sexual potency depends upon the combined action of (1) the internal secretory system, (2) the nervous system, and (3) the sexual apparatus. The glands participating in this potency are the pituitary gland, the thyroid gland, the suprarenal gland, the prostate gland, the seminal vesicle, and the epididymis. In this system the spermatic gland preponderates" (32).[29] Döblin was no physiological reductionist, because this "explanation" is clearly ironic, but it nevertheless shows that he drew on current science and invoked it to help make more intelligible acts of sexual brutality such as Reinhold's beating to death of Franz's lover in a fit of sexual frustration and rage (370).

Aldous Huxley's *Brave New World* (1932) shows further evidence of popular belief in the potency of hormones to control reproduction and regulate life. Huxley also envisioned its use in simulating murder to discharge the aggression that the narcotic soma cannot dispel. In this world, hatcheries use hormones to create different biological types, female embryos are given "male sex-hormone" to be "decanted as freemartins," adult female reproductive urges are quelled with mammary gland extract and injections of placentin, and adults refresh themselves with "sex-hormone chewing gum." Aggressive impulses are activated and discharged by hormonal treatment, as, the Controller explains, once a month "we flood the whole system with adrenalin. It's the complete physiological equivalent of fear and rage. All the tonic effects of murdering Desdemona and being murdered by Othello, without any of the inconveniences."[30]

Such tongue-in-cheek theorizing was refined by more rigorous research, which, since the early 1970s, attempted to reconstruct more precisely and even to measure the causal role of hormones, especially testosterone, in the commission of violent acts. These studies found no significant correlation between testosterone levels and individuals who commit violent acts while incarcerated or score high on self-evaluation hostility tests, but they did find significant the slightly higher testosterone levels of individuals with records of rape and murder. For example, one study in 1972 of adolescent prisoners with and without violent records concluded cautiously that "within a population that is predisposed by virtue of social factors to develop antisocial behaviors, levels of testosterone may be an important additional factor in placing individuals at risk to commit more aggressive crimes in adolescence."[31] Subsequent studies suggested that there are slightly significant higher testosterone levels in individuals inclined to commit rape and murder, although even in them the levels are within normal range.[32] Quantifying the causal role of hormone-specific violent behaviors has proved difficult. On the basis of a survey of literature in the late 1980s, L. Ellis concluded that at least twelve human and animal behaviors are influenced by male hormones: assertive erotic sexual behavior, status-related aggressive behavior, spatial reasoning, territoriality, pain tolerance, retarded acquisition of aversive conditioning, diminished fearful emotional responses to threats, task control-oriented tenacity, transient bonding tendencies, peripheralization, sensation seeking, and predatory behavior.[33]

The increasing analytical detail and methodological rigor of research have sharpened the specificity of causal understanding of the role of hormones, but the specific causal function of testosterone remains imprecisely measured and uncertain. Researchers interested in its relative role in violent behavior debated presuppositions and methods, including such questions as: When and how often should its levels be measured? Which specific elements of it are causally active in aggression? Does it play more of a role in the development of the central nervous system or in current violent acts? Does it work gradually or at a threshold level as an on/off switch? What is the role of different testosterone receptor sensitivities in different subjects? What sorts of violent behaviors are to be studied? And are self-report inventories of hostility reliable, and do they measure inherited trait hostility or acquired state hostility? One survey of research on the correlation between testosterone levels and acts of violence up to the mid-1980s concluded that most research has shown "no relation between circulating testosterone and the behavioral measures, although a few intriguing studies have revealed higher testosterone levels in groups of especially violent persons, such as incarcerated rapist-murderers."[34] The increasing specificity of questionnaire surveys of hostility and of methods for collecting and measuring testosterone levels have raised more questions than they have answered, and the answers they have provided were based on only marginally significant statistical evidence.

Researchers found more significant correlations between criminal activity and endocrine disorders in women suffering from postpartum psychosis and premenstrual tension.[35] The Dutch novelist Renate Dorrestein commented on the recent history of endocrinological explanations of behavior in her novel *A Heart of Stone* (1998), about a woman who kills three of her children as a result of the "hormonal pandemonium" of a postpartum psychosis (177). This explanation is offered by another of the woman's children who survived and grew up to study medicine. Her narration registers indignation at the doctors who erroneously diagnosed her mother with hysteria or hypochondria and failed to make the correct hormonal diagnosis. In a comment on the genesis of the novel, Dorrestein explained that she first learned about the connection between hormonal disorders and murder in the early 1970s, when she was working as a journalist in Holland and "postpartum depression was suddenly 'discovered.'"[36]

A rare hormonal disorder, Addison's disease (which John F. Kennedy had), is part of the causal history of a female serial killer in Lawrence Sanders's novel *The Third Deadly Sin* (1981).[37] The story begins with a description of thirty-six-year-old Zoe Kohler suffering from premenstrual syndrome with bloating, dizziness, back pain, and terrible cramps. She works for the security section of a New York hotel where her male colleagues treat her as if she did not exist, just as her husband had done until their divorce. In their showdown argument he had shouted: "You're not definite! You're just not *there!*" Now the city itself is a collective masculine enemy that reduces her to a cipher by ignoring her existence. Years earlier she had been traumatized when invited guests also treated her as a nonentity when they failed to show up at her thirteenth birthday party, the same day she had her first painful menstrual cramps.

Her sexual desire has degenerated into a hatred of men. She loathes her husband for neglecting her most of the time and for lusting after her when he felt like it with "that reddish, purplish, knobbed thing poking out, trembling in the air" (17). She resents men collectively because they do not experience the crucifying monthly flow and the dark, gummy stains and because they all potentially threaten her with their dumb phallic "clubs." In her mind the main reason for murdering is men's revolting lust, which she avenges by dressing like a prostitute, luring them to a hotel room, arousing them sexually, slitting their throat, and, when they are dying and helpless, repeatedly stabbing their genitals. She feels no sexual pleasure in her adventures but does feel vindicated and "charged with the hot stuff of animal existence" (233). She kills to counter her disgust over her sexuality and monthly bleedings by flaunting her sexuality to set up monthly bloodlettings.

The timing of her half-dozen murders at twenty-seven-day intervals is a clue to the hormonal disorder, which causes her homicidal rage as well as many other symptoms, including loss of pubic hair, nausea,

PMS, skin discoloration at the knuckles and elbows, and inability to tolerate stress. As a result of a struggle with one victim she is cut and leaves some blood at the murder scene. It is analyzed by a national diagnostic computer center which hypothesizes that the murderer might have Addison's disease.

A hematologist explains to the lead detective why the blood sample suggests Addison's and what that diagnosis means. The killer's blood contained high levels of adrenocorticotropic hormone (ACTH) and melanocyte-stimulating hormone (MSH). The pituitary gland, which produces ACTH and MSH, also stimulates the adrenal cortex to produce cortisol, which in turn helps keep ACTH and MSH at normal levels. When the adrenal cortex is damaged, those hormones build up in the blood. Because MSH controls melanin, or the dark pigmentation in the skin, when its levels rise, melanin accumulates, causing the discoloration that indicates Addison's. The hematologist speculates that the killer is being treated for the disease, but that the treatment is not working perhaps because of the stress of the killings (353). Thus her hormonal disorder may be causing the murders, which are in turn exacerbating her hormonal disorder.

Such a causal explanation for a female serial killer is unthinkable in a Victorian novel, not only because Victorian hematological, endocrinological, and gynecological knowledge as well as laboratory techniques had not advanced to a point where such a diagnosis and explanation would have been possible, but also because the explanation goes far beyond what Victorians could accept about the force and brutal violence that can be unleashed by female sexual desire. Zola's Thérèse Raquin (1867) was motivated by sexual desire to kill, but she did not enjoy killing for its own sake, her lover carried out the murder, neither of them mutilated the victim, hormones played no causal role, and she was eventually tormented by guilt. Zola explains Thérèse as dominated vaguely, if intensely, by "nerves and blood," with sexual desire corrupted from "a simple organic disorder, a revolt of the nervous system," which he elaborates in no greater detail. Modern novelists were willing to dig deeper into the specifics of sexual desire as a motive for murder and reconstruct them in their works. Since the Romantic period, femmes fatales such as Eve, Circe, Medusa, Judith, and Salomé had been capable of great cruelty and indeed lured men to their death, but those females did not kill strangers, let alone repeatedly stab their genitals, and their behavior was not explained by underlying hormonal disorders that caused inelegant symptoms such as bloating, menstrual cramps, loss of pubic hair, and gummy vaginal bleeding.

Nothing remotely like that appears in the 670-page textbook from 1848 on female sexual disorders by the professor of midwifery at Jefferson Medical College in Philadelphia, Charles D. Meigs. In a brief discussion of woman's "erotic state," Meigs emphasized "the more delicate, gracile and impressionable nature of her whole economy."[38] He explained female psychosexual pathology (without, of course, using such a term) entirely as a result of hysteria, which is caused not just by the uterus, as was formerly believed, but by the entire female sexual organs and radiated to the mind by an "aura." Female "aphrodisiac force," he theorized, can be "exaggerated into erotomania," which "drives from the conscience of the woman the last vestige of female purity; and from her cheek the faculty to blush." The consequences of this condition fill one evasive sentence: "The feats of Messalina are nothing to the manifestations of this power, sometimes met with in medical practice" (466–67). Ten years later a British surgeon developed the technique of surgical clitoridectomy to treat epilepsy and supposed disorders of female sexual desire such as masturbation and nymphomania. Victorian scientific ignorance of the causes and effects of female sexual desire was matched by scientific intolerance for its "abnormal" intensity. By the 1920s surgical removal of the clitoris for any reason ceased to be performed anywhere in the Western world, and masturbation and nymphomania ceased to be classified as illnesses.

SEXUALLY MOTIVATED MURDERS

Victorian murderers in fact and fiction were capable of fulminating with desire, although descriptions of such intensity were generalized with metaphorical descriptions of them as devils, monsters, or animals. Victorian psychiatrists rendered this desire as a generalized instinct that dominated the entire personality in a condition that Esquirol first identified and coined as *monomania* around 1810 and that came into widespread use by the 1820s. Compared with moderns, Victorian writers depicted fewer details about sexual sources, aims, and objects. In a history of murder in American gothic imagination, Karen Halttunen argued that the acts described in these works are not "sex-murders," such as began to appear in newspaper articles and fictional stories after

Jack the Ripper, but rather sexual tales that include murder. Such tales reveal "no depth-psychological understanding of a 'lust to kill.'" Halttunen surveyed the typical themes: rapists murder their victims, rejected lovers kill scornful sweethearts, seducers kill pregnant cast-offs, clients kill prostitutes, jealous husbands murder unfaithful wives, and adulterous husbands kill faithful wives to be free to love other women.[39] While the motivation for such murders is ultimately sexual, writers describe it indirectly through sublimation and displacement.

In *Notre-Dame of Paris*, Hugo highlighted Frollo's monomaniacal desire for Esmeralda but disguised all references to its sexual sources with metaphor and innuendo. Frollo feels "a burning vitality" when he sees Esmeralda dance; his desire is "a seething, raging lava" (83, 275). From the cathedral tower he directs his fixed look at her with rigid eyebrows and a petrified smile (258). Hugo gave physiological details, but they are displaced from their sexual sources, as Frollo's arteries throb, and the blood pounds in his temples (298). The only reference to self-stimulation is when Frollo stabs himself while watching Esmeralda being tortured. Frollo's forbidden sexual desire is a product of *fatality*, a word that Hugo had seen written in Greek on a wall in Notre-Dame and that became the ultimate explanation for Esmeralda's murder. Hugo concluded his introduction confidently: "This book was written about that word." Fatality suggests a transcendent immaterial cause, not direct sexual arousal.

Victorians frequently uncoupled the link between sex and murder by having someone other than the sexually aroused person do the killing. Frollo has his executioners kill Esmeralda, while Thérèse has her lover Laurent strangle her husband Camille. In a study of homicide in American fiction, David Brion Davis documented the Victorian conviction that woman's nature was essentially sexual, that evil was essentially sexual corruption, and that most homicides were sexually motivated by women but carried out by men.[40] Such indirection occurs in Hawthorne's *The Marble Faun* (1860), where Miriam has Donatello kill her tormentor, Brother Antonio. Her desire for Donatello causes the murder indirectly as she flashes her eyes tellingly at the crucial moment, indicating that he is to throw Antonio over a cliff. Immediately afterward, "her eyes blazed with the fierce energy that had suddenly inspired him" (172). Here sexual desire is sublimated into the couple's love for art prior to the murder, then communicated indirectly by a glance just before the murder, and finally given only metaphorical expression ex post facto when "she pressed him close, close to her bosom, with a clinging embrace that brought their two hearts together, till the horror and agony of each was combined into one emotion, and that, a kind of rapture" (173–74).

Modern novelists described more precisely a greater number of interacting sexual sources, aims, and objects of sexual desire involving fetishism, rape, sadism, masochism, voyeurism, pedophilia, necrophilia, and cannibalism. They also tracked more precisely their manifestation in killings but at the same time expressed less certainty about how the causal connections between them works. Although modern sex murderers are sexually obsessed, modern novelists avoided totalizing explanations of them with diagnostic categories such as monomania or degeneration or other tags for their entire being such as "monster" or "maniac." They believed rather that perverse sexual desires can erupt from isolated corners of the mind without governing it entirely and that even impotence can play a potent causal role in murder. Finally, modernist explanations of sex murders were more uncertain and even, as in *Gravity's Rainbow*, probabilistic.

In *La bête humaine* Zola dramatized sexually motivated murder for the late Victorian period far more explicitly than did his midcentury predecessors, but even he avoided any specific reference to genital stimulation in his sex murderer or his victim. Jacques's homicidal rage is triggered by seeing naked breasts, never genitals, as, for example, while making love to Flore he has a compulsion to stab her "between her rose-tipped white breasts" (64). At first, he feels a kinship with Severine when he learns that she herself has murdered, but he becomes acutely aroused and murderous as she tells him about that murder and becomes even more destabilized when she suggests that they stab her husband Roubaud in the neck and decapitate him on the railroad tracks, and do so while naked to avoid getting incriminating blood on their clothes. Later, when she comes toward Jacques "quite naked, neck and breasts bare," his resistance collapses and he stabs her in the throat. For all the intensity of his pathology, it is inconceivable that he would have stabbed any woman in the vagina. Zola strained to evoke the intensity and chronicity of Jacques's sexually triggered urges but avoided any details about their specific sexual sources or aims beyond a deranged desire to kill women when he sees a naked breast or becomes sexually aroused.

The erotogenic role of trains in *La bête humaine* contrasts with the modern erotogenic role of automobiles in J. G. Ballard's novel *Crash*

(1973). Zola's "human beast" refers to Jacques's killer instinct as well as the train he engineers. The train's incessant running throughout the novel symbolizes irresistible sexual desire that is linked to irrepressible homicidal compulsion: Severine and her husband Roubaud kill her former childhood molester while riding on a train, she plots with Jacques to decapitate Roubaud under a train's wheels, Flore avenges her jealousy against Jacques and Severine by derailing their train, Jacques's murderous impulse intensifies when he hears a train whistle while making love to Severine, and Jacques and his fireman Pecqueux are hacked to death by the wheels of their train after being sucked under it during a fight over a woman. But Zola's novel about a murderer aroused by speeding trains is less specific as to sexual sources, aims, and objects than is Ballard's novel about the erotic charge a murderer gets from fatal car crashes.

Crash is narrated by a character named James Ballard, who becomes obsessed with the perverse sexuality of deadly crashes under the inspiration of Robert Vaughan, a married man who eventually becomes Ballard's homosexual lover. Vaughan is a former computer specialist who is turned on by the ecstasies of head-on collisions that reveal to him the "eroticism of wounds: the perverse logic of blood-soaked instrument panels, seat-belts smeared with excrement, sun-visors lined with brain tissue."[41] He re-enacts the deaths of Albert Camus, James Dean, Jayne Mansfield, and John F. Kennedy with stunt drivers in costume, and he fantasizes about the entire world dying in a simultaneous automobile disaster with "millions of vehicles hurled together in a terminal congress of spurting loins and engine coolant" (16). His own crashes left his penis mangled by gear shifts and his face scarred by shattering instrument dials that inscribed in his flesh an elaborate "language of pain and sensation, eroticism and desire" (90).

Vaughan's lover Gabrielle has been turned into "a creature of free and perverse sexuality" by the crushed body of a sports car. Ballard apprentices as Vaughan's lover by sharing Gabrielle and having sex with her deformed body. As Ballard narrates, "My orgasms took place within the scars below her breast . . . in the wounds on her neck and shoulder, in these sexual apertures formed by fragmenting windshield louvers and dashboard dials in a high-speed impact" (179). As Vaughan taught him, Ballard learns to visualize "extraordinary sexual acts celebrating the possibilities of unimagined technologies" (179). Ballard explores myriad causal connections between sexual desire and crashes that create new sexual orifices out of wounds and mix sexual and automobile fluids. As he theorizes, "these unions of torn genitalia and sections of car body and instrument panel formed units in a new currency of pain and desire" (134).

Vaughan's desire hatches a final murder plot to kill Elizabeth Taylor in a head-on collision with himself at the wheel. He simulates in slow-motion film the anticipated crash, envisioning wounds to them both, especially their genitalia with "her uterus pierced by the heraldic beak of the manufacturer's medallion, his semen emptying across the lumines-cent dials" (8). Ballard assists in the preparation for this burlesque sex murder, anticipating that "the cars in which she moved would become devices for exploiting every pornographic and erotic possibility, every conceivable sex-death and mutilation" (136). Ballard as the author of the novel is relentless in imagining new combinations of eroticized technology, physical mutilation, sexual stimulation, and moral transgression, venturing ever deeper into psychosexual territory that was off-limits to serious Victorian novelists.

The historical record abounds with evidence that modernists explored the causal function of sexual sources, aims, and objects with greater specificity than did Victorians. Modernists also affirmed the breakdown of the determinist causality that motivated Victorian murderers. That part of my argument is documented in novels in which sexual inadequacy or impotence plays a causal role and those in which authors admit the uncertainty of knowing precisely how or why these deficiencies lead to murder.

Sexual Impotence and Murder

Victorians were reluctant to talk about impotence, but in the 1890s a spate of publications on it began to appear. Their explanations of it were rooted in the all-purpose causality of degeneration. Kraft-Ebbing explained impotence as a result of "excesses practiced in youth," which were "usually dependent upon spinal weakness."[42] He did not relate impotence to murder, even though he discussed it in the section on sadism just prior to his discussion of lust-murder. Although Victorians envisioned impotence causing many problems, such as declining birth rate, marital failure, and cultural exhaustion, sex murder was not one of them. Such a motivating circumstance would have seemed acausal to

Victorians, because they could not have conceived of the quintessentially positive action of a sex murder being caused by a lack of active capability, by sexual insecurity or impotence. Among all the explanations offered for Jack the Ripper, none was that he was impotent. Victorian sex murderers were thought to be driven by uncontrolled animalism and savagery, by sexual excess. The modernization of sex initiated by Ellis, as Robinson argued, shifted explanations of "the sexual problem" from sexual excess to sexual failure, and modern novels depicted a number of murderers who were driven by that latter problem. In these, as compared with Victorian murder novels, the causal role of potent sexual desire became less clearly deterministic and knowledge of it became more uncertain.

The positive link between impotence and aggression was first explored in Freud's influential essay of 1912, "The Most Prevalent Form of Degradation in Erotic Life." He argued that some men are impotent with gentle and loving middle-class women who remind them of their mothers and therefore conjure up forbidden incest fantasies and paralyze their sexuality. These men attempt to overcome such fantasies and achieve potency by degrading their sexual objects and choosing women from the lower classes, who were thought to be "ethically inferior," and by seeking to have perverse and sometimes aggressive sex with them. Freud added that in modern civilization most men are not fully potent precisely because they are unable to link the aggressive and tender components of erotic life.

In many men this deficiency leads from sexual failure to sexual aggression. In a few it leads to murder. In Francis Iles's *Malice Aforethought: The Story of a Commonplace Murder* (1931), the commonplace Dr. Bickleigh is rejected by his wife and becomes sexually insecure. Fear of impotence from sexual inactivity lies behind his plot to murder his wife in hope of recharging his libido with someone else. He even wonders, "Was this the first time that murder was directly traceable to an inferiority complex?" Although he rejects that historical role for himself, he concedes that he had been "a little worm" (134). The psychiatrist consulted in *The Pledge* speculates that the sort of men who sexually molest and murder little girls are usually "impotent and display feelings of inferiority toward women" (86). Both child killers in *Compulsion* are sexually deficient. "From deep in childhood, Judd had the feeling that the entire female mechanism was nauseating" (97). Artie had been impotent with a prostitute while his fraternity brothers looked on and laughed. A psychiatrist speculates that Artie chose a taped chisel for a murder weapon because it was a big, hard phallic substitute. In Faulkner's *Sanctuary* (1931), the impotent bootlegger Popeye is attempting to force himself on Temple Drake when he is interrupted by his mentally deficient flunky Tommy. Popeye shoots and kills Tommy before raping Temple with a corncob. He then installs her in a whorehouse and gets a local gangster to ravage her as he looks on from the foot of the bed while "whinnying" with impotent lust. When Temple develops a passion for the gangster, Popeye, whose name suggests impotent gazing, kills his rival in a state of what one critic calls "the vulnerable anguish of an oral-ocular and impotent despair."[43] In Graham Greene's *Brighton Rock* (1938), another criminal lowlife, Pinkey Brown, commits two murders to compensate for sexual inadequacy. This virgin hoodlum, nicknamed "the boy," is sickened by the very idea of sex. His disgust goes back to his having to watch as a child from his bed "the frightening weekly exercise of his parents." At age seventeen he sees all women as whores and is angry that people judge manliness by sexual prowess and "not by whether you had the guts to kill a man" (90). Trapped in a world where the measure of a man is his list of sexual conquests, not his list of victims, Pinkey wonders, "Was there no escape—anywhere—for anyone? It was worth murdering a world" (92). In *A Demon in My View* (1976), Ruth Rendell created a serial murderer who had been teased for being cowardly as a child and "had never known how to talk to women" (2). He displaces his compulsion to discharge his deficient sexuality and kill onto a full-size plastic doll, his "patient white lady," that he repeatedly strangles to "death" during staged hunts for her in his dark basement. When that ritual no longer provides relief, he turns to real women.

Some of the most brutal serial killers of modern fiction are driven by sexual inadequacy and terrified about being impotent. In *Red Dragon* Dolarhyde is so afraid of being seen with his harelip and being exposed for his sexual inadequacy (from grandma threatening to cut off his penis with a scissors) that he smashes the mirrors in his murder scenes and reinserts shards of them in the eyes of his female victims only after he has rehabilitated his sexuality during and immediately after the murders. He is incapable of normal sexual relations and so kills women to be potent with their dead bodies. His is able to have "normal" sexual relations with his coworker Reba McClane only because she is blind. In what may be the most perverse attempt at sexual rehabilitation in all of modern literature, he projects a silent home movie of his next intended victim, Mrs. Sherman, stolen from the photo processing lab where he works, while Reba cozies up beside him. As the movie plays, Reba unzips his pants and begins to fondle him. Then, as Harris narrates, "A stab of fear in him; he has never been erect before in the presence of a living woman. [But] he is the Dragon, he doesn't have to be afraid" (261). The Dragon is his potent alter ego, symbolized by William Blake's dragon with a muscular tail that is also tattooed on his chest. While Reba alternately rubs the tatoo and strokes his penis he squeezes the arm of his chair, instead of her neck, and then, as he becomes more aroused, addresses unspoken thoughts to the moving image of dead Mrs. Sherman on screen fused in his mind with blind Reba beside him: "You see me now, yes. That's how you feel to see me, yes" (261). After climaxing he's still potent enough to have coitus with Reba, which he does upstairs in grandma's bed, with grandma's false teeth (which he uses to bite his victims) rattling in a glass on a table beside the bed. Each time he slays as the dragon, he becomes more sexually dependent on its potency, until the dragon threatens to take over his personality entirely.

Four other sexually inadequate serial killers from the modern period are a blank, a minus, a lack, and a devoid. In *The First Deadly Sin*, the last name of the murderer Daniel Blank suggests the sexual impotence which motivate his killings. He begins having sex with Celia Montfort (strong mountain), who cultivates his perversity by inspiring him to kill. After one random ax murder of a man, he attempts to make love to her but is impotent, so she takes his scrotum in her hand while he describes his emotions during the murder. He explains that he was not aroused before or after murdering but felt a godlike power when he chose the victim. He again tries to enter her and is again impotent, so she takes his limp penis in her mouth as he explains how he felt an intense love toward and union with his victim as he buried an ax in his skull. A few more post-murder sex sessions with Celia restore Blank's libido, which, now brimming with lust and the first deadly sin of pride, motivates him to murder Celia herself, the threatening witness of his earlier sexual failures.

While Blank kills out of insecure desire, Vann Siegert in Lew McCreary's *The Minus Man* (1991) kills from utter lack of desire. He is the minus man—minus friends, morals, interests, direction, or libido. Flashbacks reveal a hodgepodge of childhood traumas from his overbearing mother and weak father that drained his character more than produced it. As the novel opens he has already killed thirteen people, not out of strong desire but, as he narrates, "a readiness in them that drew me." He is the killer of opportunity par excellence, without any clear motive. He does experience an urge to kill, but it is ill-defined. The first time he felt it he killed a man who picked him up hitchhiking. Afterward he took the man's cash, which, he explains, "made me feel more like a thief, as though I had a reason that someone could understand" (203). He does not have reasons for killing but kills to have reasons. His ego is a caricature of Sartrean concrete nothingness, entirely hollow at its core. He kills mostly strangers by giving them poisoned liquor from a flask that his mother once used to drink her "pick-me-ups." He is moderately picked up by killing, but not sexually aroused. As the poison takes effect in one victim, he explains, "Slowly the strength flows out of him and into me. . . . I am nothing but energy. Beams could shine from my eyes" (80). But the energy soon dissipates and the emptiness returns. He imagines the frustration of the detectives who will solve his case, because he is "a deep disappointment of a killer" (83). He will tell them about the childhood traumas, but these will not explain the murders. Psychiatrists will search for causal links, but his story will reveal mainly causal gaps.

In Harris's *The Silence of the Lambs*, the serial killer Jame Gumb is described by an acquaintance as someone who is "not anything really just a sort of total lack that he wants to fill." The sketch continues, "You always felt the room was a little emptier when he came in" (172). In Derek Van Arman's novel *Just Killing Time* (1992), Jack Scott is the director of the Violent Criminal Apprehension Team and the author of a study titled *The Devoid, the Psychopathology of Recreational Killers*. He tells detective Frank Rivers, whom he selects to find the recreational killer Zak Dorani, that such a man is incapable of having sex and so finds other means. "There's not a glimmer of emotion left in his soul. . . . He's what we call devoid." Such types are born with "a puny emotional base," then suffer some trauma that drives out that base. Their emotional life goes flat, and their existence becomes a torturous monotony. To stimulate feeling they rely on intellect and learn to mimic emotions. "The tiny spark of emotion left in them only ignites when they experience the most extreme of human behaviors such as killing," which stimulates changes in blood pressure, blood chemistry, respiration, gastrointenstinal activity, erection of hair, and pupil size (239). They become hooked on this brief emotional high.

Zak's childhood trauma was his mother's coercing him to fake emotions. She compelled him to stand for hours at her bedroom mirror, where she coached his efforts to enact what feelings should look like, slapping him for every mistake: "'Not like that, baby,' she would say. 'Now, laugh for Mommy!'" (279). His childhood "had deadened his core to wood" (292). Zak became a "mannequin man, his face moving with conscious efforts only, muscles tugging into an alien mask" (292). He killed victims slowly and cruelly to maximize the duration and intensity of his momentary respites from an emotional void.

These modern sexual anxieties and failures contrast sharply with the powerful, albeit sometimes bottled-up, sexual excesses that motivated Victorian killers. While Hugo and Dickens raised questions about the wisdom of overbearing religious training and internalized sex-negative moral strictures, they were confident that these features of their world adequately explained the murders by Frollo and Headstone, just as Zola was confident that hereditary taints and pent-up sexual desires explained the murders by Jacques and Thérèse. While modern novelists explored in far greater detail the specific sources, aims, objects, and grisly outcomes of sexually motivated murders, they also created new uncertainties about the complex social and psychological dynamics that produced them.

An early story about the complexity of multiple causes and the consequent difficulty of understanding them in a sexually motivated murder is Alfred Döblin's *Two Girlfriends and Their Poison Murders* (1924).[44] This novel was based on an actual arsenic poisoning of one husband and an attempted poisoning of another by their lesbian wives in 1922, and it became the subject of widespread expert legal testimony and journalistic coverage. Döblin told the story through conflicting psychiatric, medical, and legal experts testifying about general causes of women's problems from neglected education, economic dependency, and sexual inhibition as well as specific causes from the defendants' hereditary dispositions, childhood traumas, and husbands' brutality. Another doctor claims that their ovaries are to blame. The famous expert on homosexuality Magnus Hirschfeld ("Dr. H" in the novel) testifies about the women's developmental retardation and deep hatred of men stemming from suppressed lesbian urges and the role of society in making divorce so difficult.

Döblin emphasized the difficulty of finding a main cause, or even a guiding thread, to the multiperspectival narrative he had just related because of the case's complexity. As he explained: "The whole thing is a tapestry made out of scraps of cloth or silk, pieces of metal, and bits of clay. It is stuffed with straw, wire, threads. In some places the pieces aren't joined together. . . . Yet everything is nevertheless complete and carries the stamp of truth. It has been pressed into the forms of our thoughts and feelings. It happened that way; even the actors believe that. But it also didn't happen that way." In an epilogue to this case history Döblin argued, "We know nothing about psychic continuity, causality, the psyche and its concentrations of elements. We must accept the facts of this case, the letters and actions, and programmatically refuse to explain them."[45] Döblin wanted to dispel the illusion that one can know anything conclusive about mental continuity or causality. In contrast to earlier psychiatric case histories and psychological novels that attempted to find a single traumatic causal trigger, Döblin presented a borderline case (*Grenzfall*) with causality emerging out of the network of interactions between self and others, self and society. Döblin dramatized a shift from a linear causal model to one of increasingly complex causal interactions and epistemological uncertainties that raised new questions about the distinction between criminality and legality. This case history appeared as one in a series of book-length studies of recent sensational crime cases under the title *Aussenseiter der Gesellschaft: Die Verbrechen der Gegenwart* (Outsiders of Society: The Crimes of Today) (1924–25). In a study of these works Todd Herzog concluded that Döblin's contribution, "like the other volumes in the *Aussenseiter* series had its origins in a series of crises arising from confrontations with criminality that had long been developing but that seemed to intensify in the early twentieth century: the breakdown of belief in clearly definable distinctions between criminal and noncriminal, the loss of faith in the possibility of narrative coherence, the ultimate irreconcilability of competing causal explanations, the uncertain boundaries between inside and outside."[46]

A modern novel about probabilistic sexual desire and the lack of certainty in understanding its causal role is Pynchon's *Gravity's Rainbow* (1973). In it the killing is by rockets, first by V-2s toward the end of World War II and then by an imaginary rocket launched in 1945 that is screaming across the sky as the novel opens and is plummeting toward a packed movie theater in Los Angeles circa 1972 as the novel ends. The causal role of sexuality centers on the American Lieutenant Tyrone Slothrop, whose job is to study V-2 rocket hits. British intelligence officials discover an exact correlation between maps showing the location of rocket hits and maps showing the distribution of Slothrop's sexual conquests in London, and they therefore assume that his erections somehow determine where the rockets come down. This impossible sexual causality is a conundrum that Pynchon uses to critique scientific arrogance, behaviorist stimulus-response conditioning, and cause-and-effect reasoning.

Slothrop's powers are probably the result of a botched Pavlovian conditioning experiment performed on him as a child. The unconditioned stimulus was stroking his penis with a cotton swab, the unconditioned response was an erection, the conditioned stimulus was x, and the conditioned response was an erection whenever x is present. The purpose of the experiment was to cause an erection by stimulus x instead of the swab. The experimenter should have extinguished the erection reflex when the experiment was over, but investigators speculate that the extinction must have gone "Beyond the Zero" (the title for the first part of the novel) and created a reverse sexual potency that enabled him to condition the world around him. How his erections determine rocket trajectories the experts can only guess.

The novel's title is ironic in that the rocket's trajectory cannot be a true rainbow or a parabola precisely determined by gravity and the laws of motion, because it is thrown off by perturbations due to atmospheric disturbances, fuel loss, and changing gravitational pull. Some rockets explode on launch, while others turn and fall according to their unique "madness." Behind their random killings are a miscellany of persons and institutions with interacting and often conflicting motives: Hitler, Werner von Braun, rocket engineers, explosives manufacturers, intelligence officers, statisticians, behaviorists, and bureaucrats. In this world "decisions are never really *made*—at best they manage to emerge, from a chaos of peeves, whims, hallucinations and all-round assholery" (676).

The rocket explosions violate classical notions of cause and effect in several ways. The victims experience what seems to be a reversal of cause and effect because the rockets travel faster than sound and so kill before their sound is audible. The reflex arc explanation of Slothrop is that loud noises cause his erections, but the theory of the rocket hits has his erections causing the hits and therefore the noises that accompany them. Most important, in interpreting the pattern of rocket hits, which fall in a random distribution, the Pavlovian behaviorist Edward

Pointsman and the statistician Roger Mexico debate the uncertainty of cause-and-effect reasoning in the modern world.

In the realm of zero to one, Pointsman can only accept as real the zero or the one. He imagines the brain as a mass of on/off elements with nothing in between. Mexico, on the other hand, flourishes in that in-between domain of probabilities, which explain events not by cause and effect but by statistical distributions of random events. Pointsman is troubled by this probabilistic realm of the in-between, as revealed in an interior monologue: "How can Mexico play, so at his ease, with these symbols of randomness and fright? [He] threatens the idea of cause and effect itself. What if Mexico's whole generation have turned out like this? Will Postwar be nothing but 'events,' newly created one moment to the next? No links? Is it the end of history?" (56). When Mexico declines to speculate about any specific causal stimulus for Slothrop's erections or their effect on the rockets, Pointsman hopes that some such cause will be discovered that must determine the erections and the rocket hits every single time. When we find such a cause, he insists, "we'll have shown again the stone determinacy of everything, of every soul" (86).

Their final exchange marks a historical shift in thinking about causality in the modern world. Pointsman pleads the ideal of mechanical causality. "Pavlov believed that the ideal, the end we all struggle toward in science, is the true mechanical explanation. . . . His faith ultimately lay in a pure physiological basis of the life of the psyche. No effect without cause, and a clear train of linkages." Mexico projects the end of that ideal in responding that there's a feeling in the air "that cause-and-effect may have been taken as far as it will go. That for science to carry on at all, it must look for a less narrow, a less . . . sterile set of assumptions. The next great breakthrough may come when we have the courage to junk cause-and-effect entirely, and strike off at some other angle" (89).

Pynchon offered a vision of that angle through Leni Pökler, the wife of a German filmmaker, whom she accuses of being a "cause-and-effect man" himself. When her husband mocks her belief that the stars produce changes on earth, she replies "Not produce . . . not cause. It all goes together. Parallel, not series. Metaphor. Signs and symptoms" (159). Pynchon's novel works Leni's way. It does not explain causally the craziness of the postwar world but evokes that world with parallel plots, wild metaphors, and a dazzling parade of signs and symptoms. It blows the hyphens out of cause-and-effect with time reversals, impossible spatial leaps, and identity changes. Like many postmodern novels, it not only resists closure but intentionally confounds it. As it explains on the first page, "this is not a disentangling from, but a progressive knotting into" (3). Pynchon solved no mysteries but elaborated a chaotic world in which at least one power to decide life and death is located in the penis of a character whose name changes several times during the novel and who disappears well before the end. The causal role of sexual desire in *Gravity's Rainbow* is embodied in a character with an impossible libidinous power, who may be responsible for thousands of random deaths resulting from a possible causal action of which he is entirely unaware. The more experts attempt to fathom that specific action, the more probabilistic and uncertain their knowledge becomes.

THE MOST SIGNIFICANT historical causes of changing ideas about the causal role of sexual desire are the growing complexity and interdependence of sexual relations; new technologies of transportation, communication, and sexual engineering; and the increasing division of labor and specialization among sex researchers and professionals.

Sexual relations are inherently interdependent, but they became more varied and complex in the generation after 1900, as women's roles and opportunities for sexual expression began to change dramatically. Women campaigned for the vote, were admitted to institutions of higher education, entered new professions, achieved greater control over their money and property, assailed the sexual double standard, made divorce laws more equitable, learned more about their own sexuality, and showed more initiative in satisfying it. The entry of women into new professions, which was accelerated during World War I, increased the contact points where men and women met. While working as postal clerks, munitions makers, ambulance drivers, railroad guards, and front-line nurses, far from the watchful eye of parents or chaperons, women enjoyed more independence in finding men and exploring their own sexuality. Across these years women were the more historically dynamic sex, and men concentrated on reacting to them.

The crush of populations in cities brought men and women together in more varied circumstances where they could meet at new resorts, skating rinks, dance halls, theaters, city parks, museums, and cabarets. These new circumstances created new sexual dynamics to which some men reacted violently. Prostitution was an outlet for men's frustrations and a focus for sexual violence spread onto the streets. The city was the breeding ground for sex murder, in which men acted out perverted desires in brutal acts against women, driven by fears about their own sexual inadequacies as well as women's new eroticism. Serial killing, primarily an urban phenomenon, began in crowded London with Jack the Ripper, whose victims were streetwalkers. His story was the centerpiece for Walkowitz's study of "sexual danger" in late Victorian London. (On the causal role of urban life see chapter 7.)

New transportation technologies, first the bicycle and then the automobile, changed the locations in which sexual desire could be acted out, as well as its paces and modes. During the 1920s American men with fast automobiles and eager libidos were called "speeds." Later in the century, "jet-setter" connoted ways of traveling, pacing life, and making love. New communication technologies also transformed gender roles and accelerated sexual interdependence. Joshua Meyrowitz documents how in the twentieth century, electronic media penetrated and intermixed formerly exclusive male and female spheres by liberating women from the home's informational confines and leading men back into it to create a "situational androgyny": men could "hunt" for information and shop at home, whereas women could pump and freeze breast milk while talking on the phone at work.[47]

World War I was a testing ground for new technologies of transportation, communication, and warfare as well as for ways of reacting to the "New Woman." Some men volunteered for war to escape sexual problems at home. In the trenches the soldiers' sex life was mixed up with violence of unprecedented intensity, state-sanctioned killing, bitter resentment against civilians, and the vulnerability of their bodies to filth, pain, and mutilation. Prostitution, pornography, and venereal disease were rampant, while privacy and tenderness were scarce. In brothels and later at home, soldiers often experienced premature ejaculation and impotence.[48]

Women's sexuality was also transformed. Nurses in military hospitals witnessed the ravages of war and saw more of men's bodies than the typical Victorian woman had been allowed to see. Women at home were forced to compete for the few remaining men by becoming more sexually aggressive and wearing more makeup and suggestive clothing. Hemlines rose and colored underwear replaced traditional white linen. Some women became aroused by men's uniforms, suggesting the new diagnostic category of *Uniformfetischismus*, which made its way into German psychiatric textbooks. One woman aroused herself with the braids on her husband's uniform, another became excited when viewing her husbands wounds, while another masturbated to the sound of marching troops. These exceptional cases reflect new pressures for female sexuality that came out of the war.

War created new modes of sexual violence. Newspapers reported an increase in abortions and infanticides by women who conceived a child while their husband or lover was at war and then sought to get rid of it before he returned. A few women castrated dead soldiers.[49] Soldiers on leave who murdered their unfaithful wife or her lover were usually acquitted on the grounds of justifiable homicide. War propaganda controlled by the Allies included stories of German soldiers cutting off the breasts of Belgian women. Acts of disemboweling and rape, though wildly exaggerated, were reported by all belligerents. While such atrocities may have erupted in earlier wars, the invention of the halftone process in the late 1880s and wireless telegraphy and cinema in the 1890s, along with a spate of new publications thereafter, increased the speed of reporting, the size of the audience, and the vividness of the imagery.

Another corruption of sexual desire during the war years, intensified by urban life, was the sex murder, especially conspicuous in postwar German art, literature, and cinema. In *Sex Murder in the Ackerstrasse* (1916–17), George Grosz depicted a bloodied, headless woman lying on a bed next to a bloody hatchet, while the killer washes his hands in a sink as he looks back at her, horrified by his act.[50] Even more degraded are the three repugnant killers in Grosz's *After It Was Over, They Played Cards* (1917), who are indeed playing cards after hacking a woman to pieces that lie scattered on the floor. One of the men holds his cards while sitting on the lid of a box out of which protrudes a severed leg. Grosz associated such crimes with postwar German city life in other images depicting a rape or sex murder in progress that is visible through a window, outside of which the street teems with prostitutes, pimps, syphilitics, thieves, drunks, and war casualties.

Otto Dix painted even more explicit sex murders, one with himself as the killer. *The Sex Murderer: Self Portrait* (1920) shows Dix dressed like a flashy lady's man and holding a bloodied butcher's knife in one hand and a hacked-off leg in the other. Blood spurts out of dismembered limbs, an eye in the victim's severed head bulges out in mortal terror, a breast lies on the floor, and the artist/killer's bloody handprints mark other body parts which are spinning in the air as if tossed up in frenzied delight. By depicting himself as an out-of-control killer, Dix suggests that we are all capable of such madness. Dix's *Sexual Murder* (1922) was based on police photographs of a Hamburg prostitute murdered in 1900 but is energized by postwar violence and sexual anxiety.[51] The bloodied victim, with legs wide apart, hangs head down over the edge of a bed to expose her eviscerated lower abdomen, which looks as if she were hacked open by someone looking desperately for the source of her beguiling sexuality. Again we are invited to ask, Why would anyone do this? What did he hope to find or feel? What did the victim experience in her last moments of terror? Nineteenth-century images of murder, such as Cézanne's early paintings of men strangling women, are emotionally schematic by comparison. They do not invite the sort of probing questions about pathological sexual desire as does Dix's crystal-clear depiction of the ordinary and the extraordinary features of the prostitute's murder: her toes poking through stockings and her single bloody tooth, her three parallel throat slashes and savaged torso. The more effects we see, the more we realize how many motives remain obscure.

In addition to the sexually disorienting technologies of warfare and urban life, the twentieth century also yielded the development of disorienting technologies of sexual control and engineering. New contraceptive techniques blocked the natural cause-and-effect scenario of sexual desire, coitus, and pregnancy, culminating in the invention and distribution of the first widely available birth control pill, Enovid, in 1960. Other sex technologies—such as in vitro fertilization, surrogate mothering, sperm banking, prenatal gene therapy, sex-change surgeries, and cloning—revolutionized the causality of sexual reproduction and sexual identity. By giving new answers to such questions as what is a mother, a father, a man, a woman, or a child, they raised a host of new questions about the sex-gender distinction, sexual desire, and parenthood. In summarizing these developments, John Money identified ten additive stages of sexual development that go into the making and shaping of sexual desire: chromosomal sex, gonadal sex, fetal hormonal sex, internal morphologic sex, external morphologic sex, hypothalamic sex, sex of assignment and rearing, pubertal hormonal sex, gender identity and role, and procreative sex impairments.[52] The complexity of sexual constitution implied by the these stages distinguished new specific sources of sexual dysfunction and pathology and new areas of uncertainty about their causes.

Especially relevent historically is the increasing division of labor in sex research. Developments in sexology, psychoanalysis, and endocrinology that began to emerge around 1900 were drawn on after 1970 by three groups of researchers with driving political agendas and research interests who did the most to sharpen understanding of the causal role of sexual desire. Criminologists refined analyses with the new investigatory technique of profiling, while feminist and gay and lesbian theorists traced the history of their sexual experiences and sharpened the sex-gender distinction.

Victorians believed that the personality of the sex murderer was essentially a unified whole that permeated a thoroughly degenerate individual and separated him or her mind and body from everyone else. Modern criminologists identified more precisely the specific origins and causal unfolding of the propensity for sex murder and were more inclined to see the motives as not swamping the entire personality. Aside from particular compulsions, which in serial murderers surface sporadically, sex murderers may have otherwise "normal" social relations and blend into the surroundings. As the crime writer Joel Norris concluded, "Like John Wayne Gacey and Ted Bundy, the overwhelming majority of serial killers seem on the surface to be normal-looking individuals who go to work or school, come home, and blend into their environments."[53] Such thinking marks a change from the Victorians' biological and psychological determinism, which reached a high point with Lombroso's born criminal, who was thought to act consistently in the criminal manner to which he was born and to exhibit the unmistakable bodily markings of an underlying evil evident from the structure of his brain to the shape of his ears.

In the face of modern ideas about the complexity and inconsistency of criminal behavior, criminologists began to use statistical data and probabilistic reasoning to identify, locate, and predict the behavior of serial killers by means of character profiling. An early model for statistical analyses of sexual behavior were the 18,000 interviews that Alfred Kinsey and his associates conducted for his *Sexual Behavior in the Human Male* (1948). However inaccurate his database and statistical analyses were, Kinsey popularized the idea that they were a reliable basis for probabilistic understanding of sexual experience.

In the early 1970s, agents of the FBI's Behavioral Science Unit (BSU) began making statistical analyses of crime scene information to profile sex offenders. Their basic categories were the *organized* criminal, who plans and controls his act and usually removes the victim, and the *disorganized* criminal, who plans and controls the killing with less efficiency and leaves the body and the crime scene in disarray. Following the success of those early analyses, a team of researchers at the BSU studied thirty-six convicted sexual murderers between 1979 and 1983 to create a more detailed and complex motivational model of sexual homicide. They studied the crime scene (point of abduction, locations held, murder scene, and final body location) as well as current research in neurology, genetics, psychology, sociology, and criminology. Their final "Motivation Model for Sexual Homicide" began with a detailed inventory of typical pathogenic childhood experiences—ineffective social environment, parental abandonment or nonprotection, sexual and physical abuse, negative social attachments, deviant parental models, social isolation, fetishes, rebellion, lying, and entitlement. These factors produce weak cognitive mapping and logical processing, which leads to elaborate fantasies and nightmares, a tendency to deal in absolutes and generalizations, and powerful internal dialogues about dominance, revenge, rape, death, torture, and mutilation. Children with such backgrounds tend to be aroused by aggressive experiences requiring high levels of stimulation. Often they are cruel to animals and other children and enjoy setting fires, stealing, and vandalism. In adolescence they move up to assault, burglary, arson, abduction, rape, and murder, sometimes sex murders involving rape, torture, mutilation, or necrophilia.[54]

In 1984 the United States established the NCAVC (National Center for the Analysis of Violent Crime), which used computer analysis of statistical data on unsolved crimes to find patterns and assist law enforcement in identifying, locating, and apprehending violent sex offenders. Information about these crimes from media reports, crime scene analyses, other crime reports, and crime pattern theory was processed to find matches with past profiled incidents and identify known or unknown offenders on the basis of their past modus operandi including choice of victim, method of killing, and behavior before and after the crime.[55]

Researchers continued to refine their profiling of sex killers. Joel Norris summarized their findings in 1988, based on his own extensive interviews with more than a dozen serial killers as well as neurologists, endocrinologists, surgeons, psychiatrists, social workers, medical examiners, and research chemists.[56] His approach differed markedly from that of Victorian phrenologists and criminal anthropologists because he was not looking for "criminal types" but rather for provisional generalizations on the basis of empirical findings about what makes actual criminals do what they do. He analyzed twenty-one indices of aggressive behavior, including genetic disorders, neurological impairment, biochemical symptoms, memory disorders, compulsivity, deviate sexual behavior, and hypersexuality. He also identified their masks of sanity, ritualistic behavior, suicidal behavior, alcohol and drug abuse, cruelty to animals, arsonous tendencies, and feelings of inadequacy. In the end he remained acutely aware of the provisional nature of his "Serial Killer Profile" and the difficulty of using it to identify or locate such a killer or to explain his actions, even after a confession. In contrast to the classical model of the genius detective who solved crimes solo and explained them completely in the final chapter of a story, the teams of specialists at the BSU became increasingly aware of the provisional nature of their motivational model, the unpredictability of even the most obsessive-compulsive serial murderers, and the spotty nature of any explanations of them.

The increasing expertise of feminist as well as gay and lesbian scholarship has transformed understanding of sexuality in the modern world. That research fills countless publications and new sections of bookstores, while universities have established faculty positions and, in some places, whole departments devoted to it. Feminist scholars demolished Victorian ideas about female intuition, hysteria, prostitution, vapors, menstruation, masturbation, passionlessness, orgasms, pregnancy, motherhood, marriage, and the double standard. This research has immensely enriched the scope and accuracy of knowledge about sexual desire and at the same time created lively debates concerning it.

Some feminists have been fascinated by serial sex murderers because of many intriguing contradictions and unanswered questions. While these murderers are regulated by a narrowly channelled sexual pathology, the meaning of their acts is open-ended and puzzling. They choose victims according to rigid criteria, but among those who fit them, anyone will do. They kill according to fixed, predetermined scenarios as if they know exactly what they are doing, but their acts lead back to the original homicidal impulse, which remains a mystery to themselves and others. The causal role of their sexual desire is irresistible, but understanding it is fraught with obstacles beginning with their self-deception and lying. Most intriguing is how an impulse that begins with loving, or at least with the basic impulse toward human relatedness, can lead to torture and killing. The most sophisticated research is stopped dead by that question. The more closely feminists look, the more complex that causal scenario seems and the more uncertain their knowledge of it. The feminists Deborah Cameron and Elizabeth Frazer explain "the lust to kill" as a consequence of "modern patriarchal society," but their explanation is circular—men rape and kill women because they live in a patriarchal society, and one reason for that society being patriarchal is that in it men rape and kill women.[57] In fact, most men love and respect women and are horrified by rape and sex murders, and the male contribution to the formation of society is made by that vast majority of men, not by rapists and serial killers. Still, feminists scholars have played a leading role in probing the causal role of sexual desire in normal love relations as well as murder.

The increasing specificity and complexity, as well as probability and uncertainty, of causal understanding of sexual desire applies especially to knowledge of homosexuality. The analytically clumsy Victorian prejudices that homosexuality was a sin, a crime, or a disease so confused analysis that many experts believed that one could be born to homosexuality, be seduced into it, *and* catch it like some disease.[58] The pioneer sexologist Krafft-Ebing viewed it as a sign of hereditary degeneration, which could lead to sex crimes by a causal scenario he did not understand and could not explain. While Ellis was researching sexual inversion with reformist-minded values, his country was pillorying its leading playwright, Oscar Wilde, for homosexuality. After a British court found Wilde guilty, he was imprisoned for two years, which ended his literary career and, shortly thereafter, his life. Contributing to the general medicalization of mental illness in the twentieth century, Freud viewed homosexuality as an illness rather than a sin or a crime, but although this change allowed for more precise research, understanding continued to be plagued by confusion and bias.

In later years gays were suspected as child molesters and sex criminals and then held responsible for a global deadly plague. When on July 3, 1981, the *New York Times* broke the story on what became the AIDS epidemic, it associated the disease with homosexuals. The first headline read, "Rare Cancer Seen in 41 Homosexuals." The first name of the disease was "gay-related immunodeficiency" (GRID), which in 1982 became more precisely named acquired immune deficiency syndrome (AIDS). While the sexual promiscuity widespread among gays did contribute to its spread, the disease was not caused by anything fundamentally homosexual. Since the early eighties an army of researchers around the world have enormously sharpened understanding of the human immunodeficiency virus (HIV) that causes AIDS and its manifold and complex mutations in order to find a vaccine, treatment, or cure. While their focus is on the causal role of the virus, they are also concerned with the sexual desire that creates the sexual promiscuity through which it infects and kills.

The division of labor in sex research has shaped the efforts of gay and lesbian researchers in particular. They have worked passionately to understand the origin, meaning, and possibilities of sexual desire. Together with the massive research of feminist scholars and the more narrowly focused efforts of criminal profilers, they have explored the causal role of sexual desire with increasing precision and a growing appreciation for its malleability and complexity. Although sexual nonconformists continue to be stigmatized and misunderstood, modern researchers show more toleration for sexual experimentation and greater appreciation of the limits of their findings and of the vast amount they do not know. Both the increased causal precision of modern knowledge and its modesty contrast sharply with Victorian theories about the all-purpose causality of sexual degeneration in hysterical women, nymphomaniacs, and perverts.

5

Emotion

In *The Birth of Tragedy*, Nietzsche probed two fundamental human spirits that were synthesized in Greek tragedy, where they generated ever more powerful art forms. The spirit of reason, symbolized by the god Apollo, was embodied in Socrates' philosophy and was revered throughout Western culture. The spirit of emotion, symbolized by the god Dionysus, was embodied in festivals of music and dance and became suspect ever since. The Greeks depicted Dionysus as a satyr—part god, part goat. Nietzsche hoped to retrieve the bold spirit behind that ennobling of passion as at least partly godly. His philosophy was a call to resurrect the Dionysian spirit out of a pervasive anti-emotionalism that since antiquity had castrated the intellect. Throughout Western history, Nietzsche argued, thinkers viewed emotions as a source of imperfection, irrationality, temptation, and sin. Plato celebrated the life of the mind and denigrated as imperfect everything that is subject to change, especially the life of the senses. Aristotle believed that the essence of human existence is the rational soul and gave reason a privileged position among mental functions. Christendom condemned sensuousness as the source of sins.

Nietzsche found emotion at the heart of the Dionysian spirit, which enables people to lose themselves in the passion of the moment and be intoxicated by music, dance, and desire. Emotion is essential to human existence, a powerful engine to action and a necessary ingredient of the fullest cultivation of the intellect. He urged that we experience life as a passionate affirmation of the here and now, with its myriad uncertainties and without regrets for past actions or hopes of future redemption. With this celebration of emotion, Nietzsche expanded the agenda of philosophical inquiry.

Nietzsche inspired two modern statements of existential philosophy which began with emotions. Heidegger's *Being and Time* starts with an examination of moods, such as boredom and fear, which engulf us and reveal the entirety of our existence in a way that no rational concept or formal theory can. Moods penetrate to the core of existence and extend to its outer reaches. We can never fully understand the meaning of these moods, and so existence is centered in overpowering moods that feel distinctive but elusive. Sartre's *Being and Nothingness* begins with emotions, such as anxiety and shame, which reveal the essential freedom of human existence. For both Heidegger and Sartre, moods or emotions create a specific feeling but at the same time generate a unique sense of uncanniness and uncertainty.

Nineteenth-century psychologists followed philosophers in dividing the mind into three main faculties: intellect, will, and emotion. Across the years of this study, emotion gained significance as definitions of insanity moved beyond mere defects of the intellect to include defects of the will and emotion. Psychiatrists and lawyers sharpened their analyses of the causal function of emotions in disputing the role they play in determinations of criminal responsibility.

Emotions include a wide range of human experiences, from basic sensational emotions (such as pleasure and pain) to simple object-oriented emotions (such as fear and anger) to more complex object-oriented emotions (such as jealousy, revenge, and greed). In novels since 1830 these last emotions were the most frequently mentioned ones leading to murder. All three involve anger over a perceived loss, injury, or lack that the murderer links to others. Jealousy comes from a loss of love to a rival, revenge comes from an injury to oneself by an enemy, and greed comes from a lack of wealth typically as compared with those who have more. The history of thinking about these emotions reveals a growing understanding of their precise nature in that the losses, injuries, and lacks are somewhat illusory, and their sources are not entirely located in others but stem from deficiencies within one's own self. That insight into the projective nature of these emotions shifted thinking from a linear causal model of them as emerging from some inherent defect or sin to the ways they are generated in complex feedback networks involving oneself and others; it also subverted conventional notions that jealousy and revenge were directed by some transcendent destiny or justified by God.

JEALOUSY

Victorian moralists and psychologists had surprisingly little to say about jealousy. As Peter Stearns documented in a history of jealousy in America based on advice books, psychological studies, and legal cases, "the most striking feature of the actual record of romantic jealousy in the nineteenth century was the absence of frequent comment."[1] Passionless women were not supposed to feel it, and if they did, decorum dictated that they were not supposed to complain about it. Jealousy was an embarrassment to men, because passionless women were not supposed to give them cause for it. Darwin's *The Expression of the Emotions in Man and Animals* (1872) affirmed the atavistic nature of jealousy, but classic psychologies of the emotions such as Théodule Ribot's *La psychologie des sentiments* (1896) and Alexander Bain's *The Emotions and the Will* (4th ed. 1899) scarcely mention the subject. When they do it is in terms of evolutionary theory as a hereditary survival of animalistic mating rivalries, distanced from human responsibility by their remote origins.

The treatment of jealousy in advice literature absolved Victorians from responsibility by using imagery that suggested its external source. A marriage column of 1847 warned of an invasion of the "demon" of jealousy; a housewife's manual of 1858 called it a "cloud" that shaded her otherwise happy marital life.[2] For Victorians jealousy was a disease that attacked from without, a blight that descended from somewhere else, and so they avoided acknowledging its source in their own bad choices and fears. A few Victorians saw jealousy as adding spice to a faltering love, but their strategies for exploiting it to galvanize love were nothing but trickery.

Graphic evidence of Victorian men's flight from personal responsibility for their feelings of jealousy is the value attached to dueling with other men rather than confronting their own shortcomings. They were more willing to face the barrel of a gun at twenty paces than to face their own jealousy. The more men learned to take responsibility for their deficiencies in loving, the less "satisfaction" they got from killing a rival. The decline of dueling coincided with an increasing acceptance of inner responsibility for jealousy and its disastrous effects. England abolished dueling in 1844, while America outlawed it after the Civil War in 1865. In the early twentieth century, Russia, Italy, Spain, and Austria-Hungary supported the international Anti-Dueling League. In the Third French Republic, the duel began to stagnate in the 1880s and was more pretense than serious confrontation. In Germany it survived as a deadly showdown until 1918, when it was abolished along with the Hohenzollern monarchy and the cult of honor on which the feudal tradition had been based.[3] The "satisfaction" from killing an offender was supposed to compensate for an insult to a man's honor, especially to his wife or lover, but at a deeper level it satisfied men who projected personal responsibility for any romantic or marital deficiency away from themselves and onto others who threatened them.

By the late nineteenth century, novelists began to expose the futility of the duel. Theodor Fontane treated the duel in *Effi Briest* (1894) as a senseless archaic heritage. Unable to acknowledge his own responsibility for a loveless marriage, Innstetten kills a man who cuckolded him six years before because Innstetten had told a friend about the incident and was therefore obliged to go through with it to preserve his honor before this witness, no matter what. By the time of *The Magic Mountain* in 1924, Mann mocked the tradition with a burlesque duel between two dying tubercular men on the eve of World War I. When the rational optimist Settembrini fires his pistol into the air, the mystical cynic Naptha shoots and kills himself. Neither upholds the "honor" of the duel.

Some men did not wait for a duel but killed their rival on the spot in a fit of jealous rage. In America an attorney in 1859 made the first full use of the "unwritten law" to justify homicide by a jealous husband. He argued that the husband "would have been false to the instinct of humanity if that rage of jealousy had not taken possession of him," and the jury accepted his plea.[4] Fewer than thirty such cases were brought before American courts by the end of the century, but the logic of the legal ruling strengthened the notion that homicidal jealousy was an acceptable way of rooting out the evil intruder in defense of marriage. "The power of these arguments about justifiable (if insane) jealousy began to diminish after 1900," argued Stearns, "just as jealousy standards underwent further reappraisal."[5] By the 1920s that reappraisal was based on a growing appreciation of the universality of sibling jealousy among children, a more detailed examination of the inner causes and destructive effects of the emotion, and a crescendo of criticism of its value in a society that viewed women as the property of men. As moderns came to appreciate the jealous person's own responsibility for the emotion, they withdrew the legal justification for homicides motivated by it.

JEALOUSY AND MURDER NOVELS

A prime example of a Victorian character driven into a homicidal rage by monomaniacal jealousy is Bradley Headstone in *Our Mutual Friend*, who "walked with a bent head hammering at one fixed idea"

(341). His jealous love for Lizzie is fueled largely from without by her charms and by his rivalry with Eugene Wrayburn, who calls him "a curious monomaniac" (294). Headstone's declaration of desperate love abdicates personal responsibility for his jealousy, as when he cries, in textbook language of projection, "You are the ruin of me" (395). When Lizzie rejects his offer of marriage, he smashes his fist into a stone and falls into a rage. Even after his attempted murder of Wrayburn, Headstone remains chained to his jealousy. In Hardy's *Far from the Madding Crowd* (1874), Farmer Boldwood becomes obsessed over his rival for Bathsheba's love, whom he eventually kills in a fit of jealousy with a frenzied look in his eye and a face of gnashing despair (439). Boldwood's obsessive jealousy makes it impossible for him to see its sources in his own protective upbringing, his lack of experience with women, and his narcissistic love for Bathsheba.

In Tolstoy's "The Kreutzer Sonata" (1889), jealousy turns Pozdnyshev into "a wild animal," driven insane with jealousy by his wife and her music tutor, especially when they play Beethoven's *Kreutzer Sonata* together. Pozdnyshev explains that he was driven to stab his wife to death by a series of motives, all of which project responsibility away from himself, beginning with his sexual awakening at age sixteen. He further projects the cause of his jealousy onto married life in general, women's provocative clothing, his wife's piano playing, her tutor, and even Beethoven's music. Some causes come from within—his immoral fornicating and, as he explains, "some devil inventing the most abominable notions and suggesting them to me against my will." But these causes are typical of all men, not of anything unique to himself or indicative of his own responsibility. Besides, as he rationalizes, the devil made him do it.

A scene of desperate jealousy opens Zola's *La bête humaine*, when Roubaud learns that his wife had been seduced by her godfather when she was sixteen. Instead of understanding her vulnerability, let alone his own brutishness, he takes out his rage against her in a warmup for murdering her godfather. He bangs her head against a table and drags her across the floor by her hair, "gasping through clenched teeth, in savage, mindless fury" (36). Other characters are also consumed by homicidal jealousy after Roubaud kills Severine's godfather. Jacques's admirer Flore attempts to kill Jacques and his lover Severine, and Jacques and his rival Pecqueux kill each other in a fight over another woman. None of them seriously looks for the cause of their misery in their own deficiencies but rather sees a rival or an unfaithful lover as the only cause and sees killing as the only relief.

Documenting an argument about the increasing awareness of the causes and effects of jealousy (or any other causal factor) based on the thinking and actions of fictional characters raises a methodological problem about authors' distance from their characters. Zola's characters may have been blind to the causes and effects of jealousy, but surely Zola was not entirely blind; nor were Dickens, Hugo, Hardy, and Tolstoy. The literary effectiveness of their jealous characters was a function of their ability to understand and reconstruct the destructive potential of their characters' ignorance about jealousy and inability to accept responsibility for it. What, then, are the grounds for believing that modern novelists had more specific and precise understanding of jealousy than Victorian novelists had?

I found three grounds for such a claim. First, the claim is supported by many other sources, including advice manuals, psychological studies, and legal cases such as those that Stearns used to support his related argument about how in America between 1890 and 1920 jealousy moved "front and center" with more careful expert scrutiny of marital and sibling jealousies.[6] In an earlier study I surveyed representations of jealousy in literature and art from the Victorian to the modern period in Europe and America and came to similar conclusions.[7] Second, the authorial distance between novelists and their fictional characters itself differed in the two periods. While Victorian novelists understood that their fictional characters were destroyed by lack of insight, the novelists' thinking aligned more with some of their characters' own projections, and they made more excuses for them than did modern novelists. Zola believed that Jacques's jealousy was indeed conditioned by a hereditary taint, Dickens believed that Sikes's jealousy was caused by a miserable upbringing and surroundings, Hardy believed that Farmer Boldwood's monomaniacal jealousy was directed by destiny, and Tolstoy made it painfully clear that Pozdnyshev's jealousy was conditioned by current marital conventions. Third, Victorian novelists were not able to draw on theoretical analyses of behavior in bodies of thought that emerged in the modern period, such as existentialism and psychoanalysis.

While Victorian novelists indeed dramatized the devastating results of being blind to the inner causes of jealousy, they never questioned, as did modern existentialists, to what extent someone could actually *be* jealous. When Sikes killed Nancy he was full of nothing but feelings of betrayal and jealousy. Modern existentialists questioned the possibility of such existential plenitude. For Sartre jealousy is an inescapable feature of love but still an emotion that one can never experience fully. We are jealous because we desire absolute affirmation of our meaning from someone else, but that external witness is necessarily distracted by other people and things. In *Dirty Hands* (1948), Sartre created a character who plays at being a jealous husband in order to justify himself as an assassin. To prove his value to the Communist party during World War II, Hugo Marine agrees to assassinate the party member Hoederer, who is viewed as a traitor to the party because he wants to share power with fascists. While working as Hoederer's secretary, Hugo grows to admire him, as does Hugo's wife Jessica. Their marital problems also center on the difficulty of achieving sincerity. Hugo accuses her of playing at being a housewife, and she accuses him of playing at being a revolutionary. When she asks why he wants to kill a man he does not know, he replies, "So that my wife will take me seriously." Underlying that desire is the more important need to take himself seriously.

The killing is a climax of playacting, and the motive for it is jealousy. Or is it? Jessica becomes infatuated with Hoederer, who alone seems to be real. Hugo senses her infatuation and begins to get jealous. She confesses her love to Hoederer and tells him that her husband is plotting to murder him. When she complains to Hoederer that she could never kiss without laughing, he kisses her, and she does not laugh. Just then Hugo breaks in, concludes that his wife and Hoederer are lovers, and shoots his rival. While dying, Hoederer covers for Hugo by lying to his bodyguards, "He was jealous. That's why he shot me. I've been sleeping with his wife" (239). The dying Hoederer faked a betrayal of Hugo that made Hugo's quasi-sincere jealousy seem legitimate.

Released from prison two years later, Hugo visits another party member Olga, who asks why he killed Hoederer. He has been tormented by that question since the murder and struggles to answer: "I—I killed him because I opened the door. That's all I know." When she asks if it was because of jealousy, he gropes for understanding. "Jealous? perhaps . . . Did I even do it? . . . Where is my crime? Does it exist? . . . I loved Hoederer more than I ever loved anyone in the world . . . I don't know why I committed it" (241–42). Jealousy was an excuse, but, Sartre implies, the motives for all acts are excuses and partial explanations that include everything from cruel parents and capitalist oppression to chance events like the opening of a door. For Sartre jealousy could not generate the sort of emotional plenitude and singular motivational force that Dickens imputed to Sikes and Headstone, or that Zola imputed to Roubaud and Flore.[8] Jealousy involves obsession with another, but ironically it is caused largely by deficiencies within the self, and its causal role in murders stems from those powerful but incomplete inner sources.

Psychoanalysis is the most important explanatory theory that Nabokov drew on in *Lolita* (1955) to explain a murder motivated by jealousy. In 1917 Freud interpreted the unconscious determinants of jealousy in the case history of a "happily married" woman.[9] She became insanely jealous and accused her husband of having an affair because of an anonymous letter, which she knew was forged. Freud viewed her jealousy as a result of her own forbidden love for her son-in-law which she only allowed to reach consciousness inverted as her husband's infidelity. That transformation involved several unconscious mechanisms. She had to *deny* the sexual content of her feelings for her son-in-law, *repress* its libidinal energy, and *disguise* the rest as an innocent affection. The repressed forbidden impulses were *displaced* onto her husband and *converted* into a delusion of jealousy. Thus every time she experienced jealousy she was unconsciously expressing a repressed sexual desire for her son-in-law. Freud's analysis of jealousy emphasized the unconscious determination of its causes.

Nabokov did not invoke the unconscious to explain Humbert's jealousy of his male rival, Claire Quilty, who also seduced Lolita and stole her from him. But Nabokov did draw on psychoanalysis indirectly to explain the murder, although sometimes with tongue in cheek. The seed of Humbert's penchant for nymphets was the traumatic death of his first beloved, Anabelle, from typhus when he was thirteen. As narrator, Humbert interprets his murder weapon, a pistol, as "the Freudian symbol of the Ur-father's central forelimb" (219). Humbert interprets psychoanalytically his own poems and dreams as well as Quilty's pseudonyms and sexual proclivities, but he also recalls with disdain the way "psychoanalysts wooed me with pseudoliberations of pseudolibidoes" (18). Nabokov further mocked psychoanalysis when recounting how Humbert as a patient in a mental hospital had "an endless source of robust enjoyment in trifling with psychiatrists: cunningly leading them on; never letting them see that you know all the tricks of the trade; inventing for them elaborate dreams ... teasing them with fake 'primal scenes'; and never allowing them the slightest glimpse of one's real sexual predicament" (34). Despite his fun at Freud's expense, Nabokov explored Humbert's passion for Lolita and his murderous rage against Quilty with the probing spirit and uncompromising candor of psychoanalytic inquiry.

When Humbert leaves Lolita's home after learning who stole her from him, determined to kill his rival, he is as single-minded as Sikes was and even more tortured with explicit sexual imagery of jealousy. But Humbert is far more aware of the origins of his jealousy—the absurdity and hopelessness of his passion—and more willing to assume responsibility for it. He is candid about his "despicable and brutal" nature, the misery it causes him, and the corruption it works on Lolita from out of the "cesspool of rotting monsters behind his slow boyish smile" (284, 44). His frank self-analysis also includes ordinary qualities such as his being "innocuous, inadequate, passive, [and] timid" (88). He even acknowledges an identification between himself and Quilty, as when the two act out their lecherous similarities by rolling around on the floor during a brief physical struggle before Humbert begins shooting. In contrast to the deadly serious resolution of jealous Victorians hell-bent on murder, Humbert's execution of his rival is a farce beginning with a soused Quilty trying to dismiss Humbert as a pesky visitor, interrupted by a bizarre interlude when Quilty, already bloodied by several gunshots, begins frantically playing the piano, and ending with Quilty's desperate pleadings and bizarre sexual offerings to Humbert (including a woman with three breasts) in exchange for sparing his life.

Humbert is determined that Quilty understand why he is being killed and so makes him read a poem he composed to clarify the reasons. It uses the word "because" repeatedly but rambles and fails to explain precisely who is responsible for Humbert's suffering, as in the concluding lines, "because of all you did / because of all I did not / you have to die" (300). Throughout this exchange Quilty emerges as an increasingly unworthy rival, because he barely remembers Lolita and reveals to Humbert that he was usually impotent with her and did not appreciate her charms. The deeper Humbert digs, the more unfocused and unjustified his jealousy becomes. After Quilty is dead, Humbert acknowledges the haziness of his own motivation and the futility of vengeance. "Far from feeling any relief, a burden even weightier than the one I had hoped to get rid of was with me, over me" (304).

Jealousy is deformed and diffused by technological waves and radiations in DeLillo's *White Noise* (1985), a novel about how modern culture and modern emotions are deadened by the incessant white noise of supermarkets, shopping malls, and especially television. The title of the first section, "Waves and Radiation," refers to television's incessant commercials that deaden us to thoughtful choice, its news disasters that deaden us to suffering, and its predictable plots that deaden us to human possibility. The narrator is Jack Gladney, whose son warns him that TV radiations deform babies and destroy brain cells. His neighbors cannot fully experience the toxic railroad spill that threatens their town because it does not get live TV coverage. He becomes jealous after learning about an affair his wife was having with a "staticky" creation of TV culture, a man whom she calls Mr. Gray. He had extorted sex from her in exchange for the drug Dylar, a pharmacological equivalent of a TV dialer, that interacts with neurotransmitters in the brain and reduces her fear of death.

Jack's jealousy breaks up like bad TV reception when he first sees Gray, who appears as "a hazy gray seducer moving in ripples across a motel room." Jack's murder plan is like a plot from a bad TV movie. "Drive past the scene several times, park some distance from the scene, go back on foot, locate Gray under his real name or an alias, shoot him three times in the viscera for maximum pain," and so forth (304). To validate his actions, which become increasingly aimless, Jack repeats to himself this plan, which gets increasingly muddled. He locates Gray, whose real name is Mink, in a shabby motel room with a TV floating in the air, pointing down at Mink like the supermarket security cameras that make commodities out of shoppers. Mink seems more pathetic than threatening as Jack finds him with a concave face and skin the color of a Planter's peanut, sprawled in a chair and wearing plastic sandals, Budweiser shorts, and a Hawaiian shirt. He is thus a hollowed out man of peanut shells and empty beer cans, a product of cheap commercialism and TV advertising. During Jack's attempted murder of Mink, his jealousy turns to pity for his wife whose last hope, he realizes, had been "this weary pulse of a man" (307).

Dylar (and dialing) has wiped out Mink's ability to distinguish between TV and reality, and he directs himself with instructions quoted from TV jingles. As he becomes afraid, he begins popping Dylar pills while watching the flickering screen, eventually throwing them at it as the picture begins to roll. Knowing that the drug confuses words with actions, Jack shouts "hail of bullets," and Mink hits the floor and wriggles behind the toilet bowl. There Jack shoots him twice. Then, to make it look like suicide, he puts in Mink's hand a gun which Mink uses to shoot Jack in the wrist. Stunned, Jack bandages himself and drags Mink to his car, stopping en route to perform mouth-to-mouth resuscitation before taking him to a hospital. In the end Jack identifies with Mink; as he explains, "I did honor to both of us, to all of us, by merging our fortunes, physically leading him to safety" (315). His jealousy further disintegrates with this final identification. As John N. Duvall concluded, "Jack, who comes to the motel room in hopes of confronting origin—the origin of his male rage . . . finds instead only an Oz-like shell of power and authority. Mink, a pill-popping wreck, offers no satisfying target of vengeance because there is no core or center to his personality."[10] Jack's jealousy is also dispersed in a mass culture. DeLillo acknowledged no single explanation for even murder motivated by jealousy and no single source of American culture. He rather saw everyone's fortune as merged in a system that is stripped of its core by television and shopping malls, with emotions drowned in a sea of programmed white noise, which makes everyone deaf to individual utterances and incapable of original thoughts.

The more Hugo, Humbert, and Jack probe their jealousy, the more unreliable and unsatisfactory the emotion becomes as a motive for murder. By the time they pull the trigger their convictions are gone, their purposes confused. Sartre, Nabokov, and DeLillo were influenced by philosophies distinctive of the modern period in dramatizing how a close look at jealousy undermines its motivational role. Sartre analyzed jealousy through his own existential philosophy, and Nabokov drew on psychoanalysis, while DeLillo incorporated modern systems theory. *White Noise* concludes with the bitterly ironic reassurance that shoppers' confusion will ultimately be rectified. "In the end it doesn't matter what they see or think they see. The terminals are equipped with holographic scanners, which decode the binary secret of every item, infallibly." Scanners will save them from the errors of individual choice. If they are confused about what they have chosen, feedback technologies will read their minds and print out accurate receipts.

"DeLillo's orientation toward the world, as well as toward fiction," argued Tom LeClair, "is influenced by and parallels the ideas of 'systems theory,' a contemporary scientific paradigm that concentrates on the reciprocal—looping—communications of ecological systems (including man)."[11] Systems theory offered a framework for depersonalizing and distributing the causal action of jealousy among many sources in a way that challenged the linear causality of psychological determinism. DeLillo's characters act on one another and on the world and are acted upon in systems of mutually interdependent causal agencies for which no one person is responsible. It is a world in which jealousy becomes diffuse in general systems of causal action. DeLillo elaborated this action through Jack's vision of his own thinking as a network of interacting forces: "With each separate step, I became aware of processes, components, things relating to other things" (304). While television is the main medium for communication loops in *White Noise*, DeLillo's work generally explored many other feedback systems: ecological, physiological, psychological, social, economic, and linguistic. These systems include market fluctuations in economics, self-fulfilling prophecies in sociology, homeostasis in biology, vicious circles in logic, and various mechanical, electrical, and human communication networks in cybernetics. They represent a defining feature of causal understanding in the twentieth century and provide abundant evidence of the increasingly complex and probabilistic field-based causality that is central to my argument about the specificity-uncertainty dialectic.

REVENGE

Revenge has been a motive for murder from Greek tragedy to the modern age. Nothing galvanizes a plot more than some horrendous evil done to a virtuous character. While modern popular culture is rife with such stories, serious literature reveals an increasing reluctance to accept the sort of monomaniacal determination and conviction of some transcendent, if not divine, sanction that justified revenge in many earlier novels. This cultural shift resulted from the related declining literary authorities of melodramatic style and religious faith.

In Victorian melodrama, emotions were writ large on faces and acted out in overt behavior split between good heroes and evil villains. As Winifred Hughes noted, "Mid-nineteenth-century acting technique, like the scripts themselves, remained inflated and exaggerated, often to the point of frenzy, with heavy reliance on gesture and tableau. . . . Both good and evil, heroes and villains, remained unexamined and unexplained, dramatized in terms of their visible results rather than their motives or origins."[12] English sensation novelists of the 1860s (e.g., Wilkie Collins, Charles Reade, and Mary Braddon) introduced some conscience and depth to their villains, but Victorian novelists generally continued to portray quintessentially virtuous heroes fighting thoroughly evil enemies. Acts of revenge involved minimal self-inquiry about the origin of the emotion within the self and concentrated rather on the wicked deeds of villains. Victorian avengers were also often sustained by the conviction that they were carrying out a higher purpose of destiny or God. Melodramatists portrayed a world based on moral certainties that came ultimately from God. In contrast modernist novelists resisted the melodramatic triumph of good over evil and questioned the divine justification of revenge.

David Brion Davis related the popularity of murderous revenge in nineteenth-century fiction to other public enactments of vengeance, such as dueling, lynching, and capital punishment, where good and evil are clearly divided between oneself and others. In William Gilmore Simms's *The Partisan* (1835), a man kills Tory soldiers in revenge for the suffering of his pregnant wife at the hands of a gang of Tories who tortured and brutally killed her. In Robert Montgomery's *Nick of the Woods* (1837), a Pennsylvania farmer, in a gesture of friendship, gave some Indians his knife and gun, which they used to kill his wife, mother, and five children. In revenge he murdered and scalped subhuman "Injuns," convinced of his divine mission. "In his maddened state," Davis concluded, "revenge was holy, [and] plunging a knife into the breast of an Indian was a divine ecstasy." Killing offered a triumphant release from bondage, immediate annihilation of everything that threatened the ego. In typical cases of fictional revenge, "the difference between 'normal' revenge and monomania would only be one of degree," and murders for any other reason paled by comparison in the intensity of motivation and the violence of the act.[13]

Revenge is brutal and deeply satisfying against Maigrat, the hated owner of a company store in Zola's *Germinal* (1885), who exacted sexual favors from the coal miners' daughters in exchange for food when their families were starving. During a strike the women riot and force Maigrat to flee onto the roof of his store where he falls to his death. Then one of the women pulls down his trousers, another spreads his legs, and a third tears out his genitals with her bare hands. She waves the bloody mass aloft "with a snarl of triumph" and jams it on a stick, which she hoists before the line of women shouting their vindictiveness as they parade through the strike-torn town (351). Although these women are helpless to deal with the oppression of a system that puts their husbands, sons, and daughters at risk, their act of a revenge offers a moment of satisfaction without any second-guessing about its motives or value. The angry women are fully absorbed by their act and, for a brief moment, entirely satisfied.

In *Moby Dick* (1851), Ahab is the quintessence of intensity and single-mindedness, which Melville emphasizes by referring to him repeatedly as a monomaniac. Ahab lost a leg hunting Moby Dick and wants to find and kill him. He literally nails his vengeance to the mast of the *Pequod* in the form of a gold coin, which can only be retrieved by the first man who spots the whale. Ahab sleeps with clenched fists and wakes with bloodied palms. His resolve is also evident in his appearance, which reveals "an infinity of firmest fortitude, a determinate unsurrenderable wilfulness, in the fixed and fearless, forward dedication of [his] glance" (111). Nothing can swerve him from his course. As he explains, "the path to my fixed purpose is laid with iron rails, whereon my soul is grooved to run" (147).

Behind all mysteries, including Ahab's obsession with revenge, is the expectation of a guiding destiny or God's will. When Starbuck questions the wisdom of taking "vengeance on a dumb brute" who smote him from blind instinct, Ahab replies that in every event "some unknown but still reasoning thing puts forth the mouldings of its features from behind the unreasoning mask" (144). Belief in a transcendent purpose behind the whale's blind instinct sustains Ahab's belief in some divine sanction behind his own revenge. Moby Dick is an "incarnation of all those malicious agencies which some deep men feel eating in them" (160). While Ahab is unaware of these projections, Melville is not, as in explaining that Ahab "piled upon the whale's white hump the sum of all the general rage and hate felt by his whole race from Adam down" (160). Just how Ahab inherited that rage down through the ages Melville is of course unable to specify. Melville locates the ultimate explanation in some unfathomable divine causation: "To trail the genealogies of these high mortal miseries carries us at last among the sourceless primogenitures of the gods" (386). Unlike modern acknowledgments of uncertainty, which accept ultimate incomprehensibility, this Victorian confession of uncertainty is hedged by a reassurance of divine explanation. Ahab's revenge is a plenum of emotion, singularly focused and grooved to run on iron rails laid down by the fates, if not by God.

The murder solved by Sherlock Holmes in *A Study in Scarlet* (1887) is also motivated by monomaniacal vengeance sanctioned and only made possible by God's intervention. In Salt Lake City, Jefferson Hope won the love of Lucy Ferrier but was foiled by two wicked bigamist Mormon elders: Joseph Strangerson (who killed Lucy's father) and Enoch Drebber (who forced her to marry himself). She died soon afterward. Hope found her dead body, took her wedding ring, and then devoted his life to hunting down and eventually killing the two men, forcing them to view the wedding ring as they died. To Drebber he offered two pills, one of which was poisoned, saying, at the moment of confrontation, "Let the high God judge between us. Choose and eat. . . . Let us see if there is justice upon earth, or if we are ruled by chance?" Hope released years of pent-up revenge in a laugh as he saw the horror on Drebber's face when the divinely chosen poison began to act. A fight broke out when Hope offered the two pills to Strangerson. He was forced to stab Strangerson but reassured himself that "Providence would never have allowed his guilty hand to pick out anything but the poison" (115, 116). When Holmes enters Drebber's apartment and finds *Rache* written in blood on the wall, he correctly interprets it as the German word for revenge. Drebber looks his evil Lombrosian part with a "low forehead, blunt nose, prognathous jaw . . . [and] ape-like appearance" in addition to a look of terror frozen on his face, a permanent record of his climactic confrontation with his sins and of the hellish eternity of divinely sanctioned punishment that awaits him (27). In the language of Victorian psychiatry, Hope was a monomaniac. "The predominant idea of revenge had taken such complete possession of [his heart] that there was no room for any other emotion" (103).

Ahab's and Hope's unwavering motivation for revenge and their faith in divine guidance contrast in the modern period with the gaping lack of either in Camus's *The Stranger*, in which a murder is put in motion by a seedy revenge plot and carried out with abject listlessness in a godless universe. Meursault finds himself in a position to kill the Arab because he agreed to help his friend Raymond, a pimp, get even with his ex-mistress, a prostitute, whom Raymond suspects of withholding earnings from him. Raymond decides to write her a letter of apology and then, when she returns, spit in her face and throw her out. Meursault's account of his agreement to help Raymond with this lowly plot disjoins his act from any recognizable motivation: "When he told me the woman's name I realized she was Moorish. I wrote the letter." Camus does not explain the causal significance of her being Moorish, and Meursault's explanation is minimally explanatory: "I did it just as it came to me, but I tried my best to please Raymond because I didn't have any reason not to please him" (32). Apparently all motives for assisting in any revenge, however debased, are of equal value, including no motive at all—a sharp contrast to Victorian revenge plots that were triggered by evil acts against innocent characters, motivating noble hearts to act with monomaniacal focus on behalf of moral principles believed to be sanctioned by God.

The decreasing value and godliness of revenge is further evinced by contrasting Alexander Dumas's *The Count of Monte Cristo* (1845) with Friedrich Dürrenmatt's *The Visit* (1956). Both stories are about someone who was terribly harmed as a youth by several conspirators, was unjustly punished by the law, and then went away for many years and returned extremely wealthy in order to get revenge. In Dumas's novel, revenge motivates the punishment of three villains in the service of divine justice; in Dürrenmatt's play, it motivates the corruption of everyone in a godless world.

When Edmond Dantès escapes from the Chateau d'If to find Abbé Faria's fortune, he is transformed into a virtuous and fabulously wealthy instrument of divine justice. As the Christlike Count of Monte Cristo, Dantès returns, vowing "now let the avenging God make way for me to punish the wrongdoer" (260). He acts with monomaniacal determination by exploiting the unique vices of his betrayers Danglars, Mondego, and Villefort.

Danglars conspired out of greed and ambition, and so Monte Cristo plays on Danglars' greed and drives him into bankruptcy. Mondego plotted against him out of desire for his fiancée, Mercédès, and eventually succeeds in marrying her in Dantès's absence. In retaliation Monte Cristo disgraces Mondego, destroys his marriage, and drives him to suicide. At the critical moment he says to Mondego, "I can now show you a face rejuvenated by the joy of revenge" (877). Villefort betrayed Dantès to protect his own career, so Monte Cristo plots his public disgrace in court, which drives Villefort to madness and his wife to suicide. Afterward Monte Cristo concludes, "the spirit of God brought me here and takes me away triumphant" (1029). Having doubts about his revenge, he returns to the Chateau d'If and finds that

the epigraph to Abbé Faria's manuscript on the Italian monarchy justified his acts of revenge: "You will pull the dragon's teeth and trample
the lions underground, said the Lord" (1038).

The joy and triumph of Monte Cristo's revenge and the conviction
of its divine sanction are a historical epoch away from the dubious
gratification of vengeance in *The Visit*. Years earlier in the town of
Güllen, Claire Zachanassian became pregnant by her lover Alfred. He
denied paternity and bribed two men into testifying that they had had
sex with her. She was driven from town in disgrace and became a prostitute, married a rich man, and wound up a fabulously wealthy heiress.

The play begins with her expected arrival in Güllen as everyone is
hoping that Alfred will be able to persuade her to help the town out of a
depression actually inflicted by her. She says she will help, but only
in exchange for justice—a million pounds to the town if someone kills
Alfred. At first the Gülleners indignantly deny her request, but slowly
greed erodes resolve. She seduces them to buy on credit, necessitating
Alfred's execution.

Dumas and Dürrenmatt offer historically distinctive interpretations
of revenge, starting with the sources of the fortunes that make it possible. Abbé Faria is virtuous and wise, while Claire inherits her fortune
from an oil tycoon she met in a London brothel. The Isle of Monte
Cristo is named after high ground and Christ, while *Gülle* is a German
word referring to liquid manure. Dantès returns in disguise as a count,
while Claire returns old and decrepit, with a prosthetic leg and hand.
Mercédès had been faithful as long as she believed that Dantès was
alive, while Alfred betrayed Claire when she was pregnant with his own
child. Monte Cristo's enemies go down cringing in panic, while
Claire's nemesis Alfred dies with dignity, ironically the only person in
Güllen willing to accept responsibility for her mistreatment. As he concedes, "I made Claire what she is, and I made myself what I am" (76).
Dumas locates evil in the three main conspirators, while Dürrenmatt
questions the sharpness of the good/evil distinction altogether. Monte
Cristo believes that he is doing God's will, while Claire has to hire the
former Chief Justice of Güllen to pronounce her death sentence and
has to bribe an entire town to carry it out. Monte Cristo feels joy and
triumph in the confidence that his revenge is just, while Claire realizes
that her revenge subverts justice altogether for the Gülleners as she seduces them into scapegoating Alfred by corrupting them with a promise
of money. For Dumas, greed is focused in Danglars, who is justly

punished for it by bankruptcy. For Dürrenmatt, whose play is set after World War II, greed is a feedback system circulating throughout society, progressively sweeping everyone up in its degrading influence. As Claire explains, "The world turned me into a whore. I shall turn the world into a brothel" (67). Far from giving satisfaction to Claire, revenge rather hardens and dehumanizes her.

Modernists were unable to experience revenge triumphantly or believe it to be justified by God. For them the revenge became detached from its function of restoring honor or justice and was relegated to a dubious emotion that enlisted base instincts and caused messy results, with its moral justification closer to dueling and lynching than to the righting of wrongs. Dürrenmatt's novel *The Pledge* was a requiem for the criminal novel generally, just as his play *The Visit* was a requiem for literary dramatizations of revenge. In his play, the desire for murderous revenge was triggered by a betrayal, exacerbated by a miscarriage of justice, funded by prostitution, sanctioned by corrupt officials, and executed by a community that was seduced into buying death on the installment plan. More generally, into the modern period the revenge component of duels, lynchings, wars, and capital punishment became less justifiable as the underlying emotion that motivated revenge was subjected to increasing critical scrutiny.

Greed

While Victorian novelists questioned the morality of greed, they did not seriously question whether it motivated behavior, and so their murderers are typically motivated directly by the desire for money or property, often in specific amounts. Balzac's single-minded Vautrin in *Old Goriot* wants 200,000 francs to buy a farm. As he tells Rastignac, "'I consider actions as a means to an end, and the end is all I see. What is a man's life to me? Not that!' and he snapped his thumbnail against his teeth" (182). To get the money, he plots to have someone kill the brother of a woman who loves Rastignac so that she will inherit wealth and be able to marry Rastignac, who will then control her money and be able to pay off Vautrin. In Zola's *The Earth* (1887), the two Fouan sisters each inherit land from their aging father. Their greed is over acreage for which Lise Fouan fatally wounds her sister by pushing her onto an upturned scythe. In *La bête humaine* (1890), Misard is obsessed over his wife's one-thousand-franc inheritance, which she hides from him. Desperate to get her out of the way so he can hunt for the money undisturbed, he plots her murder. When she suspects that he is poisoning her salt and takes precautions to protect herself, he poisons her enema water. After her death, he tears apart their home and then digs up their property in a vain effort to find the francs. The title character in *McTeague* covets his wife Trina's five-thousand-dollar lottery prize. Her miserliness over her hoard fuels his greed, and the two fight over the money until in frustration he steals it and then kills her. Their struggle is reenacted in Death Valley when McTeague and a rival, dying of thirst, fight to the death over the same money.

In *Crime and Punishment* Raskolnikov is most famously motivated by his theory of the "exceptional man," but a number of other motives center around his need for cash. He is a poor student, his room is tiny, and at the beginning of the story he is hungry because he has eaten little for two days. Most important, he is humiliated and enraged at learning that his sister is about to make a loveless marriage to a much older man in hopes that, as his mother writes him, he "will help us assist you with money while you remain at the university" (31). Raskolnikov is further incensed when he meets Sonya and discovers that she works as a prostitute to bring home rubles to be squandered by her drunken father. Raskolnikov kills the pawnbroker to steal from her locked trunk so he can give money to others. At his trial the judge reduces his sentence on the basis of "temporary insanity" because he did not even look at the jewels he had stolen, let alone spend the proceeds. In 1860s Russia, anyone who kills for money that he does not look at or spend must be at least temporarily insane. Still, money is the immediate reason for the murder, and Dostoevsky loads the motivational picture with Raskolnikov's money worries.

In addition to murder for money or property, murder for an inheritance is another common theme in Victorian murder stories from Dickens to Doyle. Even Poe's "irrational" murderer in "The Imp of the Perverse" (1845), who intended by murdering "to do wrong for the wrong's sake" because of "a motive not *motiviert*," turns out to have been ultimately after an inheritance. Victorian novelists consistently made murderers plausible by using the desire for some specific gain as a paramount motive. Many modernists resisted that narrative strategy. Their probing of the underlying significance of the desire for money and other objects of value provides the dramatic subtext of modern novels about murders committed ostensibly for gain but in which the role of greed is ultimately traced to deeper-lying causal pressures that concern the murderer's self-worth.

In a study of the role of money in fiction, one recent scholar concluded that as compared with the late Victorian period "fewer novels dealing with money have been written in this century."[14] That decline is in part the result of an increasingly probing analysis of the power of money to forge personal identity. Behind greed, modernists see a search for self-worth doomed to failure because genuine self-worth is something that money, especially ill-gotten money, cannot buy. Modernist understanding of greed therefore becomes increasingly probing and complex, as is evident in novels where the pursuit of money or objects of value is ultimately revealed to be a superficial reason for murder behind which are deeper social-psychological forces and broader historical processes. Frank Norris and John Steinbeck found greed so pervasive in an age of corporate capitalism that no one can be held responsible for the widespread death it causes; Hermann Broch and Bret Ellis saw greed at the root of a commercial modern age that is struggling with a disintegration of human values; while William March and Truman Capote dramatized the emptiness of greed with murders carried out for trivial loot.

In Norris and Steinbeck, efforts to strike back against the dominion of greed with deadly violence are frustrated by greed's complex labyrinthine sources. In *The Octopus* (1901), the Pacific and Southwestern Railroad's monopoly enables it to charge "all the traffic will bear" and drive the farmers of the San Joaquin Valley to ruin. The profit motive generates a deadly network, symbolized by the iron tentacles of the railroad that suck up all the farmers' profits, leading to their loss of land and death. When Presley, a poet and ally of the farmers, confronts Shelgrim, the man supposedly responsible for the railroad's greed, in his San Francisco headquarters, he finds himself at the heart of a gridwork that embraces many lives. Shelgrim explains that "railroads build themselves. . . . 'You are dealing with forces, young man, when you speak of wheat and railroads, not with men'" (405). Presley staggers dumbfounded out of the office, wondering, "Was no one, then, to blame for the horror at the irrigation ditch [where some farmers were killed in a shootout with the authorities]? Forces, conditions, laws of supply and demand—were these, then, the enemies after all?" The shift in causal understanding from linear to interactive models is evinced in this novel about widespread killing indirectly caused by the corporate greed of the railroad octopus.

Similarly, in Steinbeck's *The Grapes of Wrath* (1939), huge financial corporations crush struggling farmers with foreclosures, and still no identifiable person is responsible. When one farmer, shotgun in hand, threatens the three-dollar-a-day driver of a tractor that is about to destroy his home, the driver says to the farmer that if you killed him, "They'll just hang you, but long before you're hung there'll be another guy on the tractor, and he'll bump the house down." When the farmer asks who gave him orders, the driver explains that there is a bank president and a board of directors which itself gets orders from more impersonal institutions in "the East." In despair, the farmer asks, "Where does it stop? Who can we shoot?" The driver replies, "Maybe there's nobody to shoot. Maybe the thing isn't men at all. Maybe, like you said, the property's doing it" (52). In the modern world no one person is to blame and there is no one to shoot. Whether killings are indirectly carried out by impersonal corporations or threatened directly by impotent victims, on both sides of the conflict in these novels with murder plots driven by the profit motive and its effects, the causality of greed has become increasingly multisourced, complex, and uncertain.

In the United States a new impersonal corporate greed that kills emerged in the late nineteenth century when the new railroad, telegraph, and banking industries transformed economy and society. The operation of this complex transportation, communication, and financial infrastructure necessitated the creation of vast managerial hierarchies in which even top officials were interchangeable. Railroad corporations, for example, learned to move freight cars belonging to one company across lines owned by several different railroad companies and streamlined operations by complex intercompany billing and through bills of lading. Because of the enormous expense of capital investment, railroads became the first modern high-fixed-cost industry, requiring stable and reliable rate schedules that had to be maintained, no matter what, and minimum traffic flows that had to be met for the companies to remain profitable, no matter who got in the way.[15] Railroads were inexorable. Building crews cut through every kind of terrain, and the powerful locomotives screamed through every locale. Personal loyalties to individuals, or even communities, were difficult to honor. Obstacles from anyone or anything—individual farmers to rival companies—had to be eliminated. Norris's inflated rhetoric in *The Octopus* captures the historical significance of the railroad industry that marshaled unprecedented economic and mechanical power. It was "a vast cyclopean power, huge, terrible, a leviathan with a heart of steel, knowing no compunction, no forgiveness, no tolerance; crushing out the human atom standing in its way with nirvanic calm" (406).

The first national governmental regulatory measures to attempt to control that power in the United States (the Interstate Commerce Commission Act of 1887 and the Sherman Antitrust Act of 1890) had railroad monopolies in mind, but the measures were at first ineffective, because Presidents William McKinley, Theodore Roosevelt, and William Taft refused to apply the Sherman Antitrust Act against the railroads.[16] The invisible hand was no longer working for the common good but was taking in unprecedented profits and, when necessary, had a finger on the trigger. But getting even by killing the killers was impossible because, as Steinbeck's farmer discovered with respect to banking monopolies in the 1930s, there was no one to shoot. The causal role of greed in those impersonal and indirect killings carried out by huge corporations became increasingly complex and uncertain as the interchangeable culprits disappeared into a Kafkaesque bureaucracy and became increasingly unknown even to one another.

Other novelists found greed and consumerism eating ever deeper into the modern soul and generating murder out of the need for a sense of identity. Broch's *The Sleepwalkers* (1931–32) is a panorama of the years from 1888 to 1918, characterized by a "Disintegration of Values," which is the title of ten chapters interspersed in the novel, exploring the spiritual breakdown resulting from the reign of mechanistic determinism, ethical pluralism, runaway greed, and, during the war, senseless killing. People are caught between a dying system of values based on God, nation, and duty and a new one not yet formed, sometimes justified merely by the economic catchphrase "business is business." In that sense they are sleepwalking between spiritual sleep and wakefulness.

Greed is personified by Wilhelm Huguenau, who deserts from the army in 1918 and makes his way to Kur-Trier where he finagles control of a newspaper from August Esch, whom he stabs in the back with the bayonet of his rifle. The final chapter on the disintegration of values begins with the questions: "Had he committed a murder? Had he done a revolutionary deed?" (625). Those questions cannot be answered in accord with any transcendent values in a world dominated by the supreme value of making money. He never thought about the murder again or doubted its value but did have an uneasy sense that he was living in a world like the one Nietzsche described following the death of God with "the icy breath sweeping over the world, freezing it to rigidity and withering all meaning out of the things of the world" (640).

A disturbing indictment of the connection between consumerism and murder in a failing struggle for psychic self-preservation is Ellis's *American Psycho* (1991), about some spiritually empty young men who work in a Wall Street investment firm in the early 1990s. They wear designer clothes, eat at exclusive restaurants, date only sexy "hard bodies," and make as much money as they can. One of them, the first-person narrator of the novel, Patrick Bateman, is also a serial killer whose obsession for material goods has fused with his compulsive sexual perversion and brutal killing. When he tells one potential victim that he is "into, oh, murders and executions mostly," she thinks he's talking about the mergers and acquisitions that her other dates boast about (206). Her fatal mistake underscores Ellis's fusion of greed and murder as the only things that motivate Bateman. In addition to paragraph-long lists of designer goods that Bateman and his friends wear, Bateman records the brand name on the shirt he is wearing as he brutally tortures a woman sexually and makes trophies of her body parts. He notes the make of the movie camera he uses to film her execution, the kind of CD player he uses to drown out her screaming. After sexually molesting, torturing, and disfiguring a woman who had earlier misidentified the designer of his suit, he shouts into her hacked up face, "The suit is by *Armani! Giorgio* Armani . . . And you thought it was *Henry Stuart*. Jesus!" (247). His narration includes glimmers of insight into the confusion of greed and homicidal mania that has left him empty, as he explains: "There wasn't a clear, identifiable emotion within me, except for greed and, possibly, total disgust. I had all the characteristics of a human being—flesh, blood, skin, hair—but my depersonalization was so intense, had gone so deep, that the normal ability to feel compassion had been eradicated" (282). Bateman is a distinctly modern American psycho of the early 1990s, held up only by the prestige of the designer goods he owns: Allen-Edmonds shoes, Ralph Lauren monogrammed boxer shorts, Valentino Couture trousers, Hermès ties, Brooks Brothers suits, Rolex watch, Vivagent Hair Enrichment Treatment, and so forth.

Throughout the era of classical economics, leading theoreticians believed that the value of goods came from the labor it took to produce them and was reflected in their usefulness. From Locke to Marx, some version of the labor theory of value was at the heart of economic thinking about the source of national wealth and the virtues of hard work. An alternative explanation of value emerged in the late nineteenth century as neoclassical economists, also known as marginal utilitarians or marginalists, argued that value is created not by productive labor but by consumer desire. In *Grundsätze der Volkswirtschaftslehre* (1871) the Austrian economist Carl Menger argued that value is not some quality inherent in a good, as classical economists believed, but lies in the desire for it. To compare goods that satisfy a desire, Menger devised a table of marginal utilities, showing how as a supply of goods increases, desire for it declines.

While the labor theory of value could not explain why fine art was expensive, and utilitarianism could not explain why water was cheap, marginalism could explain both, with value determined, and precisely measurable (in theory), at the margin between the desire for one unit of a product and the next. In *Theory of Political Economy*, also from 1871, the English economist William Jevons offered a theory of marginal utility using more precise mathematic calculations. The heart of his book was a theory of exchange—that utility is increased not by anything in a product but by the process of exchange itself. In contrast to the prevailing view that "labor was the *cause* of value," he showed "that we have only to trace out carefully the natural laws of the variation of utility, as depending upon the quantity of commodity in our possession, in order to arrive at a satisfactory theory of exchange."[17] Jevons also introduced mathematical calculations to measure the precise marginal utility of a good as inversely proportional to its availability and directly proportional to the desire for it.

The battle over the primacy of production or consumption in the determination of value was still being waged in the late twentieth century as Jean Baudrillard attempted to smash "the mirror of production."[18] Debate continued whether the formulation of marginalism by Menger and Jevons in 1871 was a specific turning point or was implicit in earlier classical economics and simply took hold in the 1870s or even later in the twentieth century.[19] But economists concurred that sometime after 1871 the primacy of production was superseded by the primacy of consumption, as marginalists focused on the way markets generate value when desiring individuals act and how that desire is created. As a recent historian concluded, "by the last decade of the nineteenth century, a sterile desire had replaced a productive labor as the origin of value."[20]

Greed motivates some murderers in modern novels where the objects coveted have highly illusory value, as, for example, with Clyde Griffiths, who attempts murder in *An American Tragedy* because he is mesmerized by the superficial glitz of wealthy high society. In *American Psycho*, Bateman becomes obsessed with killing superficially sexy women, many of them prostitutes, while he wears designer clothes. Ellis dramatizes the quintessential *dis*utility of Bateman's compulsive greed when, in the midst of a killing spree after shooting a cop and then being chased by two other cops, he runs down Wall Street and is overcome by consumer desire while the bullets are flying. Ellis conflates murder and consumer desire with his narration that slips from description of the chase to Bateman's inner thoughts: "he dashes past a row of Porsches, tries to open each one and sets a string of car alarm sirens off, the car he would like to steal is a black Range Rover with permanent four-wheel drive, an aircraft-grade aluminum body on a boxed steel chassis and a fuel-injected V-8 engine, but he can't find one" (350). Classic use value can make no sense of this mad consumerism in a man who, while being shot at, fantasizes about the transmission and carburation systems of the car he would like to steal. The more Bateman fucks and kills, the poorer he feels and the more he desires to own, necessitating increasingly ferocious fucking, killing, and buying. He is a horrifying embodiment of market value over use value, a dark—very dark—comic solution to the problems of unemployment, overproduction, and sluggish consumer demand.[21]

While Victorian greedy murderers were depicted as immoral (Vautrin), desperate (Lise Fouan), or obsessed (Misard and McTeague), their desire for gain remained clear, at least to them. In the modern period, that clarity itself becomes clouded and knowledge of it uncertain. In Conrad's pivotal *Heart of Darkness* (1899), Kurtz's greed turns sour and confused as his hunt for ivory requires "unsound methods," including the intimidation of enemies by head-hunting. His entire existence is suffused by emptiness and evil, ending with his final enigmatic written words, "exterminate the brutes," and his final enigmatic spoken words, "The Horror! The Horror!" This realm of darkness and ambiguity is far from Vautrin's arranging a murder to get 200,000 francs to buy a farm or from Lise's murder of her sister to keep a farm in the family. While Balzac and Zola questioned the morality of such ruthless intentions, they did not question their causal role as clear motives for murder and the bases of their plots.

The specific sums of money or acreages of land that motivated the Victorian murderers whom I have surveyed, aside from Raskolnikov, were sizable, and the plausibility of the murders committed to get them was based on those objects being of considerable value. In contrast some modern murders are committed because of trifles that highlight the superficiality of greed and point to other motives involving self-worth. In *The Bad Seed*, the objects Rhoda desires to acquire from two murders are trivial—a glass ball that an old woman had promised her and a penmanship medal that she thought she ought to have won. The novel accents the superficial nature of greed with such measly loot as the goal for two shocking murders, one by pushing an old woman down some stairs and the other by beating a boy to death with a shoe.

In Capote's *In Cold Blood*, Dick plans the robbery and murder because he thinks the Clutter family is "loaded." When he and Perry find no money their plans unravel and reveal to them the baseness of their greed, creating a strained moment that precipitates the murders. As Perry is searching through the daughter's purse, a silver dollar falls out and rolls under a chair. When he gets down on his hands and knees to look for it, he suddenly feels horribly humiliated. Then Dick says he is going to rape the daughter, and Perry stops him. As the two approach the father after these degrading experiences, Perry tells Dick that if they leave witnesses and are caught they will get a big sentence. The underlying motive of their need to preserve a shred of dignity in this debacle triggers what happens next, as Perry later revealed to a detective, "[Dick] was holding the knife. I asked him for it, and he gave it to me, and I said, 'All right, Dick. Here goes.' But I didn't mean it. I meant to call his bluff, make him argue me out of it, make him admit he was a phony and a coward. See, it was something between me and Dick. I knelt down beside Mr. Clutter, and the pain of kneeling—I thought of that goddamn dollar. Silver dollar. The shame. Disgust. . . . I didn't realize what I'd done till I heard the sound. Like somebody drowning" (276). After cutting Clutter's throat, Perry finishes him off with a shotgun and then kills the rest of his family. The initial greed that inspired the plan was so devalued in Perry's mind for a brief moment when he was down on all fours that he has to kill the witness to that humiliating self-revelation. In thinking back, he sees in that moment that both he and Dick were phonies and cowards and that he was reduced to terrorizing an entire family because of a dollar for which he had to crawl on all fours.

This crisis over the debased spoils of murder can be viewed against a broader historical crisis over the fall of the gold standard, which between roughly 1880 and 1914 provided a seemingly reliable standard for monetary value. During the nineteenth century, most accepted the intrinsic value of gold. Even Marx, who believed that money was a fetishized commodity, accommodated his study of capitalism to the representational function of gold. His chapter on money in *Capital* (1867) conceded that gold was "a universal measure of value."[22] Within a few years the Western world went onto a gold standard, which meant that currency was tied to a specific weight of gold, banknotes were convertible to gold on demand, and there were no restrictions on melting down gold coins. England fulfilled those requirements in the 1870s, as did Germany and the United States in the 1880s, and Austria-Hungary, Russia, and Japan, in the 1890s. The gold standard provided the appearance of full monetary representation as an economic transcendental signified. But the increasingly complex needs of international banking, with rapid transfer of money over vast distances facilitated by new communication technologies, made gold an impractical standard. The system collapsed in 1914 as the strain of war necessitated suspending convertibility.

After the war, Europe and the United States tried to return to the gold standard to retrieve prewar stability, but that attempt instead destabilized economies. Requiring Germany to pay war reparations in gold doomed its economy and created chronic instability with disastrous consequences. For Karl Polanyi, "belief in the gold standard was the faith of the age," and its collapse in the 1930s contributed to the collapse of the self-regulating market, balance-of-power diplomacy, and the liberal state.[23] This confluence of catastrophes brought about "the great transformation" of the liberal state.

During the postwar nostalgia for prewar stability, Gide wrote *The Counterfeiters* (1925), which was set in the months just before the outbreak of war in 1914. But unlike those who longed for the genuineness of the gold standard, Gide suggested that it was an artifice. His novel compared the representational function of money to that of language and used counterfeiting as a metaphor to suggest the unreliable representational function of all signifiers (i.e., coinages): gold, paper money, paternity, the state, religion, love, even his novel.[24] In it, characters pretend to be worth more than they are, ranging from a father and judge named *Profitendieu* (profit in God), who turns out to be neither paternal, just, nor religious, to Gide himself, who projects his role as author onto the character Edouard, who is struggling to write the novel we are reading but repeatedly subverts our belief that it refers to anything real, or even that he is its author.

In addition to the linguistic, paternal, and ethical counterfeitings, the novel is also about real counterfeiters, a group of young boys who pass counterfeit coins for kicks. When they are made to stop passing the coins they stage a counterfeit suicide that turns out to be a real murder. They tell timid Boris, who wants to join their group, that their motto is "The strong man cares nothing for life" (383). Their rite of passage is to draw slips of paper with their names on them, with the loser having to put a loaded gun to his head and fire. All the members believe that the gun will not be loaded except the one who plots the murder and puts in real bullets along with Boris who is too frightened to resist.

His murder was not motivated directly by greed but was carried out in the interest of personal gain after the conspirators were frustrated in passing counterfeit money. In place of that sport they created a counterfeit club of "strong men" (who are actually weak bullies), invented a counterfeit motto about how they cared nothing for life (while they cheated to make sure they did not pick the wrong slip of paper), and staged a counterfeit suicide with genuinely murderous consequences.

While March and Capote showed the tawdriness of murder for greed by having their murderers wind up with paltry loot, Gide decided to keep the suicide/murder out of his novel altogether, because it has such a paltry motive. As Edouard explains in the pages of his journal, "I should not like to put forward any fact which was not accounted for by a sufficiency of motive" (395). Gide could hardly have been more ironic. His early career was devoted to creating characters who act with an emphatic insufficiency of motive. Some even commit murder, as did Lafcadio. Gide/Edouard further distances himself from this debased murder by claiming that "Boris's suicide seems to me an *indecency*, for I was not expecting it" (395). The novels of Gide abound in "unforeseen" events, as, indeed, life itself is gratuitous and unforeseen. *The Counterfeiters* interrogates the causal grounding of money, motives, authorship, and murder.

Physiology of Emotions

Jealousy, revenge, and greed are complex emotions that develop over time. As such, they were well suited to motivate murder in novels, but they did not lend themselves to rigorous research by the experimental physiologists who concentrated at first on the more basic emotions, such as fear, anger, and shame. Therefore the history of that research provides a conceptually somewhat remote context for the emotions that I surveyed in this chapter. Still, by way of conclusion I will sketch that history because it is part of the broader cultural context for thinking about the causal role of emotions.

In the late nineteenth century, experimental physiologists found emotions such as fear and anger interfering with experiments designed to study other phenomena and so developed ways of working around them. As the historian Otniel Dror concluded, "Emotion signified the collapse of the laboratory's ideal of the animal-machine, of reliable control, predictability, replicability, and standardization."[25] In time, these interfering emotions became the subject of new research into how they affect phenomena such as digestion, blood pressure, metabolic rates, and blood sugar levels. This research was made possible by a series of new technologies for measuring physiological phenomena and making a visible record of the results.

In 1847 Carl Ludwig invented the kymograph to record changes in blood pressure on a revolving drum covered with sooted paper. This invention inaugurated the birth of modern physiology.[26] While earlier in the century Müller had concluded that the time between a nerve stimulus and a muscular response in frogs was "infinitely small and unmeasurable," the invention of more precise instruments and the refinement of experimental methods allowed that time to be measured. In 1850 Hermann von Helmholtz adapted an instrument patterned after Ludwig's kymograph to measure and record with unprecedented precision the velocity of a nerve impulse, a measurement that was crucial for the experimental study of the physiology of emotions.[27] Subsequent physiologists adapted other technologies to measure simple emotional reactions and create more precise permanent records of them as graphs and charts.

In the early 1860s the French physiologist Étienne-Jules Marey invented several graphic inscriptors that fulfilled four crucial requirements for more precise scientific experimentation.[28] They captured movements produced by physiological processes without interfering with them, made those movements visible without sacrificing their complexity, showed their temporal and spatial dimensions and the forces that produced them, and made a permanent and visible representation of them so they could be studied at a later time by more than one person. With these technologies Marey brought the precision of experiments in physics to physiological research. His first invention, the sphygmograph (1860), measured blood pressure by means of a lever with one end on the pulse of the wrist and the other attached to a stylus that scratched a line on a piece of moving, soot-blackened paper. It facilitated study of the precise sequence of the wrist pulse, the externally palpable heartbeat, and cardiac contractions. Other technologies Marey invented to study physiological processes include the thermograph to measure heat changes in the body (1864), the pneumograph for respiration (1865), and the myograph for muscular contractions (1864–66).[29] In 1865 Claude Bernard adapted Marey's sphygmograph to trace onto strips of paper the heart's response to emotional inputs. In 1873 Elie de Cyon drew on Bernard to explore further the connection between the heart and the brain and suggest how individual emotions leave distinctive curves on graph paper.[30] Marey's and Bernard's tracings and Cyon's curves offered the first permanent linear representations of the causal action of emotions and inaugurated a new era in the history of their scientific study.

In *The Expression of Emotions in Man and Animals* (1872), Darwin interpreted the animal origins of a wide range of emotions, such as hatred and anger, as reflected in human facial expression. He observed facial expressions of children for evidence of the human recapitulation of animal expressions. He studied the insane because, he noted, "they are liable to the strongest passions and give uncontrolled vent to them" (13). He showed photographs of the face of an old man to more than twenty "educated persons" to solicit their opinion as to what expression was represented. He studied the depiction of emotions in painting and sculpture and the expression of emotion among animals. Finally he circulated a questionnaire about emotions to missionaries for information about the expression of emotion in different races around the world. Darwin lent his great authority to the subject of emotions and stimulated widespread interest; his research was not based on experiment, however, but on highly subjective interpretations.

In 1884 the Italian physiologist Angelo Mosso published the first full-length physiological study devoted to a single emotion—fear.[31] A student of Lombroso, Mosso adapted several instruments to measure fear including a thermometer to measure changes in body temperature and a sphygmomanometer to measure and record on a graph changes in blood volume during stimulation. Mosso laid the foundation for a generation of researchers interested in the scientific study of emotions, including Charles Féré and Alfred Binet in France.[32]

Mosso also influenced the German physiologist Alfred Lehmann, whose new plethysmograph evolved into the best-known technology for measuring emotion—the polygraph, or lie detector. The prototype of the lie detector was Marey's own polygraph (1865)—a combination of several of his inventions that simultaneously measured pulse, heartbeat, respiration, and muscular contractions. The modern polygraph detects physiological phenomena produced by emotional states that accompany lying. As such it transformed understanding of the causal role of emotions in murder by detecting with unprecedented precision the most basic emotions of fear and anger that produce the most observable changes in respiration (pneumograph), electrical resistance of the skin (galvanograph), and blood pressure and pulse rate (cardiograph).

The historical significance of the polygraph embodies the specificity-uncertainty dialectic. It increased the specificity of causal knowledge by precisely measuring and recording bodily changes caused by emotions aroused by memory of the commission of a murder. The lines traced on blackened paper offered simple, precise images of linear causality, but they also suggested new questions about the complex emotions that produced them, and they were of course unable to explain any specific murder. The "poly" in polygraph referred to the multiplicity of signals that the technology could detect and record simultaneously, but the wired detectors were not hooked up to the mainsprings of past murders in real settings but merely to spots on the skin of subjects in laboratories. The causal knowledge was probabilistic in that interpretations of results were based on statistically calculated profiles of dishonesty that stemmed from all manner of guilty consciences. That statistical causal knowledge itself generated increasing uncertainty because the test results involved a large number of interacting causal factors that could be skewed by many uncontrollable circumstances. The measurable precision of the graphs was in sharp contrast with the imprecision and incompleteness of the interpretation. Even if the tests were completely reliable, which they were not, the information they supplied about the causes of a murder would have been minimal when viewed against the wide range of unanswered questions they did not even address. The lie detector indeed made the interior exterior and the private public, as many analysts noted, but this newly visible, public data represented only the hint of a complete causal explanation of the myriad interior and private causal factors involved.[33]

The most famous "discovery" of the emotions by an American researcher occurred in 1897, when Walter B. Cannon was using roentgen rays to study the digestive tract of cats and found that "reassuringly" stroking a struggling female cat altered its gastric movements.[34] Cannon subsequently elaborated his and other initially compartmentalized research into a broad synthetic study, *Bodily Changes in Pain, Hunger, Fear, and Rage* (1915). In contrast to earlier social philosophers who explained behavior in terms of the pleasure principle or a moral sense, he explained behavior as stemming from bodily functions, which humans share with lower animals. In contrast to earlier physiologists who concentrated on the function of specific organs during emotions, he focused on the emotions and drew together research on how they influenced various bodily organs and systems.

The increasing specificity of these new studies was revolutionary. As Dror concluded, during the first half of the twentieth century, physiologists elaborated these research methods and devised new instruments in "generating, releasing, inducing, amplifying, curtailing, prolonging, purifying, measuring, quantifying, temporizing, tracing, identifying, purging—controlling and manipulating the phenomenon called emotion."[35] For all the specific causal understanding that resulted from the new instrumentation and research that used them, new questions were posed and answered, creating ever more uncertainty.

MOLECULES OF EMOTION

Over the last thirty years, physiologists traced the causal role of emotions down to the molecular level where peptides and their receptors communicate the biological rudiments of emotion throughout a complex network of body systems and organs. Peptides are chains of amino acids, which are the fundamental building blocks of life. The first amino acid was isolated and analyzed in 1806. By 1936, after performing countless extractions from organic substances, physiologists had identified the remaining nineteen major amino acids in the human body. Chains of amino acids are polypeptides; those in the brain and nervous system are neuropeptides. Peptides that perform specific functions are proteins. Typical human cells may have as many as 10,000 different proteins, with an array of functions that have only begun to be identified. Receptors are protein molecules that lie on the surface of cells. They receive information from smaller molecules called ligands. These are found throughout the body, and some of them diffuse throughout it in the blood or cerebral-spinal fluid until they bind with their specific receptor. That binding with a receptor cell effects changes such as the manufacture of new proteins or the triggering of cell division. There are three types of ligands: neurotransmitters, which carry information across the gaps between nerves; steroids, which include the sex hormones that regulate sexual desire; and peptides, which in binding with their receptor cause numerous changes in the receptor's host cell and from there influence phenomena throughout the body such as pleasure, pain, attention, and emotion. Peptides and receptors are thus aptly described as *Molecules of Emotion*, the title of Candace Pert's memoir about her role in the discovery of their nature and function.[36]

The broader history of that discovery is one of ever more precise causal determination, part of a revolutionary shift in physiology from an electrical model to a more precise electrical and chemical model of the transmission of messages throughout the body. In the nineteenth century most physiologists believed that the transmission of messages along nerves and throughout the body from brain to toe and from nerve cell to nerve cell was entirely electrical, similar to the transmission of electricity through wires. An early challenge to a completely electrical model was the research of Claude Bernard on the poison curare, which causes paralysis by inhibiting the region of contact between nerves and muscles. His theory of a causally acting chemical was confirmed in 1906 by the Cambridge physiologist John Langley who experimented on the ability of curare to inhibit the stimulating action of nicotine in muscular contractions. Langley concluded that "the nervous impulse should not pass from nerve to muscle by an electrical discharge, but by the secretion of a special substance on the end of the nerve." He hypothesized that this chemical transmitter was binding to a "receptive substance" on muscle cells.[37] His theory of chemical transmission was confirmed in

1921 by Otto Loewi, who slowed the beat of a frog's heart by saturating it with juice released from the vagal nerve. He called the juice *Vagusstoff*, and a few years later demonstrated that it was the neurotransmitter acetylcholine. In subsequent experiments, acetylcholine was isolated and its chemical properties analyzed. In 1937 David Nachmansohn, a neurophysiologist at the Sorbonne, extracted and isolated acetylcholine from electric fish, and in 1972 Jean-Pierre Changeux of the Pasteur Institute of Paris first isolated its receptor.

The isolation and chemical analysis of peptides and their receptors required further technological precision and experimental refinement. In the early 1970s Pert, working at Johns Hopkins, began to study opiates that directly affect emotions. While other researchers had found receptors for chemicals made inside the body, such as insulin and acetylcholine, no one had found a receptor for drugs made outside the body, such as morphine and heroin. The search was especially important because these opiates were a major social problem, and researchers sponsored by governmental research institutes and pharmaceutical companies were avidly looking for nonaddictive substitutes. After Pert found the opiate receptor in 1972, others scrambled to find the natural opiate in the body for which the receptor existed. In 1975, working at the University of Aberdeen, John Hughes and Hans Kosterlitz isolated the brain's own morphine, an endogenous ligand that fit the opiate receptor and had the same causal impact on emotions as did exogenous opiates such as morphine. They called it enkephalin. Later, American researchers called their version of it endorphin, meaning endogenous morphine. This discovery revolutionized thinking about peptides, because it showed that enkephalin was produced in the brain and had a receptor in the brain that was responsible for pain relief in other parts of the body. These findings in turn suggested that other peptides with apparently local sources and effects might also be produced in the brain, bind with brain receptors, and influence moods and more complex behaviors throughout the body that derive from emotions.

This more networked view addressed an earlier debate about the nature of emotions between William James and his student Walter Cannon. In a famous article, "What Is an Emotion?" (1884), James argued that emotions originate in the body and visceral experience and are subsequently conceptualized and named by the mind. For example, we perceive an event (an insult), react bodily (weep), perceive our reaction, draw on memory and imagination, and finally label our reaction as an emotion (sadness). As he put it concisely, the correct argument is "that we feel sorry because we cry, angry because we strike, afraid because we tremble, and not that we cry, strike, or tremble, because we are sorry, angry, or fearful."[38] In opposition Cannon argued that emotions originate in the brain, specifically the hypothalamus, and then run down to the body through the neuronal connections and through secretions of the pituitary gland to bodily sites of emotion: pupils, salivary glands, heart, bronchi, stomach, intestines, bladder, sex organs, and adrenal glands.[39]

By the early 1980s Pert, Francis Schmitt at MIT, and others came to believe that emotions do not originate exclusively in either the body or the brain but in both together and are a manifestation of a simultaneous interaction of brain function, neurological transmission, and "information substances" including peptides. They offered a new model of "information exchange," with emotions caused by a chemical communication between cells (137). Using new autoradiographic techniques, Pert and others were able to identify where the neuropeptides were produced and bound to receptors and map how the system resembled the endocrine system, with peptides traveling like hormones to generate emotions.

While peptides do not directly cause murder, they do affect emotions, and one specific peptide, oxytocin (the first peptide to be synthesized artificially outside the body) may help prevent a class of murder—infanticide. As early as 1902 researchers knew that something in extracts from farm-animal pituitary glands helped women in labor. Over the years researchers learned further that the causally effective agent is the peptide oxytocin, which contracts uterine muscles in labor, produces uterine contractions during orgasms, stimulates maternal behavior, and stops infanticide in experimental animals and possibly also in humans.[40]

The increasingly specific knowledge of the causal role of peptides also increased uncertainties about them. Although the structure of peptides was simple, their effects could be "maddeningly complex," leading to their being classified variously as hormones, neurotransmitters, neuromodulators, growth factors, gut peptides, interleukins, cytokines, and chemokines (71). Peptides found in one part of the body were subsequently found to be produced in several other places with different functions. Peptide receptors were also distributed in various places in the body with different respective functions. Peptides that bound to kidney receptors to change blood pressure could also operate receptors in the lung to affect respiration and operate receptors in the brain to affect mood (70). Closer examination revealed that the receptors were also unstable and complex. The older view of ligands fitting into fixed and specific receptors like a lock and key proved to be overly simple. In fact receptors change shape and configuration while "vibrating and swaying rhythmically to some as yet unknown melodic key" (84). The more specific that knowledge of the causal role of peptides became, the more researchers realized the extraordinary complexity of life processes caused by them. The history of knowledge of peptides conforms to the specificity-uncertainty dialectic, just as do genes, hormones, and neurotransmitters.

The increasing specificity of knowledge about peptides did not influence novelists, but the increasing uncertainty of causal knowledge generally was shared by physiologists and novelists. Physiologists were awed by their incomplete knowledge of how the 10,000 different proteins affect the body or how the eighty or so peptides they knew about function at different binding sites, as well as what might be the function of the two hundred or so other peptides that they estimated are there to be discovered. Similarly novelists lived with their own version of increasing uncertainty in an increasingly unknowable world, where seemingly distinct emotions lie on the surface of complex underlying emotional insecurities about personal identity.

It is a long way conceptually from the simple emotional changes triggered by peptides to the complex emotions of jealousy, revenge, and greed that motivate murders in novels. That conceptual gap is evident in the novels, because while a few novelists invoked genes and hormones as part of their explanation for murders, none explained anything from peptides. While modern novelists probed deeper-lying causes of motivating emotions, that analysis led to explanations in terms of self-identity, not peptides. Characters in their novels kill out of jealousy, revenge, and greed—not, upon final analysis, to get relief by punishing an unfaithful lover, getting rid of a rival, or acquiring more money but because ultimately they are deficient and empty as human beings. After killing his enemies, Monte Cristo feels triumphant and fulfilled, confident that he has succeeded in making God's vengeance his very own. In contrast, after tricking the Gülleners to execute her former betrayer, Claire Zachanassian feels debased and empty. Dürrenmatt understood more than did Dumas that revenge may take its greatest toll on the self.

Modernist novelists made similar analyses of the underlying motives of jealousy and greed. In contrast to Victorian novelists who allowed their characters to revel in jealousy and act on it unambiguously, Sartre questioned the existential plenitude and monomaniacal focus of jealousy behind which he discerned a cluster of uncertainties about the possibility of being anything at all. His jealous assassin Hugo drags his existential doubt through the final act of *Dirty Hands*, trying unsuccessfully to salvage some reason for being anything at all. In the end he allows himself to be assassinated by party hacks in order to fabricate a politically respectable reason other than jealousy for his having killed Hoederer. Nabokov and DeLillo subjected jealousy to a trenchant analysis as their homicidal heroes wound up shooting at parodies of their own deficient selves.

Victorian novelists questioned the morality of greed but not its motivational force. Their murderers were greedy to the core and did not look for deeper-lying motives behind their desire for money, land, or gold. Modernists disclosed a desire for self-worth behind the pursuit of material gain. Broch and Ellis created characters motivated by greedy social ambition and addictive commercial desire that barely conceal profound insecurities about who they are as human beings in a world that is, in Broch's words, collapsing from a "disintegration of values." The most powerful dramatization of the existential emptiness behind greed was by Capote, who envisioned Perry wiping out the entire Clutter family because greed forced him onto his hands and knees to look for a silver dollar from a teenager's purse. It is inconceivable that Balzac's Vautrin or Norris's McTeague would have wound up in such a degrading posture over a dollar. By putting Perry in such a position Capote dramatized the lack of self-worth behind greed.

In my remaining chapters, this broad shift in thinking about causality in the direction of an increasing concern about acts of murder committed to define oneself as a self will be a central argument, along with interpretations of this shift in accord with the specificity-uncertainty dialectic.

6

Mind

AMONG THE MANY causal factors leading to murder, none is more complex than the mind. All the factors discussed in this book are rooted in the mind because its operation is necessary to their functioning. Hereditary endowment, childhood traumas, language, sexual desire, and emotions are mediated by the mind, as are social pressures and ideas—the focus of my remaining two chapters. The ubiquity of the mental aspects of experience might suggest that its function is also universal and transhistorical, but ideas about its causal role have a dynamic history. In historically distinctive ways, neuroscientists examined the brain to discover the organic seat of the mind, psychiatrists analyzed the disordered mind to understand the normal mind, jurists debated the nature of insanity and "the guilty mind" necessary to establish criminal responsibility and justify a conviction of murder, and novelists dramatized the workings of the mind behind everyday actions as well as murder.

This chapter will concentrate on concepts that were distinctive to either of the two periods I am contrasting. Nineteenth-century concepts such as craniology (Gall, c.1810), phrenology (Spurzheim, c.1819), monomania (Esquirol, c.1808), homicidal monomania (Georget, 1825), moral insanity (Prichard, 1835), impulsive insanity (Maudsley, 1874), born criminal (Lombroso, 1876), criminal brain (Benedikt, 1879), and moral epilepsy (Mann, 1883) disappeared from standard use in the modern period.[1] Conversely, in the earlier period, modern concepts were either imprecisely articulated, acknowledged but unacceptable, or unknown. Diminished responsibility was poorly understood and exerted little influence, irresistible impulse was highly suspect, and neurotransmission was unknown. Extending across these years was the increasing invocation of extenuating circumstance in murder trials, which transformed judgments of responsibility into heated debates among highly trained experts using increasingly precise explanatory systems and laboratory technologies. The movement of ideas was toward increasingly specific identifications of the cerebral location of mental functions and more precise definitions of "the guilty mind," creating new areas of study for professionals in neuroscience, psychiatry, and jurisprudence that generated more complex and probabilistic judgments of criminal responsibility and new epistemological uncertainties.

NEUROSCIENCE

Efforts to localize mental function in the brain go back to antiquity. Cerebral localization in the modern era began with the Austrian physician Franz Joseph Gall, who identified regions of the brain that he believed were the seat of specific mental faculties. He located in the brain mental functions, including the passions, which other researchers located in the heart and elsewhere. He pioneered localized cerebral anatomy, which he combined with faculty psychology to develop a theory of the mind that in 1807 he called *craniology*. It held that the human mind was divided into twenty-seven faculties whose specific functions depend on the organization of the cerebral cortex into specific "organs" that have a specific location in both cerebral hemispheres. The amount of the faculty that each organ contains varies directly with its size, which is also reflected in the shape of the skull, making it possible to infer the strength or weakness of an individual's faculties by viewing bumps on the skull in a procedure Gall called *cranioscopy*. Diagrams of these cerebral organs were therefore diagrams of the mind.

Gall's craniology was highly specific but, aside from his idea that the brain is the organ of the mind, invalid. His list of faculties of the mind is a mélange of "instincts, propensities, and talents" as well as "moral and intellectual dispositions" including firmness of purpose and veneration of the deity. In a four-volume treatise, *On the Functions of the Brain* (1822–26), he included seventy pages on the single faculty of "Destructiveness—Carnivorous Instinct; Disposition to Murder," located on the surface of the cerebral cortex across from the ears.[2] To document this location he recorded findings from prisons and asylums where he examined the heads of almost five hundred inmates, including murderers. His theory about the location of this faculty was based on anecdotal evidence, and it confused correlation with causality, as he reasoned that the organ of destructiveness was located inside the skull immediately across from the ears because this area was bigger in carnivores than in herbivores. That part of the skull was also prominent in a sadistic tyrant who delighted in watching executions, a student who liked to torture animals, an apothecary who became a public executioner, and a woman who committed infanticide. He also surveyed images of murderers in paintings that "bear the outward mark of a cruel and bloody character."[3] Gall concluded that the cerebral organ for destructiveness was more a predisposing factor than a sufficient cause of murder, but he still affirmed that the causal role of this organ, like that of all the others, was based on its size. As he wrote, "a person who has this organ large, will be more easily induced to commit homicide, than one not naturally disposed to it by his organization."[4]

Gall's main contribution to understanding the causal role of the mind was his work on cerebral localization. He performed skillful dissections of the brain to identify medullary structures, the optic tracts, and the nuclei of cranial nerves. His studies of fetuses from different gestational stages pioneered the field of developmental neuroanatomy. He insisted in principle on the importance of connecting local cerebral anatomy with associationist psychology but never managed to do so in practice and relied rather on spotty evidence to support his craniometrical speculations. He admitted being unable "to circumscribe exactly the extent of each organ," none of which conformed to the convolutions of the brain.[5] His insistence on a one-to-one correlation between brain structure and mental faculty was abandoned by later neuroscientists who came to view the connection as vastly more complex, with the entire brain participating in even the simplest cognitive functions. His location of the faculty of destructiveness was something of a lucky guess in that modern neuroscientists did have moderate success in reducing aggressive behavior by destroying areas of the amygdala and the hippocampus that were within the region of the brain that Gall designated as the organ of destructiveness.

Gall's craniological theorizing about the influence of bodily structure on mental function became extremely popular after Johann Spurzheim renamed the discipline *phrenology*, added more faculties, and took it on the road.[6] Phrenology was popularized in Great Britain by the Scottish philosopher George Combe, who emphasized its ability to reveal the complex inner secrets of the mind with easy-to-understand visual inspections. By 1832 there were twenty-nine phrenological societies in Great Britain, with Combe drawing more than a thousand listeners to some lectures. His *Constitution of Man* (1827) was a best-seller for its time, surpassed in popularity only by the Bible and *Pilgrim's Progress* in English-speaking homes.[7] During its heyday there were thousands of phrenological publications and hundreds of public lecturers on the subject, while phrenological heads adorned physicians' offices, suggesting that the practitioners knew where to locate the precise seat of mental functions and character traits. The precise lines on plaster models of skulls supposedly showing the exact location of distinct faculties, such as mirthfulness, secretiveness, and musicality, are vivid reminders of how much early nineteenth-century psychologists overestimated what phrenologists knew about the mind.

By 1840 phrenology was discredited in scientific circles, although along with physiognomy, an analogous system for reading character in the face, it continued to influence popular thinking and to aid novelists trying to express the mental makeup of their characters with easily visualizable descriptions for an expanding public of minimally educated first-generation readers. By the 1870s popularizers had illustrated the phrenological chart of mental faculties with pictures for each organ, as, for example, a tiger attacking a lamb for the faculty of destructiveness. As Roger Cooter concluded, "phrenology in the second half of the nineteenth century became in many ways more deeply entrenched than ever in everyday thought and expression."[8] In highly melodramatic Victorian sensation novels, moral and intelligent men had high brows, while criminals had low ones, although more sophisticated Victorian writers, acutely aware of the complexity of mental life, were wary of such simple reductionism, and their use of these two "sciences" was more decorative than explanatory.

Balzac drew on phrenology as well as on physiognomy to make his novels current with popular scientific theories but did not rely on the face or skull to explain character. In *Old Goriot* a medical student jokes about a "paternity bump" to explain why Goriot is devoted to his unworthy daughters, and after Vautrin's wig is knocked off, "everyone present instantly understood the manner of man Vautrin was," although no specific mention is made of character traits based on phrenological bumps (219). Phrenology influenced many other writers including Vigny, Poe, Melville, Baudelaire, Whitman, Emerson, Hawthorne, Peacock, Twain, Eliot, and Charlotte Brontë. Flaubert ridicules phrenology in *Madame Bovary* by having Emma's inept husband Charles receive a phrenological head for his birthday, symbolizing his medical incompetence, which has disastrous consequences.[9]

Victorian novelists also drew on physiognomy, although with measured credulity. In Elizabeth Gaskell's *Mary Barton* (1848), the public prosecutor explains to the court, "I am no physiognomist," but then he reads a murderous character into the face of the defendant Jem Wilson with his "low, resolute brow, his downcast eye, his white compressed lips," concluding, "I have seen a good number of murderers in my day, but I have seldom seen one with such marks of Cain on his countenance as the man at the bar." The literary critic Graeme Tytler, who documented dozens of other European novelists influenced by physiognomy, concluded than the theory was most often invoked to capture the tenor of popular thinking rather than to explain a character, and it was typically used ironically.[10]

Melville devoted two extraordinary chapters (79 and 80) to phrenological and physiognomical readings of the skull and face of "that murderous monster" Moby Dick more as a nod to current thinking about these "semi-sciences" than to capture the whale's character (155). "Such an enterprise would seem almost as hopeful as for Lavater [the theorizer of physiognomy] to have scrutinized the wrinkles on the Rock of Gibraltar, or for Gall to have mounted a ladder and manipulated the Dome of the Pantheon." Melville's application of these semi-sciences shows how unreliable they were. The whale's monstrous high forehead, which conceals a tiny brain, is physiognomically deceptive, as is the semi-crescentic depression in its middle, which is supposed to be a mark of genius. A phrenological reading of his skull would indicate poor self-esteem, whereas he in fact he cruises the seas fearlessly and strikes terror in the men who hunt him. Other serious Victorian novelists, like Melville, produced richly layered dramatizations implying a medley of causal factors that influence behavior, including economic and social pressures, moral and religious ideas, the ambient setting, and divine providence. Still, in their novels criminals were more likely to have oddly shaped skulls, low foreheads, protruding jaws, and shifty eyes than they were in modernist novels, and those phrenological and physiognomical characteristics were believed to be a sign of something about the mind within.

That historical claim is supported by further evidence from literature influenced by Lombroso, whose theory of "the born criminal" with a "criminal brain" recharged the reputation of phrenology and physiognomy and sparked interest in the new specialty of forensic psychiatry. His theory appealed to the age-old desire to read the complex mysteries of the human mind in simple bodily signs. Lombroso was an Italian physician inspired by Comte's positivism and therefore committed to empirical observation and measurement. His work and that of his followers committed to the use of science led to their work being tagged "the positivist school" of criminology. He was also influenced by evolutionary theory, from which he derived his idea that criminality was an atavism inherited from "savage" ancestors. As an army physician in the early 1860s he measured the bodies and heads of 3,000 soldiers to find anatomical differences throughout Italy. This research drew his attention to soldiers' obscene tattoos, which he correlated with crime, and then to mental patients who provided evidence for his innovative work in forensic psychiatry.[11]

In 1866 he made a breakthrough while studying the brain of the executed murderer Vilella. "At the sight of that skull," he recalled, "I seemed to see all of a sudden ... the problem of the nature of the criminal—an atavistic being who reproduces in his person the ferocious instincts of primitive humanity and the inferior animals." This insight into the evolutionary origins of the criminal type is followed by a huge leap to its explanation: "thus were explained anatomically the [born criminal's] enormous jaws, high cheek-bones, prominent superciliary arches ... excessive idleness, love of orgies, and the irresistible craving for evil for its own sake, the desire not only to extinguish life in the victim, but to mutilate the corpse, tear its flesh, and drink its blood." Vilella's brain exhibited two anomalies that Lombroso generalized into the brain of the criminal type—a depression in a part of the brain that he named the *median occipital fossa* and a vermis so enlarged that it resembled the middle cerebellum in birds.[12] He followed up his epiphany over Vilella's brain with extensive reading and research on the brains of criminals and epileptics, leading to his publication of *Criminal Man* in 1876, the grounding text for the new discipline of criminal anthropology.

At that time, local brain anatomy had made considerable progress since Gall, especially after 1861 when the French clinician Paul Broca localized the seat of spoken language.[13] Gall had localized language behind the eye orbits, based on a childhood intuition. Broca convincingly demonstrated that it was rather in the third frontal convolution, more posterior than Gall's location and off to the left side of the head, basing his findings on examination of the brain of a man who had suffered from loss of speech since childhood.[14] In 1870 the German researchers Gustav Fritsch and Eduard Hitzig discovered the location of a specific motor cortex in the brain and pioneered the new specialty of electroneurophysiology. Drawing from experiments using electrical stimulation of specific areas in the brains of dogs, they demonstrated that functions other than speech, such as motor activity, are cortically localized; that part of the cerebral cortex is electrically excitable; and that removing brain tissue can experimentally isolate and clarify precise features of brain organization and function.[15] In 1874 Carl Wernicke identified a specific cortical area that, when damaged, causes speech to be fluent but meaningless, subsequently called sensory aphasia or Wernicke's aphasia.[16]

Lombroso offered what seemed to be similarly precise anatomical evidence of criminality, which, he believed "explained anatomically" the big jaws and high cheekbones of criminals as well as their desire to kill. That conceptual leap—supported by abundant but flawed research—was the foundation for Lombroso's theory of the born criminal with atavistic physical stigmata and cerebral anomalies. It attracted considerable critical opposition almost immediately but also influenced criminologists, psychiatrists, and novelists until the early twentieth century. Throughout the 1880s criminologists contributed to these sorts of links between body type and criminal behavior with the new method of *bertillonage*, named after its inventor Alphonse Bertillon, a systematic way of identifying criminals based on multiple external measurements supplemented by photographs.

The idea of a criminal brain was suggested by earlier studies and then "confirmed" by a flood of studies following Lombroso.[17] In 1879 a French physician reported that the brains of thirty-six guillotined assassins shared pathological cerebral lesions.[18] That same year, the Austrian physician Moritz Benedikt reported that beheaded criminals revealed a deficiency of brain matter (gyrus) and a confluence of three major fissures (Rolando's, third frontal, and parietal) which tend to unite with the Sylvian fissure. His paper included extremely detailed reports and drawings of specific cerebral anatomies and concluded that "the brains of criminals exhibit a deviation from the normal type, and criminals are to be viewed as an anthropological variety of their species."[19] Numerous other Victorian anatomists supported Benedikt's specificity about the "confluent-fissure type," as it came to be known.[20]

Others dissented or equivocated. In 1882 Charles Mills doubted whether the fissure of Rolando could run into the fissure of Sylvius but did report finding in criminals' brains an excess of fissure development and deficient convolutions. He also speculated that Charles Guiteau, the assassin of President Garfield in 1881, might prove to be of "the confluent-fissure type."[21] Others found that the brains of individual murderers showed no anomalies.[22] In 1900 August Drähms, the chaplain at San Quentin Prison, summarized anthropometric studies of inmates, including forty-four murderers, along with students at Amherst College. He vacillated about a criminal type. "That defective brain organization and cranial asymmetry are oftentimes closely interrelated with moral and mental degeneration is undeniable; but that a causal relation is thereby proven to exist between such organic degeneration and the criminal propensity, or that mental alienation and moral defection necessarily verge one upon the other, is a position that cannot be maintained and [that] few would venture to affirm."[23]

Late Victorian crime novelists found Lombroso intriguing, if not fully convincing. Zola drew support for his theory of the hereditary origins of the Rougon-Maquart family's criminal propensities in Lombroso's hereditarian theory of the born criminal with telltale atavisms in the form of cranial and facial stigmata. In *La bête humaine* the most sympathetic murderer, tall and dark Jacques "with a round face and regular features," is good-looking enough to make plausible the passion that inflames his dark love for Severine, although his face is also "a little spoilt by an over-prominent jaw" (50). Signs of degeneration dominate in more thoroughly brutal or insane types. Roubaud is a walking checklist of Lombrosian criminal stigmata, with a flat head, low forehead, and eyebrows that meet over his nose (22). Pecqueux has a low brow and prominent jaw, while Cabuche, accused erroneously of a murder, still manifests immorality and mental deficiency: "The heavy face and low brow suggested the violence of a limited intelligence wholly governed by the impulse of the moment, but in the big mouth and square muzzle of a good-natured dog there was a need to be affectionate and submissive" (123–24).

The icon of Lombrosian criminality in the novel is *Dracula* (1897). As Mina Harker tells Professor Van Helsing, the Count is "a criminal type. Nordau and Lombroso would so classify him, and *qua* criminal he is of imperfectly formed mind." Van Helsing, who has studied recent philosophy of crime, explains that Dracula lacks a normal brain (439). Lombroso's characterization of the criminal included an aquiline nose (like a bird of prey's), bushy eyebrows that meet over the nose, and pointed ears. Dracula has those features. As Jonathan Harker notes: the Count's face is "aquiline, with high bridge of the thin nose and peculiarly arched nostrils." His eyebrows are "massive, almost meeting over the nose," and the tops of his ears are "extremely pointed." Evidence of his prehuman origins are hairs in the center of his palms (28). The Count's signature behavioral characteristic comes straight out of Lombroso's epiphany over Vilella's brain, which, Lombroso believed, evinced the murderer's destiny "to mutilate the corpse . . . and drink its blood." The broad impact of this rash theory in the late nineteenth century, as Daniel Pick has demonstrated, came from an effort to "represent, externalize and kill off a distinct constellation of contemporary fears," namely that the moral fiber and spiritual vigor of the Western world was degenerating.[24] Stoker adapted Lombroso to externalize and make manageable those fears in the form of a fictional monster who in the end is managed by being beheaded and stabbed through the heart.

In *The Secret Agent* (1907), Conrad used Lombroso to craft the appearance of criminalistic characters and, with some ambivalence, suggest a reason for their behavior. One of them is the mentally retarded Stevie, who had "a deep hollow at the base of his skull" and "degenerate" ear lobes—unmistakable Lombrosian signs of criminality. But this novel more importantly marked the waning of Lombroso's influence on English literature, because by the end of the story, Conrad has plunged a stake into the credibility of Lombroso's philosophy. The anarchist Comrade Ossipan is a fake doctor who espouses Lombroso with "nervous, jerky phrases" to dupe audiences. After seducing and robbing Winnie Verloc, Conrad narrates, Ossipan "gazed at her, and invoked Lombroso, as an Italian peasant recommends himself to his favorite saint. . . . He gazed at her cheeks, at her nose, at her eyes, at her ears . . . he gazed also at her teeth. . . . Not a doubt remained . . . a murdering type" (259). Demagogues like Ossipan invoke Lombroso like a religious incantation to fire their own enthusiasm and instill faith in their vulnerable followers. Another anarchist character, Karl Yundt, thinks that Lombroso was an "ass" who "made his way in this world of gorged fools by looking at the ears and teeth of a lot of poor, luckless devils" (77–78). Against the explanatory pretension of Lombroso, Conrad interprets his novel (as he explained in an author's note of 1920) in accord with Winnie Verloc's "tragic suspicion that 'life doesn't stand much looking into'" (41). She is a living refutation of Lombroso as she defies any external reading of her inner thoughts. To her husband she is an "unreadable stillness" (214). She sits under her dark veil "like a masked and mysterious visitor of impenetrable intentions." Her husband tears the veil away and finds "a still unreadable face, against which his nervous exasperation was shattered like a glass bubble flung against a rock" (230).[25] Conrad adds a final twist of complexity about the validity of Ossipan's reading of Winnie as a criminal type when she plunges a knife into her husband's chest.

The scholarly stake in the heart of Lombroso's criminal anthropology was Charles Goring's *The English Convict: A Statistical Study* of 1913.[26] This massive study of 3,000 English convicts, begun in 1902 and lasting six years, was based on statistical calculations by a team of researchers, including Karl Pearson, and it took another five years to write. In the opening sentence Goring indicted Lombroso's imprecision: "The recent application of exact and standardized methods to the study of anthropology has revealed the extent to which this science has been dominated and confused by conventional prejudices and unfounded beliefs." Lombroso's science was based on the notion that inward dispositions are revealed by outward bodily configurations. This invalid a priori assumption is akin to "the misnamed 'sciences' of phrenology, chiromancy, and physiognomy." The first specific argument Goring faulted is Lombroso's idea that the size of the head and the shape of the forehead "are reliable indices of character and intellectual worth." Goring further challenged Lombroso's sweeping generalizations based on the Vilella epiphany, his erratic definition of concepts such as criminality in confusing legal and biological terms, his inadequate controls (no comparing of criminals with the general population of the same economic and social class and level of intelligence), his impressionistic and subjective anatomico-pathological method of gathering data,[27] his confusion of correlation with causation (e.g., tattoos and criminality), and his unwarranted conclusions based on analogies and arguments from unrelated facts. Goring also assailed Lombroso's deficient statistical skills. Summarizing the techniques developed since 1876, the historian of criminology Marvin Wolfgang concluded that "Lombroso could not make use of the probable error, the significance of differences between means, the standard deviation, the coefficient of variation, the coefficient of correlation, the chi-square, the coefficient of mean square contingency."[28]

The development of these sophisticated statistical techniques constituted a revolution in the history of science. They sharpened causal understanding by identifying margins of error and discriminating more precisely the effective causal variables out of an increasing number of possible variables. In so doing they helped sort out genuine causality as a

statistical probability from the fanciful absolute causality based on anecdotal data and random correlations that compromised many earlier
thinkers. Genuine causal theorizing is testable by other researchers and
can be used as a basis for prediction, neither of which could be done successfully with Lombroso's theory of the born criminal. The application
of these new statistical techniques in criminology as well as other social
sciences is evidence of the increasing appreciation of statistical probability in causal understanding generally, one of the five major aspects
of the specificity-uncertainty dialectic. Theodore Porter has surveyed
the discovery of a number of these techniques of modern mathematical statistics, beginning in 1893 when Pearson first contacted Galton
and took up the study of statistics. "The correlation coefficient was defined mathematically in 1896, contingency analysis and the chi-square
test in 1900, the t-test and its distribution defined by W. S. Gosset
(Student) in 1908. Analysis of variance derives from a paper by Fisher
in 1918."[29] These techniques enabled modern researchers to assign a
more precise magnitude to the relative causal efficacy of each one of
an increasing number of factors in the natural and social sciences,
thereby refining but also limiting their causal explanations generally.
These more limited explanations underscored the probability of error
inherent in all causal knowledge, which also implied greater uncertainty, at least as compared with the absolute causal determinism in
Gall and Lombroso.

NEUROPHYSIOLOGY OF AGGRESSION, VIOLENCE, AND MURDER

While Goring assaulted the clinical findings of Lombrosians, other researchers were pioneering neuroscience at the cellular and molecular
level in ways that in turn revolutionized brain anatomy and understanding of the cerebral location of specific mental functions, including aggression and violence, that can lead to murder.

Until the 1880s the major techniques for studying the brain and
mind were brain lesions and ablations, clinical analysis of people with
brain injuries, electrical stimulation experiments, and autopsies of
criminals and mental patients. Victorian histologists, who studied
tissues through microscopes, were unable to identify individual nerve
cells in the brain or nervous system because tissue samples appeared to
be tangled multinucleated masses with a common pool of cytoplasm,

and so they theorized that nervous impulses travel in an interconnected reticulum or fused network.[30]

This conception was challenged by the Spanish histologist Santiago Ramón y Cajal, who refined a silver nitrate staining technique that enabled him to determine that nerve cells are discrete and to infer the existence of gaps between them.[31] At a conference in 1889, Cajal argued that nerve cells are independent entities, which he demonstrated with impressive slides made with the new stain showing in unprecedented detail that axons were elongated extensions that end discretely in terminal nobs. He also demonstrated that axons and dendrites transmit information in one direction only; axons send it to other nerve cells or muscle cells, while dendrites only receive it.[32] In 1891 Wilhelm Waldeyer called these nerve cells *neurons*, and Cajal's theory soon became known as the neurone theory.[33] In 1897 Charles Sherrington coined the term *synapsis* (later synapse) to refer to these hypothesized gaps between neurons. Cajal's neuron theory was based not on actual observation of the synaptic gap but on inferences from the one-way nature of nervous transmission and on experiments by Sherrington and others on nerve cell degeneration that seemed to preclude the reticular theory.[34] Visual evidence was not possible until the synaptic gap was actually seen under electron microscopes in the 1950s.[35]

Affirming a gap between neurons left open the question of how impulses crossed it. Theories divided between electrical and chemical processes. In the early twentieth century, physiologists began to identify chemical transmission processes that had stimulatory and inhibitory effects. Stimulation could be explained with an electrical mechanism, but inhibition could only be explained chemically. The first chemical that received serious attention was adrenaline. In 1904 Thomas Renton Elliot speculated that "adrenalin might then be the substance liberated when the nervous stimulus arrives at the periphery." Between 1906 and 1910 Henry Dale reported on further experiments with nervous transmission accelerated by adrenalin.[36] The decisive experiment that convinced the scientific community of the chemical nature of nervous transmission was performed in 1921 by Otto Loewi. He extracted the inhibitory chemical from nerves leading to a frog's heart, cut the inhibitory nerves to the heart of a second frog, applied the extracted chemical, and observed the heartbeat become slower. He repeated the experiment with the stimulating chemical leading to a frog's heart and was able to accelerate the heartbeat in another frog. This experiment offered compelling evidence for the chemical transmission of inhibiting and stimulating nerve impulses.[37]

The first neurotransmitter correctly identified was acetylcholine, following Loewi's experiments in the 1920s. In 1933 Dale proposed new terms for the two basic chemical neurotransmissional functions: cholinergic (inhibitory) and adrenergic (stimulating). In the 1940s researchers identified other important neurotransmitters that seemed to play a causal role in a number of emotions such as aggression. The neurotransmitter adrenaline was identified by the Swedish researcher Ulf von Euler in 1946 as noradrenaline (or norepinephrine). In the 1940s, researchers identified serotonin and, in the 1950s, dopamine. By 1960, four main neurotransmitters had been identified; by 1980, around fifty had been discovered.

One neurotransmitter that plays a role in aggression is serotonin. The following sketch of its production and function draws from my own limited knowledge of neuroscience and is therefore but a minute fraction of the detailed knowledge of current neuroscience, which is dwarfed by the increasingly vast realm of uncertainty and ignorance that looms around it. I offer this sketch of what neuroscientists currently know about the causal role of serotonin in greater detail than I have presented the causal role of genes, hormones, or peptides, to offer a sense of how extraordinarily detailed and precise modern science has become. This account also provides a basis for understanding the historical significance of research relating serotonin to violence and murder.

Serotonin is synthesized from the amino acid tryptophan, which humans get from protein in their diet. In the brain, tryptophan is converted to serotonin in a two-step reaction, with each step catalyzed by a different enzyme and then transferred to storage vesicles in neurons.[38] Neurons are characterized by the neurotransmitter they produce and release. Stimulation of a serotonin-producing neuron, itself a complex process, causes synaptic vesicles to fuse with the plasma membrane and release their serotonin into the synaptic gap. The rate of that release is controlled by autoreceptors that give the neuron feedback about the amount of serotonin in the gap. The released serotonin traverses the gap to bind to postsynaptic receptors. These are proteins that are specific for particular neurotransmitters and may activate signals from a single neuron or from up to 10,000 out of the approximately 100 billion neurons in the brain. Serotonin function is also affected by other chemicals that perform three main functions: they either bind to serotonin before it can stimulate its receptor, compete with it by fitting into serotonin receptors, or must be copresent with serotonin to stimulate a receptor.

The sequence of events from a stimulated receptor to gross behavior such as acts of aggression adds more specificity as well as complexity and uncertainty to the causal picture.[39] Overall, only around one in a thousand brain neurons is serotogenic. Serotogenic neurons concentrate in nine cell clusters in the base of the brain that send out three nerve pathways, one of which enters the limbic part of the brain and affects emotions in ways not well understood. The reticular formation at the top of the brain stem receives signals resulting from behavior perceived as a threat from the sensory system through a maze of hugely complicated interneuronal circuits. That part of the brain filters out the most important information for immediate response and sends it to the limbic brain for emotional action, to the cortex for cognitive action, and to the thalamus and hippocampus, setting off a danger signal in the hypothalamus, which secretes norepinephrine. At the same time, the adrenal gland secretes adrenalin, which activates norepinephrine to prepare the body for fight-or-flight responses by dilating the pupils to let in more light, accelerating the heart to make more blood available to muscles, expanding the lungs to enhance respiration, and so on—a reaction first elaborated by Walter Cannon in 1915.[40] The key role of the hypothalamus in aggression was demonstrated in experiments in the 1950s in which electrical stimulation of the anterior hypothalamus of a cornered cat caused it to manifest aggression by spitting, extending its claws, and lashing its tail. Dozens of other experiments with brain stimulations, lesions, and ablations of the hypothalamus and other parts of the brain of cats and other animals, however, have shown how variable such single-stimulus outcomes may be and therefore how probabilistic and uncertain any generalized theory of fear-induced aggression must be.[41]

Studies of the impact of serotonin on behavior are based on measurements of serotonin levels in urine, blood, and cerebrospinal fluid, each of which give different readings and offer only an approximate measure of the brain's serotonin level, which is itself an average and does not specify serotonin concentrations in critically important regions of the brain. Studies on mice, rats, and monkeys reveal that elevated levels of aggressive behavior in animals correlate significantly with low levels of serotonin. Thus serotonin acts as a brake on aggression. High serotonin levels also correlate with high social status and dominance behavior. One study reported that dominant male monkeys have twice the blood serotonin level of subordinate males. Moreover the causal arrow goes both ways, because "social experience produces changes in neurochemistry," that is, up or down changes in social status cause corresponding changes in serotonin levels. While mindful of the many limitations of these findings and the added uncertainties raised by applying them to humans, the study concludes that "there is a robust link between diminished serotonergic function and destructive aggression."[42]

These animal studies underscore the uncertainties in generalizing such findings to aggression in humans, in whom so many other biological and environmental factors are operative—including interactions among fifty neurotransmitters along with hormones, peptides, proteins, enzymes, and trace elements.[43] In addition, human aggression itself has many modes. Whereas earlier researchers believed that it was a single emotional response, recent researchers have specified a variety of aggressions: predatory, competitive, defensive, irritative, territorial, maternal protective, female social, sex-related, and instrumental. As the authors of this list concluded in 1988, "human aggression remains largely a puzzle."[44]

Elaborating this research to the causal role of serotonin in murder has been difficult. An early suggestive study in 1979 found a strong inverse correlation between serotonin levels and a life history of aggression among twenty six U.S. military men.[45] In 1983, a Finnish study of thirty six murderers and attempted murderers concluded that a low serotonin level "was more a marker of impulsivity than of violence per se," because it correlated with those who had acted impulsively as compared with those who planned a murder.[46] That hypothesis stimulated subsequent studies that raised increasingly sophisticated questions about the causal role of serotonin, including its complex interactions with norepinephrine and dopamine. A study in 1987 found that arsonists and men with a history of impulsive criminal violence had lower serotonin levels than a control group.[47] In 1998 two researchers noted that the many studies of serotonin and aggression provided only indirect evidence of its role in murder, and few related it directly to violent crime. Their survey of the research field concluded that given the small number of studies and their inconsistent findings for a direct causal influence of serotonin on violent behavior, the evidence that serotonin plays such a role "should be viewed cautiously."[48]

The history of research I have tracked, from Gall's unsupported theorizing based on correlations between gross brain anatomy and behavior to the precise research into molecules that operate across synaptic gaps of twenty to fifty billionths of a meter in a mere fraction of a second, reveals a pattern that, as I have noted, is also evident in the history of discoveries of other tiny causally acting entities such as genes, hormones, and peptides. The common pattern of those histories is one of increasingly precise knowledge of ever smaller causal entities generating at the same time increasingly vast realms of uncertainty and lack of knowledge that become more vividly delineated and sometimes actually visible, as when the electron microscope revealed new depths of inquiry about unprecedented small structures moving through ever more minute spaces as a consequence of complex biochemical and environmental interactions. Calculations of these processes also involved increasingly sophisticated statistical mathematics, producing more carefully qualified probabilistic explanations, further hedged by cautions about the enormous complexity and provisional nature of that causal knowledge as it inches its way into the expanding realm of the unknown.

Neuroscientists have sharpened the specificity of their understanding of a great deal about the workings of the brain, especially at the single neuronal level—for example, about which specific ion channels are involved in generating action potentials and propagating them along axons, or how impulses jump across synapses. But causal knowledge of single neuronal activity is an extremely long way from causal knowledge of gross behavior. A single neuron can transmit impulses to thousands of other postsynaptic neurons and in turn can receive impulses from thousands of other presynaptic neurons, and there are billions of neurons in the brain. Thus the complexity of explaining gross behavior at the neuronal level is enormous. At present neuroscientists know very little about how such cellular and molecular activities enable us to learn, remember, think, and speak. The underlying bases for emotions are even more obscure. Neuroscientists have precise knowledge of drugs that can alter emotions, stimulations that can evoke them, ablations that can distort them, and genes that can alter them, but they have no idea what these emotions are in electrochemical terms. These functions of the mind, as distinct from functions of nerve cells, are emergent properties that cannot now be predicted on the basis of the elements that make up lower levels of organization, such as ion channels, ionic currents, and ligand-receptor interactions. The increasing specificity of neuroscientific knowledge at the microscopic level underscores the vast realm of ignorance about the causal missing links that would be necessary to explain the enormously complex emergent properties of macroscopic human mental life.

The few Victorian fictional references to microscopic causes of action in the brain and nervous system of murderers are vague and imprecise. In the preface to *Thérèse Raquin*, Zola explained that his murderers were "completely dominated by their nerves and blood," although he had no idea how. Dostoevsky mocked the idea of microscopic causal agents working in the mind of the murderous Karamazov brothers. Mitya complains to Alyosha that his friend Rakitin is writing an article influenced by that "scoundrel" Claude Bernard, which will explain Mitya's supposed murder by "little nerves in the head" with "wiggly little tails." Contempt for science fuels his further exclamation that he feels "sorry for God . . . Your Holiness, shove over a little, here comes Chemistry!" (738–39). In an essay of 1890, Tolstoy speculated that Raskolnikov's action in *Crime and Punishment* was caused by "barely perceptible changes in the area of consciousness," by which Tolstoy meant incidental psychic events, not tiny biological entities.[49]

Modern novelists ventured into neuroscience tentatively. In *Lafcadio's Adventures*, neuroscientific research does not explain murders but rather causes them with "diabolical instruments." In the novel Gide denigrates such experiments designed to "reduce all animal activities to what [the researcher Anthime] termed 'tropisms,'" because they require him to blind, deafen, emasculate, skin, and brain his experimental animals by means of lesions and ablations (8). In *The Murder of Roger Ackroyd*, Agatha Christie was more respectful of the findings of modern neuroscience when she has her famous sleuth Hercule Poirot boast about his discerning "little gray cells" (92).

The only novel I found in which neurotransmitters help explain a murder is DeLillo's *White Noise*.[50] Jack Gladney's son Heinrich, who plays chess by mail with an imprisoned mass murderer, replies to Jack's question about what he wants to do with his summer: "Who knows what I want to do? . . . Isn't it all a question of brain chemistry, signals going back and forth, electrical energy in the cortex?" Motivation is "just some kind of nerve impulse in the brain . . . an accidental flash in the medulla. . . . Isn't that why Tommy Roy killed those people?" (45–46). Jack's wife becomes addicted to Dylar, a drug that, she explains, "interacts with neurotransmitters in the brain" and induces the brain to make inhibitors that deactivate the "fear-of-death part of the brain" (193, 200). The exchange closes with Jack asking rhetorically, "What about murderous rage? A murderer used to have a certain fearsome size to him. His crime was large. What happens when we reduce it to cells and molecules?" (200). Jack acts out a partial answer to that question during his attempted murder of the man who supplied his wife with Dylar, as he narrates, "I sensed molecules active in my brain, moving along neural pathways" (306). While Jack takes this pop neuroscience seriously, DeLillo was skeptical, as he distanced himself from any neuroscientific reductionism by offering a number of social and interpersonal circumstances working on both Tommy Roy and especially Jack. Still it is of considerable historical significance that he mentioned neurotransmitters as contributing to an attempted murder.

This use of neurotransmitters to explain a murder includes every feature of the specificity-uncertainty dialectic. Based on modern science, it increases the specificity of causal understanding by invoking the causal action of a recently discovered, if fictionalized, tiny biochemical substance. Dylar functions in a web of interactions among many other newly discovered causally acting substances such as neurotransmitters, hormones, and peptides. Understanding of the causal action and interaction of these entities on gross human behavior is highly probabilistic, although sharpened by increasingly reliable statistical techniques that make it possible to isolate and measure causal variables with increasing mathematical exactitude. But in spite of the impressive new theoretical and statistical techniques for dealing with these many new causal entities, the probabilistic understanding of behavior that any comprehensive account of their combined actions necessitates opens into an increasingly dark and uncharted realm. DeLillo travestied that darkness by following his account of the causal role of neurotransmitters with an attempted murder that sputters to a farcical end, narrated by a murderer who does not know what he is doing or why.

PSYCHIATRY

The thrust of Victorian psychiatry was to describe symptoms, group them into illness clusters, and classify these according to conceptual schemes derived mainly from Lockean associationist psychology or

Kantian epistemology. During the nineteenth century, psychiatric treatises became large compilations of case histories classified with increasingly complex nomenclatures. Descriptions of illnesses were the
emphasis, while causal explanations were thin on direct evidence. They
tended to be a miscellany of four kinds of causal factors—predisposing,
exciting, physical, and moral—that included such dubious specifics as
excessive brain work, luxurious habits, masturbation, gluttony, "terrifying tales in early life," and "a loaded colon."[51] In 1838 William Mosley
listed thirty-one specific causes, including lightning, gambling, and
the sight of a public execution.[52] Physiological explanations included
"cerebro-mental" hypotheses about the causal role of diseased spinal
cords, ganglia, and brains, although no one could explain how these organic disorders caused specific mental illnesses.[53] Other causal explanations were circular, as when moral insanity was explained from a
breakdown of the moral faculty. The confusion about causality is further illustrated by the profusion of treatments—many of which were
ineffective and sometimes harmful—that physicians used to treat mental illness: opiates, emetics, purgatives, enemas, blistering, bleeding,
starving, cold baths, refrigeration of the head, gyration (swinging),
fresh air, confinement, seclusion, restraint, surprise, electric shock,
ovarian pressure, clitoral cauterization, and ovariotomies.[54]

An important mental illness in the history of psychiatry is hysteria,
with its visible, bizarre, mercurial symptoms. Causal explanations
were wildly inaccurate, beginning with ancient theories of wandering
wombs and Renaissance theories of demonic possession. In the early
nineteenth century, as Mark Micale argued, physicians engaged in "a
long and largely sterile debate . . . over the precise anatomical seat of
the disease" in the female sex organs or the brain, and none successfully demonstrated any clear causal connection between either bodily
source and the symptoms. Others argued circularly that its cause was a
"hysterical constitution" or "hysterical temperament." Psychiatrists
generally concurred that hysteria was a functional nervous disorder—
that is, a disturbance of some function without an observable lesion or
organic change—but by focusing on functions they avoided having to
specify its causes. In numerous case histories relevant to hysteria published between 1878 and 1893, the eminent French neurologist Jean-
Martin Charcot argued that the malady was caused by some lesion in
the nervous system that interfered with neurological functioning, although he never found the lesion.[55] Among the assortment of other

causes that psychiatrists guessed might be etiologically significant for hysteria were temperament, climate, diet, fits of jealousy, powerful grief, unrequited love, reading novels, masturbation, sexual frustration, sexual excess, and "acute disturbances of the soul."[56]

Psychiatric explanation of the specific etiology of hysteria was transformed in the 1880s and 1890s under the influence of the germ theory of disease. Earlier in the century, as K. Codell Carter showed, medical writers "were remarkably indifferent to the *causes* of symptoms."[57] At that time, causal explanations of disease were vague and confused and therefore largely neglected. Diseases were explained by imprecise descriptions such as an inflammation of the lungs or a softening of the brain or, when even such nebulous causal speculations were not feasible, by a grouping of "morbid states" or symptoms. As Carter noted, "in 1849 the *Cyclopedia of Practical Medicine* listed more than thirty different schemes for classifying diseases, [and] not one of them was by cause" (260). The germ theory revolutionized medical thinking; it demonstrated conclusively that specific microorganisms caused specific symptoms to make possible for the first time a coherent and unified explanation of the epidemiology, symptoms, and course of a specific disease. In 1884 Adolf Strümpell urged developing a causal theory of hysteria modeled more precisely after the germ theory of disease.[58] Four years later Paul Möbius attempted such an application in suggesting that hysterical symptoms are "caused by ideas," and he urged that the means for finding these causes be modeled after the methods of investigating infectious diseases.

In the 1890s Freud adapted the new germ theory of disease as a model for explaining hysteria and devised a therapy to address specific etiological factors. He replaced Charcot's symptomatic theory with an etiological one and elaborated Möbius's causally acting simple ideas into causally acting complex repressed memories, wishes, and impulses that are transformed during specific stages of psychosexual development by a host of erotogenic stimuli, traumatic experiences, and unconscious mental process.[59] The opening sentence of *Studies on Hysteria* (1895) announced that his research had revealed that the "precipitating cause" of the many cases of hysteria was a psychic trauma. Drawing from the imagery of the germ theory, he added that "the trauma—or more precisely the memory of the trauma—*acts like a foreign body* which long after its entry must continue to be regarded as an agent that is still at work" (emphasis added).[60] Drawing from the history of germ theory, he explained that hysteria offered "a clinical picture which has been empirically discovered and is based on observation, in just the same way as tubercular pulmonary phthisis."[61]

In 1895 Freud returned to his analogy between the causes of tuberculosis and the causes of mental illness with his theory of hysteria, which was based on an "etiological equation" that formalized the relation between several kinds of causes—preconditional, specific, and auxiliary.[62] For tuberculosis, the precondition is hereditary endowment, the specific cause is the bacillus *kochii*, the auxiliary causes are anything that diminishes the body's powers to fight it, such as colds. For hysteria, the precondition is also heredity, the specific causes are sexual factors, and the auxiliary causes are emotion, exhaustion, or illness. Although Freud's subsequent analyses did not attempt to diagnose hysteria by "solving" the etiological equation, this formulation makes clear the probabilistic nature of his causal thinking, because any solution would be based on assigning magnitudes to the causal factors and then calculating the probability of a specific mental illness resulting from the confluence of their relative etiological forces.

In "Heredity and the Etiology of the Neuroses" (1896), Freud sought "to establish a constant etiological relation between a particular cause and a particular neurotic effect in such a way that each of the major neuroses [could] be attributed to a specific etiology." Each neurosis, he added, "has as its immediate cause one particular disturbance of the economics of the nervous system," which is itself caused by a disorder of a patient's recent sexual life or important past events.[63] He never succeeded in establishing a universal and specific etiology for specific neuroses, but still, with this formulation, he moved his theory clearly into the framework of the germ theory of disease with his unprecedented precise account of the etiology of mental illness. His subsequent theories of neurosis would further complicate the etiological picture by adding sexual fantasies to actual childhood sexual seductions reworked retroactively at the unconscious level. These traumatic causal germs were sometimes directly related to the subsequent symptoms but often only under disguise by means of self-deceiving symbols and other defensive measures, all under the force of repression, so that the patient not only does not recognize the connection but resists acknowledging it during therapy. Freud's causal theory was far more specific than Victorian accounts, while at the same time it suggested new questions that his predecessors never thought to ask and that proved to be increasingly difficult to answer. Thus, under Freud's influence, psychiatric understanding of the mind moved in the direction of increasing specificity, multiplicity, complexity, probability, and uncertainty.

MENTAL ILLNESS AND MURDER

The disorders most relevant to the history of ideas about the causal role of mental illness in murder in the Victorian era are monomania and split personality. Early Victorian psychiatric explanations of murder focused on monomania, specifically its subcategory, homicidal monomania. The prefix *mono-* referred not to its cause, however, but to the singular content of its motivating delusion. The disease was first named by Esquirol around 1808. By 1830 it was one of the most frequent diagnoses at French mental hospitals, although by 1870 it fell into disuse.[64] Its popularity coincided with the authority of physical causes, which for monomania Esquirol theorized to be something that no anatomist could localize—"lesions of the will." In explaining how such a lesioned will works, or fails to work, in causing monomania, Esquirol underscored the gaps of his theory: "The patient is drawn away from his accustomed course to the commission of acts which neither reason nor sentiment determine, which conscience rebukes and which the will has no longer the power to control."[65] With the cause of monomania a lack of reason, emotion, and control, studies of it bypassed its cause to focus on its symptoms and course, emphasizing the characteristic obsessive ideas and emotional agitation.

In 1819 Esquirol classified several monomanias by their ideational obsession, as with theomania (religious), erotomania (sexual), and demonomania (demons).[66] In a pamphlet of 1825, his student Etienne-Jean Georget named a variant of this malady *homicidal monomania* to explain a number of recent sensational court cases in which someone suddenly killed for no apparent reason at all.[67] Homicidal monomania was more extensive than Esquirol's other monomanias because it also involved action; like the others it was caused by a lesion of the intellect (delirium) that was responsible for the obsessional idea, but it was further caused by a lesion of the will that made it impossible to resist the impulse to kill. In the next few years psychiatrists debated its nature and function, although their theories were based on case histories that did not specify what caused the lesions of intellect or will.

Psychiatrists were also unable to explain how homicidal monomania led to a murder beyond reference to the murderer's delusion that the victim was a threat or that some voice ordered the murder. The critical focus of such speculation was the degree of criminal intent involved in murders. Such speculation was the forum for the new professional specialty that would eventually become forensic psychiatry. Georget's 1825 pamphlet defended the new profession, which he proposed should be staffed by new *médecins des aliénés*, who would play a major role in murder trials. The following year a physician used the diagnosis of *monomanie homicide* to defend a murderess, Henriette Cornier, who had suddenly and inexplicably killed a neighbor's child. His testimony was the first time this diagnosis was used in a criminal case.[68] Over the next few years several important works for and against the diagnosis of homicidal monomania appeared along with a major treatise on forensic psychiatry.[69]

Homicidal monomania was confusing. It had no clear cause, it referred to a great many symptoms and disease patterns, it caused many possible effects, and accounts of them centered on a metaphor (lesion of the will) borrowed from physiology. This confusion was magnified by the number of terms for this disorder: monomanie meurtrière, mélancholie homicide, homicidal mania, homicidal insanity, instinctive monomanie, moral epilepsy, and, beginning in the late 1880s, paranoia.[70] It nevertheless was widely used by murder novelists because the scientific jargon gave a gloss of professional expertise to their subject and, more important, because it seemed to make murders more easily comprehensible with several powerful narrative features: the implication of a unified personality, the cohesiveness of a psychiatric case history, the appearance of a single explanation, and a simple sensational label.[71]

Victorian writers routinely used monomania to explain murders. By invoking it to account for the behavior of others, Balzac's murderer Vautrin in fact sketches a self-analysis: "these people get their teeth into one idea and you can't shake them loose from it. They are thirsty, but only for water taken from one particular well. . . . To get a drink of it they would sell their very soul to the devil" (71). In Poe's "The Tell-Tale Heart" an obsession with the filmy eye of an old man leads to a murder, although the cause of the obsession remains a mystery, as the murderer himself explains. "It is impossible to say how first the idea entered my brain: but, once conceived, it haunted me day and night." Poe left the mechanism of that deeper cause of this monomania a blank, as did contemporary psychiatrists. In *Our Mutual Friend*, Eugene Wrayburn dismisses Bradley Headstone as "a curious monomaniac" (294). Lady Audley (in *Lady Audley's Secret*) diagnoses her pursuer with monomania in a thinly disguised confession of her own homicidal madness. In this condition, she explains to her husband, "the mind becomes stationary; the brain stagnates . . . the thinking power of the brain resolves itself into a monotone, . . . and perpetual reflection upon one subject resolves itself into monomania" (287). Lady Audley's explanation of monomania concentrates on the obsessive idea itself and offers no account of the deeper characterological structures and developmental experiences that make someone vulnerable to obsessions. In *Crime and Punishment* Dostoevsky tags Raskolnikov as a monomaniac, as does a physician in the story, Dr. Zosimov, whose diagnosis includes a typical Victorian miscellany of "many complex moral and material influences, anxieties, apprehensions, worries, certain ideas . . . and other things," to which he adds "a certain fixed idea, some indication of monomania" (23, 175).

The classic monomaniac is Captain Ahab. A dozen times Melville refers to him as such, for example, "his narrow-flowing monomania," "his monomaniac revenge," "his monomaniac mind" (161–62, 385). Ahab's universe is pervaded by his obsession: the crew shares it, and even the whale is a "monomaniac incarnation" of what is eating at Ahab. The ultimate source of Ahab's "monomaniac mind" is not the loss of a leg but rather "the direct issue of some former woe." Yet, like psychiatrists of that time, Melville offers no details about that woe, and of course in his time a determinative childhood trauma would have been absurdly out of scale with the immensity of Ahab's tragic character and his gargantuan nemesis. A specific etiology is, for Melville, unknowable because, as he explains through his narrator Ishmael, "to trail the genealogies of these high mortal miseries carries us at last among the sourceless primogenitures of the gods" (386). *Sourceless* means of undeterminable cause, and explanations in terms of the gods are, to say the least, unverifiable. In Victorian monomania the highly specific focus of the obsession, as well as the immediate incident that triggers it, contrasts with the unspecificity of its deeper-lying and temporally remote causes and the generative processes leading to their sequelae in the disease itself.

Moving in the direction of increasing multiplicity and complexity, Victorian explanations of the connection between mental illness and murder shifted from earlier emphases on monomania to later emphases on split personalities. In 1861 Broca's localization of language function in the left brain provided stunning experimental evidence for psychic dualism. Subsequent localizations that disclosed other asymmetrical brain functions sparked interest in the double brain for the remainder of the century. Ann Harrington reconstructed this "veritable smorgasbord of speculation" in the natural and social sciences: evolutionary theories of higher and lower types, philosophical debates about the self divided over such issues as free will versus determinism, psychiatric theories of a second unconscious self, occult belief in spiritualism and hypnotism providing access to alternative selves, clinical studies of divided personalities, and in popular thinking a sharp dichotomy between the "'good guys' and the 'bad guys' of the nineteenth-century bourgeois imagination." Drawing from the critic Masao Miyoshi, Harrington noted that Victorians often saw these polarities "in rigid pairs—all or nothing, white or black."[72] In the early twentieth century the resurgence of interest in whole brain function led to an eclipse of interest in the double brain research. Psychiatric studies focused on mental fragmentation in schizophrenia, in which the personality was in shambles rather than neatly divided between two distinct selves. The split implied by *schizo-* in modern psychiatry was not between different personalities (a separate disorder called multiple personality) but between components of a shattered personality and a confusing and threateningly complex world.

In nineteenth-century fiction a sharp human duality ranged widely from the numerous *Doppelgänger* characters in German fiction, including the two souls beating in the breast of Goethe's Faust, to the "polar twins" in the "consciousness" of Stevenson's Jekyll/Hyde. This latter duality is also manifested in the face and body, so that the change from Jekyll to Hyde is visible and so horrific that witnessing it kills Jekyll's friend Dr. Lanyon. This story is historically transitional. It reflects Victorian thinking in that the duality is between conventional categories of good and evil—as Jekyll puts it, "those provinces of good and ill which divide and compound man's dual nature" and which in his case are separated by a "deeper trench" than normal (42). It is also Victorian because those mental provinces take charge one after another not as a result of earlier traumas and developmental stress but after taking a mysterious drug. The transformation Lanyon observes is a sensational scene straight out of Victorian melodrama, because after swallowing the drug Jekyll cries out, reels, staggers, clutches, and gasps. Finally, Jekyll's explanation of Hyde's character uses moralistic evolutionary phrasing similar to the final sentence of *On the Origin of Species*, when he narrates that Hyde "bore the stamp of the lower elements in my soul."[73]

The story looks toward modernism, however, in that the explanation for murder, and for human behavior in general, points beyond the current state of thinking about a singular monomania and even beyond a basic duality to a later theorizing about greater mental multiplicity and complexity. As Jekyll himself speculates: "I say two [elements of consciousness], because the state of my own knowledge does not pass beyond that point. Others will follow . . . and I hazard the guess that man will ultimately be known for a mere policy of multifarious, incongruous, and independent denizens" (43).

Modernist murder novels abound with multifarious and incongruous denizens, a term that evokes alien inhabitants who do not belong anywhere, like Joseph K., Lafcadio, and Clyde Griffiths. They are not anchored in a wise Dr. Jekyll, and their minds are not split neatly between good and evil but fragmented under the pressure of estrangement and conflict, struggling to maintain a sense of identity in a clash of shifting and uncertain values.

In Kafka's *The Trial*, Joseph K.'s crime, his own as well as that of others against him, is not *caused by* a mental illness but *is* his mind itself, which fragments with every step he takes to discover whatever he did that might have been wrong, prove his "innocence," and learn what others might have done or will be doing to him. He is further fragmented psychically not between polar twins of good and evil but as he unravels mentally with every effort to reestablish his identity. He is also fractured hierarchically within his own mind in creating layers of conspiracy against him by all those who appear to persecute him, from the two warders who arrest him to the inspectors, lawyers, courts, and executioners whose persecutions underscore his guilt. K.'s effort to understand enacts the specificity-uncertainty dialectic. His journey into the tangled maze of the court system and the meaning of the law moves him closer to more specific understanding of whatever he may have done or whatever is being done to him but at the same time opens up one of the prototypical unfathomable spaces of modern literature, the space of the court and the law, which becomes more incomprehensible with every discovery he makes.

Gide assailed the concept of monomania along with the overbearing psychological determinism of the realist and naturalist novel with both his fictional murderer Lafcadio, who murders for the sake of murdering without a motive, and his novelist character Julius, who wants to write about such a murder. Lafcadio makes Gide's case in criticizing Julius's last book: "I should let myself die of hunger if I had nothing before me but such a hash of bare bones as the logic you feed your characters on." Lafcadio further chastises Julius for the way the hero of his last book, he charges, was "always and everywhere consistent with you and with himself—faithful to his duties and his principles— to your theories." When Lafcadio boasts that he himself is "a creature of inconsequence," Julius counters that "there is no such thing as inconsequence—in psychology any more than in physics" (82). Gide might have conceded that acting out of inconsequence is self- contradictory and therefore impossible, but in spite of this illogicality, with this exchange Gide registered his historically pointed objection to earlier novels about monomaniacal murderers as well as any other char- acters who are presented as singularly and unambiguously motivated.

Gide's stance against the deterministic psychology that lies behind the theory of monomania is further evinced in his journals. In entries of 1918 he assailed the two hundred years of psychological determinism that followed from La Rochefoucauld's reduction of all the impulses of the human heart to *amour-propre* and the consequent dominion of ex- planatory theories generally. Gide added, "Dostoevsky's greatness lies in the fact that he never reduced the world to a theory. . . . Balzac con- stantly sought a theory of passions; it was great luck for him that he never found it." In 1921, while working on the opening pages of *The Counterfeiters*, he noted, "I shall not be satisfied unless I succeed in get- ting still farther from realism."[74]

The murder plot in Dreiser's *An American Tragedy* is hatched in the mind of an unraveling personality. Clyde is not clearly divided be- tween good and evil selves and does not experience them serially dur- ing brief and discrete episodes from taking a drug; he is strained to the limit from conflicting impulses that grip him simultaneously and mount over many years as a consequence of his own shaky values and "none-too-forceful mind" (442). Dreiser crafted the slow emergence of Clyde's murder plot, beginning with his unsuccessful attempt to help Roberta get an abortion, which to Clyde means killing a fetus. Beginning with that first thought of killing, Clyde's distress grows for

more than a hundred pages packed with an ongoing interior monologue as the murder plot to get rid of Roberta emerges against layers
of tenacious resistence. "He must not allow such a thought to enter his
mind, never . . . and yet—and yet. . . . He was an excellent swimmer . . .
whereas Roberta could not swim. And then . . . Death! Murder! . . .
but he must not think of that! the death of that unborn child, too!"
(440–41). In anguish Clyde pulls away from Sondra, whose vanity
moves her to pursue him more eagerly, thereby increasing his desire
for her and his need to be rid of Roberta, "but no, no, no—not that.
He was not a murderer" (451). Slowly Clyde allows himself to think
through details of the plot. He could upset the boat, but she might
cling to it. "To prevent a thing like that he would have to—to—but
no—he was not like that—hit any one—a girl—Roberta—and when
drowning or struggling. Oh, no, no—no such thing as that! Impossible . . . and yet—and yet—these thoughts. The solution—if he wanted
one. The way to stay here—not leave—marry Sondra—be rid of
Roberta, and all—all—for the price of a little courage or daring. But
no!" (461). Then he realizes that if he thinks of such things, "he had
better think well. . . . But he was not! He could not! He, Clyde Griffiths, could not be serious about a thing like this. . . . And yet" (462).
The psychic forces come from a spectrum of conflicts that emerge out
of Clyde's past and present life—religious, moral, sexual, social, financial, familial—his tender feelings for Roberta, thoughts about the unborn child, plans for the future. The murder plot climaxes with the
death of Roberta in a boating accident that follows Clyde's plan except
that at the decisive moment he is gripped by doubt and loses his nerve.
She senses something is wrong, stands up in the boat and reaches toward him imploringly, when he pushes her away to "free himself of
her—her touch—her pleading—consoling sympathy" (492). She falls
and hits the side of the boat, causing it to shift. He reaches for her,
again in conflict, "half to assist or recapture her and half to apologize
for the unintended blow." This conflict capsizes the boat, and when he
sees her in the water he is paralyzed by more conflict and does nothing
to save her.

This reconstruction of the emergence of a murder plot in Clyde's
mind is historical in a number of respects. It contrasts with recon-
structions of the mental state of earlier fictional murderers based on
theories about monomania or the split personality, and it also evinces
the specificity-uncertainty dialectic. The emergence of Clyde's plot is

more gradual than the emergence of the murder plots for his Victorian predecessors, and its roots go back to his early childhood. Clyde is more ambivalent about murder than were his predecessors, such as Raskolnikov, who had nothing but contempt for the old pawnbroker, or Frollo, who felt nothing but lustful rage against Esmeralda. Even though Clyde becomes obsessed with ridding himself of Roberta, he is no monomaniac like Ahab—because there is no specific trigger for his obsession, because his personality is fragmented and his feelings are conflicted, and because at the decisive moment he cannot act. He is also not cleanly split like Jekyll and Hyde but crippled by a weak ego that is driven by instinctual urges and social pressures over which he has no control. The external object of his conflict is clearly represented by two women and two courses of action, but his is no dual personality. It is rather a single personality torn between two courses of action that grip him not serially but simultaneously, hence all the "and yet's" and "but no's" in his interior monologue. The moral framework of Victorian interpretations of murderers does not apply to Clyde, who has not lost his "moral faculty" but rather struggles with issues of right and wrong to the point of paralyzing him when his plan dictates that he push Roberta into the water. Dreiser captured Clyde's conflict in greater detail than was typical of Victorian murder novelists, who enlisted readers' attention with less ambivalent murderers. That ambivalence and Clyde's final paralysis are signs of his complexity, which Dreiser explored at length in the last part of the novel about Clyde's trial, which reveals the difficulty the legal system has in establishing a murderer's guilty mind.

In the modern period, murder novelists abandoned the sensational monomanias of the Victorian period and moved beyond the dichotomous villain and hero of melodrama, in particular beyond the sharp dualism that Stevenson added to the lexicon of homicide with his famous split personality of Jekyll and Hyde. For the modernists, the homicidal impulse lurks in the mind not as a raging monomania or as a defect split between personalities but as an abiding threat that emerges out of a splintered mind and sometimes also out of a traumatic past. Novelists also shy away from the moralistic framework of a dichotomous good and evil in favor of a wider-ranging descriptive and interpretive language, which they use to assail "the test" for criminal responsibility that for more than a hundred years was based on knowledge of right and wrong.

Insanity, the Guilty Mind, and Criminal Responsibility

The history of ideas about the causal role of insanity in murder is extremely complex because the two professions most concerned with it, jurisprudence and psychiatry, had clashing concepts, values, and goals. Insanity was a singular legal concept that had no place in psychiatric nosologies made up of numerous mental illnesses. As physicians, psychiatrists vowed to cure the sick, while as servants of the state, jurists vowed to judge the accused. Psychiatrists were concerned with the causes of mental illness and its treatment, while jurists were concerned with the effects of insanity and its control. Psychiatrists sought to expand understanding of the causes and effects of mental illness and liberalize the grounds for the insanity defense, while prosecutors sought to restrict those grounds to avoid allowing evil murderers to escape punishment "by reason of insanity." Law aimed for all-or-nothing judgments of innocence or guilt, while psychiatry aimed for subtle and gradational interpretations of mental health. These clashing concepts, values, and goals met in the charged forum of murder trials, where life and death were at stake. The authority of forensic psychiatrists who attempted to reconcile these differences was assailed during withering cross-examinations when they appeared in court as expert witnesses. The conceptual focus of these contests was the nature of *mens rea*, the guilty mind, which prosecutors had to establish to secure convictions. The history of thinking about this concept offers a convoluted instance of the specificity-uncertainty dialectic, because the effort of psychiatrists as well as jurists to define the causal role of insanity more precisely was met with powerful resistance, and the courts repeatedly retreated to narrow definitions of it.

The major starting point of Anglo-American legal thinking in my period of study is the "McNaughtan rule" of 1843. It held that a person is guilty of murder unless at the time of committing the act he did not know what he was doing or at least did not know that it was wrong. The narrowness of this definition can be seen against a sketch of the prehistory of attempts to define legal insanity.

Since antiquity, jurists recognized that extreme mental disorder can lead to a killing, and they were reluctant to judge and punish such acts as murder with malicious intent. The earliest recognition of exculpatory insanity in English law was by the thirteenth-century judge

Henry Bracton. He argued that the "state of mind gives meaning to [an] act, and a crime is not committed unless the intent to injure intervene."[75] Thus courts could exonerate a killer if he did not have the intent necessary for a guilty mind. For centuries, only total "madness" or "lunacy" led to such exoneration. In a trial of 1724 the presiding judge Robert Tracy instructed the jury that a killer cannot be found guilty if at the time of the killing he "could not distinguish between good and evil and did not know what he did." Tracy cautioned the jury, however, that for an accused to be exonerated the evidence must be overwhelming; he must be "totally deprived of his understanding and memory" and "not know what he is doing, no more than an infant, than a brute, or a wild beast."[76] In the early nineteenth century, English courts began to widen the grounds for the insanity defense. In the trial of James Hadfield in 1800, the defense attorney Thomas Erskine asked the judge to allow the jury to consider that not only raving madness but also delusions or derangement may lead a man to kill even though he understands what he is doing and knows that it is wrong. In instructing the jury that "if a man is in a deranged state of mind at the time, he is not criminally responsible for his acts," Judge Kenyon wrote new law, and Hadfield was found not guilty by reason of insanity.

Since 1800, thinking relevant to the insanity plea expanded to include a number of exonerating circumstances as psychiatrists and jurists attempted to define the causal role of insanity in murder and analyze more precisely the criminal mind. In 1802 the French psychiatrist Philippe Pinel introduced the diagnosis of *manie sans délire* (insanity without delusion), which expanded insanity to disorders of mental functions other than the intellect or reason. In 1835 the English alienist James Prichard introduced the new concept of *moral insanity*, which referred to a defect of the emotions and the will without any defect of the intellect, a disorder that could trigger killings during a momentary *irresistible impulse*.

In 1842 Prichard elaborated that connection. In moral insanity "the will is occasionally under the influence of an impulse, which suddenly drives the person afflicted to [commit murder]. . . . The impulse is accompanied by consciousness; but it is in some instances irresistible."[77] Making impulsive acts exculpatory raised the problem of distinguishing irresistible impulse (ground for an insanity plea) from unresisted impulse (ground for a murder conviction). That problem was dramatized when irresistible impulse became the basis for acquitting Daniel McNaughtan in 1843. While delusional, McNaughtan killed the secretary of Prime Minister Robert Peel. His lawyer drew on Isaac Ray's classic text of forensic psychiatry, *A Treatise on the Medical Jurisprudence of Insanity* (1838), in arguing successfully that "modern science has incontrovertibly established that any one of these intellectual and moral functions of the mind may be subject to separate disease, and thereby man may be rendered ... the slave of uncontrollable impulses."[78] The Queen and Parliament were incensed at the verdict of "not guilty on the ground of insanity" and urged the House of Lords to convene judges of the Queen's Bench to clarify the grounds for criminal insanity. Their findings, condensed into what became the McNaughtan rule, became the basis for insanity pleas for more than a hundred years. It held that an insanity defense must show that "at the time of committing the act, the accused was labouring under such a defect of reason, from disease of the mind, as not to know the nature and quality of the act he was doing, or if he did know it, that he did not know he was doing what was wrong." This rule, based solely on the cognitive capability of the accused with no allowance for emotional or volitional disorders, wiped out the flexibility in insanity pleas that had occasionally surfaced over the centuries and sometimes included irresistible impulse.

In subsequent years the McNaughtan rule, or the "right-wrong test," became the all-or-nothing criterion against which more flexible theories of insanity were directed. In 1855 the leading English jurist James Fitzjames Stephen backed off from an earlier strict reading of *McNaughtan*, and his draft of the Criminal Code Bill of 1879 urged extending *McNaughtan* to include irresistible impulse, "unless the absence of the power of control has been caused by [the accused's] own default." In opposition, a royal commission of 1879 argued that such a test for distinguishing an exculpatory irresistible impulse from a criminal motive was too vague to be entrusted to a jury, and the bill was defeated. Still, by the 1880s an increasing number of insanity pleas took into account innovative psychiatric testimony about the criminal's state of mind.

In the last quarter of the nineteenth century, notions of criminal responsibility shifted from a narrow interpretation to a broad one that increasingly allowed new specialized medical and psychiatric expertise to influence judgments.[79] The Criminal Lunacy Act of 1884 required examination of death sentence prisoners to ensure against executing lunatics. In 1894 a new Medico-Legal Association considered amending the McNaughtan rule. As one member of the association wrote, "the

McNaughtan rules are dying a natural death. . . . perhaps our best plan is to let them." In 1882, Home Secretary William Harcourt proposed making it necessary to prove willful intent to apply the death penalty, but his bill was defeated. "Yet," as Martin J. Wiener concluded, "if voluntarist principles had been preserved and statutory reform of murder law rebuffed, the idea of semi-responsibility was becoming ever more rooted in practice. From the late 1870s, a rising proportion of those indicted for murder were found mentally incompetent at some stage of the criminal justice process. . . . For one category of offender after another, qualifications to the norm of personal responsibility were increasingly being noted."[80] Even with the McNaughtan rule unchanged, English jurists acknowledged more exonerating circumstances for murder and applied them in an increasing number of insanity defenses, pressuring the justice system to accept an expanding range of etiological factors for an increasing variety of mental disorders.

This historical development accelerated in Scotland beginning in 1867, when its courts introduced the concept of *diminished responsibility*, which directly challenged the narrow *McNaughtan* test. Thereafter irresistible impulse was one of several kinds of mental experiences that could diminish responsibility under Scottish law. In the United States a series of trials in New Hampshire through 1871 led to a new standard, ultimately known as the New Hampshire rule, requiring juries to acquit if the killing "was the offspring or product of mental disease in the defendant."[81]

In other countries, jurists also drew from new expertise in neurology, psychiatry, and sociology to expand the list of extenuating circumstances that made more detailed and, for many, more complicated judgments of responsibility. More precise, or at least more flexible, diagnostic categories such as temporary insanity, partial insanity, irresistible impulse, and diminished responsibility in England, and *folie raisonnante* and *folie périodique* in France, replaced the more dichotomous categories of sane and insane traditionally used in determinations of responsibility.[82] Such individualization is evidence of an increasing specificity of knowledge about the causes of crime.

These more specific diagnostic categories also disclosed more gaps in the earlier notions of the causal chain of personal responsibility. For the early Victorians, as Wiener noted, "tropes of consequentialism" permeated legal discourse. Evidence of increasing nonconsequentialism includes the shift away from strict interpretations of individual responsibility based on linear and determinist explanatory models. The notion of law itself became less deterministic as legal realists shifted its basis from a one-and-only God-given law forged out of a single tradition and imposed through a rigorous chain of command to an ever-changing set of laws determined by an array of fluid social and historical developments. As a result, attributions of criminal responsibility became increasingly pragmatic, relativistic, and uncertain. In 1907 William James expressed frustration at the persistence of the ancient "common sense" equation of causality with blame: "Causal influence, again! This, if anything, seems to have been an antediluvian conception; for we find primitive men thinking that almost everything is significant and can exert influence of some sort. The search for the more definite influences seems to have started in the question: 'Who, or what, is to blame?'—for any illness, namely, or disaster, or untoward thing."[83]

An assault on *McNaughtan* began after 1945. During World War II, psychological tests had been used to choose persons for military service, assign and train them for tasks that included killing, and evaluate their ability to function under fire. The war also produced thousands of mentally ill veterans, emotionally crippled by their proximity to killing or by their role in it, who needed psychiatric diagnosis and treatment, all of which elevated dependency on and respect for psychiatry. Throughout the 1950s psychiatrists whittled away at the McNaughtan rule's narrow definition of premeditation, malice, and criminal intent and often succeeded in reducing charges from first-degree murder to manslaughter.[84] In 1954 the United States established the Durham rule, which was similar to the New Hampshire rule in that "the accused is not criminally responsible if his unlawful act was the product of mental disease or defect."[85] As in the wake of the New Hampshire rule, Durham jurists debated endlessly the meaning of *product* with all its causal possibilities, and the concept of *mental disease*, which opened up testimony to a far wider range of mental functions than the ability to know right from wrong. The Homicide Act of 1957 finally overturned *McNaughtan* in England and established by statute the principle of diminished responsibility due to mental illness. The same principle was written into American law in 1959 with *People v. Gorshen*.

The increasing specificity of psychiatric and jurisprudential analyses of the causal role of mental illness in murder drew from increasingly probing analysis of ideas about the mind, character, identity, free will, morality, and responsibility. Victorian thinkers believed that the seat of the self or soul was located in the brain or mind of human beings; it operates like the pilot in a ship and guides a person through life as an autonomous agent. Character is made up of a set of specific faculties, which, if not anatomically localizable, are present in all human beings as variable strengths or weaknesses. Personal identity evolves additively in time, as experiences are registered in consciousness, recorded in memory, and integrated into the personality. While subject to external pressures, individuals are nevertheless internally coherent agents with the capacity to choose courses of action for which they are fully responsible. As autonomous individuals capable of choosing right from wrong, they are moral agents. If they kill another with malice aforethought and at the time of the killing are cognitively aware that what they are doing is wrong, they have committed murder, for which they are responsible and must be punished, no matter how emotionally distraught their minds might be.

This view of the coherent and autonomous self was the subject of broad interrogation in the modern period. Modern thinkers concurred that the mind is centered in the brain, but they became increasingly aware of interactions among the brain, hormones, neuropeptides, neurotransmitters, and other neurobiological processes throughout the body which influenced mind, character, and emotions. They questioned the stability of individual autonomy as they became increasingly aware of impinging social and historical forces as well as linguistic conventions, unconscious mental processes, early childhood traumas, and sexual drives. For modernists, personal identity evolves in time not additively, as a sum of memories, but psychodynamically, as the outcome of traumas and crises involving challenges to the autonomy of a self that appears to be increasingly fragmented and uncertain. Individuals are not simply free to choose between good and evil but adrift in a sea of freedom, struggling to find a normative basis for action as the moral code based on a religious framework lost its earlier unimpeachable status. Individuals are not poised between good and evil but perplexed by an array of existential choices over issues that transcend morality and involve rather choosing what it means to be fully human. The Victorian image of a moral agent struggling before the witness of God to resist evil and embrace goodness is, for the moderns, a quaint self-deception that screens the vertiginous choices that modern man faces entirely alone without any divine witness, let alone savior.

These developments in thinking about the self are interwoven with a dramatic recreation of the role of the mind in murder in Musil's novel

The Man without Qualities (1933), about two outsiders who embody the characteristics of man in the modern age. The story is set just before World War I but also captures some of the building tensions of the interwar years. Ulrich is the man without qualities, that is, a man without conventional characteristics. Moosbrugger is a mentally deranged loner who commits a brutal sex-murder and then haunts Ulrich's thoughts. Musil's rendering of their interrelated lives is intended to capture modernist thinking about the character of modern man and the mind of a murderer.

Musil emphasizes the multiplicity, complexity, and probabilistic nature of the forces or qualities that shape mental life in the modern world as well as the increasing uncertainty of understanding of their interactions. Ulrich explains that things have become more complicated because people are subjected to a wider range of causally acting forces. "Just as we swim in water, we also swim in a sea of fire, a storm of electricity, a firmament of magnetism, a swamp of warmth, and so on." No mechanical deterministic explanation of this set of forces is possible, and "all that finally remains is formulas" (65). In a dissertation on Ernst Mach written in 1908, Musil had argued that in the modern world causality is no longer deterministic but is rather a probabilistic functional relation that must be expressed with formulas.[86] In the novel, Ulrich's friend Walter notes the multiplicity of causal forces that must be factored into such formulas. "Everything has a hundred aspects, every aspect a hundred connections, and different feelings are attached to every one of them. The human brain has happily split things apart, [and] what everyone of us needs today more than anything else is simplicity" (65–66).

Musil adapts the language of phenomenology, which he learned as a student of Edmund Husserl, to describe the gruesome murder of a prostitute through the mind of the murderer himself. Panicked because she would not go away and confused about the border between self and other, he slits her throat and stabs her in the abdomen more than thirty times to cut her out of himself in an act of self-definition, which Musil reconstructs with a detailed phenomenological description of the murderer's consciousness from the moment he tries to escape her clutches to his final brutal stabbings.

When the court attempts to make sense of the killing, Musil's phenomenology of a murder from within comes into sharper relief. The judge's questions—such as "Why did you wipe the blood off your hands?" and "Why did you throw the knife away?"—are intended to establish knowledge of right and wrong as a basis for a conviction. But while the judge sees those actions and Moosbrugger's guilt as a coherent whole, Moosbrugger sees them as "a series of completely separate incidents having nothing to do with one another, each of which had a different cause that lay outside [him]." In the judge's view Moosbrugger is the source of these autonomous acts for which he is responsible, while "in Moosbrugger's eyes they had perched on him like birds that had flown in from somewhere or other." Inarticulate and confused, incapable of expressing "the strange, shadowy reasonings of his mind," he is found guilty and sentenced to death (75).

In the following weeks Ulrich becomes obsessed with this case. The clarity and finality of the guilty judgment and death sentence contrasts with Ulrich's sense of the arbitrariness of all judgments and value distinctions. To him everything seems scattered and blurred. "Nothing in him was moved by cause, purpose, or physical desire, but everything went rippling out in circle after ever-renewed circle" (131). The ready-made distinctions of good and evil, innocent and guilty become unreliable as Ulrich contemplates Moosbrugger's fate, and it flashes on him that "one could just as easily devour people as build monuments" (136). Without belief in God, there is no sufficient reason why things turn out as they do. "This uncertainty gave Ulrich's personal problem a broader context. In earlier times one had an easier conscience about being a person than one does today." Nowadays personal autonomy and private experiences are swamped by impersonal forces and collective symbols.

This general confusion of self and other, personal and collective is exaggerated in Moosbrugger, who literally does not know whether his frightening voices and visions come from himself or the outside world. The judgments of Moosbrugger by the prosecutor, court, press, and local gossips are worlds apart from what he experiences from within, and Musil uses that contrast to indict the Austrian judicial system and reigning ideas about personal identity, free will, morality, and criminal responsibility. These criticisms stem from Ulrich's philosophy of "living hypothetically," which he does to avoid committing to any given order, because "no thing, no self, no form, no principle is safe, everything is undergoing an invisible but ceaseless transformation" (269).

Later he tags this philosophy "essayism," which means living experimentally by exploring life from many sides. Like pragmatism, this philosophy rejects absolute truths and single points of view and embraces partial, perspectival truths applicable to specific situations. It views causal understanding as probabilistic and uncertain. The law of world history is one of "muddling through." "The course of history was therefore not that of a billiard ball—which, once it is hit, takes a definite line—but resembles the movement of clouds, or the path of a man sauntering through the streets, turned aside by a shadow here, a crowd there, an unusual architectural outcrop, until at last he arrives at a place he never knew or meant to go to" (396). Human actions must be experienced in many ways, with understanding depending on shifting circumstances. "All moral events take place in a field of energy whose constellation charges them with meaning. They contain good and evil the way an atom contains the possibilities of certain chemical combinations" (270). Morality is not grounded absolutely in Judeo-Christian commandments but is an experimental, generative force, a provisional and unstable system of values that shifts with social and historical developments.

A fixed criminal justice system based on knowledge of Christian good and evil, patterned after the primordial discovery of that distinction in the Garden of Eden, cannot do justice to the complexity of the human mind in the modern world, even in its most obvious and brutal criminal deviations. Simple dichotomous right-wrong tests for insanity are destined to bring about injustice. "Ulrich regarded morality as it is commonly understood as nothing more than the senile form of a system of energies that cannot be confused with what it originally was without losing ethical force" (271). In the modern world, morality was losing ethical force because it lost its ground in absolute religious faith and had not found another.

Ulrich despairs of any solution to this moral crisis, as it was reflected in the Austrian criminal justice system that came down on Moosbrugger, flaunting its spiritual exhaustion and logical ineptitude. He questions that system as it is defended by his father, a professor of law, who rejects the modern concept of diminished responsibility as a dodge for the "morally feebleminded" (342). His father is suspicious of recent uses of the insanity defense by the accused who are sane but claim that at the time of the killing they were delusional. He insists that the law must hold people responsible for killings if they knew that their act was wrong, regardless of any supposed diminished responsibility from an impairment of the will because of a permanent delusion or a momentary irresistible impulse.

Musil explores this suspicion of insanity in a chapter titled "To the Legal Mind, Insanity Is an All-or-Nothing Proposition" (583–88). It

treats the clashing views about the insanity defense in a committee con-
voked by the Austrian Ministry of Justice to update the penal code. One
member, Ulrich's father, argues that a partially insane person should be
acquitted only if there is evidence that he was deluded into acting in a
way that would exempt him from liability, for example, deluded that the
victim was trying to kill him. In opposition a Professor Schwung argues
that an accused should be acquitted only if at the precise moment of the
act he was unable to control himself. The committee debates these alternatives with increasingly illogical thinking and deliberate misunderstanding until forced to disband in chaos. It reconvenes and considers other
positions. A third position is that the degree of responsibility should
vary in proportion to the degree of psychological effort that would be
necessary to maintain self-control. A fourth position is that even if the
accused was partly responsible, he must be punished with his entire person, because it is impossible to separate out only the guilty part for
punishment. A fifth position is that punishments should be modified for
"half-crazy" persons without condoning their guilt. This position generates a spilt between a "soundness of mind" faction and a "full responsibility" faction, with each splintered into subgroups. Another position
is that the accused be divided into two hypothetical parts: a "zoological-
psychological entity" created by hereditary and social factors, which
does not concern the court, and a juridical entity, which is legally free
and responsible. Ulrich's father then proposes a compromise position
from the "social school of thought," which is that the accused should be
judged not morally but solely in terms of the harm he may do to society.
Thus, the more dangerous he is, the more responsible he is for his actions, and so those who seem to be the most innocent, the mentally ill,
who are least likely to be corrected by punishment, should be threatened with the harshest penalties. This illogical position wins few supporters, and the committee disbands again in confusion and failure.

Variants of Musil's fictional travesty of jurisprudential argumentation were repeated in books and articles and embodied in court decisions to the end of the twentieth century. Movement was made toward
allowing more expert witnesses to testify and including a broader range
of extenuating circumstances in insanity defenses. These developments
involved an increasing specificity of understanding of the causal role of
mental illness in explaining behavior generally, including acts of murder. The finding in John Hinckley's trial of 1982 that in attempting to
kill President Reagan he was not guilty by reason of insanity, that his

act was a product of schizophrenia, led to a reexamination of the more tolerant criminal law that emerged in America during the 1960s and 1970s. Although such changes had been under way for some time, the Insanity Defense Reform Act of 1984 shifted the burden of proof, making insanity something that the defendant must prove by clear and convincing evidence instead of something that the prosecution must disprove; it also changed the wording of the verdict to "not guilty *only* by reason of insanity."

This seemingly insolvable debate about insanity and criminal responsibility took psychiatrists, jurists, and philosophers to the heart of one of the most perplexing questions of all time, the nature of the human mind. The historical record on assessing the causal role of insanity in murder and determining a proper judgment and punishment for individuals who commit it does not exhibit a clear forward movement according to any singular legal principle or psychiatric theory of the mind. Indeed, sometimes it seemed to backtrack. Still, efforts along that path evince general movement in the direction of increasingly detailed analyses of constituent causal elements of mental life, from neurotransmitters and childhood traumas to social forces and historical developments, assessed more precisely with diagnostic tests and new analytical technologies such as brain scans.

In 1988 Deborah Denno surveyed some of the innovative legal defenses based on biological and medical evidence allowed in American courts in the late twentieth century. Jack Ruby, who shot Lee Harvey Oswald, was diagnosed as a temporal lobe epileptic; Charles Whitman, who shot forty one people from a Texas tower, and Richard Speck, who murdered eight nurses, presented evidence of brain disease; John Hinckley presented CAT scans of his brain to prove his schizophrenia; Dan White successfully pleaded diminished responsibility for killing the mayor of San Francisco; and Ann Green invoked postpartum illness as grounds for an insanity defense in the killing her children.[87] These new legal arguments and sources of evidence were based on ever more rigorous psychiatric case histories and presented in an ongoing evolution of case law. That these findings about the causal role of mental illness in acts of murder tossed up many new questions and made some of them seem unanswerable is testimony to the overall logic of this cultural historical development in accord with the specificity-uncertainty dialectic.

7

Society

THE SIMPLEST CAUSAL analyses of human behavior distinguish between heredity and environment. While environment plays a role in most of my chapters, in this one it is central, subdivided into aspects that appear in murder novels as *ambient environment* and *social pressure*. The pivotal new social science is sociology, which emerged around the turn of the century along with studies of field theory and crowds. That investigative foundation was subsequently augmented with cybernetics, dynamic systems theory, and complexity theory, all of which involve feedback systems in which social and environmental forces play interactive causal roles. These theories were themselves influenced causally by three historical developments: new transportation and communication technologies that expanded and accelerated causal action between increasingly remote places, the growing concentration and interdependence of people in cities brought about by those technologies, and the intellectual division of labor that emerged to make sense out of an increasingly complex, hierarchical, and compartmentalized social life. In the late nineteenth century, that division of labor resulted in new academic specialties within history, anthropology, economics, and political science, along with sociology, which addressed the relative causal role of more numerous and more precisely articulated social factors in accord with the specificity-uncertainty dialectic. Though murder novels do not manifest all these developments, they do show a growing sense of the complexity of social causation and the difficulty of understanding it.

AMBIENT ENVIRONMENT

Environmental determinism was a staple of nineteenth-century positivism and materialism as well as of literary realism and naturalism, methods strongly influenced by the success of natural science. Early nineteenth-century psychiatry concentrated on the way the environment directly affected mental states and provided the ideological foundation for the emerging asylum movement of that time. This movement was based on the assumption that removing the sick from their immediate environment would cure them. Acting on this philosophy, in 1838 the French government passed laws that gave asylums professional status. Environmental determinism was also central to historians such as Henry Thomas Buckle, who emphasized the causal role of climate in history, and Hippolyte Taine, who similarly invoked the milieu. The effect of natural selection in Darwin's theory was achieved by the action of environmental pressures. The Russian critic Nicolai Chernyshevsky's popular positivistic novel *What Is to Be Done?* (1863) argued that human beings are entirely shaped by the environment. His position is presented in *Crime and Punishment* by a man who theorizes that "the environment is everything, and man is nothing" (311). Dostoevsky mocked this theory by attributing it to the brutal Lebezyatnikov, but its forceful presentation, even as a foil for Dostoevsky's own view, suggests its persuasiveness in his time.

Balzac dedicated *The Human Comedy* to Geoffroy Saint-Hilaire, and his preface endorsed the famous French zoologist's theory that every creature derives its form and functions from the environment. Balzac's novels dramatized how environmental and social forces generate the human condition, as in *Le médecin de campagne* (1833), where the respected Doctor Bernassis elaborates his theory of environmental determinism.[1] In *Le père Goriot*, the walls of Goriot's residence, the Pension Vauquer, shape the character of its residents, and so Madame Vauquer "explains the pension, and the pension implies her person." In a classic study of literary realism, Erich Auerbach concluded that for Balzac, "every milieu becomes a moral and physical atmosphere which impregnates the . . . character, surroundings, ideas, activities, and fates of men, and at the same time the general historical situation reappears as a total atmosphere which envelops all its several milieus."[2] Lee Clark Mitchell saw an environmental determinism, especially pronounced among literary naturalists in the late nineteenth century, responding to the inexorability of railroad schedules, telephone wires, and industrial production. For these writers, individuals were no longer conceived as autonomous selves but "rather like filings aligned by magnets" as they "succumbed to logics of heredity and environment."[3] Zola explained that characters in his "experimental novels" are determined by their physical and social environment just as organisms are determined by the milieu of biological experiments. Victorian obsession with the causal role of the atmosphere is evinced by the widespread scientific theory that diseases such as cholera were caused by foul-smelling air or miasma. This erroneous theory was not fully scrapped in scientific circles until the germ theory of disease gained credence toward the end of the century, when popular suspicion about the pathogenic role of stinking air was finally discredited.

The same first-generation Victorian readers and theatergoers from the middle and working classes who responded readily to characters whose inner qualities were evident on their skulls and faces (as phrenology and physiognomy held) also responded readily to the clearly evocative settings of easy-to-understand melodramas with evil villains and virtuous heroes. In Victorian melodramas about murder, a malevolent environment forecasts or even generates the evil deeds to come. As Winifred Hughes argued in *The Maniac in the Cellar*, the setting of these works "assists or controls the mood and provides the background for violence and tempestuous passion."[4] While the "sensation novels" of the 1860s added some nuance to these environmentally shaped polarities of good and evil, fictional characterizations continued to rely on a potent evil atmosphere. Such dichotomous evaluations of character reinforced by the ambient environment are frequent in Victorian literature. Some critics went so far as to argue that melodrama is a defining feature of nineteenth-century thought.[5]

The differing causal roles of the environment in Victorian and modern fictional murders can be seen through a comparison of six aspects: time, weather, location, power, direction, and value. For Victorians the time is some dramatic moment, such as an ominous winter night; the weather is threatening or stormy; the location is an urban slum or eerie rural spot; the deterministic force is strong; the direction is linear from the environment to the murderer; and the moral value is evil.

Among serious writers influenced by melodrama, Dickens is paradigmatic. In *Oliver Twist*, Bill Sikes lives in a gloomy den in the filthiest part of a London slum. His environment mirrors his immoral inner self and leaves no way out for the monomaniacal frenzy that leads to a brutal killing of his innocent lover Nancy in his room at night. In *Barnaby Rudge* (1841), Reuben Haredale is murdered on a night that was "blowing a hurricane." As Dickens elaborated, "There are times when, the elements being in unusual commotion, those who are bent on daring enterprises . . . feel a mysterious sympathy with the tumult of nature and are roused into corresponding violence. In the midst of thunder, lightning, and storm, many tremendous deeds have been committed. . . . The demons of wrath and despair have striven to emulate those who ride the whirlwind and direct the story; and man, lashed into madness with the roaring winds and boiling waters, has become for the time as wild and merciless as the elements themselves" (17). In *Martin Chuzzlewit*, Jonas contemplates his murder of Montague while they ride through a forest on a stormy night and then carries it out on a similar night as the surrounding tumult pervades his mind and body. "As the gloom of evening, deepening into night, came on, another dark shade emerging from within him seemed to overspread [Jonas's] face, and slowly change it. Slowly, slowly; darker and darker; more and more haggard; creeping over him little by little; until it was black night within him and without" (795). Dickens offered another Grand Guignol setting in *The Mystery of Edwin Drood* (1870), where murder occurs on a night when the trees toss and creak, and the wind tears the hands off the cathedral clock.

Other Victorians also invoked a threatening environment. In *Lady Audley's Secret*, the murderess and her companion lock her victim in his room before setting it on fire "with the black night above them—with the fierce wind howling round them, sweeping across a broad expanse of hidden country" (324). As with Sikes and Chuzzlewit, the menacing ambient world is reflected in the murderer's inner state, functioning causally as an inexorable external force. The murderess and her lover in Zola's *Thérèse Raquin* strangle Camille in a remote spot on the Seine at twilight as "a penetrating chill was beginning to come down from the quivering sky. . . . The countryside, dried up by the hot summer days, feels death approaching with the first cold winds as they mournfully sing in the sky of the end of hope. Night comes down from above bearing shrouds in its shadows" (92). Zola crafted the dynamic ambience for murder as literal fact and suggestive metaphor—a time of leafless trees and dying countryside, mournful cold winds, shrouds of death in the night sky, and a pervasive sense of evil. Later in the century Doyle created wicked nights for crime in London, while the foggy moor in *The Hound of the Baskervilles* became an archetypical setting for rural murder.

Even after the murder, the force of that ambience sometimes persists in witnesses who continue to plague the murderer. Sikes's dog that saw Nancy's murder tracks his master across the fields with a relentless accusatory gaze as he flees the murder scene. The dog's judgmental eyes are augmented by the terrifying eyes of Nancy herself that Sikes hallucinates as if they were following him over the countryside. The murderer in *Martin Faber* (1833), who strangles his pregnant mistress in a dark, old house, is haunted by her eyes, which proliferate in his surroundings: "The trees were hung with eyes that depended [*sic*] from them like leaves. Eyes looked at me from the water that gushed by, [and] the heavens seemed clustering with gazing thousands, all bent down terrifically upon me. . . . 'Murderer!' was the response of the trees, which had now tongues as well as eyes" (34).

In the modern period these features of melodrama persisted in popular sensation novels and horror films, but serious novelists parodied or explicitly rejected these strategies and rendered the six elements of environmental causality in distinctly new ways. The timing was less climactic and more subject to chance, the weather did not so obviously and directly portend murder, the place could be innocuous or pleasant, the deterministic force was weaker or even explicitly indeterministic, the direction was more interactive than one-way, and the value was more likely to be interpreted in aesthetic or existential terms rather than Christian moral terms.

While the timing of the environmental factor in Victorian murder was the climax of a relentless sequential buildup, for some moderns it was a matter of chance or inadvertence. Gide specifically targeted the "most tiresome" environmental determinism of Taine, who tried to explain human actions by race, milieu, and moment. In a journal entry of 1925, Gide objected that "the determinism from which it seems clear that our mind, any more than our body, cannot possibly escape is so subtle, corresponds to such diverse, multiple, and tenuous causes, that it seems childish to try to number them. . . . Man is never free; but the simplest and most honest thing is to act as if he were."[6] Gide created such a character with his spontaneous murderer Lafcadio, who tries to act as if he is free by capriciously choosing his victim in the railroad compartment. He is determined to act without a motive but lets the environment make his final "decision" to act by chance. As he reasons: "If I can count up to twelve without hurrying before I see a light in the countryside, the old sap is saved" (187). When a light fails to appear, Lafcadio slows his counting to doom his companion and sanction the murder, which he commits by pushing the man out into the night after he finally sees a light outside at the count of ten. The environment provides the signal for the murder only after Lafcadio nudges it.

The increasing role of chance in the modern novel evinces the increasingly probabilistic nature of causal understanding generally. In *Standard Deviation: Chance and the Modern British Novel*, Leland Monk related this increasing role of chance to developments in the new probabilistic sciences of the early twentieth century—genetics and quantum mechanics. But as Monk showed, it is impossible for any novelist to introduce true chance in a work that is governed by the controlling determinism of the author's mind. Chance is always being manipulated by the author, who has complete control over his story, similar to the way Lafcadio manipulated chance in killing the stranger. The main point remains, however, that even though "no novelist actually manages to represent chance in narrative, there is a history of the ongoing attempt to do so."[7] Such attempts are also evident in the way moderns render the causal role of weather.

The menacing weather for murder in Victorian melodrama implied that divine providence was expressing God's disapproval in advance of the act while his thunder and lightning stimulated its perpetrator. These factors are rare in modern novels, where chance is detached from notions of fate or God's will. Moderns generally become increasingly willing to see coincidences and accidents as evidence of the fundamentally stochastic nature of existence rather than as the result of a deity at work behind the scene.

The weather in modern murder novels is not typically stormy nights. The most famous weather is in *The Stranger*—the sunny day at the beach near Algiers where Meursault shoots an Arab. The causal influence of the heat and light at first seem to be as overpowering as the storms of Victorian melodrama. Camus made more than seventy references to the sunlight and sky, to searing heat and steamy streets, to Meursault's throbbing temples and stinging eyes, and, just before Meursault fires his gun, to the dazzling spear of light that slashes at his eyeballs from the Arab's knife. But Camus subverted the causal force of the environment during the long interrogations of Meursault's trial. After one tense exchange the examining magistrate insists on learning why Meursault fired not just once but then four more times at a body lying on the ground. "Why? You must tell me. Why?" (68). Meursault cannot answer because he himself does not know why. Before passing sentence the judge insists on an explanation, and Meursault narrates his own response: "Fumbling a little with my words and realizing how ridiculous I sounded, I blurted out that it was because of the sun. People laughed. My lawyer threw up his hands" (103). This confession does not offer nearly enough explanatory punch for Meursault's exasperated lawyer or for anyone else in the courtroom conditioned to expect the sort of strong deterministic explanations that were offered by conventional psychiatry or jurisprudence, and especially not for readers of melodrama in which bad people always do bad things in bad weather. With this "ridiculous" courtroom explanation Camus underscored the uncertainty of causal understanding generally. The novel asks in a new way what sorts of explanations are plausible and implies that all explanations of human behavior may in some ways be ridiculous. The stranger in this novel is estranged from his environment as well as from his own act.

Victorian murders typically took place in murderous locales such as eerie country spots or dangerous, filthy slums, as for example the murders in George Pitt's melodramatic classic *The String of Pearls; or, The Fiend of Fleet Street* (1847). In real life, the murders of Jack the Ripper were known as "the Whitechapel murders," because of the slum where they occurred. In contrast, modern murders take place in innocuous places: a rich woman's bedroom (*Native Son*), a calm lake (*An American Tragedy*), a pickup truck (*The Minus Man*). The murder in *Malice Aforethought: The Story of a Commonplace Crime* is conceived at a tennis party and carried out in an ordinary middle-class home, as the novel's subtitle implies. Without relying on the coercive action of a menacing locale, modern novelists could explore subtler and more unexpected and varied settings. While Victorian settings mirror the human condition, the settings of modern novels challenge and negate it. Moderns are less likely to see themselves living in a natural world created by God for their fulfillment than in an artificial world created by themselves in the imagination, in the text of novels, in the act of writing.

The strong environmental determinism of Victorian melodrama is explicitly rejected by some modern novelists who intentionally subvert determinisms of all sorts. Robbe-Grillet described the surface of objects in the environment as they are directly experienced instead of probing deeper-lying determinative forces. These objects are in the environment but do not determine behavior. Influenced by the intractable superficiality of the camera eye in modern cinema, in 1956 Robbe-Grillet clarified his idea. "The world is neither significant nor absurd. It *is*, quite simply . . . around us, defying the noisy pack of our animistic or protective adjectives. . . . Instead of this universe of 'signification' (psychological, social, functional), we must try to construct a world both more solid and more immediate. Let it be first of all by their *presence* that objects and gestures establish themselves, and let this presence continue to prevail over whatever explanatory theory that may try to enclose them in a system of references, whether emotional, sociological, Freudian, or metaphysical."[8]

Two years later Robbe-Grillet, widely criticized for "inhumanity," clarified his purpose in viewing man as detached from the world. Traditional humanism insists that the world exists to justify human existence, with God as the first cause and ultimate justification behind all of creation, which centers on a mankind created in God's image. Robbe-Grillet defined his supposed inhumanity as "the assertion that there exists something in the world which is not man, which makes no sign to him, which has nothing in common with him."[9] Such an unorthodox approach, he countered, allows a fuller openness to reality and a fuller cultivation of the freedom of the creative artist: "To reject our so-called 'nature' and the vocabulary which perpetuates its myth, to propose objects as purely external and superficial, is not—as has been claimed—to deny man; but it is to reject the 'pananthropic' notion contained in traditional humanism, and probably in all humanism. It is no more in the last analysis than to lay claim, quite logically, to my freedom." His novels work not to bridge the gap between man and world but to accentuate it. In them "everything is lacerated, fissured, divided, displaced."

He applied this notion interpretively to *The Stranger*, an important novel, but one that he believed achieved only a partial separation of man and the world. The ultimate absurdity is the impossibility of establishing between man and the world "any relation other than *strangeness*."[10] Nevertheless, Meursault remains partly influenced by an environment animated with humanizing metaphors such as the pitiless sun, the burning sand, the blinding light. In his own murder novel, *The Erasers*, Robbe-Grillet related man to the world but without such strong, humanizing metaphors and the direct environmental determinism they suggest. In this novel an ordinary eraser is part of the environment of a murder but does not directly determine it. Still, reflection on the ways the eraser erases things and in the process erodes itself reveals much about the human condition, including even the act of murder. The eraser is a functional analogy for writing (involving erasures), for criminal investigation (elimination of suspects), for the hypothetical reasoning of detectives (disproving hypotheses by counterfactual analysis), for reality (negated by false appearances), for Wallas's innocence (erased by the text), and for his accidental murder (rubbing out) of Dupont. The eraser's self-destruction through use also partially effaces its brand name, Oedipus, which is named after a character who acts in a world he misunderstands and who murders a parent, thereby eliminating one causal actor in his own procreation.

Instead of explaining murder, Robbe-Grillet used murder as a pretext for exploring the surfaces and textures of a reality that, when viewed carefully, abounds with meaning. This approach is a literary analogue of Edmund Husserl's philosophical method of the phenomenological reduction. It involves suspending or "bracketing" the "natural attitude," which seeks causes of phenomena in order to explore more fully how phenomena are constituted in consciousness. Husserl did not deny the reality of causality in the world, but he believed that preoccupation with causal knowledge distracted from more certain ways of knowing the world we experience directly. Thus, preoccupation with the causes of an eraser—who made it, how it was made, or why—would distract from careful exploration of its color, shape, and feeling. Robbe-Grillet used something similar in his novel. By "bracketing" causality, he remained open to seeing things with unexpected visions that are sharpened precisely because man is isolated from the world. His novel is about an act—murder—that cries out for a causal explanation that he refuses to offer. In so doing he remained free in historically significant ways to explore how we experience the ambient world in which seemingly innocuous objects like erasers are packed with significance. His inventive subversion of causality is a reminder of how twentieth-century crime and detective novels are full of murder suspects whose existences are truncated by criminal judgments that are always incomplete and often erroneous. For Husserl, causal analysis clutters and blunts the rigor of phenomenological descriptions; for Robbe-Grillet, it distracts and dissipates the novelist's seeing eye and sensitivity to the ambient world.

Victorian causality acts in one direction from environment to murderer. In contrast, some modern novelists target linear cause and effect itself and instead invoke nonlinear interactive systems. Tom LeClair traced the intellectual roots of these "systems novelists" to twentieth-century gestalt psychology, quantum field theory, and cybernetics as well as to Whitehead's philosophy, Saussure's linguistics, and Lévi-Strauss's anthropology. He viewed Ludwig von Bertalanffy's *General System Theory* of 1968 as the grounding text for exploring the living structures of all complex systems from individuals to ecosystems.[11] These systems cannot be broken into parts but must be considered as wholes, and their causal action is not linear but interactive with other systems in their environment, through circulations of information rather than transfers of energy. They are goal-seeking, self-organizing, self-correcting systems, as dramatized in the novels of William Gaddis, Thomas Pynchon, Robert Coover, and Don DeLillo, where the environment does not impact characters directly in a linear way but indirectly through circulating, interactive systems of new technologies and institutions that increasingly coerce individuals in ever-expanding and ultimately global exchanges of information, goods, and money.

In modern murder novels, such interactive causal networks are most evident in serial killers and terrorists who feed off an environment mediated by new communication technologies. Some are motivated by what they learn about through these media; others are stimulated by reactions to the murders they commit. In *White Noise*, titled after the pervasive feedback of sound and information in modern society, one serial killer is inspired by voices he hears on TV, which in turn reports on his killings. In *Underworld*, DeLillo speculated that serial killings "became more possible when the means of taping an event and playing it . . . became widely available. Taping-and-playing intensifies and compresses the event. It dangles the need to do it again" (159). For the northern Irish terrorists in Eoin McNamee's *Resurrection Man* (1994), "car bombings were carried out to synchronize with news deadlines," and terrorist acts were ranked on the basis of how prominently the acts were reported in the evening news, with a lead story being the ultimate triumph (58). Those news reports in turn became the inspiration for counterterrorist activities, which in turn triggered more terrorism.

The final shift concerns the moral value of environmental causation in murders, which in many Victorian novels was resoundingly evil. Moderns tended to retain a sense of evil ambience but one that is de-Christianized and de-moralized. It is still invoked metaphorically in describing individual acts, but for novelists as well as forensic psychiatrists and jurists, an evil ambience is less likely to explain murder, let alone forecast or engender it. A fuller discussion of this major shift in western culture is the subject of my final chapter on how the Western world in science and the arts transcended a fundamental Judeo-Christian moral distinction of good and evil in favor of aesthetic and existential distinctions.

SOCIAL PRESSURE

Victorians lived under an ordering of social classes with strict social norms validated by centuries of deference to status and rank. For them the force of circumstance loomed large even as it provoked protests on behalf of personal autonomy.[12] The force of those circumstances among leading thinkers mounted throughout the century such that by the 1890s, as Martin Wiener argued, "the scientific world shifted attention from acts to contexts. . . . The criminal was no longer a wicked individual but rather a product of his environment and heredity."[13]

Victorians lived in a world where crime was localized in clearly identifiable lower classes that lived in particular slums. Moderns were more likely to live in diverse urban settings with more varied social possibilities and behavioral norms. Moderns rendered the causal role of society as more problematical in novels about murderers who struck out at an increasingly enigmatic society that was rife with crime up and down the ranks and in every locale. These differences are most evident in novels about the social roots of fear and hatred.

Fear

Victorians lived under threat of exposure to society's unforgiving judgmental gaze, and their novelists created murderers motivated by fear of those who threatened to disclose their damaging secrets. In *The Red and the Black*, on the eve of Julien's wedding, Madame de Rênal sends to his prospective father-in-law, the Marquis de la Mole, a letter revealing Julien's amorous past. The Marquis had just offered Julien military rank, a title, and a fortune—keys to social success. After receiving the letter, the Marquis blocks the marriage and withdraws his offers, ensuring Julien's social ruin. Terrified at the prospect of social disgrace, Julien attempts to kill Madame de Rênal. Other Victorians committed murder or lesser crimes to protect their reputations under other pressing social circumstances. In *Bleak House* (1852–53), Tulkinghorn threatens to tell Lady Deadlock's husband that his wife has an illegitimate child, and her maid Hortense, who attempts to blackmail Tulkinghorn, murders him when he threatens her with imprisonment. Although greed is Jonas Chuzzlewit's prime motivator, the spark for murder is Montague's threat to reveal that Jonas had attempted to murder his own father. Lady

Audley attempts murder and carries out a homicidal arson to cover up socially ruinous secrets about her insane mother and alcoholic father.

Without triggering murder, threats of disclosure could still wreak havoc. Such a threat about Hester Prynne's past love life gives Roger Chillingworth his devastating hold over her and Arthur Dimmesdale in *The Scarlet Letter* (1850), as does a similar bit of information held by Winifred Hurtle over Paul Montague in Trollope's *The Way We Live Now* (1875). Even though George Eliot did not use the word, her novels abound with blackmail plots: Dunstan Cass blackmails his brother Godfrey in *Silas Marner*, Raffles blackmails Nicholas Bulstrode in *Middlemarch*, and Grandcourt blackmails Gwendolyn in *Daniel Deronda*. Gwendolyn's failure to attempt to save Grandcourt from drowning is a passive act of killing, even though Eliot provides abundant justification for her terrified inaction as the sadistic Grandcourt goes under. In *George Eliot and Blackmail*, Alexander Welsh viewed blackmail plots as a recurring motif in Eliot's corpus and a distinctive feature of Victorian literature generally.[14] Wiener added that blackmail "became for the mid- and later Victorians a greater preoccupation in law and in fiction than either before or since."[15] Later in the century Sherlock Holmes stories frequently involve scandal and blackmail. The threat of scandal drives frightened victims to Holmes, who rescues their reputation, the preservation of which is a matter of life and death. In all of these works, victims of scandal and blackmail live in a small social world and are terrified at the prospect of public disgrace.

Welsh explained why blackmail became more common under these particular historical circumstances. In small rural towns with little social or geographical movement and primitive means of communication with the outside world, blackmail was scarcely possible, because in such a society everyone knew everything about everyone else. But new transportation and communication technologies and the growth of cities gave Victorians enough social and geographical mobility to move away from past sins and gave potential blackmailers new ways to find information about their victims and threaten disclosure.[16] In the modern world these trends continued, but blackmail triggering the fear of social ruin became a less frequent motive in serious crime fiction, and the source of social pressure shifted from local gossips and specific blackmailers to an increasingly complex and alienating society.

Clyde Griffiths is indeed terrified that Roberta might disclose his role in her pregnancy and dash his chances with the wealthy socialite

Sondra and all that she represents: "this would spell complete ruin for him, the loss of Sondra, his job, his social hopes" (413). Clyde's motivation for murder is, however, distinctly modern. Roberta is no scheming blackmailer but rather a tragic a figure caught in social circumstances that make her feel trapped by the double threat of abandonment by Clyde and shame over having an illegitimate child. The frightening culprit in this *American* tragedy is not a greedy blackmailer but a spiritually bankrupt American society. That displacement of the source of fear from Roberta onto American society is behind Clyde's conflict over murdering her, which will not eliminate his social impotence, and that conflict is behind his paralysis during her accidental drowning. For the moderns, fear of society as a motive for murder breaks up in the diffuseness and complexity of social reality.

Hatred

Victorian class hatred is simple and direct. The hero of Edward Bulwer-Lytton's *Eugene Aram* (1832) kills an upper-class lout who insulted Aram about his poverty and seduced a working-class woman, driving her to suicide. Harry Carson, the wealthy murder victim in Gaskell's *Mary Barton*, is even more deserving of his fate. He exploited and starved a whole town of workers and tried to seduce one worker's daughter, Mary Barton. The workers decide to kill him, and the task falls to Mary's father. In *Germinal*, the old miner Bonnemort impulsively strangles the daughter of a mine owner's family in an act of pure class hatred that comes to a head, Zola-style, in this "broken-down animal, ravaged by a century of toil and hunger passed down from father to son" (466). In *Our Mutual Friend*, the upper-class gentleman Eugene Wrayburn treats the lower-class schoolmaster Bradley Headstone with disdain as they clash over a woman. When Headstone finally attempts to kill Wrayburn, jealousy has energized his frantic class hatred to such a pitch that he botches the job and leaves the scene unaware that Wrayburn is still alive.

Throughout Victorian literature a raging hatred of lower against upper class, often intensified by poverty and starvation, motivates single-minded acts of murder. A modern rendering of more ambivalent lower-to-upper-class hatred is Jean Genet's *The Maids* (1947). The play begins in a bedroom with an elegant lady chastising her maid Claire. As the conflict between them peaks, Claire slaps the lady. Then an alarm clock rings and the two reveal that they have been pretending.

The lady was being played by her maid Claire, whose own role was being played by Claire's sister Solange. Both admire and seek to emulate their lady, hence their wearing of her clothes and playing her role, but they also hate her, hence their make-believe drama of conflict and confrontation. The alarm reminds them that their lady will soon return, when they must resume their real-life servility. We then learn that they also have caused the arrest of the lady's lover by an anonymous letter to the police. When a telephone call alerts them that the lover is out on bail, they realize that their ruse will be discovered. They plan to kill their lady with poisoned tea when she returns, but the lady is distracted from drinking it by a phone call and rushes out. Left alone, the maids explore their feelings about the lady as they resume playacting. Claire chastises Solange for having lacked the courage to strangle the lady during an earlier murder attempt and decides to drink the poisoned tea herself, thereby "succeeding" where her sister had formerly failed. After Claire's death Solange interprets their actions. "Madame is dead. Her two maids are alive: they've just risen up, free, from Madame's icy form" (100). Every element of this speech is false and shows Solange's ambivalence and self-deception, because Madame is in fact still alive, one of her maids is actually dead, the other is half-dead of grief, they have both been beaten down, and neither is free. The fake murder was actually a suicide, which only released a fantasy of liberation locked in the icy rigidity of Solange's delusion. The sisters' class hatred is energized by deeper-lying class envy, Claire's self-affirmation is in fact an act of self-deception, and her aggression against her lady actually saves her lady.

GENERAL SOCIAL CAUSATION

Victorian society was sharply structured along class lines, and so Victorians were inclined to believe that criminals were bred in socially discrete, spatially separate, and morally inferior "lower classes." Arthur Morrison dramatized their fate in *A Child of the Jago* (1896), which pinpointed one notorious criminal breeding ground—the Jago, a ghetto in London's East End. Jack London treated the same locale in *The People of the Abyss* (1903). Maxim Gorky covered similar terrain for Russia in *The Lower Depths* (1902), while the French referred to the products of such slums as *les misérables*. Hugo's novel of that name dramatized thinking about how social pressures forge the dangerous classes at the lowest levels. Eugène Sue's popular crime novel, *The Mysteries of Paris* (1842), opens with a statement about the social and geographical isolation of the criminal classes "as far outside our civilization as are the savage populations described by [James Fenimore] Cooper."[17] Louis Chevalier summarized this notion: "'Barbarians,' 'savages,' 'vagrants,' the terms generally used by Sue and Hugo—all of them evoking a picture of a primitive race living apart from civilized people—designated a large proportion of the Paris population, all those who lived in what Sue called 'the sinister regions of poverty and ignorance,' as well as the dwellers in the lower depths and 'the great cavern of Evil.'"[18]

While moderns continued to acknowledge a link between slums and crime, they were also more likely to see crime stemming from all social strata and locales and were more interested in exploring those new pathways. Some stressed the social fluidity of the forces leading to crime (hard-boiled crime fiction), some focused on their illusory nature (Kafka and Musil), while others parodied or explicitly rejected sociological explanations in the face of increasingly complex social pressure (Döblin and McCoy). But whether they dramatized or interrogated the complex circuitry of social causation, their novels testify to the fact that it was a defining feature of modern life.

The increasingly complex nature of modern cities accelerated the movement of information and people, creating diverse modes of social interaction. These differences were strikingly evident in the varied settings and interacting social classes of the hard-boiled crime novels of the '20s and '30s. Unlike Victorian detectives such as Sherlock Holmes who found a criminal fly in the respectable social ointment and picked it out to restore order, detectives in hard-boiled crime novels were mired in a sticky criminality that pervaded all of society, typically with a corrupt police officer or politician at its source. Classic crime fiction concluded with a simple rational solution of the crime, the triumph of good over evil, and a restoration of social order; in hard-boiled fiction society is corrupt from top to bottom and all over town, every character is tainted including the police and even the detective, and understanding becomes increasingly muddled. In Dashiel Hammett's *Red Harvest* (1929), the town of *Personville*, "an ugly city of forty thousand people" which locals aptly call *Poisonville*, has been taken over by a crime syndicate and a powerful businessman. The detective hired to investigate a murder complains, "This damned burg's getting me. If

I don't get away soon I'll be going blood-simple like the natives. There's been what? A dozen and a half murders since I've been here.... I've arranged a killing or two in my time, when they were necessary. But this is the first time I've ever got the fever" (154). In Hammett's *The Glass Key* (1931), the "respectable" Senator Henry uses his daughter to seduce a rival and then kills his own son in a fit of rage. "In this novel, as in most hard-boiled fiction," Jon Thompson concluded, "society itself is essentially unknowable. Nothing is what it seems ... [and] everyone and everything is tainted in some way."[19] After World War II, film noir captured an urban space where detectives got lost and murderers got away in the darkness that was the genre's defining trait. Murder came from the endless flow of chance encounters between unreliable and unknowable persons moving in shadows.

Everyone and everything is also tainted in Kafka, and he makes knowing the causes of events highly problematic. In *The Trial*, a menacing social world may have driven Joseph K. to some guilty deed, although the actual cause may be only the workings of his own troubled mind. We are never certain. Kafka projected social causation up and down the social scale to include K.'s friends, family, lovers, professionals, artists, and officials functioning in a menacing social ambience that can only be called Kafkaesque. The novel's famous opening sentence points to such vague external forces at work—"Someone must have been telling lies about Joseph K., for without having done anything wrong he was arrested one fine morning"—but "someone" turns out to be everyone, or possibly no one, depending on whether the social circuits that he sees spinning accusations are real or imagined.

The social circuits for Musil were more tangible, although he also questioned their causal functions and our ability to know them. *The Man without Qualities* opens with an inventory of Vienna's modern social pressures. "Like all big cities it was made up of irregularity, change, forward spurts, failures to keep step, collisions of objects and interests, punctuated by unfathomable silences; it was made up of pathways and untrodden ways, of one great rhythmic beat as well as the chronic discord and mutual displacement of all its contending rhythms" (4). The man without qualities, Ulrich, is a man who resists the "qualities" (*Eigenschaften*) that history generated and that society enforces. He reflects on how the individual self became squeezed out by these socially determining qualities. In earlier times "people were like cornstalks in a field, probably more violently tossed back and forth by God, hail, fire, pestilence, and war than they are today, but as a whole . . . all this was clearly defined and could be answered for. But today responsibility's center of gravity is not in people but in circumstances. . . . Who can say nowadays that his anger is really his own anger when so many people [psychologists and sociologists] talk about it and claim to know more about it than he does? A world of qualities without a man has arisen, of experiences without the person who experiences them, and it almost looks as though ideally private experience is a thing of the past" (158–59). Ulrich's struggle against the annihilating force of social pressure aligns him with Moosbrugger, a misfit who is driven to murder because he cannot distinguish inside from outside and strikes out with a deadly knife thrust in an act of self-definition against a clinging prostitute. Moosbrugger lives in a world in which, as the title of the novel's first section indicates, "Pseudoreality Prevails."

While Musil conceived of the society of pre–World War I Vienna as an oppressive pseudoreality, Alfred Döblin conceived of postwar Berlin as an oppressive hyperreality. In *Berlin Alexanderplatz: The Story of Franz Biberkopf* (1929), the city and Franz are yoked in the title and spliced together in the text like cinematic quick cuts in alternating sections. Although Alexanderplatz is just one subway station, it stands for Berlin, which Döblin rendered seemingly verbatim from myriad urban sources: tram and bus routes, poster kiosks, weather and stock reports, police and hospital reports, mortality statistics, verbatim radio broadcasts, political speeches, descriptions of architecture building by building, vignettes of tenants floor by floor, bits of conversations street by street, and newspaper articles and advertisements with their patchwork formats that embody the complexity and discontinuity of modern urban life.[20] In place of the narrated city of realism in which an omniscient narrator explained how the city affected individuals, Berlin itself generates Franz's story in this novel with quotations from these multifarious texts to evoke the city's diverse and unpredictable social dynamics.

The murderer in Döblin's novel, as in Musil's, is alienated from the urban surroundings, but while Moosbrugger is alienated because of mental deficiency, Franz is alienated because he does not care. Corruption penetrates into every corner of Berlin, but Franz's accidental murder is committed in spite of it rather than because of it. His killing of his fiancée Ida is like a vaudeville act. During a routine argument he hit her in the stomach with a cream whipper. Döblin's scientific-sounding explanation is tongue-in-cheek: "The diaphragm of this dainty girl was not adapted to contact with cream-whippers." Döblin's further account parodies nineteenth-century determinism, as it includes "the laws of statics, elasticity, shock, and resistance," elaborated with a summary of Newton's laws of motion capped with the mathematical formulas for force and acceleration (98–99). Ida died five weeks later from complications due to "empyema, pleurisy, and pneumonia" (101). The detail of Döblin's physical explanation and medical diagnosis seems ludicrously beside the point in the messy context of Franz's accidental killing. His parody of a comprehensive causal explanation is an explanatory dead end.

Moderns increasingly identified new social forces to explain murder and mitigate responsibility. One modern fictional murderer speaks out against that trend. Paul Murphy, the killer in *Kiss Tomorrow Goodbye* (1948), is a college graduate with refined artistic taste and musical ability. He is emotionally vulnerable and morally conscientious about everything except his brutal killings. His taking personal responsibility for them and his rejection of social explanations are distinctly modern. "I didn't grow up in the slums with a drunk for a father and a whore for a mother. . . . Every other criminal I know—who's engaged in violent crime—is a two-bit coward who blames his career on society. I need no apologist or crusader to finally hold my lifeless body up to the world and shout for them to come and observe what they have wrought. This I have wrought, I and I alone" (235). Paul's impatience with sociological excuse-making echoes that of Sartre, the reigning existentialist philosopher of his time.

The hard-boiled crime novel dramatized how crime worked throughout the class structure and across the modern urban landscape. Kafka and Musil blurred the line between that menacing landscape and the inner workings of the mind. Döblin reconstructed its endless variety and causal potency while still crafting a murder that took place in spite of it. McCoy invoked the popularity of social explanations by creating a killer on the lam who bothered to rail against them. Thus, in various ways modernists dramatized current beliefs in the reality and potency of new social pressures as well as the possibility of understanding them, however incompletely.

Other writers subverted those beliefs with even more radical techniques. For postmodernists, social space is no longer a uniform expanse but an assortment of constructions with distinctive realms constituted by trains, automobiles, airplanes, and spaceships; by face-to-face conversations, letters, telephones, and newspapers; by X rays, radios, televisions, and the Internet; by mountains, seaports, rivers, and canals; and by weather, commerce, advertising, and immigration. Postmodern novelists, as Brian McHale noted, created composites of these spatial modalities in imaginary cities by juxtaposing distant places, interpolating familiar spaces with fantasized ones, superimposing two familiar places into one another, or misattributing characteristics from one region to another. In Italo Calvino's *Invisible Cities* (1972), three different cities each constitute the same vast space of the Empire of the Great Kahn in contradictory ways: Penthesilea is a continuous suburb throughout the Empire, Cecilia has engulfed surrounding territory throughout the Empire, and Trude is identical to every other city in the Empire: it is a city "that does not begin and does not end. Only the name of the airport changes."[21]

Postmodern murder novelists imagined fantasized, even self-contradictory urban spaces. In Robbe-Grillet's *Typology of a Phantom City* (1976), the setting for murder is a phantom city filled with imagery of destruction—squalid rubbish, teetering walls, and half-collapsed buildings. It is a literary construct from many historical periods that repeatedly break up and reappear in one another so that the reader is led to wonder whether the story is about a serial killing, a phantom killing, or even no killing at all. Robbe-Grillet worked to subvert conventional notions of causation. The murder(s) occur(s) in different places both before and after the narrator witnesses it (them), and he himself emerges as the main suspect, along with the reader. Robbe-Grillet mixed up historical periods and motives, along with the identity of the murderer himself, in an urban setting that is ripe for murder but has nothing to do with it. The killing zone in Pynchon's *Gravity's Rainbow* is a transhistorical construct of wartime London, where V-2 rockets cause thousands of deaths; postwar Germany, where the titular rocket is launched at the beginning of the novel; and Los Angeles around 1972, where at the end of the novel the rocket is poised to come down. This nightmarish transatlantic terrain stretches around the globe with juxtapositions of temporally and spatially diverse features from history, literature, movies, comic books, dreams, and delusions.[22]

With respect to the causal role of society, murder novels evince every element of the specificity-uncertainty dialectic. They show greater appreciation of the probabilistic nature of existence in the surprises and chance encounters of modern urban terrain, as in Musil's description of Vienna as a city of "irregularity, change, forward spurts, failures to keep step, collisions of objects and interests." Compared with Victorian novels, particularly melodramas, modern novels offered more detail about the greater variety and complex interaction of the ambient environment and societal pressure. The uncertainty of understanding these factors was dramatized in modernists such as Kafka and Musil and especially postmodernists such as Robbe-Grillet and Pynchon.

While novelists concentrated on dramatizing the processes and effects of these environmental and social factors, sociologists tried to explain them causally.

MODERN SOCIOLOGY

The pivotal social science in this chapter is sociology. It was one of several that emerged in university departments in the late nineteenth and early twentieth centuries to address problems created by capitalism (economics), imperialism (anthropology), and the state (political science).[23] Sociology became a formal discipline with scholarly journals and university status to analyze crowds, urban life, and deviant behaviors such as suicide and crime. Among all the social sciences, it was the one most concerned with understanding the causal role of society, which it did in accord with the specificity-uncertainty dialectic; that is, it specified an increasing number of interrelated causal factors that made up complex social networks. Some of these analyses involved assigning magnitudes to interrelated casual factors as dependent variables using increasingly sophisticated statistical techniques.

The rise of sociology was a response to the crowding of people in cities, the increasing division of labor, the intensification of market forces, growing interdependence, and new technologies for transportation and communication. The historical connection among these developments is the focus of Thomas Haskell's study of the emergence of American social science. The increasing division of labor in the commercial and academic worlds resulted from the concentration of populations in cities and the refinement of expertises necessitated by modern industrial society. As city dwellers specialized to establish a niche in an increasingly complex society, they became less able to carry out all the functions they needed to survive and so became more dependent on other specialists. Haskell defined this increasing inter-dependence as "that tendency of social integration and consolidation whereby action in one part of society is transmitted in the form of di-rect or indirect consequences to other parts of society with accelerating rapidity, widening scope, and increasing intensity."[24] In comparison with self-sufficient peasants, who dealt with a limited number of per-sonal acquaintances on a face-to-face basis, modern city dwellers ex-perienced greater interdependence among an expanded number of people whom they never saw. The ability of larger and more complex capitalistic enterprises to impact—and be impacted by—workers, cus-tomers, and competitors across greater distances and over longer stretches of time led to an increasing specialization of productive and commercial skills as well as scientific and scholarly knowledge. Inter-dependence and the division of labor were further intensified by the new telephone, wireless, automobile, mass newspaper, and cinema, which were themselves a result of the increasing specialization of sci-entific knowledge.

The growing interdependence also reduced the number of inde-pendent variables that could explain social phenomena simply and di-rectly. Modern social scientists were inclined to explain social phenomena less as a consequence of the autonomous action of individ-uals, in the manner of their nineteenth-century predecessors, and more as an effect of increasingly complex social networks. Tracing such causal circuitry was a major goal of the newly founded American scholarly associations: American Historical Association (1884), American Economic Association (1885), American Academy of Political Science (1890), and American Sociological Society (1905). These societies imposed new methodological rigor and identified new impor-tant subjects for study. In 1924 one founder of American sociology, Albion W. Small, recalled how "in the generation since the sociological movement began, the presumption that linear causation is the main connection of human events has given place to the presumption which we may call vortex causation." Earlier social theorists such as Comte and Spencer believed that a single principle traced chrono-logically would be the "master key to human experience." In contrast, modern sociologists believe that social life "is a resultant of causal factors which run in on that center from every point of the com-pass." Sociologists are increasingly skeptical of "one-direction causa-tion." They view causation more like "a chemical reaction than a cable transmitting an electric current straight down from the beginning of the world."[25]

The new technologies of transportation and communication also transformed how people actually experienced causation. Haskell called this phenomenon "causal recession," because causal action came from events, institutions, and people whose point of origin was increasingly remote in space as well as time. Conversely, causal reach extended outward over greater distances and farther into the future. A major consequence was the loss of vitality in the immediate milieu, as causes once attributable to the direct action of autonomous individuals whom one encountered face-to-face were thought to be reflexes of more impersonal social networks that originated and terminated farther away in space as well as time. In "The Metropolis and Mental Life" (1903), the German sociologist Georg Simmel identified a similar feature of urban life as "the blasé attitude [that] results from the rapidly changing and closely compressed contrasting stimulation of the nerves."[26] Simmel also analyzed the increasing sense of interdependence in modern society from the accelerating circulation of that depersonalized but universally recognized medium of value—money.[27] Woodrow Wilson wrote in 1913, "Yesterday, and ever since history began, men were related to one another as individuals. . . . Today the everyday relationships of men are largely with great impersonal concerns, with organizations, not with other individual men."[28] In 1920 Graham Wallas analyzed the technological underpinnings of this phenomenon. "During the last hundred years the external conditions of civilized life have been transformed by a series of inventions which have abolished the old limits to the creation of mechanical force, the carriage of men and goods, and communication by written and spoken words. One effect of this transformation is a general change of social scale. Men find themselves working and thinking and feeling in relation to an environment, which, both in its world-wide extension and its intimate connection with all sides of human existence, is without precedent in the history of the world."[29] In 1927 John Dewey added that new technologies in production and commerce had created a social revolution as local communities became increasingly conditioned by remote and invisible organizations that transformed human relations. "The invasion of the community by the new and relatively impersonal and mechanical modes of combined human behavior is the outstanding fact of modern life."[30] In this impersonal world, society itself emerged as a more potent source of causal action.

Haskell's summary of the achievements of social theory in the late nineteenth century outlines essential elements of the specificity-uncertainty dialectic: "what once had been seen as causes were shown to be symptomatic reflexes of some deeper cause; what once had been seen as a discrete area of inquiry was shown to be causally interwoven with other areas, thus requiring an expansion of the realm of inquiry; what once had been accepted as an adequate explanation was later seen as superficial, merely formalistic" (241). Society was a potent realm of causality situated "between two more familiar realms of causal attribution: it stood 'behind' personal milieu, now increasingly drained of causal potency, but 'in front of' (less remote than) Nature and God, hitherto almost the only plausible loci of remote causal influence" (43). Modern sociological explanations of indirect social causation became more complex and less certain than earlier explanations in terms of the direct action of personal acquaintances or of a singular all-knowing God.

DURKHEIM AND WEBER

The emergence of European sociology in the work of Emile Durkheim and Max Weber embodied many of these historical developments. In the 1890s Durkheim pioneered modern French sociology. In 1896 he was appointed the first full professor of social science in France, and in 1898 he founded the major French sociological journal, *L'année sociologique*. Between 1893 and 1897 he published three pathbreaking works that sharpened the precision of sociological analysis with substantive and methodological studies.

In his time the most important social developments were population increase and its concentration in cities, which were the subject of his first major work, *The Division of Labor in Society* (1893). There he argued that these developments increased the "dynamic density" of social interaction, which intensified the struggle for existence, the specialization of function, and hence the division of labor. These in turn increased social interdependence and individual autonomy. Just as Freud codified a more precise theory for unconscious mental processes and psychosexual development, Durkheim codified a more precise theory of the structure and function of society. He analyzed types of social cohesion (mechanical and organic), the elements of their respective collective consciousnesses (volume, intensity, rigidity, and content), and their ways of maintaining moral order (repressive and restitutive legal sanctions). Volume is the similarity of attitude among individuals, intensity is the hold these beliefs have over individuals, rigidity is the flexibility of those beliefs, and content is the range of activities they comprehend. Repressive sanctions are based on strict imposition of penal law to punish moral transgressions by inflicting pain on the offender, while restitutive sanctions are based on civil and commercial law and seek to restore social and moral order. Traditional societies cohere mechanically. Their collective consciousness is high in volume, intensity, and rigidity, while their content is broad because it is basically religious and reaches into many aspects of life. Individuation is low because every individual is a microcosm of the whole, and strict imposition of penal law maintains moral order. In contrast, modern societies cohere organically. Their collective consciousness is low in volume, intensity, and rigidity, while its content is limited, allowing greater individuality. Modern societies are a product of the division of labor, increasing specialization of beliefs and social roles, and greater personal individuation and interdependence. Religion plays a smaller role in them, allowing greater freedom of belief but also demanding a new basis for morality. While morality is supposed to be maintained by restitutive legal sanctions, they have not worked well. The mechanical social cohesion that once provided a uniform and rigid moral code is in disarray, but nothing has taken its place, hence the modern moral crisis evinced by rising suicide and crime.

Durkheim elaborated a way of making sociology more scientific with his treatise *The Rules of Sociological Method* (1895). It argued that such a science cannot use heredity, race, or insanity to explain social phenomena, as many social thinkers had done. While personal motives are causal for each individual, sociological explanations cannot be a summary of collective individual reasons and motives. They must explain by means of "social facts" viewed as objective things, which are "manners of acting, thinking and feeling external to the individual, which are invested with a coercive power by virtue of which they exercise control over him."[31] To clarify that coercion, one must use the method of concomitant variations; that is, one must "compare the cases where [two variables] are both simultaneously present or absent, so as to discover whether the variations they display in these different combinations of circumstances provide evidence that one depends on the other" (147). Experimental sciences can make such comparisons by controlling for all variables but one, but sociologists deal with networks of multiple causes that cannot be isolated experimentally. To approximate the relative causal force of a single cause out of many requires "the method of concomitant variations" (151). It can approximate the causal function of single variable out of a cluster of them. For example, statistics show that suicide varies directly with education, but by using the method of concomitant variations Durkheim was able to isolate another deeper lying cause of both—"the weakening of religious traditionalism, which reinforces at the same time the desire for knowledge and the tendency to suicide" (152–53).

The combination of this method with a functional and historical analysis of society are the essentials of Durkheim's sociology, which he fleshed out in *Suicide: A Study in Sociology* (1897). It identified kinds of suicide according to their distinctive social causes. This etiological classification of suicide would ground a definition of its function in society, which he elaborated by analyzing its historical roots. Focusing on suicide put his method to the test, because it required explaining sociologically an act that was thought to be quintessentially personal and more suited to individual psychological explanations, an approach that Durkheim emphatically opposed for sociology. As he argued, the suicide rate taken as a whole "is not simply a sum of independent units . . . but is a new fact *sui generis*, with its own unity, individuality and consequently its own nature—a nature, furthermore, dominantly social."[32] That social nature is determined by the distinctive forces of social cohesion that generate three modes of suicide: egoistic, altruistic, and anomic. *Egoistic suicide* occurs when those forces are weak (as in modern industrial society) and the individual lacks integrative meaning from social ties. *Altruistic suicide* occurs when social cohesion is overbearing and the individual who is governed by group pressure commits suicide so as not to be a burden to society (e.g., widows, elderly men, soldiers who have failed in battle). *Anomic suicide* occurs when the moral community breaks down (e.g., in response to rapid upward or downward economic change or from disrupted family relations, especially in divorce).

Durkheim contrasted his approach with those of others who took secondary causes for deeper-lying social causes. For example, in opposition to those who emphasized the causal role of climate, he insisted that suicide was a reflection of a more fundamental social cause. "If voluntary deaths increase from January to July, it is not because heat disturbs the organism but because [during that period] social life is more intense"

(122). In opposition to Gabriel Tarde's argument that suicide is caused by imitation, Durkheim countered that imitation is itself an incorporation of social spirit. Those who focus on religion also took secondary causality for primary. Loss of religion correlates with suicide not because religions forbid suicide or because people fear hell but because religion generates collective states of mind which are life-affirmative. "The more numerous and strong these collective states of mind are, the stronger the integration of the religious community, and also the greater its preservative value" (170). Religion preserves life not because of its ideological content but because of its social function.

Durkheim analyzed distinct social causes of suicide throughout the book, as Steven Lukes noted. These include "'states of the various social environments,' 'what is most deeply constitutional in each national temperament,' . . . 'the moral state [or] temperament [or] constitution' of 'society,' 'ideas and sentiments,' 'common ideas, beliefs, customs and tendencies,' 'currents of opinion,' 'the weakening of traditional beliefs and . . . the state of moral individualism,' 'the loss of cohesion . . . in religious society,' 'excessive individuation,' . . . 'traditionalism [when] it exceeds a certain degree of intensity,' [and] 'crises, that is, disturbances of the collective order.'" For each of these there are numerous subcategories. Lukes concluded with an overall estimate of Durkheim's contribution to understanding of the causal role of society. "His principal methodological advance over previous scholars was his handling of various factors affecting suicide rates, not one by one, but rather as jointly operative and mutually interrelated. . . . he was among the first to use multivariate analysis."[33]

Durkheim's sociology thus accords with the first three elements of the specificity-uncertainty dialectic. It offers more specifically sociological explanations of more complexly interrelated causes, which it defines more precisely than did his predecessors and puts to more fruitful analytical use. The multiplicity of causal factors listed by earlier researchers was usually a smoke screen for analytical confusion and explanatory failure, which, as Codell Carter noted, was the case for early Victorian medicine and psychiatry.[34] In 1864, for example, the French statistician André-Michel Guerry published a study of French and English "moral statistics" based on 21,322 accused murderers. From these statistics he identified 4,478 individual motives that he further grouped into ninety-seven classes of main motives.[35] But Guerry could not explain what historical or social circumstances caused the incidence of those motives or why they might change over time. As Anthony Oberschall concluded, "By the end of the century, moral statistics meant voluminous compilations of statistical data without an attempt to make sense of its contents in other than a superficial descriptive fashion. Such was the situation when Durkheim sought once more to wed moral statistics to sociological theory."[36] Durkheim's contribution was to integrate a multiplicity of causal factors drawn from statistical analysis into a functional and evolutionary framework in accord with rigorous methodological rules.

To assess Durkheim's contribution to probabilistic causality, we must consider the prehistory of Victorian statistical thinking. Around 1830, European researchers began to collect voluminous statistics on the increasing social problems of growing cities and observed statistical regularities for social or "moral" phenomena such as marriage, suicide, and crime. The influential Belgian astronomer Adolphe Quetelet tried to ground a statistical social science on the model of physics. On the basis of "moral statistics," he identified social forces or "penchants," which he believed acted like physical forces such as gravity. In 1829 he concluded that the number of criminals and their types of crime are governed by a "penchant for crime" that is constant from year to year: "We know in advance how many individuals will dirty their hands with the blood of others, how many will be forgers, how many poisoners, nearly as well as one can enumerate in advance the births and deaths that must take place."[37] This stunning claim led to a flood of statistical analyses of "moral" problems, which, following Quetelet, increasingly reified these statistical averages into actual forces, like his penchant for crime. These forces were believed to account for societal events similar to the way the force of gravity in classical physics was believed to account for falling bodies. Quetelet's biographer concluded that throughout his life "Quetelet was pursued by the idea that the entire universe is subject to laws, that nothing is left to chance."[38]

Thus, early nineteenth-century statistics of probability confirmed a deterministic view of the social world, a phenomenon that Ian Hacking called "statistical fatalism" or, as it came to be known, *Quetelismus*.[39] Dickens satirized it in *Hard Times* (1854) when Tom Gradgrind tells his father not to be shocked in learning that his own son is a thief: "So many people . . . out of so many, will be dishonest. I have heard you talk, a hundred times, of its being a law. How can *I* help laws? You have condemned others to such things, Father. Comfort yourself" (3:7). In 1857 the British historian Henry Thomas Buckle invoked a statistical fatalism to explain suicide: "In a given state of society, a certain number of persons must put an end to their own life. This is the general law; and the special question as to who shall commit the crime depends of course upon special laws; which, however, in their action, must obey the large social law to which they are all subordinate. And the power of the larger law is so irresistible, that neither love of life nor the fear of another world can avail anything towards even checking its operation."[40] The disturbing deterministic rhetoric of Tom's plea, "How can *I* help laws?" and Buckle's claim that individual persons "must obey" the larger law came from confusing statistical regularities with actual causal forces. The statistical regularities may be "irresistible" for society as a whole, but not for individuals. Throughout the century statisticians were tempted by statistical regularities to believe that individuals were driven by social forces, as inexorable as gravity, that could be formulated as laws of social behavior. Ironically, the early introduction of statistics confirmed determinism, not probability.

Durkheim resisted that reification of statistical regularities into actual social forces, although he insisted that the social forces were nevertheless real. He did not believe that those forces worked on the individual directly, as Quetelet believed, but rather through society as a whole, leaving individuals free to chose behaviors such as suicide or crime. Durkheim's later studies of religion relied less on statistics, but even at the height of his use of them, he never adopted a probabilistic causality. His sociology always accorded with the basic properties of determinism— mechanism, proportionality, and univocality. The property of mechanism is evident from his definition of social facts. "They are forces as real as cosmic forces . . . [that] affect the individual from without . . . like the physico-chemical forces to which we react" (*Suicide*, 309). They are measurable forces that can be put into social motion only by other social facts. The property of proportionality is that change in effect is proportional to change in cause, a notion that Durkheim expressed with his claim that "every proved specific difference between causes therefore implies a similar difference between effects" (*Rules*, 144, 146). The property of univocality is that each cause can have one and only one effect. While Durkheim recognized that social events are the result of many causes, he held to a variant of univocality by arguing that there was a single class of causes for every single class of effects and that sociology ought to link them one to one by the method of concomitant variation. "A given effect has always a single corresponding cause," and "if suicide depends upon more than one cause, it is because, in reality, there are several kinds of suicides. The same is true of crime" (*Rules*, 129).

Durkheim's conception of causality thus remained explicitly deterministic.[41] A bold step toward a fundamentally probabilistic view of social phenomena was made by one of Durkheim's contemporaries, Francis Galton, whose contribution was assessed by his student Karl Pearson:

> Galton turning over two different problems in his mind reached the conception of correlation: *A* is not the sole cause of *B*, but it contributes to the production of *B*; there may be other, many or few, causes at work, some of which we do not know and may never know. . . . This measure of partial causation was the germ of the broad category—that of correlation, which was to replace not only in the minds of many of us the old category of causation, but deeply to influence our outlook on the universe. The conception of causation—unlimitedly profitable to the physicist—began to crumble to pieces. In no case was *B* simply and wholly caused by *A*, nor indeed by *C*, *D*, and *F* as well! It was really possible to go on increasing the number of contributory causes until they might involve all the factors of the universe. . . . Henceforward the philosophical view of the universe was to be that of a correlated system of variates, approaching but by no means reaching perfect correlation, i.e., absolute causality.[42]

Sociological explanations would not become fully stochastic (irreducible to any underlying deterministic forces) until quantum theory influenced social thinking in the 1930s and the concept of feedback became influential in the 1940s and 1950s.[43] But Durkheim's increasing use of statistics was part of a broad discussion of the connection between statistics, probability, and causality in fin-de-siècle culture.

Another way of salvaging causality for social phenomena short of irreducible deterministic explanations was developed by Max Weber, who also pioneered modern sociology by addressing current social problems. But while Durkheim worried that modernization meant increasing division of labor, heterogeneity, and a disruption of social cohesion leading to egoism and anomie, Weber worried that modernization meant increasing bureaucratization and homogeneity, generating an oppressive social cohesion that stifled individuality and creativity. Still, Weber's contribution to modern sociology, like that of Durkheim, accorded with the specificity-uncertainty dialectic. His thinking specifically about the causal role of society was elaborated in his methods of singular causal analysis, counterfactual reasoning, interpretation, and ideal types.

Singular causal analysis offered a qualitative interpretation that was valid for its explanatory purposes even though it did not conform to a mechanistic deterministic model or offer the mathematical rigor and reductive completeness of natural science. Indeed, Weber claimed that any causal accounts of human behavior that were lawlike could not possibly be interesting, because human behavior is essentially value-oriented and meaningful, and its most important aspects do not conform to universal laws. As he noted, "an *exhaustive* causal investigation of any concrete phenomenon in its full reality is not only practically impossible—it is simply nonsense. . . . The more 'general,' i.e., the more abstract the laws, the less they can contribute to the causal imputation of *individual* phenomena."[44] Singular causal analyses do not contradict those laws but are not modeled after them. With this concept Weber forged a distinctive realm of causal understanding for the social sciences.

Social action is caused by multiple factors that are impossible to inventory, and no one factor can be isolated as in experimental science. A singular causal analysis of a social action requires isolating the circumstances that favored it. That favoring is a judgment of probability, based not on statistics but on imagining a different set of circumstances leading to an effect that would not occur without them. Such estimates of what would or would not occur are less certain than the rigorously predictive knowledge of lawlike phenomena in the natural sciences, but they may nevertheless achieve a high degree of "objective probability" by means of counterfactual reasoning based on knowledge of alternative causal scenarios.[45] For example, causal responsibility in an auto accident can be based on counterfactual reasoning about what would have happened if the driver had not been speeding, an alternative causal scenario based on accident statistics. When counterfactual reasoning leads to a high objective probability, as when an effect actually follows a set of antecedent conditions, the cause is *adequate*. When antecedent conditions contribute to an outcome without being adequate, they are said to be *accidental* causes.

The concepts of objective probability and adequate causation are at the heart of Weber's probabilistic theory of social causation. He challenged the conventional notion that causal knowledge was the exclusive province of natural science and involved only explanations of phenomena based on precise knowledge of initial conditions and an analysis of all forces acting in accordance with universal laws. For example, classical physics explains the descent time of an object with mathematical precision as a function of the law of gravitation, and so predicting when a free-falling object will hit the ground is precise, not probable. The explanatory power of such a causal account of falling motion is absolute, not merely "adequate." Weber's theory of singular causal analysis identified a distinctive kind of causal knowledge for social phenomena with a high degree of probability but still short of the deterministic model of natural science.

Singular causal analyses were not merely applicable to single experiences. Weber saw them as providing "rules of experience" that are imperfect empirical generalizations. These rules offer lawlike knowledge that is applicable to recurrent situations, but their explanatory power works better backward in time rather than forward, and so they offer little predictive capability. Those rules eventually evolved into ideal types, which Weber defined in an essay of 1904: "An ideal type is formed by the one-sided *accentuation* of one or more points of view and by the synthesis of a great many diffuse, discrete, more or less present and occasionally absent *concrete individual* phenomena, which are arranged according to those one-sidedly emphasized viewpoints into a unified *analytical* construct."[46] The accentuation, synthesis, and arrangement of these phenomena are made by interpretations. The most famous ideal types—the Protestant ethic and the spirit of capitalism—Weber elucidated in his book of that title in order to clarify the causal connection between them. Although he ran the causal arrow both ways, he saw it leading more significantly from ideology to economics: "the religious valuation . . . *must have been the most powerful conceivable lever* for the expansion of that attitude toward life which we have here called the spirit of capitalism."[47] This singular causal analysis by means of ideal types exemplified the new authority that Weber accorded to probabilistic causality, captured in the phrase "must have been the most powerful conceivable lever."

Weber's structural breakdown of the modes of social action and social domination enhanced the specificity of his analyses of complex social phenomena. His counterfactual reasoning and his theory of ideal types as inductive generalizations about behavioral patterns were probabilistic if not rigorously statistical. As he explained, "Causal explanation depends on being able to determine that there is a probability, which in the rare ideal case can be numerically stated, but it is always in some sense calculable, that a given observable event (overt or covert) will be followed or accompanied by another event."[48]

Feedback and Circular Causality in the Social Sciences

In the early twentieth century the dominant theory of causality among philosophers was limited by the Aristotelian notion that nothing could cause itself and by the Newtonian notion that causation was a function of the push-pull impact of external forces on inert matter. In conformity to these limitations, philosophers developed a theory of causal knowledge as deduction from timeless and contextless, universally valid laws. According to this theory, which in the twentieth century was known as the covering law model, knowledge of the precise initial condition of any system and the laws of motion that governed its elements made possible, in theory, predictive knowledge of its future behavior and retrodictive knowledge of its past behavior. By satisfying the important criterion of prediction, such causal knowledge was extraordinarily successful, but only in limited applications to closed and isolated systems such as the solar system or colliding balls. It was not applicable to human behavior, for which the precise initial conditions could not be determined and about which no covering laws were universally valid. Moreover, in violation of the Aristotelian and Newtonian limitations, human action was self-caused and embedded temporally in history and contextually in society.[49]

In the nineteenth century, evolutionary theory restored a measure of temporal and contextual factors to causal analysis, but it considered the environment as entirely external to the organism instead of truly interactive with it. The major assault on the classical model took off in the 1930s when a variety of researchers challenged notions that had limited causality and explanation for three hundred years. Mathematicians, biologists, engineers, logicians, philosophers, and social scientists incorporated time (history) and space (context) in revolutionizing understanding of the causal role of society by introducing the concept of feedback or interactive causal loops of action and information. These researchers explored many kinds of circular causality: homeostasis, vicious circles, hermeneutic circles, self-fulfilling prophecies, bandwagon effects, servomechanisms, cybernetics, autopoietic (self-organizing)

systems, and complex adaptive systems. In these interpretive and explanatory frameworks, circular causalities were applied to biological phenomena, such as evolution, epidemics, and ecology as well as to social
phenomena such as economic cycles, bank failures, crowd panic, race relations, cultural interactions, urban dynamics, arms races, and war games.

Causal looping first became applicable to systems analysis when the
engineering concept of feedback was combined with nonlinear mathematical models used in the biological sciences. In 1931 the Italian
mathematician Vito Volterra developed such a model of circular
causality in his analysis of a predator-prey system. It included parameters for births, deaths, and frequency of contacts between predators
and prey in a set of equations that represented several assumptions
about the relation between these two populations—for example, that
prey grow without limit in the absence of predators and that predators
die out in the absence of prey.[50] The combined nonlinear system of
differential equations for these assumptions had a loop structure, offering an early model of the mathematical foundation for circular
causality applied to biological and social systems in which unidirec-
tional cause-to-effect was replaced by circular causal action. Instead of
trying to determine a direct causal connection between a dependent
and independent variable in a linear analysis, social scientists saw interactive connections between interdependent variables in a nonlinear
analysis, as, for example, between predator, prey, and environment or
between murderer, victim, and the judicial system. Later "social constructions" of murder elaborated on this early model.[51]

Homeostasis is the process whereby an organism or an animal society maintains bodily conditions and functions based on informational
feedback about inner and external conditions. The term was coined by
Walter Cannon in *The Wisdom of the Body* (1926) to refer to a number
of self-equilibriating mechanisms in the body such as hunger, thirst,
and adrenal secretion. His final chapter on "social homeostasis" related
the concept to society.[52] An important early application of circular
causality to social phenomena was the Swedish sociologist Gunner
Myrdal's use of the vicious circle to explain racism. In *An American
Dilemma* (1944), he identified a new dynamic causation. "The mechanism that operates here is the 'principle of cumulation,' also called the
'vicious circle.' This principle has a much wider application in social relations." He continued, "Throughout this inquiry, we shall assume a
general interdependence between all the factors in the Negro problem.

White prejudice and discrimination keep the Negro low in standards of living, health, education, manners, and morals. This, in turn, gives support to white prejudice. White prejudice and Negro standards thus mutually 'cause' each other."[53] In later works, Myrdal pioneered concepts that would be elaborated in systems dynamics, as he speculated that it is useless to look for a dominant factor because "everything is cause to everything else in an interlocking circular manner."[54] In 1936 the American sociologist Robert Merton offered another type of circular causality with his concepts of the self-fulfilling prophesy and the unintended consequences of social action in an essay about how "with the complex interaction which constitutes society, action ramifies, its consequences are not restricted to the specific area in which they were initially intended to center, they occur in interrelated fields explicitly ignored at the time of action."[55]

An article of 1943 by Arturo Rosenblueth, Norbert Wiener, and Julian Bigelow on "Behavior, Purpose, and Teleology" linked the concept of feedback in engineering with social behavior in which signals from the goal modify action, as in throwing a stone at a moving target.[56] In 1946, the first Macy Conference in New York inaugurated the new field of cybernetics with its focus on "Feedback Mechanisms and Circular Causal Systems in Biological and Social Systems." The papers concentrated on negative feedback mechanisms in which goals exercise continuous restrictive control over behavior. At subsequent Macy Conferences over the next seven years, researchers applied feedback mechanisms to a variety of social phenomena. As one participant explained, "Norbert Wiener and his friends in mathematics, communication engineering, and physiology had shown the applicability of the notion of inverse feedback to all problems of regulation, homeostasis, and goal-directed activity from steam engines to human societies."[57] These researchers found feedback phenomena in social behaviors such as eating rituals, kinship practices, market fluctuations, and public opinion polls. In 1947 Kurt Lewin, a pioneer of field theory, applied feedback engineering to "social self-steering." As he noted, "Many channels of social life have not simply a beginning and an end but are circular in character.... Some of these circular processes correspond to what the physical engineer calls feedback systems, that is, systems which show some kind of self-regulation."[58] In "Toward a Cybernetic Model of Man and Society" (1948), Karl Deutsch explored "self-modifying networks" in psychology, neurophysiology, and anthropology.

Norbert Wiener applied cybernetics to society in *The Human Use of Human Beings*, subtitled *Cybernetics and Society* (1950). Cybernetics is based on the probabilistic nature of human social experience, following the pioneer work on probability theory by the nineteenth-century physicists Ludwig Boltzman and Willard Gibbs. They argued that since even the most precise measurements are imperfect, "physics now no longer claims to deal with what will always happen, but rather with what will happen with an overwhelming probability."[59] They also believed that as the universe grows older, the probabilistic nature of the world tends to increase along with entropy, the measure of disorder or randomness. As entropy increases, Wiener argued, closed systems "tend naturally to deteriorate and lose their distinctiveness, to move from the least to the most probable state, from a state of organization and differentiation in which distinctions and forms exist, to a state of chaos and sameness." But while concentrations of energy may be running down and complex structures may be coming apart in the universe as a whole, enclaves in it such as individual human beings generate organization and order out of randomness and disorder by using feedback mechanisms to resist the entropic forces of the surrounding world. The new science of cybernetics analyzes these mechanisms of circular causality in a probabilistic world. Wiener adapted this new science to study machines and individual humans as well as group phenomena in Eskimo, feudal, and modern business societies.

Some researchers argued that engineering feedback was too limited to account for the complexity of biological and social systems. In 1951 Bertalanffy charged that feedback was a mechanical concept restricted to closed systems and was therefore ill-suited explain the open systems of organic and social phenomena.[60] He offered a new general system theory to take into account the evolving circular causal dynamics of living and social systems that function as systems with properties that are not present when their components exist in isolation. In 1963 Magoroh Maruyama argued that the "first cybernetics" was based on negative feedback or deviation-counteracting processes used mainly for control, as in Wiener's machines that counteracted human errors in aiming and firing antiaircraft guns. Maruyama proposed a "second cybernetics" based on positive feedback or deviation-amplifying processes operative in social phenomena such as the growth of an economy or a city. Positive feedback was better suited to account for the increasing levels of organization and complexity in biological and social systems. To illustrate the complexity of these complex systems with greater precision, he developed "signed causal-loop diagrams" of positive and negative feedback with positive and negative signs for arrows running between these respective interactive processes.[61] These new analyses of feedback systems are also examples of the specificity-uncertainty dialectic, as increasing precision created increasing uncertainty that in turn called for further precision, and so on.

Over the past twenty-five years, theories of complex adaptive systems have elaborated interactive theories of chemical, biological, and social action in open systems of positive feedback processes that involve exchanging matter, energy, and information with the environment. Beginning with Ilya Prigogine's discovery of dissipative structures, for which he was awarded the Nobel Prize in 1977, physicists and social scientists have developed theories of dynamical systems that rely on feedback mechanisms of circular causality. Dissipative structures are different from the stable systems of the Newtonian world. They are orderly chemical structures that emerge out of nonequilibrium or chaos as a consequence of interactions with their surroundings.[62] In place of the Newtonian model, which explicates the stability, order, and equilibrium of closed mechanical systems governed by linear relationships in which small inputs yield small results, Prigogine explicates the instability, disorder, and temporal development of open chemical and biological systems governed by nonlinear relationships in which small inputs trigger enormous consequences. These self-organizing systems arise out of positive feedback and leap spontaneously to higher levels of organization, creating unstable dissipative structures that require more energy to sustain them. While these causal systems were first explored in natural and biological sciences, they were eventually applied to social processes such as economic cycles and political revolutions.

Around 1990, historians began applying nonlinear causal models to social science and history. Alan Beyerchen noted that nonlinear analysis, which proved effective in analyzing ocean currents and population ecology, was also suited to analyzing history, in which the rule of proportionality (small effects from small causes) does not hold. "It is no longer necessary," he wrote, "for historians to explain away the fact that small inputs can produce disproportionately large effects, while large-scale inputs can generate diminutive results; violation of proportionality is actually part of the natural order inherent in any interactive, nonlinear system."[63] Nonlinearity was pioneered in physics, chemistry, and biology, but it also can make sense out of history, which is a time- and context-dependent system of events in which individual choices and accidents have enormous consequences. Beyerchen subsequently applied such an analysis to Carl von Clausewitz's theory of war, a phenomenon in which outcomes are highly sensitive to initial conditions.[64] Following Beyerchen, Randolph Roth explored a nonlinear analysis in a social science not bound by the rules of proportionality, additivity (complex phenomena can be analyzed into simpler ones), or univocality (each cause has only one effect). He looked forward to the revolution in nonlinear mathematics that was transforming the physical and biological sciences and also liberating social science "from its dependence on linear metaphors and on non-reflexive empirical models."[65]

The causal theories of these systems of action evince an appreciation of the increasing specificity, complexity, and uncertainty of causal knowledge. They account more precisely for the multiple causal interactions of complex adaptive systems, but as they do so they reveal new patterns of self-activation and multilevel causality that cannot be explained with the level of certainty demanded by classical physics. Human beings are complex, dynamic systems that self-activate and interact with their environment to create novelty. Their behavior cannot be explained with Newtonian certainty but requires hermeneutic interpretations that are inescapably uncertain. As Alicia Juarrero concluded, "If we live in a dynamical universe, the novelty and creativity such complex systems display do indeed signal the end of eternal, unchanging, and universal certainty."[66] In 1995 Walter J. Freeman applied such an analysis to his own model of the human brain as a self-organizing, complex adaptive system that functions as a result of positive feedback from the entire brain in even the simplest neurological functions. He compared this theory of the brain with Foucault's theory of knowledge and power in society, arguably the most influential methodological statement in social science over the last thirty years.[67]

Foucault's analysis of circular causality in society as a field of power relations also evinces the specificity-uncertainty dialectic. His theory of power reads like a critique of the laws of mechanical and gravitational forces as applied to politics. "By power, I do not mean . . . a general system of domination exerted by one group over another, a system whose effects, through successive derivations, pervade the entire body." Power is not a single force emanating from a single source, as in politics where sovereign power emanates from a single legitimate ruler or class. It is a "multiplicity of force relations immanent in the sphere in which they operate." It is a complex network of interdependent forces that circulate throughout society from top to bottom (and bottom to top) as well as from the center to periphery and back. It is not exercised through pronouncements from positions of authority but from the endlessly protean discourses generated everywhere in society, from academic disciplines to barroom banter. "Power is everywhere, not because it embraces everything, but because it comes from everywhere." It is not transmitted in a linear manner but rather circulates in negative and positive feedback. Negatively it limits human action by dictating norms and legitimizing rewards and punishments; positively it magnifies little causes into big and unpredictable effects. It is also exercised as the dialectical interplay of positive and negative forces, an "interplay of nonegalitarian and mobile relations."[68] The discourse of power is exercised in many ways: in basic definitions of terms and scientific theories as well as in formal ideas about sickness and health, truth and falsehood, good and evil, legality and criminality. The strategic field of power relations includes those who exercise power as well those who react to it. Society defines the sexual pervert and the criminal as outsiders with discourses of power, while society itself depends on those outsiders for its own notion of normalcy and deviance.

The Foucauldian analysis of the multiplicity of discourses, their complex interaction, and the uncertain or at least unstable nature of their meaning and function in society offers a sharp contrast to positivist notions of nineteenth-century social science and even to the rationalist assumptions of those pioneers of modern sociology, Durkheim and Weber. While in recent years Foucault's authority has waned from its highpoint in the 1980s, his philosophy was a centerpiece of postmodern social science. Its assault on the authority of any single source of power or legitimacy underscored the extent to which late twentieth-century social theory embraced the highly probabilistic and uncertain nature of our knowledge of the causal role of society. The death of the author (in addition to the death of God); skepticism about objectivity, progress, and grand historical narratives; the conflation of the real and the fake; postcolonialism, multiculturalism, and globalism; deconstruction, dispersal, and indeterminism; the end of certainty, the assault on the canon, and the proliferation of texts into discourses of knowledge and power are historically distinctive elements of the modernist and postmodernist world that shattered Victorian notions about authority, sovereignty, morality, and causality. At the heart of that shift was a new take on the causal role of ideas, the subject of my final chapter.

8

Ideas

To MAKE MURDERS intelligible, novelists sometimes present ideas as the mainspring for action. This chapter tracks the history of those ideas.

Throughout the period of my study, the act of murder from literary classics to potboilers was consistently judged to be wrong. What does change is the explanatory role of moral and religious concepts based on Judeo-Christian ideals that motivated those acts. As I have noted in previous chapters, psychiatrists increasingly replaced the explanatory function of moral and religious judgments with medical and psychiatric diagnoses, while jurists replaced them with forensic and social analyses. This chapter focuses on how philosophers and novelists replaced them with aesthetic and existential interpretations. Accordingly, murders were accounted for less in terms of evil and sin and more in terms of creativity and self-definition. This shift conforms to the specificity-uncertainty dialectic insofar as critical analysis of the causal role of moral and religious ideas involved increasingly detailed understanding of their specific historical and psychological origins, while interpretations of aesthetic and existential ideas germane to understanding the cause or motivation for murder in novels became increasingly heterodoxical, probabilistic, and uncertain.

NIETZSCHE

Throughout the nineteenth century, artists and intellectuals experienced a growing crisis in religious faith. A particularly combustible contribution to this spiritual turmoil was Nietzsche's announcement of the death of God, his assault on the Christian moral distinction between good and evil, his critical genealogy of Western morality, his affirmation of aesthetic and ultimately existential values beyond moral values, and his positive philosophy of the self. His writings are central to the modernist transition from the causal role of religious and moral ideas to that of aesthetic and existential ideas, and they are therefore the intellectual pivot for this chapter.

Nietzsche's assault on religion was from deep personal experience originating in a pious German Protestant family. His father and both grandfathers were Lutheran ministers, and after the death of his father at age four he was raised by his devout mother and aunts in Naumburg, which was dominated by a glorious cathedral. Thus, early on he was immersed in an intense Christian faith against which he reacted passionately. He respected Jewish and Christian spiritual leaders for their discipline and introspection that deepened self-awareness, but he loathed their otherworldliness, asceticism, and sense of sin. He admired Jesus's moral courage but rejected the belief that he could save others and the symbolism of his crucifixion, which Nietzsche believed signified the enormous human burden of guilt that required such a horrific redemption.

In *Thus Spoke Zarathustra* (1883–85), Nietzsche announced the death of God through his spokesman Zarathustra, named after the ancient Persian philosopher Zoroaster. As Nietzsche subsequently explained, Zarathustra "was the first to consider the fight of good and evil to be the very wheel in the machinery of things." Zarathustra transposed morality "into the metaphysical realm as a force, cause, and end in itself" and in so doing produced "this most calamitous error, morality."[1] Although the ancient Zoroaster consistently reexamined the basis of that morality, his followers lost sight of his critical approach and posited his good/evil distinction as the foundation for a formal religion and fixed moral code. In speaking through the persona of a modern Zarathustra, Nietzsche reclaimed the ancient philosopher's critical spirit, which bursts on Zarathustra's listeners with the announcement of the death of God. This extraordinary claim identifies a turning point in philosophical inquiry into the basis of Western religion and morality. It signifies that in the modern world, traditional belief has been fatally weakened by the achievements of positivism, materialism, rationalism, and science. In response, some traditional believers are tempted to abandon all values and give themselves over to nihilism, which Nietzsche viewed as the greatest spiritual danger in his time. That danger was famously carried to deadly terminus in *The Brothers Karamazov* by the murderer Smerdyakov, who rationalizes his act on the basis of Ivan Karamazov's repeated contention that the realization that there is no God implies that "everything is permitted," even murder.

Nietzsche believed that Christian morality may be, ironically, the greatest threat to human excellence.[2] Morality itself might be to blame for preventing man from attaining "the *highest power and splendor* actually possible."[3] He proposed that the way to a more meaningful life involves transvaluating all values, including Christian morality, by going "beyond good and evil." His book of that title urges readers to become more profound and self-aware by moving into an "extra-moral" realm in order to overcome a dispiriting Christianity that undermines freedom, pride, and self-confidence while encouraging self-mockery and self-mutilation.[4] Christianity preaches a herd morality that cultivates submissiveness and mediocrity at the expense of assertiveness and excellence. Nietzsche also targeted the utilitarian goal of maximizing pleasure, which cultivates ordinary physical pleasures and common artistic sensibilities. He called for a new morality and a new kind of human being, a "higher man" whose goal is not ordinary pleasures and philistine tastes, but greatness. "He shall be greatest who can be loneliest, the most concealed, the most deviant, the human being beyond good and evil, the master of his virtues, he who is overrich in will" (139).

Such a philosophy of transvaluating the everyday moral code invited misinterpretation, especially among those looking to justify immoral acts such as murder. But even as a self-described "immoralist," Nietzsche was not advocating breaking moral codes. He revered courage, honesty, generosity, and even courtesy. In urging others to go beyond good and evil he intended them not to do evil but to re-examine the basis for the good/evil distinction and see its life-negating meaning in a Christianity that is held together by a restrictive list of "thou shalts" and "thou shalt nots" enforced by the fear of eternal hell. Christian morality acts as a brake on human existence, while he calls for a new spirit to drive it. Going beyond the good/evil distinction requires seeing its limits, looking beyond it, embracing other life-enhancing values, and improving oneself.

Nietzsche's *On the Genealogy of Morals* (1887) traces the historical, psychological, and physiological roots of the Judeo-Christian morality. His historical analysis goes back to "the slave revolt in morals" initiated by the Jews during their enslavement in Egypt. The morality of their overlords was based on the good/bad distinction that was derived from the positive values that kept the overlords in power (riches, strength, health, and willfulness), which they called "good" in opposition to values associated with their servile slaves (poverty, weakness, sickness, and passivity), which they called "bad." The slave revolt was led by Jews, who were filled with resentment and hungering for revenge. They based their new morality on those same values that sustained and justified the oppression of their overlords, but which they inverted and called "evil," in opposition to the new notion of "good" grounded on the values that exalted their own debased condition. Thus, the slave revolt in morals made it evil to be passionate, proud, powerful, and self-assertive while making it good to be chaste, humble, weak, and self-denying. Nietzsche traced this moral revolution initially to the Jews, whom he held responsible for the derivative self-negating message of Christianity that praises those who are meek, humble, downtrodden, prudent, chaste, and simple.

His psychological analysis turned the supposed divine origin of Christian morality topsy-turvy by viewing it as stemming from the ordinary and most debasing human psychological processes of resentment, guilt, and self-denial. His physiological analysis probed Christianity's assault on sensualism. Although Christianity presented itself as a life-affirming religion of hope, its powerful hold on believers was achieved with a life-denying message of asceticism and sin. It purported to offer strength and resolve to the weary but actually glorified weakness and helplessness, symbolized by the image of Jesus on the cross. It purported to offer hope for joy and divine justice, but actually induced suffering and injustice by a painful reminder of God's sacrifice of his quintessentially innocent son for lowly human sins going back ultimately to the original sin—a disobedience of God's command by willfully eating the fruit of the tree of knowledge of good and evil and trying to be wise like God. This first sin (of disobedience and daring to know) and its biologically determined reenactment in every subsequent sex act constitute the indelible historical, psychological, and physiological origins of Christian morality, which account for its powerful hold on the Christian faithful.

In urging his followers to go beyond good and evil, Nietzsche prescribed a new mode of existence that includes being moral but is not fundamentally defined by it. The "beyond" of his exhortation refers to a next stage for human existence and another basis for judging it–namely the aesthetic—and beyond that, what came to be called the existential. To illustrate this revolutionary act in the history of philosophy, I offer a hypothetical example. If one asked a nineteenth-century philosopher to evaluate someone's existence, he would have been obliged to answer in terms of the defining philosophical distinctions and categories of his time from metaphysics, epistemology, and ethics. That is, he could have said what kind of an entity the person was and whether that person was free or determined (metaphysics), what the source of that person's knowledge was and whether it was valid (epistemology), and how that person behaved toward others and whether that behavior was good or bad (ethics). Nietzsche proposed a new way of evaluating the *meaning* of existence, one suggested by the aesthetic distinction of beauty and ugliness but applied to the artist's will and spirit. By artist, in this context, he meant one who freely fashions his own self and its values. He was himself an artist with words, as well as a composer who used artistic terminology figuratively with reference to how to live. He also suggested another distinction analogous to the aesthetic distinction but, more basic still, defined in terms of greatness versus impoverishment of existence. In place of the model of the Christian saint, Nietzsche proposed the model of the great artist, and beyond that the "higher man," who lives the more meaningful life.[5] This philosophy of the higher man was the focus of a new field of philosophical inquiry that concerned the meaning of existence, a field that became modern existentialism.[6]

Nietzsche introduced the aesthetic distinction in *The Birth of Tragedy* (1872), which celebrated Greek drama as a source of meaning in life against the excessively rational philosophy of Socrates. In a new preface to that work in 1886, he elaborated its historical significance. "Already in the [first] preface addressed to Richard Wagner, art and *not* morality, is presented as the truly *metaphysical* activity of man." By metaphysical, Nietzsche meant that which constitutes its fundamental nature. "In the book itself," wrote Nietzsche, "the suggestive sentence is repeated several times, that the existence of the world is justified only as an aesthetic phenomenon."[7] He did not mean that existence is to be justified by artistic judgments or by beautiful or ugly external appearances but by modes of living analogous to artistic achievements that pose the greatest challenges in life and offer its greatest fulfillments. Christian art, as Christian exegesis, is not true art. Genuine artists are iconoclasts. They have "uncanny access to everything that seduces, allures, compels, overthrows," [and they are] "born enemies of logic and straight lines, lusting after the foreign, the exotic, the tremendous, the crooked, the self-contradictory."[8] Artists are spiritual Antichrists, which is how Nietzsche described himself. While he respected Jesus, he rejected his supposed role as Christ, the Messiah, because no one can save people ultimately but themselves. Nietzsche was an Antichrist in that his message was the impossibility of divine salvation through Jesus Christ. Artists are Antichrists in that by demonstrating the possibilities of human creativity they remind us of the necessity of taking responsibility for fashioning our own salvation. Divine salvation is impossible because there is no God and because we always remain uncertain and at risk, facing the endlessly blank canvas of life.

In *The Gay Science*, Nietzsche elaborated the fusion of aesthetic and existential qualities central to those "higher types" who have achieved greatness: "To 'give style' to one's character—a great and rare art! It is practiced by those who survey all the strengths and weaknesses of their nature and then fit them into an artistic plan until every one of them appears as art and reason and even weaknesses delight the eye."[9] This passage qualified the overemphasis on brute strength suggested by Nietzsche's concept of the will to power, which he proposed as life's driving force. The will to power is not exercised over others but is rather exercised by the self with reference to the surrounding world and, more important, over the self in making or creating, as suggested by the German word for power—*Macht*, from *machen* (to make). Examples of the importance of artistic accomplishment in Nietzsche's existential philosophy of the self are those accomplished artists whom Nietzsche mentioned most often as "higher types": Homer, Sophocles, Shakespeare, Goethe, Beethoven, and the early Wagner.

In *Thus Spoke Zarathustra*, Nietzsche's philosophy of the self centers on the figure of the higher man, or overman. The main problem in communication that Nietzsche faced was like the one that Zarathustra himself faced in confronting listeners who resisted serious examination of the meaning of their moral code and religious faith. To illustrate the difficult existential choice inherent in that examination Nietzsche introduced two contrasting types: the "last man," an unreflective type driven by the desire to be happy and conform to social mores, and the "overman," who courageously probes the meaning of his existence by creatively interrogating all existing values and endlessly seeking to fashion more creative and meaningful ones. In using these types to teach the way to the overman, Nietzsche offers not a blueprint for becoming a better person but a new way to think critically about the meaning of one's own existence as a way to choose becoming more fully and more deeply what one is. Subsequently Nietzsche abandoned the term "overman," except for passages in *Ecce Home* that refer to *Zarathustra*.

Nietzsche's negative goal was to analyze critically and block the powerful causal role of Christian religion and morality in human existence that he believed fostered otherworldliness and self-denial and was inimical to greatness. In its place he offered a life-affirming way of being that activated the will to power in the service of greatness. Both his negative and positive philosophy embodied elements of the specificity-uncertainty dialectic. In opposition to the conviction that Judeo-Christian morality was a unified and divinely inspired sacred dogma, he critically analyzed it as a multifaceted ideological construction of specific secular origins—historical, literary, philological, psychological, and physiological. He used classical philosophy, ancient history, and even economic theory to trace the origin of words for good and evil to the creditor-debtor relationship; he used psychology to explore the resentment and guilt of the early spiritual leaders; and he used physiology to elucidate Christianity's asceticism and repressive moral code. While theologians held that coincidences were ordained by an omniscient God and were evidence of an ultimate design in life, Nietzsche denied any such design and insisted rather that existence is fundamentally probabilistic. He also rejected the idea that actions are rationally willed to achieve clearly envisioned goals along with any Hegelian-style absolute rationality governing history and insisted rather that understanding of existence must include prankish folly. Zarathustra taught how "over all things stand the heaven Accident, the heaven Innocence, the heaven Chance."[10] Nietzsche proposed to liberate his followers from "their bondage under purpose" and restore the ancient virtues of chance. The path to the overman, like artistic creation, is full of surprises and risks. Nietzsche's affirmation of accidents was not, however, a celebration of haphazard types but of those who will to take risks. Ironically, "the most necessary soul" is the one who wills contingency, like a musician who introduces whimsy into music. Great artists exercise an accomplished orchestration of chance, not a poverty of options. Nietzsche's critique of Christian morality and his affirmation of the higher man also embraced uncertainty. "God is dead" meant that there is no certain ground for human experience, no ultimate first or final causes, no reliable moral standard, and no absolute truth. As he announced in *Zarathustra*, there are a thousand and one values, none of which has an absolute philosophical grounding or is absolutely right. His philosophy of the higher man is an urging to find one's way on a path that becomes increasingly mystifying as one proceeds.

Nietzsche had an enormous cultural impact on major thinkers such as Spengler, Freud, Buber, Heidegger, Sartre, Camus, Jaspers, Foucault, and Derrida as well as writers such as Wedekind, Kafka, Hesse, Mann, d'Annunzio, Gide, Malraux, Bataille, Shaw, Lawrence, Joyce, and Dreiser. He influenced feminists (Hedwig Dohm and Helene Stöcker), dancers (Isadora Duncan and Vaslav Nijinsky), composers (Richard Strauss and Gustav Mahler), and sociologists (Ferdinand Tönnies and Georg Simmel). He inspired German expressionists, Italian futurists, and French surrealists along with socialists, anarchists, and imperialists. Proponents of racism, fascism, and Nazism created an erroneous reputation for the philosopher that scholars since Walter Kaufmann have had to address.[11]

His philosophy was also a major source for the eclipse of moral and religious explanations of murder in modernist novels. Although Gide's Lafcadio does not mention Nietzsche directly, his iconoclasm is Nietzschean.[12] Francis Iles's Dr. Bickleigh tries to elevate his "commonplace" murder by citing the philosopher of greatness directly. Meyer Levin's young murderers Judd Steiner and Artie Strauss spout a vulgarized Nietzschean philosophy of the "superman" to each other, their lawyers, and the court. While the murderers who cite Nietzsche to justify their actions are invariably depicted as misguided, many of the authors who created such characters, as well as others who made no reference to Nietzsche, took him seriously as their own explanations of murder moved beyond the earlier explanatory concepts of moral degeneration and religious apostasy to aesthetic notions of murder as an art or even to existential notions of murder as an act of self-definition.

NINETEENTH-CENTURY MORALISM

The nineteenth century was deeply moralistic, as normative values dominated thinking about human nature. Physicians included in their etiologies of disease long lists of morally inflected causal factors: "drunkenness, intemperance, gluttony, luxury, indulgence, debauchery,

dissipation, vicious habits, solitary vice, excessive venereal indul-
gences, lustful excesses, indolence, sloth."[13] Victorian social science was
essentially moral indoctrination. As Craig Haney noted, "In the first
part of the [nineteenth] century, American college students learned
the 'facts' of human nature in courses in moral philosophy that were
often taught by college presidents and always with a heavy religious
emphasis."[14]

The permeation of moralism in Victorian thought was especially evident in the array of psychological theories about the nature, causes, and
effects of the moral faculty and its disorders. Among early English and
American psychiatrists, "moral" was roughly equivalent to what we currently mean by "psychological," but it also had normative connotations.
In 1786 its psychological function was conflated with normative behavior in Benjamin Rush's definition of the "moral faculty" as "a power in
the human mind of distinguishing and chusing [sic] good and evil; or, in
other words, virtue and vice."[15] Variants of that faculty were called the
"moral sense" or "moral feeling." In 1835 James Prichard identified the
disorder of that faculty as "moral insanity" to distinguish defects of
the emotions and the will from defects of the intellect.[16] This moralized
concept was accepted in France by Esquirol and Georget and in
Germany by Johann Heinroth, who extended it to include religious
connotations in arguing that its cause was sin.[17] In popular culture all
across Europe and America the morally insane were believed to be possessed by the devil, and so the alarm over moral insanity was magnified
by its association with religious failings. Jurists judged murderers who
exhibited no clear motives such as greed or revenge as acting as out of
"moral insanity," which for some notorious killers was renamed "moral
imbecility" or "moral monstrosity."[18]

Psychiatrists had no idea what caused moral insanity. Instead of a specific etiology they offered speculation about its telltale signs. In 1854 the
French psychiatrist J.-P. Falret argued that "madness is more often engendered by moral causes than by physical causes," although his moral
causes were not really causes at all but merely outward signs of socially
deviant behavior.[19] The many possible effects of this multicausal
disorder included any antisocial behavior, which made it a convenient
catchall diagnostic tool for baffled experts to use in explaining, circularly, why the "morally alienated" willfully chose to do evil. Vagueness
also characterized assessments of the causal role of moral insanity in
crime. In the first half of the nineteenth century, as David Brion Davis

concluded, a typical American judge "might have defined legal guilt as a causal connection between an unlawful act and the malicious disposition of an inner, nonintellectual faculty, which might variously be called the heart, will, or moral sense."[20] The circularity of explaining willful malicious acts as a result of malicious dispositions of the will or moral sense closed off any specific causal determination.

Around 1870, as researchers applied more rigorous methods, the broadly defined and emotionally charged concept of the moral faculty began to lose its explanatory authority. A shift away from moralizing in the study of crime took off in the late nineteenth century as experts in psychiatry and law purged it from explanations and diagnoses. In England moral judgments gave way to naturalistic explanations in terms of cause and effect, contributing to what Martin Wiener tagged "the de-moralizing of criminality." The interpretation of behavior "as good or evil was replaced by analyses of constitutions and dispositions that differed from one another only in degree." This new discourse blurred the previously sharp line between criminality and normalcy as the gradational continuum of "causalism" replaced the either-or disjunct of "moralism."[21] This causalism served the increasingly complex bureaucratic society which, as Christie Davies argued, turned more on "questions of cause and effect and of accountability and liability rather than praise and blame."[22] In America a dramatic challenge to moral insanity occurred during the trial of Charles Guiteau, who used it unsuccessfully in defending himself during his 1881 trial for assassinating President James Garfield, as reports of that legal defense enraged the public as well as legal experts.[23] After the turn of the twentieth century, psychiatrists began to substitute for the general and moralistic social judgments of earlier analyses the sort of detailed and individualized etiological analyses that Freud pioneered with psychoanalysis.

More recently Michel Foucault challenged the completeness of that achievement in arguing that the explicit moralizing of Victorian psychiatry remained as a morally judgmental subtext in modern psychiatry. That challenge was the focus for many histories of psychiatry over the past two decades, but in noting similarities between nineteenth-century moralizing and twentieth-century diagnosing, these works also distinguished the differences and demonstrated that the larger sweep of this history was in the direction of increasingly detailed and precise causal analyses of mental life.

Beyond Moralism in Murder Novels

While in the social sciences moralism gave way to causalism, in the murder novel moral and religious interpretations gave way to aesthetic and existential interpretations. The beginning of this shift is reflected in the disappearance of the classic villain of melodrama after the mid-nineteenth century and in the flourishing of the art-for-art's-sake movement in the 1890s. In Victorian popular literature, as Beth Kalikoff showed, murder was associated with "moral decay," and the typical villain was wall-to-wall evil.[24] In a preface to *Martin Faber* (1833), William Simms explained that "the design of this work is purely moral." It was intended to show "the injurious consequences directly flowing from each and every aberration from the standard of a scrupulous morality" (4). His titular murderer is infused with immorality throughout every fiber of his being, as he kills his lover and her fetus when she threatens to tell his fiancée and foil an advantageous marriage. "The secretions of my malignity," he narrates, "jaundiced my whole moral existence" (21). His existence was defined entirely in moral terms. As he explains, "To do wrong was to be myself" (25). Dickens's early villains were almost as thoroughly evil, and his murderers were immoral and demonic. As one commentator concluded, Dickens "never escaped from the moral categories of his age."[25]

While in the late Victorian period simpler moral dichotomies of good and evil were evolving into more complex and uncertain aesthetic and existential interpretations, in 1886 a dichotomized moral faculty still played a defining causal role. In *The Strange Case of Dr. Jekyll and Mr. Hyde*, a drug liberates "the evil side" of Jekyll's character to commit murder as Mr. Hyde, who is "pure evil" (45). In this struggle between dichotomized faculties of good and evil, the latter is more "original" and stronger when released by the drug. The defining duality of man, Jekyll realizes, is essentially moral.

That dichotomy is far less sharp four years later in Wilde's *The Picture of Dorian Gray*. This work is pivotal in the art-for-art's-sake movement that had been gaining momentum throughout the nineteenth century. The term derives from Kant's definition of art as "purposiveness without purpose." It was first used in 1804 to indicate disinterestedness in art, and by the late 1820s it designated general hostility to moral or socially useful ideas in art.[26] In the preface to *Mademoiselle de Maupin* (1835), Théophile Gautier railed against moralistic art with utilitarian goals: "There is nothing really beautiful save what is of no possible use. Everything useful is ugly, for it expresses a need, and man's needs are low and disgusting, like his own poor wretched nature." The midcentury poetry of Charles Baudelaire was infused with *l'art pour l'art*. The concept appeared in Walter Pater's *Studies in the History of the Renaissance* (1873), with the famous concluding exhortation for artists to pursue great passion that yields a quickened, multiplied consciousness: "Of such passion, the poetic passion, the desire for beauty, the love of art for its own sake, has most, for art comes to you proposing frankly to give nothing but the highest quality to your moments as they pass, and simply for those moments' sake." Although some interpreted Pater's aestheticism as advocating the elimination of morality in art, he intended to cultivate moral development through art. By that time artists were tiring of the precise descriptions of realism with its commitment to utilitarian goals and began instead to use amoral, if not immoral, symbolism and later stylistic *décadence*. Joris-Karl Huysmans's substantively decadent novel *Against Nature* (1884) shocked readers with the insistent aestheticism and immorality of a main character who celebrates the death of his virility, prefers the artificial to the natural, and intentionally corrupts a young adolescent with expensive prostitutes in the hope that he will eventually commit murder to fund his new sexual needs.

Studies of the shift from moralizing about murder to the "aesthetics of murder" typically begin with Thomas De Quincey's famous essay, "On Murder Considered as a One of the Fine Arts" (1827, with supplements in 1839 and 1854). For John G. Cawelti, De Quincey is evidence of a "new attitude toward crime," one that constitutes "a shift from an essentially religious and moral feeling about crime to what might best be called an aesthetic approach."[27] For Joel Black, De Quincey used "the adverb *aesthetically* . . . for the first time in the English language . . . for the preposterous purpose of evaluating acts of murder."[28] These historical judgments are about a new way of interpreting murder narratives aesthetically as artful or creative, made by readers of those narratives who depict murders as spectators from without, but these judgments miss the more important new way that writers attribute aesthetic and, subsequently, existential motives for the murderer himself. That is, they note a shift in the way readers of murder stories interpret the act of murder in texts but not a shift in the actual motives and purposes for the murderer himself acting as a creative force in those texts. That shift in thinking about murder is post-Nietzschean.

The philosophical foundation for this crucial distinction was noted by Nietzsche in criticizing Kant, from whom nineteenth-century aestheticism and the art-for-art's-sake movement derived. He wrote: "Kant, like all philosophers, instead of envisaging the aesthetic problem from the point of view of the artist (the creator), considered art and the beautiful purely from that of the 'spectator,' and unconsciously introduced the 'spectator' into the concept 'beautiful.' 'That is beautiful,' said Kant, 'which gives us pleasure *without interest.*' Without interest!"[29] Nietzsche's outrage over Kant's disinterested aesthetic judgments aligns with his outrage over Christianity's paralyzing asceticism in turning against sensuousness. Aesthetic experience for Nietzsche is not the passionless contemplation of a spectator from without but the passionate act of creation from within. A murder genuinely motivated by aesthetic concerns would have to be generated from within by energies and sensibilities akin to those that drive artistic creation. While such acts do violate public morality and are in no sense to be condoned, least of all by Nietzsche, they can be understood as perverse deflections of energies that resemble artistic creation more than energies stimulated by violating a public moral code. Insofar as they resemble the struggle to define oneself, they also have existential meaning.

Oscar Wilde's *The Picture of Dorian Gray* (1890) is a transitional document about murder in which artistic concerns play a causally significant role. Wilde ventures beyond good and evil in the provocative generalizations of his preface: "There is no such thing as a moral or an immoral book. Books are well written, or badly written. That is all." And in the same vein, "An ethical sympathy in an artist is an unpardonable mannerism of style." On the other hand, Wilde's aestheticism includes the possibility of treating ethical themes, as he adds, "vice and virtue are to the artist materials for an art." The novel is about an immoral murder, but one that is also partly motivated by a historically innovative interplay of artistic and existential objectives.

The murderer is the beautiful seducer Dorian Gray, whose aestheticism is his superficial good looks and his pleasure in exploiting them. He is encouraged in his immoralism by the homosexual aesthete Henry Wooton, who expresses Wilde's most radical aestheticism: "beauty is the wonder of wonders" (27). He also has existential concerns. The goal of life, he tells Dorian, is to realize one's nature. "People are afraid of themselves, nowadays. They have forgotten the highest of all duties, the duty that one owes to one's self." In a similar spirit to Nietzsche's critique of religion and morality, accented by a rousing aestheticism, Wooton rails against two paralyzing fears: "the terror of society, which is the basis of morals, the Terror of God, which is the secret of religion." Wooton also proposes a philosophy of life similar to Nietzsche's philosophy of the overman: "If one man were to live out his life fully and completely, were to give form to every feeling, expression to every thought . . . the world would gain such a fresh impulse of joy that we would forget all the maladies of medievalism and return to the Hellenic ideal—to something finer, richer, than the Hellenic ideal" (23). That ideal is, of course, a society in which homosexuality, is neither immoral nor criminal. Wilde's iconoclasm toward conventional ethical concerns, like that of his contemporary Gide, is energized by his own homosexuality, which the wider public at that time judged to be immoral, sinful, and illegal. He is contemptuous of these judgments about homosexuals but uses them in characterizing Dorian's murder of the artist Basil Hallward. In addition, Wilde weaves into his account of that murder some historically significant aesthetic and existential concerns, complicated by the powers of Dorian's portrait which miraculously registers on his face signs of the evil he does in life, while his actual face remains unchanged.

The existential motivation is Dorian's effort to define himself as a self. Early on he distances himself from simplistic views of selfhood. "He used to wonder at the shallow psychology of those who conceive the Ego in man as a thing simple, permanent, reliable, and of one essence. To him, man was a being with myriad lives and myriad sensations, a complex multiform creature that bore within itself strange legacies of thought and passion, and whose very flesh was tainted with the monstrous maladies of the dead" (157). This existential pride turns to panic when his cruel acts become visible on the image of his ego in the painting and are verbally decried by the artist who created it. When Dorian refuses to pray with Basil, the artist replies, "don't say that. You have done enough evil in your life" (173). For the man who cooly rejected moral evaluations of the ego, this biting moral judgment from the artist who put his ego on canvas cuts to the quick, and the painting itself miraculously urges him to commit murder. "Dorian glanced at the picture, and suddenly an uncontrollable feeling of hatred for Basil Hallward came over him, as though it had been suggested to him by the image on the canvas, whispered into his ear by those grinning lips" (174). Filled with loathing for Basil, he grabs a knife and stabs him to death to protect his fragile ego from dissolution in the judgmental gaze of the man who projected it into art. Formerly Basil had encouraged Dorian to exploit his beauty, but in seeing at what cost, he condemns him as an evil sinner in the language of the morality and religion that they had both arrogantly spurned.

Even with Basil dead, his judgment sticks. Dorian cannot recapture his former blithe disregard and increasingly sees himself in conventional terms of good and evil. In a final desperate act of self-definition to preserve his image as the beautiful subject of artistic inspiration, he stabs the painting itself with the same knife he had used to stab Basil. "As it had killed the painter, so it would kill the painter's work." He tries to kill Basil's indelible judgment of him by destroying the artist's representation of himself but in the process somehow kills himself. Friends find Dorian with a knife in his heart, lying on the floor in front of the painting, "withered, wrinkled, and loathsome of visage" (245–46).

The motives for Dorian's murderous acts are moral, aesthetic, and existential. He was an immoral sinner who drove his female lover and another friend to suicide and then killed an artist who judged him to be evil. His aesthetic motive was superficial—to preserve his physical beauty in accord with the aestheticism he learned from Wooton. His effort to appropriate the creative power of art by destroying it failed because artistic impulses cannot be seized forcefully from without but must be cultivated patiently from within. In the end, art takes revenge against his destructive purposes, perhaps literally, because Wilde does not reveal what power drove that knife into Dorian's heart; either Dorian stabbed himself, which is unlikely, or the stabbing came somehow from the painting itself to bring about a uniquely visceral poetic justice. Dorian's existential motive for murder was to preserve his ego from Basil's annihilating judgment. With these interwoven moral, aesthetic, and existential motives, Wilde explored new ways of rendering the causal role of ideas.

In the modern period, novelists explicitly rejected a moral framework. Lawrence parted company with earlier novelists, including Dostoevsky, who Lawrence believed worked within a rigid "moral scheme." In a letter written a month before the outbreak of war in 1914, he explained that in his writing he was rejecting the "old-fashioned" literary impulse "to conceive a character in a certain moral scheme and make him consistent. The certain moral scheme is what I object to. In Turgenev, and in Tolstoy, and in Dostoevsky, the moral scheme into which all the characters fit—and it is nearly the same scheme—is, whatever the extraordinariness of the characters themselves, dull, old, dead."[30] That same year, Joyce dramatized the shift from a moral and religious to an aesthetic framework with his hero in *A Portrait of the Artist as a Young Man* (1914–15). Stephen Dedalus's first efforts to fashion a meaningful life are religious, but eventually he rejects "the inhuman voice that had called him to the pale service of the altar" and instead envisions becoming "the great artificer whose name he bore," as he hopes to find a greater role in life "foraging anew in his workshop out of the sluggish matter of the earth a new soaring impalpable imperishable being."[31] Similar affirmations of an aesthetic over a moral or religious grounding of existence are made by other canonical novelists of the period.[32]

Murder novelists also opted for aesthetic over moral and religious explanations of murder. To clarify the historical significance of the operative motive for the "motiveless" murder in *Lafcadio's Adventures*, Gide had one of his characters, the novelist Julius, explain it to the eventual victim, Amédée: "ever since the days of La Rouchefoucauld we have all followed in his footsteps like blundering idiots; I contend that self-advantage is *not* man's guiding principle—that there *are* such things as disinterested actions, . . . [and] by *disinterested* I mean gratuitous. Also that evil actions—what are commonly called evil—may be just as gratuitous as good ones." When Amédée asks, then why do evil, Julius says, "Out of sheer wantonness—or from love of sport" (171). In rejecting self-advantage, Gide rejects hedonistic-utilitarian motives, and in bypassing the constraints of good and evil he drains the moral distinction of its privileged role in the determination of action. In offering love of sport as a reason for being evil, he grounds morality itself in the wide-ranging freedom of creative activity, although still tainted morally by the frisson he gets from doing something forbidden.

Lafcadio warms up to the dizzying freedom of human possibility in reflecting on what might have happened one day when he helped an old woman with her sack: "I could just as easily have throttled her." One always imagines "*what would happen if*, but there's always a little hiatus through which the unexpected creeps in. . . . That's what makes me want to act. . . . 'Let all that can be, be!' That's my explanation of the Creation. . . . In love with what might be" (178–79). In this exchange,

Lafcadio opts to replace religious creation with artistic creation. Later he murders Amédée during one such "creative" hiatus in a train compartment. Afterward Julius explains to Lafcadio the links between disinterested action, freedom, and creativity in criminal acts: "An erroneous system of ethics can hamper the free development of one's creative faculties." His old novels were about ethically directed, consistent characters, but his new one, he promises, will range beyond those constraints to cultivate creativity and freedom. "The hero is to be a young man whom I wish to make a criminal [but] I don't want a motive for the crime—all I want is an explanation of the criminal. Yes! I mean to lead him into committing a crime gratuitously—into wanting to commit a crime without any motive at all" (196–97). This is what Lafcadio has just done, except that he *was* motivated—to kill without a motive. He does not kill out of self-interest to maximize his pleasure or out of a desire to break moral codes by doing evil, but rather to see if he could do something forbidden by deeply ingrained moral rules that constrain most everyone. In doing that, Lafcadio seeks to go against the grain of tradition and replicate the daring creativity that is art.

Other writers connect murder and art in different ways. Ibsen's Hedda Gabler tells Eilert Lovborg to commit suicide and "do it beautifully." In *Malice Aforethought*, Francis Iles related the rationale of Dr. Bickleigh, who had read De Quincey's *Murder as a Fine Art*, and he "had no doubt whatever that in murder he had qualified not only as an artist, but as a superman" (178). The novels and plays of Jean Genet are a collective self-portrait of the author as a criminal and of criminals as artists.[33] The murderer in Nabokov's *Despair* (1936, rev. 1965) rationalizes his crime after the fact in the language of aesthetics in addition to the original motive which was money. Hermann Karlovich runs across a tramp, Felix, who is his double. Hermann crafts this accidental meeting into a murder plot for himself as the pretended victim, but with the double as the actual victim, so that he can collect life insurance, with his wife as an unwitting accomplice. Within this plot he identifies an aesthetic inspiration for his murder of Felix: "If the deed is planned and performed correctly, then the force of creative art is such that were the criminal to give himself up on the very next morning, none would believe him, the invention of art containing far more intrinsical truth than life's reality" (122). People would not care to apprehend him because his murderous masterpiece would be so magnificent. The plot fails and he is apprehended, but in a final artistic flourish he finishes up the narrative of his plot accordingly, so that his captors can read about it. To do this he shifts from third person to first person narration in order to turn his artful story into an artful experience as he concludes with the open-ended line, "I'm coming out now."

While Hermann struggled to win readers over with his artful murder, Patricia Highsmith succeeded in delighting readers with her "talented" Tom Ripley. He was so likable that Highsmith reprised him in four more novels in which the moral categories of good and evil seem passé. In the first one, *The Talented Mr. Ripley* (1955), Tom, like Hermann, also happens upon a double of sorts—Dickie Greenleaf. Dickie's American parents hire Tom to bring their errant son back from Europe. Once in Italy, Tom ensconces himself in Dickie's life and begins to assume his identity. Tom is courteous and civilized, but his real talent is for taking on characteristics of others, facilitated by his lack of a clearly defined ego. When asked to leave, Tom is threatened with financial ruin but more importantly with loss of identity, so he plots to murder Dickie and take over his identity. "This was the real annihilation of his past and of himself . . . and his rebirth as a completely new person" (127). He turns his creative talents to replicating Dickie's speech, writing, and mannerisms in order to fool those who had not met him personally. His transformation is so complete that he resents "going back to himself" as ordinary Tom Ripley when circumstances require (192). In the end he is rewarded for his artistry by being made the beneficiary of Dickie's inheritance. With this conclusion Highsmith ignores the moral context of conventional murder novels and shatters the myth that crime does not pay. Tom's murder of Dickie pays handsomely and more significantly rewards him with a new ego. Unlike his predecessors in fictional murder, he is not troubled by his violation of the moral code, but what makes this novel strikingly modern is that Highsmith almost makes her readers forget about that code. She does not condone murder but raises some modernist notions about the aptness of a moral framework for interpreting human existence.

The substitution of aesthetic for moral interpretations by surrealist artists accented probability and uncertainty. Surrealists questioned rational motives for behavior. They adapted Freud's methods of dream interpretation and free association in creating "irrational" compositions with hyperrealistic technique. In René Magritte's painting *The Murderer Threatened* (1927, cover illustration), ambiguity abounds. Three witnesses to the murder at the window look away from the scene of the crime. Two detectives waiting to apprehend the murderer resemble him and the three witnesses as well as the artist Magritte himself. This painting subverts conventional motivation in several ways. The murderer is dressed not for a murder, but for a business trip, with his hat, suitcase, and overcoat nearby. He is emotionally detached from the savage decapitation he has just performed, as the victim's throat is slit and her head is misaligned with her body. His demeanor is reflective rather than impassioned, aesthetic rather than moral or criminal. The focus of his contemplation is not a corpse or a bloody weapon but a gramophone, an instrument associated with the mechanical reproduction of art. If he is threatened by anything, it must be the gramophone itself—a new technology that suggested death to a number of artists and writers in Magritte's time, because it symbolized death of the living voice (the victim's throat is severed) or life after death in the way it preserves sounds of the past, beyond the grave. As the critic Sebastian Knowles notes, for writers such as "Eliot, Woolf, Joyce, and Lawrence . . . and for later writers like Beckett, Huxley, and Greene, the gramophone brought death, was a kind of death, the opposite of what they were writing for. . . . [They were] afraid of this new technology, distrustful of its disembodied voice and its claims to immortality."[34] The murderer may be menaced by the possibility of the voice of his dead victim coming from this new invention, which preserves voices beyond the grave and might torment him forever, if it has not already begun to do so. That interpretation is further suggested by Robbe-Grillet's novel *La belle captive* (1975), illustrated with seventy-seven of Magritte's paintings, including *The Murderer Threatened*. Referring to that image, Robbe-Grillet's narration suggests that the man in the room, who "may be the murderer," is listening to "the cry of the victim" (21–22).

NINETEENTH-CENTURY RELIGION

Victorian moral philosophy was based on a variety of psychological principles and systems of thought. Utilitarians based their philosophy on Lockean sensationist psychology and the pleasure principle, while deontologists based theirs on Kantian categorical imperatives and respect for duty and law. Alongside these secular premises was the moral grounding of Christian faith. By the early nineteenth century it had been shaken by a number of historical developments that made it increasingly difficult to believe in the absolute truth of Jesus Christ and the divine authority of the Judeo-Christian moral code. While the Victorians experienced profound crises of faith and made a variety of assaults on organized religion, a majority still adhered to the essentials of Christianity, namely, belief in God, a history monitored by divine providence, and the promise of some afterlife including reunion with deceased loved ones. Victorians increasingly rejected the doctrines of predestination and eternal damnation but continued to believe in divine justice.

The cultural record abounds with evidence of this ongoing struggle between belief and disbelief. Victorians warmed to the findings of astronomy, geology, paleontology, and evolutionary biology, but even leaders in these fields retained their belief in a God whose causal functions were evident in his roles as Father, Maker, Creator, and Prime Mover. God was a first cause of creation, a final cause of history as the goal toward which everything was moving and to whom alone history made ultimate sense, and a providential cause in his power to watch over everyday life and now and then suspend conventional causal laws.

Evidence for a substratum of religiosity can be found throughout the sciences. Early on, William Paley's *Natural Theology, or Evidence of the Existence and Attributes of the Deity Collected from the Appearances of Nature* (1802) provided a classic statement of the argument from design, according to which a powerful god created a universe of creatures and monitored their improvement in response to changing environmental conditions. For Paley, divine benevolence mixed with adaptation explains the progress of living forms to their pinnacle in human beings. Belief in such a god is supported by the evidence of his designing action in the "appearances of nature." In 1837 the geologist William Buckland insisted that "no reasonable man can doubt that all the phenomena of the physical world derive their origin from God."[35] In a history of nineteenth-century psychology, Edward S. Reed wrote, "even some of the most 'advanced' and 'radical' of scientists endorsed the use of science to support the notion of God as the organizer of the universe."[36] The Victorian philosopher of science William Whewell invoked the "Supreme Cause" of God behind all other more specific causes in the physical world and concluded, in accord with a quotation from Newton, that "this beautiful system could have its origin no other way than by the purpose and command of an intelligent and powerful Being, who governs all things, not as the soul of the world, but as the Lord of the universe; who is not only God, but Lord and Governor."[37] Still in

Darwin's time, as Peter Bowler argued, "religious debates constituted a framework within which all scientists at the time had to function. All theories had some religious component."[38] This judgment was echoed by Ernst Mayr, who concluded that "in all the writings of the naturalists, geologists, and philosophers of the period, God played a dominant role. They saw nothing peculiar in explaining otherwise puzzling phenomena as being caused by God, and that included the question of how species originate."[39] Leading scientists continued to believe that God personally created each species at a specific moment in time for a divinely conceived purpose and continued to watch over the countless details of natural history. "Among Victorian men of science," concluded A. N. Wilson, "Christian commitment was not the exception but the rule," a claim he supports with a list of twenty-five leading scientists in that category, including Michael Faraday, James Clerk Maxwell, William Thomson (Lord Kelvin), and Sir Charles Lyell.[40]

In a cultural history of Victorian England, Walter Houghton maintained that although Victorians had serious religious doubts, some fundamentals of Christian faith were secure: "they instinctively looked for the hand of God in the events of life, [and they] thought of death quite literally as a reunion with the loved ones who had gone ahead."[41] "To explain significant (but not mundane) events in their lives," wrote Diane Bjorklund, "many nineteenth-century autobiographers (including secular ones) used Divine Providence—meaning God's determination of a person's fate."[42] Providence was invoked most predictably to explain misfortunes and tragedies. Many Victorians were comforted that, however senseless and chaotic their life seemed, it made sense to God and was in some important way shaped by him. Evidence of the legal context of such belief is the fact that there were two hundred prosecutions for the crime of blasphemy in nineteenth-century England.[43] In an address to the American Social Science Association in 1880, Benjamin Peirce (father of Charles Sanders Peirce) said: "Let the tower be built in obedience to God's laws, and it will reach unto heaven. . . . science and religion will coincide; the one universal speech will be God's word written on the sun, moon, and stars . . . and in the Gospel."[44]

Throughout the century, but especially after the 1840s, a crisis of faith surfaced in the form of freethinking, skepticism, secularism, scientism, materialism, rationalism, positivism, agnosticism, and atheism.[45] These challenges to religion resulted from a series of historical developments that gained momentum from the Enlightenment onward. Political revolutions assailed the authority of monarchs whose sovereignty had been based on the doctrine of the divine right of kings, which derived legitimacy to rule ultimately from God. Social revolutions eroded the authority of a hereditary aristocracy whose privileges were originally authorized by divine-right sovereigns. Scientific revolutions challenged the causal role of God throughout the universe and, after Darwin, especially in the creation. Theological authorities who explained the creation based on a single "infallible" revealed truth were challenged by scientific authorities who explained it on the basis of fallible scientific truths. The growing separation of church and state throughout the Western world accompanied a secularization of life and thought that eroded religiosity in the earliest grades of public school. The rise of modern universities with theology marginalized to its own department, or eliminated entirely, underscored the value of truth by empiricism and rationalism as opposed to dogma and revelation, while new industries relied on secular science and technology.

Among leading thinkers, Christian dogma played a reduced role in explaining the universe and providing values and direction in life, while ecclesiastical authority was compromised from exposés of its abuse in organized religions. Early in the century, romantics celebrated the individual, whose religiosity became a deeply personal matter, independent of established churches and institutionalized ritual. Philosophy and psychology separated from theology as independent university departments and offered increasingly secular explanations of the subject of their disciplines. Historical contexts replaced theological contexts in the major systems of nineteenth-century philosophy and social science. In the 1830s Comte demoted theological explanations to the most primitive stage of knowledge. A generation later, Darwinism underscored the role of chance in the evolution of species and challenged Christian beliefs in a world designed by a divine creator and in the unique position of human beings in creation.[46] In *Das Leben Jesu* (1835–36) the German biographer David Friedrich Strauss questioned the miraculous and supernatural in the life of Jesus, while thirty years later in *La vie de Jésus* (1863) the French biographer Ernest Renan identified Jesus's divinity as an occasional inspiration, if not a part-time job. As he wrote, "Divinity has its intermittent lapses; one cannot be Son of God through a lifetime without a break."[47] Ludwig Feuerbach's *Essence of Christianity* (1841) argued that God is an anthropomorphic projection of human characteristics into a sacred object. Humans create gods in their own image and in worshiping them celebrate these projections of their own alienated characteristics elaborated into a condition of absolute perfection. Marx dismissed religion as a mystifying ideology that kept the proletariat from achieving revolutionary class consciousness. Hardy's late poem "God's Funeral" (1908–10) recalled how sweet it was to begin every day with a "trustful prayer" and go to sleep feeling "a blest assurance he was there!" Such belief, however, became impossible to sustain in his age of spiritual crisis as "Uncompromising rude reality / Mangled the Monarch of our fashioning, / who quavered, sank; and now has ceased to be." The connection between these historical developments and thinking about causality has been assessed by Thomas Haskell: "The gradual decay in the West of the ancient practice of construing the events of this world as the effects of divine will is the most dramatic change in the game of causal attribution that history records."[48]

THE CAUSAL ROLE OF RELIGION IN VICTORIAN MURDER NOVELS

In Victorian novels religious faith or lack of it was more relevant to understanding murder than it was in the modern period. The argument that follows is not always about the religiosity or irreligiosity of the authors of these novels, only about the motivation of their fictional murderers. In some instances authors share their characters' religiosity or irreligiosity; in others they do not. These considerations aside, I will argue that Victorian novelists were more inclined than moderns to explain murders from (1) an outburst resulting from excessive religious zeal, (2) belief in or direct incitement by the devil, (3) a failure of religious conviction to stem murderous impulses, (4) divine justice, or (5) divine providence.

Religion plays a causal role in the murders committed by the "austere, solemn and forbidding priest" Claude Frollo in Hugo's *Notre-Dame of Paris* and the similarly uptight cleric Bradley Headstone in Dickens's *Our Mutual Friend*. Both men internalize religious strictures so much that they are unable to control the rage that erupts as jealousy when the women they desire love someone else. These men are not inspired to kill by any specific religious instruction, but religiosity is central to the genesis of their actions.

The causal role of religious thinking was more direct in novels with murders carried out by someone in thrall to the devil. In a study of homicide in American fiction, David Brion Davis argued that by the early nineteenth century most theologians had rejected the notion that Satan instigated acts of evil, but popular culture and fiction were full of characters with satanic motives, if not actual walking-around devils.[49] During the Romantic period, Satan had a resurgence of popularity. In Goethe's *Faust* (1808, 1832), he appears as a man, a poodle, and an old woman. By one count there were ninety treatments of the Faust legend in nineteenth-century fiction.[50]

In James Hogg's *The Private Memoirs and Confessions of a Justified Sinner* (1824), a strict Calvinist minister preached to his son Robert Wringham that every unrepented sin produced a new sin with every breath. By that calculation, Robert concludes, he had already generated 150,000 sins. Convinced of his impending damnation, Robert will do anything to achieve salvation. A living caricature of the self-hatred and helplessness that Nietzsche would later identify as central to Christianity, Robert came to believe that he "depended entirely on the bounty of free grace, holding all the righteousness of man as filthy rags, and believing in the momentous and magnificent truth that, the more heavily laden with transgressions, the more welcome was the believer at the throne of grace" (89). In such a state he is prey to Satan, who convinces him that his destiny as one of the elect is to kill evil people, who turn out to include a reverend and Robert's brother George. With Robert's father praying for him "to cut off the enemies of the Lord" and Satan showing the way, Robert carries out his religiously inspired "predestined" murders. As he boasts, "I would be as a devouring fire among the workers of iniquity!" (96).

Belief in possession by the devil continued to influence Victorian culture. At midcentury a leading British manual of psychiatric medicine affirmed that "there is a latent devil in the heart of the best men, and when the restraints of religious feeling, of prudence and self-esteem, are weakened or removed by the operation of mental disease, the fiend breaks loose."[51] In *Oliver Twist*, Fagin goads Sikes into murdering Nancy, and both are associated with the devil: Sikes is repeatedly depicted as diabolical, and Fagin appears as "the old gentleman" with a red beard.[52] In Stevenson's classic, Dr. Jekyll explains that "my devil had been long caged, and he came out roaring" (49). In *The Picture of Dorian Gray*, when Dorian impulsively shows Basil the miraculous portrait that he had kept secret for years, Basil recoils in horror, exclaiming that "it has the eyes of a devil" (172). Until late in the century the dual fear of the bodily presence of the devil and of eternal punishment in hell energized Christian morality, and its disappearance was invoked to explain the reasons for crime. By the 1880s journalists lamented the "passing of the devil" as a restraint on evil and crime.

Religion was also at work when a failure to believe was responsible for a murder. Stevenson begins *Dr. Jekyll and Mr. Hyde* with the epigraph, "It's ill to loose the bands that God decreed to bind." In *Crime and Punishment*, Raskolnikov's loss of faith allows the motives for murder to work unchecked by a morality sanctioned in religion. Early on, a letter from his mother reads, "Do you pray to God, Rodya, as you used to, and do you believe in the mercy of our Creator and Redeemer?" (33). But Raskolnikov does not pray or believe and for that reason is open to the exceptional-man philosophy that helps him rationalize killing. His religiosity evolves from a lapsed state prior to the murder, to a tormenting skepticism when he tries to evade capture, to an acknowledgment of his faith as he works himself up to confessing, and finally to a willingness to consider embracing Christianity in the end. When he awakens from a dream of killing a horse and realizes he is about to kill the old woman, he appeals to God for help: "Lord!" he prayed, "show me the way, that I may renounce this accursed fantasy of mine!" (33). As he moves closer to the murder he asks Marmeladov's daughter Polenka to pray for him. During his interrogation for the murders he tells the examining magistrate that he does believe in God, and finally his love for the devout prostitute Sonya prepares him to believe. She tells him, "You have strayed away from God, and God has stricken you, and given you over to the devil!" to which he replies, "I know myself that it was the devil dragging me along" (353). In the end he struggles to be reborn spiritually by believing in God and acknowledging responsibility, which prepares him to accept punishment and hope for redemption. With this ending Dostoevsky implies that in his novel Raskolnikov killed, at least in part, because he strayed from God.

Religion also plays a causal role when murderers dispense divine justice. The Count of Monte Cristo, after saving kindly Morrel and his son Maximilien from ruin, turns to revenge. "I have taken the place of Providence to reward the good; now let the avenging God make way for me to punish the wrongdoer!" (260). Monte Cristo's machinations begin to plague his former enemy Villefort, who thinks he is in the hands of a vengeful God. After Villefort is publicly disgraced, Monte Cristo appears disguised as the Abbé Busoni, reveals his identity, and explains that God showered him with riches to enable him to carry out divine justice. In a final exchange with Mercedes, the woman he had loved and lost to the jealous conspirator Morcerf, Monte Cristo explains that "behind me was God, an invisible, unknown and jealous God, whose envoy I was." "I felt myself driven like a cloud of flame through the sky to destroy the cities of the plain" (1032–34). Religion plays multiple causal roles as Monte Cristo's motive to bring about revenge directly in the form of divine justice and as an indirect divine providence driving action behind the scenes, articulated by a narrator who is as certain of divine intervention as he is of his hero's just actions.

The most pervasive causal role of religion is in the action of providence, the name for God's involvement in human affairs. Its prevalence in the early Victorian novel is the subject of Thomas Vargish's study, which argues that "most major English novelists before George Eliot assumed the existence of a providential order to the cosmos and found evidence for a providential intention at work in it."[53] In such an order God foresees all events, cares for his creatures, and directs their lives for some ultimate purpose. Nothing occurs by mere chance. Coincidences are humans' partial interpretations of an overall deterministic design that only God sees fully, one that includes the ultimate triumph of good over evil and the corresponding just rewards and punishments.

In most of Dickens's novels, argues Vargish, "the existence of providence itself is explicitly challenged . . . usually first by certain nihilistic villains," but they cannot disrupt it entirely.[54] Sikes's murder of Nancy is part of the divine plan and cannot escape God's justice, as the narrator in *Oliver Twist* notes, "Let not man talk of murderers escaping justice, and hint that Providence must sleep" (428). In *Martin Chuzzlewit* Dickens invokes providential design before and after Jonas's murder of Montague, manifested in both the murderer and his victim. The description of the setting implies that the entire ambient universe "knows" of Jonas's evil plot, that providential forces stir with indignation over it, and that the murder had been determined somehow by ancient precedent: "When he looked back, across his shoulder, was it to see if his quick footsteps . . . were already moist and clogged with the red mire that stained the naked feet of Cain!" The entire ambient world was witness: fish, beasts, trees, moon, stars, wind, countryside. Even the victim Montague had "a vague foreknowledge of impending doom" (797–800).

Providence also works behind the murderous rage that motivates Ahab in *Moby Dick*. When Starbuck urges Ahab to give up his obsession and think of his family, Ahab wonders, after Starbuck leaves, "What nameless, inscrutable unearthly thing is it; what cozening, hidden lord and master, and cruel, remorseless emperor commands me; that against all natural lovings and longings, I so keep pushing. . . . Is Ahab Ahab? Is it I, God, or who, that lifts this arm?" If the great sun is moved by some invisible power, he wonders, then how can his small heart beat and his small brain think "unless God does that beating, does that thinking, does that living, and not I" (444). Providence also brings about those causal links across generations that are behind the ancestral causes I discussed in chapter 1. In *Tess of the d'Urbervilles*, while Hardy's fatalistic sense of destiny is not explicitly religious, the deep Victorian cultural equation of the two suggests an association. Tess lives in a culture "steeped in prefigured traditions." Her brother tells her that she moves under a "blighted star." Her destiny is anticipated by omens, her rape is foretold, and her marriage "doomed." Regarding the night she was raped, the narrator wonders, "where was the providence of her simple faith?" (119). Tess has a presentiment that her wedding coach is strangely familiar, and Angel tells her the legend of the d'Urberville Coach, that some "dreadful crime" was committed in it centuries earlier. The force of providence is clearly at work behind Tess's murder of Alec, as is first suggested on her wedding night when her husband notes a similarity between Tess and a portrait of one of her ancestors who killed out of some mysterious failed passion. Later Alec clarifies part of the mystery: "One of the family is said to have abducted some beautiful woman, who tried to escape from the coach in which he was carrying her off, and in the struggle he killed her—or she killed him—I forgot which" (437).

These various modes of religiosity characteristic of Victorian culture set it apart from the more secular thought and literature of the modern period. The Victorian crises of faith provided the spiritual context for these works of fiction in which acts of murder are variously motivated from varieties of religious faith, its lack, or behind-the-scenes operations of divine providence. In modern novels characters' preoccupations were more with aesthetic and ultimately existential ideas and motives; if they could explain their actions, they might well do so with the maxim, "I kill, therefore I am." Before turning to these distinctly modernist interpretations of the causal role of aesthetic and existential notions, I must first survey those modernist novels in which the causal role of religion is present but with less force, less credibility, less authority, and occasionally less dignity than it had in the Victorian novel.

The Causal Role of Religion in Modern Murder Novels

A defining aspect of modernist novels is the diminished role that religion plays, as shown in the way modernists rendered the five themes on religiosity that I have documented for Victorian murder novels.

The first Victorian rendering of the significant causal role of religion is the example of Frollo and Headstone, whose homicidal impulses stemmed from early religious indoctrination that stamped their natural sexual desire with the stigma of sin. These deficiencies, however, were depicted as the product of unusually oppressive and aberrent religious indoctrination, not the essential spirit of Christianity. Hugo and Dickens did not assail religion per se, only those odd types who came out of religious instruction emotionally deformed in suppressing their natural sexual desire.

Modernist novels about characters corrupted by early religious discipline are more inclined to target the substance and institutions of religion itself. The evangelical Protestantism that forms the boyhood of Clyde Griffiths in *An American Tragedy* is shaped by the unique perspective of his parents, but Dreiser nevertheless implied that it is a defining feature of American Protestantism—strong on eruptive emotion and short on humility and charity, a volatile religiosity that ultimately leads Clyde to impulsiveness without moral centering. As Dreiser explained, "the principal thing that troubled Clyde up to his fifteenth year, and for long after in retrospect, was that the calling or profession of his parents was the shabby thing that it appeared to be in the eyes of others" (14). When Clyde is awaiting execution for the murder of Roberta, "there was still lingering in him that old contempt of his for religion and its fruits,—the constant and yet fruitless prayers and exhortations of his father and mother" (782). His final reconciliation with religion is crudely pragmatic. He waits to make his confession until the court of appeals rules on his conviction for murder, because, he reasons, "why jeopardize his case when God already knew what the truth was" (788). He finally signs a confession only when urged by the pleading of his mother and the prison chaplain, who also alters sentences in Clyde's final draft. Religion fails to explain the universe or provide a moral direction until Clyde is in a state of mortal terror. Under these circumstances his confession is bogus, and the substance of his religiosity nil.

While Clyde's "shabby" religion fails to keep him from murdering, the early evangelical upbringing of Joe Christmas in *Light in August* leads directly to his murder of Joanna Burden. As a child Joe is sent from an orphanage to live with the God-fearing fanatic McEachern, who whips him into memorizing the Presbyterian catechism. Joe's stubborn refusal to accept McEachern's religion fires up later as the mainspring for murder. Years later he becomes sexually involved with Joanna, and their tortuous affair comes to a crisis when she begins insisting that he pray with her. When one night she draws a gun and threatens to kill him for refusing to kneel with her in prayer, he cuts her throat. Later on he notes what sparked him to commit murder: "It's because she started praying over me" (116). The destructive role of religion in leading to murder also has broad historical aspects. As one critic noted, Faulkner's surrounding Joe with five obsessive religious types (Doc Hines, McEachern, Joanna Burden, Gail Hightower, and Percy Grimm), "enables him to suggest that various warped and vicious religious assumptions have strongly contributed to the predicament of the South."[55] Several features of the Calvinism that governs these characters led the South to ruin and are implicated in Joanna's murder: a belief that people are naturally depraved by original sin that is endlessly resurgent as sexual desire, a fear of women as vessels of temptation, and a conviction of predestination. In lashing out with a knife at Joanna's throat, Joe silences her repeated insistence on his praying, destroys the instrument of her own prayers, and symbolically cuts down the religiosity that inspires them.

Another oppressive religious upbringing motivates the murderer in Capote's *In Cold Blood*. Perry was raised in a California orphanage by nuns who whipped him for bed-wetting. After one brutal beating he dreamt about a parrot, "a warrior-angel who blinded the nuns with its beak, fed upon their eyes, slaughtered them as they 'pleaded for mercy,' then so gently lifted him, enfolded him, winged him away to 'paradise'"

(110). The religious fanaticism that leads Frollo and Headstone to homicidal rage obviously stemmed from early religious upbringing, but neither Hugo nor Dickens recounts anything about their characters' childhood, nor do the authors impugn the child-rearing practices of religious fanatics or the oppressive sexual ethics of religion. In contrast, modernists offer more specific accounts of what happened during these religiously inspired traumatic childhoods and trace a direct causal line from them to adult murder.

The quintessential modern character who kills directly from religious inspiration is the librarian Jorge in Eco's *The Name of the Rose*, who believes that he is doing God's work by killing everyone who might be able to use a newly discovered book on comedy by Aristotle to question the literal truth of the Bible. One can only speculate about Jorge's childhood, but somewhere along the line he must have been psychologically wounded by some pathological exaggeration of widespread abuses in the church. In him these aberrations take over, but they are more importantly characteristic of medieval religion as Eco elaborates them in a series of religious disputations that present church leaders as materialistic, corrupt, intolerant, and, when necessary, willing to use torture to secure false confessions that will justify executing the innocent.

In a richly documented study of "Christian survivals in post-Christian culture" Rudolph Binion argues that as Christianity lost its credibility, its chief tenets persisted into the modern period in post-Christian guises. "A discarded set of beliefs that old, that deep, that impassioned, does not simply die. It persists on lower levels of awareness."[56] He focuses on de-Christianized renderings of three articles of Christian faith—the afterlife, original sin, and the doctrine of absolute truth— which were reinterpreted throughout modern culture. To these I add belief in the devil, a Christian character whom Victorians occasionally rendered with some degree of embodied actuality. By the modernist period, writers instead crafted the devil as metaphor as in William Golding's *The Lord of the Flies* (1954). The title itself is a name for the devil, but he does not appear in person. In this story about a group of British schoolboys marooned on an island after a plane crash, one of them, Jack, commits savage murders, but the evil character of the devil makes an appearance only as characteristics distributed throughout the group. The boys see the rotting body of the downed flier and think it is the devil, "the beast," but eventually discover that the beast is in all of them. The devil is allegorized in a post-Christian context as universal instinctual aggression, a dramatization of human behavior that Golding saw running wild during his service in World War II.

The third rendering of the causal role of religion is its failure to prevent murderous impulses. Raskolnikov murders in a state of lapsed faith, but not anti-faith, and when he returns to the church, that faith and the institution behind it commands his respect and is still worthy of the highest devotion. With the moderns religious faith itself and the institution behind it are discredited. In Graham Greene's *Brighton Rock* the young murderer Pinkie Brown is a believing Catholic, but his belief is opportunistic and shallow, and the church itself seems commercialized and profaned. After winning a prize in a shooting gallery, he chooses a doll of "the Mother of God," and then grabs it by the hair and swings it about irreverently (22). In *Crime and Punishment* Dostoevsky's Raskolnikov strayed from religion but never demeaned it. Later Pinkie boasts, "I don't take any stock in religion," but, as Greene narrated, "he was praying even while he spoke to someone or something" (91). His final murder plot involves the abuse of a Christian sacrament, as he marries Rose solely to prevent her from testifying against him. Then, fearing her testimony anyway, he tries to get her to commit suicide. Pinkie's Catholicism is a worn-out religiosity that serves the purposes of brutality, misogyny, and murder. Even after he is dead his bitterness taints confession and absolution. A priest cannot offer absolution to Rose but consoles her with the thought that Pinkie loved her. She leaves the confessional with the hope that a gramophone recording Pinkie made at her urging will pick up her spirits. The final line of the novel explains that she hurried home to listen to what will be "the worst horror of all." Previously the reader learned what Pinkie recorded: "God damn you, you little bitch, why can't you go back home for ever and let me be?" (177). Even posthumously Pinkie's irreligiosity will murder Rose's spirit and kill any loving memories as it travesties, with a modern communication technology, the hallowed convention of deathbed wishes.

Monte Cristo committed murder and coerced men into suicide in the service of a divine justice that he questioned only to reaffirm. This fourth function of the causal role of religion, murder in the service of divine justice, is travestied in Jim Thompson's *Pop. 1280* (1964). In this novel set in a small town in Texas, the sheriff Nick Corey carries out a rude divine justice by killing two pimps, his lover's husband, and an innocent black man who witnesses this last murder. Whereas Monte Cristo's divinely sanctioned revenge is elegant and chivalrous, Nick's is brutal and cowardly. Before killing Tom, Nick tells him that he is going to have sex with his wife, as he has been doing for some time. Then he says, "The second thing I'm gonna do [is] give you both barrels of this shotgun right in your stupid stinking guts." He shoots, but, as he narrates, "I didn't quite kill him, although he was dying fast. I wanted him to stay alive for a few seconds, so that he could appreciate the three or four good swift kicks I gave him."(70). To a detective investigating these murders, Nick speculates that maybe "I'm the savior himself, Christ on the Cross come right here to Potts county, because God knows I was needed here, an' I'm goin' around doing kindly deeds—so that people will know they got nothing to fear" (179). His justice is on behalf of young girls molested by their fathers, wives beaten by drunken husbands, the poor, the hungry, and the helpless. As he explains, "I shuddered, thinking how wonderful was our Creator to create such downright hideous things in the world, so that something like murder didn't seem at all bad by comparison" (200). God's beneficence has here deteriorated to the level of creating so much misery that murder looks good. Nick knows that he should be carrying out God's justice against the rich and powerful, but, he confesses, "I ain't allowed to touch them, so I've got to make up for it by being twice as hard on the white trash an' Negroes. . . . Yes, sir, I'm laborin' in the Lord's vineyard, and if I can't reach up high, I got to work all the harder on the low-hanging vines" (207). His divine justice does not target the high and mighty, as did Monte Cristo's, but the low and powerless. As he explains: "I ain't supposed to do nothing that really needs doing, nothin' that might jeopardize my job. All I can do is follow the pointin' of the Lord's finger, striking down the pore sinners that no one gives a good god-dang about" (210). In this novel, divine justice is mostly unjust.

The fifth causal role of religion is the action of divine providence, which moderns omit or explicitly deny. The murderer in Nabokov's *Despair* charges that "all this divine business is . . . a huge hoax" (101). Divine providence is emphatically absent from *Lafcadio's Adventures*, which is set in a world of widespread religious fraud where the devout are hypocritical, believers are duped, and religious icons and personalities are fake. The novel's French title, *Les caves du Vatican*, refers to labyrinthine caves under the Vatican where the popes are buried, as well as the underlying tangle of subterfuge that sustains the church. At the outset Anthime Armand-Dubois suffers from rheumatism and is a vehement atheist. In an angry gesture he swings his crutch and breaks off the arm of a statuette of the Virgin Mary made out of a fake marble called Roman plaster. That night Anthime has a dream in which Mary appears with a broken arm and strikes him with her empty sleeve. He awakens cured of his rheumatism and immediately reverts to Catholicism. The devious character Protos invents a story about a fake pope in Rome and solicits money on the pretext of funding a conspiracy to restore the "real" pope. To recruit the unwitting Amédée to bring money to Rome and fund the conspiracy, Protos disguises himself as an abbé and a cardinal. While returning from Rome Amédée is murdered by Lafcadio. Anthime becomes disillusioned and returns to his role as critic of the church, suggesting to the author Julius that when Amédée gets to heaven he might find "that his Almighty isn't the *real* God either" (230). In this novel a wild dream inspires a hasty conversion, and religion appears to be a world of hypocritical believers, fake marble, fake icons, fake clerics, a fake conspiracy about a fake pope, and possibly a fake god. Gide's specific view of the contrast between the lapsed Christian Raskolnikov and the dyed-in-the-wool atheist Lafcadio is indicated by a comment he made in 1923: "Dostoevsky's heroes inherit the Kingdom of God only by the denial of mind and will and the surrender of personality."[57]

Divine providence works through psychotic delusions in Dürrenmatt's *The Pledge* when a voice from Heaven tells the mentally disturbed Albert to kill little girls. As Albert explains: "The voice from Heaven . . . ordered me to play with the girl and then the voice from Heaven told me to giver her chocolate, and then I had to kill the girl, it was all the voice from Heaven" (137). Thomas Harris travesties divine providence through the traumatized mind of Hannibal Lecter, who soured on faith in God as a boy when his prayers to see his sister Mischa again alive after she was taken away by hungry German deserters in World War II were ignored and he subsequently discovered that the soldiers had cannibalized her. In *Hannibal* he notes that "his own modest predations paled beside those of God, who is in irony matchless, and in wanton malice beyond measure" (256). In Hannibal's mind, divine miracles are replaced by divine malice, spectacularly evident in collapsed churches that kill hundreds of the faithful. Divine intervention otherwise fails to work miracles and, if anything, brings about the reverse throughout *The Silence of the Lambs*, which parodies Christian belief and practice. Hannibal is a lector, a reader of human beings who instructs not the faithful on how to lead Christian lives but the FBI agent Clarice on how to catch a serial killer. She reverses the parable of the good shepherd in fantasizing about saving lambs from slaughter rather than leading them back to the fold. Her nightmare of their sacrifice parodies the Book of Revelation in that she is not washed in the blood of heavenly lambs but is herself, along with other female victims, a sacrificial lamb, while the serial killer has a pet white poodle that looks like a little lamb, and he performs a black mass with a moth-as-wafer in the mouth of his victims. The main clue to his capture is that he covets his women, recalling the biblical commandment not to "covet thy neighbor's wife."[58] Secularized, post-Christianized, parodied, or mocked, the causal role of religious belief paled in the twentieth century as novelists offered instead aesthetic and existential motives.

THE HISTORY DOCUMENTED by these five contrasting modalities of the causal role of religion is a gradational shift across the years of my study in accord with the specificity-uncertainty dialectic. Christianity is a complex, many-faceted faith, but it is nevertheless *a faith*, an integral dogma that comes from God as a divinely conceived, coherent system. It is to be taken as a whole on faith, not taken apart with rational analyses into the validity of its cosmology, history, ethics, or beliefs. While biblical commentary goes back to antiquity, a "science" of biblical interpretation or hermeneutics was developed in the early nineteenth century, beginning with the work of Friedrich Ast, Friedrich August Wolf, and Friedrich Schleiermacher. Although these thinkers were religious, their analyses portended an attenuation and fragmentation of religious authority that grew as hermeneutics and biblical exegeses continued to be refined into the late Victorian and modern periods. The attenuation continued with the direct assaults from Marx's characterizaton of religion as an opiate of the masses and Freud's likening it to an illusion resulting from a temporal protraction and spatial projection of infantile dependency from the biological father onto the heavenly father. Even religious existentialists such as Gabriel Marcel, Martin Buber, and Paul Tillich de-emphasized the literal truth of divine creation and miracles in favor of an individualized and therefore pluralized spirituality. Fragmentation of faith was exacerbated by scholarly studies of religious pluralism: William James, *The Varieties of Religious Experience* (1902) and

Emile Durkheim, *The Elementary Forms of the Religious Life* (1912). The driving motive of Eco's homicidal librarian was the prospect of any fragmenting interpretation of biblical texts. For Jorge, unless Christianity is literally, infallibly, and totally true, the entire edifice would collapse. Although his fanaticism is set in the fourteenth century, its critical dramatization is illustrative of twentieth-century anticlericalism.

In the modern world the unified ideological edifice of religious texts was up for grabs in the broad cultural-historical development that Nietzsche tagged "the death of God." It included probing historical studies of the "historical Jesus," which desacralized the Christian narrative and impugned its divine authority. The effect of this divine postmortem was an erosion of the causal grounding that Christianity had provided since antiquity. In its place were a variety of post-Christian literary survivals as metaphor and parody, sometimes as mockery or outright rejection. In these works, characters showed an increasing willingness to live in a godless world of fundamental probability and uncertainty, which became particularly evident as the motivations for actions and their interpretations shifted from earlier moral-religious frameworks to others based on artistic creativity and self-definition. Zarathustra envisioned a fuller existence in a world of creative risk-taking and chance. The more philosophers and novelists abandoned faith in revealed truth and probed the causal grounding of Christian morality and religious belief, the more they proclaimed the causal inadequacy of orthodox faith. The traumatic core of Darwin's message struck at the heart of Christian causality, centered in the divine creation of the world and God's continuing involvement in it.

The pairing of moral and religious authority in Victorian life and letters offered a formidable interpretive framework for evaluating human behavior, especially for judgments about murder. The critiques to which that edifice was subjected throughout the late Victorian period accelerated into the twentieth century, especially after the brutalizing effects of World War I followed by Nazism, Auschwitz, and Hiroshima. These events shattered the notion that the history of the world culminated in a morally superior and divinely inspired Western civilization. With the loss of that previously unquestioned normative authority and historical teleology, morality and religion also lost explanatory authority. While acts of murder continued to be judged as immoral and in violation of religious law, the paired interpretive frameworks of morality and religion on which these judgments were based were increasingly viewed as too limited to explain why human beings committed murder. "The moral faculty" and "moral insanity" disappeared from serious etiological analyses along with atheism, blasphemy, and thralldom to the devil.

The limits of the religious framework are dramatized in Camus's *The Stranger*. The examining magistrate stakes his own religious faith on convincing Meursault of the existence of God and getting him to repent and seek God's forgiveness. Meursault does not merely reject this offer but finds it unintelligible, annoying, boring. He cannot follow the magistrate's reasoning "because," he explains, "I was hot and there were big flies in his office" (68). For a believer, such an explanation is a non sequitur and a long way down the road of disbelief or nonbelief from the rational critiques of Christian faith by Feuerbach and Marx, the deadly serious debate about Jesus Christ in the "Grand Inquisitor" section from *The Brothers Karamazov*, or even Nietzsche's white-hot anger over Christianity's "will to nothingness." Meursault agreed to help a pimp torment a woman, and then he killed another man largely because he was feeling hot and the sun was in his eyes. He is a loner and a loser, but his exchanges with the magistrate offer a blunt rebuff of the magistrate's unquestioning religious faith and a forceful expression of Camus's impatience with people who explain behavior in terms of relationships to God.

Meursault rejects the causal grounding of religious faith in a subsequent confrontation with the prison chaplain who enters his cell uninvited and unwelcome. Meursault explains that he does not believe in God, that religion seems "unimportant," that he is simply not interested in religion, and that the little time he has left he does not want to "waste" on God (120). When the chaplain asks Meursault to call him "father" instead of "monsieur" Meursault shouts angrily that he is not his father. Meursault finds most outrageous the chaplain's absolute certainty. He grabs him by the collar and accuses him of living like a dead man, adding that "none of his certainties was worth one hair of a woman's head" (120). Alone again, he reiterates the irrelevancy of morality and religion in his existential choice: "I had lived my life one way and I could just as well have lived it another." He killed "because of the sun," and he was found guilty of murder because he did not cry at his mother's funeral. Such causal thinking is a world away from Victorian notions of a destiny directed by divine providence.

We expect big events, like disbelief in God or a decision to kill, to have big causes. Camus shattered that expectation and offered a new approach to causality in general. The notion of big events having big causes is unintelligible in an absurd world where any event can carry enormous existential significance and any experience, however trivial it may seem, can carry enormous causal clout. The modernist novels I surveyed impugned Victorian attributions of causal force to lofty and infallible moral and religious ideas by giving unprecedented causal significance to trivial incidents like the hiatus Lafcadio experienced just before deciding whether to help or throttle the old woman, the shame that Perry felt when he found himself crawling on the floor looking for the Clutter girl's silver dollar, or the rage that Joe Christmas felt when Joanna asked him to kneel and pray with her. In a godless and ultimately absurd world anything can be normative and causal, and that revelation creates a dizzying sense of freedom, which is a defining feature of existentialism. Along with a conviction of that freedom, moderns were more willing than Victorians to accept the stochastic nature of human existence centered around difficult choices and the uncertainty of lives creatively fashioned around the search for meaning.

Selfhood in Modernism and Postmodernism

Throughout Western history, beginning with Socrates and continuing with Augustine, Montaigne, Pascal, Descartes, Rousseau, and Kierkegaard, leading thinkers probed the nature of the self. In the eighteenth century, Hume encountered difficulty with the subject. "When I enter most intimately into what I call *myself*," he noted, "I always stumble on some particular perception or other, of heat or cold, light or shade, love or hatred, pain or pleasure. I never can catch *myself* at any time without a perception, and never can observe anything but the perception."[59] Existential skepticism turned into existential crisis in the modern period, as thinkers began to question seriously whether at the core of human existence there was any unified self at all. That crisis intensified after "the death of God," as existential responsibility and causal agency fell increasingly on the individual. Modernists found multiple, complex, and uncertain aspects of the self, although they still retained some unifying subject of thought and actions. Postmodernists rejected traditional metaphysics of the self as some "originary" entity and rejected traditional epistemology of the self as a mind in a body. These writers interpreted various aspects of the historical significance of this crisis in terms of the divided self (Laing), the problematic self (Tennenbaum), the vanishing subject (Ryan), the decentered subject (Dean), the simulated self (Baudrillard), the deconstructed self (Derrida), the death of man (Foucault), and the death of the author (Barthes).[60]

The target of these views was the unexamined presupposition of selfhood that grounded Victorian lives, autobiographies, and novels. Victorians thought deeply about the meaning of their lives but did not question the presence of a self at its center. They believed that the mind was made up of separate faculties but were convinced that these components cohered in a unifying subject. While they acknowledged that the mind could be split in illness, they believed that its alternating selves or souls were themselves unified wholes. They underwent tumultuous changes but assumed that an abiding self grounded them over the passage of time. The economic model was the individual capitalist entrepreneur. Americans believed in rugged individualism, the pioneer spirit, and the "self-made man" who related to others but also possessed "self-reliance," a quality celebrated in Emerson's famous essay on the subject in 1841. In urging readers to "trust thyself," he was aware that some might not, but he did not consider that there might be no self to be trusted. Similarly, in England, Samuel Smiles's *Self-Help* (1859) surveyed ways that one might evade responsibility and rely on others, but he never considered that one might be without a self altogether. The major moral achievements of the century included a new recognition of the selfhood of serfs in Russia and of slaves in America and of new civil and electoral rights all across the Western world. Victorians celebrated individuals with resolute wills and strong characters, and while they acknowledged that some people lacked these qualities, they did not question whether a self existed to underlie them in their different levels of strength. The Victorian legal system was strongly voluntarist throughout most of the nineteenth century, as jurists located criminal responsibility in the individual self.[61] Late Victorians increasingly explained aspects of the personality from social factors but still retained a notion of a unified and responsible self at its core.

Among modernist thinkers, traditional conceptions of selfhood were assailed in several ways. Nietzsche argued that the traditional self is a fiction required by grammar.[62] Sentences such as "I think" must have a subject, but the *I* has no real existence. In *Thus Spoke Zarathustra* he allowed the existence of a self, but the force of his argument was on self-overcoming, a process of endless self-negation analogous to the repeated self-corrections of the artist. The secret of life is the realization that "I am that which must overcome itself" (115). The higher man is the most fully realized self, a product of unending, creative self-renewals. In *The Analysis of Sensations* (1885), the German physicist and psychologist Ernst Mach also viewed the ego as a fiction, or at best a "practical unity" that is needed for purposes of discussion. "The ego is not a definite, unalterable, sharply-bounded entity," and so it ought to be "given up." He proposed in its place a bundle of sensations that was distributed throughout the field of experience.[63] William James argued that the self was "a stream of thought, of consciousness," a notion adapted by some important modernist writers.[64] Freud never gave up the notion of the self; indeed, psychoanalysis was an ambitious self-reeducation, but he challenged Victorian notions of the self as a fully intact mental agent pulling mental strings from a central headquarters, and he saw the self rather as a fragmentary ego prone to self-deception. He also displaced the ego from sovereignty in the mind by showing that "the ego is not even master of its own house."[65] By this he meant that the mind is governed by unconscious mental processes over which it has no conscious control and is constituted substantially out of multifarious elaborations of repressed childhood experiences to which it does not have access by normal psychological means, that is, without psychoanalysis.

Modernist fictional writers also queried the traditional self. Strindberg's characters are fragmentary and disjointed, although real, as he explained in the foreword to *Miss Julie* (1888): "My souls (characters) are conglomerations of past and present stages of civilization, bits from books and newspapers, scraps of humanity, rags and tatters of fine clothing, patched together as is the human soul." D. H. Lawrence outlined his intention to do away with "the old stable ego." He proposed to craft "another ego" that did justice to the transitive and multiple nature of human personality in passing through various "allotropic states" to reveal a deeper sense of the self than his predecessors had achieved.[66] In *Ulysses* (1922), Joyce constituted the self out of sensations, memories, dreams, and fantasies tumbling about the mind simultaneously in interaction with the buildings and streets of Dublin and with other persons, fictional and real. For Virginia Woolf no person was just one thing. Her heroine Mrs. Dalloway "would not say of herself, I am this, I am that."[67]

In Woolf's novels persons come in and out of focus in the fluidity of consciousness without any single stable identity. Mrs. Dalloway experiences herself as a streaming of her own consciousness with the consciousnesses of a shell-shock victim and a stranger she sees alone in a room along with everyone attending her party, even people she has never met. In *The Waves* (1931), the voices of six characters cannot be clearly differentiated from each other. As one of them wonders, "Am I all of them? Am I distinct? I do not know?"[68]

Modernist poets also struggled to hold on to a stable self. Yeats worried that the center would not hold. In *The Waste Land*, T. S. Eliot offered a final image of his self as so many "fragments I have shored against my ruins." Rilke's fictionalized journal *The Notebooks of Malte Laurids Brigge* (1910) is about an artist trying to integrate himself with memory and fantasy. For Malte there is no clear boundary between himself and external reality; he is what he sees and hears so much so that rain seems to penetrate his body and trams run over him. In a study of "early psychology and literary modernism," Judith Ryan interpreted Rilke, along with Hermann Bahr, Franz Kafka, Hugo von Hoffmansthal, Alfred Döblin, and Hermann Broch as a central figures in the struggle of modern psychologists and literati with "the vanishing subject."[69]

While modernists strained to keep the self from breaking up or disappearing, postmodernists welcomed its dissolution, even as they articulated its complex modalities and found ways to resurrect it. Postmodernists objected to the unexamined notion of the self as an entity at the heart of human existence, a necessary subjectivity, an interpretive orientation that is supposed to be a sovereign source of truth and meaning. This logocentric disposition, as Derrida called it, generates a blindness about the historicity, social embeddedness, and linguistic generation of human existence. Postmodernists assaulted these ideas about the self in their opposition to Eurocentrism, colonialism, racism, patriarchy, sexism, and other manifestations of the arrogance of unexamined subjectivity and the myth of wholeness that vitiated more precise understanding of the unstable and fragmentary, if not entirely illusory, nature of selfhood.[70]

As postmodernists questioned the unity, stability, and very existence of the self, they also made possible a deeper probing of its nature. This interpretive dialectic accords with my argument about the specificity-uncertainty dialectic in that the more rigorously thinkers interrogated the self, the more indeterminate and uncertain it seemed. An analogous dialectic characterizes the so-called death of the author, because the postmodernist subversion of authors had the effect of intruding them into the narrative. "Paradoxically," noted Brian McHale, "the more [authors] sought to efface themselves, the more they made their presence conspicuous. Strategies of self-effacement, while ostensibly obliterating surface traces of the author, in fact call attention to the author as *strategist*."[71] In this vein, Foucault argued that the author remains alive and well, not as the older function of a singular entity but as a plurality of functions. His approach does not seek "to re-establish the originating subject, but to grasp the subject's points of insertion, modes of functioning, and systems of dependencies."[72]

Murder for Selfhood

For all their skepticism, the modernists and even the postmodernists affirmed some sort of self at the heart of human existence, however much it was negated, repressed, alienated, fragmented, floating, discontinuous, imaginary, or deconstructed. This modern self was not a mind in a body like a pilot in a ship but a site of actions, socially constructed, historically contextualized, and mediated by language. Among those actions, murder offered distinctly modernist modes of the causal role of selfhood in four ways: as defensive self-definition in separating from others, in overcoming a sense of inferiority, in fulfilling selfhood, and in realizing self-identity in the aftermath of a murder.

Some characters kill defensively to realize or protect a sense of self carved (sometimes literally) out of a threatening relationship with others. In *The Secret Agent*, Winnie stabs her husband, Mr. Verloc, in the chest in an act of self-affirmation in response to his attempt to quash her protective instincts toward her brother Stevie, who was killed when Verloc's anarchist bomb blew him up by mistake. After learning of the accident Winnie's anger mounts slowly over thirty pages of text. The more silent she remains, the more crudely Verloc makes excuses and blames others. Her murderous instincts take over after he dares to say that "if you will have it that I killed the boy, then you've killed him as much as I" (234). When he attempts to seduce her, she stabs him in the chest. Her murder is an act of self-protection and self-definition against a man who threatened her first by intimating her guilt and then by a crude sexual advance intended to silence her.

A knife attack is intended to carve out a similar defensive self-definition in *The Man without Qualities* when Moosbrugger slashes at a prostitute who had been pursuing him in the streets, threatening his fragile ego. When she persists, he senses that he will never get rid of her, because in his deluded mind "it was he himself who was drawing her after him." As he kept walking, "that creature, trailing him, was himself again." When she persisted he began stabbing her "until he had completely separated her from himself" (1:73–74). Moosbrugger's alter ego, Ulrich, also struggles to maintain his identity in a world that has created qualities without a self to ground them. "Probably the dissolution of the anthropocentric point of view, which for such a long time considered man to be at the center of the universe but which has been fading for centuries, has finally arrived at the 'I' itself" (1:159). As a man without qualities, Ulrich struggles to resist dissolution into a composite of dehumanized qualities. Even his emotions are not his own, as he wonders, "Who can say nowadays that his anger is really his own anger when so many people talk about it and claim to know more about it than he does?" (1:158) Moosbrugger's murderous act dramatizes the threatened selfhood of Ulrich, who suspects "that the given order of things is not as solid as it pretends to be; no thing, no self, no form, no principle, is safe, everything is undergoing an invisible but ceaseless transformation" (1:269). Ulrich's struggle to resist the inundation of his selfhood by external forces is dramatized by Moosbrugger's confrontation with the prostitute, whom he kills in a desperate act of self-preservation, albeit in a deluded state.

Another murder in the service of defensive self-definition is in Toni Morrison's *Beloved* (1987). The main story takes place in 1873–74, and centers on the ex-slave Sethe, who eighteen years earlier slit the throat of her infant to keep her from being taken away by white men. In that antebellum world the selfhood of slaves was always in the hands of whites. The men Sethe knew "who hadn't run off or been hanged, got rented out, loaned out, bought up, brought back, stored up, mortgaged, won, stolen or seized" (23). The selfhood of women was equally precarious. Her mother was allowed to nurse Sethe only for a couple of weeks before the infant was given to another woman to nurse. After the birth of Sethe's first child, some white men held Sethe down in a barn and sucked her milk while her husband watched in horror from the loft. He lost his mind, and she lost her vital essence along with her dignity. Later she contemplates telling Beloved, a mysterious character who she believes is the ghost of her dead child, that "if I had not killed [my baby] she would have died [as a self] and that is something I could not bear to happen to her" (200). Sethe's life centers around the fear "that anybody white could take your whole self for anything that came to mind. Not just work, kill, or maim you, but dirty you. Dirty you so bad you couldn't like yourself anymore. Dirty you so bad you forgot who you were and couldn't think it up" (251). Sethe kills to prevent white men from taking away her child's selfhood and along with it her own in an intolerable reenactment of the self-negating crimes that were the essence of slavery. Although the novel is set in the Victorian period, it offers a distinctly modernist rendering of a murder committed to protect the self from annihilation by others.

Selfhood also functioned causally in novels about murders intended to overcome a sense of inferiority or earn self-respect. The short stature of Dr. Bickleigh in *Malice Aforethought* is the basis for his sense of inferiority. As the narrator notes, in the early 1930s there were "glib references to complexes, repressions, and fixations on every layman's lips," and Bickleigh was able to diagnose his own "inferiority complex." He is reminded of his "wormhood" by his wife who has a knack for making him feel "inexpressibly small" (27–30). While Bickleigh kills his wife to salvage a selfhood defined by his physical stature, Henry Sutpen in *Absalom, Absalom!* kills his half-brother to salvage a selfhood defined by his social status, which is threatened by the impending marriage of his sister to Charles Bon. Henry's self-image would be trashed if his family was tainted by incest (as well as by bigamy and miscegenation, because Charles is already married and is part black). Henry murders Charles at the gate of the family mansion.

The theme of self-esteem tied to tradition and public opinion that Henry attempts to salvage runs throughout Faulkner's work. Faulkner himself struggled to forge an identity between the Victorian-style old Southern conviction of the self as distinct, certain, and stable and the modernist sense of the self as multiple, partial, and shifting.[73] His solution was to create characters with changing qualities and motives depicted from the multiple points of view of their own minds as well as those of other characters. In *The Sound and the Fury* (1929), one narrator's struggle for self-identity leads to suicide. Just before drowning himself, Quentin Compson concludes a self-searching interior monologue "lying neither asleep nor awake looking down a long corridor of gray halflight where all stable things had become shadowy paradoxical . . . thinking I was I was not who was not was not who" (170).

The motive for Joe's murder of Joanna in *Light in August* also involves a defensive act of self-preservation, because it occurs as she tries to make him into something he is not. Both Joe and Joanna search for a way to unify their own personalities, which are a mixture of opposites; his are white and black, while hers are sexual repression and sexual liberation. When Joanna goes through menopause her focus shifts from sexuality to religiosity, and she emerges as a female reincarnation of the cruelly manipulating religious fanatic McEachern, who raised Joe and deformed his sexuality. She also shifts her relationship with Joe from sexual muse to academic tutor, as she encourages him to study law and change his identify from a black lover into a black lawyer. Her manipulation of his religiosity and racial identity are especially threatening because Joe's self-image is fractured by his own racial mixing. As she attempts to manipulate his religiosity, he silences her demanding voice by cutting her throat and decapitating her—a symbolic castration that removes the seat of her authority over his own shaky selfhood. In a lecture, Faulkner summed up Joe's character in terms of selfhood: "I think that was his tragedy—he didn't know what he was, and so he was nothing. He deliberately evicted himself from the human race because he didn't know which he was." "The most tragic condition a man could find himself in," Faulkner added, is "not to know what he is and to know that he will never know."[74]

The insecure hero of George Simenon's *The Man Who Watched Trains Go By* (1942) feels especially empty when he watches trains go by because they are full of people going somewhere, while he is going nowhere. He lives in an ordinary Dutch town, married to an unloving wife, with a menial job as a clerk. He is a conformist who repeatedly looks at himself posing in mirrors and is preoccupied by what others think. He is motivated to murder his boss's mistress after she laughs off a sexual overture, and he becomes even more outer-directed in the aftermath of his crime in obsessively following newspaper accounts of him with paranoid responses to the analyses of him by editors, detectives, and psychiatrists. On the run he meets and eventually kills a cabaret dancer who also laughs at his sexual advances. Before sinking into madness he has a moment of insight into the existential motive for his homicidal acts: "I am merely a man who at the age of forty has determined to live as he thinks fit, without bothering about convention or the laws; for I have discovered, if somewhat late in life, that I was the dupe of appearances" (116).

Sartre explored how individuals work to defend themselves against the existentially threatening gaze of others. In *No Exit* the murderess Estelle, who is imprisoned in a mirrorless hell, attempts unsuccessfully to use the eyes of the other female inmate, the lesbian Inez, as mirrors in which she can see herself as a fixed, constituted self. The problem is that Inez's eyes also look back and make it impossible for Estelle to see herself without Inez's intrusive lusting gaze staring through the eye-mirror image of herself. Estelle is unable to lose herself in the loving arms of the male inmate Garcin because jealous Inez watches her trying to make love to him. His anguished cry, "Hell is other people," captures the predicament of an existentially vulnerable self condemned to perpetual surveillance and definition by the consciousness of others. In Genet's *Deathwatch* (*Haute surveillance*), Lefranc murders in order to have an identity of a murderer like that of Green Eyes, but in so doing subverts the authenticity of his act. In a discussion of sincerity, Sartre had argued that the intention to *be* something or someone makes it impossible to lose oneself in that mode of existence and experience it fully, because self-consciously intending to act in a certain way interferes with authentic commitment to the act itself. Green Eyes was a more authentic murderer because he was not trying to be one. When he killed, he explains to Lefranc, he never knew he was strangling the girl, he was just carried away. To Lefranc's plea, "I wanted to become what you were," Green Eyes replies, contemptuously, that he didn't choose his fate, "it fell on my shoulders and clung to me. I tried everything to shake it off." When Green Eyes realized he could not shake it off, he settled down with misfortune and made it his heaven, but, he counters, "you try to get there by fraud" (161–62).

In Bernhard's *The Lime Works*, Konrad killed his wife because she belittled him and interfered with the completion of his book, although the murder was doubly ironic because in the end we learn that he may have killed her instead of finishing the book and because his capture and punishment ensured that he could not possibly finish it. Bernhard's account of the evidentiary sources of reasons for the murder underscores the probability and uncertainty of modernist understanding of causality. The text of the novel is a defective transcript of a verbal report about a murder investigation, presumably taken from a dictaphone by an anonymous insurance salesman, based on hearsay, gossip, and eaves-dropping from witnesses who are misinformed, biased, or delusional. Some have poor eyesight, and others are hard of hearing. Four witnesses at four different locations testify that Konrad killed his wife in four different places at four different times. Bernhard found a quagmire of complexity where most people sought unrealistic simplicity, as he noted, "People are always looking for a simple basic cause behind a lot of chaotic circumstances" (150). Evidence for the causal role of his wife's insult to his self-esteem is equally uncertain. For example, the witness Wieser "surmises" that Konrad's wife "might have happened to call her husband a fool on that catastrophic day . . . as she had done so often before. . . . Konrad probably killed his wife because she had just once too often called him a fool or a madman" (18). Bernhard further subverted his characters' explanations with a report given in the passive voice and based on hearsay: "Konrad is supposed to have told Fro [a witness] . . . [that] the real cause can never be found; whatever cause you think you spot will turn out be be a fake" (150–52).

In Patrick Süsskind's *Perfume* (1985), Jean-Baptiste Grenouille's inferiority stems from his lack of a body odor. Born in a stinking garbage heap, he has an acute sense of smell, but no body odor. This deficiency leads him on a quest to find the ultimate smell, the secret of beauty and meaning in life that would become his own captivating body odor and give him irresistible power over others. He discovers a hint of it in a young girl and longs "to emboss this apotheosis of scent on his black, muddled soul" (49). After murdering her and feasting on her smell "he felt as if he finally knew who he really was" (51). He resolves to create a superior human smell, which he does by murdering twenty-four beautiful girls and extracting their odor. He is captured, but on the day of his execution his odor works its magic and everyone worships him. His quest is futile, however, because he cannot smell himself. "Though his perfume might allow him to appear before the world as a god—if he could not smell himself and thus never know who he was, to hell with it" (306). Although the murders enable him to overcome the external source of his sense of inferiority by making others worship him, he is still lacking. He killed others to compensate for a deficient inner sense of self but in the end kills himself in existential despair, intensified to an intolerable level by the idolatry of others.

The final example of homicide motivated by existential deficiency is the serial killer in *Red Dragon*, Dolarhyde, who was born with a cleft palate, abandoned by his mother, sexually traumatized as a child, and ridiculed by his stepbrother. He also looks to find himself existentially rehabilitated in mirrors, which play a crucial role in his serial killings. He puts pieces of broken mirrors into the mouth, vagina, and eyes of his victims so they can "see" him powerful, in control, and fully potent. He records the scenes for video playback in his room, where he is further inspired by a reproduction of Blake's painting *The Red Dragon*. Dolarhyde's identification with the Red Dragon intensifies as he kills again to emulate his powerful alter ego, but it is threatened when he takes blind Reba McClane as a lover. As his feelings for her intensify, he hallucinates that he is fighting over her with the Red Dragon, whose image is tattooed on his chest. His brief moments of hallucinated existential wholeness occur when he feels the dragon to be part of his identity, but Reba's presence drives them apart, because the dragon part of his personality wants to kill her while the other part wants to save her. To resolve this inner struggle he eats the original image of the Red Dragon at the Brooklyn Museum. Driven by intolerable feelings of inadequacy, he kills to feel existentially whole, although each murder erodes his ego as it becomes more dependent on his hallucinated identification with the Red Dragon.

A third group of fictional characters kill to realize themselves as selves. Gide's Lafcadio contemplates killing the stranger in an act of self-realization. He reflects. "It's not so much about events that I'm curious, as about myself. There's many a man who thinks he's capable of anything, who draws back when it comes to the point. . . . What a gulf between the imagination and the deed!" (186). Lafcadio kills in the service of selfhood for reasons unrelated to conventional self-interest. The existential significance of such an act is interpreted by the novelist Julius. He wants to write a novel about a new kind of character who is free from conventional motives and ethical considerations and acts without "logic and consistency," qualities that governed the lives of characters in his earlier novels and hampered their creative faculties (195).

Sartre's murderers act to prove that they exist as authentic murderers, which in his world is no easy task. In Sartre's philosophy the central core of freedom and possibility at the heart of human existence makes it impossible to be any type of person fully, even a murderer. He dramatized that problem in *Dirty Hands*, about the political activist Hugo, who must prove himself as a communist by carrying out an order to kill another party member. This assignment symbolizes a perverse variation on the general human assignment of constituting oneself as a self. His wife puts the matter to him bluntly: "if you want to convince me that you're going to become a murderer, you should start by convincing yourself" (181). By the time he carries out the murder, jealousy has complicated his motivation, and afterward he is plagued by doubt whether his act was actually a murder, as he wonders, "Did I even do it? . . . Where is my crime? Does it exist?" (242). Sartre's characters toil in hells of existential doubt, trying to discover who they are, but the more they search, the more existence eludes them, whether that search is into the depths of someone's eyes or in the act of an assassin.

The existential theme of Sanders's *The First Deadly Sin* is implied by the title, which refers to the sin of pride that is integral to selfhood. Daniel Blank is as existentially as empty as his surname and lives in an apartment filled with mirrors. The existential function of his murders starts with the choosing of victims. When he chose one of them, he explains, "I was God on earth. . . . I have never had such a feeling of being myself. You know? It was a sense of *oneness*, of *me*" (183). Murder swells his pride and affirms his selfhood. "I need, most of all, to go deeper and deeper into myself, peeling layers away—the human onion" (321). He sees killing as a unique intimacy in which the murderer enters into the being of the victim. Empty Daniel Blank fills himself up existentially as if he can draw vital essence from victims to inflate his impoverished ego. During the act of killing, a unique fusion with the other allows him to penetrate deeply into himself. "What this is, the final mystery, is what I'm searching for. . . . I want to go into myself, penetrate myself as deeply as I possibly can." Murder for him is also an art form, which he choreographs like a dance routine: "Murder as a fine art: all sensual kinetics. Weight onto the right foot now. Right arm rising. Lover sensing, hearing, pausing, beginning his own turn in his dear *pas de deux*. And then. Oh. Up onto his toes. His body arching into the blow" (332).

The epigraph to DeLillo's *Libra* is a letter from Oswald that locates his search for selfhood in a social context: "Happiness is taking part in the struggle, where there is no borderline between one's own personal world and the world in general." That borderline remains fuzzy for Oswald because in trying to craft his identity on the world-historical stage he becomes swamped by fantasies that detach him from historical reality even as he becomes a notorious actor in it. Oswald's ego is a postmodern concoction, fashioned by a number of people, beginning with his overbearing mother. "He had two existences, his own and the one she maintained for him" (47). His unstable ego is easily manipulated by a group of ex-CIA operatives who had been involved in the Bay of Pigs fiasco and were plotting to turn the American public against Castro once again by staging a fake assassination attempt against JFK that could be traced to pro-Castro organizations. Win Everett devises the overall plan: "He would put someone together, build an identity, a skein of persuasion and habit," and then encourage his creation to fantasize about killing the president (78). Everett's coconspirators recruit Oswald and manufacture a fake persona out of bogus documents: an address book with ambiguous leads, phony travel papers, altered photographs, counterfeit signatures.

Oswald himself tries to fabricate an identity. He is obsessed with making something impressive out of himself, but these efforts further distance him from any secure sense of self. In applications he fakes his address, education, employment, and military record. He becomes enamored with movie assassins (Frank Sinatra in *Suddenly* and John Garfield in *We Were Strangers*), and while watching them feels as if he were in the middle of his own movie (369). He identifies with JFK after seeing him on television and begins to think of himself as the president's double. He learns that the president liked James Bond novels and the works of Mao Tse-tung and Che Guevara, so he begins to read these works. He takes heart in learning that, like himself, the president had poor spelling and handwriting. They both did military service in the Pacific, had brothers named Robert, had wives pregnant at the same time, and were known to history by their three names. The conspirators play on Oswald's obsession with these similarities to persuade him that he is destined to kill the president.

Murder plays a causal role in literature in a fourth way, also evinced in *Libra*, in which the murderer defines himself as a self after the fact. Sitting in his cell, Oswald begins to construct his identity as an assassin. As DeLillo narrates, he will have "time to grow in self-knowledge, to explore the meaning of what he's done." For the first time Oswald's life will come into focus with the singularity of his deed. He will reconstruct his entire past leading up to the assassination as a destiny unfolding, unaware of the myriad forces, including the plotting of conspirators behind the scenes, that shaped his identity and historical role. But for him, "his life had a single clear subject now, called Lee Harvey Oswald," and "everybody knew who he was now" (435).

In *Native Son* the life of Bigger Thomas was haphazard prior to his two murders. Afterward it took on a clear identity generated by his own self-reflection and by the reduction of his life to that of a murderer in the eyes of the detectives who pursue him, the journalists who report his case, and the court that judges him. Thinking about the murder "formed for him for the first time in his fear-ridden life a barrier of protection between him and the world he feared. He had murdered and had created a new life for himself. It was something that was all his own, and it was the first time in his life he had anything that others could not take from him" (118–19). As Wright explains, "his whole life was caught up in a supreme and meaningful act" (131). He killed Mary Dalton by accident but afterward accepted it as the defining event of his life. Wright narrates this transformation in modern existentialist terms. "It was the most meaningful, exciting and stirring thing that had ever happened to him. He accepted it because it made him free, gave him the possibility of choice, of action, the opportunity to act and to feel that his actions carried weight" (461).

A final character whose actions dramatize the formula, "I killed, therefore I exist," is Conrad Castiletz in Heimito von Doderer's *Every Man a Murderer* (1938). The title suggests that anyone can commit a murder, in contrast to the Victorian notion of murderers as a breed apart, born to kill or corralled into the role by crushing social, natural, or historical forces. Conrad's act of murder is an accident, and he only discovers his responsibility for it at the end of a long search that is the main story. His first self-discovery is partial; its significance will be clear to him only years later. One day he looks at himself in a mirror (another modernist attempt at self-discovery in a mirror), and slowly recognizes his image with empty eye sockets, a portent of the murder weapon—a skull. In 1921, at age sixteen, he is traveling on a train with some friends and a medical student who has a skull. The others suggest as a prank that they put a turban on the skull and stick it on a cane, so that one of them can stick it in front of the window of the next compartment to frighten anyone in it. Conrad volunteers. There is a scream in the next compartment, but his friends who investigate do not tell him what they saw.

Seven years later he marries Marianne Veik, but his love increasingly goes toward a picture of her older sister, Luison, whose murder seven years earlier was never solved. Upon learning this, Victorian readers might well expect that some divine destiny or supernatural force would drive Conrad's pursuit of the woman in the picture, but in a post-Freudian world Doderer suggests that Conrad's feelings about her are projections of his own emotions and that his pursuit of her is a search for himself. Conrad first discovers her identity while examining his wife's sleeping face one night as a train whistles, a reminder of the setting for his first "encounter" with the dead woman at the time of his prank. Conrad progressively detaches himself from his wife and connects with his past, which seems increasingly disjoined from his present self. His love and energy flow away from his wife and into an image of Luison, who becomes the key to his identity. His search for her murderer leads to one of his fellow students who tells him what really happened—Luison saw the skull, cried out, reeled toward the window, pitched through it, and struck her head fatally on some object outside the speeding train. This discovery restores a sense of wholeness and liberation similar to the postmurder reactions of Bigger and Oswald. "He had, as it were, caught up with himself, comprehended, seen through himself down to his weakest point, and was therefore freed of himself and deliciously enjoying his freedom" (357). While the medical student complains that the prank ruined his life, Conrad claims that "it was his life (what else had his life consisted of?)." Everything else had been "piled up rubbish concealing his true life." In a final exchange, a friend explains to Conrad the meaning of the road along which he has traveled. "That the road had to end with yourself is the eternal law— which we spend a considerable portion of our life's efforts trying to evade." At the end of that road, Conrad found what is revealed to few persons: "the knowledge of who they really are" (361).

THE ARGUMENT of this chapter centers on an impossible occurrence—the death of God. If God exists, by definition he cannot die. If he does not exist, then he also cannot die. Nietzsche's stunning overstatement of the early 1880s is, of course, not intended as a literal truth but as a metaphor for the demise of the spiritual, moral, and causal grounding that Christianity offered. To substantiate my interpretation of Nietzsche's pronouncement, I surveyed evidence that a crisis of religious belief began at least a century before the 1880s and that articles of conventional belief continued into the modern period usually as parodies, post-Christian survivals, or even shadows of religiosity in the counterpositions of secularism and atheism. Still, a transformation of the ideological focus of life and thought did take place in the modern period. Accordingly, modernists shifted their explanations of murder away from moral and religious judgments in the direction of increasingly aesthetic and existential ones. They continued to believe that murder was wrong and violated religious precepts but did not find such factors compelling in accounting for why it occurred, and so they increasingly invoked aesthetic and existential motives for those who kill in degraded and even, in the case of Moosbrugger, delusional modes of creation or self-affirmation. This shift accords with every element of my larger argument about the specificity-uncertainty dialectic.

Literary dramatizations of the causal role of aesthetic and existential ideas are more specific, or at least more specifically varied, than dramatizations based on moral and religious ideas because they explore a fuller range of scenarios and causal determinants. Victorian murders that center on the violation of uniform codes of behavior tend to be more uniform in both motivation and explanation. Legal judgments in terms of good versus evil simplified interpretive possibilities and blunted distinctions about the uniqueness of particular causal factors, as is evinced by the struggle to overcome the limitations of the McNaughtan rule, with its oversimplified "right-wrong test." The causal function of evil in Victorian melodrama tended to be formulaic and did not lend itself to varieties of motivational detail. The more monstrous a character, the less nuanced and differentiated he tended to be. A similar uniformity and predictability of behavior applies to religious orthodoxy. The word *religious* suggests scrupulous fidelity to a single dogma that closes off open inquiry and ideological alternatives. Modern murderers who act out of aesthetic or existential concerns exhibit greater varieties of motivation, which modern novelists elaborated with greater detail. The literary record abounds with modern fictional murderers who either reject religion (Clyde Griffiths, Joe Christmas, Perry Smith, Hermann Karlovich, Hannibal Lecter), travesty it (Jorge of Burgos, Pinkie Brown, Nick Corey), or are beyond it (Lafcadio, Moosbrugger, Dr. Bickleigh, Meursault, Hugo Marine).

Aesthetic and especially existential undertakings are also more multifaceted and complex than moral and religious ones, because they are not based on an orthodoxy. Morality is based on a distinction of right versus wrong, while religion is based on sacred precepts. The many new sects in the nineteenth century zealously followed their new orthodoxies, while in contrast modern artists zealously sought the endlessly varied meanings of life and mainsprings of behavior. Moral and religious activities are based on ideological routines, while aesthetic and existential activities are based on ideational experimentation. The greater multiplicity of aesthetic concerns is strikingly evident in the endless variety of subject matter in modern novels and figurative paintings, unconstrained by the need to follow a specific moral code or religious dogma. Existentialists celebrated the open-endedness of life and sought to pursue its radiation in many directions. They responded to Nietzsche's call for a transvaluation of all values and an existence beyond good and evil. While some misinterpreted those notions as an invitation to moral laxity, even murder, Nietzsche and those who read him correctly believed that nothing could be further from the life of the higher man, which he modeled after great artists and thinkers who celebrated the diverse and creative life. One major goal of art is to capture the complexity of life in aesthetically unified wholes. A major goal of existentialism it to experience the open-endedness of life as fully as possible without the guidelines of any specific moral code or religious doctrine.

The Victorian frame of mind was structured around determinism and predictability, while the modernist orientation allowed for probability and uncertainty, aspects of causal thinking that the more aesthetically and existentially minded modernists embraced. Virginia Woolf's observation that one could not correctly say of anything that it was just one thing could be a motto for modernists. In the modernist period, uncertainty was applied to everything from Woolf's account of a lighthouse and personal identity to Niels Bohr's account of subatomic indeterminacy and wave-particle duality. Sartre's existential murderer Hugo captured that sense of uncertainty when he wondered about his killing of Hoederer, "Did I even do it? . . . Where is my crime? Does it exist?" Victorians did not question in such a manner whether crimes were crimes or whether murders existed. Victorian jurists did shift the focus of their causal analyses from the crime to the criminal as they probed increasingly complex and mitigating aspects of the criminal act, but that development came late in the century and so accords with my rough periodization. It is easier to judge an act as violating a fixed law based on a fixed moral code than to evaluate the degree of responsibility of the perpetrator. That shift in legal analysis is further evidence of the transformation in thinking about the causal role of ideas generally in the direction of increasing probability and uncertainty.

By way of conclusion I survey a few technological and social developments that were inimical to the authority of religion and the fixed morality it legitimized and that tended to cultivate aesthetic and existential possibilities.

New transportation and especially communication technologies revolutionized religion and morality. The new media technologies enabled individuals to draw moral and spiritual ideas from many distant places without the direct enforcement of face-to-face interactions that traditionally communicated and sustained religious orthodoxies and moral codes. The originary authority of a single holy text or moral code could not wield the unified authority that it formerly was able to do. The notion of the sacred lost the status of unimpeachability in a world increasingly constituted by myriad varieties of different orthodoxies if not the profane. The death of God was driven by the dizzying fluidity of modern moral and spiritual determinants. The singular text of the Bible competed with the increasing publications of all sorts and the cultural pressures from movies, television, and the Internet. Televangelists increased the number of faithful, especially in America, but that religiosity did not impact high culture in any significant way. Religion in the modern world was unable to shape the causal thinking of serious scientists the way it had done for the Victorians. Individuals were forced to create their own moral and spiritual identities, and those undertakings fell increasingly into the realm of the aesthetic and existential as values became increasingly relative, probabilistic, and uncertain.

New means of transportation and communication created more fluid spatial divisions that eroded traditional distinctions between sacred and profane spaces and increased a sense of globalism, destabilizing religious conventions and moral values based on local practices. This expansive process also eroded local authorities that had been traditionally legitimized and consecrated by the union of altar and throne. The effect of this transformation on individuals was what Anthony Giddens called *disembedding*, that is, "the 'lifting out' of social relations from local contexts and interaction and their restructuring across indefinite spans of time-space."[75] Removing individuals ideologically from local contexts undermined the spatial basis of the argument from tradition, which tended to ground religion and morality in the soil of ancient ancestors. This uprooting reworked values and institutions that modern individuals increasingly undertook as artistic and existential projects.

Social organizations were also revolutionized by these technologies and by the crowding of people into cities. Those changes, along with the increasing division of labor, made social life increasingly dependent on anonymous and expertly trained others. Marx stated the case bluntly that in modern capitalist societies traditional and moral connections between people were replaced by the cash nexus of all human relations. Georg Simmel offered a similar analysis of this development when around 1900 he argued that money reduces quality and individuality to the question of "how much?" Under such circumstances the authority of moral and religious precepts gave way to commercial exigencies, not aesthetic or existential projects. Still the urban environment fostered a tough individuality and versatile sociability that cultivated creative energies and self-reliance. Modern social organization, as Daniel Bell argued, shifted the basis of selfhood from tradition and community to the isolated and independent self.[76] Bell bemoaned the fact that this development engendered depersonalization and alienation, but others made more positive interpretations in assessing the challenge of creative self-definition necessitated by these changes. The positive yield of that transformation is a world in which the individuals are separated from a grounding in traditional narratives and value systems and must work to ground themselves. Under such circumstances the causal role of ideas shifts fundamentally from the religious and moral to the aesthetic and existential.

I BEGAN THIS PROJECT by reading studies of the revolutionary thinking about causality that emerged from quantum theory.[1] The enormity of this theoretical development led to my identification of the five main elements of my argument. Particularly germane were my findings that as quantum physicists probed the atom ever more precisely, they discovered a complex world of subatomic particles that behaved in individually unpredictable ways while knowledge of the causes of such behavior became increasingly, indeed historically, uncertain. To give this study an interpretive focus I combined these five elements into the concept of a specificity-uncertainty dialectic. That formulation was suggested with particular force by quantum physics, because the more researchers learned about the causes and processes of subatomic events, the more they learned how much more there was to find out and, most important, they also learned that there were some things they could never know. Such a limit on possible knowledge was unprecedented in the history of science. In 1934 Max Born described the quantum revolution in terms of the uncertainty that emerged from increasingly precise research when he wrote that a major conclusion of his probing into the depths of matter was that "the deeper we penetrate, the more restless becomes the universe, and the vaguer and cloudier."[2]

Quantum theory forced researchers to limit the applicability of the extraordinarily successful classical model, which was based on classical physics developed from Galileo and especially Newton and was believed to have universal application from the microcosmic world of atoms to the macrocosmic world of ordinary objects. The classical model dominated thinking about causality in the physical world until the late nineteenth century, when physicists began to encounter phenomena it could not explain, such as the discrete spectra of excited atoms observed by Johann Balmer in 1885, blackbody radiation in the 1890s, and the photoelectric effect analyzed by Einstein in 1905. Classical physics also could not explain the stability of the atom that Ernest Rutherford hypothesized in 1911, elaborated as a miniature solar system with electrons orbiting around a nucleus like planets around a sun.[3] According to classical electrodynamics, however, such orbiting electrons should steadily radiate electromagnetic waves, lose energy, and crash into the nucleus in a fraction of a second. Therefore, atoms should not exist as stable entities. But electrons do not crash into the nucleus, and atoms do exist and are stable. Efforts to explain such phenomena fed into quantum theory, which, in accounting for subatomic events, limited the universal applicability of the classical model that was grounded in a causal theory that for more than two hundred years had satisfied the requirements of determinism, predictability, continuity, objectivity, and visualizability. Each of these features was undermined by quantum theory.

The deterministic aspect of classical physics maintained that events were determined according to the formula, cause c is always followed by effect e, but according to quantum theory, subatomic events are indeterministic in that cause c is not always followed by effect e, or, put more strongly, the cause of a given event cannot be established at all. The widest and most easily visualizable application of the classical model was for the mechanistic determinism of objects such as billiard balls and projectiles that move in response to forces that obey Newton's laws of motion and gravitation. According to this theory, the position and momentum of an object at one moment determine its position and momentum at the next instant or indeed at any other moment in its trajectory. Classical mechanics was able to map such behavior (within its proper limits), thus enabling it to make predictions concerning the behavior of the object. By contrast, quantum theory maintained that in dealing with microscopic quantum objects, the measurements necessary to make such predictions cannot be taken with sufficient accuracy in view of the so-called uncertainty principle, discovered by Werner Heisenberg, and the uncertainty relations implied by it.

According to the uncertainty relation, the numerical product of the error in the measurements of an electron's position and momentum cannot be less than Planck's constant. This constant is an extremely small magnitude that does not significantly affect the measurement of macroscopic objects such as bullets, but it does significantly affect the measurement of objects such as electrons. The inability to determine simultaneously the precise initial position and momentum of subatomic objects limits the predictability necessary for reliable causal knowledge of the behavior of those objects in accord with the determinist classical model.

Quantum indeterminism does not refer merely to the inability to make precise measurements and predictions based on them. According to Niels Bohr, it extends to the nature of objects themselves, or at least to the way this nature allows, or disallows, us to interact with it, and in this sense quantum indeterminism is ontological as well as epistemological. An example of such ontological indeterminism is radioactive disintegration. Physicists can determine to a precise degree the half-life of a mass of radium atoms based on the average rate of radioactive disintegration of all the atoms in it, but they cannot predict precisely when any specific atom will emit an electron and disintegrate or fully explain why. Bohr believed that quantum theory cannot, in principle, offer a deterministic causal description of the physical behavior of subatomic entities such as electrons but can only offer statistical predictions defined by the yield of certain experimental conditions. Therefore, he reasoned, events such as radioactive disintegration are fundamentally indeterministic.

Another related limit on the classical model was the replacement of a deterministic causality by a probabilistic one. Classical physics held that masses of particles, such as molecules in a confined gas, behave probabilistically but that individual molecules in that gas behave in a deterministic fashion. Quantum theory concurred with those findings for macroscopic events, but it also held that the behavior of *individual* subatomic particles is fundamentally or, as just explained, ontologically probabilistic.[4] Some physicists refused to accept such irreducible probability. Einstein continued to believe that nature is causal in its ultimate constitution and that physicists would someday discover a theory that accounts for quantum phenomena in a classical-like way. He expressed his skepticism about irreducible probability in a famous remark to Max Born in 1926 that God "does not play dice."[5] But for Born and Heisenberg, metaphorically speaking, God plays dice and does not know how they will fall.

Along with determinism and predictability, quantum theory undermined other aspects of causal knowledge in classical physics—continuity, objectivity, and visualizability. An example of quantum discontinuity is the behavior of electrons around the nucleus. In the classical model, objects change their position continuously and occupy every position along their trajectory. In describing the motion of subatomic objects such as orbiting electrons, however, quantum physics replaced continuous pathways with the probability of an object being in some region of space. In his 1913 model of the atom, Bohr introduced the notion of quantum "jumps" between energy levels that spelled the end of the classical notion of cause and effect.[6] He argued that electrons in orbit can change their position around the nucleus only *dis*continuously in absorbing or emitting discrete amounts of energy while jumping from one allowable energy level to another. They can give off only specific light frequencies visible as specific colors when jumping between allowable levels and are unable to be at levels in between those levels or emit light frequencies distinctive to jumps between them. The frequencies of the emitted light in the jumps between those levels are whole-number multiples of Planck's constant and cannot be any fraction of those multiples. Thus Planck's constant expresses the fundamental graininess and quantized nature of the subatomic realm. It also accounts for the discontinuous light spectra of different atoms and therefore contradicts another aspect of causality in classical physics—continuity. Eventually Bohr was compelled to reject continuous orbits and maintain rather that electrons occupy energy levels at specific distances from the nucleus. As Planck wrote in 1925, "Either the quantum of action was a fictitious quantity . . . or [it] must play a fundamental role in physics and proclaim itself as something quite new and hitherto unheard of, forcing us to recast our physical ideas, which, since the foundation of the infinitesimal calculus by Leibniz and Newton, were built on the assumption of continuity of all causal relations."[7] But throughout his life Planck remained reluctant to recast entirely his physical ideas about determinism, continuity, and causality. Einstein was also troubled by this aspect of quantum theory, because it did not explain what caused the electron to jump, when the jump will take place, or the direction of the emitted energy.[8]

Classical physics also maintained that the causal knowledge of physical behavior it provided was objective. Its experiments were thought to distinguish clearly between subject and object and to reveal an objective reality of causal actions unaltered by experiments. But in view of the uncertainty principle, some quantum experiments make this type of objective knowledge concerning quantum objects difficult, if not impossible. For example, experiments to determine the nature of subatomic objects and their behavior show that all quantum objects, such as electrons (classically believed to be particles) or photons (classically believed to be waves), exhibit either type of behavior, particle-like or wavelike, depending on the experimental setup used to detect them. As Heisenberg noted, "what we observe is not nature in itself but nature exposed to our method of questioning."[9] In experiments to determine the nature of light, researchers discovered that when the experiment is set up to test for light's wavelike properties, the light behaves in a wavelike way, and when it is set up to test for particle-like properties, it behaves like particles. Quantum physics blurred the distinction between subject and object for certain kinds of experiments and, in so doing, limited the attainability of objective causal knowledge that was fundamental to the classical model.

In classical physics, mechanical causal action can be easily visualized as one billiard ball striking and moving another. The necessity of visualizability in classical physics was underscored by William Thomson (Lord Kelvin), who, in 1884, as classical electromagnetic field theory began to dispense with mechanical models, is believed to have remarked, "I am never content until I have constructed a mechanical model of the object I am studying. If I succeed in making one, I understand; otherwise I do not. Hence I cannot grasp the electromagnetic theory of light."[10] Quantum theorists had to learn to understand certain phenomena without mechanical models and visualizability. By 1923 Bohr abandoned the visualizable model of the atom as a miniature solar system when he realized that it could not give a quantitative account of atoms more complex than hydrogen with its single electron. Then Heisenberg took the lead by proposing an entirely unvisualizable conception of the atom based on purely mathematical entities known as matrices, which could be used to obtain proper statistical predictions concerning the outcomes of relevant experiments. A partly visualizable model was restored in 1926 with Erwin Schrödinger's theory of atomic entities as wave packets, with electrons surrounding the atom's nucleus like vibrating strings charged with electricity.[11]

The impossibility of visualizing or conceptualizing certain subatomic events is strikingly illustrated by the double-slit experiment to determine the nature of light. When a beam of light is projected through two slits in an opaque surface, the light passing through the slits behaves like a wave, as indicated by the interference pattern registered on the other side of the slits by a detection device designed to register wavelike properties. If one slit is closed, however, the same beam behaves like a stream of particles, as indicated by the pattern of hits of individual photons on another device designed to register particle-like properties. Even if the photons are propagated toward the two openings slowly, one at a time, they create a particle pattern if one slit is open but eventually create a wave pattern if both are open. It is impossible to visualize or adequately conceptualize these latter experimental results, because they rely on an inconceivable notion—that individual photons "know" whether the other slit is open and modify their behavior and their characteristics accordingly.[12] As Richard Feynman warned quantum physicists with an exuberant mixed metaphor, "Do not keep saying to yourself, if you can possibly avoid it, 'But how can it be like that?' because you will get 'down the drain,' into a blind alley from which nobody has escaped. Nobody knows how it can be like that."[13] In addition to the wave/particle duality of light, other quantum phenomena are similarly difficult if not impossible to visualize or conceptualize: an alpha particle flying out of a nucleus spontaneously without any deterministic cause, an atom spinning clockwise and counterclockwise simultaneously, or a quantum object propagating in space without a classical trajectory.

Confronted with all these broken classical rules, some physicists argued that the concept of causality might as well be abandoned altogether. Friedrich Waismann tagged 1927 (when Heisenberg announced his quantum theory) as "the year which saw the demise of the notion of causality as men of science came, . . . almost against their will, to recognize the impossibility of giving a coherent causal description of happenings on the atomic scale."[14] Bohr himself argued that quantum physicists "have been forced step by step to forego a causal description of the behavior of individual atoms in space and time."[15] But he rejected causal thinking only at the atomic level, while retaining both causality and determinism at the classical level.

Quantum theory is not unconditionally acausal. It attempts to answer causal questions as far as possible, it functions in accord with the logic of cause and effect, and it relies on a deterministic causality, at least for experiments, to produce predictable consequences in which light travels from objects onto or through instruments to cause visible results for the observer reading them. Some experiments exhibit both classical and quantum causality. For example, in the double-slit experiment, the spot where the photons hit the detector is indeterminate, while the exchange of energy between the photons and the detector is determinate. Quantum physics makes excellent predictions, but these are probabilistic—not the absolutely precise predictions that classical physics claimed to be able to make, at least in theory.

Quantum theory shattered the goal of explaining causally all events from the microcosm to the macrocosm as the action of simple entities moving continuously according to deterministic forces that could be accounted for with unlimited precision by a few simple laws of motion. While few physicists seriously believed that such a deterministic reductionism obtained throughout the physical and natural world, let alone for human behavior, it still provided a standard of the highest sort of causal knowledge. Quantum theory offered a new standard. The discontinuity, probabilistic causality, and uncertainty of quantum theory, even though limited to subatomic phenomena, had considerable impact on some thinkers and imaginative writers concerned with human behavior. They reasoned that if the most basic entities and events were irreducibly discontinuous and if knowledge of them was probabilistic and uncertain, then causal knowledge of more complex composites of them, such as human beings, might reflect even more pronounced manifestations of those characteristics.

Although my understanding of the impact of quantum theory on causality shaped the original formulation of the five main elements of my argument, the remainder of my research revealed that quantum theory itself was not adapted widely to account for murders or any other human behavior. In the final analysis, my book is primarily about changing ideas about what causes the behavior of human beings, not the behavior of electrons or photons. Modern historians, like modern novelists, rejected absolute objectivity, and they could deal with a measure of uncertainty, probability, and perhaps even discontinuity, but they could not interpret or explain and most certainly could not effectively dramatize human behavior in a world of indeterminacy and unvisualizability. For these reasons quantum theory played only an infrequent and marginal, if occasionally highly suggestive role in my other historical and literary evidence.

Nevertheless, some modern writers outside of physics were intrigued by aspects of quantum theory, which they believed might hold the key to understanding human experience. The concepts they found most relevant were probability (or randomness), discontinuity, and especially the uncertainty principle, although this last was frequently misunderstood. Heisenberg did not maintain that the observer always interferes with the observation, making accurate and objective measurements impossible. In fact, he argued the opposite, because, for example, objective experiments can measure the position or momentum of an electron with unlimited precision. What cannot be measured with such precision is both position and momentum simultaneously. The most important consequence of the uncertainty principle for general cultural history is that it introduced an unavoidable and irreducible error (i.e., uncertainty) in certain kinds of knowledge, signified by a universal constant that was as absolute and inviolable as the speed of light. Whereas classical physics offered the possibility of exhaustive predictive knowledge (at least in Pierre Laplace's extreme version of it[16]), quantum theory proved that some errors in measurement were unavoidable and that absolutely certain predictive knowledge of subatomic events was therefore impossible.

Directly or indirectly, quantum theory did influence some novelists, including Kafka, Woolf, Joyce, Faulkner, Durrell, Robbe-Grillet, Pynchon, Beckett, Gaddis, Coover, Barth, Nabokov, and Vonnegut, who were intrigued by a sophisticated theory that successfully explained many phenomena in the physical world and yet radically questioned the conceptual foundations of life and thought.[17] By way of conclusion I will consider one novelist who explicitly acknowledged his debt to quantum theory and related it directly to his understanding of human behavior, as dramatized in a murder novel.

Don DeLillo is not so much typical of the modern period as he is distinctive to it, in that his rendering of the causes and motives for murder drew on uniquely modern notions that would have been inconceivable in the Victorian period. In an article of 1983 on the cultural context of his fictional reinterpretation of the Kennedy assassination in *Libra*, he claimed that "all the paradoxes and illusions that scientists have found in the microsystem among electrons and other forms of quantum matter—the bizarre interactions, the sense of indeterminacy, the lack of cause and effect—these now constitute our daily bed and board."[18] Following the Kennedy assassination, our entire world unraveled. "We seem from that moment to have entered a world of randomness and ambiguity, a world totally modern in the way it shades into the century's 'emptiest' literature, the study of what is uncertain and unresolved in our lives." The assassination was a network of inconsistencies made up of "loose ends, dead ends, small mysteries of time and space." It also signified discontinuity: "jump cuts, blank spaces, an instant in which information leaps from one energy level to another." Analyses of the bullet fragments and trajectories suggest quantum experiments on the collision of subatomic particles streaming through a cloud chamber. Analyses of the Zapruder film illustrate the difficulty of visualizing events even when filmed. This closely scrutinized record of eighteen seconds was subjected to enhancement and blur analyses to establish distances, locations, and speeds, but ultimately it became a "major emblem of uncertainty and chaos" and raised more questions than it answered. DeLillo concluded that in the end, the assassination "is a story about our uncertain grip on the world."[19]

Without referring to it explicitly, DeLillo also loosely adapted Bohr's principle of complementarity (announced in 1927), which states that the most complete account of phenomena must include seemingly contradictory interpretations such as wave/particle duality. DeLillo's novel, as he explained, is a weave of complementary interpretations— "the right-wing theme, the left-wing theme, the soviet and Cuban themes, the double-agent theme, the theme of renegade CIA men, the organized-crime theme."[20] Complementarity applies to Lee Harvey Oswald's characteristics and actions as well as to DeLillo's text. According to contrasting reports, Oswald is solid and frail, extroverted and shy, a grim killer and a baby-faced hero. In *Libra* the explanatory grasp of the assassination comes from conflicting sources: Oswald's limited sense of why things are happening, the plotting of ex-CIA operatives who shape Oswald's outlook and motivation, DeLillo's third-person narration, and the findings of the retired CIA analyst Nicholas Branch, who has spent fifteen years researching a secret history of the assassination.

If I were to suggest a single literary rendering of causal understanding that is symbolic of the modern period, it would be that of Branch, whose research experience evinces the unfolding of the specificity-uncertainty dialectic and whose conclusions embody several aspects of quantum theory. He is mired in the uncertainty of his analysis far more than was true of the rigorous modern scientists I have surveyed, but his efforts do suggest the modern combination of ever more precise analytical evidence generating new complexities and uncertainties.

For historical purposes, it is illustrative to compare his approach with that of Poe's detective C. Auguste Dupin in "The Murders in the Rue Morgue" (1841). Both try to solve a murder by discovering who did it and why, but their methods and conclusions are ages apart. Dupin's evidence is limited to a few newspaper reports and one visit to the murder scene. He makes "legitimate deductions" as "reason feels its way" in tracing the "links of the chain" in his "search for the true." His solution includes no motive because the immediate impulse for the killings turns out to have been the terrified reaction of a runaway orangutang, but the murders are fully solved, the uncertainties are removed, and an innocent man accused of the crime is released so that justice can prevail—a typically tidy Victorian closure.

Far different is the web of uncertainties that multiply precisely as Branch's investigation proceeds. His murder is never solved, uncertainty mounts, no one is entirely innocent, and justice is a shadowy ideal. In contrast to Dupin's modest apartment and a few newspaper articles that he probes with a swift and successful intuitive style, Branch has a room with bookshelves along three walls and piles of documents, tape cassettes, and files gathered during fifteen years of plodding research, where he works "frustrated, stuck, self-watching, looking for a means of connection" (181). At his disposal are numerous modern technologies and highly trained experts to provide precise analyses relevant to the investigation—spectrographic tests of bullet fragments, acoustical analyses of the sound of gunshots. The attempted search from "bullet trajectories backwards to the lives that occupy the shadows" is a forensic analogue to quantum physicists' search for hidden variables to explain the trajectories of electrons emitted by radioactive substances (15). Branch also uses the findings of numerous experts—linguists, photo analysts, fingerprint and handwriting experts, hair and fiber specialists—but their findings only expand the realms of inquiry into which Branch must probe. Dupin knew at all times where he was going and what he was doing; Branch routinely "wakes up suddenly, wondering where he is" (15).

No murder investigation in history produced such an avalanche of documents and complex analytical problems. In addition to the homicide reports, autopsy diagrams, polygraph reports, floor plans, biographies, and letters, there is that monument of investigative miscellany—the twenty-six volume Warren Report with "baptismal records, report cards, postcards, divorce petitions, canceled checks, daily time sheets, tax returns, property lists, postoperative x-rays, photos of knotted string, thousands of pages of testimony . . . [and] a microphotograph of three strands of Oswald's pubic hair" (181). In this report, Branch finds the thousands of photographs particularly disturbing: "Flat, pale, washed in time, suspended outside the particularized gist of this or that era, arguing nothing, clarifying nothing, lonely" (183).

The description of Branch's frustrated investigation is crafted in the language of the uncertainty principle: "He questions everything, including the basic suppositions we make about our world of light and shadow, solid objects and ordinary sounds, and our ability to measure such things, to determine weight, mass and direction, to see things as they are" (300).

The more he scrutinizes the data, the more uncertain it seems, as if his own investigations jarred the position and momentum of objects. The action of chance further displaces his confidence in determinism. Dupin had invoked the "theory of probabilities," not to affirm some irreducible probabilistic phenomenon but rather to rule out unlikely suspects. For Branch the substance of reality becomes probabilistic, as he concludes that the conspiracy against the president "was a rambling affair that succeeded in the short term due mainly to chance. Deft men and fools, ambivalence and fixed will and what the weather was like" (441).

Oswald's motives also become more uncertain with each new piece of evidence. Branch's research is compromised by the falsification of documents, self-deception and lies, plots within plots, spies and counterspies. Witnesses are unreliable because their senses are dulled, their memories faulty, or their motives corrupted. In the CIA, "everyone was a spook or dupe or asset, a double, courier, cutout or defector." They were "all linked in a fast and rhythmic coincidence, a daisy chain of rumor, suspicion, and secret wish" (57).

The novel is emphatically historical in capturing a new sense of the complexity and uncertainty of causal understanding. DeLillo is especially sensitive to the significance of the new technologies of transportation, communication, and investigation that transformed causal understanding in modern society. Sophisticated investigative technologies generate higher levels of uncertainty for Branch, who discovers that with every new link uncovered comes another tangle of causal chains leading into a "plot that reaches flawlessly in a dozen directions" (58). His tenacious but futile investigation captures the Sisyphean nature of modern causal inquiry, although for Branch each time the rock rolls down the mountain, the mountain grows higher. The more he learns, the more he realizes how much more there is to know and how little he understands what he thought he knew. His struggles do have a positive yield, however, because through them DeLillo reveals a more sober appreciation of the limits of human knowledge.

In spite of the similarities between Branch and the quantum physicists, the differences are striking. DeLillo traces many deceptions behind Oswald's actions, weaves them into a complex pattern that includes the working of chance, and accents the uncertainty introduced by the investigatory process; but these difficulties do not reach the level of the fundamental indeterminacy, probabilism, and uncertainty that quantum theory reveals as operative in the subatomic world. In his novel, a bullet is nothing but a bullet with a precise linear trajectory, not a wave function or a probability distribution, and the driving force for the assassination is strongly deterministic, however much complicated by multiple motives and meddling plotters. DeLillo traces the actions of different people with contrasting motives who come into conflict, as well as ambivalent individuals pulled this way and that with conflicted inner motives, but he does not attempt to dramatize Bohr-style complementarity with the same person exhibiting contradictory properties and behaving in contradictory ways at the same time.

These differences between quantum theory and DeLillo's fiction point to a larger evidentiary problem—the relative probative value of my three main sources and their respective roles in support of the five aspects of my main argument. The most historically dynamic and significant of the developments I trace is the increasing specificity of causal knowledge, as is especially clear in the history of the sciences. Increasing specificity drove the other four developments. Thus, the increasingly specific causal investigations identified a multiplicity of causal factors, which when combined generated causal complexity. The effort to analyze numerous interrelated causal factors necessitated the refinement of statistical techniques and fueled the probabilistic revolution around the turn of the century. Finally, the specification of those factors also opened up vast realms of uncertainty, as in the discovery of DNA and later the mapping of the human genome, which raised many new and unanswered questions.

The evidence for increasing specificity is compelling. Compared with Victorian sciences, modern sciences such as genetics, endocrinology, physiology, and neuroscience had more investigators working in more specialized university departments, research institutes, and professional fields with more precise technologies and laboratory techniques. The argument about increasing specificity is less compelling for the systems of thought—psychoanalysis, linguistics, language philosophy, sexology, economics, sociology, psychiatry, cybernetics, systems theory, and existentialism—although these systems did produce sharper causal understanding of various aspects of human experience. Psychoanalysis, for example, specified more precisely than previous child psychology (first defined as a new field only around 1880) the childhood origins of adult mental life.

The argument about increasing specificity that holds most convincingly for the sciences and somewhat less for the systems of thought cannot, however, be extended to fiction, nor can any claim about the progress of causal understanding. The six "considerations" I surveyed in my introduction do justify combining novels with science and systems of thought in support of an argument about the progress of causal understanding but without applying that argument directly to novels. Science and literature make for an uneasy mix rather than a seamless integration. Novelists do not explain their characters' behavior with scientific theories, let alone genes, hormones, peptides, or neurotransmitters, and most certainly not with subatomic particles. When novelists do refer to scientific theories, the reference is incidental to the larger narrative that brings the characters to life. DeLillo was inspired by quantum theory and adapted his interpretive language from popularizations of it to fill out the novel's intellectual setting and give it historical verisimilitude, but the theory contributes only marginally to his rendering of what makes Oswald tick. The same could be said for Zola's use of hereditary taints, Huxley's use of hormones, Dreiser's use of tropisms, Levin's use of child sexual traumas, DeLillo's use of neurotransmitters, and Dürrenmatt's use of "altered metabolism or a few degenerate cells." The invocation of scientific discoveries lent a sense of currency to novels but was rarely used to explain behavior. Scientific explanations aim to reduce complex behavior to simple, ideally single, causes, while literary dramatizations aim to elaborate the fuller complexities of life with all its "loose ends, dead ends, [and] small mysteries of time and space." Such features are deficiencies in science; they are the soul of literature.

Of my three main sources, novels offer the most vivid and compelling evidence. The history of the sciences conforms to an overall logic of development, if not progress, in that the sciences explicitly reject old theories and seek to refine new ones. In contrast, novels provide a fuller sense of what it was to be alive at a specific historical moment, and their collective history offers no single overall sense, let alone a record of progress. Even in novels where scientific discoveries are acknowledged directly as a source of understanding, the occasional references to science do not carry nearly as strong an explanatory load as the vast stretches of dialogue and description that make characters' motives and actions comprehensible, believable, and, occasionally, unforgettable. DeLillo drew on quantum theory for the conceptual foundation of his story, but he drew far more on his eye and ear for imagery and dialogue that captured the sights and sounds of the modern world.

His historical role in comparison with that of Victorian novelists derives more from his unique stylistic abilities than from his superior scientific explanations. Quantum theory, along with the other sciences and systems of thought I have surveyed, broadened and deepened modern understanding of human experience in accord with the specificity-uncertainty dialectic, but the literary works that drew directly on these sources rendered modern human experience with more detail, comprehensiveness, and force.

Even though scientists and novelists made different contributions to the five elements of my argument, they both conformed to the basic contours of the specificity-uncertainty dialectic. Scientists labored to identify specific causally acting entities and make causal understanding more precise, while novelists worked to weave causality into the fabric of life and make the revelation of causal understanding more artistically dynamic. As a group, scientists discovered many new causal factors, although individually their goal was to reduce causal understanding to single factors, in some instances to specific causally acting entities. Novelists occasionally identified such entities but were reluctant to simplify motives reductively. Characters whose behavior could be explained by a single trait were caricatures. Victorian melodrama abounded in such types, who sometimes killed out of monomaniacal obsession. In contrast, modernist literature repudiated melodrama as well as the naturalists' biological, psychological, and social determinisms. Complexity became more integral to scientific explanation in the modern period with feedback systems and ultimately complexity theory. In novels, the network of causal factors also became increasingly complex as novelists attempted to incorporate the causal roles of many intrapsychic layers, beginning with childhood traumas and their consequences and followed by emotional needs, social pressures, and existential concerns, although nineteenth-century novelists such as Dostoevsky, Flaubert, and Eliot in particular remain second to none in depth of insight, subtlety of expression, and complexity of characters. While Victorian murderers were generally intact as individuals thoroughly devoted to what they were doing, modern murderers were beset with identity crises as they killed to establish a sense of self.

The probabilistic revolution that spanned the middle years of my study transformed causal understanding in the natural and social sciences, as researchers sharpened statistical techniques and applied probabilistic thinking to more complex causal problems. On this element of my argument, scientists and novelists produced a similar historical shift, in that both identified the action of chance as fundamental to observed phenomena. Physicists installed probability as a defining feature of the knowledge of subatomic entities (as well as their fundamental nature), sociologists used probability increasingly to assign more precise magnitudes to a variety of interacting causal factors, while novelists dramatized it as a defining feature of human thought and action. Whereas for the Victorians chance was typically thought to be determined by destiny or God, for the moderns, notions of destiny and divine providence lost much of their explanatory force. While it is impossible to represent genuine chance in a novel whose every word is determined before the reader picks it up, modernist writers nevertheless attempted to capture the fundamental chanciness of life in increasingly inventive ways. A turning point in literary recognition of the fundamentally probabilistic nature of life and art was Mallarmé's famous line in *Un coup de dés* from 1897: "A throw of the dice will never abolish chance." No matter how many times researchers roll the dice and record the outcome, the future always remains probabilistic and uncertain.

For a final example of new literary renderings of uncertainty I return to the novelist who first suggested my focus on murder and whose life and art so broadly and intentionally subverted conventional ideas about causality. André Gide established his historical role by challenging the consistency and predictability of the naturalists' characters. In contrast he created Lafcadio, who in pushing a stranger out of a railroad car into the night for no other reason than to kill without a reason subverted earlier modes of more deterministic causality.

After the murder, Lafcadio explains to Julius that he wanted to kill without a reason, but the underlying reason is his desire to affirm his free will amidst the restrictive pressures of conventional values and customs. In a gesture toward that freedom, Lafcadio puts his act in the hands of chance—within certain limits—by deciding that if he can count to twelve before a light appears outside the window, the stranger is saved. In the Victorian novel a light would shine before he counted to twelve, or not, depending on the will of God or the forces of destiny, but in Gide's godless world no external controlling agency exists. Lafcadio takes charge of chance by slowing his count, in a sense trying to fix the dice, although he still relies somewhat on chance. At last a light shines, and he gives his victim a fatal push. By meddling with chance, Lafcadio detaches himself from the faith in some transcendent guiding force that sustained many of his predecessors and undertakes a murder for which he alone is responsible. Chance plays a role, but he limits and in that sense partially determines its range of influence.

This murder, which at first seems to be senseless, is actually full of historical significance in dramatizing a new sense of ambiguous freedom with the murder's uncertain causality and negative justification. Lafcadio's willingness to commit murder on a whim impugns his moral sense, but his single bold act vividly expresses Gide's desire to dramatize an act of free will. Its significance is not so much what drives Lafcadio to it, but what does not. With this murder Gide crafted a new kind of "unmotivated crime" that subverted the stronger determinism of many typical nineteenth-century novels. That negative motive and philosophy of "inconsequence" undermined any positive explanation of the sort that earlier novelists offered with their deterministic consequences and resounding conclusions. A few years later, in *Journal of "The Counterfeiters,"* Gide further distanced himself from that convention by calling for a new kind of novel in which the ending "must not be neatly rounded off, but rather disperse, disintegrate" (449).

An image of that open-endedness and uncertainty is the darkness that surrounds Lafcadio's train and his meddling with chance. Gide intended for this act to reflect his own historical role in liberating literature from the deadening determinism of consistent characters whose actions had predictable consequences. He commented explicitly on his intention through the novelist Julius, who explains to Lafcadio that he wants to create characters who commit crimes "gratuitously," by which he means "without a motive." Subsequently Gide addressed the obvious impossibility of a character who is motivated to kill without a motive, especially after critics attempted to explain Lafcadio's act as an example of Gide's famous notion of the *acte gratuit*. Human existence is anything but gratuitous, especially not for a novelist who intentionally sought to change the course of fiction. Gide explained that by gratuitous acts he meant those that cannot be accounted for by "ordinary psychological explanations" and therefore seem to be more "disinterested" than most.[21] Lafcadio's act is not ordinarily motivated and is offered as a gesture toward transcending conventional motivation and predictable behavior. The anonymity of his victim, the darkness of the night, and the rigged probability of the light that shines out in it together express Gide's gesture on behalf of human caprice and freedom.

Lafcadio's act dramatizes that ambiguous realm between determinism and freedom that modern novelists struggled to capture. It plays out on the free side of determinism and on the determinist side of chance. It falls short of any conventional deterministic explanation based on conventional interests in that it is emphatically "disinterested." Still, Lafcadio is highly motivated to perform such a "motiveless" act and does it with intense focus, enough to fix the dice, in a sense, by slowing the count. The murder is not determined by conventional motives such as greed or revenge, but is determined by his determination to do it without a reason. The act also falls short of being determined solely by chance, a notion that itself embodies a contradiction. Lafcadio tries get chance under his control but is still drawn to its thrilling action and so turns over the final "decision" to the "chance" appearance of a light in the night. This dialectic of determinism and freedom offers us a final graphic image of the specificity-uncertainty dialectic. The more we as readers attempt to understand the reasons for Lafcadio's action, the more we realize how little we understand it, how much more there always is to know. That lack of knowledge is precisely what sustains our interest as readers. Our limited knowledge of human causality plunges into the darkness surrounding our own inquiries as Lafcadio's train plunges into the night.

Notes

INTRODUCTION

1. William A. Wallace, *Causality and Scientific Explanation*, 2 vols. (Ann Arbor, 1972); Mario Bunge, *Causality and Modern Science* (New York, 1959); David Bohm, *Causality and Chance in Modern Physics* (New York, 1957); John Hicks, *Causality in Economics* (Oxford, 1979); Ernest Gellner, *Cause and Meaning in the Social Sciences* (London, 1973); Mervyn Susser, *Causal Thinking in the Health Sciences* (Oxford, 1973); Alfred S. Evans, *Causation and Disease: A Chronological Journey* (New York, 1993); H.L.A. Hart and Tony Honoré, *Causation in the Law* [1959], 2d ed. (Oxford, 1985); Sarnoff A. Mednick, Terrie E. Moffitt, and Susan A. Stack, *The Causes of Crime: New Biological Approaches* (Cambridge, 1987); Roy Jay Nelson, *Causality and Narrative in French Fiction from Zola to Robbe-Grillet* (Columbus, Ohio, 1990); Brian Richardson, *Unlikely Stories: Causality and the Nature of Modern Narrative* (Cranbury, N.J., 1997); K. Codell Carter, *The Rise of Causal Concepts of Disease: Case Histories* (Hants, England, 2003).

2. Henri Ellenberger, "A Clinical Introduction to Psychiatric Phenomenology and Existential Analysis," in Rollo May et al., eds., *Existence: A New Dimension in Psychiatry and Psychology* (New York, 1967), 114ff. That seminal article also surveyed modes of time and space, which was the inspiration for my earlier book *The Culture of Time and Space: 1880–1918* (Cambridge, Mass., 1983).

3. Nelson mentioned this novel (in French, *Les caves du Vatican*) only briefly in a comment on Gide. See *Causality and Narrative*, 35.

4. On these see Alfred R. Mele, "Introduction" in Alfred R. Mele, ed., *The Philosophy of Action* (New York, 1997), 2–16. Gilbert Ryle rejected a causal approach to actions in *The Concept of Mind* (Chicago, 1949), and it fell into philosophical disrepute until revived in Donald Davidson's important paper, "Actions, Reasons, and Causes," *Journal of Philosophy* 60 (1963): 685–700; and again in Alvin Goldman, *A Theory of Human Action* (Englewood Cliffs, N.J., 1970).

5. André Gide, *Lafcadio's Adventures* (New York, 1953), 194–96.

6. André Gide, "Faits-divers," *La nouvelle revue française* 30 (June 1, 1928): 841. See also Y. Davet, "Notice" to *Les caves du Vatican* in *Romans d'André Gide* (Paris, 1958), 1571. Robert Musil offered a similar critique of the "pseudoexplanation" of the psychological novel of the Naturalist period, which amounted to the "tracing of phenomena back to other complexes of phenomena that had been personally selected as useful. The only necessity in this [is] that after a certain number of steps the explanation necessarily got bogged down." "Psychology and Literature" (c. 1920), *Precision and Soul: Essays and Addresses* (Chicago, 1990), 66–67.

7. Gide, "Faits-divers," 841.

8. Nelson argues that *Lafcadio's Adventures* "stigmatizes . . . not the principle of causation but, as he made clear [in "Faits divers," 841–42] the naive belief in obvious,

mechanistic causes and in the predictability of human behavior which lay at the base of some social sciences and of literature with ethical pretensions." *Causality and Narrative*, 21–22.

9. André Gide, *The Counterfeiters; with Journal of "The Counterfeiters"* (1927; trans., New York, 1973).

10. This interpretation of Gide is the centerpiece for Jean-Joseph Goux, *The Coiners of Language* (1984; trans., Norman, Okla., 1994).

11. See note 6.

12. On the postmodern "anti-detective story" that refuses to solve the crime in order to liberate the reader from "the rigid deterministic plot of the well-made fiction," see William V. Spanos, "The Detective and the Boundary: Some Notes on the Postmodern Literary Imagination," *Boundary* 2 (1972): 147–68. Similarly David Richter found postmodern detective novels full of "the impossibility of solving mysteries, the inadequacy of the epistemology inherent in the detective process, the nausea-provoking contrariness of objects and clues." See "Murder in Jest: Serial Killing in the Post-Modern Detective Story," *Journal of Narrative Technique* 19 (Winter 1989): 108ff.

13. In a famous definition of positivism, Comte addressed the role of discovering certain kinds of causes. "In the positive state, the human mind, recognizing the impossibility of obtaining absolute notions, gives up knowing the origin and purpose of the universe and the ultimate causes of phenomena, in order to focus on discovering, by reason and observation, the actual laws of phenomena, that is, their invariable relations of succession and likeness." *Cours de philosophie positive* [1830], 5th ed. (Paris, 1892), 1:4. Although Comte excluded first, final, and ultimate causes, he grounded positivism in a search for causal understanding of empirically verifiable, lawlike phenomena based on correlations.

14. "The rigorous observation of facts has become, quite rightly, the starting point and the foundation of our knowledge.... Moral facts ... obey ... laws as positive as those that reign in the physical world." Pierre-Egiste Lisle, *Du suicide: Statistique, médicine, histoire et legislation* (Paris, 1856), quoted in Ian Hacking, *The Taming of Chance* (Cambridge, 1990), 78.

15. Honoré de Balzac, *Pensées, sujets, fragmens*, préface et notes de Jacques Crépet (Paris, 1910), 136; quoted in Charles Affron, *Patterns of Failure in La comédie humaine* (New Haven, 1966), 8.

16. Review of Robert Mackay, *The Progress of the Intellect* [1851], in *Essays of George Eliot* (London, 1963), 31.

17. Quoted in Paul F. Cranefield, "The Organic Physics of 1847 and the Biophysics of Today," *Journal of the History of Medicine and Allied Sciences* 12 (1957): 408–9.

18. On the varieties of midcentury positivism, see D. G. Charlton, *Positivist Thought in France during the Second Empire, 1852–1870* (Oxford, 1959).

19. Frank Miller Turner, *Between Science and Religion: The Reaction to Scientific Naturalism in Late Victorian England* (New Haven, 1974), 13. See also Frederick Gregory, *Scientific Materialism in Nineteenth Century Germany* (Boston, 1977), 148–59, 164–65.

20. Henry Maudsley, *Responsibility in Mental Disease* (1874; reprint, New York, 1896), 28.

21. Paul Bourget, *The Disciple* (1889; trans., London 1898), 32. In *Essai philosophique sur les probabilités* (1814), Laplace wrote, "An intelligence which at a given moment knew all the forces that animate nature, and the respective positions of the beings that compose it, and further possessing the scope to analyze these data, could condense into a single formula the movement of the greatest bodies of the universe and that of the least atom: for such an intelligence nothing would be uncertain, and the past and future alike would be before its eyes." Quoted in Jonathan Powers, *Philosophy and the New Physics* (London, 1982), 138.

22. H. Stuart Hughes's chapter, "The Decade of the 1890's: The Revolt against Positivism," is still a compelling survey of this development. *Consciousness and Society: The Reorientation of European Social Thought, 1890–1930* (New York, 1958), chap. 2.

23. New applications of highly specialized productive skills were evident in the postmodern commercial world, with small-batch production, flexible production, just-in-time production, consultancy, rapid turnover, instant data analysis, subcontracting, outsourcing, and highly specialized small-scale market niches. David Harvey, *The Condition of Postmodernity: An Enquiry into the Origins of Cultural Change* (London, 1989), 155.

24. Thomas Haskell, *The Emergence of Professional Social Science: The American Social Science Association and the Nineteenth-Century Crisis of Authority* (1977; reprint, Baltimore, 2000), 1.

25. Henry Adams, *The Education of Henry Adams* completed in 1907 (1918; reprint, Boston, 1973), 461, 457.

26. Henri Poincaré, *Science and Hypothesis* (1902; reprint, New York, 1952), 173.

27. Ibid., 456, 487, 497. In a similar vein, Robert Musil noted that "the truth is not a crystal that can be slipped into one's pocket, but an endless current into which one falls headlong.... Sun, wind, food brought it there, and illness, hunger, cold or a cat killed it, but none of this could have happened without the operation of laws, biological, psychological, meterological, physical, chemical, sociological, and all the rest." *The Man without Qualities* [1930/31], trans. Sophie Wilkins (New York, 1995), 1:582.

28. Gerald Holton, *Thematic Origins of Scientific Thought: Kepler to Einstein* (Cambridge, Mass., 1973), 96.

29. Alan D. Beyerchen, "Nonlinear Science and the Unfolding of a New Intellectual Vision," *Papers in Comparative Studies* 6 (1989): 28.

30. Victor Turner, "Process, System, and Symbol: A New Anthropological Synthesis," *Daedalus* 106 (1977): 61–80. On this see Randolph Roth, "Is History a Process? Nonlinearity, Revitalization Theory, and the Central Metaphor of Social Science History," *Social Science History* 16 (Summer 1992): 199–200 and passim.

31. David Lodge, "The Language of Modernist Fiction: Metaphor and Metonymy," in Malcolm Bradbury and James McFarlane, eds., *Modernism: A Guide to European Literature, 1890–1930* (Harmondsworth, England, 1976), 481.

32. Virginia Woolf, "Modern Fiction," in *The Common Reader* (1925; reprint, New York, 1953), 154. Gig lamps are located on either side of a gig, or one-horse carriage, so at night a line of such carriages would appear as line of symmetrically arranged lights.

33. Ford summarized a view he shared with Conrad: "It became very early evident to us that what was the matter with the Novel, and the British Novel in particular, was that it went straight forward, whereas in your gradual making acquaintance with your fellows you never do go straight forward. . . . To get . . . a man in function you could not begin at his beginning and work his life chronologically to the end. You must first get him with a strong impression, and then work backwards and forwards over his past." *Joseph Conrad: A Personal Reminiscence* (Boston, 1924), 192–95.

34. N. Katherine Hayles, *The Cosmic Web: Scientific Field Models and Literary Strategies in the Twentieth Century* (Ithaca, N.Y., 1984).

35. In 1924 the German psychiatrist Hans Berger made the first electroencephalogram recording in a process he called *Electroencephalogram*. It enabled him to measure and record alpha and beta brain waves through an intact skull. M. E. Raichle, "Positron Emission Tomography," *Annual Review of Neuroscience* 6 (1983): 249–67; on CAT, MRI, and PET technologies, see entries in Robert Bud and Deborah Jean Warner, eds., *Instruments of Science: An Historical Encyclopedia* (New York, 1998).

36. Thomas Vargish, *The Providential Aesthetic in Victorian Fiction* (Charlottesville, 1985).

37. On chance in Conrad and Joyce, see Leland Monk, *Standard Deviation: Chance and the Modern British Novel* (Stanford, 1993).

38. Lorenz Krüger, Lorraine J. Daston, and Michael Heidelberger, eds., *The Probabilistic Revolution*, 2 vols. (Cambridge, Mass., 1987); Theodore M. Porter, *The Rise of Statistical Thinking, 1820–1900* (Princeton, 1986), 315.

39. John Dewey, *The Quest for Certainty* (1929; reprint, New York, 1960). Paul Jerome Croce periodizes the "eclipse of certainty" earlier in the nineteenth century but tracks the same cultural-historical logic in the development of philosophical, scientific, and religious thought. He repeatedly phrases his argument in accordance with what I have called the specificity-uncertainty dialectic: "Paradoxically, the more people knew of religion or science, the less certain they felt. . . . An expanding base of knowledge seemed to the public to offer ever more definite answers, but when experts knew more, they simply multiplied the questions to be asked." *Science and Religion in the Era of William James*. Vol. 1, *Eclipse of Certainty, 1820–1880* (Chapel Hill, 1995), 5.

40. Vargish, *Providential Aesthetic*.

41. Karl Pearson, *The Grammar of Science* (1892; reprint, London, 1911).

42. Bertrand Russell, "On the Notion of Cause" [1912], in *Mysticism and Logic* (New York, n.d), 174. Pearson's skepticism was challenged in the later twentieth century. Wesley C. Salmon, for example, cited it as a historical low point from which modern science has emerged far more confident about its ability to comprehend and explain. See his article, "Why Ask 'Why'?" in *Causality and Explanation* (New York, 1998), 126 and passim.

43. Uncertainty sometimes includes discontinuity, although this concept was used primarily in physics and then applied to human experience, also rather loosely. An exception is William R. Everdell, who makes a compelling case for a spectrum of new discontinuities in modern thought. *The First Moderns: Profiles in the Origins of Twentieth-Century Thought* (Chicago, 1997), 346–60 and passim.

44. Oliver Wendell Holmes, "Border Lines of Knowledge in Some Provinces of Medical Science" [1861], in *Medical Essays, 1842–1882* (Boston, 1899), 211.

45. Quoted in Elizabeth Kolbert, "Ice Memory," *New Yorker* (January 7, 2002): 35. Referring to knowledge of oceanographic ecosystems, the marine biologist Peter Franks claimed that "the more data we get, the less we know." *Christian Science Monitor* (September 16, 1997). An article in *The Economist Times* on information overload was titled "The More We Learn, the Less We Know" (November 16, 1998). Applied to mathematics, see Piotr Ejdys and Grzegorz Góra, "The More We Learn the Less We Know? On Inductive Learning from Examples," *Lecture Notes in Computer Science* 1609 (1999): 262–70.

46. Arkady Plotnitsky, *The Knowable and the Unknowable: Modern Science, Non-classical Thought, and the "Two Cultures"* (Ann Arbor, 2002), xiii.

47. Ibid., 21.

48. The articles in M. Norton Wise's edited collection *The Values of Precision* (Princeton, 1995) abundantly document how new technologies and techniques throughout the nineteenth century increasingly improved scientific precision and affirmed its value.

49. K. Codell Carter, "The Development of Pasteur's Concept of Disease Causation and the Emergence of Specific Causes in Nineteenth-Century Medicine," *Bulletin of the History of Medicine* 65 (1991): 528–48; "Essay Review: Toward a Rational History of Medical Science," *Studies in the History and Philodophy of Medical Science* 26 (1995): 493–502.

50. The London Benevolent Medical Society, cited by K. Codell Carter, "The Concept of Quackery in Early Nineteenth-Century British Medical Periodicals," *Journal of Medical Humanities* 14 (1993): 89.

51. Virginia Woolf, "Modern Fiction," in *The Common Reader* (London, 1925), 151.

52. Christopher Butler, "Progress and the Avant-Garde," in *Early Modernism: Literature, Music, and Painting in Europe, 1900–1916* (Oxford, 1994), 250–61. He cautioned, however, that "it is quite mistaken to believe that innovative change by artists can plausibly be seen as part of a unilinear historical process (and in this respect the arts contrast drastically with science)" (256).

53. Charles Darwin, *On the Origin of Species* (1859; reprint, Cambridge, Mass., 1964), 489.

54. In *Modernism* (see note 31, above), the editors Malcolm Bradbury and James McFarlane made a similar argument in defining the modernist novel's use of narrative introversion in contrast to the analogous techniques in the earlier realist novel. "Whereas the former versions of self-conscious narration functioned usually for humorous effect, the later ones were normally serious and 'literary' in a way that would have been incomprehensible a century or so previously" (396).

55. Joel Black documented the interaction between murderous fact and fiction: "Whereas authors like De Quincey, Stendhal, and Balzac based their criminal literature on actual murderers, real-life murderers like Pierre-François Lecenaire and Jean-Baptiste Troppmann were inspired by their readings of popular romantic fiction, and they in turn provided fresh models for more of the same." *The Aesthetics of Murder: A Study of Romantic Literature and Contemporary Culture* (Baltimore, 1991), 11.

56. See also Carter's commentary on two circular attempts to define causality in medicine which support this spirited claim. *The Rise of Causal Concepts*, 199 n. 1.

57. A fine example of the integration of understanding of molecules and cells with understanding of human behavior as documented in fiction is Laura Otis's *Membranes: Metaphors of Invasion in Nineteenth-Century Literature, Science, and Politics* (Baltimore, 1999).

58. In an appendix to *Native Son* titled "How 'Bigger' Was Born," Wright explained that Bigger "was trying to react to and answer the call of the dominant civilization whose glitter came to him through the newspapers, magazines, radio, movies, and the more imposing sight and sound of daily American life" (513).

59. For more examples of the causal role of technology in murder, see chapter 7.

CHAPTER 1: ANCESTRY

1. Carl E. Schorske, *Thinking with History: Explorations in the Passage to Modernism* (Princeton, 1999), 4.

2. Michael Kammen documents the surge of filiopiety in America between 1870 and 1915, including the formation during the 1890s of many organizations based on ancestry, such as the Daughters of the American Revolution and the Society of Mayflower Descendants. *Mystic Chords of Memory: The Transformation of Tradition in American Culture* (New York, 1991), 215–23.

3. Thomas Hardy, *A Group of Noble Dames* [1891]; quoted in Sophie Gilmartin, *Ancestry and Narrative in Nineteenth-Century British Literature: Blood Relations from Edgeworth to Hardy* (Cambridge, 1999), 11.

4. Patricia Tobin, *Time and the Novel: The Genealogical Imperative* (Princeton, 1978), 7. The critic George Levine noted that the word *origin* "spoke directly to an apparently insatiable Victorian urge to determine origins—of language, of the Nile, of the human species, of the cosmos (or, in novels from *Oliver Twist* to *Daniel Deronda*), of parenthood." *Darwin and the Novelists: Patterns of Science in Victorian Fiction* (Chicago, 1988), 95.

5. Timothy Lenoir's *The Strategy of Life: Teleology and Mechanics in Nineteenth-Century German Biology* (Chicago, 1982) defines "teleo-mechanism" and documents the elaborate theorizing and extraordinary detail produced in functional anatomy, embryology, and cell theory by early biologists Johann Meckel, Karl Ernst von Baer, and Johannes Müller, among many others, who attempted to explain biological phenomena with teleological models that were based on mechanical principles rather than divine or occult forces. On the development of recapitulation theory, see Stephen Jay Gould's *Ontogeny and Phylogeny* (Cambridge, Mass., 1977).

6. Johann Meckel, *System der vergleichenden Anatomie* (1821), 1:345; quoted in Ernst Mayr, *The Growth of Biological Thought: Diversity, Evolution, and Inheritance* (Cambridge, MA, 1982), 471.

7. Mayr, *Growth*, 215.

8. Quoted in Mayr, *Growth*, 474.

9. "The rapid and brief ontogeny [of each organism] is a condensed synopsis of the long and slow history of the stem," and therefore "phylogeny is the mechanical

cause of ontogeny." Ernst Haeckel, *The Evolution of Man* (1874; reprint, London, 1905), 415; quoted in David J. Depew and Bruce H. Weber, *Darwinism Evolving* (Cambridge, Mass., 1955), 179.

10. Henry Maudsley, *Body and Mind: An Inquiry into Their Connection and Mutual Influence* (London, 1870); quoted in William Greenslade, *Degeneration, Culture and the Novel, 1880–1940* (Cambridge, 1994), 69.

11. Charles Darwin, *On the Origin of Species* (1859; reprint, Cambridge, Mass., 1964), 488.

12. His theory drew from the disciplines of comparative anatomy, embryology, and biogeography. "These biological disciplines, which up to 1859 had been primarily descriptive, now became causal sciences, with common descent providing an explanation for nearly everything that had previously been puzzling." Ernst Mayr, *One Long Argument: Charles Darwin and the Genesis of Modern Evolutionary Thought* (Cambridge, Mass., 1991), 23.

13. Darwin, *Origin*, 412.

14. Charles Darwin, *The Expression of the Emotions in Man and Animals* (1872; reprint, Chicago, 1965), 251.

15. Darwin, *Origin*, 202–3.

16. As Gillian Beer notes, "Lamarck's theory was in its way deeply satisfying: it gave primacy to mind—to intention, habit, memory, a reasoned inheritance from generation to generation in which need engendered solution and solutions could be genetically preserved by means of an act of will, rendered independent of consciousness as habit." *Darwin's Plots: Evolutionary Narrative in Darwin, George Eliot and Nineteenth-Century Fiction* (London, 1983), 25.

17. Laura Otis examines organic memory and its development in Victorian literature in *Organic Memory: History and the Body in the Late Nineteenth and Early Twentieth Centuries* (Lincoln, Nebr., 1994).

18. Samuel Butler, *Life and Habit* (London, 1878), 297.

19. Butler, *Unconscious Memory* (London, 1880), 80. In France, Théodule Ribot popularized the theory with *L'hérédité: Étude psychologique sur ses phénomènes, ses lois, ses causes, ses conséquences* (Paris, 1873).

20. In Charles Darwin, *The Variation of Animals and Plants under Domestication* (1868), 2:35–66, quoted in Otis, *Organic Memory*, 44.

21. Charles Darwin, *The Descent of Man and Selection in Relation to Sex* (1871; reprint, New York, 1897), 137.

22. J. B. Thomson, "The Hereditary Nature of Crime," *Journal of Mental Science* 72 (January 1870): 487–98. Thomson and several others are discussed in C.H.S. Jaywardine, "The English Precursors of Lombroso," *British Journal of Crime* 4 (1963): 164–70.

23. Maudsley, *Body and Mind*: quoted in Vieda Skultans, *Madness and Morals: Ideas on Insanity in the Nineteenth Century* (London, 1975), 207.

24. W. Bevan Lewis, "The Origins of Crime," *Fortnightly Review* 54 (1893): 329–44.

25. See e.g., Karl Landsteiner, "Ueber Agglutinationserscheinungen normalen menschlichen Blutes," *Wiener Klinische Wochenschrift* 14 (1901): 1132–34; translated in *Transfusion* 1 (Jan.–Feb. 1961): 5–8.

26. For the influence of Weismann on English culture and on Hardy, see Peter Morton, *The Vital Science: Biology and the Literary Imagination, 1860–1900* (London, 1984), 196–208. On the five successive drafts of the novel showing ever stronger hereditary influence, see John Turner Laird, *The Shaping of "Tess of the d'Urbervilles"* (Oxford, 1975), 31. On the social, sexual, historical, and hereditary causes of Tess's "blight," see Jules Law, "A 'Passing Corporeal Blight': Political Bodies in *Tess of the d'Urbervilles*," *Victorian Studies* 40 (Winter 1997): 260ff.

27. Interview with Raymond Blaythwayt in 1892; cited in F. R. Southerington, *Hardy's Vision of Man* (London, 1969), 132.

28. William Thomson, "On a Universal Tendency in Nature to the Dissipation of Mechanical Energy," *Philosophical Magazine*, ser. 4, 4 (1852): 304–6; quoted in Stephen Brush, *The Temperature of History: Phases of Science and Culture in the Nineteenth Century* (New York, 1978), 30.

29. Quoted by Daniel Pick, *Faces of Degeneration: A European Disorder, c. 1848–c. 1918* (Cambridge, 1989), 72.

30. Robert Nye, "Heredity, Pathology and Psychoneurosis in Durkheim's Early Work," *Knowledge and Society* 4 (1982): 104ff.

31. B. A. Morel, *Traité des dégénérescences physiques, intellectuelles et morales de l'espèce humaine* (Paris, 1857).

32. Charles Féré, "La famille névropathique," *Archives de neurologie* 7 (1884): 1–43, 173–91. See also Marandon de Montel, "De la criminalité et de la dégénérescence," *Archives d'anthropologie criminelle* 7 (1892): 221–44.

33. Pick, *Faces of Degeneration*, 8.

34. A. E. Carter, *The Idea of Decadence in French Literature, 1830–1900*, (Toronto, 1958). For the emphasis on heredity, see Jennifer Birkett, *The Sins of the Fathers: Decadence in France, 1870–1914* (London, 1986).

35. Charles Brace, *The Dangerous Classes of New York*, (New York, 1872), 44.

36. Nicole Hahn Rafter, *Creating Born Criminals* (Chicago, 1997), 38ff.

37. The first public recommendation for such a negative eugenics policy was made by Orpheus Everts, superintendent of the Cincinnati Sanitarium. "Asexualization, as a Penalty for Crime and the Reformation of Criminals," *Cincinnati Lancet-Clinic* 20 (1888): 377–80; cited in Arthur E. Fink, *Causes of Crime: Biological Theories in the United States, 1800–1915* (Philadelphia, 1938), 188.

38. August Drähms, *The Criminal* (New York, 1900), 141–42. Fink surveys dozens of American somatic-hereditarian theories in *Causes of Crime*.

39. S.L.N. Foote, "An Address on Crime and Its Prevention," *Kansas City Medical Index* 18 (July 1897): 244; quoted in Fink, *Causes of Crime*, 192.

40. Max Nordau, *Degeneration* (1893; reprint, New York, 1895). The causes included malnutrition, environmental poisoning, overwork, overstimulation, fatigue, "railway spine," "railway brain," vertigo, hysteria, neurasthenia, realism, naturalism, "decadentism," and neomysticism.

41. William Greenslade, *Degeneration*, 5.

42. George Henry Lewes, "Hereditary Influences, Animal and Human," *The Westminster Review* 66 (1856): 79ff.

43. Henry Maudsley, *Body and Mind: An Inquiry into Their Connection and Mutual Influence, Specially in Reference to Mental Disorders* (1873; reprint, New York, 1898) 63.

44. Ancestry in *The Hound of the Baskervilles* is analyzed in James Kissane and John M. Kissane, "Sherlock Holmes and the Ritual of Reason," *Nineteenth-Century Fiction* 17 (1962–63): 353–62.

45. "In regard to conceptions of human heredity, only comparatively minor differences distinguished the elite within the profession from their less educated and articulate colleagues." Charles Rosenberg, "The Bitter Fruit: Heredity, Disease, and Social Thought," in *No Other Gods: On Science and American Social Thought* (Baltimore, 1976), 26.

46. Georgiana Kirby, *Transmission; or, Variation of Character through the Mother* (New York 1877), 11. See also the American phrenologist O. S. Fowler, who argued that "the mental and physical character then existing is fully and completely transmitted to offspring," by means of "magnetism" and "through the instrumentality of the secretions, and their intimate relation to body and mind." *Love and Parentage Applied to the Improvement of Offspring* (New York, 1846), 25.

47. J. H. Kellogg, *Plain Facts for Old and Young* (1879; reprint, Burlington, Iowa, 1881), 109, 112.

48. Fowler, *Love* 74.

49. There is no reference to any aspect of the biology of pregnancy, let alone its effect on the fetus, in any of the forty major Victorian novels that I read for *The Culture of Love: Victorians to Moderns* (Cambridge, 1992). That omission highlights the historical significance of the detailed account of the pregnancy of Anna Victrix in D. H. Lawrence's *The Rainbow* (1915), a victory over the Victorian conspiracy of silence about sex.

50. William A. Hammond, "On the Influence of the Maternal Mind over the Offspring during Pregnancy and Lactation," *Quarterly Journal of Psychological Medicine* 2 (1868): 7, 16, 20. J. H. Kellogg also warned that "if during gestation the mother is fretful, complaining, and exacting; if she requires to be petted and waited upon. . . . the result will surely be a peevish, fretful child, that will develop in to a morose and irritable man or woman, imperious, unthankful, disobedient, willful, gluttonous, and vicious." Kellogg, *Plain Facts*, 67, 112.

51. On the history of this notion, especially among the Romantics, see Marie-Hélène Huet, *Monstrous Imagination* (Cambridge, 1993), 8 (quoting Holmes).

52. Richard W. Burkhardt, Jr., "Closing the Door on Lord Morton's Mare," in William Coleman and Camille Limoges, eds., *Studies in the History of Biology* (Baltimore, 1979): 1–21.

53. August Weismann, *The Germ-Plasm* (1892; reprint, London, 1898), 383.

54. Harriet Ritvo, *The Platypus and the Mermaid* (Cambridge, Mass., 1997), 108–9.

55. Quoted by Arthur Shipley, "Zebras, Horses, and Hybrids," *Quarterly Review* 190 (1899): 406. Burkhardt quoted the same passage and reported being unable to find the statement in Agassiz's writings. "Closing the Door," 5 n. 16.

56. Charles Darwin, *The Variation of Animals and Plants under Domestication* (London 1868), 2:388. Darwin accepted the possibility of telegony and cited ten sources for it, including Lord Morton's mare. He also cited twenty more sources on parallel phenomena in plants. Burkhardt, "Closing the Door," 18 n. 14.

57. Prosper Lucas, *Traité philosophique et physiologique de l'hérédité naturelle* (Paris, 1847–50), 1:58ff.

58. Jules Michelet, *L'amour* (Paris, 1895), 325–26. On Michelet's influence, see Marcel Cressot, "Essai sur la genèse de deux romans de jeunesse: 'La Confession du Claude', 'Madeleine Férat,' "*Revue d'histoire littéraire de la France* 35 (1928): 382–89; and Hilde Olrik, "La théorie de l'imprégnation," *Nineteenth-Century French Studies* (Fall-Winter, 1986–87): 128–40.

59. "La petite Lucie ressemblait à Jacques. . . . A coup sûr le sang de Jacques entrait pour beaucoup dans la fécondation de Madeleine." Émile Zola, *Oeuvres complètes* (Paris, 1962), 812–13.

60. Otto Weininger, *Sex and Character* (New York, 1906), 233.

61. Hammond, "Influence of the Maternal Mind," 21–22.

62. Alexander Harvey, *On the Foetus in Utero as Inoculating the Maternal with the Peculiarities of the Paternal Organism* (London, 1886), 6. This view was endorsed in a standard physiology text, William B. Carpenter, *Principles of Physiology* (London, 1851), 977, cited by Burkhardt, "Closing the Door," 19 n. 22.

63. August Strindberg, *A Madman's Defense* (1895; reprint, New York, 1967), 232.

64. Marvin Carlson, "Ibsen, Strindberg, and Telegony," *PMLA* 100 (October, 1985): 777, 781.

65. Eduard von Hartmann, *The Sexes Compared* (London, 1895), 12.

66. For basic concepts on the history of biology, I have drawn from personal conversations with Gerald Karp and information in his book, *Cell and Molecular Biology: Concepts and Experiments* (New York, 1999).

67. Peter J. Bowler, *The Mendelian Revolution* (Baltimore, 1989), 103ff. Robert Olby, "Mendel No Mendelian?" *History of Science* 17 (1979): 53–72; Elizabeth Gaskin, "Why Was Mendel's Work Ignored?" *Journal of the History of Ideas* 20 (June 1959): 60–84.

68. Ernst Mayr, *The Growth of Biological Thought* (Cambridge, Mass., 1982), 665–66.

69. August Weismann, *Die Continuität des Keimplasmas als Grundlage einer Theorie der Vererbung* (Jena, 1885).

70. George J. Romanes, "Weismann's Theory of Heredity," *Contemporary Review* 57 (1890): 695.

71. Gregor Mendel, "Versuche über Pflanzen-Hybriden," *Verhandlungen des naturforschenden Vereines in Brünn* 4 (1865): 3–47; Walter S. Sutton, "The Chromosomes in Heredity," *Biological Bulletin* 4 (1902): 231–51; T. H. Morgan, "Sex Limited Inheritance in Drosophilia," *Science* 32 (1910): 120–22; Alfred H. Sturtevant, "The Linear Arrangement of Six Sex-Linked Factors in Drosophilia as Shown by Their Mode or Association," *Journal of Experimental Zoology* 14 (1913): 43–59; Theophilus Painter, "A New Method for the Study of Chromosime Rearrangements and Plotting Chromosome Maps," *Science* 78 (1933): 585–86; O. T. Avery, C. M. MacLeod, and M. McCarty, "Studies on the Chemical Nature of the Substance Inducing Transformation of Pneumococcal Types," *Journal of Experimental Biology* 79 (1944): 137–57; M. W. Nirenberg and J. H. Matthaei, "The Dependence of Cell-Free Protein Synthesis in *E. Coli* upon Naturally Occurring or Synthetic Polyribonucleotides," *Proceedings of the National Academy of Science USA* 47 (1961): 1588–1602.

72. Horace Freeland Judson, "A History of the Science and Technology behind Gene Mapping and Sequencing," in Daniel J. Kevles and Leroy Hood, eds., *The*

Code of Codes: Scientific and Social Issues in the Human Genome Project (Cambridge, Mass., 1992), 72ff.

73. Richard Preston, "The Genome Warrior," *New Yorker*, June 12, 2000, 68.

74. For a gold mine of information about the discovery of causality in medicine or "the etiological research program," see K. Codell Carter, *The Rise of Causal Concepts of Disease: Case Histories* (London, 2003). For this particular fact see "Causes of Disease in Early Nineteenth-Century Practical Medicine" in ibid., 10–13. See also Bruno Latour, *Pasteurization of France* (Cambridge, Mass., 1988), 20.

75. Carter, *Rise of Causal Concepts*, 63.

76. "The Etiology of Tuberculosis" [1882], in K. Codell Carter, trans. and ed., *Essays of Robert Koch* (New York 1987), 95.

77. Carter, *Rise of Causal Concepts*, 74.

78. C. R. Scrivener, A. L. Beaudet, W. S. Sly, and D. Valle, eds., *The Metabolic and Molecular Bases of Inherited Disease* (New York, 1995).

79. John C. Avise, *The Genetic Gods: Evolution and Belief in Human Affairs* (Cambridge, Mass., 1998), 56–61.

80. Ibid., 825.

81. The gene has come to signify the ultimate biological causal agent. Dorothy Nelkin and M. Susan Lindee surveyed the pervasiveness of this concept across late-twentieth-century popular culture in movies, cartoons, advertisements, musical lyrics, radio talk shows, jokes, child-care books, and biographies. They concluded that the gene has become "the key to human relationships and the basis of family cohesion." *The DNA Mystique: The Gene as a Cultural Icon* (New York, 1995), 198.

82. Stephen J. Kunitz, "Explanation and Ideologies of Mortality Patterns," *Population and Development Review* 13 (1987): 379–408; Mervin Susser, *Causal Thinking in the Health Sciences* (Oxford, 1973), 22–24; cited in Carter, *Rise of Causal Concepts*, 4.

83. Burkhardt, "Closing the Door," 16.

84. Ethological studies such as Konrad Lorenz, *On Aggression* (1966), and Robert Ardrey, *The Territorial Imperative* (1966), documented similarities in basic instincts such as aggression and territoriality, but not in complex acts such as murder. While this burst of research in the mid-1960s remained speculative and controversial, these authors made a strong argument that much of our own social behavior can be traced through genetic lineages to our nonhuman ancestors. Those and current similar studies do not deal with specific genes, however, so their verification or refutation is difficult to accomplish, and any precise causal account at the genetic level is far beyond the capacities of current understanding.

85. Quoted in William Greenslade, *Degeneration, Culture and the Novel, 1880–1940* (Cambridge, 1994), 66.

86. Emile Durkheim, *The Division of Labor in Society* (1893; reprint, New York, 1964), 308, 317.

87. Francis Galton, *Hereditary Genius: An Inquiry into Its Laws and Consequences* (Cleveland, 1962), 45.

88. L. C. Dunn, "Cross Currents in the History of Human Genetics," *American Journal of Human Genetics* 14 (1962): 7.

89. P. A. Jacobs et al., "Aggressive Behavior, Mental Subnormality and the XYY Male," *Nature* 208 (1965): 1351–52. The XYY chromosome was first reported in 1961 in A. A. Sandberg, et al., "The XYY Human Male," *Lancet* 2 (1961): 488–89.

90. Reed Pyeritz et al., "The XYY Male: The Making of a Myth," in Ann Arbor Science for the People Editorial Collective, *Biology as a Social Weapon* (Ann Arbor, 1977): 86–100; Dorothy Nelkin and M. Susan Lindee, "Evil in the Genes," in *DNA Mystique*, 83–94.

91. D. Borgaonkar and S. Shah, "The XYY Chromosome, Male—Or Syndrome," *Progress in Medical Genetics* 10 (1974): 135–222; quoted in Pyeritz, "The XYY Male," 89. The idea that criminality is directly heritable has persisted, but largely at the margins of popular culture in talk-show wisdom, nonscholarly publications, and sensationalist movies. A psychiatrist on *The Donahue Show* in 1993 explained that one of his patients was driven by his extra Y chromosome to kill eleven women. That same year a made-for-TV movie with Raquel Welch, titled *Tainted Blood*, advertised its important message as showing that "some girls are born killers." Nelkin and Lindee, *DNA Mystique*, 84ff.

92. Jean-Paul Sartre, "François Muriac and Freedom," in *Literary and Philosophical Essays* (New York, 1955), 7.

93. Jean-Paul Sartre, "Camus' *The Outsider*," in *Literary and Philosophical Essays*, 42, 44.

94. Jacques Guicharnaud, "Man and His Acts," in Edith Kern, ed., *Sartre: A Collection of Critical Essays* (Englewood, N.J., 1962), 62.

95. John E. Atwell interpreted Sartre as akin to action theorists, who believe that "human actions are not subject to causal determinism and cannot possibly be causally explained, that is, explained by appeal to antecedent events or conditions." "Sartre and Action Theory," in Hugh J. Silverman and Frederick A. Elliston, eds., *Jean-Paul Sartre: Contemporary Approaches to His Philosophy* (Pittsburgh, 1980), 3.

96. Karl Pearson, *Life, Letters and Labours of Francis Galton* (Cambridge, 1930), 3:309; quoted in Dunn, "Cross Currents," 7.

CHAPTER 2: CHILDHOOD

1. Diana Fuss, "Monsters of Perversion: Jeffrey Dahmer and *The Silence of the Lambs*," in Marjorie Garber, Jann Matlock, and Rebecca L. Walkowitz, eds., *Media Spectacles* (New York, 1993), 195.

2. I wrote to Thomas Harris and asked when he himself came up with the childhood trauma that explains Hannibal's actions, specifically whether he had it in mind from the late 1970s when he was working on *Red Dragon* (which would mean that he intentionally kept it from readers until the publication of *Hannibal* in 1999) or whether he hit upon it sometime later, and if so when. He replied, enigmatically, "I can't give you an answer because I don't know myself." Communication to the author, April 26, 2000. In an intriguing "Forward to a Fatal Interview," which Harris added to a new edition of *Red Dragon* in 2000, he explained that in writing a novel "you begin with what you can see and then you add what came before and what came after" (ix). Then he added in a final comment addressed

presumably to the reader, "By the time I undertook to record the events in *Hannibal*, the doctor, to my surprise, had taken on a life of his own. You seemed to find him as oddly engaging as I did" (xiii).

3. "The assumption that the cause of compulsive violence resides ultimately in childhood trauma has become canonical in criminological and popular accounts. . . . Such explanation has become virtually automatic in the literature (factual and fictional) on serial killing." Mark Seltzer, *Serial Killers: Death and Life in America's Wound Culture* (New York, 1998), 256.

4. Wordsworth, "Intimations of Immortality from Recollections of Early Childhood."

5. Wordsworth, "Our simple childhood," *The Prelude*, 5.508.

6. Charles Darwin, *The Descent of Man and Selection in Relation to Sex* (1971; reprint, New York, 1897), 127.

7. Preyer wrote: "The mind of the new-born . . . is already written upon before birth, with . . . countless sensuous impressions of long-gone generations." *The Mind of the Child* (1881; reprint, New York, 1892), xiv. Preyer inspired others to observe children and record their evolutionary development: Bernard Perez, *L'enfant de trois à sept ans* (Paris, 1886); Adolf Matthias, *Wie erziehen wir unsern Sohn Benjamin?* (Munich, 1904).

8. Alexander Chamberlain, *The Child: A Study in the Evolution of Man* (London, 1900), 70.

9. In a history of traumatic neurosis, E. Fischer-Homburg traced the "psychologization" of trauma from the mid-1880s to Freud's complete psychologization after 1897. *Die traumatische Neurose: vom somatischen zum sozialen Leiden* (Bern, 1975), 79.

10. Draft A, sent to Wilhelm Fliess, in Jeffrey Masson, ed., *The Complete Letters of Sigmund Freud to Wilhelm Fliess, 1877–1904* (Cambridge, Mass., 1995), 38.

11. Sigmund Freud, "An Autobiographical Study" [1925], in *Standard Edition of the Complete Psychological Works of Sigmund Freud* (London 1957), 20:33.

12. On this see Stephen Kern "Freud and the Emergence of Child Psychology: 1880–1910," (Ph.D. diss., Columbia University, 1970); and my article, "Freud and the Discovery of Child Sexuality," *History of Childhood Quarterly* (Summer 1973): 117–41.

13. S. Lindner, "Das Saugen an den Fingern, Lippen etc. bei den Kindern. (Ludeln)," *Jahrbuch für Kinderheilkunde* 14 (1897): 77.

14. In 1904 Sanford Bell concluded that the sucking impulse "entirely disappears from most children . . . [but] it is reclaimed in a number of sexual and other perversions in adults." "An Introductory Study of the Psychology of Foods," *Pedagogical Seminary* 11 (1904): 57. Less moralistic was a German handbook for parents that advised that nursing generates orderliness, self-control, and abstinence. Matthias, *Wie erziehen wir*, 6.

15. Marius Feyat, *De la constipation et des phénomènes toxiques qu'elle provoque* (Paris, 1890); H. Illoway, *Constipation in Adults and Children* (New York, 1897). In *Handbuch der privaten und öffentlichen Hygiene des Kindes* (Leipzig, 1881), the German pediatrician Julius Uffelman argued that regular toilet training instilled a sense of cleanliness and regularity (365). In *Die Charakterfehler des Kindes* (Leipzig, 1892), Friedrich Scholz recommended rigorous toilet training, which he associated with

orderliness, cleanliness, and pedantry (112). Matthias recommended early and regular toilet habits to instill orderliness, regularity, and temperance (197).

16. Charles Féré, *L'instinct sexuel* (Paris, 1899); Hans Rau, *Der Geschlechtstrieb und seine Verirrungen* (Berlin, 1903).

17. Richard von Krafft-Ebing, *Psychopathia Sexualis* (Berlin, 1886); Albert Moll, *Untersuchungen über die Libido Sexualis* (1898); Iwan Bloch, *Beiträge zur Aetiologie der Psychopathia Sexualis* (1902).

18. Letter to Wilhelm Fliess, December 6, 1896, in Masson, ed., *Complete Letters*, 212. The following year he added that "in infancy the release of sexuality is not yet so much localized as it is later, so that the zones which are later abandoned (and perhaps the whole surface of the body as well) also instigate something that is analogous to the later release of sexuality." Letter to Fliess, November 14, 1987, in ibid., 279. Although Freud was most original with this conception, Christian Stratz hinted at something like it in *Der Körper des Kindes* (Stuttgart, 1903): "The sensitivity of children is deeper, purer, simpler, and more rapid than that of adults" (39).

19. Sigmund Freud, "Three Essays on the Theory of Sexuality," in *Standard Edition*, 7:191.

20. Ibid., 220.

21. John Ruskin, "Of Queens' Gardens" (1865), sec. 68.

22. Stephen Kern, "Explosive Intimacy: Psychodynamics of the Victorian Family," *History of Childhood Quarterly* 1 (Summer 1974): 437–60; Rudolph Binion, "Fiction as Social Fantasy: Europe's Domestic Crisis of 1879–1914," *Journal of Social History* 27 (Summer 1994): 679–99.

23. Masson, ed., *Complete Letters*, 141.

24. Sigmund Freud, "The Aetiology of Hysteria," in *Standard Edition*, 3:206–7, 212, 214.

25. Masson, ed., *Complete Letters*, 264, 265 (translation modified slightly).

26. In 1916 he wrote, "The childhood experiences constructed or remembered in analysis are . . . in most cases compounded of truth and falsehood." And later, "Phantasies of being seduced are of particular interest, because so often they are not phantasies but real memories." *Introductory Lectures on Psycho-Analysis* (New York, 1966), 457, 460. Subsequent researchers have concluded that Freud erred in implying than an imaginary seduction had the same unconscious effect as a real one.

27. Sigmund Freud, "Sexuality in the Aetiology of Neurosis," in *Standard Edition*, 3:280.

28. Freud, "Three Essays," 7:171–72. For Freud's nonmoral definition of perversion see chapter 4.

29. Draft N, sent to Fliess May 31, 1897, in Masson, ed., *Complete Letters*, 250, 272.

30. Letter to Fliess, October 15, 1897, which also includes: "I have found, in my own case too, [the phenomenon of] being in love with my mother and jealous of my father, and I now consider it a universal event in early childhood," Masson, ed., *Complete Letters*, 272.

31. Sigmund Freud, "Contributions to the Psychology of Love," in *Standard Edition*, 11:163–76.

32. Sigmund Freud, "Fragment of an Analysis of a Case of Hysteria," in *Standard Edition*, 7:115.

33. John Toews summarized Freud's causal explanation of this "active complicity" in her case history: "Although Freud did not deny the factual accuracy of Dora's descriptions of her external traumas and betrayals (her 'seduction'), he insisted that it was the inner psychic conflict produced by the history of her own active unconscious desires that lay at the root of her illness." "Historicizing Psychoanalysis: Freud in His Time and for Our Time," *Journal of Modern History* 63 (September 1991): 513–14. My interpretation is indebted to Toews's analysis of Freud's rejection of the seduction theory. See also Gerald N. Izenberg, "Seduced and Abandoned: The Rise and Fall of Freud's Seduction Theory," in Jerome Neu, ed., *The Cambridge Companion to Freud* (Cambridge, 1991), 25–43.

34. *Moses and Monotheism* (1939), *Leonardo Da Vinci and a Memory of His Childhood* (1910), and "Dostoevsky and Parricide" (1928). Also in 1910, Ernest Jones elaborated Freud's explanation of Hamlet's ambivalence in "The Oedipus Complex as an Explanation of Hamlet's Mystery," *American Journal of Psychology* (January 1910): 72–113.

35. Heinz Kohut, "Thoughts on Narcissism and Narcissistic Rage," *Psychoanalytic Study of the Child* 27 (1972): 360–400.

36. Iago Galdston, ed., *Freud and Contemporary Culture* (New York, 1957); Harold D. Laswell, "Impact of Psychoanalytic Thinking in the Social Sciences," in Leonard D. White, ed., *The State of the Social Sciences* (Chicago, 1956); 84–115; Walter A. Weisskopf, *The Psychology of Economics* (Chicago, 1955); F. J. Hoffmann, *Freudianism and the Literary Mind* (Baton Rouge, 1945); Louis Schneider, *The Psychoanalyst and the Artist* (New York, 1950); Edward N. Saveth, "The Historian and the Freudian Approach to History," *New York Times Book Review*, January 1, 1956.

37. William L. Langer, "The Next Assignment," *American Historical Review* 63 (January 1958): 283–304.

38. "In its determination to be sparing with teleological assumption," Erickson wrote, "psychoanalysis has gone to the opposite extreme and developed a kind of *originology* . . . a habit of thinking which reduces every human situation to an analogy with an earlier one, and most of all to that earliest, simplest, and most infantile precursor which is assumed to be its 'origin.'" Erik Erikson, *Young Man Luther: A Study in Psychoanalysis and History* (New York, 1958), 18.

39. Ibid., 14, 18, 122.

40. James Gleick, *Chaos: Making a New Science* (New York, 1987), 8, 23.

41. Rudolph Binion, *Hitler among the Germans* (New York, 1976).

42. The cutting off of Eastern Prussia from Germany by the Polish Corridor could appear like a diagram of a mastectomy. Binion does not offer this interpretation, but it accords with his argument.

43. David Brion Davis concluded that "Irving lost no chance to describe the young Italian as a persecuted boy, whose attempts to achieve happiness were thwarted by a malicious plot." *Homicide in American Fiction, 1798–1860* (Ithaca, N.Y., 1957), 33.

44. William Gilmore Simms, *Guy Rivers: A Tale of Georgia* (1834; reprint, New York 1970), 453.

45. Davis, *Homicide in American Fiction*, 170.

46. Ibid., 222.

47. Joseph Satten et al., "Murder without Apparent Motive—A Study in Personality Disorganization," *American Journal of Psychiatry* 117 (July 1960): 48–53.

48. Frank E. Manuel, "The Use and Abuse of Psychology in History," *Daedalus* 117 (Summer 1988): 210.

49. Walter Benjamin, "The Work of Art in the Age of Mechanical Reproduction" [1936], in *Illuminations* (New York, 1968), 235ff.

50. In *Studies in Hysteria* (1893), Freud argued, "the principal feature in the aetiology of the neuroses . . . [is] that their genesis is as a rule overdetermined, that several factors must come together to produce the result." *Standard Edition*, 2:263.

51. John Franklin Bardin, *Devil Take the Blue-Tail Fly* (1948); Georges Simenon, *Maigret Sets a Trap* (1955); Margaret Millar, *Beyond This Point Are Monsters* (1970); Kathy Reichs, *Déjà Dead* (1997).

52. Louise A. Jackson, *Child Sexual Abuse in Victorian England* (London, 2000), 2–7, 14–16.

53. C. Kempfe et al., "The Battered Child Syndrome," *Journal of the American Medical Association* 181, no. 1 (1962): 17–24. My discussion of multiple personality is indebted to Ian Hacking, *Rewriting the Soul: Multiple Personality and the Sciences of Memory* (Princeton, 1995), 59–60 passim.

54. Flora Rheta Schreiver, *Sybil* (Chicago, 1973).

55. Hacking, *Rewriting the Soul*, 195. See also K. C. Carter, "Germ Theory, Hysteria, and Freud's Early Work in Psychopathology," *Medical History* 20 (1980): 259–74.

56. Hacking concluded that "psychiatry did not discover that early and repeated child abuse causes multiple personality. It forged the connection" (85, 94). He insisted that the theoretical link was circular. Researchers defined MPD in terms of childhood traumas and then argued that the disorder was caused by childhood traumas (82). Researchers were convinced that traumatic child sexual abuse caused multiples, so they found cases of such abuse that confirmed the theory and then supported the theory with these cases. While the validity of this etiological theory remains questionable, the historical record is unambiguous in showing that child sexual traumas remain central to explanations of MPD. The seemingly precise causal role of traumatic child sexual abuse continues to attract researchers who also discover vast realms of ignorance in their increasingly detailed case histories based on initiatory childhood traumas. Hacking, *Rewriting the Soul*, 81–86, 94.

57. Richard J. Gelles, "The Social Construction of Child Abuse," *American Journal of Orthopsychiatry* 45 (April 1975): 365. See also Ian Hacking, "The Making and Molding of Child Abuse," *Critical Inquiry* 17 (Winter 1991): 253–88.

58. John M. Macdonald, "The Threat to Kill," *American Journal of Psychiatry* 120 (1963): 130.

59. See Eliott Leyton, *Hunting Humans: The Rise of the Multiple Murderer* (Toronto, 1986), 3, 4, 25, 34, 45.

60. Philip Jenkins, *Using Murder: The Social Construction of Serial Homicide* (New York, 1994); Seltzer, *Serial Killers*.

CHAPTER 3: LANGUAGE

1. Romantic poets were acutely aware of the limits of language, but that skepticism waned by 1830, especially among the realist novelists, who provide the bulk of my literary evidence. Realists told stories through trustworthy narrators, who may have questioned their own perspective but not the adequacy of language per se to communicate it.

2. *Performative* comes from J. L. Austin's notion (in *How to Do Things with Words* [Oxford, 1962] that utterances perform actions rather than describe the world and from Emile Benveniste's identification (in *Problems in General Linguistics* [Miami, 1971] of sentences that name the action they accomplish. Modern scholars debate whether the Romantics developed a performative view of language. Brigitte Nerlich and David D. Clark wrote that "what is still missing in the romantic conception of language is an insight into the performativity of language" in *Language, Action, and Context: The Early History of Pragmatics in Europe and America, 1780–1930* (Amsterdam, 1996), 60; while Angela Esterhammer countered with abundant evidence that German and British Romantic poets conceived of language generally as "action, energy, force, and creative power" in *The Romantic Performative: Language and Action in British and German Romanticism* (Stanford, 2000), 5.

3. John Fletcher and Malcolm Bradbury concluded that in the modernist novel there is "a progressive fading of that realism which has long been associated with the novel; language ceases to be what we see through, and becomes what we see." "The Introverted Novel," in Malcolm Bradbury and James McFarlane, eds., *Modernism: A Guide to European Literature, 1890–1930* (Harmondsworth, England, 1976), 401.

4. Articles on the subject were reprinted in Richard Rorty, ed., *The Linguistic Turn* (Chicago, 1967). Rorty credits the first use of the term to Gustave Bergman, *Logic and Reality* (Madison, 1964), 177.

5. Ludwig Wittgenstein, *Tractatus Logico-Philosophicus* (London, 1922) 4.0031.

6. George Steiner, *Real Presences*, (Chicago, 1989), 92.

7. Ibid., 93.

8. Richard Evans, *Tales from the German Underworld: Crime and Punishment in the Nineteenth Century* (New Haven, 1998), 6. For similar arguments about France, America, and England, see Louis Chevalier, *Laboring Classes and Dangerous Classes in Paris during the First Half of the Nineteenth Century* (1958; reprint, New York, 1973); David Brion Davis, *Homicide in American Fiction, 1798–1860* (Ithaca, N.Y., 1957); Richard D. Altick, *Victorian Studies in Scarlet: Murders and Manners in the Age of Victoria* (New York, 1970).

9. William Gilmore Simms, *Martin Faber: The Story of a Criminal* (1833; reprint, Albany, N.Y., 1990), 4–5.

10. For a study of how, as DeLillo put it, "the crux of the whole matter is language," see David Cowart, *Don DeLillo: The Physics of Language* (Athens, Ga., 2002).

11. The precedent for this torturous moral instruction is biblical. "The sin of Judah is written with a pen of iron, and with the point of a diamond: it is graven upon the table of their hearts, and upon the horns of your altars" (Jeremiah 17:1).

See also Jeremiah 31:33, "I will put my law in their inward parts, and write it in their hearts."

12. Jean-Paul Sartre, *Saint Genet: Actor and Martyr* (1952; reprint, New York, 1971), 17. Poem quoted by Sartre from Genet, *Poèmes*, 56.

13. Virginia Woolf, *A Room of One's Own.* Sandra M. Gilbert and Susan Gubar explored the dominion of patriarchal language in the war of the sexes in *No Man's Land: The Place of the Woman Writer in the Twentieth Century*, vol. 1, *The War of the Words* (New Haven, 1988), especially "Sexual Linguistics: Women's Sentence, Men's Sentencing," 227–71.

14. Julio Cortázar, *Blow-Up and Other Stories* (New York, 1963), 63–65.

15. Tom LeClair, *In the Loop: Don DeLillo and the Systems Novel* (Urbana, 1987), 192.

16. Friedrich Nietzsche, *Beyond Good and Evil* (1886; reprint, New York, 1966), sec. 20. On Nietzsche and language see Tracy B. Strong, "Language and Nihilism: Nietzsche's Critique of Epistemology," *Theory and Society*, 3 (Summer 1976): 239–63; Sander L. Gilman, Carole Blair, and David J. Parent, *Friedrich Nietzsche on Rhetoric and Language* (New York, 1989). Alan Megill calls this causal function of language *aestheticism*, defined as a "tendency to see 'art' or 'language' or 'discourse' or 'text' as constituting the primary realm of human experience," *Prophets of Extremism: Nietzsche, Heidegger, Foucault, Derrida* (Berkeley, 1985), 2.

17. Friedrich Nietzsche, "On Truth and Lies in a Nonmoral Sense," *Philosophy and Truth: Selections from Nietzsche's Notebooks of the Early 1870's* (Atlantic Highlands, N.J., 1979), 82–84.

18. Friedrich Nietzsche, *On the Genealogy of Morals* (1887; reprint, New York, 1967), 1:13.

19. *Beyond Good and Evil*, 1:21.

20. Friedrich Nietzsche, *The Will to Power*, trans. Walter Kaufmann (New York, 1967), sec. 631.

21. Friedrich Nietzsche, "On the Uses and Disadvantages of History for Life" [1874], in *Untimely Meditations* trans. R. J. Hollingdale (Cambridge, 1983), 119.

22. Friedrich Nietzsche, "Richard Wagner in Bayreuth," in Hollingdale, trans., *Untimely Meditations*, 215.

23. Friedrich Nietzsche, *Twilight of the Idols* [1889], trans. R. J. Hollingdale (Harmondsworth, England, 1968), 38.

24. Friedrich Nietzsche, *The Joyful Wisdom* [1882], trans. Thomas Common (New York, 1960), sec. 125.

25. Hermann Osthoff and Karl Brugmann, *Morphologische Untersuchungen* (Leipzig, 1878–1910), 1:xiii.

26. Geoffrey Sampson, *Schools of Linguistics* (Stanford, 1980), 17.

27. August Schleicher, *Die Darwinische Theorie und die Sprachwissenschaft* (Weimar, 1873); cited in Ernst Cassirer, *The Philosophy of Symbolic Forms* (New Haven, 1953), 1:166–67.

28. Jan Baudouin de Courtenay, *Vermenschlichung der Sprache*, quoted in Sampson, *Schools of Linguistics*, 25.

29. Sampson, *Schools of Linguistics*, 29–31.

30. Ibid., 33.

31. Ferdinand de Saussure, *Course in General Linguistics* [1915], trans. Wade Baskin (New York, 1966), 4.

32. In particular he structured the science of linguistics around four crucial distinctions: *langue/parole*, signified/signifier, diachronic/synchronic, syntagmatic/paradigmatic.

33. On the connection between Saussure's "field view of language" and uses of "field models" in physics and mathematics, see N. Katherine Hayles, *The Cosmic Web: Scientific Field Models and Literary Strategies in the Twentieth Century* (Ithaca, 1984), 22.

34. Claude Lévi-Strauss, "The Structural Study of Myth," *Journal of American Folklore* 78 (Oct.–Dec. 1955): 428–44.

35. Sartre, *Saint Genet*, 39.

36. In one study of the linguistic "production" of criminals in nineteenth-century criminology, popular press, and novels, Marie-Christine Leps summarized the positivist epistemology on which such explanations were based: "Positivist thought . . . considers truth to arise when the subject adequately represents objective reality in language; in other words, positivism rests on the epistemological presupposition that reality is a given, truth is absolute and cumulative, and language is transparent." *Apprehending the Criminal: The Production of Deviance in Nineteenth-Century Discourse* (Durham, N.C., 1992), 154.

37. Fritz Mauthner, *Beiträge zu einer Kritik der Sprache*, quoted in Linda Ben-Zvi, "Samuel Beckett, Fritz Mauthner, and the Limits of Language," *PMLA* 95 (March 1980): 186.

38. *Beiträge*, 1:176; quoted in Ben-Zvi, "Samuel Beckett," 188ff. Joyce's self-imposed exile from Ireland distanced him from his native language. Mauthner, like Kafka after him, grew up speaking German in a Czech-speaking society, and both were further marginalized by being Jewish and learning Hebrew in an education system which they held in contempt. Other analysts of the arbitrariness of language as well as its constitutive role were also marginalized Jews—Roman Jacobson, Lévi-Strauss, Emmanuel Levinas, Derrida, and Wittgenstein (by descent).

39. Mikhail M. Bakhtin, *The Dialogic Imagination*, trans. Caryl Emerson and Michael Holquist (Austin, Tex., 1981).

40. Benjamin Lee Whorf, *Language, Thought and Reality* (Cambridge, 1956). Most of the articles were written between 1936 and 1941.

41. He specifically mentioned Lucien Lévy-Bruhl's *Les functions mentales dans les sociétés inférieures* (1912) along with Freud's and Jung's equation of "primitive" and infantile minds.

42. Many American Indian and African languages, Whorf argued, "abound in finely wrought, beautifully logical discriminations about causation, action, result, dynamic or energetic quality," and "in this respect they far out-distance the European languages." "Thinking in Primitive Communities," in Whorf, *Language*, 78–85.

43. Quoted in Marjorie Perloff, *Wittgenstein's Ladder: Poetic Language and the Strangeness of the Ordinary* (Chicago, 1996), 32.

44. Ibid., xiv–xv.

45. On quantum theory and Robbe-Grillet, see Raylene L. Ramsay, *Robbe-Grillet and Modernity: Science, Sexuality, and Subversion* (Gainesville, Fl., 1992); on how complementary "constituted the essential structure of Robbe-Grillet's work" (4, 12, 21). Also see Ramsay's 1972 dissertation, "La complémentarité multiple: Une étude de l'oeuvre d'Alain Robbe-Grillet."

46. Although the exact phrase cannot be found in Bohr's writings, Aage Peterson implied that it was a frequent and typical response to the challenge that traditional philosophy viewed reality as primary and language as secondary. "The Philosophy of Niels Bohr," *Bulletin of the Atomic Scientists* 19 (September 1963): 10–11. For Bohr on language, see Hayles, *Cosmic Web*, 52–54.

47. Alain Robbe-Grillet, "A Future for the Novel," in *For a New Novel* (1956; reprint, Evanston, 1965), 22–23.

48. Bruce Morrissette, "Post-Modern Generative Fiction: Novel and Film," *Critical Inquiry* 2 (1975): 253–62.

49. Bruce Morrissette, "Oedipus or the Closed Circle: *The Erasers*," in *The Novels of Robbe-Grillet* (1963; reprint, New York, 1971), 38–74.

50. On these strategies in Robbe-Grillet and the novelists Jean Ricardou, Raymond Queneau, and Raymond Roussel, see Morrissette, "Post-Modern Generative Fiction."

51. Françoise Meltzer, "Preliminary Excavations of Robbe-Grillet's Phantom City," *Chicago Review* 28 (Summer 1976): 44–46.

52. Ursula K. Heise, *Chronoschisms: Time, Narrative, and Postmodernism* (Cambridge, 1997), 119.

53. Robbe-Grillet, "A Future for the Novel," 15.

54. Robbe-Grillet, "New Novel, New Man" [1961], in *For a New Novel*, 141.

55. Jacques Derrida, "Structure, Sign, and Play in the Discourses of the Human Sciences," in *Writing and Difference* (Chicago, 1978), 178, 179.

56. In French there is only one word for differ and defer, *différer*, but Derrida invented *différance* to suggest both, thus privileging writing, because in French the distinction is obscured in speech. The key text is "Différance" [1972], in *Margins of Philosophy* (Chicago, 1982), 1–28.

57. Jacques Derrida, "Plato's Pharmacy" [1968], in *Dissemination* (Chicago, 1981), 61–171.

58. Umberto Eco, *The Name of the Rose* (New York, 1984).

59. On the contribution of these thinkers during those conferences, subsequently called the Macy Conferences on Cybernetics, in the development of information theory and cybernetics see, N. Katherine Hayles, *How We Became Posthuman: Virtual Bodies in Cybernetics, Literature, and Informatics* (Chicago, 1999), 7 and passim.

60. Norbert Weiner, *Cybernetics* (New York, 1948).

61. Hayles, *How We Became Posthuman*, 29, 30. Donna Haraway, "A Manifesto for Cyborgs: Science, Technology, and Socialist Feminism in the 1980s," *Socialist Review* 80 (1985): 65–108.

62. Jeremy Campbell, *Grammatical Man: Information, Entropy, Language, and Life*, (New York, 1982).

63. "If mind is superseded by language as our means of knowing, then the very waywardness of language introduces a larger degree of uncertainty in our

epistemological theories of knowing." He decried the "anything goes" attitude among writers who affirm "this centrality of language as the frame of understanding." Daniel Bell, "Afterword: 1996," in *The Cultural Contradictions of Capitalism* (1976; reprint, New York 1996), 297.

64. George Lakoff and Mark Johnson, *Metaphors We Live By* (Chicago, 1980), 4.

65. Perry Anderson, *The Origin of Postmodernity* (London, 1998), 25, 89.

66. David Harvey, *The Condition of Postmodernity* (London, 1989), 46ff.

CHAPTER 4: SEXUALITY

1. *Sexology* was coined by Elizabeth Willard in 1867. Freud introduced the term *psychoanalysis* in 1896. *Sexualwissenschaft* was coined by Iwan Bloch in 1906. See Harry Oosterhuis, *Stepchildren of Nature: Krafft-Ebing, Psychiatry, and the Making of Sexual Identity* (Chicago, 2000), 58.

2. For the sources of these and numerous other coinages, see Oosterhuis, *Stepchildren of Nature*, 44–46. Jacques Donzelot reconstructed the increasing medical intervention in sexuality throughout the nineteenth century in three stages: early articles limited to onanism and refusal to breast-feed, midcentury contributions on contraception, and late Victorian beginnings of the "hygenization of sexuality" to prevent venereal diseases, alcoholism, and tuberculosis. *The Policing of Families* (New York, 1979), 173.

3. Richard von Krafft-Ebing, *Psychopathia Sexualis* [1886], English trans. of 12th ed. (1902; New York, 1965).

4. Judith R. Walkowitz, *City of Dreadful Delight: Narratives of Sexual Danger in Late-Victorian London* (Chicago, 1992), 191–228; Deborah Cameron and Elizabeth Frazer, *The Lust to Kill: A Feminist Investigation of Sexual Murder* (New York, 1987), 122–38; Maria Tatar, *Lustmord: Sexual Murder in Weimar Germany* (Princeton, 1995).

5. Quoted in Tatar, *Lustmord*, 23.

6. On these views, see Christopher Frayling, "The House That Jack Built: Some Stereotypes of the Rapist in the History of Popular Culture," in Sylvania Tomaselli and Roy Ported, eds., *Rape* (London, 1986), 174–215; and Walkowitz, *City of Dreadful Delight*, 192–228.

7. This judgment is from Colin Wilson's introduction to Donald Rumbelow, *The Complete Jack the Ripper* (Boston, 1975), vii. It is also the title for Jane Caputi's *The Age of Sex Crime* (Bowling Green, Ohio, 1987).

8. Walkowitz, *City of Dreadful Delight*, 197.

9. Paul Robinson, *The Modernization of Sex* (1976; rev., Ithaca, 1989), 2–3.

10. In 1896 Ellis published *Das konträre Geschlechtsgefühl*, translated into German by Hans Kurella. It appeared in English as *Sexual Inversion* in 1897 and was volume 1 of the six-volume edition of the *Studies in the Psychology of Sex*, completed by 1910.

11. Albert von Schrenck-Notzing, "Literaturzusammenstellung über die Psychologie und Psychopathologie der vita sexualis," *Zeitschrift für Hypnotismus* 8 (1899): 40–53, 275–91; cited in Havelock Ellis, "Love and Pain," in *Studies in the Psychology of Sex* (New York, 1942), 1:120.

12. Sigmund Freud, "Three Essays on the Theory of Sexual Theory," in *Standard Edition of the Complete Psychological Works of Sigmund Freud* (London, 1953), 7:150. All subsequent references are to this edition.

13. In sketching the breakup of this existential homogenization, Foucault lists with bitter amusement some of the outrageous names invented to differentiate specific homosexual types: "there were Krafft-Ebbing's zoophiles and zooerasts, Rohleder's auto-monosexualists; and later, mixoscopophiles, gynecomasts, presbyophiles, sexoesthetic inverts, and dyspareunist women." Michel Foucault, *The History of Sexuality: Vol. I: An Introduction* (1976; reprint, New York, 1978), 43.

14. George Chauncey, Jr., "From Sexual Inversion to Homosexuality: The Changing Medical Conceptualization of Female 'Deviance,'" in Kathy Peiss, *Passion and Power* (Philadelphia, 1989) 89, 92, 88, and passim.

15. My reconstruction of this history is drawn primarily from Nelly Oudshoorn, *Beyond the Natural Body: An Archaeology of Sex Hormones* (London, 1994).

16. On the theory of humors in Balzac see Moïse Le Yaouanc, *Nosographie de l'humanité balzacienne* (Paris, 1960).

17. Virchow cited the French physiologist Achille Chéreau. See Victor Cornelius Medvei, *A History of Endocrinology* (The Hague, 1983), 215.

18. Ernest H. Starling, "The Croonian Lectures on the Chemical Correlation of the Functions of the Body," *Lancet* 2 (1905): 339–41; quoted in Oudshoorn, *Beyond the Natural Body*, 16.

19. Quoted in Oudshoorn, 23–24.

20. O. Fellner, *Pflüger's Archiv* (1921), 189; cited in Oudshoorn, *Beyond the Natural Body*, 24.

21. Thomas Laqueur, *Making Sex: Body and Gender from the Greeks to Freud* (Cambridge, Mass., 1990).

22. Patrick Geddes and J. Arthur Thompson, *The Evolution of Sex* (London, 1889), 266.

23. The most outspoken include Gayle Rubin, Sherry Ortner, Harriet Whitehead, Julia Kristeva, Joan Scott, and Catharine MacKinnon; see Laqueur, *Making Sex*, 12–13.

24. Freud, "Three Essays on the Theory of Sexuality," in *Standard Edition*, 7:215–16. James Strachey translated *Chemismus* as *chemistry*. For Brill's influence and Freud's use of the concept, see Ellen Moers, "Chemism and Freudianism" in *Two Dreisers* (New York, 1969), 256–70.

25. In 1935, various newspapers asked Dreiser to comment about a man accused of a murder similar to the one in *American Tragedy*. His essay on that experience included a speculation that in the future such murders will be explained in "chemical laboratories." "It will probably be shown that the love emotion, the sex emotion, is a chemical or quiescent content of the human body, but one which contacted by a related something in the body of a member of the opposite sex, is set in motion and caused to become a violent force." Theodore Dreiser, "I Find the Real American Tragedy" [1935], *Resources for American Literary Study* 2 (Spring 1972): 73.

26. Jacques Loeb, *The Heliotropism of Animals and Its Identity with the Heliotropism of Plants* (1905); Jacques Loeb, *Forced Movements, Tropisms, and Animal Conduct* (1918). On these sources and Loeb's influence on Dreiser, see Moers, *Two Dreisers*,

240–42; and Louis J. Zanine, *Mechanism and Mysticism: The Influence of Science on the Thought and Work of Theodore Dreiser* (Philadelphia, 1993), 81ff.

27. Further evidence of this influence is this quotation from 1921: "The more we know, exactly, about the chemic, biologic, and social complexities by which we find ourselves generated, regulated, and ended, the better. Man has never progressed either self-defensively or economically via either blind faith or illusion. It is exact knowledge that he needs." Theodore Dreiser, "A Word concerning Birth Control," *Birth Control Review* 5 (April 1921): 5; quoted in Zanine, *Mechanism and Mysticism*, 112.

28. Max Schlapp and Edward Smith, *The New Criminology* (New York, 1928), 28. George B. Vold and Thomas J. Bernard refer to Schlapp and Smith's book as "little more than armchair speculation." *Theoretical Criminology* (New York, 1986), 96. I discuss it here because of its influence on Dreiser and as a sample of popular hormonal theory in the early years of endocrinology.

29. Döblin adds more sexual science: "Testifortan, authorized patent No. 365695, sexual therapeutic agent approved by Sanitary Councillor Dr. Magnus Hirschfeld and Dr. Bernard Shapiro, Institute of Sexual Science, Berlin. Main causes of impotence are: (a) insufficient charging through functional disorder of the internal secretory glands (b) too strong resistance through extreme psychic inhibitions" (*Berlin Alexanderplatz*, 34).

30. Aldous Huxley, *Brave New World* (New York, 1969), 8, 25, 104, 163. In *The Silence of the Lambs*, the serial killer Jame Gumb takes the hormones premarin and then diethylstilbestrol in an attempt to become a woman (136).

31. Leo E. Kreuz and Robert M. Rose, "Assessment of Aggressive Behavior and Plasma Testosterone in a Young Criminal Population," *Psychosomatic Medicine* 34 (1972): 321ff.

32. These studies are surveyed in Robert T. Rubin, "The Neuroendocrinology and Neurochemistry of Antisocial Behavior," in Sarnoff A. Mednick et al., eds., *The Causes of Crime: New Biological Approaches* (Cambridge, 1987), 246–47. See also Saleem A. Shah and Loren Roth, "Biological and Psychophysiological Factors in Criminality," in Daniel Glaser, ed., *Handbook of Criminology* (Chicago, 1974), 101–73.

33. L. Ellis, "Evidence of Neuroendrogenic Etiology of Sex Roles from a Combined Analysis of Human, Nonhuman, Primate and Nonprimate Mammalian Studies," *Personality and Individual Differences* (1987); summarized in Hans J. Eysenck and Gisli H. Gudjonsson, *The Causes and Cures of Criminality* (New York, 1989), 130–31.

34. Rubin, "Neuroendocrinology," 257.

35. K. Dalton, "Menstruation and Crime," *British Medical Journal* 2 (1961): 1752–53.

36. "A Conversation with Renate Dorrestein," quoted in Renate Dorrestein, *A Penguin Readers Guide to a Heart of Stone* (Harmondsworth, England, 2000), 7.

37. This disease was named after the English physician Thomas Addison, who described its symptoms in an article, "On the Constitutional and Local Effects of Disease of the Suprarenal Capsules" (London, 1855).

38. Charles D. Meigs, *Females and Their Diseases* (Philadelphia, 1848), 50–51.

39. "The late eighteenth and early nineteenth-century discourse on murder did not yet conceptualize any crimes as 'sex-murders' in this sense" (175). Karen

Halttunen, *Murder Most Foul: The Killer and the American Gothic Imagination* (Cambridge, Mass., 1998), 176, 173.

40. David Brion Davis, *Homicide in American Fiction, 1798–1860* (Ithaca, 1957), 169, 205ff.

41. J. G. Ballard, *Crash* (New York, 1973), 10, 12.

42. Krafft-Ebing, *Psychopathia Sexualis*, 57.

43. Greg Forter, *Murdering Masculinities: Fantasies of Gender and Violence in the American Crime Novel* (New York, 2000), 118.

44. Alfred Döblin, *Die beiden Freundinnen und ihr Giftmord. Aussenseiter der Gesellschaft*, ed. Rudolf Leonhard (Berlin, 1924), vol. 1. My reading of this novel is indebted to Todd Herzog, "Crime Stories: Criminal, Society, and Modernist Case History," *Representations* 80 (Fall 2002): 34–61. See also Todd Herzog, "Criminalistic Fantasy: Imagining Crime in Weimar Germany" (Ph.D. diss., University of Chicago, 2000).

45. Quoted in Herzog, "Crime Stories," 53, 51.

46. Ibid., 56.

47. Joshua Meyrowitz, *No Sense of Place: The Impact of Electronic Media on Social Behavior* (New York, 1985), 224.

48. On sexuality in World War I, see Stephen Kern, "Eros in Barbed Wire," in *Anatomy and Destiny: A Cultural History of the Human Body* (New York, 1975), 191–206.

49. Erich Wulffen, *Woman as a Sexual Criminal* (New York, 1934), 186.

50. Offset lithograph in George Grosz, *Ecce Home* (Malik Verlag, 1923), plate 32. Beth Irwin Lewis emphasized the causal role of urban life, the new woman, and the horrors of war in "*Lustmord*: Inside the Windows of the Metropolis," in Charles W. Haxthausen and Heidrun Suhr, eds., *Berlin: Culture and Metropolis* (Minneapolis, 1990), 111–40.

51. Oil on canvas, 165 × 135 cm, whereabouts unknown. The photos appeared in Erich Wufflen, *Der Sexualverbrecher: ein Handbuch für Juristen, Verwaltungsbeamte und Aertze* (Berlin, 1910); cited by Tatar, *Lustmord*, 187 n. 22. She explained images of *Lustmord* German art, cinema, and literature during and after World War I as a reaction to the burgeoning women's movement before the war and the violent disruptions of normal male-female relations during the war.

52. John Money, *Sex Errors of the Body: Dilemmas, Education, Counseling* (Baltimore, 1968), 11; cited in Robert Nye, *Sexuality* (Oxford, 1999), 232.

53. Joel Norris, *Serial Killers: The Growing Menace* (New York, 1988), 21. Rudolf Höss, commandant at Auschwitz, routinely gassed hundreds of Jews by day and led a normal homey existence off the job. Rudolf Höss, *Commandant of Auschwitz: The Autobiography of Rudolf Hoess* (New York, 1959).

54. Robert K. Ressler, Ann W. Burgess, and John E. Douglas, *Sexual Homicide: Patterns and Motives* (New York, 1988), 69–97.

55. Roger L. Depue, "The National Center for the Analysis of Violent Crime," in ibid., 99–120.

56. Norris, *Serial Killers*, 210–42.

57. Cameron and Frazer, *The Lust to Kill*, 34ff.

58. Jeffrey Weeks, *Sexuality and Its Discontents* (New York, 1985), 45ff.

CHAPTER 5: EMOTION

1. Peter N. Stearns, *Jealousy: The Evolution of an Emotion in American History* (New York, 1989), 44.

2. Ibid., 47, 23.

3. Kevin McAleer, *Dueling: The Cult of Honor in Fin-de-Siècle Germany* (Princeton, 1994), 3–9.

4. Quoted in Peter N. Stearns, *American Cool: Constructing a Twentieth-Century Emotional Style* (New York, 1994), 34.

5. Stearns, *Jealousy*, 28–30.

6. See chapter 3, "Jealousy Moves Front and Center: 1890–1920," in Stearns, *Jealousy*, 66–87.

7. Stephen Kern, *The Culture of Love: Victorians to Moderns* (Cambridge, Mass., 1992), 264–80. Modern novelists whose characters did not kill unfaithful lovers or rivals and who grew through the experience of jealousy include Henry James, E. M. Forster, Thomas Mann, Marcel Proust, and James Joyce. I concluded the chapter on jealousy with the following: "Victorians, by trivializing or projecting their responsibility for jealousy, denigrating their experience of it, and failing to resolve it inwardly, generalized jealousy into something that was alike for everyone, a 'foreign visitation' that remained distant from their very selves even though it might be eating them up with anxiety and self-pity. The moderns, by accepting responsibility for jealousy, evaluating it as constructive (if not pleasurable), and resolving it more self-consciously, experienced jealousy as a meaningful revelation of the deficiencies and possibilities of their very own ways of loving" (280).

8. For another case of jealousy interpreted from an existential perspective see Simone de Beauvoir, *She Came to Stay* (1943; trans., London, 1975), where Françoise murders her rival Xavière, not over the man, but because Xavière discovered that Françoise was jealous. Françoise kills to annihilate the power of the Other to label her with such a degrading and defining emotion.

9. Sigmund Freud, *Introductory Lectures on Psycho-Analysis* (New York, 1966), lecture 16.

10. John N. Duvall, "The (Super)Marketplace of Images: Television as Unmediated Mediation in DeLillo's *White Noise,*" *Arizona Quarterly* 50 (Autumn 1994): 145.

11. Tom LeClair, *In the Loop: Don DeLillo and the Systems Novel* (Urbana, Ill. 1987), xi–xii.

12. Winifred Hughes, *The Maniac in the Cellar: Sensation Novels of the 1860s* (Princeton, 1980), 11, 12.

13. David Brion Davis, *Homicide in American Fiction, 1798–1860* (Ithaca, N.Y., 1975), 105, 106, 211.

14. John Vernon, *Money and Fiction: Literary Realism in the Nineteenth and Early Twentieth Centuries* (Ithaca, N.Y., 1984), 194.

15. Alfred D. Chandler, *Scale and Scope: The Dynamics of Industrial Capitalism* (Cambridge, Mass., 1994), 54–55.

16. Martin J. Sklar, "Capitalism and Socialism in the Emergence of Modern America: The Formative Era, 1890s–1916," in Elizabeth Fox-Genovese and

Elisabeth Lasch-Quinn, eds., *Reconstructing History: The Emergence of a New Historical Society* (New York, 1999), 317.

17. W. S. Jevons, *The Theory of Political Economy* (1871); quoted in Robert Heilbroner, *The Worldly Philosophers: The Lives, Times, and Ideas of the Great Economic Thinkers* (New York, 1961), 210.

18. Jean Baudrillard, *The Mirror of Production* (1973; reprint, St. Louis, 1975).

19. On these issues, see Mark Blaug, *Economic Theory in Retrospect* (Cambridge, 1985), 294–308.

20. Lawrence Birkin, *Consuming Desire: Sexual Science and the Emergence of a Culture of Abundance, 1871–1914* (Ithaca, N.Y., 1988), 28.

21. On the connection between modern consumerism, stock market activity, and murder, see Don DeLillo, *Players* (1977), in which terrorists plot to blow up the stock exchange. As one of them explains, "It was this secret of theirs that we wanted to destroy, this invisible power. It's all in that system, bit-bit-bit-bit, the flow of electric current that unites money, plural, from all over the world." "It has to be shattered . . . Nothing but waves and currents talking to each other. Spirits. So, the thing should be hit to whatever extent, now" (107, 109). Caryl Churchill's *Serious Money* (London, 1987) is about the murder or suicide of an inside trader in the London Stock Exchange caught selling illegal information to an American trader.

22. Karl Marx, *Capital*, trans. Ben Fowkes (London, 1976), 1:188.

23. Karl Polanyi, *The Great Transformation* (1944; reprint, New York, 1957), 25, 3.

24. For this interpretation of Gide see Jean-Joseph Goux, *The Coiners of Language* (1984; reprint, Norman, Okla., 1994).

25. Otniel Dror, "The Affect of Experiment: The Turn to Emotions in Anglo-American Physiology, 1900–1940," *Isis* 90 (June 1999): 237. My discussion of the history of the physiology of emotions is indebted to Otniel Yizhak Dror, "Modernity and the Scientific Study of Emotions, 1880–1950" (Ph.D. diss., Princeton University, 1998); and articles drawn from it—the above cited; "Creating the Emotional Body: Confusion, Possibilities, and Knowledge," in Peter N. Stearns and Jan Lewis, eds., *An Emotional History of the United States* (New York, 1998), 173–94; and "The Scientific Image of Emotion: Experience and Technologies of Inscription," *Configurations* 7 (1999): 355–401.

26. Carl Ludwig, "Beiträge zur Kenntnis des Einflusses der Respirationsbewegungen auf den Blutlauf im Aortensysteme," *Archiv für Anatomie, Physiologie, und wissenschaftliche Medizin* (1847): 244. On its historical role, see Merriley Borell, "Instrumentation and the Rise of Modern Physiology," *Science and Technology Studies* 5 (1987): 53–62.

27. For these citations and the significance of these experiments, see Frederic L. Holmes and Kathryn M. Olensko, "The Images of Precision: Helmholtz and the Graphical Method in Physiology," in M. Norton Wise, ed., *The Values of Precision* (Princeton, 1995), 198–221.

28. On Marey's inventions, see Marta Braun, *Picturing Time: The Work of Etienne-Jules Marey (1830–1904)* (Chicago, 1992), 8–27.

29. Ibid., 24.

30. M. E. Cyon, "Le coeur et le cerveau," *Revue scientifique de la France et de l'étranger* 21 (1873): 481–89.

31. Angelo Mosso, *Fear* (1884; reprint London, 1896).

32. Charles Féré, *Sensation et mouvement: Études expérimentales de psycho-mécanique* (Paris, 1887), 108–22; Alfred Binet and J. Courtier, "Influence de la vie émotionnelle sur le coeur, la respiration et la circulation capillaire," *Année Psychologique* 3 (1896): 65–126, cited in Dror, "Affect of Experiment," 213.

33. For a historical interpretation of the polygraph as "a perfect symbol for the medicalization of the criminal body that took place during this period," see Ronald R. Thomas, *Detective Fiction and the Rise of Forensic Science* (Cambridge, 1999), 25ff.

34. W. B. Cannon, "The Movements of the Stomach Studied by Means of the Röntgen Rays," *American Journal of Physiology* 1 (1898): 359–82; cited in Dror, "Affect of Experiment," 216.

35. Dror, "Creating the Emotional Body," 173.

36. Candace B. Pert, *Molecules of Emotion* (New York, 1997). My reconstruction of the history of peptide research derives largely from this book as indicated by subsequent text references.

37. John Langley, "On Nerve Endings and on Special Excitable Substances in Cells," *Proceedings of the Royal Society of London*, ser. B 78 (1906), 183, 194.

38. William James, "What Is an Emotion?" *Mind* 9, no. 34 (April 1884): 190.

39. Walter Cannon, *The Wisdom of the Body* (1927); cited by Pert, *Molecules of Emotion*, 136.

40. Pert, *Molecules of Emotion*, 68.

CHAPTER 6: MIND

1. Henry Maudsley, *Responsibility in Mental Disease* (London, 1874), 413; Edward C. Mann, *A Manual of Psychological Medicine and Allied Nervous Diseases* (Philadelphia, 1883), 120.

2. He published his findings in two volumes in 1810, supplemented by two more volumes coauthored with Johann Spurzheim in 1819. F. J. Gall and J. Spurzheim, *Anatomie et physiologie du système nerveux en général et du cerveau en particulier* (Paris, 1810–19). Gall revised these volumes as *Sur les fonctions du cerveau* (Paris, 1822–26). They were translated into English as *On the Functions of the Brain and Each of Its Parts: With Observations on the Possibility of Determining the Instincts, Propensities, and Talents, or the Moral and Intellectual Dispositions of Men and Animals, by the Configurations of the Brain and Head* (Boston, 1835). The discussion of destructiveness is in 4:50–119.

3. Ibid., 118.

4. Ibid., 110.

5. Robert M. Young, *Mind, Brain and Adaptation in the Nineteenth Century: Cerebral Localization and Its Biological Context from Gall to Ferrier* (Oxford, 1970), 28, 24.

6. *Phrenology* was first used by Benjamin Rush in 1805, and afterward in an article by Thomas Forster on Gall and Spurzheim in 1815. Spurzheim claimed the term as his own, while Gall refused to use it. Edwin Clarke and L. S. Jacyna, *Nineteenth-Century Origins of Neuroscientific Concepts* (Berkeley, 1987), 222–23.

7. Stanley Finger, *Minds behind the Brain: A History of the Pioneers and Their Discoveries* (Oxford, 2000), 131.

8. Roger Cooter, *The Cultural Meaning of Popular Science: Phrenology and the Organization of Consent in Nineteenth-Century Britain* (Cambridge, 1884), 258. Cooter reproduced such a head from 1878 and listed Victorian thinkers influenced by phrenology: Auguste Comte, Henri de Saint-Simon, John Stuart Mill, Alfred Russell Wallace, Herbert Spencer, and Paul Broca (268, 7).

9. Ibid., 288 n. 7.

10. Graeme Tytler, *Physiognomy in the European Novel: Faces and Fortunes* (Princeton, 1982). These writers include Dickens, Eliot, Flaubert, Fontane, Hawthorne, Hugo, Maupassant, Meredith, Poe, Radcliffe, Scott, Stifter, and Tolstoy.

11. Cesare Lombroso, *La medicina legale nelle alienazioni mentali studiata col metodo sperimentale* (Padova, 1865).

12. Cesare Lombroso, *Criminal Man according to the Classification of Cesare Lombroso*, intro. Gina Lombroso-Ferrero (1911; reprint, Montclair, N.J., 1972), xxiv–xxv.

13. "We have every reason to believe that, in this case, the lesion of the frontal lobe was the cause of the loss of language." Quoted in Ian Hacking, *Rewriting the Soul: Multiple Personality and the Sciences of Memory* (Princeton, 1995), 203.

14. Paul Broca, "Remarques sur le siège de la faculté du langage articulé; suivies d'une observation d'aphémie (perte de la parole)," *Bulletins de la Société Anatomique*, 6 (1861): 330–57, 398–407.

15. G. Fritsch and E. Hitzig, "Ueber die elektrische Erregbarkeit des Grosshirns," *Archiv für Anatomie und Physiologie* (1870), 300–332.

16. Carl Wernicke, *Der aphasische Symptomenkomplex: Eine psychologische Studie auf anatomischer Basis* (Breslau, 1874); cited in Finger, *Minds behind the Brain*, 150.

17. In the 1860s the British researchers James Bruce Thompson, George Wilson, and David Nicholson published on distinctive mental characteristics and cerebral anomalies of criminals. See C.H.S. Jaywardene, "The English Precursors of Lombroso," *British Journal of Criminology* 4 (1963): 164–70.

18. A. Bordier, "Étude anthropologique sur une série de cranes d'assassins," *Revue d'anthropologie* (1879): 264–300.

19. Moritz Benedikt, *Anatomical Studies upon Brains of Criminals: A Contribution to Anthropology, Medicine, Jurisprudence, and Psychology* (New York, 1881), 157.

20. E. P. Fowler, "Are Brains of Criminals Anatomical Perversions?" *The Medical-Chirurgical Quarterly* 1 (October 1880): 1–32; William Osler, "On the Brains of Criminals," *Medical and Surgical Journal* 10 (1882): 385–98; James Weir, "Criminal Anthropology," *Medical Record* 45 (January 1894): 42–45.

21. Charles K. Mills, "The Brains of Criminals," *Medical Bulletin* 4 (March 1882): 57–60.

22. H. H. Donaldson, "The Criminal Brain; Illustrated by the Brain of a Murderer," *Journal of Nervous and Mental Disease* 19 (August 1892): 654; Edward Spitzka, "The Execution and Post Mortem Examination of the Van Wormer Brothers at Dannemore," *Daily Medical Journal* 1 (February 8, 1904): 1–2. Hugo Münsterberg, *On the Witness Stand: Essays on Psychology and Crime* (New York,

1908), 255. See also Arthur E. Fink, *Causes of Crime: Biological Theories in the United States, 1800–1915* (Philadelphia, 1938), 99–132.

23. August Drähms, *The Criminal: His Personnel and Environment* (New York, 1900), 106.

24. Daniel Pick, *Faces of Degeneration: A European Disorder, c. 1848–1918* (Cambridge, 1989), 167–75.

25. On this reading of Conrad, see Mitchell R. Lewis, "Timely Materialisms: Modernism, Subjectivity, and Language" (Ph.D. diss., University of Oklahoma, 2001), 63–86. See also John E. Saveson, "Conrad, *Blackwoods*, and Lombroso," *Conradiana* 6, no. 1 (1974): 57–62; Martin Ray, "Conrad, Nordau, and Other Degenerates: The Psychology of *The Secret Agent*," *Conradiana* 16, no. 2 (1984): 125–40.

26. Charles Goring, *The English Convict: A Statistical Study* (1913; reprint, Montclair, N.J., 1972).

27. Lombroso's anatomic-pathological method relied on subjective determinations of physical and mental anomalies that he believed indicated a criminal type. Instead, Goring argued, his own anthropometrical method with precise measurement of physical features provided more reliable and objective scientific data.

28. Marvin E. Wolfgang, "Cesare Lombroso," in Hermann Mannheim, ed., *Pioneers in Criminology* (Montclair, N.J., 1972), 270.

29. Gosset published under the name "Student," possibly as Karl Pearson's student. Theodore M. Porter, *The Rise of Statistical Thinking, 1820–1900* (Princeton, 1986), 315.

30. Joseph von Gerlach, "Ueber die Struktur der grauen Substanz des menschlichen Grosshirns," *Zentralblatt für die medizinischen Wissenschaften*, 10 (1872): 273–75; cited in Finger, *Minds behind the Brain*, 203.

31. In 1886 Wilhelm His suggested independent cells and transmission without fusing, as did August Forel in 1887, although the reticular view prevailed until Cajal. Finger, *Minds behind the Brain*, 205.

32. Wilhelm His coined the term *dendrite* in 1890, and Albrecht von Kölliker coined *axon* in 1896. Charles Sherrington, who coined *synapse* in 1897, ranked Cajal's as one of the greatest accomplishments in the history of physiology, along with Harvey's theory of the circulation of blood in 1628 and the Bell-Magendie law in 1822. L. W. Swanson, preface to the American translation of S. Ramón y Cajal, *Histology of the Nervous System of Man and Vertebrates* (New York, 1995), 1:xxv.

33. E. G. Jones, "The Neurone Doctrine, 1891," *Journal of the History of the Neurosciences* 3 (1994): 3–20.

34. C. S. Sherrington, "On Nerve-Tracts Degenerating Secondarily to Lesions of the Cortex Cerebri," *Journal of Physiology* 10 (1889): 429–32.

35. Cajal first presented the heart of his theory in *Textura del sistema nervioso del hombre y de los vertebrados*, two massive volumes of 1899 and 1904, profusely illustrated by original drawings that he made from painstaking microscopic observations.

36. Finger, *Minds behind the Brain*, 262.

37. Otto Loewi, "Ueber humorale Uebertragbarkeit der Herznervenwirkung. I Mitteilung" *Pflüger's Archiv für die gesamte Physiologie* 189 (1921): 239–42; discussed in Finger, *Minds behind the Brain*, 269–70.

38. Arthur Yuwiler, Gary L. Brammer, and K. C. Yuwiler, "The Basics of Serotonin Neurochemistry," in Roger D. Masters and Michael T. McGuire, eds., *The Neurotransmitter Revolution: Serotonin, Social Behavior, and the Law* (Carbondale, Ill. 1994), 37–46.

39. Floyd E. Bloom and Arlyne Lazerson, *Brain, Mind, and Behavior* (New York, 1988).

40. Walter B. Cannon, *Bodily Changes in Pain, Hunger, Fear and Rage* (New York, 1915).

41. These are summarized in K. E. Moyer, *The Psychobiology of Aggression* (New York, 1976), 256–70.

42. Michael J. Raleigh and Michael T. McGuire, "Serotonin, Aggression, and Violence in Vervet Monkeys," in Masters and McGuire, eds., *Neurotransmitter Revolution*, 129–45.

43. The ultimate unknowability of these processes was anticipated early on by Cajal in 1909. "The complexity of the nervous system is so great, its various association systems and cell masses so numerous, complex, and challenging, that understanding will forever lie beyond our most committed efforts. We face inevitable frustrations; the complexity seems both to mask and obscure everything." Ramón y Cajal, *Histologie* (1909; reprint, Oxford, 1995), 1:39.

44. Bloom and Lazerson, *Brain, Mind, and Behavior*, 218, 236.

45. G. L. Brown et al., "Aggression in Humans Correlates with Cerebrospinal Fluid Amine Metabolites," *Psychiatry Research* 1 (1979): 131–39.

46. M. Linnoila et al., "Low Cerebrospinal Fluid 5-Hydroxyindoleacetic Acid Concentration Differentiates Impulsive from Nonimpulsive Violent Behavior," *Life Sciences* 33 (1983): 2609–14. See also Brown et al., "Aggression in Humans," 131–39.

47. M. Virkkunen et al., "Cerebrospinal Fluid Monoamine Metabolite Levels in Male Arsonists," *Archives of General Psychiatry* 44 (1987): 241–47.

48. Mitchell E. Berman and Emil F. Coccaro, "Neurobiologic Correlates of Violence: Relevance to Criminal Responsibility," *Behavioral Sciences and the Law* 16 (1998): 303, 309.

49. Leo Tolstoy, "How Minute Changes of Consciousness Caused Raskolnikov to Commit Murder," in George Gibian, ed., *Crime and Punishment* (New York, 1989), 487–88.

50. In Harris's *Red Dragon*, postmortem serotonin levels determine how long a victim lived after she was shot (12).

51. The sources for these last two are from British psychiatric treatises from 1824 and 1853, excerpted in Vieda Skultans, *Madness and Morals: Ideas on Insanity in the Nineteenth Century* (London, 1975), 33, 55.

52. Ibid., 50.

53. Roger Smith assessed the mind-body imprecision of a leading British alienist: "Medical aetiology was strikingly incoherent in its language of mind and body. [James] Prichard, for instance, defined insanity as illness of the mental faculties, described faculties as functions of the brain, and then related the brain to the body as a whole. He did not specify what he meant by these relationships." *Trial by Medicine: Insanity and Responsibility in Victorian Trials* (Edinburgh, 1981), 43.

54. Skultans, *Madness and Morals*, 98–132.

55. Mark S. Micale, *Approaching Hysteria: Disease and Its Interpretations* (Princeton, 1995), 23–25.

56. Lawrence Rothfield, *Vital Signs: Medical Realism in Nineteenth-Century Fiction* (Princeton, 1992), 24–25.

57. The following reconstruction is indebted to K. Codell Carter, "Germ Theory, Hysteria, and Freud's Early Work in Psychopathology," *Medical History* 24 (1980): 259–74.

58. Adolf Strümpell, "Ueber die Ursachen der Erkrankungen des Nervensystems," *Deutsches Archiv für klinische Medizin* 35 (1884): 1–17, 2; quoted in Carter, "Germ Theory," 261.

59. P. J. Möbius, "Ueber den Begriff der Hysterie," *Zentralblatt für Nervenheilkunde* 11 (1888): 66–71. See also his "Ueber die Einteilung der Krankheiten," *Zentralblatt für Nervenheilkunde* 15 (1892): 289–301. Freud acknowledged his debt to Möbius in *Studies on Hysteria* [1893–95], in *Standard Edition of the Complete Psychological Works of Sigmund Freud* (London, 1953), 2:8n, 186–91, 215, 243.

60. Joseph Breuer and Sigmund Freud, "Studies on Hysteria," in *Standard Edition*, 2:3, 6.

61. Ibid., 187. For more references to the tuberculosis model, see Freud, *Standard Edition*, 3:129, 137, 209.

62. Sigmund Freud, "A Reply to Criticisms of My Paper on Anxiety Neurosis," in *Standard Edition*, 5:3, 136.

63. Sigmund Freud, "Heredity and the Aetiology of Neuroses," in *Standard Edition*, 3:149.

64. On this date and the development of monomania theory generally, see Jan Goldstein, *Console and Classify: The French Psychiatric Profession in the Nineteenth Century* (Cambridge, 1987), 153ff.

65. J.-E.-D. Esquirol, *De la monomanie*, reprinted in *Des maladies mentales* (Paris, 1838), 2:1; quoted in Raymond de Saussure, "The Influence of the Concept of Monomania on French Medico-Legal Psychiatry (from 1825–1840)," *Journal of the History of Medicine* (July 1946): 366.

66. J.-E.-D. Esquirol, "Monomania," *Dictionaire des sciences médicale* 34 (1819): 125.

67. Etienne-Jean Georget, *Examen médicale des procès criminels* (Paris, 1825).

68. Goldstein, *Console amd Classify*, 166–67.

69. A. Brierre de Boismont, *Observations médico-légales sur la monomanie homicide* (Paris, 1827); Elias Regnault, *Du degré de compétence des médecins dans les questions judiciares relatives aux aliénations mentales et des théories physiologiques des monomanies* (Paris, 1828); J.-C. Hoffbauer, *Médicine légale relative aux aliénés et aux sourds-muets* (Paris, 1827).

70. Kraepelin and Krafft-Ebing introduced paranoia in the 1880s. Fink, *Causes of Crime*, 29–30, 54.

71. On the suitability of monomania for Victorian American murder novelists, especially for creating plausible "belief in a unified personality," see David Brion Davis, *Homicide in American Fiction, 1798–1860* (Ithaca, N.Y., 1957), 116ff.

72. See Ann Harrington, *Medicine, Mind, and the Double Brain: A Study in Nineteenth-Century Thought* (Princeton, 1987), 248, 100, 105ff.; Masao Miyoshi, *The Divided Self: A Perspective on the Literature of the Victorians* (New York, 1969), xv.

73. Darwin ends *Origin* with the observation "that man with all his noble qualities, with sympathy which feels for the most debased, with benevolence which extends not only to other men but to the humblest living creature, with his god-like intellect . . . with all these exalted powers—Man still bears in his bodily frame the indelible stamp of his lowly origin."

74. *The Journals of André Gide*, (New York, 1948), 2:237–38, 271.

75. Quoted in Jacques M. Quen, "Anglo-American Criminal Insanity: An Historical Perspective," *Journal of the History of the Behavioral Sciences* 10 (1974): 314.

76. Ibid., 316.

77. James Prichard, *On the Different Forms of Insanity in Relation to Jurisprudence* (1842); quoted in Daniel N. Robinson, *Wild Beasts and Idle Humours: The Insanity Defense from Antiquity to the Present* (Cambridge, Mass., 1996), 161.

78. *Queen v. M'Naghten* (1843) 887; quoted in Robinson, *Wild Beasts*, 168.

79. Martin J. Wiener, *Reconstructing the Criminal: Culture, Law, and Policy in England, 1830–1914* (Cambridge, 1990), 12.

80. Ibid., 273–79.

81. *State v. Pike*, 49 N.H. 399 (1869); quoted in Thomas Maeder, *Crime and Madness: The Origins and Evolution of the Insanity Defense* (New York, 1985), 46.

82. In France, as Robert A. Nye noted, "in 1832 a general measure of 'extenuating circumstances' was admitted to the code, permitting judges and juries the opportunity to impose a lesser sentence . . . for a crime. This measure was the first in the general trend toward the individualization of punishment in modern criminal law that [subsequently] transformed the binding legalism of the classical code into an instrument allowing the judge to fit the punishment to the criminal." *Crime, Madness, and Politics in Modern France* (Princeton, 1984), 28.

83. William James, *Pragmatism* [1907], in *Pragmatism and Four Essays from "The Meaning of Truth"* (Cleveland, 1964), 119.

84. Bernard L. Diamond, "Criminal Responsibility of the Mentally Ill," *Stanford Law Review* (December 1961): 75.

85. Quoted in Quen, "Anglo-American Criminal Insanity," 321.

86. Robert Musil, "The Polemic against the Concept of Causality; Its Replacement by the Concept of Function," in *On Mach's Theories* (1908; trans., Washington, D.C., 1982), 44–56.

87. Deborah W. Denno, "Human Biology and Criminal Responsibility: Free-Will or Free Ride?" *University of Pennsylvania Law Review* 137 (1988): 615–71.

CHAPTER 7: SOCIETY

1. Lawrence Rothfield, *Vital Signs: Medical Realism in Nineteenth-Century Fiction* (Princeton, 1992), 25–28, 57–63.

2. Erich Auerbach, *Mimesis: The Representation of Reality in Western Literature* (1946; reprint, New York, 1953), 417.

3. Lee Clark Mitchell, "Naturalism and the Languages of Determinism," in Emory Elliott et al., eds., *Columbia Literary History of the United States* (New York,

1988), 526. "The formula of the Naturalistic narrative [of surroundings] is simple; it is one-way traffic: the description determines the action." Elrud Ibsch, "Historical Changes of the Function of Spatial Description in Literary Texts," *Poetics Today* 3, no. 4 (1982): 101–2.

4. Winifred Hughes, *The Maniac in the Cellar: Sensation Novels of the 1860s* (Princeton, 1980), 26–27.

5. Hughes noted that "Wylie Sypher has also argued, rather ingeniously, that melodrama is the single characteristic mode of nineteenth-century thought and art, that the Victorians perceived their situation in terms of extreme polarities and expressed it by means of overstatement and emphatic instances." Ibid., 13. This bold generalization is more true of drama, as Michael Booth concluded: "almost all serious nineteenth-century plays are to a greater or lesser extent melodramatic." *Hiss the Villain* (New York, 1964), 9.

6. *The Journals of André Gide* (New York, 1948), 2:376–77.

7. Leland Monk, *Standard Deviations: Chance and the Modern British Novel* (Stanford, 1993), 9.

8. Alain Robbe-Grillet, "A Future for the Novel," in *For a New Novel* (1958; reprint, Evanston, Ill., 1965), 19, 21.

9. Alain Robbe-Grillet, "Nature, Humanism, Tragedy," in *For a New Novel*, 52.

10. Ibid., 57, 62, 63.

11. Tom LeClair, *In the Loop: Don Delillo and the Systems Novel* (Urbana, Ill., 1987), 1–31.

12. One such protest was by Thomas Carlyle, who insisted that people were "not the thrall of Circumstances, of Necessity, but the victorious subduer thereof." Quoted in Walter E. Houghton, *The Victorian Frame of Mind, 1830–1879* (New Haven, 1957), 337.

13. Martin Wiener, *Reconstructing the Criminal: Culture, Law, and Policy in England, 1830–1914* (Cambridge, 1990), 162, 226.

14. The *O.E.D.* attributes the first use of *blackmail* to Macaulay in 1840, although there it refers to "extortion by intimidation or pressure." Not until 1895 did British common law criminalize threatening to reveal noncriminal misconduct. Alexander Welsh, *George Eliot and Blackmail* (Cambridge, Mass., 1985), 5, 6.

15. Wiener, *Reconstructing the Criminal*, 247.

16. Ibid., 33–38, 76.

17. Eugène Sue, *Les Mystères de Paris* (Paris, 1851), 1.

18. Louis Chevalier, *Laboring Classes and Dangerous Classes in Paris during the First Half of the Nineteenth Century* (1958; reprint, New York, 1973), 40.

19. Jon Thompson, *Fiction, Crime, and Empire: Clues to Modernity and Postmodernism* (Urbana, 1993), 147.

20. In *Reading Berlin 1900* (Cambridge, 1996), Peter Fritzsche argued that around 1900, Berliners read newspapers to learn about their city, while the newspapers helped determine the city's structure. Newspapers also made the city readable by replicating its discontinuity with their chance juxtapositions of numerous disparate items. In contrast to nineteenth-century novels about the city that were told from an omniscient point of view, were narrated as a coherent plot, and which

offered closure on the city as a whole, modern novels, and especially Döblin's, attempted to accommodate the city's "discontinuity, dissociation and unpredictability [which] steadily overruled the orderings of plot and narrative" (37). See also Klaus R. Scherpe, "The City as Narrator: The Modern Text in Alfred Döblin's *Berlin Alexanderplatz*," in Andreas Huyssen and David Bathrick, eds., *Modernity and the Text: Revisions of German Modernism* (New York, 1989), 162–79.

21. Brian McHale, *Postmodernist Fiction* (London, 1987), 45–49, 43 (Calvino quote).

22. Ibid., 45–49.

23. Immanuel Wallerstein et al., *Open the Social Sciences: Report of the Gulbenkian Commission on the Restructuring of the Social Sciences* (Stanford, 1996), 1–32; Fritz K. Ringer, *The Decline of the German Mandarins: The German Academic Community, 1899–1933* (Cambridge, Mass., 1969); Ivan Strenski, "Durkheim, Disciplinarity, and the '*Sciences Religieuses*,'" in Amanda Anderson and Joseph Valente, eds., *Disciplinarity at the Fin de Siècle* (Princeton, 2002), 153–73.

24. Thomas L. Haskell, *The Emergence of Professional Social Science: The American Social Science Association and the Nineteenth-Century Crisis of Authority* (1977; reprint, Baltimore, 2000), 28–29.

25. Albion W. Small, *Origins of Sociology* (New York, 1924), 332–33, quoted in Haskell, *Emergence of Professional Social Science*, 253.

26. Georg Simmel, "The Metropolis and Mental Life," in Kurt H. Wolff, ed., *The Sociology of Georg Simmel* (New York, 1950), 413–14.

27. Georg Simmel, *Philosophie des Geldes* (1907); the German critic Hermann Bahr observed that "one thing distinguishes modernity from all that is past and gives it its particular character . . . [the] disappearance of all things in ceaseless flight and insight into the connectedness of all things, into the dependency of each thing upon every other in the unending chain of what exists." Quoted in David Frisby, *Fragments of Modernity: Theories of Modernity in the Work of Simmel, Kracauer and Benjamin* (Cambridge, Mass., 1986), 11.

28. Graham Wallas, *The Great Society* (New York, 1920), 3.

29. Ibid.

30. John Dewey, *The Public and Its Problems* (1927); quoted in Haskell, *Emergence of Professional Social Science*, 253–54.

31. Emile Durkheim, *The Rules of Sociological Method* (1895; reprint, New York, 1982), 3. Further text references are to this edition.

32. Emile Durkheim, *Suicide: A Study in Sociology* (1897; reprint, New York, 1951), 46. Further text references are to this edition.

33. Steven Lukes, *Émile Durkheim, His Life and Work: A Historical and Critical Study* (Harmondsworth, England, 1973), 214–15, 205.

34. K. Codell Carter, *The Rise of Causal Concepts of Disease: Case Histories* (Hants, England, 2003), 10ff.

35. André-Michel Guerry, *Statististique morale de l'Angleterre comparée avec la statistique morale de la France* (Paris, 1864); cited in Ian Hacking, *The Taming of Chance* (Cambridge, 1990), 79–80.

36. Anthony Oberschall, "The Two Empirical Roots of Social Theory and the Probability Revolution," in Lorenz Krüger et al., eds., *The Probabilistic Revolution* (Cambridge, Mass., 1990), 2:115.

37. Quoted in Hacking, *Taming of Chance*, 105.

38. Joseph Lottin, *Quetelet, statisticien et sociologue* (Louvain, 1912), 276; quoted in Oberschall, "Two Empirical Roots," in Krüger, et al., *Probabilistic Revolution*, 2:117.

39. Hacking, *Taming of Chance*, 116, 127.

40. Henry Thomas Buckle, *History of Civilization in England* (London, 1857), 1:20.

41. "There is no hint in Durkheim's writings that he ever thought a chance mechanism at the individual level might generate laws at the macro level." Oberschall, "Two Empirical Roots," 117. Hacking argued that Galton brought about "the autonomy of statistical law" without making it fully irreducible to deterministic phenomena. "Statistical laws became autonomous when they could be used not only for the prediction of phenomena but also for their explanation." He attributed this achievement to Galton. *Taming of Chance*, 182.

42. Karl Pearson, *The Life, Letters and Labours of Francis Galton* (Cambridge, 1914–30), 3A:1f; quoted in Hacking, *Taming of Chance*, 188.

43. On feedback, see George P. Richardson, *Feedback Thought in Social Science and Systems Theory* (Philadelphia, 1991), ix and passim.

44. Max Weber, "'Objectivity' in Social Science and Social Policy" [1904] in *The Methodology of the Social Sciences* (New York, 1949), 78–79.

45. Fritz Ringer, *Max Weber's Methodology: The Unification of the Cultural and Social Sciences* (Cambridge, Mass., 1997), especially chap. 3, "Singular Causal Analysis." I followed Ringer in translating *objektive Möglichkeit* as "objective probability" instead of "objective possibility," 64 n. 1. See also Stephen P. Turner and Regis A. Factor, "Objective Possibility and Adequate Causation in Weber's Methodological Writings," 29, no. 1 *Sociological Review* (1981): 5–29.

46. Weber, "Objectivity," 90.

47. Max Weber, *The Protestant Ethic and the Spirit of Capitalism* (1904–5; trans., New York, 1958), 172.

48. Max Weber, *Economy and Society* (1925; trans., New York, 1968), 11–12.

49. Alicia Juarrero, *Dynamics in Action: Intentional Behavior as a Complex System* (Cambridge, Mass., 1999), 2–5 and passim.

50. Vito Volterra, "Leçons sur la théorie mathématique de la lutte pour la vie," cited in Richardson, *Feedback Thought*, 36. My discussion of feedback and dynamic systems is indebted to Richardson and to Juarrero, *Dynamics in Action*.

51. On the prehistory and current role of social constructionism in murder, see Philip Jenkins, *Using Murder: The Social Construction of Serial Homicide* (New York, 1994).

52. Richardson, *Feedback Thought*, 48–52.

53. Quoted in ibid., 80.

54. Gunner Myrdal, *Rich Lands and Poor* (New York, 1957), 31.

55. Robert Merton, "The Unanticipated Consequences of Purposive Social Action," *American Sociological Review* (1936): 894–904.

56. Arthur Rosenblueth, Norbert Wiener, and Julian Bigelow, "Behavior, Purpose, and Teleology," *Philosophy of Science* 10 (1943), 18–24.

57. Warren S. McCulloch, quoted in Richardson, *Feedback Thought*, 98.

58. Kurt Lewin, "Feedback Problems of Social Diagnosis and Action," *Human Relations* 1 (1947): 147–53; cited in Richardson, *Feedback Thought*, 99.

59. Norbert Weiner, *The Human Use of Human Beings: Cybernetics and Society* (1950; reprint, New York, 1967), 18.

60. Ludwig von Bertalanffy, "General System Theory: A New Approach to Unity of Science," *Human Biology* 23, 1 (1951): 353–54; cited in Richardson, *Feedback Thought*, 121.

61. Magoroh Maruyama, "The Second Cybernetics: Deviation-Amplifying Mutual Causal Processes," *American Scientist* 51 (1963):164–79.

62. On dissipative structures and their historical significance, see Ilya Prigogine and Isabelle Stengers, *Order Out of Chaos: Man's New Dialogue with Nature* (New York, 1984), 12 and passim.

63. Alan Beyerchen, "Nonlinear Science and the Unfolding of a New Intellectual Vision," *Papers in Comparative Studies* 6 (1989): 45.

64. Alan Beyerchen, "Clausewitz, Nonlinearity, and the Unpredictability of War," *International Security* 17, 3 (Winter 1992/93): 59–90.

65. Randolph Roth, "Is History a Process? Nonlinearity, Revitalization Theory, and the Central Metaphor of Social Science History," *Social Science History* 16, no. 2 (Summer 1992): 203ff.

66. Juarrero, *Dynamics in Action*, 223.

67. Walter J. Freeman, *Societies of Brains: A Study in the Neuroscience of Love and Hate* (Hillsdale, N.J., 1995), 51–53.

68. Michel Foucault, *The History of Sexuality* vol. 1, *An Introduction* [1976]; (trans., New York, 1978), 92–94. See also Foucault, "Lecture Two: 14 January 1976," in Colin Gordon, ed., *Power/Knowledge: Selected Interviews and Other Writings, 1972–1977* (New York 1980), 92–108.

CHAPTER 8: IDEAS

1. Friedrich Nietzsche, *Ecce Homo* [1888], trans. Walter Kaufmann (New York, 1967), 328.

2. On Nietzsche's moral philosophy, see Brian Leiter, *Nietzsche on Morality* (London, 2002); Simon Way, *Nietzsche's Ethics and His War on "Morality"* (Oxford, 1999).

3. Friedrich Nietzsche, *On the Genealogy of Morals* [1887], trans. Walter Kaufmann (New York, 1967), 20. All further references are to this edition.

4. Friedrich Nietzsche, *Beyond Good and Evil* [1886], trans. Walter Kaufmann (New York, 1966), 60. All further references are to this edition.

5. On the aesthetic emphasis in Nietzsche, see Alexander Nehamas, *Nietzsche: Life as Literature* (Cambridge, Mass., 1985); Alan Megill, "Friedrich Nietzsche as an Aestheticist," in *Prophets of Extremity: Nietzsche, Heidegger, Foucault, Derrida* (Berkeley, 1985), 29–102.

6. While philosophers since antiquity had been concerned with the meaning of existence, that inquiry was not quite as specifically centered on a philosophy of existence the way it was in modern existentialism, and over the centuries it became divided between the conventional subfields of philosophical inquiry.

7. Friedrich Nietzsche, *The Birth of Tragedy* [1872], trans. Walter Kaufmann (New York, 1967), 22. One of those passages in the book reads, "it is only as an *aesthetic phenomenon* that existence and the world are eternally *justified*" (52).

8. *Beyond Good and Evil*, 197.

9. Friedrich Nietzsche, *The Gay Science* [1882–87], trans. Walter Kaufmann (New York, 1974), 290.

10. Friedrich Nietzsche, *Thus Spoke Zarathustra* [1883–85], trans. Walter Kaufmann (New York, 1978), 166.

11. Walter Kaufmann, *Nietzsche: Philosopher, Psychologist, Antichrist* (Princeton, 1950); David S. Thatcher, *Nietzsche in England 1890–1914: The Growth of a Reputation* (Toronto, 1970); Patrick Bridgewater, *Nietzsche in Anglosaxony* (Leicester, 1972); Pierre Boudot, *Nietzsche et l'au-delà de la liberté: Nietzsche et les écrivains français de 1930 à 1960* (Paris, 1970); H. G. Kuttner, *Nietzsche-Rezeption in Frankreich* (Essen, 1984); Edith W. Clowes, *The Revolution of Moral Consciousness: Nietzsche in Russian Literature, 1890–1914* (Dekalb, Ill. 1988); Ernst Nolte, *Nietzsche und der Nietzscheanismus* (Frankfurt, 1990); Steven E. Aschheim, *The Nietzsche Legacy in Germany, 1890–1990* (Berkeley, 1992); Alan D. Schrift, *Nietzsche's French Legacy: A Genealogy of Poststructuralism* (London, 1995); Douglas Smith, *Transvaluations: Nietzsche in France 1872–1972* (Oxford, 1996).

12. For Nietzsche's influence on Gide, especially on his early novel *The Immoralist* (1902), see John Burt Foster, Jr., *Heirs to Dionysus: A Nietzschean Current in Literary Modernism* (Princeton, 1981), 145–79.

13. These were culled from Robley Dunglison, ed., *Cyclopedia of Practical Medicine*, American ed., 4 vols. (Philadelphia, 1845), by K. Codell Carter in *The Rise of Causal Concepts of Disease* (London, 2003), 20.

14. Craig Haney, "Criminal Justice and the Nineteenth-Century Paradigm: The Triumph of Psychological Individualism in the 'Formative Era,'" *Law and Human Behavior* 6 (1982): 202.

15. Benjamin Rush, *An Oration Delivered before the American Philosophical Society . . . Containing an Enquiry into the Influence of Physical Causes upon the Moral Faculty* (Philadelphia, 1786), 2.

16. Graham Richards interpreted Prichard's introduction of moral insanity as a transition point in "the way in which the term 'moral' slithers from being a descriptive to a prescriptive term between 1790 and the mid nineteenth century." *Mental Machinery: The Origins and Consequences of Psychological Ideas, 1600–1850* (Baltimore, 1992), 354.

17. Henri Ellenberger, *The Discovery of the Unconscious* (New York, 1970), 212. Robert A. Nye documented the conflation of medical and moral concepts in nineteenth-century French medicine and psychiatry. *Crime, Madness and Politics in Modern France: The Medical Concept of National Decline* (Princeton, 1984), 42, 63, 229.

18. This last pair of categories emerged at the 1881 trial of the man who assassinated President James Garfield. One psychiatric expert in support of his insanity defense explained that "some authors call that moral insanity which I term moral imbecility or moral monstrosity." Edward D. Spitzka, "Review of the Trial of Charles J. Guiteau," *American Journal of Insanity* 32 (January 1881): 303–448; quoted in Arthur E. Fink, *Causes of Crime: Biological Theories in the United States, 1800–1915* (London, 1938), 56.

19. Quoted in Robert Castel, "Moral Treatment: Mental Therapy and Social Control in the Nineteenth Century," in Stanley Cohen and Andrew Skull, eds., *Social Control and the State: Historical and Comparative Essays* (Oxford, 1983), 265 n. 12.

20. David Brion Davis, *Homicide in American Fiction, 1798–1860* (Ithaca, N.Y., 1957), 114.

21. Martin J. Wiener, "The De-moralizing of Criminality," in *Reconstructing the Criminal: Culture, Law, and Policy in England, 1830–1914* (Cambridge, 1990), 215–56, 253. On the shift from moralism to causalism see Christie Davies, "Crime, Bureaucracy, and Equality," *Policy Review* 23 (Winter 1983): 98–101.

22. Davies, "Crime, Bureaucracy, and Equality," 98–99.

23. Charles E. Rosenberg, *The Trial of the Assassin Guiteau: Psychiatry and Law in the Gilded Age* (Chicago, 1968), 71ff.

24. Beth Kalikoff, *Murder and Moral Decay in Victorian Popular Literature* (Ann Arbor, 1986).

25. Philip Collins, *Dickens and Crime* (Bloomington, Ind., 1962), 318.

26. Karl Beckson, introduction to *Aesthetes and Decadents of the 1890's* (New York, 1966), xix n. 4.

27. John G. Cawelti, *Adventure, Mystery, and Romance: Formula Stories as Art and Popular Culture* (Chicago, 1976), 54.

28. Joel Black, *The Aesthetics of Murder: A Study in Romantic Literature and Contemporary Culture* (Baltimore, 1991), 2.

29. *Genealogy of Morals*, 104.

30. Letter to Edward Garnett, June 5, 1914, in Harry T. Moore, ed., *The Collected Letters of D. H. Lawrence* (London, 1962), 281–82.

31. James Joyce, *A Portrait of the Artist as a Young Man* (New York, 1944),169–70.

32. These include Marcel Proust, Virginia Woolf, Henry James, Wyndham Lewis, and Aldous Huxley. Randal Stevenson, *Modernist Fiction: An Introduction* (New York, 1992), 155–65.

33. On these readings of Genet and other modernists, see Theodore Ziolkowski, "A Portrait of the Artist as a Criminal," in *Dimensions of the Modern Novel: German Texts and European Contexts* (Princeton, 1969), 289–331.

34. Sebastian D. G. Knowles, "Death by Gramophone," *Journal of Modern Literature*, forthcoming. Mary Mathews Gedo suggests that the painting recasts the actual suicide of Magritte's mother as a murder and in so doing redirects Magritte's hostility toward his father, who is depicted as the actual murderer. "Meditation on Madness: The Art of René Magritte," in Terry Ann R. Neff, ed., *In the Mind's Eye, Dada and Surrealism* (Chicago, 1985), 78ff.

35. William Buckland, *Geology and Mineralogy Considered with Reference to Natural Theology* (Philadelphia, 1837), 19.

36. Edward S. Reed, *From Soul to Mind: The Emergence of Psychology from Erasmus Darwin to William James* (New Haven, 1997), 2.

37. William Whewell, *The Philosophy of the Inductive Sciences* (1847; reprint, New York, 1966), 2:439.

38. Peter J. Bowler, *Evolution: The History of an Idea* (Berkeley, 1983), 22. For a more shaded interpretation of the opposition between religion and science, see David A. Hollinger, "Justification by Verification: The Scientific Challenge to the Moral Authority of Christianity in Modern America," in Michael J. Lacey, ed., *Religion and Twentieth-Century American Intellectual Life* (Cambridge, 1989), 116–35; which argues that the relation between these two disciplines

involves aggression and differentiation as well as mutual engagement and divergence.

39. Ernst Mayr, *One Long Argument: Charles Darwin and the Genesis of Modern Evolutionary Thought* (Cambridge, Mass., 1991), 12–13.

40. A. N. Wilson, *God's Funeral* (New York, 1999), 189–90.

41. Walter E. Houghton, *The Victorian Frame of Mind, 1830–1870* (New Haven, 1957), 21.

42. Diane Bjorklund, *Interpreting the Self: Two Hundred Years of American Autobiography* (Chicago, 1998), 60–61.

43. Joss Marsh, *Word Crimes: Blasphemy, Culture, and Literature in Nineteenth-Century England* (Chicago, 1998), 15.

44. Benjamin Peirce, "The National Importance of Social Science in the United States" [1880]; quoted in Thomas Haskell, *The Emergence of Professional Social Science* (Urbana, 1977), 147.

45. J. Hillis Miller, *The Disappearance of God: Five Nineteenth-Century Writers* (Cambridge, Mass., 1963); Owen Chadwick, *The Secularization of the European Mind in the Nineteenth Century* (Cambridge, 1975); James Turner, *Without God, Without Creed: The Origins of Unbelief in America* (Baltimore, 1985); Bernard Lightman, *The Origins of Agnosticism: Victorian Unbelief and the Limits of Knowledge* (Baltimore, 1987).

46. Mayr, *One Long Argument*, 38.

47. Quoted in Wilson, *God's Funeral*, 137.

48. From Thomas L. Haskell, "Persons as Uncaused Causes: John Stuart Mill, the Spirit of Capitalism, and the 'Invention' of Formalism," in *Objectivity Is Not Neutrality: Explanatory Schemes in History* (Baltimore, 1998), 331.

49. Davis, *Homicide in American Fiction*, 28.

50. J. A. Cuddon, introduction to James Hogg, *The Private Memoirs and Confessions of a Justified Sinner* (London, 1994), xxv.

51. J. C. Bucknill and D. H. Tuke, *A Manual of Psychiatric Medicine* (Philadelphia, 1858), 273; quoted in Wiener, *Reconstructing the Criminal*, 27.

52. Lauriat Lane, Jr., "The Devil in *Oliver Twist*," *Dickensian* 52 (1956): 132–36.

53. Thomas Vargish, *The Providential Aesthetic in Victorian Fiction* (Charlottsville, 1985), 1. On the persistence of a sense of providence in Eliot, see Carol Christ, "Aggression and Providential Death in George Eliot's Fiction," *Novel* 9 (Winter 1976): 130–40.

54. Vargish, *Providential Aesthetic*, 93.

55. Lawrence Thompson, *William Faulkner: An Introduction and Interpretation* (New York, 1967), 68.

56. Rudolph Binion, *After Christianity: Christian Survivals in Post-Christian Culture* (Durango, Colo., 1986), 11.

57. André Gide, *Dostoevsky* (1923; reprint, New York, 1961), 90.

58. On religious imagery in the novel, see Bill McCarron, "*The Silence of the Lambs* as Secular Eucharist," *Notes on Contemporary Literature* 25, no. 1 (1995): 5–6.

59. David Hume, *A Treatise of Human Nature* (1739; reprint, Oxford, 1978), 252.

60. R. D. Laing, *The Divided Self* (London, 1959); Elizabeth Brody Tennenbaum, *The Problematic Self: Approaches to Identity in Stendhal, D. H. Lawrence, and Malraux* (Cambridge, Mass., 1977); Judith Ryan, *The Vanishing Subject: Early Psychology and Literary Modernism* (Chicago, 1991); Carolyn J. Dean, *The Self and Its Pleasures: Bataille, Lacan, and the History of the Decentered Subject* (Ithaca, N.Y., 1992); Jean Baudrillard, *Simulacra and Simulation* (1981; reprint, Ann Arbor, 1994); Michel Foucault, *The Order of Things: An Archaeology of the Human Sciences* (1966; reprint, New York, 1970), 328–35, 386–87; Roland Barthes, "The Death of the Author," in *Music-Image-Text* (New York, 1977), 142–48.

61. Haney, "Criminal Justice," 192ff.

62. For a probing analysis of Nietzsche's deconstruction of the self, especially in *The Will to Power*, see J. Hillis Miller, "The Disarticulation of the Self in Nietzsche," *Monist* 64 (1981): 247–61. For a critique of Miller, see David Booth, "Nietzsche on 'The Subject as Multiplicity,'" *Man and World* 18 (1985): 121–46.

63. Ernst Mach, *The Analysis of Sensations* (1885; reprint, New York, 1959), 22–29.

64. William James, *Principles of Psychology* (New York, 1890), 1:239.

65. *The Standard Edition of the Complete Psychological Works of Sigmund Freud* (London, 1963), 16:285.

66. Letter to Edward Garnett, 282.

67. Virginia Woolf, *Mrs. Dalloway* (New York, 1925), 11.

68. Virginia Woolf, *The Waves* (New York, 1931), 288.

69. Judith Ryan, *The Vanishing Subject: Early Psychology and Literary Modernism* (Chicago, 1991), 51–62.

70. Richard K. Ashley, "Living on Border Lines: Man, Poststructuralism, and War," in *International/Intertextual Relations: Postmodern Readings of World Politics* (Lexington, Mass., 1989), 259–321.

71. Brian McHale, *Postmodernist Fiction* (London, 1987), 199.

72. Michel Foucault, "What Is an Author?" in Josue Harari, ed., *Textual Strategies: Perspectives in Post-Structuralist Criticism* (Ithaca, N.Y., 1979), 144.

73. Daniel J. Singal saw this struggle as central to Faulkner's writing and a reflection of cultural historical developments in his time. *William Faulkner: The Making of a Modernist* (Chapel Hill, 1997), 114ff.

74. Frederick L. Gwynn and Joseph L. Blotner, eds., *Faulkner in the University: Class Conferences at the University of Virginia, 1957–1958* (New York, 1959), 72.

75. Anthony Giddens, *The Consequences of Modernity* (Stanford, 1990), 21.

76. Daniel Bell, *The Cultutral Contradictions of Capitalism* (1976; reprint, New York, 1996), 89ff.

Conclusion

1. Friedrich Waismann, "The Decline and Fall of Causality," in A. C. Crombie, *Turning Points in Physics* (New York, 1959); Paul Forman, "Weimar Culture, Causality, and Quantum Theory, 1918–1927: Adaptation by German Physicists

and Mathematicians to a Hostile Intellectual Environment," *Historical Studies in the Physical Sciences* 3 (1971), 1–115; Mario Bunge, *Causality and Modern Science* (New York, 1979). My discussion of quantum theory generally is indebted to personal communications by Harold Brown and Arkady Plotnitsky.

2. Max Born, *The Restless Universe* (New York, 1951), 277.

3. On these and other problems in the classical model see Morton Tavel, *Contemporary Physics and the Limits of Knowledge* (New Brunswick, N.J., 2002), 167.

4. Arkady Plotnitsky, *The Knowable and the Unknowable: Modern Science, Nonclassical Thought, and the "Two Cultures"* (Ann Arbor, 2002), 34. Plotnitsky offers an extensive discussion of Bohr's views in the context of current philosophical debates.

5. Letter to Max Born, December 4, 1926, in Max Born, ed., *The Born-Einstein Letters* (New York, 1971).

6. Arthur I. Miller, "Visualization Lost and Regained: The Genesis of the Quantum Theory in the Period 1913–1927," in Judith Wechsler, ed., *On Aesthetics in Science* (Cambridge, Mass., 1978), 74–77. Of course, electrons do not jump and they do not travel in orbits. Bohr was acutely aware of the necessity of metaphorical language taken from mechanical and visualizable models, hence his belief that we are "suspended in language." On this subject, see chapter 3, above.

7. Max Planck, *A Survey of Physical Theory* (New York, 1960), 108–9; quoted in Alan J. Friedman and Carol C. Donley, *Einstein as Myth and Muse* (Cambridge, 1985), 114.

8. Heinz R. Pagels, *The Cosmic Code: Quantum Physics and the Language of Nature* (New York, 1983), 54.

9. Werner Heisenberg, *Physics and Philosophy: The Revolution in Modern Science* (New York, 1958), 58.

10. Quoted in Waismann, "Decline and Fall," 146–47. It is puzzling that Waismann gave no source for such an important quotation. Kelvin did make a similar statement, however, in 1884 in his Baltimore lecture 11: "It seems to me that the test of 'Do we or [do we] not understand a particular subject in physics?' is, 'Can we make a mechanical model of it?'" Robert Kargon and Peter Achinstein, eds., *Kelvin's Baltimore Lectures and Modern Theoretical Physics* (Cambridge, Mass., 1987), 111.

11. This historical summary based on Miller, "Visualization," 74–76. See also Arthur I. Miller, *Insights of Genius: Imagery and Creativity in Science and Art* (New York, 1996), 56.

12. On visualization see Miller, "Visualization Lost and Regained," and Arthur I. Miller, *Imagery in Scientific Thought Creating 20th-Century Physics* (Cambridge, Mass., 1986).

13. Richard Feynman, *The Character of Physical Law* (Cambridge, Mass., 1967), 129.

14. Waismann, "Decline and Fall," 84–154. See also Forman, "Weimar Culture."

15. Niels Bohr, "Introductory Survey" [1929], in *Atomic Theory and the Description of Nature* (Woodbridge, Conn., 1987), 4.

16. For Laplace quotation, see note 21 to the introduction, above.

17. On these literary influences see Plotnitsky, "Knowable and Unknowable," 26; Susan Strehle, *Fiction in the Quantum Universe* (Chapel Hill, 1992); Robert

Nadeau, *Readings from the Book of Nature: Physics and Metaphysics in the Modern Novel* (Amherst, 1981); Carol Donley, "Modern Literature and Physics: A Study of Interrelationships," (Ph.D. diss., Kent State University, 1975); Friedman and Donley, *Einstein as Myth and Muse*; Phillip F. Herring, *Joyce's Uncertainty Principle* (Princeton, 1987). For poetry, see Daniel Albright, *Quantum Poetics: Yeats, Pound, Eliot, and the Science of Modernism* (Cambridge, 1997).

18. Don DeLillo, "American Blood," *Rolling Stone* (December 1983): 21–28, 74.

19. Ibid., 22–28.

20. Ibid., 23.

21. See André Gide "Faits-divers," *La nouvelle revue francaise* 30 (June 1, 1928): 841.

Bibliography of Fictional Sources

Ballard, J. G. *Crash*. New York: Farrar, Straus and Giroux, 1973.

Balzac, Honoré de. *Old Goriot*. 1834. Translated by Marion Ayton Crawford. Reprint, Harmondsworth, England: Penguin, 1951.

Bardin, John Franklin. *Devil Take the Blue-Tail Fly*. 1948. Reprint, Harmondsworth, England: Penguin, 1988.

Bear, Greg. *Blood Music*. New York: Arbor House, 1985.

Beckett, Samuel. *Molloy*. 1955. Reprint, New York: Grove, 1989.

Bentley, E. C. *Trent's Last Case*. 1913. Reprint, Oxford: Oxford University Press, 1995.

Bernhard, Thomas. *The Lime Works*. 1970. Translated by Sophie Wilkins. Reprint, Chicago: University of Chicago Press, 1973.

Bloch, Robert. *The Scarf*. Greenwich, Conn.: Facade, 1947.

———. *Psycho*. New York: Tom Diehard Associates, 1959.

Borges, Jorge Luis. "The Garden of Forking Paths." 1941. In *Ficciones*, translated by Helen Temple and Ruthven Todd, 89–101. New York: Grove, 1962.

Bourget, Paul. *The Disciple*. 1889. Reprint, London: F. Tennyson Neely, 1898.

Braddon, Mary Elizabeth. *Lady Audley's Secret*. 1862. Reprint, Oxford: Oxford University Press, 1987.

Broch, Hermann. *The Sleepwalkers*. 1931–32. Translated by Willa and Edwin Muir. San Francisco: North Point Press, 1985.

Bulwar-Lytton, Edward. *Paul Clifford*. 1830. Reprint, Rahway, N.J.: Mershon, n.d.

Burgess, Anthony. *A Clockwork Orange*. 1962. Reprint, New York: Ballantine, 1982.

Camus, Albert. *The Stranger*. 1942. Translated by Matthew Ward. New York: Vintage, 1988.

Capote, Truman. *In Cold Blood*. New York: Signet, 1965.

Carr, Caleb. *The Alienist*. New York: Bantam, 1994.

Christie, Agatha. *The Murder of Roger Ackroyd*. 1926. Reprint, New York: Harper, 1991.

Conrad, Joseph. *Heart of Darkness*. 1899. Reprint, Harmondsworth, England: Penguin, 1973.

———. *The Secret Agent*. 1907. Reprint, New York: Penguin, 1996.

Cortázar, Julio. "Continuity of Parks." In *Blow-Up and Other Stories*, translated by Paul Blackburn, 63–65. New York: Random House, 1963.

de Beauvoir, Simone. *She Came to Stay*. 1943. Translated by Yvonne Moyse and Roger Senhouse. Glasgow: Fontana, 1975.

DeLillo, Don. *Libra*. 1988. Reprint, Harmondsworth, England: Penguin, 1991.

———. *Mao II*. Harmondsworth, England: Penguin, 1991.

———. *The Names*. 1982. Reprint, New York: Vintage, 1989.

———. *Players*. 1977. Reprint, New York: Vintage, 1989.

———. *Underworld*. New York: Scribner, 1997.

———. *White Noise*. 1985. Reprint, Harmondsworth, England: Penguin, 1986.

Dexter, Pete. *Paris Trout*. 1988. Reprint, Harmondsworth, England: Penguin, 1989.

Dickens, Charles. *Barnaby Rudge*. 1841. Reprint, Oxford: Oxford University Press, 1954.

———. *Bleak House*. 1853. Reprint, Harmondsworth, England: Penguin, 1971.

———. *Martin Chuzzlewit*. 1844. Reprint, Harmondsworth, England: Penguin, 1995.

———. *The Mystery of Edwin Drood*. 1870. Reprint, Harmondsworth, England: Penguin, 1974.

———. *Oliver Twist*. 1838. Reprint, Harmondsworth, England: Penguin, 1985.

———. *Our Mutual Friend*. 1864–6. Reprint, Oxford: Oxford University Press, 1998.

Döblin, Alfred. *Berlin Alexanderplatz: The Story of Franz Biberkopf*. 1929. Translated by Eugene Jolas. Harmondsworth, England: Penguin, 1978.

Doderer, Heimito von. *Every Man a Murderer*. 1938. Translated by Richard and Clara Winston. New York: Knopf, 1964.

Dorrestein, Renata. *A Heart of Stone*. 1998. Translated by Hester Velmans. Harmondsworth, England: Penguin, 2000.

Dostoevsky, Fyodor. *Crime and Punishment*. 1866. Translated by Jessie Coulson. New York: Norton, 1989.

———. *The Karamazov Brothers*. 1880. Translated by Ignat Avsey. Oxford: Oxford University Press, 1994.

Doyle, Arthur Conan. *The Adventures of Sherlock Holmes*. New York: Heritage Press, n.d.

———. *The Hound of the Baskervilles*. 1901. Reprint, Oxford: Oxford University Press, 1993.

———. *A Study in Scarlet*. 1887. Reprint, New York: Heritage Press, n.d.

Dreiser, Theodore. *An American Tragedy*. 1925. Reprint, New York: Signet, 1981.

Dumas, Alexandre. *The Count of Monte Cristo*. 1844–45. Translated by Robin Buss. Harmondsworth, England: Penguin, 1966.

Dürrenmatt, Friedrich. *The Pledge*. 1958. Translated by Richard and Clara Winston. New York: Knopf, 1959.

———. *Traps*. 1956. Translated by Richard and Clara Winston. New York: Knopf, 1960.

———. *The Visit*. 1956. Translated by Patrick Bowles. New York: Grove, 1962.

Eco, Umberto. *The Name of the Rose*. 1980; postscript. 1983. Translated by William Weaver. New York: Harcourt, 1984.

Eliot, George. *Adam Bede*. 1859. Reprint, Harmondsworth, England: Penguin, 1985.

———. *Daniel Deronda*. 1876. Reprint, Harmondsworth, England: Penguin, 1986.

Ellis, Bret Easton. *American Psycho*. New York: Vintage, 1991.

Faulkner, William. *Absalom, Absalom!* 1936. Reprint, New York: Vintage, 1990.

———. *Light in August*. 1932. Reprint, New York: Vintage, 1987.

———. *Sanctuary*. 1931. Reprint, New York: Vintage, 1987.

Fitzgerald, F. Scott. *The Great Gatsby*. New York: Scribner, 1925.

Fontane, Theodor. *Effi Briest*. 1894. Translated by Douglas Parmée. New York: Penguin, 1967.

Gadda, Carlo Emilio. *That Awful Mess on Via Merulana*. 1957. Translated by William Weaver. New York: George Braziller, 1984.

Gaskell, Elizabeth. *Mary Barton: A Tale of Manchester Life*. 1848. Reprint, Harmondsworth, England: Penguin, 1985.

Genet, Jean. *Deathwatch*. 1949. In *The Maids and Deathwatch: Two Plays by Jean Genet*. Translated by Bernard Fechtman. New York: Grove, 1962.

———. *The Maids*. 1947. In *The Maids and Deathwatch: Two Plays by Jean Genet*. Translated by Bernard Fechtman. New York: Grove, 1962.

Gide, André. *The Counterfeiters*. 1925. Translated by Dorothy Bussy. New York: Vintage, 1973.

———. *The Journals of André Gide*. 2 vols. Translated by Justin O'Brien. New York: Knopf, 1947, 1948.

———. *Lafcadio's Adventures*. 1914. Translated by Dorothy Bussy. New York: Vintage, 1953.

Golding, William. *The Lord of the Flies*. New York: Perigee, 1954.

Greene, Graham. *Brighton Rock*. 1938. Reprint, Harmondsworth, England: Penguin, 1970.

———. *This Gun for Hire*. New York: Pocket Books, 1971.

Hammett, Dashiel. *The Glass Key*. 1931. Reprint, New York: Vintage, 1989.

———. *Red Harvest*. 1929. Reprint, New York: Vintage, 1992.

Hardy, Thomas. *Far from the Madding Crowd*. 1874. Reprint, Harmondsworth, England: Penguin, 1986.

———. *Tess of the d'Urbervilles*. 1891. Reprint, Harmondsworth, England: Penguin, 1985.

Harris, Thomas. *Hannibal*. New York: Delacorte, 1999.

———. *Red Dragon*. New York: Dell, 1981.

———. *The Silence of the Lambs*. 1988. New York: St. Martin's, 1989.

Hawthorne, Nathaniel. *The House of Seven Gables*. 1851. Reprint, New York: Washington Square, 1961.

———. *The Marble Faun*. 1860. Reprint, Harmondsworth, England: Penguin, 1990.

Highsmith, Patricia. *The Talented Mr. Ripley*. 1955. Reprint, New York: Vintage, 1992.

Hoffmann, E.T.A. "Mademoiselle de Scudéri." 1816. In *Tales of E.T.A. Hoffman*, translated and edited by Leonard J. Kent and Elizabeth C. Knight, 173–233. Chicago: University of Chicago Press, 1969.

Hogg, James. *The Private Memoirs and Confessions of a Justified Sinner*. 1824. Reprint, London: Everyman, 1994.

Hugo, Victor. *Les Misérables*. 1862. Translated by Norman Denny. Harmondsworth, England: Penguin, 1976.

———. *Notre-Dame of Paris*. 1831. Translated by John Sturrock. Harmondsworth, England: Penguin, 1978.

Huxley, Aldous. *Brave New World*. 1932. Reprint, New York: Harper, 1969.

Huysmans, Joris Karl. *Against Nature*. 1884. Translated by Robert Baldick. Harmondsworth, England: Penguin, 1966.

Iles, Francis. *Malice Aforethought: The Story of a Commonplace Crime*. 1931. Reprint, Montreal: Pocket Books, 1947.

Kafka, Franz. "In the Penal Colony." 1919. In *The Penal Colony: Short Stories and Short Pieces*, translated by Willa and Edwin Muir, 191–227. New York: Shocken, 1964.

———. *The Trial*. 1925. Translated by Willa and Edwin Muir. New York: Shocken, 1984.

Kerr, Philip. *A Philosophical Investigation*. Toronto: Doubleday, 1992.

Koestler, Arthur. *Darkness at Noon*. 1941. Translated by Daphne Hardy. New York: Bantam, 1968.

Levin, Meyer. *Compulsion*. 1956. Reprint, New York: Carroll & Graff, 1996.

March, William. *The Bad Seed*. 1954. Reprint, Hopewell, N.J.: Ecco, 1997.

McCoy, Horace. *Kiss Tomorrow Goodbye*. 1948. Reprint, New York: Serpent's Tail, 1996.

McCreary, Lew. *The Minus Man*. New York: Grove, 1991.

McNamee, Eoin. *Resurrection Man*. 1994. Reprint, London: Picador, 1995.

Melville, Herman. *Moby Dick*. 1851. Reprint, New York: Norton, 1967.

Morrison, Toni. *Beloved*. 1987. Reprint, New York: Plume, 1988.

Musil, Robert. *The Man without Qualities*. 2 vols. 1952; 1978. Translated by Sophie Wilkins. New York: Knopf, 1995.

Nabokov, Vladimir. *Despair*. 1936; revised 1965. Reprint, New York: Putnam, 1966.

———. *Lolita*. 1955. Reprint, New York: Vintage, 1989.

Norris, Frank. *McTeague: A Story of San Francisco*. 1899. Reprint, New York: Norton, 1977.

———. *The Octopus: A Story of California*. 1901. Reprint, New York: Signet, 1964.

Puzo, Mario. *The Godfather*. 1969. Reprint, New York: Signet, 1978.

Pynchon, Thomas. *Gravity's Rainbow*. 1973. Reprint, Harmondsworth, England: Penguin, 1995.

Rendell, Ruth. *A Demon in My View*. 1976. Reprint, New York: Bantam, 1981.

Robbe-Grillet, Alain. *La belle captive*. 1975. Translated by Ben Stoltzfus. Berkeley: University of California Press, 1995.

———. *The Erasers*. 1953. Translated by Richard Howard. New York: Grove, 1964.

———. *Topology of a Phantom City*. 1976. Translated by J. A. Underwood. New York: Grove, 1977.

Royce, Kenneth. *The XYY Man*. London: Pan, 1970.

Sanders, Lawrence. *The First Deadly Sin*. 1972. Reprint, New York: Berkley, 1980.

———. *The Third Deadly Sin*. 1981. Reprint, New York: Berkley, 1982.

Sartre, Jean-Paul. *Dirty Hands*. 1948. In *No Exit and Three Other Plays*, 131–248. Translated by Lionel Abel. New York: Vintage, 1949.

———. *No Exit*. 1945. In *No Exit and Three Other Plays*, 3–47. Translated by Stuart Gilbert. New York: Vintage, 1949.

Schlink, Bernhard. *The Reader*. 1995. Translated by Carol Brown Janeway. New York: Vintage, 1997.

Simenon, Georges. *The Man Who Watched Trains Go By*. 1942. Translated by Stuart Gilbert. New York: Berkley, 1958.

Simms, William Gilmore. *Guy Rivers: A Tale of Georgia*. 1834. Reprint, New York: AMS, 1970.

———. *Martin Faber: The Story of a Criminal*. 1833. Reprint, Albany, N.Y.: New College and University Press, 1990.

Steinbeck, John. *The Grapes of Wrath*. 1939. Reprint, New York: Modern Library, 1952.

Stevens, Shane. *By Reason of Insanity*. 1979. Reprint, New York: Dell, 1980.

Stevenson, Robert Louis. *The Strange Case of Dr. Jekyll and Mr. Hyde*. 1886. Reprint, New York: Dover, 1991.

Stoker, Bram. *Dracula*. 1897. Reprint, Harmondsworth, England: Penguin, 1993.

Strindberg, August. *The Father*. 1887. In *Six Plays of Strindberg*. Translated by Elizabeth Sprigge. New York: Doubleday, 1955.

Süskind, Patrick. *Perfume*. 1985. Translated by John E. Woods. New York: Washington Square, 1991.

Thompson, Jim. *The Killer Inside Me*. 1952. Reprint, New York: Vintage, 1991.

———. *Pop. 1280*. 1964. Reprint, New York: Vintage, 1990.

Tolstoy, Leo. "The Kreutzer Sonata." 1889. In *The Kreutzer Sonata and Other Stories*, translated by David McDuff. Harmondsworth, England: Penguin, 1985.

Van Arman, Derek. *Just Killing Time*. 1992. Reprint, New York: Onyx, 1993.

Van Dine, S. S. *The Benson Murder Case*. 1926. Reprint, New York: Pocket, 1946.

Wilde, Oscar. *The Picture of Dorian Gray*. 1890. Reprint, Harmondsworth, England: Penguin, 1985.

Wright, Richard. *Native Son*. 1940. Reprint, New York: Harper, 1993.

Zola, Émile. *La Bête humaine*. 1890. Translated by Leonard Tancock. Harmondsworth, England: Penguin, 1977.

———. *Doctor Pascal*. 1893. Translated by Mary J. Serrano. New York: Macmillan, 1898.

———. *The Earth*. 1887. Translated by Douglas Parmée. Harmondsworth, England: Penguin, 1980.

———. *Germinal*. 1885. Translated by L. W. Tancock. Harmondsworth, England: Penguin, 1971.

———. *Nana*. 1880. Translated by George Holden. Harmondsworth, England: Penguin, 1972.

———. *Thérèse Raquin*. 1867. Translated by Leonard Tancock. Harmondsworth, England: Penguin, 1962.

Index

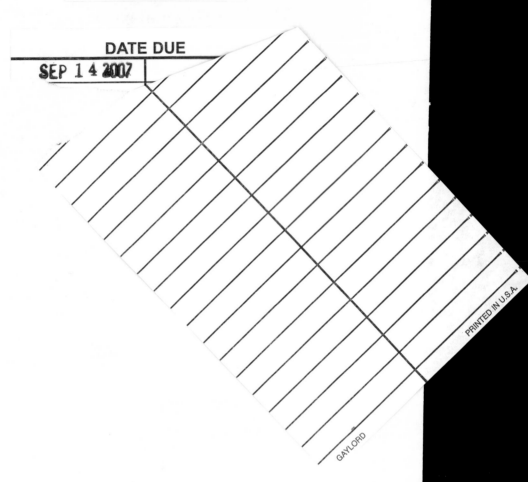